More praise for *The Triumph of Liberty*

"Jim Powell has written a fast-moving, zesty history of champions of liberty from Cicero to Thoreau, from Rabelais to Rand."

—JAMES BOVARD, author of *Lost Rights, Freedom in Chains*

"The Triumph of Liberty reads extremely well and deals with such intellectually fascinating people."

—GARY S. BECKER, Professor of Economics and Sociology, University of Chicago, and Nobel Prize–winning author of *The Economics of Life*

"Jim Powell has done yeoman's work assembling the ideas and arguments of the world's greatest liberty-oriented thinkers. *The Triumph of Liberty* is vital to the teaching and understanding of American history and fundamental to a meaning of our nation's values and origins. The writing is superb."

—WALTER E. WILLIAMS, Chairman of the Economics Department, George Mason University, and author of *The State Against Blacks*

"An inspiring chronicle that will lift the spirits of freedom lovers everywhere. As Jim Powell reminds us, liberty is not to be taken for granted. An awesome book!"

—GEORGE B.N. AYITTEY, Professor of Economics, American University, and author of *Africa Betrayed*

"A wonderful reference for any lover of liberty. Lift your spirits by reading a story each night. I am giving copies to my children."

—RANDY E. BARNETT, Austin B. Fletcher Professor, Boston University School of Law, and author of *The Structure of Liberty*

THE
TRIUMPH
OF LIBERTY

A 2,000-YEAR HISTORY, TOLD
THROUGH THE LIVES OF FREEDOM'S
GREATEST CHAMPIONS

JIM POWELL

THE FREE PRESS

New York   London   Toronto   Sydney   Singapore

*f*P

The Free Press
A Division of Simon & Schuster Inc.
1230 Avenue of the Americas
New York, N.Y. 10020

Manufactured in the United States of America

1 3 5 7 9 10 8 6 4 2

Library of Congress Cataloging-in-Publication Data

Powell, Jim
   The triumph of liberty : a 2,000-year history, told through
the lives of freedom's greatest champions / Jim Powell.
      p. cm.
   Includes bibliographical references and index.
      1. Biography. 2. Liberty—History. I. Title.
   CT104.P72 2000
   920.02—dc21

                                        00-025547

ISBN: 0-684-85967-X

FOR

MADELINE, FRANK, MARISA, JUSTIN, KRISTIN, AND ROSALYND

Major funding for this work was provided by
Commercial Tenant Real Estate Representation, Ltd.

Additional funding was provided by
Eastbridge Holdings Inc.

CONTENTS

Where liberty dwells, there is my country.

—BENJAMIN FRANKLIN (1783)

God grants liberty only to those who love it,
and are always ready to guard and defend it.

—DANIEL WEBSTER (1830)

FOREWORD

BY PAUL JOHNSON[*]

As SOMEONE WHO, in a small way, has tried his best to advance the cause of human liberty through books, articles, broadcasts, and lectures over many decades now, I commend this book to the American people. Jim Powell is a stalwart champion of liberty. He is a man of great energy, determination, obstinacy, and courage, and all of these qualities have gone into his work on behalf of liberty.

He believes, as I do, that worthwhile abstract ideas are best promoted by the study of the lives of those who embodied them. That is what he has done in this book. I do not agree with all of it. Some of the people he presents as heroes and heroines of liberty in this narrative exhibited serious flaws of character and judgment, and their lives and writings and sayings should be studied with caution. But that is how one should approach all history, not least biographical history.

What I am sure of is that anyone who reads *The Triumph of Liberty* will profit from it, emerging with a better idea of what liberty means and how it is advanced. That is something well worth doing, and Jim Powell has done it.

---

[*] Paul Johnson is author of *Modern Times, A History of the Jews, A History of Christianity, A History of the American People,* and other books.

INTRODUCTION

How did mankind ever come by the idea of liberty?
What a grand thought it was!

—G. C. Lichtenberg (1799)

LIBERTY IS A RARE and precious thing. For thousands of years, no one had ever heard of individual rights. According to historian Fernand Braudel, slavery was the norm—"a universal phenomenon, affecting all primitive societies."

In ancient Mesopotamia, prisoners of war and offenders undergoing punishment were slaves. So were children, whose destitute parents often sold them into slavery. Government officials and priests owned slaves who labored as household servants, artisans, and concubines. Egypt was substantially built on forced labor. Almost all agricultural land was tilled by serfs, usually condemned to be serfs for life. The government conscripted thousands for massive projects, and successful foreign military campaigns brought large numbers of slaves who performed a myriad of menial tasks. Government officials had households full of slaves who worked as cooks, seamstresses, and brewers. In China, slavery goes back at least to the Shang dynasty in the second millennium B.C., where it was commonplace. Slaves, typically captured during war, performed farm labor with leashes around their necks. There were slaves in ancient Crete and Greek city-states. Scholars estimate that over eighty thousand slaves lived in Athens during the fifth and fourth centuries B.C. Rome engaged in seemingly endless military campaigns, yielding hundreds of thousands of prisoners who became slaves. At the emporiums of Capua and Delos, some 20,000 slaves changed hands each day. By some estimates, three-quarters of the people living on the Italian peninsula were slaves.

Nor were slaves unique to the ancient world. By the third century A.D., as more and more peasants abandoned their farmland and headed for cities where free food was distributed, the untended land lost value and didn't yield tax revenue. In 332 A.D., as a "temporary" measure to help maintain tax collections, Emperor Constantine declared that peasants must remain on the land. They were *coloni*. Constantine decreed, "As for the coloni who attempt to run away, it shall be allowed to load them with chains, in the manner of slaves." Thirty-nine years later, this policy had become permanent.

In medieval Europe, most people were serfs, enslaved to the soil. They farmed land and performed other services for aristocratic landowners, who themselves owed military service as well as money to their kings. Serfs could not be sold apart from the land, nor could they legally leave the land. This was the era of feudalism. Forced labor aimed sometimes to mount a defense against barbarian invaders and sometimes to pillage more prosperous neighbors.

The Catholic church promoted serfdom and slavery. In 1452 and 1453, Pope Nicholas IV officially approved Portugal's efforts to enslave heathens, and in 1493, Pope Alexander VI sanctioned Spanish slavery in the Americas. Since medieval monks were so successful at convincing lords they should bequeathe their estates to the Catholic church, it became the biggest landowner in Europe, with more serfs than anyone else. Church canon law had specific provisions against freeing slaves, and the church even profited from the death of serfs who belonged to nonchurch landlords: the lord had the right to seize a deceased serf's best farm animal, and the local priest could seize the second-best animal.

There were few constraints on what feudal landowners could do. "The knight of the eleventh and twelfth centuries was no model of gentleness and refinement," reported medieval scholar Brian Tierney. "He drank himself into a stupor with considerable regularity. His castle was usually filled with prostitutes. If he got annoyed with his opponent during a chess game, he was inclined to brain him with one of the massive chessmen of the day. When a servant was slow in bringing his wine, he threw a javelin at him to speed his steps. If his wife annoyed him, he beat her savagely. . . . While he was bound not to injure his lord, his lord's immediate family, his vassal, or his vassal's family, the feudal system left him entirely free in regard to all other persons."

Slavery has continued throughout much of the world, right up to the twenty-first century. In *Slavery, a World History,* Milton Meltzer reported continuing slavery in Bangladesh, Brazil, Ghana, India, Mauritania, Mozambique, Pakistan, Saudi Arabia, Sri Lanka, and Thailand, among other places. Investigator Harry Wu exposed the *laogai* camps in China, where millions are enslaved.

Worse than slavery has been government killing on an unimaginable scale. In 1221 A.D. Mongol Tului murdered some 700,000 people in Khorassan, north of Persia. The thirteenth-century sultan of Delhi, Kutb-d Din, reportedly murdered hundreds of thousands of Indians. The fourteenth-century Mongol conqueror Tamerlane murdered an estimated 100,000 prisoners near Delhi. Aztecs conducted human sacrifices, and a Spanish conquistador reported counting 125,000 skulls; the Spanish went on to slaughter the Aztecs. During the late fifteenth century, an estimated 125,000 people were murdered or died in prison because of the Spanish Inquisition. In 1572, the government of French king Charles IX authorized the St. Bartholomew's Day massacre in which about 36,000 Protestants were murdered. About 7.5 million people were killed as European states fought for power during the Thirty Years War (1618–1648). In America, at least 2 million Indians were massacred. Between 1740 and 1897, 230 European wars and revolutions resulted in the deaths of over 20 million people. During the fifteen-year Teiping

Rebellion of the mid-nineteenth century, Chinese imperial forces killed all potential opponents, and the death toll reportedly hit 40 million.

The twentieth century was drenched in blood. Adolf Hitler murdered an estimated 21 million Balts, Czechs, Frenchmen, gypsies, homosexuals, and Slavs as well as Jews. Communist China murdered an estimated 35.2 million of its people, and another 27 million starved to death in government-induced famines. The Soviet Union established its slave labor system, the gulag, which claimed an estimated 40 million lives. Soviet governments murdered another 20 million of their people. Soviet government murders alone were about triple the number of deaths that resulted from the African slave trade.

Altogether, reported political science professor R. J. Rummel, "During the first eighty-eight years of this century, almost 170 million men, women, and children have been shot, beaten, tortured, knifed, burned, starved, frozen, crushed, or worked to death; buried alive, drowned, hung, bombed, or killed in any other of the myriad ways governments have inflicted death on unarmed, helpless citizens or foreigners. The dead could conceivably be nearly 360 million people. It is as though our species has been devastated by a modern Black Plague. And indeed it has, but a plague of Power, not germs."

How, amid such recurring horrors, did some people manage to break free? What is the role of ideas in the history of liberty? What are the essential institutions of a free society? Why do some efforts to achieve a free society go wrong? How do people let their liberty slip away? How can we best help liberty to thrive? How much difference can one person make? These are just some of the questions I address here.

The Triumph of Liberty seeks answers by exploring the lives of remarkable individuals who made crucial contributions to liberty during the past two thousand years. Although some were aristocrats, most were commoners. They include a failed corset maker, a former tanner, a disillusioned clergyman, an impoverished composer, a one-time printer's assistant, a medical doctor, an engineering draftsman, a professor, a housewife, a pencil maker's son, a handkerchief weaver's daughter, a wandering hobo, and a slave, among others. They made their mark as writers, editors, educators, political leaders, and, in a few cases, military leaders. They didn't always live up to their ideals, but their contributions were monumental, and I believe there has been more liberty because they lived.

The stories are based on biographies supplemented with letters, diaries, and speeches as well as material relating to events of their time. Sometimes I was able to draw on unpublished material. I tapped library resources at Harvard University, the University of California (Berkeley, UCLA), the University of Chicago, Cornell University, Stanford University, Yale University, and the Library of Congress. I had the help of out-of-print booksellers on both sides of the Atlantic. To help trace the continuing influence of the people whose stories I tell, I interviewed dozens of scholarly specialists throughout

North America and visited historic sites in Britain, Germany, Switzerland, Japan, and the United States.

Stories appear in chronological order within thematic groupings. There is chronological overlap within and among groupings. This helps to underscore that liberty did not advance on a single track. Some societies embraced religious toleration before they understood the case for economic liberty. In many places, people thrived with economic liberty, although they didn't have political liberty.

This book could not possibly cover all the different ways in which people have used the word *liberty* or *freedom.* I write here about only one tradition: freedom from fraud and coercion of every kind. In the history of liberty, this is the original tradition, the longest tradition, the tradition that has inspired millions to rebel against tyranny.

The individuals chronicled here were key players in one of the most thrilling stories ever told. They changed history with their extraordinary vision, skill, courage, and love. They made it possible for millions of us to do what was unthinkable in ages past: enjoy life, liberty, and the pursuit of happiness.

NATURAL RIGHTS

Liberty is the sovereignty of the individual.
—JOSIAH WARREN (1852)

IN THE BEGINNING, there was oppression. The earliest recorded civilizations were ruthlessly run by kings and priests, and government plunder, slavery, and murder were legal. Then the ancient Jews developed the idea that all people, including rulers, were subject to laws from their god, Yahweh and the vision of a law above rulers came to be called a higher law. Among the Greek dramatists who embraced the idea of a higher law was Sophocles (c.496–406 B.C.). In *Antigone*, for example, the heroine explains why she must defy the king:

> *Your edict, King, was strong.*
> *But all your strength is weakness itself against*
> *The immortal unrecorded laws of God.*
> *They are not merely now: they were, and shall be,*
> *Operative for ever, beyond man utterly.*

The idea of a higher law was expanded on by Greek and Roman Stoic philosophers. During the English Revolution, a number of thinkers developed it into the modern doctrine that each individual owns himself or herself and has the inalienable right to life, liberty, and property—and the right to rebel against rulers who deny these rights.

A HIGHER LAW

MARCUS TULLIUS CICERO expressed principles that became the bedrock of liberty in the modern world. He insisted that law is legitimate only when it is consistent with standards of liberty and justice, based on what he called natural law. He declared that government is morally obliged to protect human life and private property, and he honored daring individuals who helped overthrow tyrants. Intellectual historian Murray N. Rothbard praised Cicero as "the great transmitter of Stoic ideas from Greece to Rome. . . . Stoic natural law doctrines heavily influenced the Roman jurists of the second and third centuries A.D., and thus helped shape the great structures of Roman law which became pervasive in Western civilization."

Cicero was renowned as well for transforming Latin from a utilitarian language, serving generals, merchants, and lawyers, to a poetic language. The first century A.D. Roman writer Quintilian remarked that Cicero was "the name not of a man, but of eloquence itself." Thomas Jefferson called Cicero "the first master of the world." Historian Edward Gibbon, who elegantly chronicled Rome's decline, recalled that when reading Cicero, "I tasted the beauties of language, I breathed the spirit of freedom, and I imbibed from his precepts and examples the public and private sense of a man."

As Rome's most famous orator, Cicero prosecuted crooked politicians and defended citizens against rapacious officials. Scholar H. Grose Hodge observed that Cicero at his best offered "a sustained interest, a constant variety, a consummate blend of humour and pathos, of narrative and argument, of description and declamation; while every part is subordinated to the purpose of the whole, and combines, despite its intricacy of detail, to form a dramatic and coherent unit."

Amidst a violent age, Cicero was a man of peace. He didn't build a personal army like other leading Roman politicians, and he spoke out against violence. "It is a hard thing to say," he declared, "but we Romans are loathed abroad because of the damage our generals and officials have done. . . . There is now a shortage of prosperous cities for us to declare war on so that we can loot them afterwards. . . . Do you know of a single state that we have subdued that is still rich?" As well, he defended civilized pursuits like reading. "No other pleasure," he wrote, "suits every occasion, every age, or every place. But the study of letters is the food of youth, the delight of old age, the ornament of prosperity, the refuge and comfort of adversity, a delight at home and no burden abroad; it stays with us at night, and goes with us on our travels, near and far."

Cicero never challenged Roman slavery, which was among the most brutal in history, yet he preferred to have his farms worked by tenants rather than by slaves. And on one occasion, he remarked, "I am more upset than I ought to be at the death of a slave." He made his secretary Tiro a freedman, which brought this reply from his brother: "I am so grateful to you for feeling that he did not deserve his station in life and for preferring that he should be a friend to us rather than a slave." More is known about Cicero than any other ancient personality, because he wrote *Brutus* (46 B.C.), one of the earliest pieces of intellectual autobiography, and because hundreds of his letters were dispatched by courier throughout the Mediterranean, and many of them survive. Cicero comes across, by turns, as vain, indecisive, affectionate, charming, and generous. "It is probable that Cicero is the greatest of all letter-writers," observed classical scholar J. A .K. Thomson. "The importance of his matter, the range of his public and private interests, the variety of his moods, his facility in expressing every shade of sense and feeling, the aptness of his quotations, above all his spontaneity, have never in combination been excelled or equalled." Although he lived during an era of great sculpture, only one bust is marked as his and it has been the basis for identifying others. These sculptures tend to portray Cicero as having a high forehead, large nose, small mouth, and worried expression, as if he were agonizing over the fate of the Roman Republic.

Cicero displayed the courage of his convictions. He opposed Julius Caesar's schemes for one-man rule, and after Caesar's assassination, denounced Mark Antony's bid to become dictator. For that, Cicero was beheaded.

MARCUS TULLIUS CICERO was born January 6, 106 B.C., on his grandfather's country estate in Arpinum, about seventy miles southeast of Rome. His father, who shared all three names, was a frail aristocrat with literary interests, property in Arpinum, and a house in Rome. Cicero's mother, Helvia, was from a socially connected family in Rome. The Cicero family name does not suggest much dignity; though; in Latin, *cicer* means "chickpea."

Cicero aimed to be a defense attorney as the best bet for success in politics, and there was plenty to keep a defense attorney busy. Murder had been common in Roman politics since at least 133 B.C., when a reformer named Tiberius Sempronius Gracchus was clubbed to death by senators he had criticized. According to the biographer Plutarch, who wrote in the first century A.D., "The city was filled with murder, and there was no counting the executions or setting a limit to them."

Cicero first sought political office when he was thirty—as quaestor, the lowest major office with any administrative responsibility for a province. In the elections, which took place every July after the harvest, voters scratched the name or initials of their chosen candidate on waxed wooden ballots, then dropped these in baskets for counting. Once elected, Cicero was assigned western Sicily, where one of his jobs was to make sure corn supplies reached Rome. He also joined the Senate, which played a prestigious advisory role in the government but had little real power. Cicero started to move up the political ladder to consul, the highest office in Rome. In the election, he beat out Lucius Sergius Catiline, who tried to recruit foreign armed forces, assassinate Cicero, and take over the government. Cicero delivered powerful orations against Catiline, who was subsequently killed in battle.

Although this republic was corrupt and limited, it offered the best chance of averting one-man rule. Yet its conquests continued, and successful generals eclipsed the power of the Senate and other republican institutions. Cicero now found himself in the uncomfortable position of choosing among evils. The least dangerous, he believed, was Cnaeus Pompeius (Pompey), a highly capable military commander, remarkable administrator, and political opportunist; during his early days, he was known as the "boy executioner." He crushed Rome's adversaries in the Middle East; wiped out piracy in the eastern Mediterranean, which had disrupted Rome's vital food supplies; conquered some fifteen hundred towns and fortresses; organized four new Roman provinces that extended Roman frontiers to the Caucasus Mountains and the Red Sea; and started or rebuilt thirty-nine cities. In this process, he established a network of client rulers who helped Rome guard the eastern frontiers, and boosted Rome's revenue from the region by 70 percent, becoming himself the wealthiest Roman at the time.

But in December 62 B.C., Pompey returned to Rome and dismissed his army. He wanted fame rather than political power. All he asked was that the Senate pass a bill giving his soldiers land in the provinces, as soldiers were usually rewarded after a successful military campaign. But the Senate refused, convincing Pompey that he should consider collaborating with his rivals.

His best-financed rival was Marcus Crassus, who had inherited a small fortune and multiplied it more than twenty-fold by buying cheaply the properties of people condemned to death and then reselling the property. Until Pompey's lucrative triumph in the Middle East, Crassus had been the wealthiest Roman. He built his own army and crushed the slave revolt led by Spartacus, crucifying six thousand slaves on the Appian Way.

To strengthen his position against Pompey, Crassus bought the support of Gaius Julius Caesar, an ambitious, spendthrift demagogue who had been elected a quaestor in 68 B.C. and assigned to administer Further Spain, where he discovered his genius as a military commander. Equally important, he acquired loot for expanding his power, and gained a popular following by sponsoring lavish "free" games and banquets whose astonishing cost—almost a tenth of government revenues—were underwritten by Crassus.

In 60 B.C., Pompey, Crassus, and Caesar were frustrated by Senate efforts to thwart their ambitions, so they formed a dictatorship known as the first triumvirate. During the next decade, they controlled candidates for office and parceled out provincial loot among themselves. Crassus got the East; Pompey, Spain; and Caesar, Cisalpine Gaul (northern Italy) and Illyricum (on the eastern Adriatic coast). Cicero declined an invitation to join them.

In 58 B.C. the gangster-senator Publius Clodius Pulcher (an ally of Caesar's known as Clodius) proposed a law banishing Cicero from Rome, and plundered three of Cicero's homes. Cicero was exiled for sixteenn miserable months, spent at a friend's home in Salonika in northeastern Greece. Titus Pomponius Atticus, Cicero's banker and publisher, helped cover his expenses in exile. Cicero returned to Rome when Pompey decided he needed an ally against Clodius. But the triumvirs would not tolerate the free expression of Cicero's views.

Meanwhile, Crassus continued to pursue more wealth and military glory, now leading his army against the Parthians, a nomadic people based in western Persia, where their territory sat astride the great Silk Road that connected China with the Mediterranean. But the army was routed by Parthian bowmen, and Crassus was slain in May 53 B.C.

Caesar meanwhile had been building his personal empire in Gaul, which now included territory in France, Belgium, part of Holland and Switzerland, and Germany west of the Rhine. In the process, he reportedly sold 53,000 members of the Nervii tribe as slaves; boasted that he had slaughtered 258,000 Helvetii men, women, and children; and went on to slaughter some 430,000 Germans. He combined his tactical genius, especially surprise attacks, with effective propaganda, something the aloof Pompey had neglected. Caesar appealed for popular support as a champion of peace and repeatedly sought Cicero's backing because he needed legitimacy. Although Caesar had always been cordial to Cicero, Cicero reluctantly sided with Pompey.

In January 49 B.C., the Senate ordered Caesar to return from Gaul without his army. He refused to cooperate in what would have been his political destruction. On the evening of January 10, 49 B.C., he led a legion of soldiers across the Rubicon, a small river on the northwestern Italian peninsula, separating Gaul from Rome. This violated Roman law requiring that armies be kept in the provinces, and another civil war was on. Unable to defend himself in Italy, Pompey fled to the East on March 17, 49 B.C.

Caesar entered Rome on April 1, seizing the Roman treasury to finance his military campaigns. That month, with his deputy Mark Antony in charge of Italy, Caesar went to Spain, preventing Pompey from rebuilding an army there. He destroyed Marseilles, which had supported Pompey, then returned to Italy and defeated Pompey's larger forces at Pharsalus, north of Athens, on August 9, 48 B.C. When Pompey fled to Egypt, he was murdered upon landing by local people who had had enough of Rome's wars.

As Caesar arrived in Egypt, he was presented with Pompey's severed head. He subsequently became a lover of young Queen Cleopatra, who joined him back in Rome. Caesar crushed remnant opposition, some 10,000 people were slaughtered, and their leader, Cato, plunged a sword into his abdomen.

Cicero, almost sixty, had been offered command of Pompey's surviving forces, but wanted no part of the violence. Instead he turned to writing about philosophy and secured his immortality. He drew from his own library, since there were not public libraries in Rome, and wrote with a reed pen and ink on papyrus scrolls, using ink made from lampblack and gum. He worked to expand Latin, which, among other things, had few metaphors or compound words, and he adapted words from Greek, which had been a philosophical language for over four centuries. He introduced *essentia, qualitas*, and *moralis* to Latin, which makes him the source of the English words *essence, quality,* and *moral.* Atticus had slaves make a thousand copies of Cicero's works.

Although Cicero did not construct any new philosophical system, he interpreted his favorite Greek thinkers and made their ideas soar. He transmitted the Greek Stoic idea of a moral higher law to the modern world. In his dialogue *De Legibus (On the Laws,* 52 B.C.), he discussed the "supreme law which existed through the ages, before the mention of any written law or established state. . . . Nor may any other law override it, nor may it be repealed as a whole or in part, nor have we power through Senate or people to free ourselves from it. . . . Nor is it one thing at Rome and another at Athens, one thing today and another tomorrow, but one eternal and unalterable law, that binds all nations forever. It is the one universal lord and ruler of all, and God himself is its author, promulgator and enforcer. . . . Whoever disregards this law, whether written or unwritten, is unjust."

He also contributed some key ideas of his own. Greek philosophers had conceived of society and government as virtually the same, coming together in the *polis* (city-state). Cicero declared that government is like a trustee, morally obliged to serve society, which means that society is something larger than government and separate from it. An appreciation for the myriad wonders of civil society, where private individuals develop languages, markets, legal customs, and other institutions, did not come until the eighteenth century, but it was Cicero who began to see the light.

Cicero was the first to say that government was justified primarily as a means of protecting private property. Both Plato and Aristotle had imagined that government could improve morals, but neither had conceived of private property—an absolute claim to something over everyone else. Cicero wrote in *De Officiis (On Duties,* 44 B.C.), "The chief purpose in the establishment of states and constitutional orders was that individual property rights might be secured. . . . It is the peculiar function of state and city to guarantee to every man the free and undisturbed control of his own property."

Caesar proceeded to have himself named dictator for life. As historian John Dickinson observed, he "indulged in a lifetime of double talk, professing slogans of democracy, while debasing and destroying the powers of the electorate, and insisting on constitutional technicalities, while persistently undermining the constitution. In the end, his prescription for government turned out to be a surprisingly simple one: to reduce its mechanism to the simplest and most primitive of all institutional forms, personal absolutism, and to employ it for one of the simplest and most primitive of all purposes, foreign conquest."

Proud, hot-tempered Gaius Cassius, who hated Caesar, seems to have hatched the revolt against him. He was joined by his intense brother-in-law Marcus Brutus, who felt betrayed after Caesar had promised a new order but then pursued one-man rule. They recruited about sixty co-conspirators and on March 15—the Ides of March—stabbed Caesar to death.

Soon Caesar's hard-drinking, brawling deputy Mark Antony bid to succeed Caesar as dictator. He seized Caesar's papers and personal fortune, which Caesar had intended for his eighteen-year-old adopted son, Octavian, and pushed through a law giving him control of north and central Cisapline Gaul.

On September 2, 44 B.C., Cicero delivered a speech asserting that Antony's actions were unconstitutional, unpopular, and contrary to Caesar's intentions. On September 19, Antony countered with a scathing speech, which signaled that Cicero was a mortal enemy. Cicero then wrote a second blistering speech. It was never delivered, yet became one of the most famous political pamphlets in history. He blasted Antony, whom he portrayed as an unscrupulous opportunist, for inciting violence and provoking the civil war. "I fought for the Republic when I was young," Cicero declared. "I shall not abandon her in my old age. I scorned the daggers of Catiline; I shall not tremble before yours. Rather I would willingly expose my body to them, if by my death the liberty of the nation could be recovered and the agony of the Roman people could at last bring to birth that with which it has been so long in labor."

Cicero delivered another dozen attacks on Antony by April 21, 43 B.C. Among other things, he urged that the Senate brand Antony as a public enemy for promoting civil war and recognize the legitimacy of Octavian as the lesser of evils. These speeches became known as the *Philippics,* inspired by Demosthenes' speeches three centuries before, intended to stir Athenian against the invader Philip of Macedon. Cicero withdrew to his Arpinum estate, away from the turmoil of Rome, where he finished his final book, *De Amicitia (On Friendship,* 44 B.C.).

The rivals Antony, Octavian, and Marcus Aemilius Lepidus finally concluded that they were not in a position to crush each other or get cooperation from the Senate, so they established themselves as triumvirs for the restoration of the republic and divided the spoils in the western provinces. They also announced rewards for anyone who could produce the heads of their enemies. Cicero's name was on the list.

Cicero fled. He started sailing for Greece, where he had heard that Brutus had some armed forces, but rough winter weather soon forced him ashore, and he sought shelter at his house near Formiae, along Italy's west coast. There, on December 7, 43 B.C., assassins caught up with him. A soldier named Herennius cut off Cicero's head and hands and took them to Antony. Fulvia, Antony's wife, pushed a hairpin through Cicero's tongue, and Cicero's head and hands were nailed to the Senate Rostra where orators spoke.

This was just the beginning of renewed violence. Antony ordered the murder of some three hundred senators and a couple of thousand influential citizens. Antony and Octavian then crushed the republican forces of Brutus and Cassius at Philippi in northeastern Greece in October 43 B.C. Brutus and Cassius both committed suicide. But Antony and Octavian soon were at each other's throats. Antony lost three-quarters of his fleet at Actium in western Greece, then fled with Cleopatra to Egypt, where they committed suicide in 30 B.C. Octavian, later known as Augustus, launched the Roman Empire.

Cicero's works generally fell out of favor during the empire. In the fifth century A.D., Catholic philosopher St. Augustine confessed, "I came in the usual course of study to a work of one Cicero, whose style is admired by almost all, not so his message." By the early Middle Ages, many of Cicero's works were lost.

The Renaissance scholar Petrarch found some of Cicero's speeches (fifty-eight were eventually recovered) and then, in 1345 at the Verona cathedral library, a collection of Cicero's letters—864 altogether (90 to Cicero and the rest by him)— that had been published in the first century A.D. Half were written to his friend Atticus, mostly based in Greece. Petrarch exulted: "You are the leader whose advice we follow, whose applause is our joy, whose name is our ornament." Cicero was cherished by Erasmus, the Dutch-born champion of toleration.

In seventeenth-century England, according to one observer, it was "the common fashion at schooles" to use Cicero's De Officiis (On Duties) as a text on ethics. Philosopher John Locke recommended Cicero's works. Cicero's vision of natural law influenced natural law thinkers like Locke, Samuel Pufendorf, and Cato's Letters' authors John Trenchard and Thomas Gordon, who had the most direct intellectual impact on the American Revolution.

Cicero's defense of the Roman Republic made him a hero to many others. In Germany, he was admired by dramatist Friedrich Schiller. The French baron de Montesquieu, who urged dividing government powers, considered Cicero "one of the greatest spirits." Voltaire wrote that Cicero "taught us how to think." Inspired by Cicero during the French Revolution, journalist Jean-Baptiste Louvet de Couvray boldly attacked Maximilien de Robespierre for promoting the Reign of Terror.

Cicero's oratory influenced the dramatic speaking styles of young (libertarian) Edmund Burke, Charles James Fox, William Ewart Gladstone, and Winston Churchill. Cicero helped inspire the libertarian ideals of the great nineteenth-century historian Thomas Babington Macaulay.

Cicero's views became unfashionable again when imperial Germany emerged as a major power during the late nineteenth century. Nobel Prize–winning historian Theodor Mommsen, for instance, was an ardent admirer of Caesar and sneered at Cicero's republicanism. While Hitler did much to make Caesarism unpopular, Cicero has continued to suffer at the hands of pro-Caesar classicists like D. R. Shackleton Bailey, who belittled Cicero as "a windbag, a wiseacre, a humbug, a spiteful, vain-glorious egotist."

Cicero nevertheless remains an "absorbingly significant builder of western civilization," as historian Michael Grant put it. Cicero urged people to reason together. He championed decency and peace, and he gave the modern world some of the most fundamental ideas of liberty. At a time when speaking freely was dangerous, he courageously denounced tyranny. He helped keep the torch of liberty burning bright for more than two thousand years.

AGENDA FOR LIBERTY

A NUMBER OF TIMES throughout history, tyranny has stimulated break-through thinking about liberty. This was certainly the case in England with the mid-seventeenth-century era of repression, rebellion, and civil war. Among the tremendous outpouring of political pamphlets and tracts, by far the most influential writings emerged from the pen of John Lilburne. In more than eighty pamphlets, he attacked intolerance, taxes, censorship, trade restrictions, and military conscription. He championed private property, free trade, freedom of association, freedom of religion, freedom of speech, freedom of the press, a rule of law, a separation of powers, and a written constitution to limit government power. Lilburne helped bring these dynamic ideas together for the first time in human history.

Moreover, he risked death to put them into action. He was the first person to challenge the legitimacy of the Star Chamber, the English royal court that had become a notorious instrument for suppressing dissent. He was the first to challenge Parliament's prerogative as a law court for imprisoning adversaries and the prosecution tactic of extracting confessions until defendants incriminated themselves. He challenged the standard practice of imprisoning people without filing formal charges, and he challenged judges who tried to intimidate juries. He was imprisoned most of his adult life, enduring brutal beatings, and four times he faced the death penalty.

"I walk not, nor act, from accidents," Lilburne told a friend, "but from principles, and being thoroughly persuaded in my own soul they are just, righteous and honest, I will by God's goodness never depart from them, though I perish in maintaining them."

Dubbed a "Leveller" by his adversaries, he won the hearts of people and helped discredit criminal justice proceedings that were a bulwark of oppression. "While others supported civil liberties to gain their own freedom and denied it to their enemies," noted historian Leonard W. Levy, "Lilburne grew more and more consistent in his devotion to the fundamentals of liberty, and he was an incandescent advocate . . . he sacrificed everything in order to be free to attack injustice from any source. . . . His entire career was a precedent for freedom."

Lilburne looked like an ordinary man. Biographer M. A. Gibb described him in his twenties as "slightly built, with a delicacy of appearance which renders his powers of physical endurance the more remarkable. Plainly dressed, after the fashion of the Puritans, he wore his hair to the shoulder and was beardless; his long, oval face, with its high forehead, luminous, earnest eyes, and often melancholy expression, indicated the depth of the fanaticism which could fire his spirit, while the resolute mouth showed strength of purpose and courage to fulfil his aims."

As Levy acknowledged, "Such men as Lilburne who make civil disobedience a way of life are admirable but quite impossible. He was far too demanding and uncompromising, never yielding an inch to his ideals. He was obstreperous, fearless, indomitable, and cantankerous, one of the most flinty, contentious men who ever lived. . . . No one in England could outtalk him, no one was a greater political pamphleteer. . . . Had Lilburne been the creation of some novelist's imagination, one might scoff at so far-fetched a character. He was, or became, a radical in everything—in religion, in politics, in economics, in social reform, in criminal justice."

JOHN LILBURNE WAS born in Greenwich, England, sometime in 1614 or 1615. His parents, Richard and Margaret Lilburne, were minor officials in the royal court.

In 1625, King Charles I issued a proclamation making it illegal to publish or import a book without a license from the bishop of London, William Laud, or the vice chancellor of Oxford or Cambridge. Licensed printers, who belonged to the Stationers Company guild, helped enforce the law against unlicensed competitors. The young Lilburne became friends with many unlicensed printers. For example, he visited the Gatehouse, where Presbyterian Dr. John Bastwick was imprisoned and had his ears cut off for criticizing Church of England officials. Through Bastwick, Lilburne met William Prynne, a Presbyterian lawyer who had published many attacks on the Church of England, for which he was fined; he was disbarred as a lawyer, condemned to life imprisonment in the Tower of London, his ears were hacked off, and his cheeks were branded with the initials "SL" (for seditious libeler).

The government considered Lilburne a potential troublemaker for associating with these people, and in 1637 he went to Holland, where free presses flourished. He seems to have spent his savings printing and distributing unlicensed pamphlets. He began with *Letany* by Dr. Bastwick. But when he returned to London in December 1637, he was betrayed by one of his collaborators, arrested, and imprisoned in the Gatehouse. His case came before the Star Chamber, which was separate from the common law courts, with proceedings based on interrogating defendants. Those who incriminated themselves were declared guilty and imprisoned. "It was a court of politicians enforcing a policy, not a court of judges administering a law," noted constitutional historian F. W. Maitland.

When Lilburne was grilled about his trip to Holland and his knowledge of unlicensed Puritan pamphlets, he attacked the Star Chamber. He had never been served with a subpoena or charged with any crime. He would not pay the court clerk's fee, nor would he agree to answer all questions. The Star Chamber nevertheless fined Lilburne £500 and ordered that he be tied to a cart as it moved two miles from Fleet prison to Westminister Palace yard. Along the way, his bare back was lashed with a whip some two hundred times; the doctor who treated him reported that his wounds were "bigger than tobacco pipes." Then he was put in a pillary, where he harangued all who would listen with attacks on the government and the Church of England. After several hours under a hot sun, Lilburne was taken back to Fleet prison and chained in a cold, damp, dark cell for four months. Then Oliver Cromwell, a member of parliament who represented Cambridge, gave his first speech in which he declared that Lilburne's Star Chamber sentence was "illegal and against the liberty of the subject." Lilburne was released, and Parliament passed a bill abolishing the Star Chamber. King Charles I reluctantly agreed on July 5, 1641.

Lilburne tried to resume his private life. He married Elizabeth Dewell, who was to raise their four children on little money and provide steadfast support during her husband's subsequent imprisonments. He got a job working at his uncle's brewery and spent his spare time studying philosophy and law. In 1642, he obtained a copy of jurist Edward Coke's *Institutes*. Coke had championed common law over arbitrary royal edicts. With common law, local judges made decisions case by case, from which general rules evolved. These tended to be applied more predictably than statutes.

As the struggle between king and Parliament intensified, Lilburne was drawn into the fray, and he was named a captain in the Parliamentary Army. But he was captured in 1642 and imprisoned at Oxford Castle. He refused a pardon in exchange for recanting his principles and was sentenced to death. Lilburne's wife, Elizabeth, then addressed the House of Commons and persuaded members to execute captured royalists if any parliamentary loyalists like Lilburne were executed. Liburne was set free. But he quit the Parliamentary Army when Oliver Cromwell, by this time a lieutenant-general, ordered that everybody subscribe to the Scottish National (Presbyterian) Covenant, which called for the suppression of religious dissidents. Lilburne declared he would "dig for carrots and turnips" before he would ever support compulsory religion.

Lilburne was influenced by John Milton, who had been charged with violating Parliament's June 1643 law requiring that prior to publication, written work must be licensed by a government censor and registered with the Stationers Company, a guild that controlled the printing business. Ordered to defend himself before Parliament, Milton gave a speech that became the famous pamphlet *Areopagitica* (1644). He maintained that truth tends to prevail when markets are open and the press is free.

In January 1645, Lilburne wrote *A Copy of a Letter* about the injustices he had suffered. He criticized Puritan William Prynne who, having suffered from intolerance by Charles I and Bishop Laud, would not tolerate others of differing views. Parliamentary officials found a printing press alleged to have produced Lilburne's offending pamphlet, and one of Lilburne's eyes was poked out with a pike.

In July 19, he was imprisoned for criticizing the Speaker of the House of Commons. He refused to answer questions and demanded to know the charges against him, insisting, "I have as true a right to all the privileges that do belong to a free man as the greatest man in England." When he was sent back to Newgate prison, he wrote *England's Birthright Justified Against All Arbitrary Usurpations, Whether Regall or Parliamentary or Under What Vizor Soever* (1645). Once again he set out his beliefs: that laws should be written in English so everybody could read them and that a trial would be proper only when formal charges are filed, when they refer to known laws, and when the defendant can confront the accuser and have an adequate opportunity to present a defense. He denounced the government-granted monopoly on preaching, attacked government-granted business monopolies, and spoke out for free trade and a free press. He observed that the longer politicians remained in Parliament, the more corrupt they became, so he called for annual parliamentary elections and universal male suffrage. He urged people to do as much as they could to remedy wrongs through constitutional action, and he implied that if this failed, people have a right to rebel.

Released from prison in October 1645, he wrote *The Just Man's Justification,* which spelled out his grievances against the House of Lords. On June 11, 1646, he was summoned to appear before the House of Lords and asked if he knew about this latest seditious pamphlet. He countered by demanding to know what, if any, charges were filed against him. Then he lashed out at the Lords: "All you intended when you set us a-fighting was merely to unhorse and dismount our old riders and tyrants, that so you might get up, and ride us in their stead." The Lords committed him to Newgate prison, where he wrote another pamphlet, *The Freeman's Freedom Vindicated.*

Lilburne's friends again rallied to his defense. Elizabeth Lilburne organized groups of women who visited the House of Commons to offer her husband's petition for justice. Printer Richard Overton wrote pamphlets defending Lilburne, for which he too was sent to Newgate prison.

In October, Overton produced his brilliant pamphlet, *An Arrow Against All Tyrants and Tyranny, Shot from the Prison of Newgate into the Prerogative Bowels of the Arbitrary House of Lords.* "To every individual in nature is given an individual property by nature," he wrote, "not to be invaded or usurped by any. For every one as he is himself, so he hath a self propriety, else could he not be himself. . . . No man hath power over my rights and liberties and I over no man's. . . . For by natural birth all men are equally and alike born to like propriety, liberty and freedom."

As historian G. P. Gooch noted, "By its injudicious treatment of the most popular man in England, Parliament was arraying against itself a force which only awaited an opportunity to sweep it away." Lilburne's ideas inspired army radicals to draft the *Agreement of the People, for a Firme and Present Peace, upon Grounds of Common-Right*, the forerunner of modern constitutions making clear that sovereignty rests with the people. It called for holding parliamentary elections every two years, specified that representation should be proportional to population, provided freedom of religion, barred military conscription, and envisioned a rule of law: "That in all Laws made, or to be made, every person may be bound alike, and that no Tenure, Estate, Charter, Degree, Birth or place, do confer any exemption from the ordinary Course of Legall proceedings, whereunto others are subjected."

The *Agreement of the People* was the issue at the "Army debates" in Putney on October 28 and 29, 1647, where ordinary people discussed the future of their country. These radical ideas, however, threatened to undermine the harsh discipline that accounted for Cromwell's military success, so he broke up the debates. *Agreement of the People* nevertheless was a historic achievement. Never before had there been such a serious effort to resolve fundamental issues through discussion.

Lilburne, granted time away from prison while still serving a term, began organizing the first political party. His supporters identified themselves publicly by wearing sea-green ribbons. As House of Lords informer George Masterson reported, Lilburne's agents went "out into every city, town and parish (if they could possibly), of every county of the kingdom, to inform the people of their liberties and privileges, and not only to get their hands to the Petition." In January 1648, tipped off by Masterson, Parliament ordered Lilburne to stand trial for sedition and treason—and he was again imprisoned. Lilburne reported that he was saved when his wife defiantly stood between him and soldiers brandishing their swords. While in prison, he churned out more pamphlets: *A Defiance to Tyrants* (January 28), *The People's Prerogative* (February 6), *A Whip for the Present House of Lords* (February 27), *The Out-cryes of Oppressed Commons* (with Richard Overton, February 28), *The Prisoners Plea for a Habeas Corpus* (April 4), and *The Oppressed Mans Importunate and Mournfull Cryes to be Brought to the Barre of Justice* (April 7).

The Levellers presented petitions with over eight thousand signatures demanding Lilburne's release. Now, facing the prospect of renewed civil war, the House of Commons needed support from the Levellers, and on April 18, it voted to drop charges against him. Parliament voted him £3,000 as compensation for his wrongful imprisonments, but Lilburne would not accept taxpayer money.

By November 1648, Cromwell had crushed the king's forces, and many in the army wanted to execute the king. Lilburne, however, declared that liberty depended on checks and balances because he observed that the king, Parliament, and army were all pursuing their interests at the expense of everybody else. By contrast, John Milton favored hanging the king, which took place on January 30, 1649, and Milton rushed into print with a pamphlet defending the deed. Milton worked as a secretary in Cromwell's military dictatorship.

On March 28, army officers dispatched about a hundred soldiers to seize Lilburne and Overton on suspicion of writing radical pamphlets. Cromwell reportedly thundered, "I tel you, Sir, you have no other Way to deale with these men, but to break them in pieces." Sentenced to the Tower of London, they issued a new *Agreement of the People.*

Levellers circulated petitions for "honest John o' the Tower," signed by some forty thousand people. They held rallies where people displayed their sea-green ribbons and sang about "the bonny Besses in the sea-green dresses." Cromwell fumed that "the Kingdome could never be setled so long as Lilburne was alive," and he crushed the Levellers at Burford in May 1649, apparently fearing a dangerous backlash if Lilburne were executed.

Cromwell now moved to suppress the Irish, who had been revolting against English rule since 1641. In Drogheda and Wexford, on Ireland's east coast, he ordered a massacre Irish rebels would never forget, and he transferred title for vast Irish lands to English owners. Historian George Macaulay Trevelyan observed, "In Ireland as Oliver left it and as it long remained, the persecuted priests were the only leaders of the people because the English had destroyed the class of native gentry. The Cromwellian settlement rendered the Irish for centuries the most priest-led population in Europe."

Lilburne, still imprisoned in the Tower, issued another pamphlet, *The Legal Fundamentall Liberties* (June 1649), this one attacking army officers for ruling "over us arbitrarily, without declared Laws, as a conquered people." Out on bail to visit his family (two of his sons were dying from smallpox), he escalated attacks in his pamphlet *An Impeachment of High Treason against Oliver Cromwell* (July 1649), warning that with Cromwell there would be "nothing . . . but Wars, and the cutting of throats year after year."

On September 14, Attorney General Edmund Prideaux demanded to know if Lilburne had written *An Outcry of the Young Apprentices of London.* When Lilburne denied the government's right to question him, a warrant for his arrest was issued, and he was charged with high treason. Biographer Pauline Gregg reported, "There was nothing at first glance to indicate the struggle he had been through. It was apparent, however, that strife over the years had coarsened his features, that the delicacy of the young man's face had gone. The disfigurement caused by his eye injury many years before gave his face in repose a slightly saturnine look. He no longer curled his hair back from his ears, as he had done as a young man, but let it hang to his shoulders, slightly grizzled and somewhat unkempt . . . It was perhaps in the eyes and the mouth that the greatest difference showed. At twenty-three Lilburne held the simple belief that the demonstration of an injustice led to its abrogation. Seven years later disillusionment and bitter struggle had left their mark in the set of his mouth and the challenge in his eyes."

As always, Lilburne handled his own defense. Despite the judge's objections, he repeatedly told the jury that they were empowered to issue a verdict on laws as well as the facts in his case. This doctrine became known as jury nullification, meaning that an independent jury should acquit an individual guilty of breaking a law if the law is unjust. Lilburne won a stunning acquittal on October 26, 1649. But in December 1751, Parliament ordered that Lilburne be fined £7,000, banished from England, and threatened with execution if he ever returned. He crossed the English Channel on June 14, 1653, was captured by sheriffs and brought to Newgate prison. Awaiting a likely trial, he wrote another pamphlet, *Plea in Law*, in which he harangued the court about his right to see the indictment and challenged the legitimacy of the law that was the basis for it. The jury verdict was that "John Lilburne is not guilty of any crime worthy of death." He was returned to the Tower of London, then to the Castle Orgueil on the Isle of Jersey, and later to Dover Castle. At Dover Castle, he gained some peace of mind by talking with Quakers—followers of George Fox, a shoemaker's apprentice who had become convinced that divine revelation ("inner light") could come without preacher, prayer book, or ceremony.

During August 1657, while he was on parole in Eltham and visiting his wife, his health began to fail. On August 29, he died in Elizabeth's arms. He was about forty-three years old. "I shall leave this Testimony behind me," he had remarked, "that I died for the Laws and Liberties of this nation." Some four hundred people followed his plain wood casket for burial in a Bethlehem churchyard near Bishopsgate.

Although the Stuart monarchy was restored in 1660, King Charles II did not regain all the powers that his father had possessed. Royal prerogative courts like the Star Chamber never came back. Parliament, not the king, controlled taxation. This was part of John Lilburne's lasting legacy. Many of his daring demands for criminal justice reform were realized too. Historian George Macaulay Trevelyan observed, "The Puritan Revolution had enlarged the liberty of the accused subject against the prosecuting Government, as the trials of John Lilburne had shown. . . . Questions of law as well as of fact were now left to the Jury, who were free to acquit without fear of consequences;

the witnesses for the prosecution were now always brought into court and made to look on the prisoner as they spoke; witnesses for the defense might at least be summoned to appear; and the accused might no longer be interpellated by the King's Counsel, entangled in a rigorous inquisition, and forced to give evidence against himself. Slowly, through blood and tears, justice and freedom had been advancing." Added historian H. N. Brailsford, "Thanks to the daring of this stripling, English law does not aim from the first to last at the extraction of confessions. To Americans this right appeared so fundamental that they embodied it by the Fifth Amendment in the constitution of the United States." But Lilburne became a forgotten man. His pamphlets were unsigned and easily lost, and his many stirring lines were buried amid voluminous prose about specific legal cases that later generations did not care about. The next thinker to develop a bold vision of liberty was the philosopher John Locke, but Oxford University scholar Peter Laslett concluded that it was "from conversation and casual contact, not from documentary acquaintance, that Locke inherited the fruit of the radical writings of the Civil War."

In 1679, more than twenty years after Lilburne's death, the earl of Shaftsbury (Anthony Ashley Cooper), Algernon Sidney, Richard Rumbold, and their compatriots in London's Green Ribbon Club (the name recalled Leveller days) contemplated a general insurrection against tyrannical King Charles II. Shaftsbury fled to Holland, but other rebels were caught and condemned to die. In his scaffold speech, Rumbold, who had been a Leveller, affirmed Leveller principles. "I am sure there was no man born marked of God above another," he declared, "for none comes into the world with a saddle upon his back, neither any booted and spurred to ride him." Thomas Jefferson adapted Rumbold's phrasing in one of his last letters, written on June 24, 1826: "All eyes are opened, or opening, to the rights of man. The general spread of the light of science has already laid open to every view the palpable truth, that the mass of mankind has not been born with saddles on their backs, nor a favored few booted and spurred ready to ride them legitimately, by the grace of God."

English historian John Richard Green was among the few nineteenth-century authors to recognize the crucial importance of the Levellers. "For the last two hundred years," he wrote, "England has been doing little more than carrying out in a slow and tentative way the schemes of political and religious reforms which the army propounded at the close of the Civil War."

Behind many of our most fundamental civil liberties stood John Lilburne, a mere apprentice who helped develop a bold new vision of liberty, took a principled stand, risked his life, defied tyrants, and got his story out.

LIFE, LIBERTY, AND PROPERTY

DURING THE POLITICAL upheavals of the seventeenth century, when the first libertarian agenda developed, the most influential case for natural rights came from the pen of scholar John Locke. He expressed the radical view that government is morally obliged to serve people by protecting life, liberty, and property; explained the principle of checks and balances to limit government power; and favored representative government and a rule of law. He denounced tyranny and insisted that when government violates individual rights, people may legitimately rebel. These views were most fully expressed in his famous *Second Treatise Concerning Civil Government*, and they were so radical that he never dared sign his name to it. (He acknowledged authorship only in his will.) Locke's writings did much to inspire the libertarian ideals of the American Revolution, setting an example that inspired people throughout Europe, Latin America, and Asia.

Thomas Jefferson ranked Locke, along with Locke's compatriot, Algernon Sidney, as the most important thinkers on liberty. Locke helped inspire Thomas Paine's radical ideas about revolution. He fired up George Mason. From Locke, James Madison drew his most fundamental principles of liberty and government. Locke's writings were part of Benjamin Franklin's self-education, and John Adams believed that both girls and boys should learn about Locke. The French philosopher Voltaire called Locke "the man of the greatest wisdom. What he has not seen clearly, I despair of ever seeing."

Yet when Locke set out to develop his ideas, he was an undistinguished Oxford scholar. He had a brief experience with a failed diplomatic mission and was a physician who lacked traditional credentials and had just one patient. His first major work was not published until he was fifty-seven. He was distracted by asthma and other chronic ailments.

There was little in Locke's appearance to suggest greatness. He was tall and thin. According to biographer Maurice Cranston, he had a "long face, large nose, full lips and soft, melancholy eyes." Although he had a love affair which "robbed me of the use of my reason," he died a bachelor.

Nevertheless, some notable contemporaries thought highly of Locke. Mathematician and physicist Isaac Newton cherished his company. Locke helped Quaker William Penn restore his good name when he was a political fugitive, as Penn had arranged a pardon for Locke when he had been a political fugitive. The famous English physician Dr. Thomas Sydenham called him

"a man whom, in the acuteness of his intellect, in the steadiness of his judgement, in the simplicity, that is, in the excellence of his manners, I confidently
declare to have, amongst the men of our time, few equals and no superiors."

JOHN LOCKE WAS born in Somerset, England, on August 29, 1632. He was the
eldest son of Agnes Keene, daughter of a small town tanner, and John Locke,
an impecunious Puritan lawyer who served as a clerk for justices of the peace.

Locke was seventeen when parliamentary forces hanged King Charles I,
ushering in Oliver Cromwell's military dictatorship. In 1652, after graduating
from the prestigious Westminister School, Locke won a scholarship to Christ
Church, Oxford University, which trained men mainly for the clergy. In
November 1665, as a result of his Oxford connections, Locke went on a
diplomatic mission in Brandenburg. The experience was a revelation because
Brandenburg had a policy of toleration for Catholics, Calvinists, and Lutherans, and there was peace.

During the summer of 1666, the rich and influential Anthony Ashley
Cooper, earl of Shaftsbury, visited Oxford. There he met Locke, who was
then studying medicine. Cooper, a defender of religious toleration (except for
Catholics), suffered from a liver cyst that threatened to become swollen with
infection, and he asked Locke to be his personal physician. Accordingly,
Locke moved into a room at Cooper's Exeter House mansion, Westminister,
London, and when Shaftsbury's liver infection worsened, Locke supervised
successful treatment.

Shaftsbury retained Locke to analyze toleration, education, trade, and
related issues, and among other things Locke opposed government efforts to
restrict interest rates. Locke was in the thick of just about everything Shaftsbury did. Shaftsbury formed the Whig party, and Locke carried on a correspondence to help influence parliamentary elections. Shaftsbury was imprisoned
for a year in the Tower of London; then he helped pass the Habeas Corpus Act
(1679), which made it unlawful for government to detain anyone without filing
formal charges and specified that no one could be put on trial for the same
charge twice. Shaftsbury pushed exclusion bills aimed at preventing the king's
Catholic brother from royal succession.

In March 1681, Charles II dissolved Parliament, and it soon became clear
that he did not intend to summon Parliament again. Consequently, the only
way to stop Stuart absolutism was rebellion. Shaftsbury was the king's most
dangerous opponent, and Locke was at his side. He prepared an attack on
Robert Filmer's *Patriarcha, or The Natural Power of Kings Asserted* (1680),
which claimed that God sanctioned the absolute power of kings. The attack
was risky; it could easily be prosecuted as an attack on King Charles II. Pamphleteer James Tyrrell, whom Locke had met at Oxford, left unsigned his

own substantial attack on Filmer, *Patriarcha Non Monarcha or The Patriarch Unmonarch'd*, which had merely implied the right to rebel against tyrants.

Locke worked in his bookshelf-lined room at Shaftsbury's Exeter House, drawing on his experience with political action. He wrote one treatise that attacked Filmer's doctrine, denying the claim that the Bible sanctioned tyrants and that parents had absolute authority over children. He then wrote a second treatise that presented an epic case for liberty and the right of people to rebel against tyrants. He drew his principles substantially from Tyrrell, then pushed them to their radical conclusions: an explicit attack on slavery and a defense of revolution.

As Charles II intensified his campaign against rebels, Shaftsbury fled to Holland in November 1682 and died there two months later. On July 21, 1683, Locke might well have seen Oxford University burn books considered dangerous in the Bodleian Quadrangle. It was England's last book burning. Locke owned some of the outlawed titles, and when he feared his rooms would be searched, he hid his draft of the two treatises with Tyrrell. He moved out of Oxford, checked on country property he had inherited from his father, then fled to Rotterdam on September 7. The English government tried to have him extradited for trial and presumably hanging. He assumed the name Dr. van der Linden and signed letters as "Lamy" or "Dr. Lynne." Anticipating that the government might intercept mail, he protected friends by referring to them with numbers or false names.

Charles II died in February 1685, and his brother became James II. The new king began promoting Catholicism in England. He replaced Anglican church officials and sheriffs with Catholics and staffed the army with Catholic officers. All this was a threat to the English, who cherished their independence from the pope as well as from Catholic kings.

Meanwhile, Locke, still in Holland, worked on his philosophical masterpiece, *An Essay Concerning Human Understanding*, which urged people to base their convictions on observation and reason. He also worked on a letter advocating religious toleration (except for atheists, who would not swear legally binding oaths, and Catholics, loyal to a foreign power).

In June 1688, James II announced the birth of a son—and suddenly the specter of a Catholic succession loomed. Tories, the English defenders of royal absolutism, now embraced Whig ideas of rebellion. The Dutchman William of Orange, agreeing to recognize the supremacy of Parliament, crossed the English Channel on November 5, 1688, and within a month, James II fled to France. This Glorious Revolution helped secure Protestant succession and parliamentary supremacy without violence.

Locke returned home, and during the next twelve months, his major works were published. Suddenly he was famous. His *Letter Concerning Toleration*, published in October 1689, opposed persecution and called for toleration of

Anabaptists, Independents, Presbyterians, and Quakers. "The Magistrate," Locke declared, "ought not to forbid the Preaching or Professing of any Speculative Opinions in any Church, because they have no manner of relation to the Civil Rights of the Subjects. If a *Roman Catholick* believe that to be really the Body of Christ, which another man calls Bread, he does no injury thereby to his Neighbour. If a *Jew* do not believe the New Testament to be the Word of God, he does not thereby alter any thing in mens Civil Rights. If a Heathen doubt of both Testaments, he is not therefore to be punished as a pernicious Citizen." Locke's *Letter* brought replies, and he wrote two further letters in 1690 and 1692.

Locke's two treatises on government were also published in October 1689 (with a 1690 date on the title page). Although later philosophers have belittled them because Locke based his thinking on archaic notions about a state of nature, his bedrock principles endure. Locke was concerned about arbitrary power which "becomes *Tyranny,* whether those that thus use it are one or many." He defended the natural law tradition whose lineage goes back to the ancient Jews: the tradition that rulers cannot legitimately do anything they want, because moral laws apply to everyone. "Reason, which is that Law," Locke declared, "teaches all Mankind, who would but consult it, that being all equal and independent, no one ought to harm another in his Life, Health, Liberty, or Possessions." Locke envisoned a rule of law: "have a standing Rule to live by, common to every one of that Society, and made by the Legislative Power erected in it; A Liberty to follow my own Will in all things, where the Rule prescribes not; and not to be subject to the inconstant, uncertain, unknown, Arbitrary Will of another Man."

Locke established that private property is absolutely essential for liberty: "Every Man has a *Property* in his own *Person.* This no Body has any Right to but himself. The *Labour* of his Body, and the *Work* of his Hands, we may say, are properly his . . . The great and *chief end* therefore, of Mens uniting into Commonwealths, and putting themselves under Government, *is the Preservation of their Property.*" Locke believed that people legitimately turn common property into private property by mixing their labor with it, and improving it. Marxists liked to claim this meant that Locke embraced the labor theory of value, but he was talking about the basis of ownership rather than value.

He insisted that people, not rulers, are sovereign. Government, he wrote, "can never have a Power to take to themselves the whole or any part of the Subjects *Property,* without their own consent. For this would be in effect to leave them no *Property* at all." He makes his point even more explicit: rulers "must *not raise* Taxes on the Property of the People, *without the Consent of the People,* given by themselves, or their Deputies." Then he affirmed an explicit right to revolution: "Whenever the *Legislators endeavor to take away, and destroy the Property of the People,* or to reduce them to Slavery under

Arbitrary Power, they put themselves into a state of War with the People, who are thereupon absolved from any farther Obedience, and are left to the common Refuge, which God hath provided for all Men, against Force and Violence. Whensoever therefore the *Legislative* shall transgress this fundamental Rule of Society; and either by Ambition, Fear, Folly or Corruption, *endeavor to grasp* themselves, *or put into the hands of any other an Absolute Power* over the Lives, Liberties, and Estates of the People; By this breach of Trust they *forfeit the Power,* the People had put into their hands, for quite contrary ends, and it devolves to the People, who have a Right to resume their original Liberty."

To help ensure his anonymity, he dealt with the printer through a friend, Edward Clarke, who might have been the only person to know the author's identity. Locke denied rumors that he was the author and begged his friends to keep their speculations to themselves. He cut off those like James Tyrrell who persisted in talking about Locke's authorship. Locke destroyed the original manuscripts and all references to the work in his writings. His only written acknowledgment of authorship was in an addition to his will, signed a couple of weeks before he died. Ironically, the two treatises caused barely a stir during his life. Nobody bothered to attack it, as happened with Locke's by-line on religion.

Locke's byline did appear with *An Essay Concerning Human Understanding,* published in December 1689, and it established him as England's leading philosopher. He challenged the traditional doctrine that learning consists entirely of reading ancient texts and absorbing religious dogmas. Understanding the world, he maintained, requires observation. He encouraged people to think for themselves and urged that reason be the guide. This book became one of the most widely reprinted and influential works on philosophy.

In 1693, Locke published *Some Thoughts Concerning Education,* which offered many ideas as revolutionary now as they were then. He declared that education is for liberty. He believed that setting a personal example is the most effective way to teach moral standards and fundamental skills, which is why he recommended home schooling. He objected to government schools and urged parents to nurture the unique genius of each child.

Locke's friends Francis and Damaris Masham invited him to spend his last years at Oates, their manor house in North Essex, about twenty-five miles from London. He had a ground-floor bedroom and an adjoining study containing most of his 5,000-volume library. He insisted on paying: a pound per week for his servant and himself, plus a shilling a week for his horse. Locke gradually became infirm, and by October 1704, he could hardly arise to dress. Around 3:00 in the afternoon, Saturday, October 28, he died while sitting in his study with Lady Masham. He was seventy-two years old. He was buried in the High Laver churchyard.

During the 1720s, two English radical writers, John Trenchard and Thomas Gordon, popularized Locke's political ideas in *Cato's Letters,* a series of essays published in London newspapers that had a direct impact on American thinkers. Locke's influence was most apparent in the Declaration of Independence, the constitutional separation of powers, and the Bill of Rights.

Meanwhile, in France, Voltaire, the witty critic of religious intolerance, had promoted Locke's ideas in France. Baron de Montesquieu expanded on Locke's ideas about the separation of powers. Locke's doctrine of natural rights was embodied in the Declaration of the Rights of Man, but his belief in the separation of powers and the sanctity of private property never took hold in France.

Then Locke virtually vanished from intellectual debates. A conservative reaction engulfed Europe as people associated talk about natural rights with rebellion and Napoleon's wars. In England, Utilitarian philosopher Jeremy Bentham ridiculed natural rights, proposing that public policy be determined by the principle of the the greatest happiness for the greatest number. But both conservatives and utilitarians proved intellectually helpless when governments demanded more power to rob, jail, and even murder people in the name of doing good.

In the twentieth century, novelist-philosopher Ayn Rand and economist Murray Rothbard, among others, revived a compelling moral case for liberty based on natural rights and provided a meaningful moral standard for determining whether laws are just. They inspired millions as they sounded the battle cry that people everywhere are born with equal rights to life, liberty, and property. They stood on the shoulders of John Locke.

A RIGHT TO REBEL

LIKE NOBODY BEFORE him, Thomas Paine stirred ordinary people to defend their liberty. He wrote the three top-selling literary works of the eighteenth century, which inspired the American Revolution, issued a historic battle cry for individual rights, and challenged the corrupt power of government churches. His radical vision and dramatic, plainspoken style connected with artisans, servants, soldiers, merchants, farmers, and laborers alike. Paine's work breathes fire to this day.

Paine's devastating attacks on tyranny compare with the epic thrusts of Voltaire and Jonathan Swift, but unlike these authors, there was not a drop of cynicism in Paine. Ever earnest in the pursuit of liberty, he was confident that free people would fulfill their destiny. These ideas provoked explosive controversy. The English monarchy hounded him into exile and decreed the death penalty if he ever returned. Egalitarian leaders of the French Revolution ordered him into a Paris prison, and he narrowly escaped death by guillotine. And because of his critical writings on religion, he was shunned and ridiculed during his last years in America.

The founding fathers, however, recognized Paine's rare talent. Benjamin Franklin helped him get started in Philadelphia and considered him an "adopted political son." He served as an aide to George Washington and was a compatriot of Samuel Adams. James Madison was a booster, James Monroe helped spring him from French prison, and his most steadfast friend was Thomas Jefferson. Even bitter Federalist foes acknowledged Paine's contributions. "As a political gladiator," James Thomson Callender wrote, "his merit is of the highest kind. He knows, beyond most men, both when and where to strike. He deals his blows with force, coolness and dexterity."

Paine was vain, tactless, and untidy, but he nevertheless charmed people. Pioneering individualist feminist Mary Wollstonecraft wrote that "he kept everyone in astonishment and admiration for his memory, his keen observation of men and manners, his numberless ancedodes of the American Indians, of the American war, of Franklin, Washington, and even of his Majesty, of whom he told several curious facts of humour and benevolence."

Some of Paine's ideas were half-baked. To remedy injustices of the English monarchy, he talked about "progressive" taxation, "universal" education, "temporary" poor relief, and old age pensions. He naively assumed such policies would do what they were supposed to. Yet in the same work containing these proposals (*Rights of Man, Part II*) he repeatedly affirmed his libertarian principles—for example: "Great part of that order which reigns among mankind is not the effect of government. It has its origin in the principles of society and the natural constitution of man. It existed prior to government, and would exist if the formality of government was abolished."

Paine stood five feet, ten inches tall, with an athletic build. He dressed simply. He had a long nose and intense blue eyes. His friend Thomas Clio Rickman noted that "his eye, of which the painter could not convey the exquisite meaning, was full, brilliant, and singularly piercing. He had in it the 'muse of fire.'"

THOMAS PAINE WAS born on January 29, 1737, in Thetford, England. His mother, Francis Cocke, came from a local Anglican family of some distinction. His father, Joseph Pain, was a Quaker farmer and shoemaker. Although Thomas Paine was not a practicing Quaker, he endured some of the intolerance directed against Quakers.

It took Paine a while to find his calling. He left school at age twelve and began apprenticeship as a Thetford corset maker, but the work was not to his liking. Twice he ran away from home. He tried his hand as an English teacher and as a Methodist preacher, and then, in a puzzling decision, became an excise tax collector. In this job, he witnessed the resourcefulness of smugglers, resentment against tax collectors, and the pervasiveness of government corruption.

With a couple of brief interludes, Paine was a loner. Believing that marriage should be based on love, not social status or fortune, he wed Mary Lambert, a household servant, in September 1759; within a year, she died during childbirth. In March 1771, he married Elizabeth Ollive, a twenty-year-old teacher. But in 1774, while trying to earn a living as a grocer and tobacconist, he went bankrupt, and most of his possessions were auctioned off. Two months later, Paine and his wife went their separate ways.

Intellectually curious, Paine liked to browse in bookstores, attend lectures on scientific subjects, and meet thoughtful people. He befriended a London astronomer who introduced him to Benjamin Franklin, then representing colonial interests in England. Franklin seems to have convinced Paine that he could make a better life in America, and Franklin provided Paine with a letter of introduction to his son-in-law in Philadelphia.

Paine arrived in the colonies on November 30, 1774, and rented a room that looked out on the Philadelphia slave market. He spent his spare time in a bookstore operated by Robert Aiken and must have impressed the bookseller as a lively and literate man, because he was offered the job of editing Aiken's new publication, *Pennsylvania Magazine*. Paine produced at least seventeen articles, some of them vehemently attacking slavery and calling for prompt emancipation.

When a British major in Lexington, Massachusetts, ordered his troops to fire on American militiamen who gathered in front of a meeting house on April 19, 1775, the outraged Paine resolved to defend American liberty. In early September, he began making notes for a pamphlet and completed the draft in early December. Astronomer David Rittenhouse, brewer Samuel Adams, and Benjamin Franklin (who had returned from London) reviewed his work, which Paine wanted to title *Plain Truth*, but Rush recommended *Common Sense*. On January 10, 1776, *Common Sense*, written anonymously "by an Englishman," was published. Paine signed over royalties to the Continental Congress.

With simple, bold, and inspiring prose, Paine launched a furious attack on tyranny. He denounced kings as inevitably corrupted by political power. He broke with previous political thinkers when he distinguished between government compulsion and civil society where private individuals pursue productive lives. He envisioned a "continental union" based on individual rights. He answered objections from those who feared a break with England and called for a declaration to stir people into action.

Common Sense crackled with unforgettable lines: "Society is produced by our wants, and government by our wickedness." "The sun never shined on a cause of greater worth." "Now is the seed-time of Continental union." "We have every opportunity and every encouragement before us to form the noblest, purest constitution on the face of the earth." "O! ye that love mankind! Ye that dare oppose not only the tyranny but the tyrant, stand forth!" "We have it in our power to begin the world over again." "The birthday of a new world is at hand."

The first edition sold out in a couple of weeks. Soon rival editions began appearing. Printers in Boston, Salem, Newburyport, Newport, Providence, Hartford, Norwich, Lancaster, Albany, and New York issued editions. Within three months, an estimated 120,000 copies had been printed. Dr. Rush recalled that "its effects were sudden and extensive upon the American mind. It was read by public men, repeated in clubs, spouted in Schools, and in one instance, delivered from the pulpit instead of a sermon by a clergyman in Connecticut." George Washington declared that *Common Sense* offered "sound doctrine and unanswerable reasoning."

Paine's incendiary ideas leaped across borders. An edition appeared in French-speaking Quebec. John Adams reported that "Common Sense was received in France and in all Europe with Rapture." There were editions in London, Newcastle, and Edinburgh and translations into German and Danish. Copies even got into Russia. Altogether, some 500,000 copies were sold.

"Thomas Paine's *Common Sense*," reflected historian Bernard Bailyn, "is the most brilliant pamphlet written during the American Revolution, and one of the most brilliant pamphlets ever written in the English language. How it could have been produced by the bankrupt Quaker corset-maker, the some-time teacher, preacher, and grocer, and twice-dismissed excise officer who happened to catch Benjamin Franklin's attention in England and who arrived in America only fourteen months before *Common Sense* was published is nothing one can explain without explaining genius itself."

Before the publication of *Common Sense,* most colonists had hoped that their grievances with England could be resolved, but this pamphlet inspired increasing numbers of people to speak out for independence. Then the Second Continental Congress asked Thomas Jefferson to serve on a five-person committee that would draft the kind of declaration Paine had suggested in *Common Sense.*

When independence brought war, Paine enlisted as a military secretary and by year-end 1776 was with General George Washington. In the evenings, Paine began writing a new pamphlet. When he returned to Philadelphia, he took his manuscript to the *Philadelphia Journal,* which published it on December 19 as an eight-page essay, *American Crisis.* On Christmas Day 1776, George Washington read it to his soldiers, untrained, poorly paid Americans, each typically serving in the army for a year, who had already been routed by well-trained British soldiers and ruthless Hessian mercenaries. Paine's immortal opening lines: "These are the times that try men's souls. The summer soldier and the sunshine patriot will, in this crisis, shrink from the service of their country; but he that stands it *now,* deserves the love and thanks of man and woman. Tyranny, like hell, is not easily conquered; yet we have this consolation with us, that the harder the conflict, the more glorious the triumph." Within hours, Washington's fired-up soldiers gained a much-needed battle victory against British forces in Trenton.

Paine wrote a dozen more *American Crisis* essays, dealing with military and diplomatic issues as he promoted better morale. In the second essay, published on January 13, 1777, Paine coined the name "United States of America."

After the British surrendered at Yorktown, Paine was broke and wanted a government stipend for what he had done to help achieve American independence. New York State gave him a 300-acre farm in New Rochelle, about thirty miles from New York City, and Congress voted him $3,000 for war-related expenses he had paid out of pocket.

In France, he renewed his friendship with Marquis de Lafayette who had helped win the victory at Yorktown. Lafayette introduced Paine to the marquis de Condorcet, a French mathematician and influential libertarian. In England, Paine met Charles James Fox and Edmund Burke, both of whom had opposed the war against America.

The outbreak of the French Revolution in July 1789 horrified Burke, who began writing his counterrevolutionary manifesto that defended monarchy and aristocratic privilege, *Reflections on the Revolution in France,* which appeared on November 1, 1790. When Paine, who had been working on a new book about general principles of liberty, learned the gist of Burke's manifesto, he decided to revise his book as a rebuttal. He moved into a room at the Angel Inn, Islington, where he could concentrate on the project. He started work November 4th. He worked steadily, often by candlelight, for about three months, and finished the first part of *Rights of Man* on January 29, 1791—his fifty-fourth birthday. He dedicated the work affectionately to George Washington, and it was published on Washington's birthday, February 22.

While Burke impressed people with purple prose, Paine replied with plain talk. He lashed out at tyranny, denounced taxes, denied the moral legitimacy of the English monarchy and aristocracy, and declared that individuals have rights regardless of what laws might say. He embraced the Declaration of the Rights of Man and the Citizen, which affirmed, in part, "The right to property being inviolable and sacred, no one ought to be deprived of it, except in cases of evident public necessity, legally ascertained, and on condition of just indemnity." The first printing sold out in three days, the second printing within hours. There was a third printing in March 1791; a fourth printing appeared in April. Some 200,000 copies sold in England, Wales, and Scotland, and another 100,000 copies in America.

Rights of Man convinced many people to support the French Revolution and dramatic reform in England. On May 17, 1792, the British government charged Paine with seditious libel, which could be punished by hanging. Paine fled to Dover and boarded a boat for Calais, France, in September 1792, twenty minutes before a warrant for his arrest reached the port.

In France, Paine was elected Calais representative to the National Convention, which was supposed to carry out reforms; he was an ideological ally of the so-called Girondins who favored a republican government with limited powers. His adversaries were the ruthless, xenophobic Jacobins. Incredibly, Paine was considered suspect because he was born in England—even though he could be hanged if he returned there. On Christmas Eve 1793, Jacobin police hauled him away to Luxembourg Prison where he was held without trial in a cell about ten feet long by eight feet wide. On July 24, 1794, Paine's name was added to the list of prisoners who would be beheaded, but prison guards mistakenly passed by his cell when they gathered the night's victims. Three days later, rebels beheaded Maximilien-François-Marie-Isdore de Robespierre, the most fanatical promoter of Jacobin violence, and the worst of the Terror was over.

Before Paine was imprisoned, he had started his most controversial major work, *Age of Reason,* and he continued writing it behind bars. Although he commended Christian ethics, believed that Jesus was a virtuous man, and opposed the Jacobin campaign to suppress religion, he nevertheless attacked the violence and contradictions of many Bible stories. He denounced the incestuous links between church and state, insisted that authentic religious revelation came to individuals rather than established churches, defended the deist view of one God and a religion based on reason, and urged a policy of religious toleration.

Age of Reason written in a dramatic, plainspoken style that stirred strong emotions, had enormous impact. The book became a hot seller in England, and government efforts to suppress it only spurred demand. *Age of Reason* was much sought after in Germany, Hungary, and Portugal, and there were four American printings in 1794, seven in 1795, and two more in 1796. People formed societies aimed at promoting Paine's religious principles.

The U.S. minister to France, James Monroe, demanded that government officials bring Paine to trial or release him, and by November 6, 1794, gray-bearded and frail, Paine was free at last. First Consul Napoleon Bonaparte invited Paine to dinner, hoping for insights about conquering Britain. Paine recommended peace, the last thing Napoleon wanted to hear about, and they never met again. He returned to America on September 1, 1802, at age sixty-five. A Massachusetts newspaper correspondent observed: "Years have made more impression on his body than his mind. He bends a little forward, carries one hand in the other behind, when he walks. He dresses plain like a farmer, and appears cleanly and comfortably in his person. . . . His conversation is uncommonly interesting; he is gay, humorous, and full of anecdote—his memory preserves its full capacity, and his mind is irresistible."

After Napoleon gained control of Louisiana in 1800 and the Mississippi was closed to American shipping, Paine encouraged President Jefferson to propose purchasing the Louisiana territory. Alexander Hamilton thought Napoleon would never agree, but Paine knew Napoleon needed funds. In May 1803, Napoleon sold the Louisiana territory to the United States for $15 million.

Although Federalist critics savaged President Thomas Jefferson for defending Paine, he courageously invited his friend to the White House. When Jefferson's daughters, Mary and Martha, made it clear that they would rather not associate with Paine, Jefferson replied that Paine "is too well entitled to the hospitality of every American, not to cheerfully receive mine."

Paine spent his last years in poverty, finally moving into the home of his friend Marguerite de Bonneville in New York City, and he died there on June 8, 1809. She arranged for burial at his farm because no cemetery would take him. But he did not rest in peace. A decade later, English journalist William Cobbett secretly dug up the casket and shipped it to England. According to some accounts, he thought that by making it part of a shrine, he could inspire large numbers of people to push for reform of the government and the church of England. But people were not much interested in Paine's bones, and when Cobbett died in 1835, they were dispersed with his personal effects and lost.

Paine remained a forgotten founder for decades. Theodore Roosevelt summed up the prevailing view when he referred to Paine as a "filthy little atheist." The first big biography of Paine did not appear until 1892, and there remains no authoritative edition of Paine's complete work. The American bicentennial helped revive interest in him. Paperback collections of his major writings became widely available for the first time, and at least eight biographies have appeared since the late 1970s.

Perhaps a new generation is rediscovering this marvel of a man. He did not have much money, and he never had political power, yet he showed how a single-minded private individual, by making a moral case for natural rights, can arouse millions to throw off their oppressors.

A SOPHISTICATED, RADICAL VISION

WHEN VIRGINIANS REFLECT on the American Revolution, they often describe George Washington as its sword, Patrick Henry as its tongue, and Thomas Jefferson as its pen. Jefferson expressed a sophisticated, radical vision of liberty with grace and eloquence. He affirmed that all people are entitled to liberty, regardless of what laws might say. If laws do not protect liberty, he declared, then the laws are illegitimate, and people should rebel. Although Jefferson did not originate this idea, he put it in a way that set afire the imagination of people around the world. Moreover, he articulated a doctrine for strictly limiting the power of government, the most dangerous threat to liberty everywhere.

Jefferson was among the most learned men of his time. He understood historic struggles for liberty and he drew on his practical experience of serving as a representative in the Virginia House of Burgesses, the Virginia Convention, Continental Congress, and Confederation Congress, and as Governor of Virginia, Minister to France, Secretary of State, Vice President, and President of the United States.

With his gifted pen and meticulous script, Jefferson drafted more reports, resolutions, legislation, and related official documents than any other founding father. Above all, he wrote letters, probably more than his illustrious contemporaries, and a large number of these letters survive—some eighteen thousand. He corresponded with many other leading lights of liberty, including Thomas Paine, John Adams, Benjamin Franklin, Patrick Henry, marquis de Lafayette, James Madison, George Mason, Jean-Baptiste Say, Madame de Staël, and George Washington. Most of the famous Jefferson quotations are from letters.

Jefferson was among the most instantly recognizable founding fathers. He stood about six feet two inches tall, was thin, and had reddish hair, hazel eyes, and a freckled complexion. As a young man, he was a snappy dresser, but in later years he neglected his appearance, reportedly greeting morning visitors in worn slippers and a worn coat when he was president.

He had a reserved manner, even with his children, but he was a steadfast friend, counting James Madison, Thomas Paine, and John Adams among his friends. In an affectionate letter, Adams commended him for "friendly warmth that is natural and habitual to you."

Jefferson set a new individualist standard for virtue. The old standard, deriving from ancient Greece and Rome, was that virtue depended on one's role as a citizen—voting, running for office, doing public work. Although Jefferson enjoyed a distinguished public career, he had an entirely different idea: that what counts most is the way individuals conduct their private lives—their contribution to civil society, that is, rather than politics. He was industrious, honest, kind, and discreet, with few exceptions keeping critical opinions of people to himself. He set aside political differences to nourish relationships with people he loved. Jefferson pursued beauty by designing his home and gardens at Monticello, and knowledge by collecting books and exploring scientific discoveries. He helped others improve their lives by establishing the University of Virginia.

For four decades after he left the White House, Jefferson's ideas dominated U.S. government policy, and he was revered as the "Sage of Monticello." Then during the Civil War, public opinion turned against Jefferson, because he had defended the right of secession and independence. He fell even further out of favor during the "progressive" era, when reformers imagined that every problem could be fixed by giving the federal government more power. President Theodore Roosevelt scorned Jefferson as a "scholarly, timid, and shifting doctrinaire." Hamilton, apostle of government power, took over his place as the most revered founder.

The bicentennial of Jefferson's birth, 1943, got many Americans thinking about his life, and his reputation experienced a comeback, marked by construction of the Jefferson Memorial in Washington, D.C., emblazoned with his stirring oath: "I have sworn upon the altar of God eternal hostility against every form of tyranny over the mind of man." Historian Merrill D. Peterson explained, "The man glorified in the monument had transcended politics to become the hero of civilization. He had come to stand for ideals of beauty, science, learning, and conduct, for a way of life enriched by the heritage of the ages yet distinctly American in outline. The range of his appeal, if not its intensity, increased with the disclosure of his varied and ubiquitous genius."

But since about 1960, Jefferson has again come under attack. Constitutional historian Leonard Levy, for instance, cited episodes when Jefferson suppressed civil liberties, especially during his terms as Virginia governor and U.S. president. Historian J. G. A. Pocock portrayed him as a backward-looking country aristocrat who feared cities and commerce and was out of touch with the modern world. Historian Bernard Bailyn called Jefferson an unthinking "stereotype." DNA testing seems to confirm charges that Jefferson fathered children with his attractive young slave, Sally Hemings. And many historians expressed disgust that Jefferson owned slaves, bred slaves, gave away slaves as wedding presents, and never liberated any slaves. He reportedly owned 180 slaves when he wrote the Declaration of Independence and had 260 when he died. Historian Page Smith claimed that because Jefferson did not always live up to his expressed ideals, he was a fraud, and his ideals were no good.

Although Jefferson had personal failings—in the case of slavery, a monstrous one—they do not invalidate the philosophy of liberty he championed (any more than Einstein's personal failings are evidence against his theory of relativity). Jefferson's accomplishments and philosophy of liberty must be recognized for their monumental importance.

THOMAS JEFFERSON WAS born April 13, 1743, on a plantation along the Rivanna River in Virginia. He was the third child of Peter Jefferson, who seems to have been a self-educated, enterprising man—surveyor, plantation operator, judge, and representative in the Virginia House of Burgesses. His mother, Jane Randolph, brought aristocratic blood from a prosperous Virginia family. Peter Jefferson died at age fourty-nine, when Jefferson was fourteen. The estate consisted of properties totaling 7,500 acres, 53 slaves, 21 horses, and other farm animals, but his son did not become involved in managing the properties until he turned twenty-one. His business was learning.

Jefferson was tutored by Anglican ministers in Latin, Greek, science, and natural history. For two years, he attended William and Mary, America's second-oldest college (after Harvard), located in Williamsburg, Virginia. Then he began studying English common law. He wrote summaries of English legal classics, such the seventeenth-century scholar Edward Coke's *Institutes of the Laws of England,* and began practicing law in 1767. Each year he handled more cases. Jefferson based his briefs on natural law as well as written law, writing in a 1770 case, for example, that "under the law of nature, all men are born free, every one comes into the world with a right to his own person, which includes the liberty of moving and using it at his own will." He was influenced as well by John Locke's *Two Treatises on Government,* Adam Ferguson's *An Essay on the History of Civil Society,* and baron de Montesquieu's complete works.

Williamsburg was the capital of Virginia, the largest and richest colony, and Jefferson was drawn to politics. His political career began when he was twenty-five years old in December 1768. Elected to the Virginia House of Burgesses, Jefferson helped form a committee of correspondence for coordinating resistance to British taxes. Early on, he displayed a facility for expression. His first effort was a reply to a speech by Virginia's imperious royal governor, John Dunmore. Angered at the contentious proceedings, Dunmore declared on May 26, 1774, that the House of Burgesses was no longer in session. The next day, legislators met at Raleigh Tavern, in what became known as the "Williamsburg convention," to continue their deliberations.

In 1774, Jefferson published his first work. The twenty-three-page pamphlet, *A Summary View of the Rights of British America,* was a legal brief that boldly declared that Parliament did not have the right to rule the colonies. He asked, "Shall these [colonial] governments be dissolved, their property annihilated, and their people reduced to a state of nature, at the imperious breath of a body of men whom they never saw, in whom they never confided, and over whom they have no powers of punishment or removal, let their crimes against the American public be ever so great?"

The Williamsburg convention considered Jefferson too junior for the delegation to the First Continental Congress, which met from September 5 to October 26, 1774, but delegates read and were surely influenced by *A Summary View.* They affirmed the individual right to "life, liberty and property," insisted that only American legislatures could legitimately levy taxes on Americans, and demanded an end to British taxes and trade restrictions imposed since war with France had ended in 1763.

By March 1775, Jefferson was named a delegate to the Second Continental Congress in Philadelphia and shortly after set to work drafting documents. With John Dickinson, he drafted the *Declaration of the Causes and Necessity of Taking Up Arms,* which George Washington would issue, and he worked with Benjamin Franklin, Richard Henry Lee, and John Adams on a report about responding to Parliament's latest proposals. Both documents were published in colonial newspapers without Jefferson's by-line, but within a month and a half after he had arrived, members of the Continental Congress recognized he was a leading figure.

When Richard Henry Lee urged the Continental Congress to adopt his resolution for independence on June 7, 1776, Jefferson, Franklin, John Adams, Roger Sherman, and Robert K. Livingston were assigned to prepare a statement announcing and justifying independence. The thirty-three-year-old Jefferson spent the next seventeen days drafting it on the second floor of a Philadelphia home belonging to bricklayer Jacob Graff, where he rented several rooms. They were at Market and Seventh streets. Jefferson wrote in an armchair pulled up to a dining table. He probably scratched away with a goose quill pen, a writing implement that is quite difficult to use. By habit, he did most of his writing between about 6:00 P.M. and midnight. He was done in seventeen days.

Like *A Summary View,* the Declaration of Independence was mostly a legal brief listing a succession of complaints against England. Jefferson directed his case against George III rather than Parliament, and he provided a philosophical justification for the revolution. In just 111 words, he expressed ideas that would inspire people everywhere: "We hold these truths to be self-evident, that all men are created equal, that they are endowed by their Creator with certain unalienable rights, that among these are Life, Liberty and the pursuit of Happiness. That to secure these rights, Governments are instituted among Men, deriving their just powers from the consent of the governed. That whenever any Form of Government becomes destructive of these ends, it is the Right of the People to alter or abolish it, and to institute new Government, laying its foundation on such principles, and organizing its powers in such form, as to them shall seem most likely to effect their Safety and Happiness." This was radical stuff—radical for Jefferson's day, as subsequent struggles with Federalists made clear, too radical for Abraham Lincoln, who forcibly resisted the secession of southern states; and still radical today, since few Americans talk much about the right of armed rebellion against government.

Jefferson later explained his aims: "To place before mankind the common sense of the subject, in terms so plain and firm as to command their assent, and to justify ourselves in the independent stand we are compelled to take. Neither aiming at originality of principle or sentiment, nor yet copied from any particular and previous writing, it was intended to be an expression of the American mind, and to give to that expression the proper tone and spirit called for by the occasion."

All colonial delegates except those from New York, who initially abstained, voted for Lee's independence resolution on July 2. In the ensuing three-day debate on the draft of the Declaration, the Continental Congress voted to cut about a quarter of the text and insisted on many minor changes. Deferring to delegates from Georgia and South Carolina, and perhaps delegates from some northern colonies that had engaged in the slave trade, the Continental Congress cut Jefferson's extended attack on George III for not outlawing the slave trade. On July 4, the delegates approved the Declaration of Independence, and on August 2, fifty men officially signed what was to become the most important document in American history. (Five more men added their signatures later.) The Declaration proclaimed the birth of a nation and expressed a passion for liberty with unforgettable eloquence.

Jefferson served as Revolutionary War governor of Virginia, raising money and cobbling together defenses against the British. Moreover, thanks to his efforts, Virginia became the first to achieve complete separation of church and state.

Amid these public crises, Jefferson endured shocks at home. He and his wife, Martha, had three children die in infancy. On September 6, 1782, Martha died at age thirty-three from childbirth complications; they had been married ten years. Deeply depressed, Jefferson stayed in his room for three weeks. Then for several more weeks, he spent nearly every day alone, riding his horse through the woods around Monticello. It was fellow Virginian James Madison who coaxed Jefferson back into public life.

Jefferson went on to do much more for liberty during his phenomenal career. He represented American interests in Paris while the Constitutional Convention conducted its epic debates, but through correspondence he helped convince James Madison, architect of the Constitution, to support adoption of a bill of rights. As secretary of state in George Washington's cabinet, Jefferson was horrified at Alexander Hamilton's scheming to subvert the Constitution and expand federal power. Jefferson became convinced that he must seek the presidency. After a bitter campaign against president John Adams, he won in 1800. He cut taxes and spending and paid off a third of the national debt. When Spain blocked access to the Mississippi and ceded it to Napoleon, then conquering Europe, Jefferson moved to purchase the Louisiana territory, although he could not defend the policy on constitutional grounds. His presidency closed on a sour note: frustrated by British seizures of American sailors and goods, he declared a trade embargo, which backfired.

After his second term, Jefferson retired to Monticello, his beloved mountaintop mansion near Charlottesville, Virginia. Here he planned the University of Virginia, played with his thirteen grandchildren, struggled with his money-losing properties, and wrote many luminous letters. He explained his exhilarating vision of liberty, perhaps his most precious legacy to the world. He insisted that liberty is impossible without secure private property: "A right to property is founded in our natural wants, in the means with which we are endowed to satisfy these wants, and the right to what we acquire by those means without violating the similiar rights of other sensible beings." He gracefully rejected envious appeals to seize wealth: "To take from one, because it is thought his own industry and that of his fathers had acquired too much in order to spare to others who, or whose fathers have not exercised equal industry and skill, is to violate arbitrarily the principle of association, the guarantee to everyone a free exercise of his industry and the fruits acquired by it." And he urged Americans to pursue peace through free trade. "It should be our endeavor," he wrote, "to cultivate the peace and friendship of every nation. . . . Our interest will be to throw open the doors of commerce, and to knock off all its shackles."

Personally, the most heartening experience of Jefferson's last years was his reconciliation with John Adams. It was the idea of Benjamin Rush, a Philadelphia physician and fellow signer of the Declaration of Independence. In January 1811, Rush wrote to Jefferson, reminiscing about Revolutionary days and Adams's contributions. Although Jefferson and Adams became bitter rivals for the presidency, Adams had later defended Jefferson against attacks from fanatical Federalists. Jefferson, almost sixty-nine, told Rush that although he was wary of the suspicious and envious Adams, then seventy-six years old, he recognized what Adams had done for American liberty. Not long afterward, a couple of Jefferson's Virginia friends visited Adams and heard him declare: "I always loved Jefferson, and still love him." Word got back to Jefferson, who was thrilled.

Adams ended up writing the first letter, on January 1, 1812, and Jefferson replied: "I now salute you with unchanged affections and respect." Soon correspondence was flowing between Quincy, Massachusetts, Adams's home, and Monticello. The two men talked about their health, books, history, and current affairs. They touched on past political disagreements, Adams's persistent pessimism, and Jefferson's enduring optimism. Above all, they talked about the American Revolution, which both men were immensely proud of. "Crippled wrists and fingers make writing slow and laborious," Jefferson confided in October 1823. "But, while writing to you, I lose the sense of these things, in the recollection of ancient times, when youth and health made happiness out of every thing."

Before Jefferson slipped into a coma on July 3, 1826, he asked: "Is it the Fourth?" He died on July 4, at about 12:20 P.M., a half-century after the glorious Declaration. In Quincy, some five hundred miles away, John Adams was fading too. Around noon on July 4, some six hours before he died, he managed a few words: "Thomas Jefferson still survives." Indeed he does, in the hearts and minds of millions everywhere who cherish liberty

EQUAL RIGHTS

IN WESTERN EUROPE during the late eighteenth century, single women had little protection under the law, and married women lost their legal identity. Women could not retain a lawyer, sign a contract, inherit property, vote, or have rights over their children. As Oxford law professor William Blackstone noted in his influential *Commentaries on the Laws of England* (1758), "The husband and wife are one person in law; that is, the very being or legal existence of the woman is suspended during the marriage or at least is incorporated and consolidated into that of the husband: under whose wing, protection and cover, she performs every thing."

Then along came passionate, bold Mary Wollstonecraft, who caused a sensation by writing *A Vindication of the Rights of Woman* (1792). She declared that both women and men are human beings endowed with unalienable rights to life, liberty, and the pursuit of happiness. She called for women to get educated, and insisted that women should be free to enter business, pursue professional careers, and vote if they wished. "I speak of the improvement and emancipation of the whole sex," she declared. "Let woman share the rights, and she will emulate the virtues of man; for she must grow more perfect when emancipated."

Wollstonecraft spoke from the heart. Although she was reasonably well read, she drew more from her own tumultuous experience: "There is certainly an original defect in my mind," she confessed, "for the cruelest experience will not eradicate the foolish tendency I have to cherish, and expect to meet with, romantic tenderness."

She dared do what no other woman had done: pursue a career as a full-time professional writer on serious subjects without an aristocratic sponsor. "I am then going to be the first of a new genus," she reflected. It was a harsh struggle, because women were traditionally cherished for their domestic service, not their minds. Wollstonecraft developed her skills on meager earnings. She dressed plainly and seldom ate meat, and when she had wine, it was in a teacup, because she could not afford a wine glass.

Contemporaries noted Wollstonecraft's provocative presence: thin, medium height, brown hair, haunting brown eyes, and a soft voice. "Mary was without being a dazzling beauty, yet of a charming grace," recalled a German admirer. "Her face, so full of expression, presented a style of beauty beyond that of merely regular features. There was enchantment in her glance, her voice, and her movements."

MARY WOLLSTONECRAFT WAS born on April 27, 1759, in London, the second child and eldest daughter of Elizabeth Dixon, who hailed from Ballyshannon, Ireland. Mary's father, Edward John Wollstonecraft, was a handkerchief weaver. The family moved seven times in ten years as their finances deteriorated and Edward drank to excess.

Mary's formal schooling was limited, but one of her friends in Hoxton, outside London, had a respectable library, and Mary spent considerable time exploring it. Through these friends, she met Fanny Blood, two years older and skilled at sewing, drawing, watercolors, and the piano, and she inspired Mary to take the initiative to cultivate her mind.

Spurred by family financial problems, Wollstonecraft resolved somehow to make her own way. At age nineteen, she got a job as live-in helper for a widow. She then tried, but failed, to establish a school at Islington, North London. Then she, her sisters Eliza and Everina, and Fanny Blood started a school nearby at Newington Green, but it too eventually failed.

Wollstonecraft's discouraging experiences were compounded by the death of her mother and Fanny Blood. She then assumed primary responsibility for taking care of her alcoholic father. Through the Newington school experience, however, Wollstonecraft had met many local Dissenters whose religious beliefs put them outside the tax-supported Anglican church. Among them was minister and moral philosopher Richard Price, who was in touch with Thomas Jefferson, Benjamin Franklin, marquis de Condorcet, and other radical thinkers.

She was in desperate shape. As biographer Claire Tomalin explained, "Mary was homeless again, without a job or a reference; she had nothing to live on, and she was in debt to several people. She had no marriage prospects."

Finally Wollstonecraft wrote a pamphlet on education and submitted it to Joseph Johnson, the radical publisher and bookseller with a shop at St. Paul's Churchyard. Johnson was a forty-nine-year-old, slight-of-build, modest, asthmatic bachelor who told Wollstonecraft that she had talent and could succeed if she worked hard. He published her pamphlet in 1786 as *Thoughts on the Education of Daughters; with Reflections on Female Conduct, in the More Important Duties of Life*. Sales were negligible, but the work launched Wollstonecraft's literary career. She sent her author's fee to the impoverished Blood family and redoubled her efforts.

Johnson helped Wollstonecraft find lodgings, advanced her money when needed, dealt with her creditors, helped her cope with her father's chaotic situation, and calmed her bouts of depression. By 1788, he offered her steady work. She translated books from French and German into English and served as an assistant editor and writer for his new journal, *Analytical Review*. She contributed to it until her death, perhaps as many as two hundred articles on fiction, education, sermons, travelogues, and children's books. In the course of working for Johnson, she met more radicals who visited him, including William Blake, Swiss painter Henry Fuseli, Johnson's publishing partner, Thomas Christie, philosopher William Godwin, and passionate pamphleteer Thomas Paine. Wollstonecraft dominated the conversations. "I heard her very frequently," Godwin recalled, "when I wished to hear Paine."

The outbreak of the French Revolution in July 1789 triggered explosive controversy. In November, radical political philosopher Richard Price gave a talk before the Society for Commemorating the Glorious Revolution of 1688, defending the right of French people to rebel and suggesting that the English should be able to choose their rulers—an obvious challenge to the hereditary monarchy. He alarmed Edmund Burke, a member of Parliament known for having defended the American Revolution. Now Burke wrote *Reflections on the Revolution in France* (November 1790), a rhetorically brilliant attack on natural rights and a defense of monarchy and aristocracy.

Burke's ideas, as well as his swipes at Price, made Wollstonecraft indignant. Drawing on the ideas of John Locke and Price, she rushed into print with *A Vindication of the Rights of Men*, among the earliest of some thirty replies to Burke. Although this polemic was repetitious and disorganized and Wollstonecraft overdid her attacks on Burke as vain, unprincipled, and insensitive, she had an impact. She faulted Burke for being blind to poverty—"Misery, to reach your heart, I perceived, must have its cap and bells"—and denounced injustices of the British constitution, which had evolved during the "dark days of ignorance, when the minds of men were shackled by the grossest prejudices and most immoral superstition." She lashed out as well at arbitrary government power: "Security of property! Behold, in a few words, the definition of English liberty. . . . But softly—it is only the property of the rich that is secure; the man who lives by the sweat of his brow has no asylum from oppression; the strong man may enter—when was the castle of the poor sacred?—and the base informer steal him from the family that depend on his industry for subsistence. . . . I cannot avoid expressing my surprise that when you recommended our form of government as a model, you did not caution the French against the arbitrary custom of pressing men for the sea service." Wollstonecraft's work (and everyone else's for that matter) was later dwarfed by Thomas Paine's far more powerful reply to Burke, *The Rights of Man*, but she had established herself as an author to reckon with.

Wollstonecraft had generally supposed that when revolutionaries spoke of "man," they were using shorthand for all humanity. But on September 10, 1791, Tallyrand, former bishop of Autun, advocated government schools that would end at eighth grade for girls but continue for boys. It was clear to Wollstonecraft that despite all the talk about equal rights, the French Revolution was not intended to help women much. She began planning her most famous work, *A Vindication of the Rights of Woman*, which went for beyond previous authors on women's issues. Johnson published it in three volumes on January 3, 1792. It sold out within a year, and Johnson issued a second edition. An American edition and translations into French and German followed. "Taxes on the very necessaries of life," she wrote, "enable an endless tribe of idle princes and princesses to pass with stupid pomp before a gaping crowd, who almost worship the very parade which costs them so dear." She specifically cited laws that "make an absurd unit of a man and his wife; and then, by the easy transition of only considering him as responsible, she is reduced to a mere cipher . . . how can a being be generous who has nothing of its own? or virtuous who is not free?"

Wollstonecraft issued the first call for woman suffrage: "I really think that women ought to have representatives, instead of being arbitrarily governed without having any direct share allowed them in the deliberations of government." And she attacked those like collectivist Jean-Jacques Rousseau who wanted to keep women down. Education, she believed, could be the salvation of women: "The exercise of their understanding is necessary, there is no other foundation for independence of character; I mean explicitly to say that they must bow only to the authority of reason, instead of being the modest slaves of opinion." She insisted that women be taught serious subjects, like reading, writing, arithmetic, botany, natural history, and moral philosophy, and she recommended vigorous physical exercise to help stimulate the mind. In a call to eliminate obstacles to the advancement of women, she asserted, "liberty is the mother of virtue, and if women be, by their very constitution, slaves, and not allowed to breathe the sharp invigorating air of freedom, they must ever languish like exotics, and be reckoned beautiful flaws of nature."

She envisioned a future when women could pursue virtually any career opportunities: "Though I consider that women in the common walks of life are called to fulfill the duties of wives and mothers, by religion and reason, I cannot help lamenting that women of a superior cast have not a road open by which they can pursue more extensive plans of usefulness and independence. . . . How many women thus waste life away the prey of discontent, who might have practiced as physicians, regulated a farm, managed a shop, and stood erect, supported by their own industry, instead of hanging their heads surcharged with the dew of sensibility."

When Wollstonecraft crossed the English Channel so she could see the French Revolution for herself, she was welcomed by Thomas Paine. She sided with liberal Girondins, who, including Condorcet, favored a constitutionally limited government and equal rights for women. But she was horrified at how fast the totalitarian Jacobins pursued the Reign of Terror.

Wollstonecraft had a hard time applying her liberating ideas to her own life. She became infatuated with the eccentric genius Henry Fuseli, but he was married and brushed her off after an extended flirtation. While in France, she fell in love with an adventurer named Gilbert Imlay, a schemer always seeking to strike it rich. They had a daughter, Fanny, but he lost interest in both of them and walked out. Wollstonecraft attempted suicide twice.

While recovering from despair over Imlay, she took a three-month break with Fanny in Scandinavia and produced one of her most poignant works, *Letters Written During a Short Residence in Sweden, Norway and Denmark,* addresssed to the unnamed American father of her child. They provide a travelogue laced with commentary on politics, philosophy, and her personal life. For example, she tempered her hopes for social change after the terror and wrote: "An ardent affection for the human race makes enthusiastic characters eager to produce alterations in laws and governments prematurely. To render them useful and permanent, they must be the growth of each particular soil, and the gradual fruit of the ripening understanding of the nation, matured by time, not forced by an unnatural fermentation." William Godwin remarked, "If ever there was a book calculated to make a man in love with its author, this appears to me to be the book."

Wollstonecraft decided to pursue her acquaintance with Godwin, calling on him in April 1796. He had a large head, deep-set eyes, and a thin voice. "He seems to have had some charm which his enemies could not detect or his friends define, but which had a real influence on those who attained his close friendship," reported Godwin biographer George Woodcock. Like Wollstonecraft, he had started a school, but his ideas were too radical, and the effort failed. His literary career had begun with a dull political biography, a book of sermons, and some potboiler novels. Then London publisher George Robinson offered to pay Godwin enough of an advance that he could work out his philosophy, and the result was *Enquiry Concerning Political Justice* (1793), which described his vision of a harmonious society without laws or war and established him as England's foremost radical thinker. He couragously spoke out against the British government's campaign to suppress the corresponding societies, which were debating clubs interested in revolutionary ideas, wrote public letters supporting defendants, and charged that the government's campaign was illegal since none of the defendants had committed revolutionary acts of violence. His writings won widespread sympathy for the defendants, and further prosecution was abandoned.

At the time Wollstonecraft called, Godwin was a forty-two-year-old bachelor courting Amelia Alderson, a doctor's daughter. But he was intrigued with Wollstonecraft despite his initial impression that she talked too much, and he invited her to a dinner party the following week. Included were James Mackintosh and Dr. Samuel Parr, both of whom had written rebuttals to Burke's *Reflections on the Revolution in France.*

After Alderson rejected Godwin, he became more responsive to Wollstonecraft, and her passion overwhelmed him. "It was friendship melting into love," he recalled. Wollstonecraft was haunted by fear of another betrayal, but Godwin reassured her that he longed for a relationship between equals, and her passion surged again. "It is a sublime tranquility," she wrote him, "I have felt it in your arms." By December, she was pregnant. Both Wollstonecraft and Godwin had criticized marriage as a vehicle for exploitation, but they nevertheless married on March 29, 1797. She rejoiced that she had found true love at last.

She went into labor during the early morning of Wednesday, August 30th. She was attended by one Mrs. Blenkinsop, an experienced midwife. After 11 P.M. that night, a daughter was born—Mary, who grew up to be Mary Shelley, author of *Frankenstein.* For a while, it appeared things were alright, but three hours later, Mrs. Blenkinsop notified Godwin that the placenta still hadn't come out of the womb. The longer the placenta remained, the greater the risk of infection. Godwin called a Dr. Poignand who reached into the womb, removing much of the placenta. Wollstonecraft reported that the procedure was excruciatingly painful.

That Sunday, she began suffering chills, an ominous sign of infection. Doctors offered wine to help ease the pain, and they had puppies draw milk from her breasts—presumably an effort to stimulate her body to eject the remains of the placenta. Wollstonecraft continued to decline. She died Sunday morning, September 10, a little before eight. Godwin was so overcome that he did not attend the funeral, held at St. Pancras Church where they had been married just five months before. She was buried in the churchyard.

Soon afterward, ever-loyal publisher Joseph Johnson issued Godwin's edition of the *Posthumous Works of the Author of a Vindication of the Rights of Woman,* together with Godwin's candid memoir about her. Although Godwin believed that telling all would boost her reputation, it unleashed a firestorm of controversy, and her unsettled personal life became an easy excuse to belittle her ideas.

Decades later Virginia Woolf remarked about Wollstonecraft, "We hear her voice and trace her influence even now among the living." American crusaders for equal rights like Margaret Fuller, Lucretia Mott, and Elizabeth Cady Stanton were all inspired by *A Vindication of the Rights of Woman.*

Wollstonecraft established the individualist roots of equal rights. She took responsibility for her life and educated herself, and she showed how women can succeed. She urged everyone to achieve their human potential. She spoke out for vital economic liberties, demanded justice, and championed relationships based on mutual respect and love.

THE SIN OF SLAVERY

⚜

WILLIAM LLOYD GARRISON was the greatest publicist for the emancipation of American slaves. He did more than anybody else to make slavery a burning issue.

While Anthony Benezet, Thomas Paine, and others had spoken out against slavery long before Garrison was born, there had never been an American abolitionist movement. Indeed, in the late eighteenth century, it appeared that American slavery was dying out. Starting with Vermont in 1777, one northern state after another abolished slavery. Then demand for cheap cotton soared, Eli Whitney's gin (1793) provided a more efficient way to process it, the Louisiana Purchase (1803) increased the amount of land to grow it on— and the number of American slaves soared from around 500,000 during the Revolutionary War to about 4 million by the Civil War.

When Garrison resolved to fight slavery, two antislavery views prevailed: that slavery should be ended gradually and that slaves should be colonized back to Africa. He focused on immediate emancipation without compensation to slaveholders, and in a few years that became the battle cry of American abolitionists. As his compatriot Wendell Phillips explained, "Garrison was the first man to begin a movement designed to annihilate slavery. He announced the principle, arranged the method, gathered the forces, enkindled the zeal, started the argument, and finally marshalled the nation for and against the system."

Garrison was a bold man of action. With just a few dollars in his pocket, he founded and for thirty-five years edited the best-known abolitionist newspaper, *The Liberator,* which *Uncle Tom's Cabin* author Harriet Beecher Stowe praised for "its frankness, fearlessness, truthfulness, and independence." Garrison organized the New England Anti-Slavery Society, which launched the abolitionist movement; was a founder of the American Anti-Slavery Society; and traveled continuously to speak about the horrors of slavery. He brought over the great English antislavery orator George Thompson, and recruited Wendell Phillips and Frederick Douglass, who became the most famous abolitionist orators.

Garrison needed considerable courage, because most people in the North did not want to hear about the slavery issue. Antislavery talk threatened to disrupt business and split the Union; and besides, even people who opposed slavery did not generally like blacks. Garrison was jailed in Baltimore; North

Carolina indicted him for provoking slave revolts; the Georgia legislature offered $5,000 for anybody who brought him back to their state for trial and probable hanging; six Mississippi slaveholders offered $20,000 for anyone who could deliver Garrison; proslavery advocates put up a nine-foot-high gallows in front of Garrison's house; and a Boston mob tried to lynch him.

Nobody else blasted slavery like Garrison. "And what has brought our country to the verge of ruin," he wrote, "THE ACCURSED SYSTEM OF SLAVERY! To sustain that system, there is a general willingness to destroy LIBERTY OF SPEECH and of the PRESS, and to mob or murder all who oppose it. In the popular fury against the advocates of a bleeding humanity, every principle of justice, every axiom of liberty, every feeling of humanity—all the fundamental axioms of republican government are derided and violated with fatal success." This provocative language, however, dismayed many people, and he was accused of setting back the abolitionist movement. But proposals for gradual emancipation had been voted down everywhere in the South. Historian William E. Cain observed, "There is no proof that Garrison slowed down reforms by slave owners of their system. . . . It was not the kind of discussion of slavery that Garrison fostered, but any discussion at all, that proslavery forces were concerned about."

Garrison had an exhilarating vision: natural rights. He frequently cited the Declaration of Independence, and declared that "black children possess the same inherent and unalienable rights as ours." He crusaded as well for women's rights and peace, and the emancipation of slaves. He defended persecuted Chinese immigrants. And he wrote: "I avow myself to be a radical free trader, even to the extent of desiring the abolition of all custom-houses, as now constituted, throughout the world. That event is far distant, undoubtedly, but I believe it will come with the freedom and enlightenment of mankind."

Garrison affirmed the harmony of social cooperation in a free society: "There is a prevalent opinion that . . . the poor and vulgar are taught to consider the opulent as their natural enemies. Where is the evidence that our wealthy citizens, as a body, are hostile to the interests of the laboring classes? It is not in their commercial enterprises, which whiten the ocean with canvas and give employment to a useful and numerous class of men. It is not found in the manufacturing establishments, which multiply labor and cheapen the necessities of the poor. It is not found in the luxuries of their tables, or the adornments of their dwellings, for which they must pay in proportion to their extravagance."

Liberty was the keynote of his personal life. His wife, Helen, whom he married in 1834, was the daughter of a Connecticut abolitionist. They moved to a little place they called "Freedom's Cottage" in Roxbury, near Boston, and they named most of their children after abolitionists: Wendell Phillips,

George Thompson, Charles Follen, Francis Jackson, and Elizabeth Pease. Another son was named after Garrison, a daughter after Helen. Garrison and his wife were together until her death in 1876.

Garrison had a big bald head and blue eyes behind steel-rimmed glasses. Essayist Ralph Waldo Emerson described him as "a virile speaker." Joseph Copley, editor of a Pittsburgh religious newspaper, recalled that Garrison "was a quiet, gentle and I might say handsome man—a gentleman, indeed, in every sense of the word." English abolitionist Harriet Martineau thought he "had a good deal of the Quaker air; and his speech is deliberate like a quaker's but gentle as a woman's. . . . Every conversation I had with him confirmed my opinion that sagacity is the most striking attribute" Wendell Phillips avowed, "Such is my conviction of the soundness of his judgment and his rare insight into all the bearings of our cause, that I distrust my own deliberate judgment, when it leads me to a different conclusion from his."

WILLIAM LLOYD GARRISON was born in Newburyport, Massachusetts, on December 10, 1805, the son of Frances Maria Lloyd and Abijah Garrison. His mother was descended from Irish immigrants, and his father was a red-bearded, hard-drinking sea captain who was seldom at home and left for good after he lost his job because of the 1807 Embargo Act. Garrison's mother struggled to make ends meet as a nurse, and she taught her children moral values.

In 1818 Garrison began an apprenticeship at the *Newburyport Herald.* He seems to have been horrified by newspaper advertisements, placed by slave owners, that told how to identify runaway slaves—for instance; "From being whipped, has scars on his back, arms and thighs . . . stamped N.E. on the breast and having both small toes cut off . . . seriously injured by a pistol shot . . . branded on the left cheek, thus 'R' . . . a ring of iron on his left foot . . . a large neck iron."

Southern slavery was enforced by Black Codes, which, writes historian Milton Meltze, "surrounded the slave with a wall of prohibitions. [A slave] could not leave the plantation without a pass. He could not carry arms. He could not gamble. He could not blow a horn or beat a drum. He could not smoke in public or swear. He could not assemble with other slaves unless a white were present. He could not walk with a cane or make a 'joyful demonstration.' He could not ride in a carriage except as a servant. He could not buy or sell goods except as his master's agent. He could not keep dogs, horses, sheep, or cattle. He could not visit a white or a free black's home or entertain them in his home. He could not live in a place separate from his master. He could not be taught to read or write. He could not get, hold, or pass on any 'incendiary' literature." The pro-slavery Illinois senator Stephen A. Douglas admitted, "Slavery cannot exist a day or an hour anywhere, unless it is supported by local police regulations."

In 1826, Garrison became editor of the *Newburyport Free Press*, and on June 8, he published a poem by a shy, eighteen-year-old John Greenleaf Whittier from Haverhill, Massachusetts. Whittier was proud of his Quaker heritage: German Quakers from Philadelphia had organized the first protest against slavery back in 1688, and no Quakers had owned slaves since 1777. Whittier was inspired by John Milton's *Areopagetica* (1643), the eloquent early case for freedom of the press, and by the poems of Lord Byron who had died fighting for Greek independence.

In March 1828, Garrison met a thin, stoop-shouldered, red-haired Quaker saddle-maker, Benjamin Lundy, who promoted colonization—as shipping blacks back to Haiti and Africa—and invited Garrison to edit his newspaper, *The Genius of Universal Emancipation*, when it moved to Baltimore.

Since Baltimore was a slave port, Garrison would have seen notices like this: "To be sold, a cargo of ninety-four prime, healthy NEGROES, consisting of thirty-nine men, fifteen boys, twenty-four women, and sixteen girls, just arrived." Garrison hid a runaway slave who had been lashed 37 times for failing to load a wagon fast enough. He learned that if blacks were colonized, it would be against their will, and consequently, he abandoned the colonization idea and embraced immediate emancipation: the right "to make contracts, to receive wages, to accumulate property, to acquire knowledge, to dwell where he chooses, to defend his wife, children, and fireside." Garrison denounced two slave traders as "highway robbers" and was fined $100 for libel. Since he couldn't raise that much money, he went to jail. He was released after forty-nine days when the New York Quaker merchant Arthur Tappan paid the fine.

Meanwhile, as the fast-growing North gained seats in the U.S. House of Representatives, many southerners concluded they must promote the expansion of slavery—a contrast with founders like Thomas Jefferson, James Madison, Patrick Henry, and George Washington who, although they owned slaves, acknowledged that slavery was evil. Virginia senator John Randolph ridiculed the Declaration of Independence, and South Carolina senator John C. Calhoun called slavery "the most safe and stable basis for free institutions in the world."

Garrison decided he must launch an antislavery newspaper. With financial backing from Arthur Tappan and the Boston lawyer Ellis Gray Loring, Garrison rented an 18-square-foot office in Merchants Hall. It had just enough room for a desk, a table, two chairs and a mattress. He bought a cheap press and borrowed type during the night when another publisher was not using it. The first issue of *The Liberator* appeared on January 1, 1831. It was a four-page weekly, appearing every Friday, and its masthead displayed a phrase adapted from Thomas Paine: "Our Country is the World—Our Countrymen Are Mankind." Garrison declared his views with this editorial: "I will be as harsh as truth, and as uncompromising as justice. On this subject, I do not wish to think, or speak, or write, with moderation. No! No! Tell a man whose house is on fire, to give a moderate alarm; tell him to moderately rescue his wife from the hands of the ravisher; tell the mother to gradually extricate her babe from the fire into which it has fallen—but urge me not to use moderation in a like cause like the present. I am in earnest—I will not equivocate—I will not excuse—I will not retreat a single inch—AND I WILL BE HEARD."

The Liberator was always a shoestring venture. After a year, there were only fifty white subscribers, a year later, just four hundred. Three-quarters of subscribers were free blacks. Total circulation never exceeded three thousand. Although *The Liberator* lost money and nearly bankrupted Garrison, he published it for thirty-five years without missing a single week—1,820 issues altogether.

Garrison was blamed for inciting the August 1831 rebellion led by slave Nat Turner against slaveholders in Southampton County, Virginia, where about sixty whites were killed. Southern states made it illegal to speak or write about abolition. In Mississippi, men suspected of being abolitionists were hanged.

Garrison established the New-England Anti-Slavery Society, which started January 1, 1832, in the basement of the African Baptist Church on Boston's Joy Street. Later, as other states formed abolitionist societies, the name was changed to Massachusetts Anti-Slavery Society.

Garrison was convinced that, as long as colonization was considered a respectable cause, it would paralyze the antislavery movement. He wrote a pamphlet, *Thoughts on African Colonization* (1832), which insisted blacks had the right to choose where to live. Garrison went to England, where agents of the American Colonization Society were trying to raise money, and he persuaded English abolitionist heroes William Wilberforce and Thomas Clarkson to repudiate colonization. He saw Daniel O'Connell, the great champion of Irish freedom. Garrison eliminated colonization as a factor in the abolitionist movement.

Garrison still faced stubborn opposition throughout the North. Influential Unitarians thought slavery was no concern of northerners. Presbyterians refused to preach against slavery, as did a majority of Baptist ministers. In 1836, the General Conference of the Methodist Church ordered members not to participate in antislavery agitation. Bills to restrict abolitionist literature were introduced in the legislatures of Connecticut, Maine, New Hampshire, and Rhode Island, and free blacks were banned in Illinois, Iowa, Indiana, and Oregon. The opposition turned violent at times. A Marblehead, Massachusetts, mob wrecked the printing press and home of publisher Amos

Dresser, who had previously suffered a public lashing for abolitionist agitation in Nashville. In New Canaan, New Hampshire, local people used oxen to drag a school into a nearby swamp, because the teacher there was educating black children. A proslavery mob in Philadelphia burned down Pennsylvania Hall, an abolitionist gathering place, and then torched an orphanage for black children. And when Garrison appeared at the hall where the Boston Female Anti-Slavery Society was meeting in 1835, a lynch mob threw a noose around his neck and dragged him away. He was rescued by valiant friends.

Nevertheless, he gained supporters. One of them was twenty-four-year-old Harvard-educated Wendell Phillips, who saw the attempted lynching from his law office on Court Street. According to biographer Ralph Korngold, he was "six feet tall, deep-chested, broad-shouldered and with a soldierly bearing." Phillips joined the abolitionist movement, becoming its greatest orator and one of Garrison's closest associates. Theodore Weld, who had organized over a hundred antislavery societies in Ohio, was another stalwart who helped Garrison. Weld married Angelina Grimké who, with her sister, Sarah, toured the antislavery lecture circuit. Many ministers were upset to see women speaking out in public, but Garrison exulted in the struggle "against wind and tide, against the combined powers of Church and State."

Runaway slave Frederick Douglass was another of Garrison's recruits. After he had escaped from Maryland in 1838, he discovered *The Liberator*, which "sent a thrill of joy through my soul, such as I had never felt before!" Douglass, an eyewitness to slavery, became one of the most effective antislavery speakers.

Garrison developed more radical views. He wrote the *Declaration of Sentiments of the Non-Resistance Society* (1838), which, among other things, proclaimed: "Every human government is upheld by physical strength and its laws are enforced virtually at the point of a bayonet. . . . We cannot acknowledge allegiance to any human government, neither can we oppose any such government by a resort to physical force. . . . The history of mankind is crowded with evidences proving that physical coercion is not adapted to moral regeneration. . . . We register our testimony, not only against all war, but against all preparation for war."

Although an estimated 200,000 people belonged to antislavery organizations by the 1840s, the movement was losing momentum. Then came the Compromise of 1850 and the Fugitive Slave Act, which required the return of runaway slaves. Any northerner could be accused by a slave hunter of helping an alleged runaway slave, be brought before a federal commissioner, and be imprisoned down South. Alleged runaways were denied a jury trial and could not testify in their defense. Federal commissioners who decided cases were paid five dollars if they freed the accused and ten dollars if they ordered him or her sent South. The Fugitive Slave Law spurred Cincinnati housewife

Harriet Beecher Stowe to write a novel. *Uncle Tom's Cabin,* published in March 1852, chronicled the suffering and dignity of black slaves. English-language editions sold 2 million copies, and the book was translated into twenty-two languages.

Garrison now denounced the Constitution as a bulwark of slavery. On July 4, 1854, at an outdoor meeting of the Massachusetts Anti-Slavery Society, several speakers, including Henry David Thoreau, attacked slavery. Then Garrison lit a candle and used it to burn a copy of the Fugitive Slave Law and the Constitution.

Subsequent events moved the country to war. In 1857, Supreme Court Chief Justice Roger B. Taney held in the *Dred Scott* decision that blacks were not citizens and could not become citizens, and Congress that could not ban slavery in any new U.S. territory. John Brown's October 1859 raid on the federal arsenal at Harper's Ferry, intended to stir a slave rebellion, triggered a backlash against blacks and abolitionists. Six weeks after Lincoln was elected president in 1860, South Carolina seceded from the Union, and Garrison urged that it be permitted to go peacefully. "All Union-saving efforts are simply idiotic," he wrote. The April 16, 1861, Confederate assault on U.S. Fort Sumter, Charleston, however, convinced Garrison that slaves could not be freed peacefully.

Lincoln was not an abolitionist; In fact he favored gradual emancipation and colonization. But on January 1, 1863, he issued the Emancipation Proclamation. Aimed at encouraging black rebellion in the South, it declared that slaves there were free. It did not apply to slaves in border states still part of the Union, but it made freeing the slaves a war aim.

After the Civil War ended in April 1865, Garrison toured America. He told Charleston blacks: "It was not on account of your complexion or race, as a people, that I espoused your cause, but because you were the children of a common Father, created in the same divine image, having the same inalienable rights, and as much entitled to liberty as the proudest slaveholder that ever walked the earth."

In 1867, Garrison sailed with his daughter Fanny (Helen) and son Harry to Europe. They met British free trade crusader John Bright, economist John Stuart Mill, philosopher Herbert Spencer, and Liberal Member of Parliament William Ewart Gladstone.

Garrison began to suffer excruciating pain from his kidneys. He went to New York so he could stay with his daughter Fanny Garrison Villard at Westmoreland Apartment House, 100 East 17th Street, on Fifth Avenue near Union Square. He lapsed into a coma and died a few minutes after 11:00 P.M., Saturday, May 24, 1879. He was seventy-three.

Garrison's remains were moved to Roxbury, Massachusetts, where a funeral service was held on May 28 at the church of the First Religious Society. John Greenleaf Whittier, in a poetic tribute, called Garrison "a hand to set the captive free." Wendell Phillips and Theodore Weld gave addresses, as did feminist Lucy Stone, who remembered how "nothing could induce him to place himself with those who did not recognize the equal rights of all." Garrison was buried next to his wife at Forest Hills Cemetery, Roxbury.

Garrison's friends published books praising his moral vision, and he was revered for decades. But during the twentieth century, the tendency has been to disregard him. For instance, Gilbert H. Barnes's *The Anti-Slavery Impulse* (1933) made a case that the key abolitionist was the shy political organizer Theodore Weld, not the flamboyant publicist Garrison, a view maintained by Dwight L. Dumond in *Antislavery: The Crusade for Freedom* (1961). Historian John L. Thomas, in *The Liberator* (1963), blamed Garrison for the Civil War, and English professor Walter M. Merrill's *Against Wind and Tide* (1963) belittled Garrison's ideological views by suggesting they were a consequence of his unhappy childhood. Yet historian Aileen S. Kraditor had this to say: "I turned to Garrison's own writings. . . . and the more I read the more I became convinced that I was meeting the man for the first time. . . . Most of all I was increasingly struck by the logical consistency of his thought on all subjects."

Henry Mayer, in *All on Fire* (1998), affirmed the view that William Lloyd Garrison is an authentic American hero who, with a Biblical prophet's power and a propagandist's skill, forced the nation to confront the most crucial moral issue in its history.

Before Garrison, there was not much of a debate on American slavery, and slaveholders dominated both sides of it. Garrison framed the issues more clearly and dramatically than anybody else, stayed focused on the moral evil of slavery, and was an eloquent champion of natural rights for all. He took giant steps to help millions live free.

SELF-OWNERSHIP

THE GREATEST NATURAL rights thinker of the nineteenth century was the American lawyer and maverick individualist Lysander Spooner. He responded to the tumultuous events of his era, including the panic of 1837 and the Civil War, with pamphlets about natural rights, slavery, money, trial by jury, and other timely subjects. "Lysander Spooner deserves a place of honor," declared law professor Randy E. Barnett, "both for the principles for which he stood against the crowd and for the brilliance with which he defended those principles." Intellectual historian George H. Smith called Spooner "one of the greatest libertarian theorists."

Spooner spoke with bold clarity: "The enactment and enforcement of unjust laws are the greatest crimes that are committed by man against man. The crimes of single individuals invade the rights of single individuals. Unjust laws invade the rights of large bodies of men, often of a majority of the whole community; and generally of that portion of community who, from ignorance and poverty, are least able to bear the wrong." As he grew older, he became more radical. In 1885, two years before his death, he wrote: "All taxes, levied upon a man's property for the support of government, without his consent, are mere robbery; a violation of his natural right to property. . . . The monopoly of money is one of the most glaring violations of men's natural right to make their own contracts, and one of the most effective—perhaps the most effective—for enabling a few men to rob everybody else. . . . The government has no more right to claim the ownership of wilderness lands, than it has to claim the ownership of the sunshine, the water, or the atmosphere. . . . By its conscriptions, the government denies a man's right to any will, choice, judgment, or conscience of his own, in regard either to being killed himself, or used as a weapon in its hands for killing other people."

According to biographer Charles Shively, Spooner was "gruff, direct, and impatient with any hypocrisy. His correspondence includes cantankerous and not entirely creditable disputes with friends who failed to understand him." He found romance awkward and never married. But his friend Benjamin Tucker, editor of *Liberty* magazine, hailed him for his "towering strength of intellect, whose sincerity and singleness of purpose, and whose frank and loving heart would endear him to generations to come. . . . On any day except Sunday, for as many years back as the present writer can remember, a visitor at the Boston Athenaeum Library between the hours of nine and three might have noticed, as nearly all did notice, in one of the alcoves . . . the stooping figure of an aged man, bending over a desk piled high with dusty volumes of history, jurisprudence, political science, and constitutional law, and busily absorbed in studying and writing. Had the old man chanced to raise his head for a moment the visitor would have seen, framed in long and snowy hair and beard, one of the finest, kindliest, sweetest, strongest, grandest faces that ever gladdened the eyes of man."

LYSANDER SPOONER WAS born on January 19, 1808, at his father's farm near Athol, Massachusetts. He was the second of nine children born to Asa Spooner and Dolly Brown. He took a while to find his calling, working on the family farm, doing clerical work, practing law, and speculating (unsuccessfully) in Ohio land.

Then came the panic of 1837, which got Spooner thinking about the causes of booms and busts. In his *Constitutional Law Relative to Credit, Currency and Banking* (1843), he explained how government intervention disrupted the banking business, and he made a case for repealing legal tender laws (which required that government paper money be accepted for debts) and the requirement that banks be chartered by the government.

His next business venture was mail delivery. He decided to challenge federal laws awarding a monopoly to the U.S. Post Office and in January 1844 established the American Letter Mail Company to carry mail between Boston and Baltimore. In 1845, Congress forced Spooner and other private mail carriers out of business. In response, he wrote a pamphlet, *The Unconstitutionality of the Laws of Congress Prohibiting Private Mails*.

Spooner became caught up in the great debate about American slavery. Although southern lawyers claimed that slavery was supported by the Constitution, and abolitionist William Lloyd Garrison agreed (which is why he denounced the Constitution as "an agreement with hell"), Spooner thought constitutional arguments could be used against slavery. With some financial assistance from New York philanthropist Gerrit Smith, a major backer of the abolitionist movement, Spooner wrote *The Unconstitutionality of Slavery* (1845), in which he maintained that slavery was not supported by American colonial charters, the Declaration of Independence, the Articles of Confederation, or the Constitution. He did not convince Garrison or his associate Wendell Phillips, but he did win over the runaway slave and abolitionist orator Frederick Douglass, in the process contributing to the split in the abolitionist movement between those for and against political action.

The Unconstitutionality of Slavery was perhaps more interesting for Spooner's affirmation of natural law: "Man has an inalienable right to so much personal liberty as he will use without invading the rights of others.

This liberty is an inherent right of his nature and his faculties. It is an inherent right of his nature and his faculties to develop themselves freely, and without restraint from other natures and faculties, that have no superior prerogatives to his own. And this right has only this limit, viz., that he do not carry the exercise of his own liberty so far as to restrain or infringe the equally free development of the natures and faculties of others. The dividing line between the equal liberties of each must never be transgressed by either. This principle is the foundation and essence of law and civil right."

Back at the family farm at Athol, he wrote *Poverty: Its Illegal Causes, and Legal Cure* (1846). Again, the most interesting passages are about natural rights: "Nearly all the positive legislation that has ever been passed in this country, either on the part of the general or state governments, touching men's rights to labor, or their rights to the fruits of their labor . . . has been merely an attempt to substitute arbitrary for natural laws; to abolish men's natural rights of labor, property, and contract, and in their place establish monopolies and privileges . . . to rob one portion of mankind of their labor, or the fruits of their labor, and give the plunder to the other portion."

In 1852, Spooner produced *Trial by Jury*, which doubled as a scholarly work and a political tract. Tracing the history of trial by jury since medieval times in England, he showed how it provided crucial protection against oppressive government. He cited legal documents and legal authorities from the Magna Carta to his own time, affirming that a jury must be free to hear all facts in a case without constraint by capricious rules of evidence. Moreover, a jury must be free to render a decision not just on the facts but also on the legimacy of the law that the defendant was charged with violating, and it must be able to nullify an unjust law.

Spooner's case for jury nullification came when juries were playing an important role in the movement to liberate American slaves. The Fugitive Slave Law (1793) had mandated the return of runaway slaves to their "owners," but when juries increasingly refused to enforce that law, political pressures resulted in the Fugitive Slave Act (1850), which aimed to avoid jury trials. It permitted a summary process before federal judges; slave hunters who provided "satisfactory proof" of ownership could take possession of the runaways, who were not permitted to testify in their behalf.

United States v. Morris (1851) was among the jury trials involving individuals charged with helping runaway slaves. A slave known as Shadrach had escaped from Norfolk, Virginia, and reached Boston, where, known as Frederick Jenkins, he served as a waiter. In February 1851, he was discovered by a slave hunter, who took him to a federal judge for summary proceedings under the Fugitive Slave Law, but a crowd burst into the courtroom and escorted Shadrach out and over to Cambridge, where he vanished and eventually made his way to Canada. Eight individuals—four whites and four blacks—

were charged with rescuing him and thereby violating the Fugitive Slave
Law. The jury trial began May 1851.

Defense counsel went beyond challenging the facts in the case and
declared "the jury were rightfully the judges of the law, as well as the fact;
and if any of them conscientiously believed the act of 1850 . . . commonly
called the 'Fugitive Slave Act,' to be unconstitutional, they were bound by
their oaths to disregard any direction to the contrary which the court might
give them." Judge Benjamin Curtis was so shocked by this line of argument
that he cut off the defense counsel and instructed the jurors that they "have
not the right to decide any question of law. . . . [They must] apply to the facts,
as they may find them, the law given to them by the court." He then issued an
opinion warning of chaos if jurors could reject whatever laws they wanted to.
The jury nevertheless disregarded the judge's opinion and acquitted the
defendants.

Without jury nullification, Spooner warned, "The government will have
everything its own way; the jury will be mere puppets in the hands of the government; and the trial will be, in reality, a trial by the government. . . . If the
government may dictate to the jury what laws they are to enforce . . . the jury
then try the accused, not by any standard of their own—not by their own
judgments of their rightful liberties—but by a standard dictated to them by
the government. And the standard thus dictated by the government becomes
the measure of the people's liberties. . . . The government determines what
are its own powers over the people, instead of the people's determining what
are their own liberties against the government. In short, if the jury have no
right to judge of the justice of a law of the government, they plainly can do
nothing to protect the people against the oppressions of the government; for
there are no oppressions which the government may not authorize by law."

He rejected the claim that people are adequately protected by the right to
vote. Voting, he observed, "can be exercised only periodically; and the
tyranny must at least be borne until the time for suffrage comes. Besides,
when the suffrage is exercised, it gives no guaranty for the repeal of existing
laws that are oppressive, and no security against the enactment of new ones
that are equally so. The second body of legislators are liable to be just as
tyrannical as the first. If it be said that the second body may be chosen for
their integrity, the answer is, that the first were chosen for that very reason,
and yet proved tyrants."

To the question of whether jury nullification would introduce more uncertainty, undermining a rule of law, Spooner countered by observing that the
principal sources of uncertainty in the legal system come from "innumerable
and incessantly changing legislative enactments, and of countless and contradictory judicial decisions, with no uniform principle of reason or justice running through them. . . . So great is this uncertainty, that nearly all men,

learned as well as unlearned, shun the law as their enemy, instead of resorting to it for protection. They usually go into courts of justice, so called, only as men go into battle—when there is no alternative left for them. And even then they go into them as men go into dark labyrinths and caverns—with no knowledge of their own, but trusting wholly to their guides."

Spooner was alarmed at the vast expansion of federal power during the civil war: military conscription; paper money inflation ("greenbacks"); tariffs as high as 100 percent; excise, sales, inheritance, and income taxes; censorship of mail, telegraphs, and newspapers; and jailing people without filing formal charges—many of these measures taken without congressional approval. After the war, the federal government maintained a standing army 50 percent higher than before the war began; federal spending as a proportion of the national economy was twice as high after the war than before; the national debt, about $65 million when the Civil War began (largely a consequence of the Mexican War), skyrocketed to $2.8 billion, and interest on it accounted for about 40 percent of the federal budget through the mid-1870s.

Increasingly radicalized, Spooner drew closer to some ideas of American inventor and social philosopher Josiah Warren (1798–1874) and in perhaps his most important work, *No Treason No. 6, Constitution of No Authority* (1870), Spooner attacked the dishonesty of government, which, "like a highwayman, says to a man: *Your money, or your life.* And many, if not most, taxes are paid under the compulsion of that threat. The government does not, indeed, waylay a man in a lonely place, spring upon him from the road side, and, holding a pistol to his head, proceed to rifle his pockets. But the robbery is none the less a robbery on that account; and it is far more dastardly and shameful. The highwayman takes solely upon himself the responsibility, danger, and crime of his own act. He does not pretend that he has any rightful claim to your money, or that he intends to use it for your own benefit. He does not pretend to be anything but a robber. He has not acquired impudence enough to profess to be merely a 'protector,' and that he takes men's money against their will, merely to enable him to 'protect' those infatuated travellers, who feel perfectly able to protect themselves, or do not appreciate his peculiar system of protection. He is too sensible a man to make such professions as these. Furthermore, having taken your money, he leaves you, as you wish to do. He does not persist in following you on the road, against your will; assuming to be your rightful 'sovereign,' on account of the 'protection' he affords you."

Spooner got to know the eloquent journalist and editor Benjamin Tucker, who believed government is so incompetent, dishonest, and violent that people would be better off without it. Tucker was born in South Dartmouth, Massachusetts, April 17, 1854. He described his parents as "radical Unitarians." After three years at the Massachusetts Institute of Technology, he decided he was more interested in politics than science, and plunged whole-heartedly into the movements for both alcohol prohibition and woman suffrage. He embraced free banking, the view that market competition is more effective than government regulation at maintaining sound banking practices. His path crossed with the radical libertarian author and entrepreneur Joseph Warren (1798–1874), whose ideas had an impact on Spooner's thinking.

Tucker asserted his independence in his new publication, *Liberty*, where he welcomed a wide range of radical views. He helped make better-known the ideas of individualist Josiah Warren, the egoist ethics of German author Max Stirner and the liberating vision of Norwegian dramatist Henrik Ibsen. All this must have helped Tucker clarify his own thinking, because after a few years he insisted that secure private property is essential for liberty, and he attacked communism. Tucker edited *Liberty* for twenty-seven years. As independent scholar James J. Martin noted, "*Liberty* preserved sufficient vitality to become the longest-lived of any radical periodical of economic or political nature in the nation's history, and certainly one of the world's most interesting during the past two centuries."

Spooner's major contribution to *Liberty* was "A Letter to Grover Cleveland," to which he added a cantankerous subhead: "His False Inaugural Address, the Usurpations and Crimes of Lawmakers and Judges, and the Consequent Poverty, Ignorance, and Servitude of the People." There were nineteen installments beginning on June 20, 1885, and they were gathered into a book published in July. Spooner eloquently lashed out against military conscription. "The government does not even recognize a man's right to his own life," he protested. "If it have need of him, for the maintenance of its power, it takes him, against his will (conscripts him), and puts him before the cannon's mouth, to be blown in pieces, as if he were a mere senseless thing, having no more *rights* than if he were a shell."

Spooner lived out his life quietly as a scholar in a boarding house on Boston's Beacon Hill, at 109 Myrtle Street. Tucker reported that he was "surrounded by trunks and chests bursting with the books, manuscripts, and pamphlets he had gathered about him in his active pamphleteer's warfare over half a century ago."

In early 1887, he became seriously ill but, skeptical about doctors, he delayed seeking medical attention. With Tucker apparently by his side, he died Saturday, May 14, 1887, around 1:00 P.M. Tucker and abolitionist Theodore Weld were among those who spoke at the memorial gathering, in Wells Memorial Hall, Boston. Spooner, Tucker declared, had a mind that was "keen, clear, penetrating, incisive, logical, orderly, careful, convincing, and crushing, and set forth withal in a style of singular strength, purity, and individuality." Spooner was buried in Boston's Forest Hills Cemetery.

Spooner seemed to be a forgotten man, but, as a number of thinkers have explored the moral basis for liberty, his writings have been rediscovered. Six volumes of his collected works were reprinted in 1971, and *The Lysander Spooner Reader* appeared in 1992. Now there's a Spooner website, *http://www.lysanderspooner.org*, which makes available information about the man and his writings. His ideas on liberty are soaring through cyberspace into the new millennium.

CREATORS AND PRODUCERS

AYN RAND, MOST famous for her dramatic philosophical novels *The Foun-tainhead* (1943) and *Atlas Shrugged* (1957), did more than anybody else to develop a compelling moral case for individualism, liberty, and free markets and won over millions to the philosophy of natural rights, which had fallen out of fashion more than a century before. She developed a coherent view of ethics, economics, and politics. According to a survey by the Library of Congress and the Book-of-the-Month Club, *Atlas Shrugged* ranked second after the Bible as the book that most influenced people's lives. Rand wrote much more—nonfiction as well as fiction. Some 20 million copies of her books have been sold, and new collections of her writings and books about her continue to pour off the presses.

The Russian-born Rand spoke with a thick accent and didn't seem entirely comfortable in the public spotlight, but she made the most of it. She appeared on television with the likes of Mike Wallace and Phil Donahue, and *Playboy* published an interview with her.

Rand framed issues with refreshing clarity. For instance, she wrote: "What is the basic, the essential, the crucial principle that differentiates freedom from slavery? It is the principle of voluntary action *versus* physical coercion or compulsion. . . . The issue is *not* slavery for a 'good' cause versus slavery for a 'bad' cause; the issue is *not* dictatorship by a 'good' gang versus dictatorship by a 'bad' gang. The issue is freedom versus dictatorship. . . . If one upholds freedom, one must uphold man's individual rights; if one upholds man's individual rights, one must uphold his right to his own life, to his own liberty, to the pursuit of his own happiness. . . . Without property rights, no other rights are possible. Since man has to sustain his life by his own effort, the man who has no right to the product of his effort has no means to sustain his life." And she disagreed with friends of liberty who hoped to gain influence with free market economics alone: "Most people know in a vague, uneasy way, that Marxist economics are screwy. Yet this does not stop them from advocating the same Marxist economics. . . . The root of the whole modern disaster is philosophical and moral. People are not embracing collectivism because they have accepted bad economics. They are embracing bad economics because they have embraced collectivism."

It is true that Rand lost patience with those who could not understand her and with compatriots who deviated from her views. In part, perhaps, this was because she had spent so many years struggling to escape from Russia, establish herself in Hollywood, overcome publisher rejections, and endure harsh reviews.

Biographer Barbara Branden described Rand on her arrival in America at age twenty-one: "Framed by its short, straight hair, its squarish shape stressed by a firmly set jaw, its sensual wide mouth held in tight restraint, its huge dark eyes black with intensity, it seemed the face of a martyr or an inquisitor or a saint. The eyes burned with a passion that was at once emotional and intellectual—as if they would sear the onlooker and leave their dark light a flame on his body." Later in life, chain smoking and sedentary habits took their toll, but Rand was still unforgettable.

RAND WAS BORN Alissa Rosenbaum on February 2, 1905, in St. Petersburg. Her father, Fronz Rosenbaum, had risen from poverty to the middle class as a chemist. Her mother, Anna, was an extrovert who believed in vigorous exercise and a busy social life, but Alissa was interested in neither. After school, she studied French and German at home. Inspired by a magazine serial, she began writing stories, and at nine years old resolved to become a writer.

The Rosenbaums' comfortable world ended when the czar entered World War I. The war devastated the nation's economy, and within a year, more than a million Russians were killed or wounded. Bolsheviks seized power.

The Russian Revolution spurred Rosenbaum to invent stories about heroic individuals who battled kings or communist dictators. At this time, too, she discovered novelist Victor Hugo, whose dramatic style and towering heroes captivated her imagination. "I was fascinated by Hugo's sense of life," she recalled. "It was someone writing something important. I felt this is the kind of writer I would like to be, but I didn't know how long it would take."

At the University of Petrograd, she took courses with the stern Aristotelian Nicholas Lossky who, scholar Chris Sciabarra showed, had an enormous impact on her thinking. She read plays by Friedrich Schiller (she loved him) and William Shakespeare (hated him), philosophy by Friedrich Nietzsche (provocative thinker), and novels by Feodor Dostoevsky (good plotter), and she was utterly captivated by foreign movies. She had her first big crush, on a man named Leo, who risked his life to hide members of the anti-Bolshevik underground.

In 1925, the Rosenbaums received a letter from relatives who had emigrated to Chicago more than three decades before so they could escape Russian anti-Semitism. Alissa desperately wanted to see America, and the relatives agreed to pay her passage and be responsible for her. Miraculously, Soviet officials granted her a passport for a six-month visit. On February 10, 1926, she boarded the ship *De Grasse* and arrived in New York with fifty dollars.

Alissa soon joined her relatives in a cramped Chicago apartment. She saw a lot of movies and worked at her typewriter, usually starting around midnight (which made it difficult for others to sleep). She settled on a new first name for herself, Ayn (after a Finnish writer she had never read, but she liked the sound) and a new last name, Rand (after her Remington Rand typewriter). Biographer Branden says Rand might have adopted a new name to protect her family from possible recrimination by the Soviet regime.

Determined to become a movie script writer, she moved to Los Angeles and worked as an extra at the Cecil B. DeMille Studio. And she fell in love with a tall, handsome, blue-eyed bit actor named Frank O'Connor. They got married on April 15, 1929. Rand no longer had to worry about going back to the Soviet Union, and she applied for American citizenship.

When the DeMille Studio closed, Rand found odd jobs. Finally, in 1935, she had a taste of success: her play *Night of January 16th*, about a ruthless industrialist and the powerful woman on trial for his murder, ran for 283 performances on Broadway. In 1936, her novel, *We the Living*, about the struggle to find liberty in Soviet Russia, was published. Macmillan printed three thousand copies, but the book languished. Although word of mouth gave it a lift after about a year, Macmillan had destroyed the type, and *We the Living* went out of print. Rand had earned just $100 in royalties.

In 1937, while struggling to work out the plot of *The Fountainhead*, Rand wrote a short, lyrical futurist story, *Anthem*, about an individual versus collectivist tyranny. *Anthem* offered a bold affirmation of liberty, going far beyond more famous anti-totalitarian novels like Aldous Huxley's *Brave New World* (1932), Arthur Koestler's *Darkness at Noon* (1941), and George Orwell's *Animal Farm* (1945) and *1984* (1949). In *Anthem*, a man rediscovered the word "I." He explained, "My happiness is not the means to any end. It is the end. It is its own goal. It is its own purpose. Neither am I the means to any end others may wish to accomplish. I am not a tool for their use. I am not a servant of their needs." Rand's literary agent sold it to a British publisher but could not find a U.S. publisher. But about seven years later, Los Angeles Chamber of Commerce general manager Leonard Read visited Rand and O'Connor, then living in New York, and remarked that somebody ought to write a book defending individualism. Rand told him about *Anthem*, and Read's small publishing firm, Pamphleteers, made a U.S. edition available in 1946. It has since sold some 2.5 million copies.

Meanwhile, Rand finished plotting *The Fountainhead* in 1938 after nearly four years of work and then began writing it. The hero, architect Howard Roark, expressed her vision of an ideal man. He battled collectivists all around him to defend the integrity of his ideas, even when it meant dynamiting a building because its plans were altered in violation of his contract. He defended his action by saying, in part: "The great creators—the thinkers, the artists, the scientists, the inventors—stood alone against the men of their time. Every great new thought was opposed. Every great new invention was denounced. The first motor was considered foolish. The airplane was considered impossible. The power loom was considered vicious. Anesthesia was considered sinful. But the men of unborrowed vision went ahead. They fought, they suffered and they paid. But they won."

Selling *The Fountainhead* proved tough. Rand's editor at Macmillan expressed interest and offered another $250 advance, but she insisted the company agree to spend at least $1,200 on publicity, so Macmillan bowed out. By 1940, a dozen publishers had seen finished chapters and rejected the book. One influential editor declared the book would never sell, and even Rand's literary agent turned against it. Her savings were down to about $700.

Rand suggested that the partial manuscript be submitted to Bobbs-Merrill, an Indianapolis-based publisher that had issued *The Red Decade* by anti-Communist journalist Eugene Lyons. Bobbs-Merrill's Indianapolis editors rejected *The Fountainhead,* but the company's New York editor Archibald Ogden loved it and threatened to quit if they didn't take it. They signed a contract in December 1941, paying Rand a $1,000 advance. With two-thirds of the book yet to be written, Rand now focused on making her January 1, 1943, deadline for completion.

She found herself in a friendly race with her friend Isabel Paterson, the hot-tempered, sometimes tactless journalist then working to complete *The God of the Machine.* Paterson wrote novels and some twelve hundred newspaper columns, but it was *The God of the Machine* that secured her reputation. The book mounted a powerful attack on collectivism and explained the extraordinary dynamics of free markets. Paterson was nineteen years older than Rand and for several crucial years served as her mentor. English professor Stephen Cox of the University of California (San Diego) believed that with Paterson, Rand had "what may have been the closest intellectual relationship of her life." Rand and Paterson got together when Paterson was proofreading typeset pages of book reviews she wrote for the *New York Herald Tribune.* She introduced Rand to many books about history, economics, and political philosophy, helping Rand develop a more sophisticated world view.

The Fountainhead was published in May 1943, the same month as *The God of the Machine.* From conception to publication had taken Rand about nine years. Paterson promoted it in a number of *Herald Tribune* columns. *The Fountainhead* generated many more reviews than *We the Living,* but most reviewers either denounced it or misrepresented it as a book about architecture. One of the most surprising reviews came from the *New York Times,* where Lorine Pruette wrote: "Miss Rand has taken her stand against collectivism. . . . She has written a hymn in praise of the individual."

Rand was thrilled to get a letter from famed architect Frank Lloyd Wright. "I've read every word of *The Fountainhead*," he wrote. "Your thesis is the great one. . . . The individual is the Fountainhead of any Society worthwhile. The Freedom of the Individual is the only legitimate object of government: the Individual Conscience is the great inviolable." Although Roark wasn't modeled after Wright, he was reported to have kept a copy of *The Fountainhead* by his bed at Taliesin West, Arizona. (He designed a house for Rand, but it was never built because Rand and her husband decided to stay in New York City. The drawing remains in the Wright collection.)

For a while, the book moved slowly. But word of mouth stirred a groundswell of interest, and the publisher ordered a succession of reprintings, most of them small, in part because of wartime paper shortages. The book gained momentum and hit the best-seller lists. Two years after publication, it had sold 100,000 copies, and by 1948, 400,000 copies. Then came the New American Library paperback edition, and *The Fountainhead* went on to sell over 6 million copies.

The day Warner Brothers agreed to pay Rand $50,000 for movie rights to *The Fountainhead*, she and O'Connor splurged and each had a 65-cent dinner at their local cafeteria. Rand fought to preserve the integrity of the script and was largely successful, though some of her most cherished lines were cut. The movie, starring Gary Cooper, Patricia Neal, and Raymond Massey, premiered in July 1949 and propelled the book onto the best-seller lists again.

Earlier, when the book had just been published, Rand told her friend Isabel Paterson how disappointed she was with its reception. Paterson urged her to do a nonfiction book and added that Rand had a *duty* to make her views more widely known. But Rand rebelled at the notion that she owed people anything. "What if I went on strike?" she asked. "What if *all* the creative minds of the world went on strike?" This became the idea for her last major work, tentatively called *The Strike*.

As Rand worked on the book for some fourteen years, much of that time in her New York City apartment, everything about the story became larger than life. It featured her most famous hero, mysterious John Galt, the physicist-inventor who organized a strike of the most productive people against taxers and other exploiters. The book introduced Dagney Taggart, Rand's first ideal woman, who found her match in Galt. A friend suggested that the tentative title might make many people think the book was about labor unions, and she abandoned it. O'Connor urged her to use one of the chapter headings as the book title, and it became *Atlas Shrugged*.

The book overflows with provocative ideas. For example, copper entrepreneur Francisco d'Anconia, in a conversation with steel entrepreneur Hank Rearden, expresses Rand's vision of sex: "A man's sexual choice is the result and sum of his fundamental convictions. Tell me what a man finds sexually attractive and I will tell you his entire philosophy of life. Show me the woman he sleeps with and I will tell you his valuation of himself." Anconia talked about the morality of money: "Money rests on the axiom that every man is the owner of his mind and his effort. . . . Money demands of you the recognition that men must work for their own benefit, not for their own injury, for their gain, not their loss. . . . The common bond among men is not the exchange of suffering, but the exchange of goods." Rearden defends achievement in this way: "I have made my money by my own effort, in free exchange and through the voluntary consent of every man I dealt with. . . . I refuse to apologize for my ability. . . . I refuse to apologize for my success." And from John Galt's climactic radio broadcast to the oppressors is this compelling line: "We are on strike against the dogma that the pursuit of one's happiness is evil."

Rand's ideas were as controversial as ever, but sales of *The Fountainhead* had impressed publishers, and several big ones courted her for *Atlas Shrugged.* Random House co-owner Bennett Cerf was most supportive, and Rand received a $50,000 advance against a 15 percent royalty, a first printing of at least seventy-five thousand copies, and a $25,000 advertising budget. The book was published on October 10, 1957.

Most reviewers were savage. The old-line socialist Granville Hicks sounded off in the *New York Times,* and others were similarly offended by Rand's attacks on collectivism. The most hysterical review of all turned out to be in conservative *National Review,* where Whittaker Chambers, presumably offended by Rand's critique of religion, likened her to a Nazi "commanding: 'To a gas chamber—go!'" Word of mouth proved too strong for these naysayers, though, and sales began to climb, eventually passing 4.5 million.

With *Atlas Shrugged,* Rand had fulfilled her dreams, and she became depressed. She no longer had a giant project to focus her prodigious energies, and she leaned increasingly on her Canadian-born intellectual disciple, Nathaniel Branden, with whom she had become intimate. To serve the growing interest in Rand and help revive her spirits, he established the Nathaniel Branden Institute (NBI), which offered seminars, marketed taped lectures and began issuing publications about Rand's philosophy, called Objectivism. Branden was sometimes a ruthless enforcer of Objectivist orthodoxy, but he displayed remarkable skills promoting the ideals of individualism and free markets. An estimated twenty-five thousand people went through NBI courses.

Good times continued until August 23, 1968 when Branden told Rand about his affair with another woman. Rand denounced him publicly, and they split, although the reasons weren't fully disclosed until Branden's ex-wife Barbara wrote a biography that was published eighteen years later. Nathaniel Branden went on to become a bestselling author about self-esteem.

Meanwhile, Rand turned to nonfiction writing. *For a New Intellectual* (1961) gathered selections on her philosophy from *We the Living, Anthem, The Fountainhead,* and *Atlas Shrugged.* She edited and published *The Objectivist Newsletter* (1962–1966), *The Objectivist* (1966–1971) and *The Ayn Rand Letter* (1971–1976). A number of her essays, together with essays by Nathaniel Branden, Alan Greenspan, and Robert Hessen, were reprinted in *Capitalism: The Unknown Ideal* (1962). With a flair for controversy, she titled one essay collection *The Virtue of Selfishness* (1964). Her essays on culture appeared in *The Romantic Manifesto* (1969). Outraged at youthful rebellion against capitalism, she issued another essay collection, *The New Left: the Anti-Industrial Revolution* (1971).

Rand kept more to herself after Frank O'Connor's death in November 1979, nearly oblivious to how her ideas inspired millions. She did make two appearances on Phil Donahue's nationally syndicated TV talk show. The following year, knowing that Rand loved trains, precious metals entrepreneur James U. Blanchard III arranged for her travel in a private rail car from New York to New Orleans where, on November 21, 1981, four thousand people cheered her as she delivered "The Sanction of the Victims." She talked about how businesspeople perform the vital service of transforming new knowledge into improved products and services. Yet they are generally despised as greedy capitalists and—what's worse—they finance universities, Hollywood studios and other institutions that spew out propaganda for suppressing liberty. She urged businesspeople to defend the morality of liberty.

Rand's heart began to give out in December, and she died in her 120 East 34th Street, Manhattan apartment on March 6, 1982. She was buried next to O'Connor in Valhalla, New York, as some 200 mourners tossed flowers on her coffin. She was seventy-seven.

Publishers have since been busy with new Rand titles. Her closest associate, Leonard Peikoff, who founded the Ayn Rand Institute, brought out *Philosophy: Who Needs It* (1982), largely material drawn from *The Ayn Rand Letter; The Early Ayn Rand: A Selection from Her Unpublished Fiction* (1984); and *The Voice of Reason: Essays in Objectivist Thought* (1988). Ayn Rand Institute executive director Michael S. Berliner edited *Letters of Ayn Rand* (1995), and scholar David Harriman edited *Journals of Ayn Rand* (1997). Then came *Marginalia* (1998), *The Ayn Rand Column* (1998), and *The Art of Fiction* (2000).

At a fiftieth anniversary celebration of *The Fountainhead,* English professor Stephen Cox observed, "Rand's courageous challenge to accepted ideas was rendered still more courageous by her willingness to state her individualist premises in the clearest terms and to defend the most radical implications that could be drawn from them."

The fortieth anniversary of *Atlas Shrugged* was marked in October 1997 at a day-long event sponsored by the Cato Institute and the Institute for Objectivist Studies. "The message of *Atlas Shrugged*," remarked Institute for Objectivist Studies executive director David Kelley, "is that capitalism . . . allows and rewards and celebrates the best in human nature. And socialism, or any form of collectivism, is not just inefficient, it is immoral. It is a degrading expression of envy, of malice, of the lust for power in the few who rule and the fear of freedom in the many who submit."

Rand's books continue to sell some 300,000 copies a year. Although she has had the greatest impact in the United States, she has readers around the world. *Atlas Shrugged* is in German. There are editions of *The Fountainhead* in French, German, Norwegian, Swedish and Russian. *We the Living* is available in French, German, Greek, Italian and Russian editions. French and Swedish translations of *Anthem* are under way.

There has been an outpouring of books about Rand. Barbara Branden's biography, *The Passion of Ayn Rand*, appeared in 1986. Nathaniel Branden told his story in *Judgment Day* (1989). Peikoff wrote *Objectivism: The Philosophy of Ayn Rand* (1991). That same year brought Los Angeles entrepreneur Ronald E. Merrill's *The Ideas of Ayn Rand*. Scholar Chris Matthew Sciabarra's *Ayn Rand, the Russian Radical*, published in 1995, placed her ideas in the context of Russian philosophy. As *Newsweek* reported, "She's everywhere."

The 1997 release of Michael Paxton's documentary film *Ayn Rand: A Sense of Life* was nominated for an Academy Award. In May 1999, Showtime aired *The Passion of Ayn Rand*, starring Helen Mirren as Rand, Peter Fonda as Frank O'Connor, Eric Stoltz as Nathaniel Branden, and Julie Delpy as Barbara Branden.

Ayn Rand came out of nowhere to challenge a corrupt, collectivist world. She single-mindedly seized the high ground, affirming the moral imperative for liberty and showing that all things are possible

TOLERATION

Live and let live.
—SCOTTISH PROVERB

FOR THOUSANDS OF years, it was thought necessary for rulers to enforce religious orthodoxy in order to make people virtuous and preserve the social order. Allowing people to pick their own religion seemed to risk chaos. St. Augustine (354–430) was among the first to say that people should be persecuted for deviating from Christian doctrines. By the High Middle Ages, the Catholic church had targeted Jews, and they were expelled from Vienna, Linz, Cologne, Milan, Florence, and other European cities. In 1480, King Ferdinand and Queen Isabella began the Spanish Inquisition; by the time it ended in 1808, it was estimated to have killed over 31,900 people; another 125,000 victims died in prison. Thousands more were burned to death in the New World. Amid all this, there came an insistent voice for toleration.

A TOLERANT MIND

DURING THE EARLY sixteenth century, an era of religious persecution and frequent wars, Desiderius Erasmus emerged as the first modern champion of toleration and peace. "I am a lover of liberty," he wrote with his only weapon, a quill pen. He denounced persecution by both Catholics and Protestants and was among the first to say that different religions should flourish peacefully. He urged an end to burning heretics, witches, and books. When Martin Luther declared that human beings cannot choose their destiny, Erasmus defended free will. Just two decades after the Spanish established a colony in America, Erasmus came out against colonialism which he called "nothing but robbery masquerading as the propagation of Christianity."

Erasmus's *Dulce bellum inexpertis* (1515) was the first book in European history to make a case for peace, and the theme of peace runs throughout his writings. He attacked "the vengeful furies whenever they let loose their snakes and assail the hearts of men with lust for war."

He was an outspoken critic of monarchy. A king, Erasmus wrote, is "carnivorous, rapacious, a brigand, a destroyer, solitary, hated by all, a pest to all." Ahead of his time, Erasmus urged a "limited monarchy, checked and decreased by an aristocracy and by democracy."

Individualist Albert Jay Nock hailed Erasmus as the "citizen of the world and native of all countries." Lord Acton called him "the greatest figure of the Renaissance. . . . He lived in France and Belgium, in England and Italy, in Switzerland and Germany, so that each country contributed to his development, and none set its stamp upon him. He was eminently an international character; and was the first European who lived in intimacy with other ages besides his own, and could appreciate the gradual ripening and enlargement of ideas." French literary genius François Rabelais wrote that Erasmus was his spiritual father, and Swiss religious reformer Ulrich Zwingli said, "It is impossible not to love Erasmus."

Historian Paul Johnson noted that "Erasmus made himself into a scholar with high academic standards; he was also a popularizer and a journalist who understood the importance of communication. He wanted his books to be small, handy and cheap, and he was the first writer to grasp the full potentialities of printing. He worked at top speed, often in the printing shop itself, writing and correcting his proofs on the spot. He was exhilarated by the smell of printer's ink, the incense of the Reformation." Erasmus himself said, "My home is where I have my library."

Historian Will Durant remarked that Erasmus "wrote bad French, spoke a little Dutch and English, 'tasted Hebrew only with the tip of the tongue,' and knew Greek imperfectly; but he mastered Latin thoroughly, and handled it as a living tongue applicable to the most un-Latin nuances and trivia of his time. A century newly enamoured of the classics forgave most of his faults for the lively brilliance of his style, the novel charm of his understatements, the bright dagger of his irony. His letters rival Cicero's in elegance and urbanity, surpass them in vivacity and wit."

Biographer George Faludy: "Erasmus wrote with great speed and ease, occasionally completing thirty to forty pages a day, and even more when writing a polemic. He worked standing behind a lectern to stay alert, and seems to have enjoyed the act of writing, adapting himself in it from this period until the end of his life to the speed of the printing presses. When questioned about the number of books he was turning out, he replied that they were to be attributed to his insomnia."

Although Erasmus was a prolific author—some 750,000 copies of his books were sold during his lifetime—he gained immortality for a single work, *The Praise of Folly* (1511). "It is this folly which produces states," wrote historian Johann Huizinga, "and through her, empires, religion, law-courts. The state with its posts of honour, patriotism and national pride . . . the stateliness of ceremonies, the delusion of caste and nobility—what is it but folly? War, the most foolish thing of all."

Durant described Erasmus as "short, thin, pale, weak in voice and constitution. He impressed by his sensitive hands, his long, sharp nose, his blue-gray eyes flashing with wit, and his speech—the conversation of the richest and quickest mind of that brilliant age. The greatest artists among his northern contemporaries were eager to paint his portrait, and he consented to sit for them because such portraits were welcomed as gifts by his friends."

"His faults leaped to the eye," Durant continued. "He could beg shamelessly, but he could also give, and many a rising spirit expanded in the warmth of his praise. . . . He lacked modesty and gratitude, which came hard to one courted by popes and kings. He was impatient and resentful of criticism, and sometimes answered it in the abusive manner of that polemic age. He shared the anti-Semitism of even the scholars of the Renaissance. . . . He loved flattery, and agreed with it despite frequent disclaimers."

Biographer Cornelis Augustijn remarked on "Erasmus' toughness, his undaunted tenacity, in spite of all obstacles, in holding to the goal he wanted to attain. He did not let himself be held back by poverty. His far from robust health and his numerous illnesses could not keep him from the work he had chosen."

Many historians, especially German historians, have promoted the view that Erasmus's rival Martin Luther was a great defender of liberty, even though Luther defended persecution, tyranny, slavery, and mass murder. Ron Schoeffel, editor of the University of Toronto Press, which is publishing the first English language edition of Erasmus's complete works, observed that "Erasmus is perhaps the least known of the chief architects of modern thought. . . . [H]is intellectual and spiritual legacy is only now, in our own time, beginning to manifest itself fully."

DESIDERIUS ("THE DESIRED ONE") Erasmus was born October 27, in either 1466 or 1469, in Gouda, just northeast of Rotterdam, Holland. He was the second son of a priest whom he referred to as Gerard. His mother was a washerwoman named Margaret. Throughout his life, he was embarrassed by his origins. He grew up at the rectory, though perhaps to get away from scandalized parishioners, Margaret took Erasmus and his older brother, Peter, east to Deventer, a small town, for schooling. The region was then embroiled in wars, and when Erasmus was eight, he saw some two hundred war prisoners pulled apart on the rack by order of the local bishop.

Around 1484 Erasmus lost both parents to the bubonic plague. Apparently to get rid of the children, the principal guardian, a schoolmaster, consigned them to monasteries and squandered the family assets. Erasmus ended up at an Augustinian monastery in Steyn. During his six years there, he spent a lot of time in the library, where he read the works of Marcus Tullius Cicero and other Roman authors. Once he was ordained as a priest in April 1492, he left the monastery and ended up at the Sorbonne, but the rector in charge of the place modeled himself after St. Francis of Paula, an ascetic who ate roots and never bathed. By 1496, Erasmus had enough.

In 1500, he published a little volume called *Adagia collectanae*, containing 818 Latin sayings and some commentary. The theme of republican liberty and peace runs through this, as through so many of Erasmus's other works— for instance: "Do we not see that noble cities are erected by the people and destroyed by princes? That a state grows rich by the industry of its citizens and is plundered by the rapacity of its rulers? That good laws are enacted by representatives of the people and violated by kings? That the commons love peace and the monarchs foment war?"

His next book, *Enchirdion militis christiani* (*The Handbook of the Christian Soldier*), was a practical guide to Christianity. In it he insisted that people save their souls not by performing religious rituals but by cultivating faith and goodness. The book, which helped set the stage for the Reformation, was translated into English (after 1518), Czech (1519), German (1520), and then French, Italian, Polish, Portuguese, and Spanish.

In May 1509, Erasmus was invited to England, and he stayed in Thomas More's house in London. He composed a satire, *Moriae Encomium* (*The Praise of Folly*)—an oration by Folly, who chronicles the foolishness of contemporary life. Erasmus ridiculed the "merchant, soldier or judge who believes . . . all his perjury, lust, drunkenness, quarrels, killings, frauds, perfidy and treachery he believes can be somehow paid off . . . in such a way that he's now free to start afresh on a new round of sin." Erasmus scorned those "whose belief in communism of property goes to such lengths that they pick up anything lying about unguarded, and make off with it without a qualm of conscience as if it had come to them by law."

Some of Erasmus's most passionate passages were about war—for instance: "Since the Christian Church was founded on blood, strengthened by blood and increased in blood, they continue to manage its affairs by the sword as if Christ has perished and can no longer protect his own people in his own way. War is something so monstrous that it befits wild beasts rather than men, so crazy that the poets even imagine that it is let loose by Furies, so deadly that it sweeps like a plague through the world, so unjust that it is generally best carried on by the worst type of bandit, so impious that it is quite alien to Christ; and yet they leave everything to devote themselves to war." Erasmus arranged for *The Praise of Folly* to be published in Paris in 1511, and it was reprinted thirty-nine times during his lifetime. It was translated into Danish, Dutch, English, French, German, Icelandic, Italian, and Swedish, and it inspired the great French satirist François Rabelais, among many others.

In 1513, "the warrier pope," Julius II, died, and Erasmus wrote *Julius exclusus,* a satire in which the pope finds the gates of heaven closed. St. Peter tells him, "You are Julius the Emperor come back from hell. . . . With your treaties and your protocols, your armies and your victories, you had no time to read the Gospels. . . . Fraud, usury, and cunning made you pope. . . . The people ought to rise with paving stones and dash such a wretch's brains out."

Erasmus's next book, *Familiarium colloquiorum formulae* (*Forms of Familiar Conversation,* 1514), generally referred to as *Colloquies,* offered a racy guide about religion and life. Erasmus ridiculed greedy clergymen, phony miracles, and meaningless rituals and declared that married love was better than celibacy. Authorities in France ordered the book burned. Charles V, emperor of Spain, the Netherlands, Austria-Hungary, much of Italy, and South America, decreed that anybody using the *Colloquies* would be executed. Yet some twenty-four thousand copies of the *Colloquies* were sold during Erasmus's lifetime, and according to Lord Acton, it was "the most popular book of his age." George Faludy remarked that "neither More's *Utopia,* Montaigne's *Essays* nor Rabelais' *Gargantua* and *Pantagruel* was so widely influential or left such a lasting impression."

Because of all the errors in the official Latin Vulgate edition of the Bible, Erasmus went back to Greek manuscripts—fourteenth-century copies as it turned out—and produced a fresh Latin translation of the New Testament with annotations and commentary. His translation, published in Basel, inspired others to translate the New Testament: Martin Luther's German translation (1522), William Tyndale's English translation (1525), Benedek Komjati's Hungarian translation (1533), and Francisco de Enmzinas's Spanish translation (1543).

In response to Niccolò Machiavelli's *The Prince,* which held that the business of a state is to expand its power and fight wars, Erasmus countered with *Institutio principis Christiani (Education of a Christian Prince),* the very title of which was intended as a contrast to Machiavelli's book title. In it, Erasmus urged a policy of peace and tranquility. Erasmus must have been uneasy about his friend Thomas More's *Utopia,* written in 1515 or 1516, which described an ideal society where "everything's under state control."

Meanwhile, as Charles V and Francis I prepared for war, Erasmus wrote *Querela pacis (The Complaint of Peace).* "Where is the river that has not been dyed with human blood?" he asked. "All [the wars] were undertaken at the caprice of princes, to the great detriment of the people, whom these conflicts in no way concerned." Thirty-two Latin editions of *The Complaint of Peace* appeared during the next century and a half, and it was translated into seven languages. Biographer Faludy noted, "When rigid intolerance slowly gained the upper hand throughout Europe in the wake of the Reformation and Counter Reformation, no other book of Erasmus's was to suffer so much reviling. It was condemned by the Sorbonne in 1525 and publicly burnt. The Spanish translation was banned by the chief inquisitor Juan Valdes, in 1559, and it was burnt in the Spanish Netherlands."

On March 15, 1517, Pope Leo X, son of the Florentine merchant and politician Lorenzo de' Medici, announced the biggest of all indulgences, which meant the church would forgive as many sins as believers were willing to pay for. The goal was to raise money so officials could enjoy lavish living and church monuments. Martin Luther attacked the indulgences in *Disputatio pro declaratione virtutis indulgentiarum (Disputation for Clarification of the Power of Indulgences);* the famous ninety-five theses circulated in Wittenberg on October 31, 1517. By 1520 the pope concluded that Luther's defiance was causing his indulgence revenue to go down, and his inquisitor Hieronymo Aleandro, had people burned for advocating Luther's doctrines. When Erasmus protested the killings, Aleandro vowed to wipe out this "lousy man of letters."

Luther had also made clear that he was an enemy of liberty. "Those who sit in the office of the magistrate," he wrote, "sit in the place of God, and their judgment is as if God judged from Heaven." He believed slaves had no right to rebel against their masters. In response to Erasmus's *Discussion of Free Will* (1524), which maintained that God's grace is meaningless unless individuals have the capacity to make choices, Luther countered with a savage attack, *On the Bondage of the Will,* in which he denounced Erasmus as "a piece of filth." And when German peasants who rebelled against the princes in 1525 expected Luther's support since he had defied the church, he urged that the peasants be slaughtered because he depended on the favor of the princes. About 100,000 peasants were hanged or impaled. Erasmus protested, "The princes know no remedy but cruelty." Historian William Manchester commented, "No other figure on the European stage saw the religious crisis so clearly; if he was vain to suppose that he could impose his solution [tolerance] on it, the fact remains that no other solution made sense."

Despised by Catholics and Lutherans alike, Erasmus was a discouraged man, but he continued to display prodigious industry. In three works— *Against the Theological Faculty of Paris, Refutations of the Errors of the Inquisitor Beda,* and *Against the Holy Inquisition*—he renewed his attack on the Inquisition and on the practice of burning books and heretics. In *Advice to the Senate of Basel,* he warned about coming religious wars and recommended toleration. One of his last works, *On the Sweet Concord of the Church,* expressed the desperate hope that Catholics and Protestants would find a way to live in peace. He wrote to the duke of Saxony, "Tolerating the sects may appear a great evil to you, but it is still much better than a religious war; if the clergy should succeed in entangling the rulers, it will be a catastrophe for Germany and for the Church."

Erasmus moved to Basel, Switzlerland, which he hoped would be free from religious strife. Suffering from painful kidney stones, gout, ulcers, pancreatitis, and rheumatism, he died a little before midnight on July 11, 1536, after a three-week struggle with dysentery. He was about sixty-seven. He was buried in the Basel cathedral.

"Erasmus," noted William Manchester, "died a martyr to everything he despised in life: fear, malice, excess, ignorance, barbarism." The Spanish Inquisition excommunicated him as a heretic, and, Manchester continued, "everything Erasmus had ever published was consigned to the *Index Expurgatorius,* which meant that any Catholic who read the prose which had once delighted a pontiff would be placing his soul in jeopardy." In 1546, the Council of Trent condemned Erasmus's edition of the New Testament, and Pope Paul IV called him "the leader of all heretics" and urged people to burn his writings.

Then came religious persecutions and wars. In Geneva, ruled by theologian John Calvin, people were burned when their church attendance was considered slack. In 1567, the Spanish duke of Alva sentenced thousands of

Dutch Protestants to death, and Protestants retaliated by destroying four hundred Catholic churches. England's Queen Elizabeth I executed some eight hundred rebellious Catholics. In 1572, French Catholics seized and slaughtered thousands of French Protestants, triggering a quarter-century of religious conflicts. And in Germany, bloodshed over religion climaxed during the Thirty Years War (1618-1648), which annihilated about a third of the people.

All of this carnage brought a renewed appreciation for Erasmus. Denis Diderot, the eighteenth-century French dramatist and encyclopedist, wrote, "We are indebted to him, principally for the rebirth of the sciences, criticism and the taste for antiquity." Voltaire's biographer, Alfred Noyes, noted that Erasmus's influence was evident in the Frenchman's satires.

It was in the United States that people began to fulfill Erasmus's vision of tolerance. "Thus for the first time since the Dark Ages," wrote historian Paul Johnson, "a society came into existence in which institutional Christianity was associated with progress and freedom, rather than against them. The United States was Erasmian in its tolerance, Erasmian in its anti-doctrinal animus, above all Erasmian in its desire to explore, within a Christian context, the uttermost limits of human possibilities."

During terrible wars, people remembered Erasmus. In 1813, for instance, amid the Napoleonic Wars, a selection of his commentary was published as *The Plea of Reason, Religion and Humanity Against War*. His *Complaint of Peace* was reprinted in 1917 during World War I. Biographies published in the aftermath of World War I, such as those by Johann Huizinga and Pre-served Smith, stressed Erasmus's commitment to peace. The popular Dutch historian Hendrik Willem Van Loon recalled how, during World War II, the Nazis invaded Holland and destroyed a statue of Erasmus in Rotterdam. Van Loon cried, "Turn me loose in a universe re-created after the Erasmian principles of tolerance, intelligence, wit, and charm of manner and I shall ask for no better."

Clarendon Press published a twelve-volume Latin edition of Erasmus's correspondence, *Opus Epistolarum* (1906–1958), which historian Myron Gilmore called "the single most important source for the intellectual history of the Renaissance and Reformation." In 1969, North-Holland Publishing Company began issuing a comprehensive Latin edition of Erasmus' works, *Opera Omnia,* and twenty-five volumes have thus far been published. Also during the 1960s, University of Toronto Press editor Ron Schoeffel wanted to read some of Erasmus's correspondence, only to discover there was not any standard edition in English. He arranged financing, contacted about a hundred Erasmus scholars, and in 1974 issued the first of a projected eighty-nine volumes of *The Collected Works of Erasmus,* which would include twenty-two volumes of correspondence. Forty-four volumes have appeared.

Erasmus never had much money and never held political office, but he courageously challenged powerful institutions that had dominated Europe for a thousand years. He championed reason over superstition, tolerance over persecution, and peace over war. With his mighty quill pen, this frail man, who complained about bad wine and kidney stones, established intellectual foundations for liberty in the modern world.

AN OPEN SOCIETY

THE MOST DRAMATIC opportunities for religious liberty opened up in the New World as persecuted people fled England. Roger Williams was the greatest of these pioneers. He went beyond toleration and insisted that people be free to worship according to their conscience. "It is impossible for any man or men to maintain their Christ by the sword," he wrote.

Williams established the American colony of Rhode Island, the first sanctuary for religious liberty. "The creation of Rhode Island was," wrote historian Paul Johnson, "a critical turning point in the evolution of America. It not only introduced the principles of complete religious freedom and the separation of church and state, it also inaugurated the practice of religious competition." Moreover, Williams got along peacefully with the Indians, from whom he bought rather than expropriated land, and spent much of his career as a trusted peacemaker between Indians and whites. "Williams could treat Indian culture with respect," observed biographer Perry Miller. "He was the only Englishman of his generation who could do so."

Nevertheless, critics abounded. One, the Scottish Presbyterian Robert Baillie, ridiculed Williams's idea that the English government should be subject "to the free will of the promiscuous multitude." Massachusetts minister William Hubbard called him "a man of a very self-conceited, unquiet, turbulent, and uncharitable spirit." Plymouth historian Nathaniel Morton referred to "the great and lamentable Apostacy of Mr. Williams." Other critics attacked Williams as "divinely mad." Massachusetts officials derided Rhode Island as "the Sewer of New England."

For decades, intolerant neighbors in Massachusetts and Connecticut schemed to seize Rhode Island's territory, but Williams remained an effective defender. Rhode Island people told him in 1652. "Wee may not neglect any opportunity to salute you . . . [who] make firme the fabricke under us."

No portrait of Williams survives, and we have only a vague idea what he looked like. Biographer Cyclone Covey reported that "it is almost certain that he would have been clean-shaven. Beards, goatees, and heavy mustaches were common among Puritan magistrates, but not the fashion for . . . Puritan preachers, who wore no more than a thin mustache, if that. . . . But no matter how much modern commentators may wish to make him into a secular attacker of Puritan religiosity, he remained a devout Puritan preacher and his mental habits always preacher-oriented. Remembering this fact of his primarily being a preacher will more than anything else clarify his perplexing career."

Williams was respected by those who knew him best, including his adversaries. Massachusetts's first governor William Bradford described him as "a man godly and zealous, having many precious parts." After he was banished from Massachusetts, one associate wrote to another Massachusetts governor, John Winthrop: "I am sorry to heare of Mr. Williams separation from you. . . . He is passionate and precipitate, which may transporte him into error, but I hope his integrity and good intentiones will bring him at last into the waye of truth." For years after Williams's banishment from Massachusetts, in which Winthrop played an important role, the two men carried on a warm correspondence. And Williams got along well with Winthrop's son, John, who later became governor of Connecticut.

Williams, who never had much money and died destitute, wrote this about his greatest achievement: "It was not price nor money that could have purchased Rhode Island. Rhode Island was purchased by love."

ROGER WILLIAMS WAS born in a rented house in London around 1603, the third child of James Williams, who might have been a cloth importer. His mother, Alice Pemberton, came from a family of landowners, merchants, and goldsmiths. It was remarkable that Roger survived infancy, since in that year about one in six London children died from the bubonic plague. Accordingc to biographer Ola Elizabeth Winslow, "London became a ghost city."

Williams acquired religious zeal and became aware of religious persecution. When he was about eight, the young London cloth merchant Bartholomew Legate was convicted of being a heretic and "burned to ashes." Roger's home was near Austin Friars, a church attended by Dutch and French refugees who, scorned by Londoners, rejected rituals of the Church of England. Williams developed a facility with both Dutch and French languages.

Perhaps at the church where he worshipped, Williams met Sir Edward Coke, chief justice of the King's Bench, an outspoken champion of common law against Kings James I and Charles I. Apparently Coke observed that Williams took shorthand notes of the sermons and hired him as a secretary in 1617, then sponsored him for admission to Charterhouse School, which he attended for three years, and for Pembroke Hall, Cambridge University, which he entered in June 1623. At the time, Cambridge and Oxford universities offered the only higher education available in England. Williams objected to government influence there. The universities, he wrote, "changed their taste and colour to the Princes eye and Palate."

On December 15, 1629, at High Laver Church (where natural rights philosopher John Locke was later buried), Williams married Mary Barnard, who worked as an aristocrat's companion.

Soon the government began intensifying its suppression of religious dissent. The clear signal came in July 1629, when King Charles I named intolerant William Laud to be bishop of London. Dissenter Alexander Leighton had his nose slit, his face branded, and his ears cut off. Thomas Hooker escaped to Holland.

America loomed as a promising refuge, and in December 1630, Roger and Mary Williams boarded the *Lyon* for Salem, Massachusetts. Fifty-seven days later, they anchored in Boston Harbor. Williams was quickly offered the honored position of teacher at the Boston church, which observed the rituals of the Church of England, but by this time he had apparently come to believe it was wrong for government to enforce religious beliefs, and he turned down the job. "The Civil Magistrate's power," he wrote, "extends only to the Bodies and Goods, and outward state of men."

As Williams became acquainted with Indians, he traded and learned their language. For a while, his primary aim was converting them to Christianity. But in listening to the Indians and hearing their grievances, especially about settlers taking their land, he determined that New England land belonged to the Indians unless they sold it, and he objected to English settlers who justified taking land from the Indians on the grounds that they had no property rights. In his Treatise, he countered that "the Natives are very exact and punctual in the bounds of their Lands, belonging to this or that Prince or People." These were shocking views to English people, who were proud of explorers like John Cabot who had claimed land in the New World for their king.

On July 5, 1635, the General Court of Massachusetts charged Williams with holding "dangerous opinions." He was told he had eight weeks to "give satisfaction to the court, or else to expect the sentence." On October 9, the General Court ordered him to leave the colony within six weeks. And sometime in January 1636, he headed south into the wilderness, amid a bitter-cold winter. Joined by a dozen friends, he reached the headwaters of Narragansett Bay and began to build a settlement and plant crops on the east bank of the Seekonk River. But Plymouth Colony governor Edward Winslow told him he was still on Plymouth territory and would have to start over, building a settlement on the other side of the river.

Williams had little time to prepare for a harsh winter, but as biographer Edwin S. Gaustad observed, "The hardness of that first year was mitigated chiefly by the trusting relationship Williams had developed with the Narragansett Indians. He had traded with them, lived with them, respected them, and they had confidence in him. Now they came to his aid." They agreed to sell him land, seeds, and food. On March 24, 1637, or 1638, there was a ceremony at Pettaquamscutt Rock to confirm officially that Williams had properly purchased land from the Narragansetts. The resulting deed, known as The Towne Evidence, shows that Providence began as Williams's private land purchase. He gave the land to the town fellowship, which included thirteen of his associates, and Providence was officially incorporated on August 20. Settlers who followed him established Portsmouth, Newport, and Warwick.

Apparently Williams intended to retain ownership of the land, but some of his associates demanded squatters' rights for the parcels they worked. In return, he asked that his associates contribute toward community improvements—roads, bridges, and schools—and there do not seem to have been any objections. Williams himself made a living by planting crops and trading with Indians.

The colony became known as a sanctuary for religious toleration, attracting all kinds of immigrants and Williams became uncomfortable with many: riotous Samuel Gorton, mystic Ann Hutchinson with her own religious following, and, most disturbing to Williams, the Quakers. To his credit, as John Winthrop noted, "Mr. Williams and the rest did make an order, that no man should be molested for his conscience."

Despite the agreement with the Narragansetts, Providence was vulnerable. At any time, Massachusetts or Connecticut could have sent forces to seize his colony. If Williams had gone back to England as a recent exile from Massachusetts, he would not have secured a royal patent legitimizing the settlement, so he stayed and defended his position as a squatter.

Massachusetts needed his expertise dealing with Indians, and officials called on him a number of times. Besides the Narragansetts, reported biographer Winslow, "he knew Massasoit, chieftain of the Wampanoags, and also understood something of the long story of family feuds, inter-tribal jealousies, and lusty revenges which slumbered among the Pequots, fiercest and most unscrupulous of all the Indians in the region. An Indian to him was not just an Indian; he was a Pequot, a Cowsett, a Mohawk, a Nyantic, a Wampanoag, a Nipmuc, a Shawomet. In his trading operations along the Cape and inland thus far, he had dealt with members of the rank and file of all these tribes, but fortunately for what was yet to come, he had seen to it that he knew them also at the top level through their chieftains. By all this previous knowledge and direct acquaintance, he had laid foundations that would serve him well as ambassador of peace between red and red, as well as between white and red. . . . Among his acquired qualifications for such a role, his ease with the Indian language was by all odds the most important. . . . The sachems [Indian chiefs] soon discovered that they could not deceive this man, and would not be deceived by him through misinterpretation. . . . In their personal need his friendliness knew no limits. Indians as well as English found their way to his door in confidence at all times."

As more people settled in Providence, internal disputes arose, and these triggered disputes with Massachusetts and Connecticut. When in 1643 several men asked Massachusetts to uphold their land claims in Providence, it became clear that Providence must seek a royal patent to help secure its independence, so Williams sailed to London from New Netherlands in March 1642 or 1643. He spent his time on board ship writing a book, *A Key into the Language of America,* in which he offered about twenty-five hundred Indian phrases relating to greetings, food, shelter, land, weather, trading, religion, and other topics, and in which he shared his many insights about Indians. The book was published in London in 1643, and proved to be quite popular, because there was much interest in American Indians—especially how to make them into Christians.

This a was bad time to get action on Providence, because England was embroiled in civil war, and King Charles I was fighting to save his throne and feared that freedom of conscience would mean chaos—a "stupendous innundation of Heresie," as one pamphleteer put it. Williams did have some friends in England, though. One was twenty-two-year-old Henry Vane who, after having been governor of Massachusetts, had returned to Parliament and supported religious toleration. Williams also befriended John Milton, whose speech, published as *Areopagetica* (1644), was a plea to abolish the prelicensing of printed works. (At that time, any book published without a government license could be burned.) Williams helped Milton learn Dutch, and Milton helped Williams learn Greek.

On December 10, 1643, two agents for the Massachusetts colony secured what became known as the Narragansett Patent for the territory that Williams had purchased from the Indians. It was a phony document without proper signatures or seals, but unless Williams secured an authentic patent, the phony document might gain acceptance, and he would lose everything. Less than ten months after he had arrived in England, on March 14, 1644, Williams was awarded the Free Charter of Civil Incorporation and Government for the Providence Plantations in the Narragansett Bay in New England, which joined the four towns of Providence, Portsmouth, Newport, and Warwick in a single colony. The charter further empowered people in Providence Plantations to govern themselves. Williams wrote, "The form of government established in Providence Plantations is DEMOCRATICAL, that is to say, a government held by the free and voluntary consent of all, or the greater part, of the free inhabitants." In Newport, the court of elections adopted Rhode Island as the name of the colony.

Meanwhile, Williams plunged into religious controversies. In February 1644, he wrote *Mr. Cotton's Letter Lately Printed, Examined and Answered,* venting his anger at John Cotton, who had played a role in banishing him from Massachusetts. Then he wrote *Queries of Highest Consideration,* in which he appealed to Parliament, saying, "Remember that religion is not your care. The Bodies and Goods of the Subject is your charge. Leave their Souls to the Messengers and Embasssadors sent from Heaven." On July 15, his provocatively titled *The Bloudy Tenant of Persecution, for Cause of Conscience* was published in London, presenting a case that religious toleration was not enough; there must be unqualified religious liberty "to diverse and contrary consciences, either of Jew or Gentile. . . . God requireth not an *uniformity* of Religion to be *inacted* and *inforced* in any *civill state.*" Parliament voted "for the publick Burning of one Williams his Booke, intitled, &c. the Tolerating of all Sorts of Religion." Fortunately, some of Williams's friends in Parliament had copies, and he brought copies back to America.

Williams certainly was not the first to call for religious liberty. Earlier pamphlets, such as *The Compassionate Samaritan* and *Liberty of Conscience,* advocated religious liberty, but Williams was the one who defended it. One Robert Baillie had denounced religious liberty as "so prodigious an impiety." Richard Baxter called religious liberty "soul-murder." Thomas Edwards attacked it as the "grand design of the devil, his masterpiece, and chief engine he works by at this time to uphold his tottering kingdom." Nathaniel Ward could not conceive a "worse Assertion than that men ought to have liberty of Conscience."

Williams arrived back in Boston on September 17, 1644, and proceeded to Providence, where he was named the "chiefe officer." Three years later, in May 1647, Portsmouth and Newport agreed to join with Providence in a "democratical" arrangement based on "the free and voluntary consent of all, or the greater part of the free inhabitants."

During the next two decades, there were more efforts to destroy Rhode Island as a sanctuary for religious toleration, and fending each of them consumed Williams's energies. He wrote more pamphlets, including *The Examiner Defended,* which affirmed his defense of "Soul-freedom." Not until July 18, 1663, did all the challenges end as King Charles II granted Rhode Island its first royal charter. It specified that "no person within the said colony, at any time hereafter, shall be in any wise molested, punished, disquieted or called in question, for any difference of opinion in matters of religion." Oppressed people flocked to the colony.

During the late 1670s, Williams's health began to fail. By now he was destitute, having long since sold his trading business and his properties to help the colony. He died in 1683 sometime between January 16 (when he signed a deed) and April 25 (when William Carpenter signed a deed, referring to himself as the last survivor from the original thirteen proprietors of Pawtuxet). Williams was buried behind his house, which subsequently burned.

Intolerant Puritans nevertheless considered him a mortal enemy. Cotton Mather, for instance, wrote in 1702, "There was a whole country in America like to be set on fire by the rapid motion of a windmill in the head of one particular man, Roger Williams." Mather warned that his ideas menaced "the whole political, as well as the ecclesiastical, constitution of the country."

During the nineteeth century, historian George Bancroft interpreted Williams as a Jeffersonian, and this view prevailed through the 1920s. Vernon L. Parrington, for instance, wrote, "The just reknown of Roger Williams has too long been obscured by ecclesiastical historians. . . . He was primarily a political philosopher rather than a theologian—one of the acutest and most searching of his generation of Englishmen, the teacher of Vane and Cromwell and Milton, a forerunner of Locke and the natural-rights school, one of the most notable democratic thinkers that the English race has produced." Other historians have countered that Williams was primarily concerned with religious, not political, principles.

Modern critics like biographer Perry Miller carped at Williams's personal failings. "Roger Williams was exiled as much because he was a nuisance as because he was subversive," Miller wrote. He conceded, however, that "the American character has inevitably been molded by the fact that in the first years of colonization there arose this prophet of religious liberty . . . as a figure and a reputation he was always there to remind Americans that no other conclusion than absolute religious freedom was feasible in this society."

Roger Williams championed religious toleration; he showed that separating church and state would bring peace. The ideas practiced in his fragile colony ultimately prevailed in the United States and inspired people around the world.

BROTHERLY LOVE

❦

DURING THE LATE seventeenth century, when Protestants persecuted Catholics, Catholics persecuted Protestants, and both persecuted Quakers and Jews, William Penn established the largest American sanctuary for freedom of conscience. Everywhere except Rhode Island, colonists stole land from the Indians, but Penn traveled unarmed among the Indians and negotiated peaceful purchases. He gave Pennsylvania a written constitution that limited the power of government, provided a humane penal code, and guaranteed many fundamental liberties.

For the first time in modern history, a large society offered equal rights to people of different races, genders, and religions. Penn's dramatic example caused a stir in Europe. The French philosopher Voltaire, a champion of religious toleration, offered lavish praise: "William Penn might, with reason, boast of having brought down upon earth the Golden Age, which in all probability, never had any real existence but in his dominions."

Penn was the only person who made major contributions to liberty in both the New and the Old Worlds. Before he conceived the idea of Pennsylvania, he became the leading defender of religious toleration in England and was imprisoned six times for speaking out. While in prison, he wrote one pamphlet after another that gave Quakers a literature and attacked intolerance. He alone proved capable of challenging oppressive government policies in court; one of his cases helped secure the right to trial by jury. Penn used his diplomatic skills and family connections to get large numbers of Quakers out of jail and saved many from the gallows. Yet despite the remarkable clarity of his vision for liberty, he had a curious blind spot about slavery and even owned some slaves, probably to help clear his estate near Philadelphia. Antislavery did not become a widely shared Quaker position until 1758, forty years after Penn's death.

Only two portraits of Penn were painted in his lifetime, one depicting him as a handsome youth, the other as a stout old man. A biographer described young Penn's "oval face of almost girlish prettiness but with strong features, the brusqueness of the straight, short nose in counterpoint to the almost sensuous mouth. What gives the face its dominant character are the eyes, burning with a dark, luminous insistence. . . . It is known from verbal descriptions that Penn was fairly tall and athletic. . . . the young man must have been both handsome and impressive."

❖   ❖   ❖

WILLIAM PENN WAS born on October 14, 1644, in London. His father, William Penn, Sr., was was a much-sought-after naval commander because he knew the waters around England, could handle a ship in bad weather, and got the most from his crew. He also had a good personal relationship with Stuart kings and for a while served their most famous adversary, the Puritan Oliver Cromwell. William's mother, Margaret, was said to be Dutch.

Left mostly to himself, young William become interested in religion. He was thrilled to hear a talk by Thomas Loe, a missionary for the Society of Friends, derisively known as Quakers. Founded in 1647 by the English preacher George Fox, Quakers were a mystical Protestant sect emphasizing a direct relationship with God. An individual's conscience, not the Bible, was the ultimate authority on morals. Quakers did not have a clergy or churches; rather, they held meetings where participants meditated silently and spoke when the spirit moved them. They favored plain dress and a simple life rather than aristocratic affectation.

After Penn was expelled from Oxford University for protesting compulsory chapel attendance, he went to study at Lincoln's Inn, a prestigious law school in London. He learned important lessons about legal arguments and court-room strategy. He next served his father as a personal assistant. Admiral Penn rebuilt the British Navy for war with the Dutch. Young William must have gained a valuable inside view of high command, and because his father used him as a courier to deliver military messages to King Charles II, he developed a cordial relationship with the king and his brother, the duke of York and the future King James II.

Penn's quest for spiritual peace led him to attend Quaker meetings, even though the government considered this a crime. In September 1667, police broke into a meeting and arrested everyone. In jail, Penn drew on his legal training to prepare a defense and began writing about freedom of con-science.

His father now disowned him, and he lived in a succession of Quaker households. In 1668, one of his hosts was Isaac Penington, a wealthy man in Buckinghamshire. There he met Pennington's stepdaughter, Gulielma Springett. A friend noted her "innocently open, free and familiar Conversa-tion, springing from the abundant Affability, Courtesy and Sweetness of her natural Temper." Penn and Springett got married April 4, 1672, in a small house. They had seven children, four of whom died in infancy.

Penn began to question the Catholic-Anglican doctrine of the Trinity, and the Anglican bishop had him imprisoned in the Tower of London. Ordered to recant, Penn declared from his cold isolation cell: "My prison shall be my grave before I will budge a jot; for I owe my conscience to no mortal man." By the time he was released seven months later, he had written pamphlets defining the principal elements of Quakerism. His best-known work from this period, *No Cross, No Crown* (1669), presented a pioneering historical case for religious toleration.

He was not free for long. To curb the potential power of Catholics, notably the Stuarts, Parliament had passed the Conventicle Act that aimed to suppress religious dissent as sedition. But the law was applied mainly against Quakers, perhaps because few were politically connected. Thousands of Quakers were imprisoned for their beliefs and the government seized their properties. When Penn decided to challenge the Conventicle Act by holding a meeting on August 14, 1670, the Lord Mayor of London arrested him and his fellow Quakers. At the historic trial, Penn insisted that since the government refused to present a formal indictment—officials were concerned the Conventicle Act might be overturned—the jury could never reach a guilty verdict, and he appealed to England's common law heritage: "If these ancient and fundamental laws, which relate to liberty and property, and which are not limited to particular persuasions in matters of religion, must not be indispensably maintained and observed, who then can say that he has a right to the coat on his back? Certainly our liberties are to be openly invaded, our wives to be ravished, our children slaved, our families ruined, and our estates led away in triumph by every sturdy beggar and malicious informer—as *their* trophies but *our* forfeits for conscience's sake."

The jury acquitted all defendants, but the lord mayor refused to accept this verdict. He fined the jury members and ordered them held in Newgate prison. Still, they affirmed their verdict. After the jury had been imprisoned for about two months, the Court of Common Pleas issued a writ of habeas corpus to set them free, and they sued the lord mayor for false arrest. The lord chief justice of England, together with his eleven associates, ruled unanimously, in a key precedent protecting the right to trial by jury, that juries must not be coerced or punished for their verdicts.

Penn had now become a famous defender of liberty who could attract several thousand people for a public talk. In his travels to see how Quakers were faring, Holland made a strong impression on him because it was substantially free. The pursuit of profit led people to disregard religious differences, and persecuted Jews and Protestants flocked to Holland. Penn began to envision a community based on liberty.

After Parliament refused to embrace religious toleration, Penn asked the king for a charter enabling him to establish an American colony. Perhaps the idea seemed like an easy way to get rid of troublesome Quakers. On March 4, 1681, Charles II signed a charter for territory west of the Delaware River and north of Maryland, approximately the present size of Pennsylvania, where about a thousand Germans, Dutch, and Indians lived without any particular government. The king proposed the name "Pennsilvania," which meant

"Forests of Penn"—honoring Penn's late father. Penn would be proprietor owning all the land, accountable directly to the king. According to traditional accounts, Penn agreed to cancel the debt of 16,000 pounds that the government owed his father for back pay, but no surviving documents speak to such a deal. At the beginning of each year, Penn had to give the king two beaver skins and a fifth of any gold and silver mined within the territory.

Penn sailed to America on the ship *Welcome* and arrived on November 8, 1682. With assembled Friends, he founded Philadelphia, which means "city of brotherly love" in Greek. He approved the site between the Delaware and Schuylkill rivers and envisioned a 10,000-acre city, but his more sober-minded Friends thought that was overly optimistic and accepted a 1,200-acre plan.

Penn was most concerned about developing a legal basis for a free society. In his First Frame of Government, which he and initial land purchasers had adopted on April 25, 1682, he anticipated the Declaration of Independence: "Men being born with a title to perfect freedom and uncontrolled enjoyment of all the rights and privileges of the law of nature. . . . no one can be put out of his estate and subjected to the political view of another, without his consent."

Penn provided that there would be a governor—initially himself—whose powers were limited. He would work with a council (seventy two members), which proposed legislation, and a general assembly (up to five hundred members), which either approved or defeated it. Each year, about a third of members would be elected for three-year terms. As governor, Penn would retain a veto over proposed legislation.

First Frame of Government was the first constitution to provide for peaceful change through amendments. A proposed amendment required the consent of the governor and 85 percent of the elected representatives. It also provided for secure private property, virtually unlimited free enterprise, a free press, trial by jury, and, of course, religious toleration. Whereas the English penal code specified the death penalty for some two hundred offenses, Penn reserved it for just two: murder and treason. As a Quaker, Penn encouraged women to get an education and speak out as men did. He insisted on low taxes and actually suspended all taxes for a year. Pennsylvania, he said, was his "Holy Experiment."

Benevolent though Penn was, people in Pennsylvania were disgruntled about his executive power as proprietor and governor and sought to make the limitations more specific and provide stronger assurances about the prerogatives of the legislature. The constitution was amended several times. The version adopted on October 28, 1701, endured for three-quarters of a century and then became the basis for Pennsylvania's state constitution, adopted in 1776.

Collecting rent due Penn as proprietor was always a headache. He never earned enough from the colonies to offset the costs of administration, which he paid out of his personal capital. He estimated that his total losses from Pennsylvania exceeded £30,000.

Penn achieved peaceful relations with the Indians—Susquehannocks, Shawnees, and Leni-Lenape—who respected his courage because he ventured among them without guards or personal weapons. He was a superior sprinter who could outrun Indian braves, and this helped win him respect. He took the trouble to learn Indian dialects, so he could conduct negotiations without interpreters, and from the beginning acquired Indian land through peaceful, voluntary exchange. Reportedly Penn concluded a "Great Treaty" with the Indians at Shackamaxon, near what is now the Kensington district of Philadelphia. Voltaire hailed this as "the only treaty between those people [Indians and Christians] that was not ratified by an oath, and that was never infringed." His peaceful policies prevailed for about seventy years.

Penn's practices contrasted dramatically with other early colonies, especially Puritan New England, a vicious theocracy. The Puritans despised liberty. They made political dissent a crime; whipped, tarred, and hanged Quakers; and stole what they could from the Indians.

Penn faced tough challenges defending Pennsylvania back in England. There was a lot at stake, because Pennsylvania had become the best hope for persecuted people in England, France, and Germany. Charles II tried to establish an intolerant absolutism modeled after that of the French king, Louis XIV; concerned that Pennsylvania's charter might be revoked, Penn turned on his diplomatic charm and he helped convince the king to proclaim the Acts of Indulgence, which released more than a thousand Quakers, many imprisoned for over a dozen years. He also worked as a remarkable diplomat for religious toleration. Every day as many as two hundred petitioners waited outside his London lodgings, hoping for an audience and help. He intervened personally with the king to save scores of Quakers from a death sentence and got Society of Friends founder George Fox out of jail.

Penn's fortunes collapsed after James II had a son, which meant a Catholic succession. The English rebelled and welcomed the Dutch king, William of Orange, as William III, who overthrew the Stuarts without having to fire a shot. Suddenly Penn's Stuart connections were a terrible liability. He was arrested for treason, and the government seized his estates. Although he was cleared by November 1690, he was marked as a traitor again and became a fugitive for four years, hiding in London's squalid slums. His friend John Locke helped restore his good name, in time to see his wife, Guli, die on February 23, 1694, at age forty-eight.

Harsh experience had taken its toll on Penn. As biographer Hans Fantel put it, "He was getting sallow and paunchy. The years of hiding, with their enforced inactivity, had robbed him of his former physical strength and grace. His stance was now slightly bent, and his enduring grief over the death of Guli had cast an air of listless abstraction over his face." His spirits revived two years later when he married thirty-year-old Hannah Callowhill, the plain and practical daughter of a Bristol linen draper.

Unfortunately, Penn did not attend to administrative details, and his business manager, fellow Quaker Philip Ford, embezzled substantial sums from Penn's estates. Worse, Penn signed papers without reading them. One of them turned out to be a deed transferring Pennsylvania to Ford, who demanded rent exceeding Penn's ability to pay. After Ford's death in 1702, his wife, Bridget, had Penn thrown in debtors' prison, but her cruelty backfired. In 1708 the lord chancellor returned ownership of Pennsylvnia to Penn and his heirs.

In October 1712, Penn suffered a stroke while writing a letter about the future of Pennsylvania. Four months later, he suffered a second stroke. Although he had difficulty speaking and writing, he spent time catching up with his children, whom he had missed during his travels. He died on July 30, 1718. He was buried at Jordans, next to Guli.

Long before his death, Pennsylvania ceased to be a spiritual place dominated by Quakers. Penn's policy of religious toleration and peace, and no military conscription, attracted all kinds of war-weary European immigrants: English, Irish, and Germans; Catholics, Jews, and an assortment of Protestant sects including Dunkers, Huguenots, Lutherans, Mennonites, Moravians, Pietists, and Schwenkfelders. Liberty brought so many immigrants that by the American Revolution, Pennsylvania had grown to some 300,000 people and became probably the second-largest colony after Virginia. Pennsylvania was America's first great melting pot.

Philadelphia was America's largest city, with almost eighteen thousand people, and a major commercial center; sometimes more than a hundred trading ships anchored there during a single day. People in Philadelphia could enjoy any of the goods available in England. Merchant companies, shipyards, and banks flourished. Philadelphia thrived as an entrepôt between Europe and the American frontier, and with an atmosphere of liberty, it emerged as an intellectual center. Between 1740 and 1776, Philadelphia presses issued an estimated eleven thousand pamphlets, almanacs, and books. In 1776, it had seven newspapers reflecting a wide range of opinions. No wonder Penn's "city of brotherly love" became the most sacred site for American liberty, where Thomas Jefferson wrote the Declaration of Independence and delegates drafted the Constitution.

By creating Pennsylvania, William Penn set an enormously important example for liberty. He showed that people who are courageous enough, persistent enough, and resourceful enough can live free. He showed how individuals of different races and religions can live together peacefully when they mind their own business. He affirmed the resilient optimism of free people.

THE SANCTITY OF PRIVATE LIFE

THE FRENCH THINKER Benjamin Constant was, according to respected Oxford University scholar Isaiah Berlin, "the most eloquent of all defenders of freedom and privacy." Constant insisted that individual liberty is a moral principle. "Tell a man," he wrote, "you have the right not to be put to death or despoiled. You give him an entirely different sense of security and guarantee than if you tell him: it is not useful that you should be arbitrarily put to death or despoiled."

Before the French Revolution, monarchy was generally considered the big enemy of liberty. After the revolution turned into totalitarian terror and Napoleon introduced the modern police state, Constant became perhaps the first to recognize that the most serious threat to liberty is political power itself. He understood that the key issue is not who exercises power or how they acquired it but how much power they have over people's lives. "For forty years," he reflected, "I have defended the same principle: freedom in everything, in religion, in philosophy, in literature, in industry, in politics—and by freedom I mean the triumph of the individual both over an authority that would wish to govern by despotic means and over the masses who claim the right to make a minority subservient to a majority. . . . The majority has the right to oblige the minority to respect public order, but everything which does not disturb public order, everything which is purely personal such as our opinions, everything which, in giving expression to opinions, does no harm to others either by provoking physical violence or opposing contrary opinions, everything which, in industry, allows a rival industry to flourish freely—all this is something individual that cannot legitimately be surrendered to the power of the state."

A cosmopolitan man, Constant moved easily among intellectuals in France, Germany, Holland, Belgium, and Britain, as well as his native Switzerland. He absorbed the ideas of baron de Montesquieu about law and those of Adam Smith and Jean-Baptiste Say about markets. He was a friend of the German political thinker Wilhelm von Humboldt and the German literary geniuses Johann Wolfgang von Goethe and Friedrich Schiller. In the French Chamber of Deputies, Constant championed civil liberties with the legendary Lafayette. Novelist-playwright Victor Hugo believed that Constant was "one of those rare men, who furbish, polish, and sharpen the general ideas of their times." Lafayette remembered Constant, "Endowed with one of the most extensive and varied esprits which has ever existed . . . the master of all the languages and literatures of Europe, he united to the highest degree sagacity . . . and the faculty, especialy attributable to the French school, of making clear abstract ideas."

Constant was an eyeful. "His appearance was striking," noted biographer J. Christopher Herold, "tall and gangling, in his late twenties; a pale, freckled face surmounted by a shock of flamboyant red hair, braided at the nape and held up by a small comb; a nervous tic; red-rimmed myopic [blue] eyes; ironic mouth; a long, finely curved nose; long torso, poor posture, slightly pot-bellied, long-legged, wearing a long flapping riding coat—a decidedly gauche, unhandsome, yet interesting and attractive figure of a man, certainly somebody altogether out of the ordinary."

By his fifties, Constant had become a familiar member of the Chamber of Deputies, the French elected legislative body, where he was an outstanding champion for liberty, especially freedom of speech and freedom of the press. According to historian Paul Thureau-Dangin, "He showed great skill in argument, rare presence of mind, he had a way of saying everything, despite legal restrictions, so that even the most intolerant audience understood what he was implying, and he was nimble enough to slip through his opponent's fingers and to stand up for himself even in the tightest corner."

AS CONSTANT BEGAN the story of his life, he wrote, "I was born on 25 October 1767, in Lausanne, Switzerland, the son of Henriette de Chandieu, who was from a formerly French family which had taken refuge in the Pays de Vaud for religious reasons, and Juste Constant de Rebecque, a colonel in a Swiss regiment in the service of Holland. My mother died as a result of giving birth, a week after I was born."

After a succession of tutors, he went to the University of Erlangen (Bavaria) where he began learning German (and became addicted to gambling) and then transferred to the University of Edinburgh, whose faculty included such distinguished friends of liberty as Adam Smith, Adam Ferguson, and Dugald Stewart. Constant mainly studied history and Greek. After two years he went to Paris and studied with the intellectual Jean-Baptiste-Antoine Suard, whose friends included philosopher marquis de Condorcet and the freedom fighter Lafayette.

On September 18, 1794, Constant met twenty-eight-year-old Germaine de Staël, who emerged as the most influential woman in Europe—brilliant, bold, vain, and sensuous. "She was not adverse to displaying those physical advantages which she undeniably had," noted biographer J. Christopher Herold. "Her voluptuous arms, which she always left bare; a generous bosom, which she did not cover even when traveling; and a pair of legs whose substantial proportions seemed to assert the presence of the flesh, lest anyone should suspect her of being pure intellect."

She launched a fabled salon that attracted the leading lights of French life, including Condorcet and Lafayette (who abandoned his "marquis" title during the Revolution). Constant admired Madame de Staël for operating a remarkable network to help friends escape from the French Reign of Terror. One of her friends, Jean Lambert Tallien, launched the political attack on Maximilien Robespierre that brought his overthrow and execution on July 27, 1794, ending the Reign of Terror. The following year, Constant and Staël ventured to Paris and witnessed the ruins of revolution amid runaway inflation. There was unrest because of high taxes, forced loans, military conscription, and the seizure of gold, silver, and art works. Poor people resented greedy government officials, who seized their crops and their sons. There were price controls, chronic shortages, and endless lines for the simplest things like bread. In once-prosperous Lyons, an estimated thirteen thousand out of fifteen thousand shopkeepers were driven out of business. The government responded by ordering dissidents arrested, suppressing newspapers, and deporting editors. On November 9, 1799, the bold and resourceful Napoleon Bonaparte seized power and proceeded to establish a police state.

To appear as if he were establishing representative government, Napoleon established a tribunate whose members received a salary and were expected to support his policies. Constant was appointed a tribune, but in his first address, on January 5, 1800, he presented a case for freedom of speech and denounced Napoleon's absolute power. He was dismissed and fled with Madame de Staël to Coppet, her family estate near Geneva. Then they traveled to Weimar, Germany, where he got to know Goethe and Schiller. "With Benjamin Constant," Goethe noted in a memoir, "I enjoyed many hours of the most pleasurable and profitable intercourse. . . . The efforts he made to attune my ideas to his conceptions and as it were to translate them into his own language—all this was of the greatest help to me."

Constant's autobiographical novel *Adolphe,* which chronicled the ups and downs of an affair between Adolphe and a Polish woman named Ellenore, was presumed to be based on his affair with Staël that ended in 1808. By the time the novel was published in 1816, Constant had married Charlotte von Hardenberg, who offered him the closest thing he would ever know to domestic harmony.

Meanwhile, Napoleon had emerged as a world-class monster. As historian Paul Johnson wrote, Napoleon "created the first modern police state, and he exported it. Austria, Prussia, and Russia all learned from the methods of Joseph Fouche, Bonaparte's minister of police, from 1799 to 1814. . . . Over 2 million people died as direct consequence of Bonaparte's campaigns, many more through poverty and disease and undernourishment. Countless villages had been burned in the paths of the advancing and retreating armies. Almost every capital in Europe had been occupied—some, like Vienna, Dresden, Berlin and Madrid, more than once. Moscow had been put to the torch. . . . The wars set back the economic life of much of Europe for a generation. They made men behave like beasts, and worse. . . . In Spain, French stragglers were stripped and roasted alive, and in Russia the serfs buried them up to their necks in mud and ice for the wolves to feed on."

In late November 1813, Constant started writing a pamphlet, *De l'esprit de conquête et de l'usurpation (The Spirit of Conquest)*, which told how a police state crushes private life. The Hanover edition appeared on January 30, 1814. This was followed by a London edition (March) and two Paris editions (April, July).

The British and their allies finally entered Paris on March 31, 1814. On April 6, the Senate, whose members were nominated by Napoleon, voted to depose him, and he fled to the island of Elba, between Corsica and western Italy. The British favored the restoration of the Bourbon monarchy as the best bet for peace, and the Bourbon heir became Louis XVIII. He issued the *Charte*, another French constitution, which promised religious toleration, equality before the law, freedom of the press, and a two-chamber legislature. But ultraroyalists, led by the king's brother, the comte d'Artois, were outraged that the king would embrace such liberal ideas. Among those defending ultra views was Felicité Robert de Lamennais, whose *Essai sur l'indifférence en matière de religion* (1817) attacked individualism and liberalism as he asserted the supreme authority of the infallible pope. The vicomte de Bonald (Louis Gabriel Ambroise) maintained that sovereignty belonged not to the people but to an absolute monarch. The leading European conservative thinker was Joseph de Maistre who denounced reason, liberty, and democracy, insisting that the only alternative to chaos was a Catholic king.

Constant responded to the ultras by writing pamphlets that emphasized the importance of limiting government power. For instance, in *Les Réflexions sur les Constitutions (Reflections on Constitutions and the Necessary Guarantees,* 1814), he insisted on the primacy of civil liberties. When censors suppressed this pamphlet, Constant wrote another, *De la liberté des brochures, des pamphlets et des journaux (Freedom of Pamphlets and Newspapers).*

On March 1, 1815, Napoleon escaped from Elba and landed on the Cap d'Antibes, near Cannes, with about 800,000 gold francs and 1,100 soldiers, and they marched toward Paris. As they proceeded north, more soldiers joined them. Although Constant loathed the Bourbon kings, he gave Louis XVIII credit for acknowledging some liberal principles, and he wrote an attack on Napoleon, published in *Journal de Paris* on March 11, followed with a March 19 attack in *Journal des débats.* The next day Napoleon entered

Paris, and Constant went into hiding at Angers, about 150 miles southwest of Paris. Napoleon declared a general amnesty. The two men met on April 14, and Napoleon told him, "I need the support of the nation. In return, the nation will ask for liberty; she shall have it."

Constant adapted the constitution that Louis XVIII had accepted, and on April 24 Napoleon accepted a modified version with a two-chamber legislature, civilian control of the military, an independent judiciary, freedom of the press, freedom of association, free trade, and trial by jury. The Acte Additionnel aux Constitutions de l'empire, known as La Benjamine, was approved in a plebiscite and proclaimed June 1.

Constant had been working on a book, *Principes de politique (Principles of Politics)*, and it was published in May as an analysis of constitutional principles. "The citizens possess individual rights independently of all social and political authority," he wrote, "and any authority which violates these rights becomes illegitimate. . . . No authority can call these rights into question without destroying its own credentials." Constant explained that unlimited power is dangerous whether exercised in the name of a king or the people: "Arbitrary power destroys morality, for there can be no morality without security; there are no gentle affections without the certainty that the objects of these affections rest safe under the shield of their innocence. . . . When sovereignty is unlimited, there is no means of sheltering individuals from governments." Referring to totalitarian thinker Jean-Jacques Rousseau, Constant added, "It is in vain . . . to submit governments to the general will. It is always they who dictate the content of this will, and all your precautions become illusory. . . . What matters to us is not that our rights should not be violated by one power without the approval of another, but rather than any violation should be equally forbidden to all powers alike."

Before anything could come of the new constitution, the Prussian general Marshal Blucher and the British duke of Wellington (Arthur Wellesley) gathered 213,000 British, Prussian, Dutch, and Belgian soldiers and on June 18 routed Napoleon at Waterloo, near Brussels. Napoleon tried to stay in power, but Lafayette, a member of the Chamber of Deputies, demanded Napoleon's abdication. He was banished to a shabby house he shared with his top officers and families on St. Helena, a British-controlled volcanic island in the South Atlantic Ocean about 1,140 miles east of South Africa, where he died a half-dozen years later. Allied armies entered Paris on July 7, 1815, and the following day Louis XVIII was back in power.

In 1817, the liberal-leaning Minister Elie Decazes pushed through an extension of the voting franchise to every Frenchman over age thirty who paid more than three hundred francs of taxes—about eighty-eight thousand out of an estimated 30 million people. Constant and Lafayette were elected to the Chamber of Deputies from Sarthe, a district in central France, and emerged as leaders of the new Liberal party. Constant edited the newspaper *Minerve française.*

Constant defied laws that prohibited seditious speech and writing, denied court appeals, and required sentences to be carried out within twenty-four hours. He produced dozens of newspaper articles and pamphlets and delivered hundreds of speeches. Nobody was as steadfast a champion of freedom of speech and freedom of the press. He went on to launch a campaign against the African slave trade and attacked slavery for years through articles and speeches.

In 1819, Constant delivered a lecture at the Athénée Royal, Paris, *"De la liberté des anciens comparée à celle des modernes"* ("On liberty ancient and modern"), in which he discussed the vision of liberty that had developed in England and the United States: "It is for every one to have the right to express his opinion, to choose and exercise his occupation, to dispose of his property and even to abuse it, to go and come without having to obtain permission, and without having to give an accounting of his motives or actions. It is the right of each person to associate with other individuals, either to discuss their interests, or to practice the form of worship they prefer, or simply to fill the days and hours in a way which best suits their inclinations and fancies." He hailed commerce, which "inspires in men a vivid love of individual independence. Commerce supplies their needs, satisfies their desires, without the intervention of the authorities. . . . Every time collective power wishes to meddle with private speculations, it harasses the speculators. Every time governments pretend to do our own business, they do it more incompetently and expensively than we would."

In 1822, Constant wrote a remarkable essay, *Commentaire sur l'ouvrage de Filangieri* (*Commentary on the work of Filangieri*). Gaetano Filangieri was an eighteenth-century lawyer and economist from Naples, author of *La scienza della legislazione* (*Science of Legislation,* 1780), who imagined that political power might do good if it were in the right hands. Constant, like Montesquieu, believed laws should be limited to protecting liberty and peace. Therefore, he urged that government policy should be *"laissez-faire, laissez-passer,* and *laissez-aller."*

When Louis XVII died on December 22, 1825, he was succeeded by his ultraroyalist brother, the comte d'Artois, who became Charles X. His policy was to imprison people found guilty of offending Catholic clergymen, to let Catholic clergy appoint all teachers in primary school, and to forbid anybody to question publicly the legitimacy of kings. Constant, elected to the Chamber of Deputies from a Paris district, led the opposition. Then his health deteriorated seriously during 1830. His legs became swollen, and he suffered paralysis in his feet, tongue and other parts of his body. He was confined to his house at 17 rue d'Anjou, Paris, and told a friend, "I have been unable to sustain an hour's conversation."

The French people now decided they had had enough of Charles X, and there was a revolution in July 1830. Lafayette wrote Constant, "A game is being played here in which our heads are all at stake. Bring yours!" Constant went to the Chamber of Deputies, which deposed the king and named the duc d'Orleans as the successor. Constant helped secure his agreement to protect liberties specified in the Charte of 1814.

Constant died on December 8, 1830. He was sixty-three. As his coffin was brought to the Cemetery of Père Lachaise, people waved the tricolor flags of the Liberal party, and Lafayette told the crowd, "Love of liberty, and the need of serving her, always ruled his conduct."

The duc de Broglie, a leader in the Chamber of Deputies, wrote that Constant "was the first to teach republican government to the nation." Armand Carrel, editor of the *Nationale* newspaper, commended him as "the man who during fifteen years had done the most for the constitutional education of France. He taught to every one the philosophy of Government, which had hitherto been inaccessible to ordinary minds." And there was a letter to Constant's wife, Charlotte, signed by thirteen people in the French colonies of Martinique and Guadeloupe who expressed sadness at "the loss of a man who was always the staunchest supporter of our rights."

Constant's most influential ideological successor was Alexis de Tocqueville. "The last generation in France," Tocqueville wrote, "showed how a people might organize a stupendous tyranny in the community at the very time when they were baffling the authority of the nobility and braving the power of kings. . . . When I feel the hand of power lie heavy on my brow, I care but little to know who oppresses me; and I am not the more disposed to pass beneath the yoke, because it is held out to me by the arms of a million men. . . . Unlimited power is in itself a bad and dangerous thing."

Although the French liberal journalist Edward Laboulaye brought out an edition of Constant's works in 1861, collectivism was coming into fashion, and Constant was remembered as an author of French romantic literature (mainly *Adolphe*). This view continues in some quarters; a 1993 biography of Constant by French literature professor Dennis Wood belittles his political philosophy. Elizabeth Schermerhorn's 1924 biography remains the best in English.

But twentieth-century government has brought recognition that Constant had fantastic insight. Political theorists F. A. Hayek and Isaiah Berlin helped revive interest in Constant's political writings during the 1950s, and a new Paris edition of his works was issued in 1957. In 1980, the Institut Benjamin Constant got started in Lausanne, Switzerland, and the first English-language assessment of Constant's political contributions was published: *Benjamin Constant's Philosophy of Liberalism* by political science professor Guy H. Dodge. Cambridge University Press published the first English translation of Constant's major political writings in 1988. New documents have come to light, and since 1993 the German publisher Max Niemeyer Verlag has issued the first three of a projected forty volumes of Constant's publications, memoirs, and correspondence. It it hoped that more people will discover the genius of this great thinker for liberty.

A SEARCH FOR TRUTH

JOHN STUART MILL'S essay *On Liberty* (1859), clear, concise, logical, and passionate, is the most famous work about toleration in the English language. It defends toleration—of thought, speech, and individuality—as a practical means to promote happiness for the greatest number of people. The book inspired generations of classical liberal thinkers and today is probably the only historic work about toleration that most people ever read. Yet from the standpoint of liberty generally, the philosophy behind *On Liberty*—Utilitarianism—was a terrible failure. Mill and other Utilitarians relentlessly hammered the doctrine of natural rights, a moral basis for liberty that had provided the only known intellectual barrier to tyranny. Natural rights, as explained by thinkers like Thomas Jefferson and Thomas Paine, defined what governments could not rightfully do. Neither Mill nor any other Utilitarian offered fixed principles to replace natural rights. As far as Mill was concerned, Utilitarianism became a moral plea for socialism. He did not anticipate how socialist government power could unleash horrifying intolerance during the twentieth century.

Mill was the most influential English philosopher of the nineteenth century; the author of respected books on economics, logic, and political philosophy; a prolific journalist; the editor of a widely followed journal of opinion; and a friend of leading intellectuals in Europe and the United States. People listened when he spoke.

Mill owed his influence perhaps as much to his appealing personality as to his intellectual firepower. He was a rational, positive, generous man who sincerely loved liberty. *On Liberty* resonates with moral fervor even if he could not bring himself to justify liberty for moral reasons. He was ahead of his time in insisting that women are entitled to equal rights, and he endured more hostile criticism for his book *The Subjection of Women* (1869) than for anything else he wrote.

Recalled libertarian author John Morley, who first met Mill several years after *On Liberty* was published, "In bodily presence, though not commanding, at sixty he was attractive, spare in build, his voice low but harmonious, his eye sympathetic and responsive. His perfect simplicity and candour, friendly gravity with no accent of the don, his readiness of interest and curiosity, the evident love of truth and justice and improvement as the standing habit of mind—all this diffused a high, enlightening ethos that, aided by the magic halo of accepted fame, made him extraordinarily impressive."

MILL, WHO WAS born on May 20, 1806, had humble beginnings. Not much is known about his mother, Harriet Barrow. His father, James Mill, went to the University of Edinburgh on a scholarship. James moved to London following the death of his mother and the bankruptcy of his father's meager shoemaking business. He was resourceful and got himself a succession of jobs editing small publications.

Two years later, when James Mill was thirty-five, he met the sixty-year-old philosopher and legal reformer Jeremy Bentham. This eccentric bachelor was quite a sight in an austere Quaker-cut coat, knee breeches, and white woolen stockings. Bentham had developed the doctrine of Utilitarianism, which held that government policy should aim to help achieve the greatest happiness for the greatest number of people. He promoted the expansion of the voting franchise and attacked the irrational, conflicting features of British law. Bentham's zeal inspired James Mill to become a passionate political reformer, who decided to groom his eldest son as a rationalist philosopher who could guide the next generation of political reformers. This involved an ambitious experiment in accelerated education at home. The curriculum consisted mainly of great books. John Stuart Mill started learning Greek when he was three. He learned Latin, arithmetic, algebra, geometry, and political economy by the time he was a teenager. In May 1823, when he was seventeen, he gained security for life—a six-hour-a-day administrative job at the East India Company, arranged by his father who had been working there for four years. Over the thirty-five years he worked there, he got promotions and had plenty of time for intellectual pursuits.

Mill's first effort to improve the world landed him in jail for a couple of days on an obscenity charge: concerned about overpopulation, he had distributed birth control information in a London park. Mill was defiant; his family and friends were scandalized.

He then launched his scholarly career, writing articles for the *Westminster Review*, the Utilitarian journal, which started publication in 1824 and was financed by Bentham. They debated issues with the Whig *Edinburgh Review* as well as the Tory *Quarterly Review*.

Mill seemed to be doing fine. But after all the years of absorbing facts, concentrating on his logical powers and, without a close personal relationship, he suffered a nervous breakdown in 1826, at the age of twenty, and was severely depressed for about six months. Over that time, he began to read poetry and he flirted with the ideas of French socialists Comte de St. Simon and Auguste Comte.

In the summer of 1830, when Mill was twenty-four, he had dinner at the home of London merchant John Taylor and his twenty-two-year-old wife, Harriet Taylor who, it turned out, shared his intellectual interests. According to one acquaintance, she "was possessed of a beauty and grace quite unique of their kind. Tall and slight, with a slightly drooping figure, the movements of undulating grace. A small head, a swan-like thoat, and a complexion like a pearl. Large dark eyes, not soft or sleepy, but with a look of quiet command in them. A low sweet voice with very distinct utterance emphasized the effect of her engrossing personality." Mill was enchanted. They began an affair, with a resigned John Taylor's consent, and spent time together in London and traveled through Europe together, scandalizing their friends. For about two years, Mill was her mentor, sharing his panoramic view of Western thought. Gradually, though, she gained influence over Mill. She suggested changes in his manuscripts, and he reflected her passion for women's rights and social reform.

His *Principles of Political Economy* (1848) was a collaborative effort, and it became the most influential economics book of the nineteenth century. It was sophisticated enough to satisfy the most rigorous thinkers, yet was written in language that was readily understandable by almost everyone. Mill prepared the draft, she critiqued it, and he dutifully made changes, which were significant in later editions (there were four editions before she died—eight altogether). He eliminated his most serious objections to socialism.

John Taylor died in July 1849. Two years later, Mill and Harriet Taylor married, and he gave her a written agreement foreswearing any special legal privileges as a husband. But her health was frail, and she succumbed to tuberculosis in November 1858.

Mill and his wife had collaborated on *On Liberty,* which he had started writing in 1855, and after her death he worked to complete it; the book, published in February 1859, was dedicated to her. Like most other intellectuals, Mill was mainly interested in freedom of thought and was much less concerned about freedom of action, which required secure private contracts as well as private property. The book is an eloquent plea for toleration rather than a general defense of liberty, as is commonly supposed. Nonetheless, the vigor of Mill's language makes clear that he valued liberty for its own sake and not just as one among many possible ways to achieve a Utilitarian's conception of happiness.

"The object of this Essay," he wrote, "is to assert one very simple principle . . . the only purpose for which power can be rightfully exercised over any member of a civilised community, against his will, is to prevent harm to others. . . . Over himself, over his own body and mind, the individual is sovereign." Mill's "one very simple principle" became quite controversial. Adversaries claimed everything an individual might do affected others and therefore was potentially subject to government intervention.

Mill based his case on "utility," rejecting natural rights and offering practical reasons for tolerating unorthodox opinions: "First, if any opinion is compelled to silence, that opinion may, for aught we can certainly know, be true. To deny this is to assume our own infallibility. Secondly, though the silenced opinion be an error, it may, and very commonly does, contain a portion of truth; and since the general or prevailing opinion on any subject is rarely or never the whole truth, it is only by the collision of adverse opinions that the remainder of the truth has any chance of being supplied. Thirdly, even if the received opinion be not only true, but the whole truth; unless it is suffered to be, and actually is, vigorously and earnestly contested, it will, by most of those who receive it, be held in the manner of a prejudice, with little comprehension or feeling of its rational grounds. And not only this, but, fourthly, the meaning of the doctrine itself will be in danger of being lost, or enfeebled, and deprived of its vital effect on the character and conduct."

Then Mill insisted that individuality ought to be tolerated even when eccentricities bother other people. He observed that cultivation of individuality is essential for well-developed human beings, and he reminded readers that no one ever knows which individuals will contribute valuable innovations.

Mill recognized that liberty cannot survive government takeover of the economy: "If the roads, the railways, the banks, the insurance offices, the great joint-stock companies, the universities, and the public charities, were all of them branches of the government; if, in addition, the municipal corporations and local boards, with all that now devolves on them, became departments of the central administration; if the employes of all these different enterprises were appointed and paid by the government, and looked to the government for every rise of life; not all the freedom of the press and popular constitution of the legislature would make this or any other country free otherwise than in name."

Yet, inexplicably, Mill did not see that government control is every bit as dangerous as outright government ownership. For example, although he opposed government schools, he heartily urged that government compel all children to attend schools, set educational standards, and conduct regular examinations to verify that standards are being met, and he thought that the government might have to provide education. Equally amazing, this fabled Utilitarian, as devoted as ever to reason, failed to make a reasoned case for government control. Although he disparaged natural rights philosophers for basing their views on "self-evident" truths, he claimed that government control of education was "almost a self-evident axiom." Moreover, he took the puzzling position that free trade could not be justified by his principles of liberty.

Mill did not come up with anything to take the place of natural rights, which clearly define human liberty and set specific, enforceable limits to government power. His cherished principle of utility turned out to be a slippery slope. Without the anchor of natural rights, Mill found himself advocating steep inheritance taxes, nationalization of land, local government takeover of gas companies, and—most astounding—universal military conscription. Utilitarian James Fitzjames Stephen went much further, advocating an authoritarian government to improve human behavior forcibly by applying Bentham's pleasure-pain principle on a grand scale. During the twentieth century, intellectuals and mobs alike swept aside practical considerations as they plunged into socialism.

In later writings, Mill made clear that he did not think socialism or communism would work. For example, in *Chapters on Socialism,* a partial draft of a book he started in 1869 and published posthumously by his stepdaughter in 1879, he recognized that socialism does not give people any incentive to improve their performance. Mill dismissed talk about central planning.

Although Mill presented a compelling practical case for liberty, he avoided a moral defense of it. Indeed, he made it clear that he believed socialists occupied the moral high ground. Mill died on May 5, 1873, still trying to reconcile the seeming desirability of socialism with its evident dangers.

Despite critical limitations, Mill's essay did much to stimulate continuing debate about liberty. He expressed his practical case more passionately than anyone else, especially his declaration that there is a significant sphere of individual action that should never be restricted by government. Mill's work survived his death and penetrated mainstream opinion like few other writings about liberty before or since. For that, he achieved immortality.

PEACE

Peace,
Dear nurse of arts, plenties and joyful births.
—SHAKESPEARE, HENRY V (1599)

SINCE THE BEGINNING of history, people have tried to acquire wealth through war and conquest. The Old Testament chronicled a succession of terrible wars. The Roman Empire was based on conquest. The Dark Ages was a period of endemic violence. Medieval Europe was rife with violence. More often than not, established churches were an obstacle to peace; at worst, they promoted war. There was almost always a war going on in early modern Europe. During the fourteenth and fifteenth centuries, the Hundred Years War devastated much of France. In the sixteenth century, the Habsburgs and the Dutch fought each other for eighty years. Then the Thirty Years War ravaged Germany, and Britain and the Dutch Republic fought three wars. War bankrupted mighty Spain four times. From 1689 to 1815, there were seven wars between Britain and France. For a long time, peace seemed like an outrageous, even an unpatriotic, idea.

NATURAL LAW AND PEACE

❧

RULERS HAVE JUSTIFIED wars to spread their religion, gain territory, seize assets, or in other ways expand their power. The Florentine political thinker Niccolò Machiavelli had described war as a perfectly legitimate government policy. Then the early seventeenth-century Dutch legal scholar and philosopher Hugo Grotius declared that war was wretched and harmed all participants. If war cannot always be avoided, he pleaded that at least the killing and destruction must be limited: "It is folly, and worse than folly, wantonly to hurt another. . . . War is a matter of gravest importance, because so many calamities usually follow in its train, even upon the head of the innocent. So, where counsels conflict we ought to incline toward peace. . . . It is often a duty, which we owe to our country and ourselves, to forbear having recourse to arms. . . . [The] conquered should be treated with clemency, in order that the interests of each may become the interests of both."

Historian John Neville Figgis observed, "The danger of Machiavelli was not that he dissected motive and tore the decent veil of hypocrisy from statesmen, but that he said or implied that these facts were to be the only ideal of action; the service of Grotius, his forerunners and successors is . . . that they succeeded in placing some bounds to the unlimited predominance of 'reason of state.'"

Grotius originated international law as we know it, refining principles to help improve the prospects for peace. He declared: "On whatever terms peace is made, it must be absolutely kept, from the sacredness of the faith pledged in the engagement, and every thing must be cautiously avoided, not only savouring of treachery, but that may tend to awaken and inflame animosity." His great aim, explained biographer Liesje van Someren, "was to develop, and insist upon, the idea of justice among nations. With that in mind, he hoped that the widest international differences could be met, if not by the parties themselves then by mediators, arbitrators, or international conferences. If the world would only follow Grotius' rules and principles, war may become less frequent, and less horrible."

Grotius championed a natural law philosophy that derived from the higher law doctrine of Marcus Tullius Cicero and other ancient Roman and Greek philosophers: that the legitimacy of government laws must be judged by standards of justice—natural law. Grotius defended natural law without appealing to the Bible or organized religion, insisting instead that it followed from the nature of things and was discovered by human reason. He wrote, "Now the Law of Nature is so unalterable, that it cannot be changed even by God himself. For although the power of God is infinite, yet there are some things, to which it does not extend."

Natural law, Grotius maintained, is the basis of natural rights: "Civilians call a faculty that Right, which every man has to his own. . . . This right comprehends the power, that we have over ourselves, which is called liberty. . . . It likewise comprehends property. . . . Now any thing is unjust, which is repugnant to the nature of society, established among rational creatures. Thus for instance, to deprive another of what belongs to him, merely for one's own advantage, is repugnant to the law of nature." In the process of working out these ideas, intellectual historian Murray N. Rothbard pointed out, Grotius "brought the concepts of natural law and natural rights to the Protestant countries of northern Europe."

Grotius displayed an extraordinary passion for knowledge throughout life. He was considered a child prodigy and achieved impressive things as a young man. He managed to continue learning when he was in prison. His most famous work, *De Jure Belli ac Pacis* (*The Law of War and Peace*) was written when he was an impoverished refugee, and it cited about 120 ancient authors (Cicero was his favorite). Grotius's learning helped him make friends among Catholics and Protestants, although Catholics and Protestants were killing each other.

He had the misfortune of being a Protestant persecuted by Protestants because he defended the view that human beings have free will. It is no wonder, van Someren reported, that "his friends found him often moody and irritable, and not as tactful as he might have been; yet they all liked him. His own family were devoted to him despite the fact that he was sometimes inconsiderate and quarrelsome."

Grotius was apparently an impressive-looking man—tall and handsome. "His features were finely chiseled," wrote biographer Hamilton Vreeland, "his nose slightly aquiline, his eyes blue and sparkling, his hair brown. His person was tall and well formed. Active both in mind and in body."

Grotius influenced the English natural rights philosopher John Locke. The Scottish economist and philosopher Adam Smith observed, "Grotius seems to have been the first who attempted to give the world anything like a regular system of natural jurisprudence, and his treatise [*De Jure Belli ac Pacis*], with all of its imperfections, is perhaps at this day the most complete work on the subject." Thomas Jefferson and James Madison considered Grotius a leading authority on resolving international disputes. Lord Acton declared, "It would be easy to point out . . . a sentence of Grotius that outweighs in influence the Acts of fifty Parliaments."

Historian John U. Nef wrote, "What is most significant for subsequent history in his work on war and peace is the insistence that legal principles exist in the human reason, independent of any actual worldly authority, political or religious, yet binding in the world—principles which should govern in all contingencies arising out of breaches of the peace between sovereign states. Before recourse to arms, a country should make a formal declaration of its grievances, and should go to war only if satisfaction could not be obtained through diplomatic negotiations. Wars should be fought according to accepted rules providing for humane treatment of the wounded and the prisoners. Treaties ending wars should also be drawn according to accepted rules which, in effect, precluded the conquest of one of the antagonists by the other and the subjugation of the enemy population."

HUIG VAN GROOT, Latinized to Hugo Grotius, was born in Delft, Holland, on April 10, 1583. He was the oldest of four children, the son of Jan de Groot and Alida van Oerschie. Jan de Groot was a lawyer and a trustee of the University of Leyden.

This was a perilous time. In 1568, Protestants in the seven northern Dutch provinces had begun their struggle for independence from Spain, whose Catholic king, Philip II, pursued religious intolerance and high taxes. The Dutch, fortunately, were served by able leaders, beginning with William of Orange (William the Silent) and, after his death, his second son, William of Nassau, in partnership with the lawyer Johan van Oldenbarnevelt. William of Nassau proved to be a resourceful military commander, while Oldenbarnevelt kept the provinces politically together.

When Grotius was eleven, he entered the University of Leyden, where he studied Greek and Roman history, philosophy, mathematics, astronomy, law, and religion. As a student, he lived in the home of Franciscus Junius, who passionately believed in religious toleration and peace. Grotius studied for a year in France, earning a bachelor of laws degree at the University of Orléans. Back in Holland, he was sworn in as a lawyer on December 1, 1599, and began practice with a government official. He began his writing career with a book on logic, and he translated a work about using the compass. In 1601, the United Provinces asked eighteen-year-old Grotius to write the history of their valiant struggle against Spain.

Around 1604, the Dutch East India Company, formed to handle Dutch trade in the Indian Ocean, asked Grotius for a brief explaining why they ought to be able to do business with territories claimed by the Portuguese. When he made a case that everybody had the right to use an ocean, regardless of who explored it, the company decided against publishing the brief, *De*

Jure Praedae (*The Law of Spoils*), and it did not come to light until it was discovered in The Hague more than two and a half centuries later.

While visiting Veere, Zeeland, with his lawyer friend Nicholaas van
Reigersbergen, Grotius stayed at the home of Reigersbergen's parents and
met their beautiful, self-assured eighteen-year-old daugher Maria. When she
fell for Grotius, her father recognized marriage possibilities and began negotiations with Hugo's father. The wedding took place in mid-July 1608. They
were to have six children: Cornelius, Pieter, Diederic, Frances, Mary, and
Cornelia.

The Dutch East India Company now asked Grotius for a book about freedom of the seas, and he submitted the twelfth chapter of *De Jure Praedae*,
which was published as *Mare Liberum* (*The Free Sea*). Grotius drew on it
when he prepared a brief against Britain's King James I, who banned foreigners from fishing in the waters around Britain and Ireland. Grotius wrote: "No
prince can challenge further into the sea than he can command with a cannon, except gulfs within their land from one point to another." Cannon-shot
range—about three miles—became an international standard defining territorial waters.

Grotius became a good friend of Jacobus Arminius, a University of Leyden
theology professor who believed that individuals have free will. He disputed
the prevailing Calvinist doctrine of predestination—that God determines
what everybody's fate will be, regardless of how virtuous they are—and
believed instead that anybody could achieve eternal happiness with faith.

Controversy intensified after Arminius's death on October 19, 1609, at age
forty-nine, and Grotius tried to resolve issues peacefully. Elder statesman
Johan van Oldenbarnevelt proposed that city officials should be able to raise
armed forces for maintaining order. On August 29, 1618, Grotius, Oldenbarnevelt and their compatriot Gillis van Ledenberg were arrested, although the
particular charge was not specified, and a special tribunal of twenty-four
judges was set up to hear these cases. Guilty verdicts were a foregone conclusion. Ledenberg, fearing torture, stabbed himself in the stomach and cut his
throat. Oldenbarnevelt, a Founder of the United Provinces, was convicted of
treason and beheaded. Grotius feared the same fate, but on November 19,
1618, he drew a sentence of life imprisonment and forfeiture of all his goods.
Soldiers escorted him to the massive fortress of Loevestein, near Gorcum, with
two moats and walls about six feet thick. Grotius was kept in a two-room cell.

Nine months into his sentence, Grotius's wife, Maria, was given permission
to visit him, and he was allowed to get books from the library of his friend
Adrian Daatselaer, a ribbon and thread merchant. The books were brought
from Daatselaer's house to the prison in a trunk about four feet long. When
Grotius was through, he sent the trunk back so it could bring him more
books. Grotius translated some Greek and Latin tragedies into Dutch, and he

wrote *The Truth of the Christian Religion,* which was later translated into Arabic, Chinese, Danish, English, Flemish, French, German, Greek, Persian, and Swedish. Ironically, since his trial had violated principles of Dutch law, he wrote *Introduction to the Jurisprudence of Holland.*

Security procedures were lax at the prison, and soldiers did not bother to check the trunk as it passed back and forth. On March 22, 1621, Grotius escaped in it, accompanied by their twenty-year-old maid, Elsje van Houwening. Several times, soldiers expressed suspicion because of the unusual weight of the trunk, but Elsje assured them it was filled with books. After arriving at Daatselaer's house, Grotius dressed in stonemasons' clothes and fled to France. Daatselaer, Maria, and Elsje were interrogated, but nothing could be proved against them. Some of Europe's best-known poets celebrated Grotius's escape to freedom and the brave wife and friends who helped him. Maria joined him by September.

Amid poverty and debts—his assets had been seized, and he had few prospects for immediate income—he produced *Justification of the Lawful Government of Holland and West Friesland,* which attacked the proceedings against him. He wrote in it that he had been denied an opportunity to defend himself and that it was not true, as officials claimed, that he had confessed to crimes; he said he had never been interrogated, and he did not know what the alleged crimes were about. Then he affirmed his belief that toleration was better than persecution. When the work was published in Amsterdam in November 1622, it outraged the States-General, which denounced him for what they called "a notorious, seditious and scandalous Libel" and declared that anybody caught possessing or reading a copy of the work would be punished.

When a plague epidemic broke out, Grotius moved to the countryside and accepted an offer to live at a friend's house near Senlis. Here, in 1623, he began work on *De Jure Belli ac Pacis* (the title come from a phrase in Marcus Tullius Cicero's *Oratio pro Balbo*), which expanded on the ideas and organization he had used in *De Jure Praedae,* the unpublished brief written more than twenty years before. Grotius was able to work rapidly because another friend made available a big library, and he finished the book in about a year. It appeared in Paris in June 1625. The printer paid Grotius by giving him two hundred copies of the book.

"I am convinced," Grotius wrote, "that there is some law common to all nations, which applies both to the initiation of war and to the manner in which war should be carried on. There were many and weighty considerations impelling me to write a treatise on the subject of law. I observe everywhere in the Christian world a lawlessness in warfare, of which even barbarous nations would be ashamed. And arms once taken up, there would be an end to all respect for law, whether human or divine, as though a fury had been let loose with general license for all manner of crime."

Grotius was influenced by Thomas Aquinas, Francisco Suarez, and other Scholastic thinkers, but he developed principles of justice independent of organized religion or the Bible. He believed nations should be guided by natural law, which meant "the dictate of right reason showing the moral terpitude, or the moral necessity, of any act from its agreement or disagreement with a rational nature." He did not follow the logic of natural law all the way. He accepted slavery, which clearly violated the natural principle that individuals own themselves, and did not see all the radical implications of natural rights.

Grotius recognized the right of self-defense and the right to be compensated for injuries inflicted by an adversary, but he encouraged restraint. He believed that everything should be done to resolve disputes peacefully, because all sides are sure to suffer grievous losses from war. He advised limiting what might be seized from an adversary. He wrote, "The law of nature indeed authorizes our making such acquisitions in a just war, as may be deemed an equivalent for a debt, which cannot otherwise be obtained, or as may inflict a loss upon the aggressor, provided it be within the bounds of reasonable punishment." Similarly, he insisted that retaliation "must be directly enforced upon the person of the delinquent himself."

De Jure Belli ac Pacis provoked controversy. Catholics were shocked because Grotius did not refer to the popes by their Catholic titles. Accordingly, *De Jure Belli ac Pacis* was placed on the Papal Index in March 1626, and Catholics were forbidden to read it. The book remained on the Papal Index until 1901.

Grotius hoped that the fame he gained from *De Jure Belli ac Pacis* would lead Dutch officials to forgive his escape from prison. He traveled to Rotterdam and visited a statue of Erasmus that had been put up while he was away, but officials issued an order for his arrest, and he fled on March 17, 1632. He now headed for Hamburg because it was reasonably close to Sweden, whose king, Gustavus Adolphus, was emerging as a leading Protestant champion and might retain his services.

Grotius was miserable in Hamburg. He had no money, he met no intellectually interesting people, and he was unable to find a library where he could work. Then Gustavus Adolphus was killed in the battle of Luetzen in November 1632 and was succeeded by his six-year-old daughter, Maria Christina. The regent was Axel Oxentierna who had more important things to think about than Grotius. Then another blow came: Grotius's son Cornelius was killed in battle.

In 1634, largely on the strength of the knowledge and wisdom displayed in *De Jure Belli ac Pacis,* Grotius was asked to be Sweden's ambassador to France. In this capacity, he helped to promote peace between Sweden and France.

When he retired in 1645, he was ill and headed back to Paris. He boarded a ship that got caught in a storm and came ashore on the Pomeranian coast, in northern Germany east of Denmark. He was carried by farm cart about 60 miles to Rostock. He arrived, quite frail, at a lodging house on August 26, 1645. He asked for a minister, and the only one available was John Quistorpius, a Lutheran. Quistorpius remained by Grotius' side and heard his despairing last words: "By undertaking many things I have accomplished nothing."

He died around midnight, August 28, at age sixty-two. According to biographer Charles Edwards, "The vital organs were removed from Grotius' body, sealed in a copper container, and buried in the cathedral at Rostock. His mortal remains were sent to Delft where they were entombed in the Nieuwe Kerk, or New Church, situated on the public square. Ironically, Grotius was laid to rest amidst the tombs of the princes of Orange, one of whom had compelled him to live for so many years as a fugitive from justice."

Biographer W. S. M. Knight reported that "during the century succeeding the first publication [of De Jure Belli ac Pacis] edition after edition issued from the press, almost always in Germany or Holland, at the rate of about one in every third year." Gradually, though, people came to rely on more recent works. By the twentieth century, according to Steven Forde in an article in the American Political Science Review, Grotius's "reputation suffered a severe decline due to the rise of positivism in international law and the disfavor of natural law thinking in moral philosophy." Positivist thinkers insisted that whatever government does is acceptable as long as it is legal. But the positivist view was discredited when twentieth-century governments murdered millions legally. There is renewed interest in Grotius—for instance, many Grotius sites on the Internet.

Grotius couragously spoke out against war, upheld moral standards independent of rulers, and told how to improve the prospects for peace. The greatest peace settlements, like those ending World War II and the Cold War, displayed his wisdom and generous spirit as they helped turn enemies into friends.

HORRORS OF WAR

❧

FEW OTHER ARTISTS have depicted the horrors of war as dramatically as the Spanish painter Francisco Goya who lived during the violence of the Napoleonic wars. Goya, wrote historians Pierre Gassier and Juliet Wilson, portrayed "scenes of murder, shooting, prisoners, rape and fire, besides those almost indecipherable scenes, certainly among the finest, where figures molded from light and shadow seem to writhe or fly from the threat of some unknown, monstrous horror. In these, Goya goes beyond the conventional limits of a painting or a print to cry aloud. . . . It should be noted that he never painted a single scene to glorify the regular Spanish army, still less the forces of Wellington; the only heroes in his eyes were the common people, the brave women and the men without uniforms, almost without arms, who fought in the shadow of the crushing boot of the conqueror."

Goya's paintings and prints, historian José Lopez-Rey observed, show "the sufferings, and humiliations undergone by creative, upright, or simply innocent tyranny and fanaticism. They also record the radiant moment, in Goya's time, when men, deluded into optimism though they may have been, saw freedom and truth turning the course of history." Goya lived at the time and place where the word *liberales*—liberalism—came into the modern world.

Like Beethoven, Goya created his most important works after he suffered his worst heartbreaks. He went competely deaf at forty-six and lived another thirty-six years in silence. When his satirical works became known, he went from being the toast of royalty to a target of police. He is believed to have had nineteen children, but only his son Francisco Javier survived him.

Goya was among the most sought-after artists of his age. He was asked to paint portraits for King Charles III; his successor, Charles IV; Joseph Bonaparte, who overthrew him; the duke of Wellington, who drove Bonaparte out of power; and Ferdinand VII, who followed Bonaparte. Yet Goya created his most enduring works—especially those expressing antiwar views—in his spare time. Many circulated underground to avoid trouble with the authorities.

Biographer Antonina Vallentin described Goya during the 1790s when he began his spiritual transformation into a great master: "The face had grown very much thinner. The hollow cheeks were underlined by the collar of a heavy beard. . . . His thick black hair was disheveled, its short locks falling in disorder over his vast forehead and piling up heavily around the ears that would never hear again. . . . His big nose thrust itself powerfully forward between the shrunken surfaces of his cheeks, in the elongated oval of his face. The wide mouth was marked by his illness: the sinuous upper lip was slightly twisted, as if the rigidity of paralysis were lingering there still. At the corners of the mouth deep creases met the wrinkles that furrowed the cheeks. . . . Those immense eyes were ringed by deep circles, as if their sadness overflowed in shadows on the cheeks. . . . The heavy gaze is directed within, but with the force of a knockout blow."

Growing up wretchedly poor fired Goya's ambition. He was a maverick determined to make his own way—but cautiously. Critic Richard Schickel added, "He had the vigorous, inflammable nature of a rebel, but his deep need for security and affluence taught him to curb his tongue. Material success and personal prudence, however, never dulled the thrust of his art. He remained to his dying day, at the age of 82, a passionate Spaniard who drew and painted with intense veracity those things he saw around him and the emotion he felt for them."

FRANCISCO JOSÉ DE GOYA y Lucientes was born in Fuendetodos, Aragon province, northern Spain, on March 30, 1746. His mother, Gracia Lucientes, was a *hidalgo,* the lowest rank of the nobility. His father, José Goya, was a notary's son who never made much money as a gilder of church altarpieces, and the family lived in a dark stone hut. Goya had two brothers, Camillo and Tomas.

Spain was then a backwater of Europe where bandits terrorized the countryside, and aristocrats lived off their landed estates and had a prejudice against doing any useful work. Crafts were controlled by medieval guilds, which prevented the emergence of innovative entrepreneurs. Members of the politically powerful Mesta sheep ranchers' association let flocks eat their way through farmland, which discouraged farmers from making improvements. The Inquisition enforced religious orthodoxy.

Not much is known about Goya's youth. Attending a school run by Father Joaquin, who was in the order of the Scolopes, Goya apparently gained little more than knowledge of Catholic rituals, which remained with him all his life. He barely learned how to read or write. He set his mind on becoming an artist, evidently because he wanted to express himself and because he could see that artists were able to travel more easily than other commoners. He learned how to paint the human figure by copying sculpture because it was against the law in Spain to paint a nude person.

Goya began to get commissions for religious painting and decided it was time to become respectable. On May 23, 1773, he married Josefa Bayeu, the younger sister of the painter Francisco Bayeu, who worked at the Spanish royal court. The one portrait believed to be of her shows a woman with large eyes, thin lips, and reddish-blond hair. It is not known how many children they had, but all except one son died in infancy.

A big breakthrough came when Goya was offered a commission from the Royal Tapestry Manufacture, where he produced thirty dynamic designs about everyday life in Madrid. Then he did a series of well-received portraits of aristocrats, for which he often got paid, and was appointed a painter for King Charles IV in April 1789.

While Goya was establishing himself as an artist of royalty, the French Revolution awakened his ideals of justice. In particular, he sympathized with those who wanted to end the Spanish Inquisition, which ruthlessly suppressed heresy. Defendants were brought before judges without being told the names of their accusers. They were commonly tortured until they told the inquisitors something incriminating, and then they were convicted. Sentences were read publicly to humiliate defendants before they were burned.

In 1792, Goya suffered a collapse because of the syphilis that had cost him his hearing. Cut off from people and forced to draw inspiration from within, his art changed dramatically. He embraced shocking realism, portraying the royal family as a bunch of homely people.

Goya began creating uncommissioned works. In February 1799, he finished *Caprichos,* eighty etchings caricaturing the irrationality of life around him. "The word *capricho,*" explained art historian A. Hyatt Mayor, "refers to the goat (*cabra*) who scorns the huddle of sheep on the valley floor to browse dangerously on the cliffs. Goya's Caprichos comment outwardly on the hobbles of ignorance in Spain's medievalism, then being revealed by new ideas from France and England." Among other subjects, Goya depicted a fickle woman, a harsh mother, stupid aristocrats, and brutal inquisitors. One image seems to say it all: *El sueño de la razón produce monstruos* (The sleep of reason produces monsters). Apparently because Goya was afraid of the Spanish Inquisition, he withdrew *Caprichos* from the market just two weeks after they had been offered.

Soon Spaniards had much more to worry about than the Inquisition. Napoleon Bonaparte, expanding his power through Europe, interpreted squabbling at the Spanish royal court as an opportunity to seize direct control of Spain. In March 1808, he banished King Charles IV to Italy, imprisoned his rival Ferdinand, and made his older brother Joseph Bonaparte the king of Spain.

Like many other Spaniards disgusted with the bloody Inquisition and corrupt monarchy, Goya must have hoped Napoleon would bring needed reforms. Napoleon, after all, had reformed the hodgepodge of civil laws in France, abolishing medieval practices. But French soldiers were behaving like conquerors, raping, robbing, and pillaging. Throughout Spain, clergymen, aristocrats, merchants, tradesmen, and others formed committees to help organize what came to be called *guerrilla* (little war) resistance. They constantly changed their tactics and practiced sabotage and terrorism against the foreign invaders. This struggle was the Peninsular War.

Napoleon dispatched some 300,000 soldiers to maintain control, and Spaniards retaliated against the escalating brutality. "French corpses piled up in the mountain ravines, reported biographer Antonina Vallentin," . . . Drunk with fury against the servants of Christ who preached hatred, the French soldiers sacked the churches, carried away the objects of veneration, profaned the House. The village priests slaughtered the French who sought refuge among them. Farms were left burning like torches when the French had passed by. The wounded and the ill were murdered as they were being taken from one place to another. The roads were strewn with denuded corpses; the trees were weighed down with the bodies of men hanged; blind hate was loosed against hate, a nameless terror roamed the deserted countryside, death came slowly through the most frightful mutilations . . . Goya had seen the ravages of war with his own eyes."

The Napoleonic wars, reported Paul Johnson, "set back the economic life of much of Europe for a generation. They made men behave like beasts, and worse. The battles were bigger and much more bloody. The armies of the old regimes were of long-service professional veterans, often lifers, obsessed with uniforms, pipe clay, polished brass, and their elaborate drill—the kings could not bear to lose them. Bonaparte cut off the pigtails, ended the powdered hair, supplied mass-produced uniforms and spent the lives of his young, conscripted recruits as though they were loose change. His insistence that they live off the land did not work in subsistence economies like Spain and Russia, where if the soldiers stole, the peasants starved. So in Spain, French stragglers were stripped and roasted alive. . . . Throughout Europe, the standards of human conduct declined as men and women, and their growing children, learned to live brutally."

Goya lay low for a while. In 1810 he began a series of eighty-five dramatic etchings, *Los desastres de la guerra* (*The Disasters of War*), that he continued to work on for a decade (although they were not gathered together and published until 1863). The title might have referred to the *Les misères et les malheurs de la guerre* (*The Miseries of War*), etchings by the French printmaker Jacques Callot, who had illustrated the monstrous killing of the Thirty Years War (1618–1648). Goya's proofs circulated, but publishing them would have brought harsh reprisals from church and government officials. They leave little to the imagination as they show people being shot, castrated, beheaded, and hanged. Women were ravished by soldiers, the dead were picked clean of valuables, and bodies piled up for the vultures. To avoid singling out the French, Goya only did a sketchy rendering of military uniforms; the soldiers could have been from any army. "The *Disasters*," wrote Elie Faure, "constitute the most terrible document, because it is the truest, which has remained to us of the Spanish war of independence, or for that matter of any war, past, present or future."

In 1812, the year Goya's wife, Josefa, died, the Cortes (representative body) of Cadiz issued a liberal constitution. It provided for a monarch with limited powers and affirmed the principle of popular sovereignty, establishing a single-chamber legislature, with no reserved seats for the Catholic church or aristocrats. This Constitution of Cadiz abolished the inquisitorial powers of the Holy Office, provided for an independent judiciary without interference from the executive power, and decreed a free press.

"The first Liberals, calling themselves by that name, arose in Spain among certain opponents of Napoleonic occupation," observed historian Robert R. Palmer. "The word then passed to France, where it denoted opposition to royalism after the restoration of the Bourbons in 1814. In England many Whigs became increasingly liberal, as did even a few Tories, until the great Liberal party was founded in the 1850s." But this spark of liberalism was soon snuffed out in Spain. In 1813, after Napoleon's stunning losses in Russia, the duke of Wellington, the brilliant Irish-born British general, forced the French out of Spain and subsequently defeated Napoleon at Waterloo. When Ferdinand, supported by the Spanish army and the Catholic church, gained the Spanish crown in March 1814, he imprisoned liberals, reestablished the Spanish Inquisition, and dissolved the Cortes, saying, "Not only do I refuse to swear to observe the Constitution, or to recognize any decrees of the Cortes, but I declare the Constitution and decrees alike null and void, today and forever."

Goya poured volcanic passions into immortalizing the struggle against tyranny, singling out the Napoleonic nightmare rather than Ferdinand, who had just come to power. In 1814, he painted *The Second of May, 1808, in Madrid: The Insurrection against the Mamelukes* and especially *The Third of May, 1808, in Madrid: The Shooting on Principe Pio Mountain.* Although Goya almost certainly did not witness these events, he saw many stabbings and shootings during the years of guerrilla warfare. Art historian H. W. Janson wrote, "The picture has all the emotional intensity of religious art, but these martyrs are dying for Liberty, not the Kingdom of Heaven; and their executioners are not the agents of Satan but of political tyranny."

Historian Fred Licht wrote, "If one regards Goya's total *oeuvre* from the point of view of civilization as a whole, then certainly there can be no doubt that *The Third of May* is Goya's most important achievement. . . . No visitor to the Prado has failed to experience a marked and shocking disparity between it and all the other paintings housed in the same museum. Without exception, all the other pictures declare themselves as composed realities. Raw facts have been contemplated, rearranged, and then presented to us. Art was meant for our pleasure or for our instruction; someone has taken us by the hand and guided us. With *The Third of May* we are suddenly thrust unguided into a brutal scene of murder and anguish. The true force of the picture lies in its ferocious shock value."

At *Quinta del Sordo* (house of the deaf man), a two-story adobe house he had bought outside Madrid in February 1819, Goya painted the walls of two rooms in fresco—fourteen paintings of terrible savagery, which became known as his "Black Paintings." One of the most striking images was a giant Satan devouring a child. "During and after the Peninsular War," explained historian Priscilla Muller, "many considered Napoleon just such a Colossus, as they did too the combined forces of war, bloodshed, famine and irreligion which came to devastate in the wake of Napoleonic intervention. Another highly destructive Colossus, however, long had more than equally menaced the well-being of Spaniards, the uniquely Spanish 'monster,' the Inquisition. Although Inquisition and Napoleon alternately imposed life-destroying reigns of terror, affecting first one faction and then another in the Spain of Goya's time, the Spanish Inquisition was the more immediate painful memory. . . . [It] could not be dismissed entirely or be forgotten, for it would return if Spain's liberal government were to fail, as it soon did."

During a new wave of repression, Goya joined many of his friends who had become exiles in Bordeaux. His friend Leandro Fernandez de Moratin, a dramatist, reported that Goya was "deaf, old, slow and weak." At age seventy-five, he learned the technique of lithography and created some memorable works, but he began showing symptoms of lead poisoning, a consequence of being exposed for years to the lead in white pigment used for priming canvases. Then on April 2, 1848, he awoke partially paralyzed—presumably from a stroke. He died on April 16 around 2 A.M. His long-time companion Leocadia Zorrilla, his grandson Mariano, and liberal Spanish painter Antonio de Brugada by his side.

Goya's friend Don Martin de Goicoechea arranged to have Goya interred the next day in his family's tomb at La Chartreuse cemetery, Bordeaux. In 1899, Goya's remains were brought back to Spain and buried in the chancel of San Antonio de la Florida Church, where he had done some acclaimed fresco paintings.

By this time, Goya's sketchlike style and fantasy subjects were long out of fashion. Academicians favored formal renditions of respectable subjects. When the growth of Madrid threatened *Quinta del Sordo*, a French banker, Frédéric-Emil d'Erlanger, bought it and had Goya's "Black Paintings" transferred to canvas and preserved. They went to the Prado museum.

Out of fashion though he was, Goya had some admirers. One was Eugène Delacroix, the great French romantic artist who painted *Liberty Leading the People* (1830), which celebrated the overthrow of the oppressive Bourbon dynasty.

Bloodbaths of the twentieth century inspired some dramatic antiwar art. The best-known work undoubtedly is *Guernica* (1937), which Pablo Picasso painted after fascists bombed that Basque town during the Spanish Civil War. Nobody, though, has surpassed Goya in his depiction of war horrors. He made clear that war involves senseless slaughter and destruction. Only when people fear the barbarism of war are they likely to refrain from military adventures and cherish peace.

HARMONIOUS INTERESTS

THE NINETEENTH CENTURY was the most peaceful period in modern history. There were no general wars between the fall of Napoleon in 1815 and the outbreak of World War I in 1914. This extraordinary peace followed centuries of endless wars and preceded the colossal carnage of the twentieth century.

Peace prevailed, in large part, because nations seldom tried to push each other around, and economic policy was a major reason for this situation. There was unprecedented freedom of movement for people, goods, and capital. By reducing intervention in economic affairs, governments reduced the risks that economic disputes would escalate into political disputes. There was little economic incentive for military conquest, because people on one side of a border could tap resources about as easily as could people on the other side of a border. Trade expanded, strengthening the stake that nations had in the continued prosperity of one another as customers and suppliers. Free trade was never a guarantee of peace, but it reduced the danger of war more than any public policy ever had.

In all this, one name towers above the rest: Richard Cobden, the straight-talking English textile entrepreneur who gave up his business to crusade during three crucial decades. In pursuing the most successful political strategies for free trade, he articulated the moral case that proved decisive. He traveled throughout Europe, the United States, North Africa, and the Near East, spreading the gospel of free trade to kings and commoners alike and inspiring thousands of people.

"He had no striking physical gifts," noted biographer John Morley. "In his early days, he was slight in frame and build. He afterwards grew nearer to portliness. He had a large and powerful head, and the indescribable charm of a candid eye. His features were not of a commanding type; but they were illuminated and made attractive by the brightness of intelligence, of sympathy, and of earnestness. About the mouth there was a curiously winning mobility and play. His voice was clear, varied in its tones, sweet, and penetrating; but it had scarcely the compass, or the depth, or the many resources that have usually been found in orators who have drawn great multitudes of men to listen to them. Of nervous fire, indeed, he had abundance, though it was not the fire which flames up in the radiant colors of a strong imagination. It was rather the glow of a thoroughly convinced reason, of intellectual ingenuity, of argumentative keenness. It came from transparent honesty, thoroughly clear ideas, and a very definite purpose."

Biographer Wendy Hinde: "Apart from his personal charm and his intellectual liveliness, what most impressed contemporaries was his single-mindedness, his simplicity, his complete disinterestedness and his ability to exclude bitterness and rancour from fierce political controversy."

COBDEN WAS BORN June 3, 1804, the fourth of eleven children, near Heyshott, Sussex, England. His father, William Cobden, was apparently an inept farmer, and he and his wife, Millicent Amber, went bankrupt.

In 1819, Richard started working as a clerk at his uncle's textile warehouse. He became a traveling salesman, and a dozen years later he and two partners launched a textile warehouse business, specializing in calicos and muslins. By 1831, they were doing well enough to take over an old calico-printing factory in Sabden and print their own calicos. Family burdens fell on Cobden when his mother died, his father remained idle, a brother and sister died, and another brother's business failed. He took care of everybody and helped start the first school in his town.

Recognizing that he needed knowledge to get ahead, he began educating himself. He sent away for books on mathematics, and read European history and English and European literature. In 1835, he wrote his first political pamphlet, *England, Ireland and America,* which, among other things, made a case for not starting wars or getting involved in other wars, and in 1836 he wrote *Russia* (1836), a pamphlet that attacked the popular British view that Russia posed a national security threat justifying a big boost in the military budget.

During the next several years, Cobden traveled to France, Switzerland, Spain, and the United States, observing how all kinds of people cooperate peacefully in markets. For example, in Gibraltar he observed "English, French, Spanish, Italian, Mahometans, Christians, and Jews, all bawling and jostling each other, some buying, others selling or bartering."

In 1836 or 1837, Cobden was asked by a man named John Bright to give a talk on education, and the two hit it off. Bright was born on November 16, 1811, the son of a Rochdale cotton spinner. According to one biographer, he had a "beautiful, mild, and intelligent eye, fringed with long and dark lashes, an expansive and noble forehead, over which hung in thick clusters his rich brown, naturally curly hair." Like Cobden, Bright's formal education had ended with grammar school, but he pursued his love for English literature. As a Quaker whose ancestors had been imprisoned for their Nonconformist (non–Church of England) views, Bright expressed a passion for liberty. He honed his speaking abilities in public squares, church meetings, and other gatherings.

Cobden and Bright together attacked the Corn Laws, as grain tariffs were called, and spearheaded a successful national movement. They began by setting an inspiring goal of repealing the Corn Laws. Cobden convinced supporters that every shilling of tariff inflicted misery on people, so modifying the tariffs, a position favored by compromise-minded chamber of commerce people, was out. Free trade could capture the imagination of people as a moral issue. "It appears to me," Cobden wrote an Edinburgh publisher, "that a moral and even a religious spirit may be infused into that topic [free trade], and if agitated in the same manner that the question of slavery has been, it will be irresistible." Success, however, would require a national campaign to coordinate anti–Corn Law associations throughout England—the mission of the Anti-Corn-Law League, launched in March 1839. A national campaign would call for vigorous fund raising, so Cobden made arrangements to turn his calico printing and marketing business over to his partners.

Cobden's mastery of facts helped win supporters. For example, he noted that although farmers in Chester, Gloucester, and Wiltshire wanted high tariffs to protect their cheese, they had to pay needlessly high costs for tariff-protected commodities they wanted, such as oats and beans. Similarly, farmers in the Lothians supported high tariffs on wheat, but this was offset by the extra cost of tariff-protected linseed cake and other foodstuffs for their cattle.

Cobden hammered the Corn Laws for making people miserable. "He knew of a place," noted biographer Morley, "where a hundred wedding-rings had been pawned in a single week to provide bread; and of another place where men and women subsisted on boiled nettles, and dug up the decayed carcase of a cow rather than perish of hunger."

Increasingly, Cobden and Bright appeared together on the same platform, and they achieved far greater impact than either could alone. "Cobden always spoke first," explained Bright's biographer George Macaulay Trevelyan, "disarming prejudice and exposing with clear economic arguments set off in homely illustration the wrongs that farmers and labourers, or manufacturers and operatives, suffered through the working of Protection. When the audience had thus been brought round into a sympathetic state of mind, then—to use Bright's own words—'I used to get up and do a little prize-fighting.' . . . His characteristic and vital contribution was the passion with which he reinforced reason, and the high tone of moral indignation and defiance which he infused into his listeners. And this was exactly where Cobden, the persuader, was necessarily weakest. Each supplied the defects of the other's qualities."

Cobden and Bright were on the road almost nonstop. "We spoke to about two thousand persons in the parish church [Aberdeen]," he wrote his brother, "travelled thirty-five miles, held a meeting at Montrose, and then thirty-five miles to Dundee, for a meeting the same evening. Tomorrow we go to Cupar

Fife, next day, Leith, the day following, Jedburgh. . . . I got here [Newcastle-on-Tyne] last night from Jedburgh, where we had the most extraordinary meeting of all. The streets were blocked up with country people as we entered the place, some of whom had come over the hills for twenty miles."

While the free trade campaign was still a long way from its climax, Cobden married Catherine Anne Williams, a charming Welsh woman who was one of his sister's friends. They went on a honeymoon through France, Switzerland, and Germany—the last time they saw much of each other in quite a while, as it turned out.

Although Cobden and Bright generated increasing popular support for free trade, Tory-dominated Parliament moved slowly. Tories—and probably most Whigs for that matter—were notorious protectionists representing landlords who were convinced that the Corn Laws helped maintain the value of their agricultural land. But pro–free trade historian Thomas Babington Macaulay noted in his diary in 1839, "The cry for free trade in corn seems to be very formidable. If the Ministers play their game well, they may now either triumph completely, or retire with honour. They have excellent cards, if they know how to use them."

Cobden concluded he was not likely to succeed if he were only an outside agitator; he had to work within Parliament too. After an unsuccessful bid, Cobden won election in 1841. He exerted considerable influence because of his ability to get popular support.

Bright's wife, Elizabeth, died of tuberculosis on September 10, 1841. They had been married less than two years, and he was devastated. Three days later, his partner was by his side. "Mr. Cobden," recalled Bright, "called upon me as his friend, and addressed me, as you might suppose, with words of condolence. After a time he looked up and said, 'There are thousands of houses in England at this moment where wives, mothers, and children are dying of hunger. Now,' he said, 'when the first paroxysm of your grief is past, I would advise you to come with me, and we will never rest till the Corn Law is repealed.' I felt in my conscience that there was a work which somebody must do, and therefore I accepted his invitation, and from that time we never ceased to labour hard on behalf of the resolution which we had made."

By September 1845, as torrential rains swept across the British Isles, Cobden told Bright that he was worn out. They had been on the road almost non-stop for more than five years, addressing large crowds night after night. He had not seen much of his wife, and his business was in trouble. He wanted to quit. Bright replied: "Your retirement would be tantamount to a dissolution of the League; its mainspring would be gone. I can in no degree take your place. As a second I can fight; but there are incapacities about me, of which I am fully conscious, which prevent my being more than second in such work as we have laboured in."

The rains continued, accelerating the spread of a potato blight that had recently ruined crops in the United States, Holland, and France. A signs of the blight appeared in England, informed people worried about what might be going on in miserable Ireland where nearly everyone depended on potatoes to survive. Except for northeastern Ulster, Ireland had never gone through an industrial revolution, and Irish peasants were believed to be the poorest in Europe—even worse off than American black slaves. As historian Cecil Woodham-Smith reported, "All nostrums were useless. Whether ventilated, dessicated, salted, or gassed, the potatoes melted into a slimy, decaying mass." Peasants began dying from famine and related epidemics of typhus, cholera and other diseases. Eventually over a million Irish perished, and many more emigrated.

Cobden and Bright intensified the pressure, holding Anti-Corn-Law League meetings in Manchester, London, and other cities, and attracting many thousands of people. They began holding meetings every night, raising as much as £60,000 in just two hours.

Finally Tory Prime Minister Robert Peel reluctantly announced his bill for total repeal of the Corn Laws, phased over a three-year period, by February 1, 1849. In the House of Commons, though, Whigs were split. The House of Lords, overwhelmingly against repeal, had the power to delay any consideration of Peel's bill. Cobden and Bright denounced proposals for some kind of compromise that would keep the Corn Laws.

On May 16, Cobden recalled, he "had the glorious privilege of giving a vote in the majority for the third reading of the bill for the total repeal of the Corn Law. . . . Macaulay and others came and shook hands with me, and congratulated me on the triumph of our cause." The House of Commons passed the bill by a vote of 327 to 229. Against such sustained support for repeal, opposition in the House of Lords faded, and repeal won, 211 to 164.

Repeal ushered in an era of trade liberalization and goodwill. In 1849, England abolished the two-hundred-year-old Navigation Acts, opening its ports to foreign ships. Between 1853 and 1879, Prime Minister William Ewart Gladstone cut the number of dutiable imports from 1,152 to 48. Duties—low ones at that—were retained mostly on luxury items like sugar, tea, coffee, tobacco, liquor, wine, and chicory. Everything else came into England duty free. Free trade boosted incentives for English entrepreneurs to adapt in changing markets. When entrepreneurs failed to deliver what was needed, customers were free to protect their interests by seeking alternatives elsewhere. Problems were not spread from moribund businesses to millions of people.

Although European countries retained their prohibitive tariffs, England prospered. Cheap food poured into the country, and workers shifted out of agriculture into manufacturing. Then as other countries industrialized, many workers shifted into services. England became the leader of world shipping, commerce, insurance, and finance. From 1846 until the outbreak of World War I, its industrial output soared 290 percent. Imports were up 701 percent and exports 673 percent. Money wages in England increased about 59 percent for agricultural workers and 61 percent for industrial workers.

Philosopher Bertrand Russell observed, "If the Corn Laws had remained in force, much more agricultural labor would have been required to feed the increasing population, and less food would have been secured by a given amount of labor on British land than by exchanging manufactures for food produced abroad." Cobden, Russell added, "certainly desired to improve the condition of the working classes, and he certainly did improve their condition most remarkably."

Cobden and his family toured Europe. "His reception," reported biographer Morley, "was everywhere that of a great discoverer in a science which interests the bulk of mankind much more keenly than any other, the science of wealth. He had persuaded the richest country in the world to revolutionize its commercial policy. People looked on him as a man who had found out a momentous secret." In Europe Cobden met friends of liberty like Wilhelm von Humboldt in Prussia and Alexis de Tocqueville and Frédéric Bastiat in France.

Soon after his return to England, Cobden became alarmed by those like Lord Palmerston who believed Britain should get more involved with global politics. As Cobden wrote to Bright in September 1847, "In all my travels, three reflections constantly occur to me: how much unnecessary solicitude and alarm England devotes to the affairs of foreign countries; with how little knowledge we enter upon the task of regulating the concerns of other people; and how much better we might employ our energies in improving matters at home." He continued, "It will be a happy day when England has not an acre of territory in Continental Asia." Finally, he sounded this warning: "If we do not draw in our horns, this country, with all its wealth, energy, and resources, will sink under the weight of its extended empire."

In 1854, Britain entered the Crimean War, purportedly to maintain the balance of power by preventing Russia from grabbing the Turkish empire. Cobden and Bright stood virtually alone for nonintervention and for setting Britain's colonies free. During the next parliamentary elections, in 1857, both were defeated. The two-year war turned out to be a pointless bloodbath that cost the lives of some twenty-five thousand English soldiers.

For the next several decades, English foreign policy returned to nonintervention, as Cobden and Bright had advocated. England stayed out of the Franco-Austrian War, the American Civil War, the Danish War, the Franco-German War, and later wars between Turkey and Russia. By 1859, both Cobden and Bright had been reelected to Parliament.

On July 21, 1859, Bright gave a speech in which he suggested that Britain could cut its military spending (much of which was to protect against a possible attack from France) and that both countries should open their markets. This idea inspired French government trade adviser Michel Chevalier who had met Cobden through Bastiat. Chevalier urged Cobden to try converting the French emperor, Louis-Napoleon, since Cobden had been so successful at converting England to free trade. "We came to the conclusion," Cobden recalled, "that the less we attempted to persuade foreigners to adopt our trade principles, the better; for we discovered so much suspicion of the motives of England, that it was lending an argument to the protectionists abroad to incite a popular feeling against the Free Traders, by enabling them to say—'See what these men are wanting to do; they are partisans of Englishmen, and they are seeking to prostrate our industries at the feet of that perfidious nation'. . . . To take away this pretense we avowed our total indifference whether other nations became free traders or not: but we should abolish Protection for our own sakes, and leave other countries to take whatever course they liked best."

The resulting commercial treaty provided that Britain would end its tariffs on French goods and cut its tariffs on French wines 85 percent. France would convert its import bans to tariffs, which would be reduced to less than 25 percent within five years. The initial term of the treaty would be ten years. The treaty signed by Louis-Napoleon on January 23, 1860, had a dynamic impact. Between 1862 and 1866, the French negotiated trade liberalization treaties with the Zollverein (German customs union), Italy, Belgium, the Netherlands, Switzerland, Spain, Portugal, Sweden, Norway, the Papal States, and North German commercial cities, and most of these in turn liberalized trade with each other. Trade restrictions were reduced or eliminated on international waterways: the Baltic and North Sea channel (1857), and the Danube (1857), Rhine (1861), Scheldt (1863), and Elbe (1870) rivers. Even Russia lowered tariffs somewhat in 1857 and 1868. Because each treaty accepted the most-favored-nation principle, subsequent commercial treaties would offer newcomers the best terms available. Never before in European history had people been able to go about their daily business so freely.

"To the surprise of adamant protectionists," noted economic historian David Landes, "all nations saw their volume of exports grow. Home industries did not collapse before British competition, but rather changed and grew stronger in the process. Marginally inefficient firms, vegetating in the shelter of protective duties, were compelled to retool or close. In France especially, where the high tariff had long been a fetish, the effect of the commercial treaties, coming as they did on the heels of a severe commercial crisis (1857–59), was to purge manufacturing enterprise and hasten its relocation along rational lines."

On one occasion during his last years, Cobden strolled with a friend through St. Paul's Cathedral cemetery, burying ground for many of England's most famous heroes. The friend suggested Cobden might find an honored place there. Cobden replied: "I hope not. My spirit could not rest in peace among these men of war. No, no, cathedrals are not meant to contain the remains of such men as Bright and me."

Approaching his sixty-first birthday, Cobden suffered serious asthma attacks. Breathing became a deadly struggle. In a London lodging house, where he went to relax near the House of Commons, he died on Sunday, April 2, 1865. John Bright was among those by his side. "I have only to say that after twenty years of most intimate and almost brotherly friendship," Bright mourned, "I little knew how much I loved him until I had lost him.

MORAL IMPERATIVE FOR PEACE

❧

WILLIAM EWART GLADSTONE dominated British politics in the heyday of classical liberalism. He entered Parliament at age twenty-three, first held a cabinet post at thirty-four, and delivered his last speech as a member when he was eighty-four. He served as prime minister four times. Nobel laureate F. A. Hayek ranked Gladstone among the greatest friends of liberty, and Lord Acton believed Gladstone's "supremacy was undisputed." Historian Paul Johnson declared, "There is no parallel to his record of achievement in English history."

As chancellor of the exchequer in four ministries, Gladstone fought the most powerful interest groups. He helped abolish more than one thousand—about 95 percent—of Britain's tariffs, and he cut and abolished other taxes year after year. Imagine the U.S. income tax with a single rate of 1.25 percent. That is what was left of the British income tax when Gladstone got through hammering it down. He was not satisfied, though, because he wanted to eliminate it.

Gladstone believed the cost of war should be a deterrent to militarism and insisted on a policy of financing war by taxation. He opposed borrowing money for war, because this would make conflict easier and future generations would be unfairly burdened.

Gladstone's most glorious political campaigns, to stop British imperialism and to give the oppressed Irish self-government, came late in life. Gladstone showed that even in such lost causes, friends of liberty had the strength and courage to put up a tremendous fight that would never be forgotten.

Gladstone towered above his rivals. His most famous was Benjamin Disraeli, the Tory who promoted higher taxes, more powerful government, and imperial conquest. Gladstone's liberal rivals were mostly fans of Viscount Palmerston, best known for his bullying of weaker countries. During the late nineteenth century, Gladstone's chief liberal rival was Joseph Chamberlain, a socialist who became a big imperialist. If Gladstone hadn't been around, there probably would have been fewer gains for liberty, and losses probably would have come faster.

Gladstone's enduring contribution was to stress the moral imperative for liberty. Influential British philosophers Jeremy Bentham and John Stuart Mill had almost banished morality from political discussion as they touted the principle of the greatest good for the greatest number, but Gladstone brought out the moral dimension of taxes, trade, and everything else. "Whatever he did," remarked historian A. J. P. Taylor, "was a holy cause." Gladstone's moral fervor was a key to his popular appeal. As historian J. L. Hammond observed, a "It is safe to say that for one portrait of anybody else in working-class houses, there were ten of Gladstone."

He accomplished much in part because he had prodigious energy. He worked fourteen-hour days to become England's leading expert on government finance. As biographer Richard Shannon noted, "Gladstone spoke copiously. He is estimated to have filled fifteen thousand columns of *Hansard* and to have featured in 366 volumes of that publication in over sixty years as a member of Parliament. . . . Nor was he much less copious 'out of doors' . . . thirty-eight volumes of *Speeches and Pamphlets* and eleven volumes of *Speeches and Writings,* mostly press clippings. In his spare time, Gladstone wrote books, mostly about Greek and Roman literature (he loved Homer); he enjoyed riding horses; and chopping down trees was a favorite pastime. He went on long walks—up to twenty-five miles—well into his seventies, which is why Roy Jenkins remarked that, for him, attempting a biography of Gladstone "is like suddenly deciding, at a late stage in life and after a sedate middle age, to climb the rougher face of the Matterhorn."

Gladstone gained strength from his Anglican faith and happy home life. He married the passionate Catherine Glynne on July 25, 1839. They had four sons and four daughters and remained together more than a half-century, until his death. They lived at Carlton House Terrace in London and at Hawarden, the turreted castle where she was born, on a hilltop overlooking Liverpool. There Gladstone had a library that grew to twenty-seven thousand books. Hawarden had been heavily mortgaged to help finance his brother-in-law's business venture, which failed, and Gladstone spent years paying down debt and saving the property for the family.

Gladstone took charity to heart, even when this exposed him to ridicule. For some forty years, he spent about three nights every week working to help London women quit prostitution, and he helped establish the Church Penitentiary Association for the Reclamation of Fallen Women, which raised money for homes where these women could turn their lives around. He also started the Newport Home of Refuge (Soho Square) and the St. Mary Magdalen Home of Refuge (Paddington) and served on the Management Committee of the Millbank Penitentiary, where arrested prostitutes were sent. He often worked with his wife, and together they established the Clewer Home of Mercy. He spent £83,500 on these missions.

Gladstone's commanding manner made him seem like a giant, yet he was only average height (5 feet, 10¾ inches), with broad shoulders, a pale complexion, and large eyes that were nearly black. During his fifties, his thick black hair thinned and began to turn gray. He let it grow around his face in the popular bewiskered style. His strong, musical voice was a major asset as a public speaker.

Although he was sometimes long-winded (one of his speeches went on for five hours), he could rise to great eloquence. He combined a mastery of facts with an ability to inspire moral indignation. During one election campaign when he faced a hostile crowd of twenty thousand, his stirring two-hour speech climaxed with a unanimous vote of confidence.

Biographer H. C. G. Matthew summed up his importance: "In offering freedom, representative government, free-trade economic progress, international co-operation through discussion and arbitration, probity in government and in society generally, as the chief objectives of public life, and in an ideology which combined and harmonized them, Gladstone offered much to the concept of a civilized society of nations."

WILLIAM EWART GLADSTONE was born December 29, 1809, at 62 Rodney Street, Liverpool. His father, John Gladstone, was a Scottish politician and investor who owned plantations in the West Indies. His mother, Anne Robertson, was a frail woman from Scotland.

Gladstone had a proper education, initially learning from a local clergyman, then at age eleven attending prestigious Eton, where he acquired a lifelong taste for Greek and Latin literature. In October 1829, he enrolled at Christ Church, Oxford.

His father was determined that he become a statesman, so a family friend, the duke of Newcastle, nominated him as a candidate to represent Newark in Parliament. He won the election in December 1832 and the following year began studying law at Lincoln's Inn.

A devout supporter of the Church of England, Gladstone in 1838 wrote *The State in Its Relation with the Church*, which expressed the view that there could be only one religion in society, and government must enforce it. The book is remembered mainly because Thomas Babington Macaulay denounced it in the *Edinburgh Review* (April 1839), and the essay was reprinted in Macaulay's hugely popular collections.

Despite his Tory beliefs, Gladstone instinctively rose to the defense of oppressed people. In 1840, he spoke out against the British government's Opium War, intended to help politically connected merchants sell opium in China. After Gladstone visited Naples in 1850 and discovered that Ferdinand II, king of the Two Sicilies, had some twenty thousand political prisoners, he wrote an angry letter, which circulated throughout Europe.

It was tall, reserved Tory Robert Peel, founder of the Conservative party, who recognized Gladstone's capabilities and named him to the cabinet position of junior lord of the treasury. In a succession of ministries, Gladstone mastered government finances better than anyone else and held many important posts including undersecretary for war and the colonies, vice president of the Board of Trade, president of the Board of Trade, and master of the Mint.

Meanwhile, Benjamin Disraeli, the clever conservative politician, came to the fore. He was a thin, dark-complexioned member of Parliament with long ringlets of black hair. For years, he was known as a dandy who wore jeweled shirts and rings over his gloves. His taste for high living exceeded his modest means, and he spent much of his life struggling to avoid embarrassment because of overdue debts. He was born December 1804 to a Jewish man of letters but later baptized into the Church of England. He denounced the free market views of Adam Smith and felt most comfortable among protectionist aristocrats, despite the anti-Semitism of many of them. Disraeli rejected the principle of religious toleration.

Disraeli made a name for himself during the June 1846 debates about the Corn Laws (grain tariffs) in speeches noted for their controlled, low-key delivery, clever phrasing, and savage personal attacks. Disraeli spearheaded successful efforts to bring down the Tory government of Robert Peel, who had backed repeal of the Corn Laws. When he became Tory chancellor of the exchequer in February 1852, he proposed a budget that supposedly would be balanced by doubling taxes on houses. Gladstone delivered a compelling speech against the budget, intensifying their rivalry, the most memorable in British politics since that between William Pitt the Younger and Charles James Fox. The Tory ministry resigned on December 17, 1852.

Gladstone launched a great campaign for tax cuts when he was appointed chancellor of the exchequer in the coalition government of Lord Aberdeen. His first budget speech, in April 1853, called for income tax cuts, repeal of the soap tax, and reductions in taxes on tea and advertisements. He cut income taxes further in 1863, 1864, and 1865 (that year, he also halved the tax on fire insurance), ultimately bringing the income tax down from 10 percent during the Napoleonic Wars and 6.6 percent during the Crimean War (1854–1856) to 1.25 percent.

In 1860, as chancellor of the exchequer in Lord Palmerston's ministry, Gladstone approved Richard Cobden's plan to negotiate a trade liberalization treaty with France, and it inspired a trend toward freer trade throughout Europe. Disraeli led Tory opposition to tariff cuts, but overall Liberals prevailed, and the number of tariffs was reduced from 1,163 in 1845 to 460 in 1853 and 48 in 1859—only fifteen of any consequence. Between 1861 and 1864, Gladstone persuaded Parliament to abolish the paper tariff, the hops tax, and tariffs on timber and pepper, and he lowered tariffs on sugar, tea, bottled wine, and taxicabs. He announced trade liberalization treaties with Austria, Belgium, and the German states.

The policies were a stupendous triumph. Every effort to cut income taxes, tariffs, and other taxes involved a fight with affected interest groups, yet Gladstone persisted, and the more he cut the cost of government, the more people prospered. "The improved living standards of manual workers," reported economic historian Charles More, "were paralleled by improved living standards both for the middle class and for the very rich."

In 1864, Gladstone had startled many people by declaring, "Every man who is not presumably incapacitated by some consideration of personal unfitness or political danger, is morally entitled to come within the pale of the constitution." Disraeli scoffed that Gladstone "revived the doctrine of Tom Paine." Gladstone was not able to expand the voting franchise, but two years later Disraeli switched positions and maneuvered a more ambitious version of Gladstone's bill through the House of Commons, adding about a million people to the voter rolls.

Now Gladstone focused on injustices in Ireland. The situation there had festered for centuries and became inflamed after Parliament assumed direct control of Ireland in 1800. At the time, libertarian Member of Parliament Charles James Fox had warned "that we ought not to presume to legislate for a nation with whose feelings and affections, wants and interests, opinions and prejudices we have no sympathy." In 1868, Gladstone introduced a resolution that poor Catholic peasants should not be taxed for the (Protestant) Church of Ireland. Prime Minister Disraeli objected that an attack on the Church of Ireland invited attacks on the Church of England. But the House of Commons adopted the resolution, and Disraeli offered his resignation. Liberals won the subsequent elections, and Gladstone became prime minister in December 1868. The following year, Parliament enacted Gladstone's Disestablishment Bill for the Church of Ireland. Then came his Irish Land Act (1870): a paying tenant farmer, evicted from land he worked, was entitled to compensation for buildings and other improvements he made.

After six years as prime minister, Gladstone had offended a host of powerful interest groups; Disraeli accused Gladstone of attacking "every institution and every interest, every class and calling in the country." When Liberals were routed in the February 1874 election, Disraeli, now seventy years old, became prime minister. He pushed through Factory Acts in 1874 and 1878, increasing government regulation of business. His Trade Union Act essentially put labor union bosses above the law. With the Sale of Food and Drugs Act, Disraeli's government assumed responsibility for the health of people. The Artisan's Dwelling Act authorized local governments to seize private property for housing projects.

More distressing for Gladstone, Disraeli promoted imperialism. He spent more money on armaments, got involved in a war between Russia and Turkey, occupied Cyprus, and had British forces invade Transvaal, South

Africa, and Kabul, Afghanistan. He guaranteed to protect three states on the Malay Peninsula and claimed about two hundred Pacific islands. Then he acquired a controlling interest in the Suez Canal, a move that afforded more secure access to British India but became an eighty-year occupation of Egypt, including wars, big military expenditures, and political embarrassments. Disraeli flattered Queen Victoria by naming her empress of India, and she cherished the thought that the sun never set on the British Empire.

But an empire brought trouble. Between April and August 1876, Turkish forces slaughtered some twelve thousand rebellious Bulgarian Christians. Disraeli played this down, because he supported the Turkish regime to offset Russian influence. Gladstone insisted that moral standards apply to everyone, including allies, and his pamphlet, *The Bulgarian Horrors and the Question of the East,* soon sold 200,000 copies. Disraeli snarled, "There may be more infamous men [than Gladstone] but I don't believe there is anyone more wicked."

Gladstone warned against good intentions that end up squandering blood and treasure in foreign wars. On May 7, 1877, he declared: "Consider how we have conquered, planted, annexed, and appropriated at all the points of the compass, so that at few points on the surface of the earth is there not some region or some spot of British dominion at hand. . . . And then I ask you what quarrel can arise between any two countries or what war, in which you may not, if you be so minded to set up British interests as a ground of interference."

The warnings came true. Disraeli tangled with the emir of Afghanistan, who refused to let British diplomats into the country. In South Africa, about eight hundred British soldiers were killed by Zulus, and European pressures led Disraeli to ask for an expanded British naval presence in the Mediterranean. As prime minister, Disraeli hiked taxes by £5 million and incurred £6 million of budget deficits versus Gladstone's previous five years marked by £12 million of tax cuts and £17 million of budget surpluses.

But imperialism was popular, and Gladstone recognized he could not stop it by debating political issues only within Parliament. On November 24, 1879, he launched a campaign for a parliamentary seat in Midlothian, Scotland, long held by Tories. This was the first British political campaign that started before an election date was set. Gladstone urged that foreign policy be based on six principles. First, keep government small so people can prosper. Second, promote peaceful relations among nations. Third, maintain cooperation in Europe. Fourth, avoid "entangling engagements." Fifth, try to treat all nations equally. Sixth, "The foreign policy of England should always be inspired by the love of freedom. . . . In freedom you lay the firmest foundations both of loyalty and order." Disraeli called Gladstone an "Arch Villain," but in March 1880 the Liberals swept out the Tories, and Gladstone was prime minister again. Although he withdrew from Afghanistan, overall he failed to reverse Disraeli's imperialist policies. Nevertheless, he resisted embroiling Britain in more overseas conflicts. The bitter rivalry ended with Disraeli's death on April 19, 1881.

The 1884 Reform Act, which Gladstone engineered, expanded the number of voters from about 3 million to 5 million, but Ireland became the biggest issue during the long sunset of his career. He believed peace would come to Ireland only when feudalism ended, and peasants had a meaningful stake in their work. He thus threw his energies into the 1881 Irish Land Act, which extended protections for tenants who paid rent and obeyed the laws.

Charles Stewart Parnell, an Irish Protestant landowner and influential member of Parliament, called the new Irish Land Act a fraud and urged continued Irish resistance. His bloc voted against Gladstone, forcing the prime minister's resignation on June 9, 1885. But because Tories did not get enough support in the subsequent election, they refused to form a new government, and Gladstone formed his third ministry in January 1886. Parnell's followers had won eighty-five seats during the parliamentary elections, and this seems to have convinced Gladstone the time was ripe for bold action. On April 8, he announced he was for home rule, which would have meant setting up an Irish Parliament to handle domestic policy. Ireland would have remained part of the British Empire, and British Parliament would have handled international relations. Ireland would have contributed some tax revenue to help cover imperial expenses. There would be no more Irish representatives in the British Parliament, which offered the prospect of an end to Irish obstructionist tactics.

Home rule split the Liberal party apart. Many opposed what they considered concessions to violent peasants. In June 1886, ninety-four Liberal members of Parliament voted against Gladstone's home rule bill, defeating it and leading to a general election that the Liberals lost. Gladstone, however, retained his leadership position because he was the "Grand Old Man," the most famous political personality in the land. He still viewed Irish home rule as the top priority and a prelude for home rule in England, Scotland, and Wales. Liberals won the July 1892 general elections, and Gladstone formed his fourth ministry.

He began his last political battle on February 13, 1893. "Never did Gladstone speak more ably than on the introduction of the second Home Rule bill," reported biographer Walter Phelps Hall. "The old familiar thumping on the treasury box was renewed; the magic voice, so grave, so eloquent, now rose and fell in musical cadence, exhorting Englishmen." On September 1, 1893, the House of Commons passed the bill. A week later the Tory-dominated House of Lords rejected it, forcing Gladstone's resignation as prime minister. He told his loyal associate and biographer John Morley, "I was brought up to hate and fear liberty. I came to love it. That is the secret of my whole career."

Gladstone died of cancer at Hawarden on May 19, 1898, surrounded by his wife and children. He was eighty-eight. The coffin was placed in Westminster Hall, and an estimated 250,000 people came to pay their respects. He was buried in Westminster Abbey near his mentor, Robert Peel, who had converted to free trade. "The only comparable non-royal funerals of the past 150 years," reported biographer Roy Jenkins, "have been those of the Duke of Wellington and of Churchill."

As Gladstone anticipated, the Irish seized their destiny. The Irish Free State was established on December 6, 1921. Then came the 1937 constitution for the Republic of Ireland. Northern Ireland, still subject to British rule, remains a source of chronic violence.

Recent biographers have been most fascinated by the publication of *The Gladstone Diaries* (1825–1896, 14 volumes), abounding with detail about his intense religiosity and his determination to help prostitutes find another line of work. There have been biographies by historian Richard Shannon (1984, 1999), historian H. C. G. Matthew (1986, 1995), and Labourite Jenkins (1997).

Gladstone achieved much for liberty. He was a world-class tax cutter who slashed government spending and gave taxpayers a greater voice in their government. He secured the triumph of free trade. He advanced the cause of Irish liberty. He courageously spoke out against imperialism, urging people to embrace liberty and peace rather than power and prestige, and he displayed the kind of moral fervor that could help liberty rise again.

THE FALLACY OF
TERRITORIAL EXPANSION

❧

As LEADING AMERICAN intellectuals clamored for bigger government and war during the late nineteenth century, William Graham Sumner emerged as perhaps the most important American defender of liberty and peace. This popular economics and sociology professor at Yale University for thirty-seven years boldly spoke out when there were serious assaults on liberty. He fought protectionists who robbed people with tariffs enriching special interests, socialists who clamored for power over people's lives, and imperialists who provoked wars. Despite fierce denunciations by major newspapers and repeated efforts to have him dismissed from Yale, he persisted in expressing his libertarian views.

With a mighty pen, he sounded his themes: "All institutions are to be tested by the degree to which they guarantee liberty . . . The history of states has been a history of selfishness, cupidity, and robbery . . . War is never a handy remedy, which can be taken up and applied by routine rule. No war which can be avoided is just to the people who have to carry it on, to say nothing of the enemy . . . If we look back for comparison to anything of which human history gives us a type of experiment, we see that the modern free system of industry offers to every living human being chances of happiness indescribably in excess of what former generations have possessed." And in his essay "War" (1903), he made this epic prediction: "There is only one limit possible to the war preparations of a modern European state; that is, the last man and the last dollar it can control. What will come of the mixture of sentimental social philosophy and warlike policy? There is only one thing rationally to be expected, and that is a frightful effusion of blood in revolution and war during the century now opening." Best-selling economic journalist Henry Hazlitt observed that "few men have ever exposed the fallacies of state paternalism with more gusto and devastating logic." Sumner believed free competition was the only reliable way to identify superior talents and better ways of doing things, to build capital and raise living standards.

Sumner brought impressive scholarship to bear on his work. He studied at leading European universities; read Dutch, French, German, Hebrew, Italian, Polish, Portuguese, Russian, Spanish, and Swedish; and studied thousands of documents. His published work includes biographies of Alexander Hamilton, Andrew Jackson, and Robert Morris, and books about American financial history and sociology. But he achieved immortality through his passionate, polemical books and essays such as *What Social Classes Owe to Each Other*, "The Forgotten Man," "The Fallacy of Territorial Expansion," "The Conquest of the United States by Spain," and "War," all still in print.

Sumner was blunt and plainspoken. At a Yale University faculty meeting, after President A. T. Hadley had disagreed with him, Sumner protested: "But it's the truth." Hadley replied, "It is not always necessary to tell the truth butt-end first." Sumner insisted, "I always tell the truth butt-end first."

Sumner had an unforgettable presence. His student Albert Galloway Keller recalled that "at a time when emulation of Homer and Socrates seemed to go with age, Sumner wore no beard. His close-clipped mustache and fringe of hair were not gray; his complexion was ruddy. He looked powerful in body, though his legs seemed to be a little unsteady. He wore no glasses, except that he clapped on a *pince-nez*, rather fiercely, when he had something to read. He was immaculately groomed and clad—a little old-fashioned sometimes with his tie drawn through a gold band. . . . He was not at all sensitive about his baldness. . . . Once, when we moved offices, I asked him whether a small mirror on the wall was his. 'What do I need of a mirror?' he replied, passing his hand over his head."

WILLIAM GRAHAM SUMNER was born on October 30, 1840, in Paterson, New Jersey. He was the eldest of three children of Thomas Sumner, who had emigrated from Lancashire, England, to Hartford, Connecticut, where he repaired locomotive wheels for the Hartford and New Haven Railroad. His mother was Sarah Graham, whose parents had also come from Lancashire. She died, probably from appendicitis, when William was eight. By the time William was a teenager, he was spending considerable time in the library of the Hartford Young Men's Institute. He read Harriet Martineau's *Illustrations of Political Economy* and other books that emphasized the importance of economic liberty. Early on, he displayed an ability to write well. He produced some adventure stories, such as "Adventures at the Convent of the Great St. Bernard," about the rescue of a political prisoner. He graduated from Yale College in 1863, eighth in his class of 122.

The outbreak of the Civil War brought military conscription, and Sumner was summoned for the army, but at the time it was possible to pay a volunteer substitute, and Sumner's friends raised the needed funds. They also contributed money so he could pursue graduate studies abroad. He studied French and Hebrew in Geneva and then enrolled at the University of Göttingen in Germany, studying German and history for two years.

In December 1867, Sumner was ordained a deacon in Trinity Episcopal Church in New Haven and served in two more churches during the next five years. Meanwhile, he had fallen in love with lively Jeannie Whittemore Elliott, daughter of New York merchant Henry Hill Elliott and Elmira Whittemore Elliott. They were married on April 17, 1871, and eventually had two sons, Eliot and Graham.

Sumner soon decided he would rather teach than preach, and in 1872 he accepted a professorship in political and social science at Yale. His mission, reported biographer Harris E. Starr, was "to make men, to develop the critical faculties of the youth committed to him, to create in them hatred of shams and love of truth."

In 1872, an English publication, *Contemporary Review*, serialized *The Study of Sociology* by the English philosopher Herbert Spencer, and Sumner embraced his idea that free people can achieve unlimited human progress without government direction as private individuals find ways to make money serving others. Spencer cited plenty of experience showing that the major obstacle to progress is government interference. Sumner assigned Spencer's book to his students, but Yale president Noah Porter objected because Spencer downplayed the role of religion. Sumner refused to drop the book and offered to resign, but an uproar among students caused Porter to drop the matter. University officials were embarrassed when the Spencer controversy made the front page of the *New York Times*.

Like Spencer, whom Sumner met on an 1882 visit to Yale, he recognized socialism as an evil. In the modern world, socialism went back to the Swiss-born theorist Jean-Jacques Rousseau, but during the nineteenth century, socialist ideals were tried in voluntary communes like those promoted by Charles Fourier and Robert Owen. Because these voluntary communes collapsed, a number of intellectuals concluded that socialism must be imposed by force. In his essay "Socialism" (probably 1880), Sumner warned that human progress occurs only when everybody has strong incentives to work hard, save money, and improve their property.

Sumner explained how laws backfire in his essay "The Forgotten Man" (1883): "As soon as A observes something which seems to him to be wrong, from which X is suffering, A talks it over with B, and A and B then propose to get a law passed to remedy the evil and help X. Their law always proposes to determine what C shall do for X or, in the better case, what A, B and C shall do for X. As for A and B, who get a law to make themselves do for X what they are willing to do for him, we have nothing to say except that they might better have done it without any law, but what I want to do is to look up C. . . . I call him the Forgotten Man. . . . He is the simple, honest laborer, ready to earn his living by productive work. . . . We shall, before we know it, push down this man who is trying to help himself."

In 1883, Sumner wrote *What Social Classes Owe to Each Other*. "If any one think that there are or ought to be somewhere in society guarantees that no man shall suffer hardship," he explained, "let him understand that there can be no such guarantees, unless other men give them—that is, unless we go back to slavery, and make one man's effort conduce to another man's welfare." Sumner explained how progress occurs spontaneously when people are free: "The modern industrial system is a great social co-operation. . . . The parties are held together by impersonal force—supply and demand. They may never see each other; they may be separated by half the circumference of the globe. Their co-operation in the social effort is combined and distributed again by financial machinery, and the rights and interests are measured and satisfied without any special treaty or convention at all. . . . This great co-operative effort is one of the great products of civilization."

During the Civil War, the federal government had enacted high tariffs (import taxes) to help cover military costs, and these tariffs persisted long afterward. "Import duties of forty, fifty, sixty, even a hundred percent," reported historian Frank W. Taussig, "came to be advocated as a good thing in itself by many who, under normal circumstances, would have thought such a policy preposterous." Sumner insisted that free trade—the right to buy and sell as one wishes—is a key economic liberty. For this, he was denounced by the Republican press, especially the *New York Tribune*, and Republican alumni demanded that Yale fire him.

Sumner counterattacked with *Protectionism—the Ism That Waste Makes Wealth*, which appeared in 1885. "If a protectionist shows me a woolen mill and challenges me to deny that it is a great and valuable industry," Sumner wrote, "I ask him whether it is due to the tariff. . . . If he says 'yes,' then I answer that the mill is not an industry at all. We pay sixty percent tax on cloth simply in order that that mill may be. It is not an institution for getting us cloth, for if we went into the market with the same products which we take there now and if there were no woolen mill, we should get all the cloth we want. The mill is simply an institution for making cloth cost per yard sixty per cent more of our products than it otherwise would. . . . Protectionism is now corrupting our political institutions just as slavery used to do. . . . There is only one reasonable question now to be raised about it, and that is: How can we most easily get rid of it?"

During the 1890s, nations around the world pursued imperialism. In his 1896 essay "Earth Hunger, or the Philosophy of Land Grabbing," Sumner exploded: "Earth hunger is the wildest craving of modern nations. They will shed their blood to appease it. . . . The notion is that colonies are glory. The truth is that colonies are burdens—unless they are plundered, and then they are enemies."

An increasing number of Americans felt they had to have some kind of empire. Hawaii (then known as the Sandwich Islands) had made treaties with the United States, encouraging American investors to develop sugar plantations, and they thrived. Almost 100 percent of Hawaiian sugar was exported to the United States. But the 1890 McKinley tariff threatened to keep it out, jeopardizing all the investments there. Accordingly, the sugar planters lobbied in Washington to have the United States make Hawaii a U.S. territory, since this would nullify the effect of the McKinley tariff as far as Hawaii was concerned. In 1893, the U.S. Marines invaded Hawaii, and the queen was deposed. Sumner protested such military intervention with his essay "The Fallacy of Territorial Expansion," which appeared in the June 1896 *Forum*.

But American imperialists wanted more. Admiral Alfred Thayer Mahan's *The Influence of Sea Power upon History, 1660–1783* (1890), claimed that the future belonged to nations with big navies, and Republican politicians like Henry Cabot Lodge, Albert J. Beveridge, and Theodore Roosevelt aggressively promoted Mahan's ideas. The *Washington Post* reported, "The taste of Empire is in the mouth of the people even as the taste of blood in the jungle."

In 1895, the Cubans rebelled against their Spanish rulers, and the Spanish retaliated harshly, with newspapers like the *New York World* and *New York Journal* giving front-page coverage to the lurid horrors. On February 15, 1898, the U.S. battleship *Maine* exploded in Havana harbor, and 260 lives were lost, reportedly because the ship had struck a Spanish submarine mine. Amid cries to "Remember the Maine!" Congress authorized spending $50 million for national defense. On April 20, Congress approved a joint resolution that authorized military forces to invade Cuba. Within ten weeks, U.S. forces easily defeated the Spanish in the Philippines as well as Cuba. The U.S. ambassador to Great Britain (and soon Secretary of State), John Hay, told Theodore Roosevelt, "It has been a splendid little war."

The Spanish-American War outraged Sumner. On January 16, 1899, he delivered a defiant talk at crowded College Street Hall, Yale University. Titled "The Conquest of the United States by Spain," it subsequently appeared in the *Yale Law Journal*. He declared, "We have beaten Spain in a military conflict, but we are submitting to be conquered by her on the field of ideas and policies. . . . It is militarism which is eating up all the products of science and art, defeating the energy of the population and wasting its savings. It is militarism which forbids the people to give their attention to the problems of their own welfare and to give their strength to the education and comfort of their children." He lashed out against "war, debt, taxation, diplomacy, a grand governmental system, pomp, glory, a big army and navy, lavish expenditures, political jobbery—in a word, imperialism."

Sumner hit the hypocrisy of imperialism. "Americans," he wrote, "cannot assure life, liberty and the pursuit of happiness to negroes inside of the United States. When the negro postmaster's house was set on fire in the night in South Carolina, and not only he, but his wife and children, were murdered as they came out, and when, moreover, this incident passed without legal investigation or punishment, it was a bad omen for the extension of liberty, etc., to Malays and Tagals by simply setting over them the American flag." Democrats and Republicans alike demanded Sumner's dimissal from Yale.

Sumner recalled the American dream: "The men who came here were able to throw off all the trammels of tradition and established doctrine. . . . It was a grand opportunity to be thus able to strip off all the follies and errors which they had inherited. . . . Their idea was that they would never allow any of the social and political abuses of the old world to grow up here. . . . There were to be no armies except a militia, which would have no functions but those of police. They would have no court and no pomp; no orders, or ribbons, or decorations, or titles. . . . If debt was incurred in war it was to be paid in peace and not entailed on posterity. . . . [The citizen] was, above all, to be insured peace and the quiet while he pursued his honest industry. . . . The citizen here would never be forced to leave his family or to give his sons to shed blood for glory and to leave the widows and orphans in misery for nothing. Justice and law were to reign in the midst of simplicity, and a government which had little to do was to offer little field for ambition. . . . It is by virtue of this conception of a commonwealth that the United States has stood for something unique and grand in the history of mankind and that its people have been happy."

While Sumner was producing his antiwar essays, he also turned to academic sociology, and the result was his projected *Science of Society*. The segment on customs expanded to some 200,000 words, and he decided to issue it separately as *Folkways* (1907). He surveyed customs about marriage, sex, sports, drama, education, and so on, describing their evolution as a long, spontaneous process. *Folkways* became his best-known book.

Sumner suffered a stroke in 1907 and retired from Yale in June 1909, thereafter spending much of his time at home, 120 Edwards Street, New Haven. That September, he went to New York for a gathering of the American Sociological Society, which he served as president. He was at the Murray Hill Hotel when he suffered another stroke. With his left side paralyzed, he was taken to Engelwood Hospital, New Jersey. He was transferred to his son's home in Engelwood where he died on April 10, 1910. He was sixty-nine years old. There was a memorial service at Battell Chapel, on College Street, Yale University, and he was buried in his wife's family plot, Guilford, Connecticut.

By this time, the progressive era was at floodtide, and Sumner was very much out of fashion. Muckraking novelist Upton Sinclair, for instance, denounced him as a "prime minister in the empire of plutocratic education." But Sumner's student Albert Galloway Keller made sure his intellectual legacy would be available for future generations. He gathered Sumner's essays into four volumes: *War and Other Essays* (1911), *Earth Hunger and*

Other Essays (1913), *The Challenge of Facts and Other Essays* (1914), and *The Forgotten Man and Other Essays* (1919). Then he edited Sumner's thousands of pages of notes into the four-volume *Science of Society* (1933), a vast catalogue of human institutions as they have evolved around the world. Some passages evoked the passion of Sumner's essays. For instance, Sumner and Keller wrote, "The struggle for property is the struggle for liberty. He who feels the constraint of his situation and desires to win command of it, which is liberty, finds that he can succeed only through property. The effort to get property stimulates the social virtues. . . . Property is sacred as marriage is sacred. . . . It is the great stabilizer and equilibrator of them all." Keller went on to write *Reminiscences of William Graham Sumner* (1933), and the following year he collaborated with Maurice R. Davie, issuing a two-volume collection of Sumner's essays. "In an age of yearning after collectivism," they reflected, "the antidote of a powerful statement by a hard-hitting individualist is a good thing to have at hand."

Free markets were blamed for the Great Depression, fascism, and just about every other evil, and when anybody cared to remember Sumner, they dismissed him. Richard Hofstadter called him "a defender of the status quo," and Robert Green McCluskey sneered that Sumner had "a vision of society in which beauty, charity and brotherhood could find no place, in which wealth and self-interest were the ruling norms."

Naysayers had their way, and during the past three decades, the U.S. government spent over $6 trillion on more than seventy antipoverty programs, yet the poverty rate is higher than it was in 1965. Even the advocates of these programs have begun to admit that giving away money has backfired by encouraging dependence. It has become apparent that the most important step for poor people—as it is for recovering alcoholics and drug addicts—is to take responsibility for one's life, which is what William Graham Sumner advocated in his essays.

Moreover, some of Sumner's critics have acknowledged his steadfast support for peace. Historian Page Smith noted that "Sumner was an outspoken enemy of imperialism." He was right when he declared that political power is a dangerous thing. He correctly warned that war subverts free institutions with crushing taxes, monstrous debts, odious censorship, military conscription, and brutal deaths;. He was right that war turns civilized people into savages. He was right to say that constitutional limits on political power offer the best hope for protecting peace.

"TRUST BUT VERIFY"

COMMUNISM WAS THE worst curse of the twentieth century. Nazism lasted a dozen years, Italian fascism twenty-two years, and Soviet communism seventy-four years. Soviet boss Joseph Stalin was estimated to have killed three times more people than Hitler, and the total death toll from communism has been estimated to exceed 150 million people. The Soviets enslaved millions in Eastern Europe after World War II, stole American secrets for making nuclear weapons, and deployed thousands of nuclear missiles aimed at the United States, some from as close as Cuba—and the United States could not have stopped a single missile, whether launched intentionally or accidentally. During the 1970s, the Soviets worked to expand their influence in Asia, Africa, and the Americas.

Meanwhile, the United States and other Western countries seemed to be in decline. Inflation and interest rates hit double digits, and unemployment remained high. Intellectuals bowed to the seeming inevitability of Soviet gains and Western decline. Economics professor John Kenneth Galbraith wrote in *The New Yorker* (1984), "The Russian system succeeds because, in contrast with the Western industrial economies, it makes full use of its manpower." Paul A. Samuelson's influential textbook, *Economics* (1985), asserted, "There can be no doubt that the Soviet planning system has been a powerful engine for economic growth." Economics professor Lester Thurow in 1989 hailed "the remarkable performance of the Soviet Union." And historian Arthur M. Schlesinger, Jr., had this to say: "Those in the U.S. who think the Soviet Union is on the verge of economic and social collapse. . . . [are] only kidding themselves."

President Ronald Reagan proved them all wrong. He did much to revive American spirits and change the terms of public policy debate. He insisted that free markets work better than bureaucrats, and American individualism and liberty are things to be immensely proud of. Rather than prodding the Federal Reserve Board to print more paper money, as his predecessor Jimmy Carter had done, Reagan supported the Fed's efforts to curb the money supply; within two years, inflation disappeared as a national issue. Reagan dramatically cut and capped income tax rates, encouraging an economic boom that, with the exception of a nine-month recession two years after he left office, has continued into the next millennium, and chronic high unemployment ceased to be a national issue. Reagan stopped Soviet aggression in its tracks and intensified pressure on the Soviet Union, contributing to its stunning collapse. As Britain's prime minister Margaret Thatcher put it, "Ronald Reagan won the cold war without firing a shot."

Reagan emerged as a great champion of peace. He supported development of a defense system aimed at stopping nuclear missiles fired at the United States, and he offered to share his Strategic Defense Initiative technology, once proved effective, so it could help reduce the risks of a nuclear war. Previous U.S. presidents had pursued SALT (Strategic Arms Limitation Talks), aimed at slowing the rate of nuclear missile deployment, but Reagan launched START (Strategic Arms Reduction Talks), aimed at reducing the number of nuclear weapons deployed. His administration negotiated the Intermediate Nuclear Forces Treaty, the first to provide for the elimination of an entire category of nuclear weapons.

Many Reagan critics claimed that since the Soviet economy turns out to have been in worse shape than they imagined, his policies had little or nothing to do with the collapse. Yet in the past, disintegrating regimes like those in imperial China and the Ottoman Empire ("Sick Man of Europe") hung on for decades. Moreover, communists still rule in wretechedly poor China, Cuba, and North Korea.

Former Secretary of State Henry Kissinger observed, "Reagan's was an astonishing performance—and to academic observers, nearly incomprehensible. . . . A president with the shallowest academic background was to develop a foreign policy of extraordinary consistency and relevance. Reagan might well have had only a few basic ideas, but these also happened to be the core foreign policy issues of his period, which demonstrates that a sense of direction and having the strength of one's convictions are the key ingredients of leadership."

Policy analyst Martin Anderson wrote in the 1980s, "When you meet Ronald Reagan, the first thing you notice about him is how big he is. He is half a foot taller than most people, weighs over two hundred pounds, and is lean and muscular. He still looks and moves very much the lifeguard he was for seven years in the 1920s, when he saved seventy-seven people from drowning in the Illinois Rock River."

Reagan particularly endeared himself to the American people through his responses to the attempted assassination outside the Washington Hilton Hotel on March 30, 1981. A bullet fired by John Hinckley, Jr., stopped less than an inch from Reagan's heart, but from George Washington University Hospital came humorous quips that let everyone know he would be all right.

"We are particularly conscious of the courage of Ronald Reagan," Thatcher remarked. "It was easy for his contemporaries to ignore it; he always seemed so calm and relaxed, with natural charm, unstudied self-assurance and unquenchable good humour. . . . Ronald Reagan set out to challenge everything that the liberal political elite of America accepted and sought to propagate. They believed that America was doomed to decline; he believed it was destined for further greatness. They imagined that sooner or later there would be convergence between the free Western system and the socialist Eastern system, and that some kind of social democratic outcome was inevitable. He, by contrast, considered that socialism was a patent failure which should be cast onto the trash heap of history. They thought that the problem with America was the American people, though they didn't quite put it like that. He thought that the problem with America was the American government, and he did put it just like that."

RONALD WILSON REAGAN was born February 6, 1911, in an apartment above a bank in Tampico, Illinois. His father, John Edward Reagan, a shoe salesman whose ancestors had come from Ireland, became the town drunk. Ronald's mother, Nelle Wilson, whose ancestors were Scots-English, was the source of his sunny optimism.

Early on, Reagan took advantage of opportunities to learn public speaking, radio broadcasting, and acting. While on a sportscasting assignment in California, he landed a contract as an actor with Warner Brothers. He graduated from "B" pictures to features like *Knute Rockne—All-American* in which he played dying football hero George Gipp. Reagan was elected president of the Screen Actors Guild five times and learned how to be a tough negotiator with the big studios.

After his divorce from Jane Wyman, Reagan met actress Nancy Davis, who shared many of his views. They were married March 4, 1952, and had two children, Patricia Ann (1952) and Ronald, Jr. (1958).

During the 1950s, Reagan served as a host for the General Electric Theater, which ran for eight years on television. At GE facilities in thirty-nine states, he gave talks about the problems with government and benefits of free enterprise. As he was to do for years, he wrote his speeches longhand on legal-size yellow pads, then transferred them to four- by six-inch cards, using block letters and his own shorthand system. He could get the contents of each card at a glance and maintain good eye contact with the audience.

To help Republican presidential candidate Barry Goldwater, Reagan taped a thirty-minute television address that was broadcast on October 27, 1964, and subsequently shown at fund-raising events, generating $8 million for the Goldwater campaign. After Goldwater lost to Lyndon Johnson, Reagan entered the 1966 race for California governor against Democratic incumbent Pat Brown. Brown's TV commercials compared Reagan with actor John Wilkes Booth who assassinated Abraham Lincoln, but Reagan won 58 percent of the votes. During his term in office, he raised taxes to cover Brown's deficits, and when the state budget was in surplus, he returned money to tax-payers four times.

Reagan won the presidency on his second try, in 1980. The incumbent, Jimmy Carter, had inherited rising inflation and pressured the federal reserve system to expand the money supply, which made inflation worse. When he imposed price controls to keep gasoline prices below market levels, the results were chronic shortages and aggravating lines at gas stations. Carter harangued pro-Western governments about human rights violations, while ignoring far worse oppression by communist regimes. His dubious advice to the shah of Iran, a pro-Western autocrat, figured in the shah's downfall. Anti-Western Islamic mobs invaded the American embassy in Tehran and held fifty-two Americans hostage for a year.

Reagan, in contrast, focused on a few priorities. He ended gas lines with an executive order abolishing price controls on oil and gasoline, since the short-term surge in prices attracted new supplies on the market while encouraging consumers to economize. The biggest issue was inflation, which had sent interest rates soaring to 21.5 percent, reportedly the highest level since the Civil War. Reagan supported policies by Federal Reserve Board chairman Paul Volcker to rein in the money supply, and inflation fell dramatically. At the same time, Reagan was determined to revive the economy. His 1981 tax reform was a three-year deal that cut personal income tax rates 10 percent the first year, another 10 percent the second year, and 5 percent more the third year. Then tax rates were indexed so that inflation would stop pushing people into higher tax brackets. Reagan's 1986 tax act eliminated all but two federal income tax rates, 15 percent and 28 percent.

Reagan, however, didn't cut federal spending. Democrats controlled Congress, and Speaker of the House Tip O'Neill rejected cuts because federal spending is a primary way of paying off key constituencies and contributors. In 1983, Reagan agreed to close $98 billion worth of tax loopholes if the Democrats came through with $280 billion of spending cuts, but they reneged. Most Republicans opposed budget cuts, too, since they had their own constituencies to pay off. It would have been ideal if Reagan had focused his vast persuasive powers on spending cuts, but the political support was not there.

The Soviet buildup and aggression remained an issue. "As the foundation of my foreign policy," Reagan explained, "I decided we had to send as power-ful a message as we could to the Russians that we weren't going to stand by anymore while they armed and financed terrorists and subverted democratic governments. . . . If we hadn't begun to modernize, the Soviet negotiators . . . would know we were bluffing without a good hand, because they know what cards we hold just as we know what's in their hand." Reagan made a moral appeal to the American people: in a March 8, 1983 speech, he called the Soviet Union "an evil empire," a phrase heard round the world.

Reagan rejected the prevailing doctrine of mutual assured destruction (MAD)—that peace could best be protected by having both sides armed with deadly nuclear missiles. The theory would deter an intentional launching of missiles as long as both sides believed they could not win a nuclear war. But there is evidence that some Soviet generals believed they could win a nuclear war, and in any case MAD did nothing to protect against an accidental launching of nuclear missiles. Despite the billions that Americans had been taxed for national defense, they were helpless. The Soviets had six thousand nuclear warheads, and the United States had another two thousand; the more missiles there were, the greater the risk that poorly trained or negligent missile officers might accidentally launch a missile that could not be recalled. A Soviet missile could reach Washington, D.C, in about thirty minutes. Accordingly, Reagan sought to develop a defense system that could stop missiles, launched intentionally or accidentally.

On March 23, 1983, he delivered a speech seeking support for his Strategic Defense Initiative (SDI). "Let me share with you a vision of the future which offers hope," he said. "Let us turn to the very strengths in technology that spawned our great industrial base and that have given us the quality of life we enjoy today. . . . Current technology has attained a level of sophistication where it's reasonable for us to begin the effort. It will take years, probably decades of effort on many fronts. There will be failures and setbacks, just as there will be successes and breakthroughs. . . . But isn't it worth every investment necessary to free the world from the threat of nuclear war?"

The Soviet Union denounced the proposal. Soviet boss Yuri Andropov, who had headed the secret police, called the SDI "insane." Many Americans thought that it could not be done and ridiculed it as "Star Wars." When some critics warned that SDI would provoke the Soviets into expanding their own missile defense system or even launching a preemptive first strike against the United States, Reagan offered to share missile defense technologies with the Soviets.

As biographer Dinesh D'Souza explained, "The SDI had two political consequences that Reagan's critics did not anticipate. It destroyed the base of the nuclear freeze movement, because Reagan showed himself to be more deeply committed than its leadership to reducing the danger to Americans posed by the Soviet nuclear arsenal. Reagan seemed to have found a more imaginative way that the United States could unilaterally move closer to eliminating the nuclear threat. SDI was disarmament through technology rather than diplomacy. Moreover, to the complete amazement of the arms control establishment, the mere concept of SDI did what Reagan said it would: it brought the Soviet Union back to the bargaining table." The Soviets feared they could not keep up with American development of a missile defense system.

Events took a turn on August 31, 1983, when the Soviets shot down a South Korean commercial aircraft that had strayed into Soviet air space. The death toll was 269, including 61 Americans. Reagan condemned the incident as "an act of barbarism." Mikhail Gorbachev, acting for General Secretary Andropov, claimed the Korean passenger liner was a spy plane, and the Soviet press compared Reagan with Hitler. Reagan reflected, "If, as some people speculated, the Soviet pilots simply mistook the airliner for a military plane, what kind of imagination did it take to think of a Soviet military man with his finger close to a nuclear push button making an even more tragic mistake. . . . Yet, if somebody made that kind of mistake—or if a madman got possession of a nuclear missile—we were defenseless against it. Once a nuclear missile was launched, no one could recall it, and until we got something like the Strategic Defense Initiative system in operation, the world was helpless against nuclear missiles." Meanwhile, Reagan pushed for deployment of U.S. intermediate-range Pershing II missiles and Tomahawk cruise missiles in Europe, and they were accepted by Britain, Italy, and West Germany to counter Soviet SS-20 missiles aimed at Western European cities.

Reagan vowed he would help people resisting the Soviet Union—democrats in Poland and Czechoslovakia, Islamic fundamentalists in Afghanistan, tribal autocrats in Angola, rightists in Nicaragua. Some of these were not really friends of liberty, but Reagan's strategy undeniably put pressure on the Soviets, and they abandoned positions they had gained during the 1970s. The most dramatic success came after Reagan supplied Afghan guerrillas with Stinger antiaircraft missiles. As former Secretary of State George P. Shultz explained, "The Stingers, even when parceled out with care, made a huge, perhaps even a decisive, difference. The Soviets could no longer dominate areas by helicopter or by accurate bombing from low-flying aircraft. High-level bombers were ineffective against the dispersed and mobile forces of the Afghan freedom fighters." The Soviets pulled out of Afghanistan in 1989. Vietnam pulled out of Cambodia in 1990. That year, the Soviet-backed Sandinistas agreed to hold elections in Nicaragua, and they lost. Cuban forces pulled out of Angola in 1991.

The Reagan administration's only serious foreign policy blunder was the Iran-contra scandal—selling Iran $30 million worth of arms to secure the release of American hostages held by pro-Iranian terrorists in Lebanon and thus violating long-standing policy against paying ransom for hostages. Profits from this deal were channeled to contras fighting the communist regime in Nicaragua, which had received several billion dollars of Soviet arms. Helping the contras violated the 1984 Boland Amendment, an effort by the Democrat-controlled Congress to restrict Reagan's foreign policy. Independent prosecutor Lawrence E. Walsh found no evidence that Reagan had broken the

law, and convictions against principals in the case were overturned, but the
administration had jeopardized prudent constitutional restraints.

Andropov's successor, Konstantin Chernenko, died in March 1985, and
Soviet powerbrokers apparently realized they needed somebody who might
be better at dealing with Reagan. They picked fifty-four-year-old Mikhail
Gorbachev. Biographer Lou Cannon credited Gorbachev with better analytical skills than Reagan, yet Gorbachev thought the key problem with communism was its corruption, not its compulsion. Then he thought the key
problem was widespread alcoholism. He increased government spending on
machine tools and heavy industry, as Stalin had done, but this aggravated
shortages of consumer goods. Then he launched his so-called *perestroika*
reform, but as historian Martin Malia explained in *The Soviet Tragedy* (1994),
"there was no national market, no real prices, and no free peasantry; moreover, 90 percent of the economy remained nationalized and directly managed
by state organs under the Party's supervision." Gorbachev covered budget
deficits by printing money, which led to runaway inflation. He lamented that
"the science of economics has not yet provided a detailed concept of how to
make the transition to a dynamic, highly efficient economy." Gorbachev
seemed unaware of Adam Smith's *The Wealth of Nations,* which had provided just such a concept more than two hundred years before. He was
equally ignorant of a vast literature documenting that free people are far
more productive than bureaucrats.

Reagan met Gorbachev at their Geneva summit in November 1985. Gorbachev defended Soviet aggression in Afghanistan, but Reagan, who had seen
pictures of Afghan children maimed by Soviet bombs, denounced the aggression. Gorbachev claimed SDI would make war more likely. Reagan attacked
the MAD doctrine that the best hope for peace was to have superpowers aim
deadly missiles at each other. Gorbachev agreed to visit America, and Reagan
agreed to visit the Soviet Union. Journalist Robert G. Kaiser reported that
Gorbachev and his foreign minister, Eduard Shevardnadze, somehow
"decided that Reagan wasn't terribly bright or very knowledgeable about specific issues—they could handle him."

Then, as journalist Peter Schweizer reported, Reagan's advisors urged
Saudi Arabia to step up their daily oil production, and they did—from 2 million barrels to nearly 9 million. Crude oil prices plunged from thirty dollars
per barrel to twelve dollars by mid-1986. This was catastrophic for the Soviet
Union, since 80 percent of its hard currency earnings came from oil. The
money was desperately needed to buy food and technology. The Saudis were
producing enough oil that they grossed more than they had before, but other
oil producers, like Iran, Iraq, and Libya, were hard pressed, and they cut
back their purchases of Soviet weapons, a major source of Soviet earnings.

The explosion at the Chernobyl, Ukraine, nuclear power plant in April 1986 gave people around the world reason to distrust Gorbachev. Although he had touted *glasnost*—a limited degree of openness—he suppressed the truth. When Western Europeans detected a radioactive cloud coming from the Soviet Union, Gorbachev stonewalled. Sixty-seven hours after the explosion, the Soviets issued a brief bulletin. A radioactive cloud reached Japan by May 3. Then on May 14, amid mounting criticism, Gorbachev lashed out against an "unrestrained anti-Soviet propaganda campaign."

In October 1986, Reagan and Gorbachev held a summit meeting at Reykjavik, Iceland. After the two men offered dramatic arms cutbacks, Gorbachev demanded that Reagan abandon the SDI, and Reagan walked out of the talks. The American press condemned him for refusing to compromise, but Reagan insisted, "There was no way I could tell our people their government would not protect them against nuclear destruction." The Soviets were stunned.

Gorbachev gave up trying to stop SDI. In December 1987, he flew to Washington and signed the Intermediate Nuclear Forces Treaty, which called for both countries to phase out intermediate-range nuclear missiles. The Soviets agreed to destroy four times more nuclear weapons than the United States. Reagan cited a Russian proverb: *Dovorey no provorey*—"trust but verify."

Reagan kept up the pressure. His most dramatic moment came in Berlin. The East German Communist government had started building the Berlin Wall back on Sunday, August 13, 1961, to stop people from fleeing communism. Many East Germans were shot trying to smash their way through the Wall, dig tunnels under it or fly over it. On June 12, 1987, Reagan gave a speech at the Berlin Wall near Brandenburg Gate. He declared, "General Secretary Gorbachev, if you seek peace, if you seek prosperity for the Soviet Union and Eastern Europe, if you seek liberalization: Come here to this gate! Mr. Gorbachev, open this gate! Mr. Gorbachev, tear down this wall!" Then he traveled to Moscow for more talks with Gorbachev. On May 31, 1988, he told students at Moscow State University: "The key is freedom—freedom of thought, freedom of information, freedom of communication. . . . People do not make wars; governments do. And no mother would ever willingly sacrifice her sons for territorial gain, for economic advantage, for ideology. A people free to choose will always choose peace." Gorbachev biographers Dusko Doder and Louise Branson reported that Reagan's speeches to Russian students "were perhaps his most spectacular performances and touched the deepest chords of the Russian psyche. . . . The Russians loved him."

Gorbachev announced, on December 7, 1988, that the financially strapped Soviet Union would cut its armed forces by 10,000 tanks and 500,000 soldiers, and he indicated he would not try to prop up communist regimes elsewhere. On November 9, 1989, East Germans began tearing down the Berlin Wall, an electrifying event that inspired successful revolutions against hated communist oppressors throughout Eastern Europe.

Gorbachev nevertheless continued to defend the Communist party's political monopoly. He insisted on keeping the Five Year Plan, and he did not like the idea of a presidential election, since he would lose, so he rejected Russia's demand for sovereignty. But on December 25, 1991, the Soviet red flag was lowered from the Kremlin, and the U.S.S.R. ceased to exist. Incredibly, *Time* magazine picked Gorbachev as Man of the Year, and he got the Nobel Peace Prize, although it was Reagan who prevailed.

"What occurred," Martin Malia wrote, "was a revolution of consciousness, and not just in the former Soviet bloc but throughout the world. There was suddenly a general consensus that the market, private property, and democracy formed an organic whole; that one could not have the rule of law, human rights, constitutional government, and political pluralism without a material 'base' for civil society in personal property and freedom of economic choice"—everything Reagan had stood for.

Ronald and Nancy Reagan were cheered by thousands as they made a triumphal ten-day tour of Eastern Europe: they visited what was left of the Berlin Wall and worked on it with a chisel, he addressed the Polish Parliament in Warsaw and Polish shipyard workers in Gdansk, and he greeted enthusiastic crowds in Moscow.

Ironically, the SDI fell out of favor as defense-related interest groups scrambled for congressional appropriations. President Bill Clinton assumed that the collapse of the Soviet empire meant SDI was not needed anymore, though some research continued on a scaled-down version known as National Missile Defense. But General Lee Butler, of the Strategic Air Command, warned: "The Russian command and early warning system is in a state of great decline. . . . They're experiencing false alarms now on almost a routine basis, and I shudder to think about the morale and discipline of their rocket forces." In January 1995, for instance, Russian military officials were close to launching a nuclear attack against the United States because they thought a U.S. missile was coming at them; it turned out to be a Norwegian rocket launching a weather satellite. Moreover, many Russian bombs reportedly have been sold to rogue states. About twenty countries are believed to possess missiles capable of intercontinental ranges. There is increasing concern about North Korea and China, especially after Chinese communists stole U.S. military secrets; in 1999 Congress voted to step up development of a missile defense system.

Thus has experience underscored Reagan's wisdom. He displayed the vision and courage to help make this a freer, more peaceful world.

SELF-HELP

God helps them that help themselves.
—ENGLISH PROVERB

FREE SOCIETIES THRIVE when people take responsibility to help themselves and their neighbors. Nobody is likely to know as much about your needs as you do, and nobody will be as highly motivated to fulfill them. In addition, there is an ethical imperative to take care of your own business and as much as possible avoid imposing your troubles on others. Self-help means cultivating the virtues of hard work, discipline, thrift, and courtesy, essential for a success in life. When people are on their own, they can deal with each other as independent beings and enjoy mutual respect.

RESOURCEFUL ENTERPRISE

BENJAMIN FRANKLIN PIONEERED the spirit of self-help in America. With less than three years of formal schooling, he taught himself almost everything he knew, including how to speak French, German, Italian, Latin, and Spanish. He learned how to play the guitar, violin, and harp, for example. He made himself an influential author and editor; started a successful printing business, newspaper, and magazine; and developed a network of printing partnerships throughout the American colonies.

In Philadelphia, he helped launch the city's first police force, the first volunteer fire company, the first fire insurance firm, the first hospital, the first public library, and the academy that became Pennsylvania's first institution of higher learning (University of Pennsylvania). As postmaster, he doubled and then tripled the frequency of mail deliveries.

Franklin, who reportedly amassed early America's largest private library, helped expand the frontiers of science and invention. He started the American Philosophical Society, this country's first scientific society, and maintained the first science library, first museum, and first patent office; over ninety members of this society, still in existence, went on to win Nobel Prizes. On his eight transatlantic crossings, Franklin took measurements that helped chart the gulf stream. He pioneered the study of water flowing around a hull (hydrodynamics) and investigated meteorology. He invented bifocal spectacles. He was most famous for his experiments with electricity, especially lightning.

Franklin had more to do with founding the American Republic than anyone else. As American representative in London, he helped persuade Parliament to repeal despised Stamp Act taxes, giving America an additional decade to prepare for armed conflict with Britain. He was on the committee that named Thomas Jefferson to draft the Declaration of Independence. He went to France and secured military help as well as a formal alliance, without which America probably would not have won the Revolutionary War. He helped negotiate the peace with Britain. He crafted a compromise that helped prevent the collapse of the Constitutional Convention and moved that the Constitution be adopted.

Franklin linked emerging movements for liberty. James Madison recalled that he "never passed half an hour in his company without hearing some observation or anecdote worth remembering." Franklin dined with *Wealth of*

Nations author Adam Smith. The Scottish philosopher David Hume told Franklin: "America has sent us many good things, Gold, Silver, Sugar, Tobacco, Indigo, &c. But you are the first Philosopher, and indeed the first Great Man of Letters for whom we are beholden." Edmund Burke, who had opposed Britain's war against America, called Franklin "the friend of mankind." When the French wit Voltaire met William Temple Franklin, he quipped: "God and Liberty! It is the only benediction which can be given to the grandson of Franklin." Jacques Turgot, who implemented laissez-faire principles in France, remarked that Franklin "snatched the lightning from heaven and the scepter from tyrants."

Late-blooming radical, Franklin during his thirties brokered the sale of some slaves as a sideline for his general store. He and his wife owned two slaves. In 1758, when he was fifty-two, he suggested establishing Philadelphia's first school for blacks. At seventy, he abandoned his support for the British empire and committed himself to the American Revolution. Philadelphia Quakers had launched the abolitionist movement by organizing the Pennsylvania Society for Promoting the Abolition of Slavery (1775), but its activities ceased during the Revolution; this pioneering society revived in 1787 when Franklin became its president, at age eighty-one. Two years later he voiced his support for the ideals of the French Revolution.

Although Franklin was generous with his friends and adopted families, he could be insensitive with his own. He disregarded pleas from his dying wife, Deborah, whom he had not seen in almost a dozen years, to return home from Britain, where he represented American colonial interests. He refused to approve his daughter Sarah's proposed marriage to the man she loved. His son William's decision to side with Britain during the American Revolution provoked a bitter break that never healed.

As biographer Ronald W. Clark noted, Franklin "was only an inch or two less than six feet in height, thickset and muscular, with dark brown hair above friendly hazel eyes. He was obviously able to look after himself, a distinct advantage in the rougher eighteenth century. . . . These physical attributes were compounded by a nimbleness of mind, so that in argument as well as in action he tended to be off the mark quicker than most men. Above all, and largely concealed by his instinctive hail-fellow-well-met nature, there was a steely determination to succeed and some impatience with those who got in his way."

BENJAMIN FRANKLIN WAS born in Boston on January 17, 1706, the tenth son of Abia Folger, daughter of an indentured servant. His father, Josiah Franklin, made candles. At eight, he was sent to Boston Latin School, then a school for writing and arithmetic, and he apprenticed in his father's candle-making shop. Because he began to enjoy books, his father arranged for him to apprentice with his twenty-one-year-old brother, James, a Boston printer. "All the little money that came into my hands was ever laid out in books," Franklin recalled.

Franklin went to Philadelphia, the most exciting city in the American Colonies, where he heard a printer was looking for help. "I was dirty from my Journey," he wrote about his arrival at the Market Street Wharf, "my Pockets were stuff'd out with Shirts & Stockings; I knew no Soul, or where to look for Lodging. I was fatigued with Travelling, Rowing & Want of Rest. I was very hungry, and my whole Stock of Cash consisted of a Dutch Dollar and about a Shilling in Copper."

Franklin found a job, impressed people, and was sent to England for printing equipment. Financing for it fell through, but in 1725 and 1726 he worked for a couple of big London printers and gained valuable experience. London, an intellectual capital of Europe, expanded Franklin's vision. During the tedious seventy-nine-day voyage home, he wrote down some principles for success. His original draft was lost, but the main points were probably similar to what he remembered later: "1. It is necessary for me to be extremely frugal for some time, till I have paid what I owe. 2. To endeavor to speak truth in every instance, to give nobody expectations that are not likely to be answered, but aim at sincerity in every word and action; the most amiable excellence in a rational being. 3. To apply myself industriously to whatever business I take in hand, and not divert my mind from my business by any foolish project of growing suddenly rich; for industry and patience are the surest means of plenty. 4. I resolve to speak ill of no man whatever."

Within months after his return in late 1726, he was in business for himself. He landed a contract to print Pennsylvania's currency, printed the first novel published in America (Samuel Richardson's *Pamela*), and sold material printed by others, including Bibles and legal forms. Franklin bought a failing newspaper, changed its name to the *Pennsylvania Gazette*, and wrote many of the articles himself. The December 28, 1732, issue announced that he would be offering *Poor Richard: An Almanack*, which offered memorable aphorisms about success—for instance, "God helps them that help themselves," "Diligence is the Mother of Good-Luck," "Early to bed and early to rise, makes a man healthy wealthy and wise," and "When you're good to others, you are best to yourself." *Poor Richard's Almanack*, published annually until 1758, sold some ten-thousand copies a year and helped make Franklin a well-known name.

In 1727, Franklin started a group called the Junto, which he described as "a Club for mutual Improvement," that met weekly on Friday evenings, initially at a tavern and later in a rented room. Participants included young apprentices, and they made presentations to each other. During the next three decades, the Junto helped pioneer many of Philadelphia's institutions, starting with the city's first public library. To provide greater security against crime, Franklin started City Watch, which organized neighborhood patrols at night. He promoted the paving, cleaning, and lighting of streets and provided crucial support for Philadelphia's first hospital. He thought college education should be available in Pennsylvania, and he recommended that it focus on basic skills like writing and speaking. His proposed reading list included the seventeenth-century radical author Algernon Sidney. In 1749, Franklin was elected the first president of this new academy, which became the University of Pennsylvania.

Franklin had some romantic adventures, one of which brought a son, William. On September 1, 1730, he began a common-law marriage with Deborah Read, a carpenter's daughter, who seems to have been barely literate. They had a son, Francis, who died four years later from smallpox and a daughter, Sally (Sarah), who was born in 1743. Franklin's first son, William, lived with them. During the next forty-five years, Deborah displayed phenomenal patience as Franklin spent decades away on business throughout the colonies and Europe.

With his buoyant curiousity, Franklin pursued myriad scientific interests. He investigated weather patterns, speculated about the origin of mountains, invented a more efficient wood-burning stove, connected to a radiator, and in 1744 started popularizing this stove as the Pennsylvania Fire Place. Franklin began to experiment with electricity. In June 1752, he climbed a Philadelphia hill, flew a silk kite during a thunderstorm, touched one knuckle to a key on the wet string—and felt an electrical shock. He published *Experiments and Observations on Electricity,* and it was translated into French, German, Italian, and Latin. He developed lightning rods, which could draw lightning away from a house and protect it from fire. Lightning rods earned Franklin the gratitude of people throughout America and Europe. He was elected a fellow of the English Royal Society and the French Académie des Sciences.

By the time Franklin had become famous for his experiments on electricity, he was in the thick of Pennsylvania politics, having been elected to the Pennsylvania Assembly in August 1751. As Britain and France struggled for control of North America, the French won over many Indian tribes as allies, and Pennsylvania was vulnerable to attack. Franklin helped organize a people's militia. In 1754, he proposed a federal union of the colonies under the British crown.

He published *The Way to Wealth* (1758) which, based on *Poor Richard,* went into nine Spanish printings, 11 German printings, 56 French printings and 70 English printings. Moreover, it also appeared in Bohemian, Catalan, Chinese, Danish, Dutch, Gaelic, Greek, Polish, Russian, Swedish and Welsh. The boom helped make Franklin well known abroad, which helped later when he served as an American diplomat.

Pennsylvania politics intensified. Many people resented the Penn family because their vast landholdings were tax exempt, so they did not help pay defense costs. The Pennsylvania Assembly sent Franklin to London where they hoped he could promote their interests against the Penns. He was successful and the Penns were taxed like everybody else.

Massachusetts and Georgia asked Franklin to help them resist British taxes too. Parliament passed the Stamp Act, which became law November 1, 1765. It called for taxes on legal documents, newspapers, and playing cards in the colonies. Franklin spoke out against "the mistaken Notion . . . that the Colonies were planted at the Expence of Parliament . . . [America] was possess'd by a free People." When warned there would be armed resistance, the Stamp Act was repealed. Parliament tried again to assert its supremacy over the colonies, and Franklin worked for a compromise.

In Britain, Franklin met Anthony Benezet, the Philadelphia Quaker teacher who was one of the earliest advocates of liberating black slaves. Benezit urged Franklin to condemn the slave trade, and he subsequently spoke out against the "pestilential, detestable traffic in the bodies and souls of men." He served as well on the board of Bray Associates, an organization that established schools for black boys and girls in Newport, New York, Philadelphia, and Williamsburg.

Franklin got his hands on six explosive letters by Massachusetts governor Thomas Hutchinson who wrote, "There must be a great restraint of natural liberty." Samuel Adams saw the letters, made them public, and there was an uproar. British officials blamed Franklin and humiliated him in public proceedings. The experience ended his desire for reconciliation.

He sailed for America on March 21, 1775, soon after learning about the death of his wife, whom he had not seen in eleven years. While he was at sea, armed conflict had begun as British soldiers fired on Americans in Lexington and Concord, Massachusetts. On May 6, the day after Franklin reached Philadelphia, the Pennsylvania Assembly appointed him a delegate to the Second Continental Congress. He was asked by the Second Continental Congress to help secure war supplies from abroad. Since the government had no credit, Franklin advanced £353 in gold from his personal funds.

In October 1775, Franklin talked with an impassioned English immigrant whom he had met in London, suggesting the young man write "a history of the present transactions." The young man, Thomas Paine, was already at work on such a project and showed Franklin a draft of his pamphlet *Common Sense,* which, after publication in January 1776, convinced Americans to embrace independence.

On June 21, 1776, Franklin, John Adams, Thomas Jefferson, Robert Livingston (New York), and Roger Sherman (Connecticut) were appointed to a committee for producing a declaration that would announce American independence. The committee asked Jefferson to draft it. Franklin, for one, suggested a number of changes. When time came to sign the Declaration, on August 2, John Hancock, president of Congress, reportedly remarked: "We must be unanimous; there must be no pulling different ways we must all hang together." According to legend, Franklin added: "We must, indeed, all hang together, or most assuredly we shall all hang separately."

The best possibility for help was France, which, having lost a war with Britain, would surely like to see the British empire come apart, but the French were wary. King Louis XVI saw danger in supporting revolution, and Americans felt some uneasiness seeking help from a king who claimed absolute power.

When Franklin was asked if he would go to France, he noted his gout and other infirmities and reportedly replied, "I am old and good for nothing." But he agreed, then withdrew more than £3,000 from his bank and loaned it to Congress. French intellectuals respected him for his pioneering experiments with electricity, and ordinary people knew that his lightning rods saved homes from fire. As John Adams put it, "There was scarcely a peasant or a citizen, a *valet de chambre,* coachman or footman, a lady's chambermaid or a scullion in a kitchen, who was not familiar with [Benjamin Franklin], and who did not consider him as a friend to human kind."

On October 26, 1776, Franklin secretly left Philadelphia with his grandsons William Temple Franklin and Benjamin Franklin Bache. They reached Paris on December 22 and established headquarters at Passy, a chateau in the town of Chaillot, about one mile from Paris and seven miles from Versailles. The chateau belonged to a friendly entrepreneur. Franklin described himself as "very plainly dressed, wearing my thin, gray straight hair, that peeps out under my only *coiffure,* a fine fur cap." Pictures of Franklin appeared in paintings, engravings, and aquatints, on medallions, wall plaques, rings, bracelets, snuffboxes, and hats. He wrote his daughter, Sally: "These, with pictures, busts and prints (of which copies upon copies are spread everywhere), have made your father's face as well known as that of the moon."

On one occasion, Franklin was dining at a Paris restaurant and learned that Edward Gibbon, the British historian who chronicled ancient Rome's decline and fall, was there too. When Gibbon declined to sit with Franklin, a rebel, Franklin replied that if Gibbon ever wanted to write a history of Britain's decline and fall, he would provide "ample materials."

Despite all Franklin's savvy, he might not have accomplished much without evidence that the Americans could win the war. Washington provided that when he crossed the Delaware River on Christmas Day 1776 and won the battle of Trenton, capturing over nine hundred enemy soldiers. Franklin negotiated two treaties with France, giving important diplomatic recognition to the American Republic, and arranged a succession of shipments to America. That they included the most basic stuff suggests how desperate America was. One shipment, for instance, included 164 brass cannon, 3,600 blankets, 4,000 tents, 4,000 dozen pairs of stockings, 8,750 pairs of shoes, 11,000 grenades, 20,000 pounds of lead, 161,000 pounds of gun powder, 373,000 flints, and 514,000 musket balls.

Franklin handled many more tasks. For example, he met the Scottish-born naval captain John Paul Jones and encouraged his bold raids along Britain's coast, undermining British morale. Jones's flagship, the *Bonhomme Richard*, honored the "Poor Richard" of Franklin's *Almanack*.

Franklin's diplomacy and French support helped secure victory. The valiant Frenchman La Fayette helped George Washington corner the British general Charles Cornwallis at Yorktown, Virginia. The fleet of French Admiral François Joseph Paul de Grasse prevented British ships from rescuing Cornwallis, and the Revolutionary War ended on October 19, 1781.

Franklin had worked wonders, although London knew what he was doing. His chief assistant at Passy was his friend Dr. Edward Bancroft, an American who worked as a British spy. Jonathan Dull, author of *Franklin the Diplomat*, remarked that "the American mission was so full of people stealing information it is surprising they did not trip over each other."

Congress named Franklin to a committee that would negotiate peace terms with Britain. After eight and a half years, with the mission accomplished, he left Paris on July 12, 1785. He sailed for America with Jean-Antoine Houdon, the sculptor who had done a noble bust of Franklin and would help immortalize Jefferson, Lafayette, and Washington.

Soon after arriving home, Franklin declared, "I shall now be free of Politicks for the Rest of my Life." But at eighty he joined Philadelphia's delegation to the Constitutional Convention, which gathered in May 1787 at the State House, Philadelphia, where the Second Continental Congress had met and the Declaration of Independence had been signed. It looked as if the convention might collapse because of conflict between small states and big states over how they would be represented. Franklin recommended there be two legislative bodies—an idea others had suggested—because this made possible a compromise: states would have equal representation in one legislative body (the Senate) and representation according to population in the other legislative body (the House of Representatives). This "great compromise" assured the small states that their interests would be protected, and they were more willing to compromise on other issues, helping to move the proceedings forward. Finally, Franklin made a motion that the Constitution be adopted. He remarked that the new Constitution looked as if it might last, but "in this world nothing can be said to be certain, except death and taxes."

In late 1787, Franklin had a bad fall going down steps to his garden, and he suffered excruciating pain from a kidney stone. He wrote his will and resumed work on his autobiography, which he had started back in 1771 when he was in London. As the French Revolution exploded across the Atlantic, Franklin wrote to his friend David Hartley, "God grant that not only the love of liberty, but a thorough knowledge of the rights of man, may pervade all the nations of the earth, so that a philosopher may set his foot anywhere on its surface, and say, 'This is my country.'"

In March 1790, Thomas Jefferson visited him and reported: "I found him in bed where he remains almost constantly. He had been clear of pain for some days and was cheerful & in good spirits. . . . I pressed him to continue the narration of his life." The last letter Franklin ever wrote, nine days before his death on April 17, was to Jefferson. Franklin developed a fever and complained about pain on the left side of his chest. Then a lung abscess burst, and breathing became ever more difficult. He died on April 17, about 11:00 at night. He was eighty-four. Four days later, a funeral procession began at the state house, and he was buried at Christ Church cemetery. Some twenty-thousand people paid their respects. He had written his wry epitaph long ago: "B. Franklin, Printer; like the Cover of an old Book, Its Contents torn out, And stript of its lettering and Gilding, Lies here, Food for Worms. But the Work shall not be wholly lost, For it will, as he believ'd, appear once more, In a new & more perfect Edition, Corrected and amended By the Author."

Part One of Franklin's *Autobiography*, a pirated French edition, was published in 1791. Then came two English editions. There were 14 reprintings before 1800. Franklin's selected works, including the *Autobiography*, were not published until 1817 because of delays by William Temple Franklin who had inherited his grandfather's manuscripts. The rest of Franklin's manuscripts were stored in a stable and eventually recovered by the American Philosophical Society.

The *Autobiography* had many factual errors, since Franklin recalled events years after they happened; the story only went up to 1760; and Franklin revealed little about his feelings. But the book appealed to people because he wrote in a plain manner, chronicled his failures as well as his successes, and identified principles for building strong character. Franklin, noted American historian Carl Becker, was "a true child of the Enlightenment . . . its passion for freedom and its humane sympathies . . . its profound faith in common sense, in the efficacy of Reason for the solution of human problems and the advancement of human welfare."

German poet Johann Wolfgang von Goethe organized a "Friday Club" modeled after Franklin's Junto. Franklin inspired Simón Bolívar and José de San Martín, who helped people in South America gain independence. In Japan, author Fukuzawa Yukichi promoted Franklin's principles and inspired entrepreneurs. Florentine painter Gaspero Barbera published an Italian translation, explaining: "At the age of 35 I was a lost man. . . . I read again and again the

Autobiography of Franklin, and became enamoured of his ideas and principles to such a degree that to them I ascribe my moral regeneration. . . . Now, at the age of fifty-one, I am healthy, cheerful and rich."

During the heyday of American individualism, Franklin's story was taken up by educators whose books sold in the tens of millions. For instance, drawing on the *Autobiography*, Noah Webster included an eleven-page account of Franklin's life in his *Biography for the Use of Schools* (1830); Peter Parley wrote *Life of Benjamin Franklin* (1932); and William Holmes McGuffey included selections from the *Autobiography* in his enormously popular *Readers*.

By the 1850s, the *Autobiography* had been reprinted almost a hundred times, and between 1860 and 1890, Franklin was reportedly the most popular subject for American biographers. The *Autobiography* inspired James Harper to leave his Long Island farm and launch what became a major publishing house, now HarperCollins; Thomas Mellon was inspired to quit farming, become a banker, and make his family fortune. The *Autobiography* inspired steel entrepreneur Andrew Carnegie. Harvard University president Jared Sparks told how the *Autobiography* "taught me that circumstances have not a sovereign control over the mind." Savings banks across America were named after Franklin. Altogether, reported American historian Clinton Rossiter, Franklin's *Autobiography* has been "translated and retranslated into a dozen languages, printed and reprinted in hundreds of editions, read and reread by millions of people. . . . The influence of these few hundred pages has been matched by that of no other American book."

As individualism fell out of fashion, intellectuals belittled personal responsibility and self-help. In 1923, for instance, novelist D. H. Lawrence ridiculed Franklin for seeming to cherish reason over passion. In recent decades, some professors have claimed the *Autobiography* was an elaborate pose, covering up Franklin's "dark side."

But nobody has denied Franklin's stupendous achievements. He championed personal responsibility, intellectual curiousity, honesty, persistence, and thrift—principles that have helped people everywhere lift themselves up. He nurtured an entrepreneurial culture, one that creates opportunity and hope through peaceful cooperation. He affirmed that by improving yourself and helping your neighbors, you can make a free society succeed. His most glorious invention is the American dream.

CULTIVATING CHARACTER

SAMUEL SMILES INSPIRED people around the world to improve their lives. He produced a succession of popular books, including *Self-Help* (1859), *Character* (1871), *Thrift* (1875), *Duty* (1880), and *Life and Labour* (1887), that sold hundreds of thousands of copies in Arabic, Chinese, Croatian, Czech, Danish, Dutch, German, Gujariti, Hindustani, Italian, Japanese, Marati, Portuguese, Russian, Swedish, and Tamil as well as English. These books are still in print.

Smiles stressed the moral dimension of self-help. "The crown and glory of life is Character," he declared. "It is the noblest possession of a man, constituting a rank in itself, and an estate in the general good will; dignifying every station, and exhalting every position in society. It exercises a greater power than wealth, and secures all the honour without the jealousies of fame. It carries with it an influence which always tells; for it is the result of proved honour, rectitude, and consistency—qualities which, perhaps more than any other, command the general confidence and respect of mankind. . . . The spirit of self-help is the root of all genuine growth in the individual; and, exhibited in the lives of many, it constitutes the true source of national vigour and strength. . . . Daily experience shows that it is energetic individualism which produces the most powerful effects upon the life and action of others, and really constitutes the best practical education."

As a biographer, Smiles could have written about kings, politicians, and conquerors, but instead he illustrated fundamental truths with stirring stories about ordinary people who achieved extraordinary things. He exulted, "Great men of science, literature, and art . . . have belonged to no exclusive class nor rank in life. They have come alike from colleges, workshops, and farmhouses—from the huts of poor men and the mansions of the rich. . . . The poorest have sometimes taken the highest places." Historian Asa Briggs hailed Smiles, "who more than any other nineteenth-century writer popularized the heroes of the industrial revolution and proclaimed their values."

His granddaughter Aileen referred to "his striking figure, his massive head, his keen eye beaming benevolence." She remarked that "he committed every Victorian crime. He wore hair on his face and painted in water-colours. He believed in large families (in moderation) and thought that parents should feed and educate their children, even to their own discomfort. . . . I remember Granpa only as a kind, merry, good-tempered man."

*　　　*　　　*

Samuel Smiles was born December 23, 1812, at 62 High Street, his family's house in Haddington, a Scottish village about eighteen miles from Edinburgh. He was the third of eleven children of Samuel Smiles, who had a general store. His mother, Janet Wilson, came from a family of farmers and mechanics.

Young Samuel attended Haddington Grammar School and dreamed of growing up to be an artist, but he settled on becoming a doctor, a more practical choice. In November 1826, he began a part-time apprenticeship with two doctors. Half the day, he attended a school where he read Greek and Roman literature; the rest of the day he learned medicine. He took his medical exams, graduated in 1832, and lived at home to help care for his siblings. He could not earn much money as a doctor because many patients were paupers.

In 1837 Smiles began writing articles for the *Leeds Times*, in a center of the woolen industry, about expanding the number of people who could vote. The following year, that newspaper needed an editor, and he got the job. Smiles heard many of the leading speakers of the day, including Daniel O'Connell, the great champion of Irish liberty. Smiles became a good friend of Manchester-based Richard Cobden, who, with John Bright, led the campaign to repeal tariffs that prevented hungry people from buying cheap, imported food.

Smiles met Sarah Ann Holmes, who seems to have been the granddaughter of an earl. Her father disapproved of his humble status, and the couple eloped and were married December 7, 1843. They lived at 24 Wellington Street, Leeds. They had five children: Janet (1844), William (1846), Edith (1847), Samuel (1852), and Lilian (1854).

As England's Industrial Revolution gathered momentum, there was a railroad building boom, and in 1845 Smiles again gave up his medical practice, this time to become assistant secretary of the Leeds and Thirsk Railroad. A decade later, after consolidation of the railroad industry, he ended up with the South Eastern Railway, based in Newcastle, where he remained until 1866. As his granddaughter noted, Smiles pursued his literary work "by snatches, in odd moments with long intervals in between."

Newcastle was where one of his heroes, engineer George Stephenson, had played a key role developing the locomotive. Smiles wrote a biography of the man. The prestigious London publisher John Murray was interested in the book, and Smiles made a deal to split the profits. The book was issued in 1857, and there were five printings during the first year.

Meanwhile, in March 1845, he was invited to speak before the Mutual Improvement Society, and he titled his talk "The Education of the Working Classes." He developed the theme of self-help, talking about ordinary people who took initiative, persevered, and lifted themselves up from poverty. He celebrated the possibilities of life. "What is the great idea that has seized the mind of this age?" he asked. "It is the grand idea of man—of the importance of man as man; that every human being has a great mission to perform—his noble faculties to cultivate, great rights to assert, a vast destiny to accomplish." The audience loved the talk, and he was invited to give it before other organizations and churches. He expanded his talk with more anecdotes about people who worked hard and fulfilled their dreams, and he eventually gave up his medical practice and accepted a job as assistant to the secretary of a new railway so he could have evenings for his writing. Over the years, he expanded his material into a book-length manuscript.

"My object in writing out *Self-Help,* and delivering it at first in the form of lectures, and afterwards rewriting and publishing it in the form of a book," Smiles explained, "was principally to illustrate and enforce the power of George Stephenson's great word—PERSEVERENCE. I had been greatly attracted when a boy by Mr. [G. L.] Craik's *Pursuit of Knowledge under Difficulties.* I had read it often, and knew its many striking passages almost by heart. It occurred to me, that a similar treatise, dealing not so much with literary achievements and the acquisition of knowledge, as with the ordinary business and pursuits of common life, illustrated by examples of conduct and character drawn from reading, observation, and experience, might be equally useful to the rising generation. It seemed to me that the most important results in daily life are to be obtained, not through the exercise of extraordinary powers, such as genius and intellect, but through the energetic use of simple means and ordinary qualities, with which nearly all human individuals have been more or less endowed. Such was my object, and I think that, on the whole, I hit my mark."

Smiles certainly illustrated perseverance with dramatic stories. For instance, he told how Norway rats gnawed some two hundred of John James Aububon's precious bird drawings into bits. Audubon resolved that he would not be stopped and "went forth to the woods as gaily as if nothing had happened." An English maid thought she was throwing out a bundle of waste paper, but it turned out to be the manuscript of Thomas Carlyle's book *The French Revolution;* he wrote it all over again, and it became a classic. Isaac Newton's dog Diamond destroyed papers recording several years of calculations, but the English physicist and mathematician achieved immortality because he had the determination to redo all that work.

Smiles clearly understood that poverty cannot be eradicated by giving poor people money. "Even the best institutions can give a man no active help," he declared. "Perhaps the most they can do, is leave him free to develop himself and improve his individual condition. . . . It is every day becoming more clearly understood, that the function of Government is negative and restrictive, rather than positive and active; being resolvable principally into protection—protection of life, liberty, and property. Laws, wisely administered, will secure men in the enjoyment of the fruits of their labour, whether of mind or body, at a comparatively small personal sacrifice; but no laws, however stringent, can make the idle industrious, the thriftless provident, or the drunken sober. Such reforms can only be effective by means of individual action."

John Murray published *Self-Help* in July 1859 with an initial printing of three thousand copies, but word of mouth was so strong that advance orders led the publisher to go ahead with another printing of three thousand. During the first year, sales hit twenty thousand. The book continued to be in strong demand, and during the next forty years sales exceeded a quarter of a million. There were many pirated editions, notably in the United States.

Smiles became the biographer of men who during the Industrial Revolution worked hard to make British people the most prosperous on earth. From 1858 to 1861, he worked on the three-volume *Lives of the Engineers* (1861) that chronicled two centuries of extraordinary progress achieved by self-disciplined, largely self-taught private individuals and told the story of technology, economic progress, and social change. "It will be observed from these pages," he wrote, "that the works of our engineers have exercised an important influence on the progress of the English nation. . . . Most of the Continental nations had a long start of us in art, in science, in mechanics, in navigation, and in engineering. Not many centuries since, Italy, Spain, France, and Holland looked down contemptuously on the poor but proud islanders, contending with nature for a subsistence amidst their fogs and their mists. Though surrounded by the sea, we had scarcely any navy until within the last three hundred years. Even our fisheries were so unproductive, that our markets were supplied by the Dutch, who sold us the herrings caught upon our own coasts. England was then regarded principally as a magazine for the supply of raw materials, which were carried away in foreign ships and partly returned to us in manufactures worked up by the foreign artisans. We grew food for Flanders, as America grows cotton for England now. Even the little manufactured at home was sent to the Low Countries to be dyed.

"Most of our modern branches of industry were begun by foreigners, many of whom were driven by religious persecution to seek an asylum in England. Our first cloth-workers, silk-weavers, and lace-makers were French and Flemish refugees. The brothers Elers, Dutchmen, began the pottery manufacture; Spillman, a German, erected the first paper-mill at Dartford; and Boomen, a Dutchman, brought the first coach into England.

"When we wanted any skilled work done, we almost invariably sent for foreigners to do it. Our first ships were built by Danes or Genoese. When the *Mary Rose* sank at Spithead in 1545, Venetians were hired to raise her. . . . When an engine was required to pump water from the Thames for the supply of London, Peter Morice, the Dutchman, was employed to erect it. Our first lessons in mechanical and civil engineering were principally obtained from

Dutchmen, who supplied us with our first wind-mills, water-mills, and pump-ing-engines. . . . In short, we depended or our engineering, even more than we did for our pictures and our music, upon foreigners. . . .

"After the lapse of a century, we find the state of things has become entirely reversed. Instead of borrowing engineers from abroad, we now send them to all parts of the world. British-built steam-ships ply on every sea; we export machinery to all quarters, and supply Holland itself with pumping engines. During that period our engineers have completed a magnificent sys-tem of canals, turnpike-roads, bridges, and railways, by which the internal communications of the country have been completely opened up; they have built lighthouses round our coasts, by which ships freighted with the produce of all lands, when nearing our shores in the dark, are safely lighted along to their destined havens; they have hewn out and built docks and harbours for the accommodation of a gigantic commerce; whilst their inventive genius has rendered fire and water the most untiring workers in all branches of industry, and the most effective agents in locomotion by land and sea."

Historian Thomas Parke Hughes noted that Smiles "relied upon printed sources—especially those contemporary to his subject—and drew as well upon the memories of those who had known the late eighteenth- and early nine-teenth-century engineers. . . . The excellence of his research has been evi-denced by the heavy dependence of subsequent historians upon his biographies and the rare instances in which they have been able to justify their reworking of his material by citing his errors and setting the record straight."

Lives of the Engineers sold well and was later expanded to fill five volumes. William Ewart Gladstone, the champion of liberty and peace who served as Britain's prime minister four times, told Smiles, "It appears to me that you first have given practical expression to a weighty truth—namely, that the character of our engineers is a most signal and marked expression of British character." In *Industrial Biography* (1863), Smiles provided a similar account of the contributions of major iron workers and tool makers.

Smiles recognized the immense contributions of immigrants and became fascinated with the Huguenots, Protestants who, persecuted in France dur-ing the late seventeenth century, had emigrated to England and Ireland. Accordingly he wrote *The Huguenots: Their Settlements, Churches and Industries in England and Ireland.* His first volume appeared in 1867 and the second in 1873. They were reprinted many times.

He wrote *Character* in 1871. "Truthfulness is at the foundation of all per-sonal excellence," he wrote, "And a man is already of consequence in the world when it is known that he can be relied on—that when he says he knows a thing, he does know it—that when he says he will do a thing, he can do it, and does. . . . It is the individual men, and the spirit which actuates them, that determine the moral standing and stability of nations. The only true barrier against the despotism of public opinion, whether it be of the many or of the few, is enlightened individual freedom and purity of personal character. Without these there can be no vigorous manhood, no true liberty in a nation."

In *Thrift* (1875), Smiles insisted that "men who are paid good wages might also become capitalists, and take their fair share in the improvement and well-being of the world. . . . The principal industrial leaders of to-day consist, for the most part, of men who have sprung directly from the ranks. It is the accumulation of experience and skill that makes the difference. . . . Savings are the result of labor; and it is only when laborers begin to save that the results of civilization accumulate. . . . Thrift produces capital, and capital is the conserved result of labor. The capitalist is merely a man who does not spend all that is earned by work."

Smiles began *Duty* (1880) with a discussion of conscience, which "is the very essence of individual character. . . . Every man is bound to develop his individuality, to endeavor to find the right way of life, and to walk in it. He has the will to do so; he has the power to be himself and not the echo of somebody else. Duty, he explained, means putting sound principles into action: "Our wits are sharpened by our necessity, and the individual man stands forth to meet and overcome the difficulties. . . . A man is a miracle of genius because he is a miracle of labor. Strength can conquer circumstances."

Smiles was deluged with requests to write biographies, and despite a paralytic stroke, which he suffered in November 1871, he turned out a half-dozen. By the 1890s, though, intellectual trends were very much against Smiles. Socialism was in vogue, and authors like Edward Carpenter and Sidney Webb promoted the idea that individuals could not take care of themselves and that government could make everything right if it seized control of the economy. Sales of Smiles's books petered out. In 1898, his publisher, John Murray, declined to publish his last self-help book, *Conduct*. The manuscript was destroyed.

Smiles and his wife spent their sunset years at a house they built at 8 Pembroke Gardens, London. He had a large study, recalled his granddaughter Aileen Smiles, "and there was barely space to walk round it. The place was crammed. There were books everywhere." Smiles became increasingly feeble and died on April 16, 1904. He was ninety-two. He was buried in Brompton Cemetery. Most of his papers, including about a thousand letters, went to the Leeds Public Library.

For some time, Smiles had been working on his *Autobiography*. It was published in 1905, but there was little interest in it. Since then, there has been only one book-length biography, written by his granddaughter and published in 1956. Smiles was largely forgotten.

Yet an increasing number of researchers have concluded that Smiles was right. Industrial Revolution entrepreneurs generated prosperity that made

possible the survival of millions who otherwise would have perished. As economist Thomas S. Ashton wrote, England "was delivered, not by her rulers,
but by those who, seeking no doubt their own narrow ends, had the wit and
resource to devise new instruments of production and new methods of
administering industry. There are today on the plains of India and China men
and women, plague-ridden and hungry, living lives little better, to outward
appearance, than those of the cattle that toil with them by day and share their
places of sleep at night. Such Asiatic standards, and such unmechanized horrors, are the lot of those who increase their numbers without passing through
an Industrial Revolution."

Smiles was right to say that giving away money will never resolve social
problems. During the last three decades, the U.S. government has spent over
$6 trillion in an effort to wipe out poverty, and the result has been a chroni-
cally dependent underclass. It is again acceptable, if not fashionable, to talk
as Smiles did about the crucial importance of individual action to cultivate
character. Hence, best-sellers like William J. Bennett's *The Book of Virtues*
(1993), *The Moral Compass* (1995), *The Children's Book of Virtues* (1995),
and *The Children's Book of Heroes* (1997) have sold several million copies.

Now there is renewed interest in Smiles. A new edition of *Self-Help* has
appeared, and all his works are back in print. A number of them can be
downloaded from Internet web sites. The principles he explained help people everywhere who are intent on struggling upward.

UP FROM SLAVERY

❧

BOOKER T. WASHINGTON did more than anybody else to help blacks lift themselves up from slavery. He started a great institution, Tuskegee (now Tuskegee University), that helped tens of thousands of people gain skills they needed. The graduates have included people from Africa, Cuba, Jamaica, Puerto Rico, and other places as well as the United States. Research conducted at Tuskegee, especially by botanist George Washington Carver, helped poor Southern farmers.

Washington's influence as an educator extended well beyond Tuskegee. He directed a private campaign that led to the construction of thousands of elementary schools for blacks. As a trustee, he raised hundreds of thousands of dollars for Howard University and Fisk University, the two major institutions of higher learning for blacks.

Washington's stirring autobiography, *Up from Slavery* (1901), was translated into every major language and is still in print. Although he was born a slave, he gained a good education and found an important calling, and he helped other blacks improve their lives despite discriminatory laws. He believed that personal responsibility and a spirit of enterprise are crucial. He expressed a long-term view: "Brains, property, and character for the Negro will settle the question of civil rights."

Teaching moral behavior and competence was the best bet to promote racial harmony, he thought. He did not believe in salvation through government. The more things blacks produced that whites need, the more whites were likely to abandon their racial stereotypes and show respect. Improving racial relations required changing human hearts, which could not be done by passing laws.

Washington's efforts to cultivate the goodwill of the white majority, which controlled legislatures, courts, businesses, newspapers, universities, and other institutions, were severely criticized by northern black intellectuals like W. E. B. Du Bois who advocated confrontational tactics against racial segregation. Historian Page Smith offered this perspective: "Much of the present-day discussion about Washington's education and racial philosophy fails to take into account that he *had no alternative*. For the place and time his doctrine that blacks must win the confidence and friendship of whites in order to make even modest progress was unassailably true. Those who came to differ with him lived, almost without exception, outside the South. At the very least they did not have to protect an institution—Tuskegee—for which he had the primary, if not sole, responsibility."

Until Louis R. Harlan's authoritative biography, the first volume of which appeared in 1972, few people were aware that Washington fought racial segregation behind the scenes. He tapped contacts developed during his extensive fund-raising tours through the North and the West. He insisted on anonymity as he financed court cases that challenged the disenfranchisement of blacks, the exclusion of blacks from juries, and the improper application of the death penalty.

Washington always stayed close to his roots. According to Harlan, "When he dressed up for public occasions, it was as a prosperous peasant, wearing a brown derby instead of a top hat. The same rural southernness showed in his speech, never salty but always earthy and direct. . . . He rode horseback all his life, hunted and fished when he could, and derived psyhic healing from cultivating his own garden." Yet he became one of the most dynamic public speakers of his time as he traveled around the United States and Europe, promoting individual responsibility, self-help, hard work, thrift, and goodwill. His former teacher Nathalie Lord remembered: "I can see his manly figure, his strong, expressive face, and hear his voice, so powerful and earnest when a thought required it, yet gentle and tender . . ."

BOOKER TALIAFERRO WASHINGTON was born on a plantation belonging to James Burroughs near Hale's Ford, Virginia, probably in April 1856. His mother, Jane, almost certainly gave birth in a log cabin on a dirt floor covered with rags. He never knew who his father was. His mother was the Burroughs' cook. Washington recalled, "She snatched a few moments for our care in the early morning before her work began, and at night after the day's work was done. . . . I cannot remember a single instance during my childhood or early boyhood when our entire family sat down to the table together. . . . Meals were gotten by the children very much as dumb animals get theirs. It was a piece of bread here and a scrap of meat there."

After the Civil War, the family moved to Malden, West Virginia, where salt furnaces and coal mines offered work. Young Washington developed a burning desire to read and write, though southern laws had made it illegal to teach blacks these skills. His mother got him a spelling book, and he began attending Sunday school at the African Baptist Church where he learned from William Davis, an eighteen-year-old Ohio boy living with the pastor. A school opened in nearby Tinkerville, and Washington attended while working at the salt furnaces.

Then he got a job as a servant with Louis Ruffner and his wife, Viola, and learned to do cleaning that satisfied Mrs. Ruffner's tough standards. After about a year and a half, Washington set out for a school he had heard about—Hampton Normal and Agricultural Institute in Hampton, Virginia, where poor blacks could pay their expenses by working on campus. Washington rode part of the 500 miles on a train, then boarded a stagecoach until he had no more money. He walked the rest of the way, occasionally getting rides on passing wagons. By the time he reached Richmond, he was broke, so he had to sleep under an elevated sidewalk. He earned money for food by helping to unload pig iron from a ship and continued to do this work until he had fifty cents, which seemed enough to finish the trip.

When he arrived at the school, his clothes were rags, and he had not had a bath in quite a while. The principal, Mary Fletcher Mackie, tested his ability to work by asking him to clean the recitation room. He did a thorough job, and she accepted him. He agreed to work as a janitor for his expenses. "Life at Hampton was a constant revelation to me," Washington continued. "The matter of having meals at regular hours, of eating on a tablecloth, using a napkin, the use of the bathtub and of the toothbrush, as well as the use of sheets upon the bed, were all new to me." Washington was introduced to public speaking by a teacher who gave him private lessons in breathing, emphasis, and articulation. He participated in the debating society, which met on Saturday nights. The most outstanding part of Hampton was the thirty-three-year-old founder, Samuel Chapman Armstong, who set an inspiring example for integrity, responsibility, and enterprise.

After graduation in 1875, Washington was asked to teach at the Tinkersville school, where he displayed considerable enterprise. He taught hygienic practices as well as reading, writing, and arithmetic. Soon attendance exceeded eighty students, and he started a night school; attendance was about eighty students there too. He taught Sunday school at Zion Baptist Church and at the Snow Hill salt furnace, established a public library and debating society, and went on to establish a night school at Hampton.

In 1881, Armstrong received a letter asking him to recommend a person who might be a good principal for a new school in Tuskegee, Alabama, a small town about five miles from the nearest railroad station. The purpose of the school would be to train elementary school teachers. Armstrong recommended Washington, and he was accepted. When he arrived on June 24, he discovered the school had not even been built or financed.

He resolved that although the new school would be starting with some government money, he would gain as much independence as he could. The new school, called the Tuskegee Institute, started in the African Methodist church on July 4, 1881. Washington persuaded a local man to loan him two hundred dollars for a rundown farm that students could build into a campus, and the property was deeded to the school rather than the state. Friends donated newspapers, books, maps, knives, and forks. Washington, the only teacher, ran the place much like the Hampton Institute, with daily inspections of dress, rooms, and facilities. The initial average attendance of about thirty-seven doubled within two months, and Washington began recruiting teachers, mainly Hampton graduates.

Over the years, Washington's most illustrious recruit was the botanist George Washington Carver (1861?–1943). Born a Missouri slave, he was separated from his mother, and he never knew who his father was. While supporting himself as a household worker, laundryman, hotel cook, and farm laborer, he learned as much as he could about plants and animals. He managed to acquire a high school education by his late twenties. He entered Simpson College, Indianola, Iowa, then transferred to Iowa State Agricultural College and earned a B.A. (1894) and an M.S. (1896). He went to Tuskegee where he took over the agriculture department. The single-crop system in the South had substantially depleted the soil, so Carver encouraged farmers to restore soil nitrogen by planting soybeans, peanuts, and sweet potatoes. Because there was limited demand for these products, he conceived hundreds of new uses for them.

With merchant George Marshall looking after finances, Washington and Tuskegee teacher Olivia Davidson (mathematics, astronomy, botany) began fund-raising tours of the North, raising as much as three thousand dollars a month. Then they began tapping northern philanthropic funds like the Slater Fund and Peabody Fund. Washington organized the Tuskegee Singers, who toured the North raising money. A New England widow gave Washington a gold watch, and he pawned it many times.

On August 2, 1882, Washington married Fanny Smith, a Tinkersville student of his who had gone on to graduate from Hampton. They had a daughter, Portia, born in 1883; Fanny died the following year, at age twenty-six. In 1885, he married Olivia Davidson. They had two sons, Booker Taliaferro Washington, Jr., and Ernest Davidson Washington. Olivia's health, which had been fragile, broke down after the birth, and she died on May 8, 1889.

While at Fisk University for a speaking engagement, Washington met a senior named Margaret James Murray who had written him about a teaching position at Tuskegee. Impressed, he hired her as an English teacher. Soon she was supervising women's industries at Tuskegee. Then he asked her to become the principal. Eventually they were married. She assumed more and more responsibility at Tuskegee, giving Washington time to pursue fund raising and to address political issues.

On September 18, 1895, Washington spoke at the Cotton States and International Exhibition. He noted that a third of the population in the South was black, and so the South could not prosper unless black people prospered. He urged blacks to "cast down your bucket where you are" and make the most of available opportunities and whites to "cast down your bucket among these [black] people who have, without strikes and labour wars, tilled your fields, cleared your forests, builded[sic] your railroads and cities, and brought forth treasures from the bowels of the earth, and helped make possible this magnificent representation of the progress of the South." Then, in a bid for racial peace, he offered what came to be called the Atlanta Compromise: "In all things that are purely social we can be as separate as the fingers, yet one as the hand in all things essential to mutual progress."

Overnight, Washington became recognized as a black leader, the successor to Frederick Douglass who had died seven months earlier. This was a tough time, because trends continued to move against blacks. In 1890, Mississippi had become the first southern state to deny blacks the vote. South Carolina followed in 1895. Three years later, Washington tried unsuccessfully to stop Louisiana from disenfranchising blacks, but he won in Georgia. Then, despite his best efforts, Alabama disenfranchised blacks in 1900.

Washington did the best he could to influence political opinion, delivering as many as three talks a day. In October 1898, he warned sixteen thousand people at the Chicago Peace Jubilee, "We shall have, especially in the Southern part of our country, a cancer gnawing at the heart of the Republic, that shall one day prove as dangerous as an attack from an army without or within."

With all the traveling, he suffered from chronic fatigue, so northern supporters arranged for Washington and his wife to take a much-needed vacation in Europe. In Holland, he was impressed by how Dutch farmers made a good living efficiently working small acreage. The Washingtons were treated like celebrities in Paris and London; Queen Victoria served them tea. They met Mark Twain, Susan B. Anthony, and Henry Stanley (the British journalist who had tracked down explorer and antislavery crusader David Livingstone in Africa).

Back in the United States, Washington retained a writer to help him with his memoirs. The resulting *Story of My Life and Work* (1900) was published by a Naperville, Illinois, firm that marketed books via subscription. Reportedly it sold seventy-five thousand copies. Then he retained Vermont-based writer Max Bennett Thrasher, and Doubleday's Walter Hines Page agreed to publish a better autobiography. The book, *Up from Slavery,* appeared in 1901; it has been translated into Arabic, Chinese, Danish, Dutch, Finnish, French, German, Hindi, Japanese, Malayalam, Norwegian, Russian, Spanish, Swedish, and Zulu.

Up from Slavery had on enormous impact on contributions. Among those inspired to support Tuskegee were photography entrepreneur George Eastman, Standard Oil partner Henry H. Rogers, and steel entrepreneur Andrew

Carnegie. Realizing that Jews had suffered much too, Washington success-fully appealed to Jewish entrepreneurs like investment bankers Jacob Schiff, Paul Warburg, Isaac Seligman, and the Lehmans, Goldmans, and Sachses. Sears Roebuck chief executive Julius Rosenwald became a big contributor. Washington won the hearts of these entrepreneurs with his thrift and enter-prise. After he had built Rockefeller Hall for less than was budgeted, Wash-ington sent John D. Rockefeller, Jr., a refund for $239.

Washington was outraged that everybody was taxed for government schools but almost none of this money helped blacks. Philadelphia Quaker Anna Jeanes named Washington a trustee to spend $1 million improving the quality of southern teachers for black children. Washington was an adviser to Julius Rosenwald who began financing the construction of school buildings for black children throughout the South. He helped advance higher educa-tion for blacks when he served on the boards of Howard and Fisk universi-ties, and he used his influence with Carnegie to get a library building for Howard. Washington persuaded Carnegie to give Fisk $25,000. Washington and New York corporate lawyer Paul Cravath took charge of a $300,000 fund-raising campaign for Fisk.

Behind the scenes, Washington helped mount a legal counterattack against escalating white efforts to deny blacks their civil liberties. He paid his New York–based personal lawyer, Wilfred Smith, to bring two Alabama disenfran-chisement cases, *Giles v. Harris* (1903) and *Giles v. Teasley* (1904), before the Supreme Court. They lost. Then Washington and Smith challenged the prac-tice of barring blacks from juries with an Alabama case they took to the Supreme Court in 1904. The Court overturned the conviction of a black man who had been found guilty by a jury from which blacks were excluded. Wash-ington raised money and recruited lawyers who persuaded the Supreme Court to strike down peonage statutes, which held debtors in servitude to their creditors.

Because Washington's public persona was so accommodating and he fought segregation behind the scenes, he was bitterly criticized by radical black northern intellectuals. His most persistent critic was W. E. B. Du Bois, the Massachusetts-born sociologist who graduated from Fisk University and earned a Ph.D. from Harvard University. His critique of Washington appeared in the *Dial, The Souls of Black Folk* (1903), and elsewhere. "Mr. Washington," he charged, "represents in Negro thought the old attitude of adjustment and submission."

In November 1915, Washington began to suffer the symptoms of serious kidney trouble and high blood pressure. He went to St. Luke's Hospital in New York and consulted doctors there, but they couldn't do much. He decided to head home. "I was born in the South," he remarked, "I have lived and labored in the South, and I expect to die and be buried in the South." His wife helped him take the train from Pennsylvania Station on Friday, November 12. She arranged to have an ambulance meet them at Chehaw, the train station about five miles from Tuskegee, around 9 P.M. Saturday.

Washington had much to be proud of. Tuskegee had about two thundred teachers training some one thousand five hundred students in thirty-eight trades and professions. The campus had a hundred modern buildings. Tuskegee was debt free with over two thousand acres and a $2 million endowment. Most important was the legacy of graduates who, he noted, "are showing the masses of our race how to improve their material, educational, and moral and religious life . . . [and they are] causing the Southern white man to learn to believe in the value of educating the men and women of my race."

Washington got home, but he died at 4:45 Sunday morning, November 14, 1915. He was fifty-nine years old. A simple funeral was held Wednesday at Tuskegee. He was buried in the campus cemetery with a tremendous hunk of granite for a gravestone.

Self-help went out of fashion among black intellectuals who, like W. E. B. Du Bois, came to believe that improving the lives of blacks depended on political action and government intervention. Yet while blacks got nowhere politically from the 1890s through the 1920s, as Thomas Sowell reported in his book *Race and Economics* (1975), "for the masses of the black population, these were years of great economic advance . . . and even culturally the 1920s was a period of great development variously known as the 'black renaissance' and the arising of the 'new Negro.' Great numbers of Negroes entered industrial occupations for the first time during World War I and set in motion a mass migration to the North which transformed the history of black America."

Du Bois lived almost a half-century after Washington's death, and his belief in salvation through government had a major influence on black intellectuals, even though black income relative to whites declined during Franklin D. Roosevelt's New Deal. Du Bois discredited himself by embracing communism, including to Soviet dictator Joseph Stalin.

Blacks nevertheless continued to help themselves. After World War II, four times more southern blacks migrated North than had migrated North through the 1920s. "The Second Great Migration brought about an enormous improvement in the kinds of jobs held by African Americans and in the incomes they earned," reported Stephan and Abigail Thernstrom in their book *America in Black and White* (1997). "In many respects the pace of progress was more rapid before the civil rights legislation of the early 1960s and the affirmative action policies that began in the late 1960s than it has been since."

Booker T. Washington proved to have much better insights than Du Bois about improving people's lives, especially the poorest. He understood that dramatic progress can be achieved, even in a hostile political environment, if individuals educate themselves, work hard, and produce things other people want, and he recognized that as far as individual advancement is concerned, there is no substitute for responsibility, honesty, thrift, and goodwill. Character is destiny.

CHILDREN ACHIEVING
INDEPENDENCE

❧

WHAT DID INVENTOR Alexander Graham Bell, philosopher Bertrand Russell, actor Cary Grant, actress Vanessa Redgrave, singer Bing Crosby, comedian Bob Hope, cellist Yo-Yo Ma, and Britain's Princess Diana have in common? They all sent their children or grandchildren to schools inspired by Maria Montessori, the courageous woman who showed why freedom is absolutely essential for creativity and independence.

Despite sharp differences on political issues, people of every major culture and religion appreciate how Montessori schools set children free to learn. There are Montessori schools throughout Europe and the Americas. They are well-established in India, in mainland China, in Russia, and they are expanding fast in Japan. There's a Montessori school in remote Cambodia, both Israel and the United Arab Emirates have them, and one is reportedly is being built in Somalia. Altogether, there are Montessori schools in fifty-two nations around the world.

These schools thrive because children and parents love them. More than 90 percent of U.S. Montessori teachers, for instance, are in private schools where revenue comes from parents voluntarily—not from taxpayers. By contrast, the major U.S. teachers' colleges do their best to ignore Maria Montessori, treating her as a historical figure of little relevance now. Vast teachers' unions are uneasy about the freedom in Montessori classrooms.

This has always been a maverick movement. Defying progressive educators who molded children to fit a collectivist vision, Maria Montessori declared that the purpose of education is to help individuals fulfill their destiny. She rebelled against regimented schooling and insisted that children must have freedom to grow. She showed that children learn mainly by teaching themselves, not by having teachers drum knowledge into passive heads. Montessori established that children begin learning practically from birth, and education—the right kind—could start offering benefits much sooner than had been thought. "The fundamental principle," she wrote, "must be the *liberty of the pupil;*—such liberty as shall permit a development of individual, spontaneous manifestations of the child's nature. If a new and scientific pedagogy is to arise from the study of the individual, such study must occupy itself with the observation of free children."

Montessori had a formidable presence when, in 1906, she began making epic discoveries about how children learn. "In her late thirties," wrote biographer Rita Kramer, "she was a somewhat portly figure, still handsome but putting on weight, still self-assured but a shade more dignified. She would come into a classroom wearing a simple but stylish dark-colored dress or shirtwaist, her dark hair piled neatly on top of her head, and smile at the children." She had a "smooth, unwrinkled face and bright, clear eyes . . . poise and serenity."

Montessori was born August 31, 1870, in Chiaravalle, Italy, the year Italian states combined to form a new nation. Her father, Alessandro Montessori, was an official who managed the finances of a government-owned tobacco factory. Her mother, Renilde Stoppani, was the bookish daughter of a landed aristocrat.

When Maria was about five, Alessandro Montessori secured a job as an accountant in Rome and moved the family there, so Maria would have access to a better education. She was encouraged to set her sights on teaching, among the few professions available for women. Stubborn Maria, however, considered one profession after another that was closed to women: first engineering, then biology and medicine. In 1896, she became Italy's first woman doctor, but she was not permitted to practice because it was unthinkable to have a woman examining a man's body, so she accepted an appointment as assistant doctor at the University of Rome's Psychiatric Clinic. This gave her an opportunity to observe "defectives"—children who were retarded, learning disabled, or difficult for other reasons. These children were kept in crowded rooms without toys or much to do. As she observed them, she became convinced that their lives might be improved if they were treated more thoughtfully. Searching for ideas, she discovered the writings of Jean Itard and Edouard Seguin, French doctors who had spent their lives looking for better ways to educate such children.

In 1899, she spoke on the subject before a teachers' conference and caused quite a stir. She was invited to become a lecturer at the University of Rome and director of the new Orthophrenic School for "defective" children. For two years, 1899 to 1901, Montessori searched feverishly for teaching techniques that could help these children. She spent about twelve hours a day observing them, working with them, and trying out various ideas. She visited institutions for "defective" children in London and Paris. Incredibly, the children she taught learned to read and write as well as ordinary children.

Then came the anguish and joy of her life, which led to a new career helping children around the world. At the Orthophrenic School, she worked with a Dr. Giuseppe Montesano. They had an affair, and she gave birth to a son, Mario. Then Montesano refused to marry her and soon married another woman. Montessori's mother was horrified that scandal could destroy her daughter's career. Mario was sent to live with country cousins near Rome, and the whole business was hushed up. Biographer Kramer concluded that the pregnancy as well as breaking up with Montesano must have occurred in 1901, when Maria suddenly resigned from the Orthophrenic School, dropped out of sight for about a year, and abandoned her successful work.

Imagine the anguish of this woman who was pressured to give up her own child, unable to share with him the benefits of her extraordinary insights that would help other people's children around the world. For almost fifteen years, she visited him periodically without identifying herself. He thought of her as a mysterious "beautiful lady." Not until after Maria's mother died in 1912 did Mario come live with her.

Meanwhile, Montessori transformed her grief into a new vision for her life: improving education for normal children. She enrolled as a student at the University of Rome and studied everything that might help better understand how children learn—courses in psychology, anthropology, hygiene, and teaching. She visited elementary schools and noticed what teachers did and how children reacted. These schools had adopted the military-style method promoted in Prussia, the United States, and elsewhere: large numbers of students seated in rows before a teacher who instructed everyone at the same time. She reacted instinctively against the regimented teaching, the passivity of students, and the system of rewards and punishments.

One of her magazine articles expressing her views drew the attention of Edouardo Talamo, an executive with a residential real estate developer, the Istituto Romano dei Beni Stabili. Two of the firm's new apartment buildings, in the impoverished, squalid, violent San Lorenzo section of Rome, were being vandalized by young children living there while their parents were away at work. Talamo concluded it was in the self-interest of the firm to start a school within each building, so the children would have constructive things to do and be properly supervised. He asked Montessori for advice.

She offered to take on the project herself, despite objections from friends who considered it demeaning for a doctor to be teaching young children. Instead of the usual school desks, Montessori acquired child-sized chairs and tables for fifty to sixty-three to six year olds. She brought along the self-correcting instructional materials that she had created for "defective" children to help her students learn sorting, fitting things together, and other skills essential for independence. Her observations suggested the need for additional materials, and gradually her repertoire expanded. She found that children learned abstract concepts more readily when materials involved all of a child's senses—touch as well as sight and sound. Known as Casa dei Bambini (Children's House), the school opened January 6, 1907.

The children were an unpromising lot: sullen, withdrawn, and rebellious. Yet Montessori made a series of startling observations as she worked with them: that children have a powerful, inborn desire to learn and achieve independence, that they learn spontaneously where they have enough freedom, that they develop remarkable concentration on tasks that they choose, that they prefer exploring real things—the world of grownups—rather than conventional toys, and that they blossom in an atmosphere of dignity, respect, and freedom. Classroom order was maintained without rewards and punishments when children were happily engaged.

Although Montessori gave children considerable freedom, this did not mean they could do anything they wanted. She insisted children conduct themselves properly and treat others with respect. "The first idea that the child must acquire," she wrote, "is that of the difference between *good* and *evil;* and the task of the educator lies in seeing that the child does not confound *good* with *immobility,* and *evil* with *activity,* as often happens in the case of old-time discipline. And all this because our aim is to discipline *for activity, for work, for good;* not for *immobility,* not for *passivity,* not for *obedience.* . . . A room in which all the children move about usefully, intelligently, and voluntarily, without committing any rough or rude act, would seem to me a classroom very well disciplined indeed."

Montessori observed that children thrived when the teacher (whom she termed a "directress") showed how to do something and then encouraged free exploration. To help children develop self-confidence and become more independent, she emphasized practical life skills: personal hygiene, putting materials back where they belonged, cleaning the classroom, preparing meals, taking care of plants and pets.

Like most other people, Montessori had assumed that children would not be receptive to reading and writing until age six, but the young children in her classroom asked for instruction, so she and her assistant made sets of script letters with markers enabling the children to tell which way was up. She devised exercises to help children learn the shapes and sounds of letters. Within two months, she witnessed an explosion of writing. By Christmas, while government-school children were still struggling with their letters, two of Montessori's students—four year olds—wrote holiday greetings to building owner Edouardo Talamo. Montessori reported triumphantly: "These were written upon note paper without blot or erasure, and the writing was adjudged equal to that which is obtained in the third elementary grade."

Contrary to prevailing doctrines, Montessori found that children best learned how to read after learning how to write, so she prepared cards to label everyday objects and showed how to sound them out; the children already knew the sounds of individual letters. Within days, they were reading street signs, store signs, package labels, and just about everything else around them, as well as books.

She began training teachers, opening more schools, and writing books. Her first book, *Il Metodo della Pedagogia Scientifica applicato all'educazione infantile nelle Case dei Bambini,* appeared in English in 1912 as *The Montes-*

sori Method and became an American best-seller. She was no abstract philosopher like her contemporary John Dewey. Rather, she provided a specific model to help children learn and achieve independence. Her book was translated into Chinese, Danish, Dutch, French, German, Japanese, Polish, Rumanian, Russian, and Spanish.

Montessori was a sensation. Aspiring teachers came from thousands of miles away to be trained by her. In December 1913, she visited the United States where she met telephone inventor Alexander Graham Bell, electrical genius Thomas Edison, social worker Jane Addams, and Helen Keller who, though blind and deaf, had made herself a remarkably cultivated woman. During the next four decades, Montessori traveled throughout Europe and Asia; she trained over a thousand teachers in India alone.

Although Montessori schools were established around the world, her influence waned after initial publicity about the Casa dei Bambini. Concerned that her work was being oversimplified, she insisted on total control of teacher training and Montessori materials, and this alienated many supporters. She encountered ferocious opposition from academics, especially in the United States. The most influential adversary was William Hurd Kilpatrick, a follower of John Dewey and professor at the prestigious Columbia University Teachers College. Montessori surely encountered opposition because she was a woman at a time when school administrators and education professors were men; she was Catholic, which made a lot of Americans suspicious; her academic training was as a medical doctor, not an educator; and she was Italian. Americans had become disillusioned with President Woodrow Wilson's intervention in World War I, which failed to "make the world safe for democracy" as he had promised, and they turned inward, away from Italy and just about everything else European.

Maria and Mario Montessori and his family left Italy in 1936 when fascist dictator Benito Mussolini imposed government control over schools. They settled in Amsterdam, then spent World War II in India, and returned to Amsterdam afterward, promoting her ideas every step of the way. The most famous student of an Amsterdam Montessori school was a Jewish girl named Anne Frank whose poignant diary was published after she died in Hitler's Bergen-Belsen concentration camp.

While chatting with friends in Noordwijk aan Zee, a North Sea Village not far from the Hague, with Mario by her side, Maria Montessori suffered a cerebral hemorrhage and died on May 6, 1952. She was almost eighty-two. She considered her place wherever she happened to be, so she was buried at a Catholic church cemetery in Noordwijk. When the obituary notices appeared, few Americans had any idea who she was. Rejecting failed progressive education and rooting around forgotten doctrines, though, some enterprising individuals rediscovered Montessori.

In Greenwich, Connecticut, a feisty, outspoken educator named Nancy McCormick Rambusch was not satisfied with the local schools and remembered reading about Montessori's results from giving children freedom to learn. Rambusch went to London for Montessori teacher training. Friends asked her to educate their children, and in 1958 she opened the Whitby School, which sparked the American revival of Montessori. Four years later, at Santa Monica Montessori School (California), former public school teacher Ruth Dresser led the revival on the West Coast, attracting celebrity parents like Robert Mitchum, Yul Brynner, Michael Douglas, Cher Bono, and Sarah Vaughn. Now there are 155 American schools accredited by Association Montessori Internationale (AMI), the group established by Maria Montessori in 1929 to uphold her standards. Another eight hundred schools are accredited by the American Montessori Society (AMS), which, started by Rambusch in 1960, considers some variations appropriate for American culture. About three thousand more schools call themselves "Montessori." In a dramatic turnabout, two hundred public schools have established Montessori programs.

At a Montessori school one can see how children thrive when they are free to move about. One can see the intense, joyous concentration of children who freely choose their work. Children teach themselves important skills with Montessori materials and gain independence with the liberating spirit of Maria Montessori.

INDIVIDUALISM

Individuality is the aim of political liberty.
By leaving to the citizen as much freedom of
action and of being as comports with order and
the rights of others, the institutions render
him truly a freeman. He is left to pursue his
means of happiness in his own manner.
—JAMES FENIMORE COOPER (1838)

THERE HAS ALMOST always been enormous pressure for individuals to conform. Departing from dominant religious views, political views, manners, dress, and other conventions has often meant being treated as an outcast. But in the West during ancient times, the view began to take hold that individuals matter for themselves. Only individuals think or create, only individuals experience pain or joy, and only individuals have rights and responsibilities. It is morally proper for individuals to be mavericks if they wish and go their own way, peacefully. This philosophy of individualism has had its greatest flowering in the United States, although the idea appeals to people around the world.

"DO WHAT THOU WILT"

THE FRENCHMAN FRANÇOIS Rabelais did as much as anyone else to inspire individualism in the modern world. Born during the Renaissance, he matured amid the turmoil of the Reformation and defied the intolerance of Catholics and Protestants alike. He expressed himself freely, pursued the occupation of his choice, and befriended mavericks. His hero was Desiderius Erasmus, the Dutch-born champion of toleration.

Few other writers displayed as playful a free spirit as Rabelais did in his satiric tales about the giants Gargantua and Pantagruel. H. L. Mencken admired Rabelais's "stupendous learning . . . furious impatience of fraud . . . heroic zest for folly." The French scholar Jean Marie Goulemot observed that Rabelais's work "contains a critique of religious and political authority and embraces antiauthoritarian social forms . . . represents a choice, an affirmation of the individual's freedom to set his own standards, to reject received ideas and accepted beliefs, and to constitute a knowledge of his own." Historian Will Durant called Rabelais a "unique, inexhaustible, skeptical, hilarious, learned, and obscene author," and historian Daniel J. Boorstin said that "Rabelais made every institution and article of faith the target of his extravagant imagination."

To challenge established institutions, especially religions, took some courage. One of Rabelais's friends, the French humanist Etienne Dolet, was hanged and burned for printing a translation of Plato, and the physician Miguel Serveto was burned at the stake for heresy. When Rabelais started writing, he felt it was prudent to use a pseudonym. Indeed his work was denounced by powerful churchmen, and on more than one occasion, he secretly moved about to avoid the authorities. Although he said he just wanted to make readers laugh, scholar J. M. Cohen observed that "it was clear to everyone that he was making serious criticisms of laws, customs, and institutions, and it was no good his disguising himself as a boon companion, bent on providing pure entertainment. The entertainment probably always came first. Not only was the criticism there as well, however, but his verbal mastery made it doubly damaging."

Rabelais challenged Europe's most powerful institutions, including the Catholic church; for example, he ridiculed monks and kings and their endless wars. And then he began to envision a free society: "Men that are free, well-born, well-bred and conversant in honest companies, have naturally an instinct and spur that prompteth them unto virtuous actions and withdraws them from vice, called honour. Those same men, when by base subjection and restraint they are brought under and kept down, turn aside from that noble disposition by which they formerly were inclined to virtue."

Brave New World author Aldous Huxley adapted Rabelais's phrase about liberty for his essay collection *Do What You Will* (1929), and the American individualist Albert Jay Nock called Rabelais's vision "an entrancing picture of the humanist's dream of human society existing in a state of absolute freedom; with economic freedom as a foundation, and with political and social freedom erecting themselves naturally and inevitably upon it."

Despite the controversy he stirred up, Rabelais made friends easily with influential Catholics, and he spent time with the pope. Nock reported, "Rabelais's relations with people appear always to have been distinctly personal; he had a great gift for friendship, a fine talent for making himself loved." Some of his friends became patrons and protectors.

"Of his size and shape nothing is known," wrote biographer D. B. Wyndham Lewis. "One imagines him as above average height, ruddy, robust, vigorous and in short as he describes himself in the Prologue to the Fourth Book, 'hale', and cheery, as sound as a Bell, and ready to drink if you will'. His face we know. Its arresting features are a pair of dark, shrewd, vigilant, questing, sardonic eyes; thin brows, seeming continually about to be arched in amusement, mockery, or wrath; an aggressive nose; a firm, imperious, impatient mouth."

Lewis, an English Catholic, declared: "For every pint of wisdom he pours out a quart of nonsense, but who cares? Pen in hand, he is incomparable. He is unique. He is magic. He is magnificent. He is gigantic. . . . Once having fallen under his spell it is impossible to throw it off."

FRENCH PROFESSOR DONALD M. Frame wrote, "We do not know when he was born, or consequently his age at any point; anything about his childhood; what woman or women bore the three illegitimate children of his that we know of; how he regarded and got on with his sexual partner or partners; or why he entered and later left the monastic life." We do know that he was younger than one of his brothers and quite possibly younger than all three siblings: Antoine, Jr., Jamet, and Françoise. François's birthplace was probably La Deviniere, a stone farmhouse several miles from Chinon, south of the Loire River. His father was Antoine Rabelais, an influential lawyer and landowner.

Rabelais might have attended a Seuilly school near his birthplace that was conducted by Benedictine monks, known for their teaching. He grew up when there was mounting interest in Greek and Latin languages and literature, and he learned to write Latin as well as Greek. Thanks to Johannes Gutenberg's invention of printing from movable type around 1450, works that had existed as scarce manuscript copies became more widely available as books, and Rabelais seems to have devoured everything.

By about 1520 he chose to become a monk, perhaps because as a younger son he would not inherit his father's property and become a landed gentleman, and he did not wish to apprentice himself to a local merchant. The Catholic church offered the most promising careers and economic security of sorts, and it possessed vast libraries and afforded opportunities for travel.

Rabelais entered the monastic order founded by St. Francis of Assisi. Franciscan monks traveled about preaching and begging for bread; they did not do any teaching. As Albert Jay Nock and C. R. Wilson noted, "In carrying out their vow of poverty, they became very filthy and slovenly; notably so, even in a time when the general standard of cleanliness was low enough, and thus they did their share to strengthen the traditional relation between saintliness and squalor. . . . The majority were very ignorant; indeed, their ignorance was somewhat of a byword. . . . The work of the order put no premium upon education." Nonetheless, Rabelais went to live at the Puy-Saint-Martin monastery, Fontenay-le-Comte, Poitou, owned by Franciscan monks, where he stayed for about four years. He soon befriended Pierre Amy, the only other monk there who shared his passion for Latin and Greek.

Meanwhile, dissatisfaction with the Catholic church was spreading throughout northern Europe by people who were weary of paying high taxes to the church, especially considering all the church corruption. Many princes encouraged what became the Reformation since they wanted to gain political independence from the church, and they schemed to keep all the tax revenues for themselves. Catholic kings, too, gained power at the expense of the church; in France, François I negotiated the prerogative to name French bishops without interference from Rome. But the church struck back: in France, the Counter-Reformation was led by the faculty of theology at the University of Paris, known as the Sorbonne. They banned further study of Greek literature as subversive.

It was a sign of Rabelais's ability to make friends that in 1524 he secured a transfer from the Franciscan to the Benedictine order. Accordingly, he joined the Benedictine abbey in Maillezais, where the influential bishop Geoffroy d'Estissac presided; Pope Clement VII himself had to approve such a move. Apparently d'Estissac cherished Rabelais's knowledge, conversation, and companionship, because Rabelais accompanied him on travels around the diocese.

Rabelais left this position in 1527 and seems to have spent time in Paris studying medicine, which at the time meant reading ancient authors rather than conducting clinical tests. In September 1530, he registered with the faculty of medicine at the University of Montpellier and three months later received his medical degree. He delivered medical lectures about two ancient Greek physicians whose writings his contemporaries depended on for their medical information. The lectures were published in Latin as *Hippocrates and Galen* in 1532. He was subsequently appointed physician in the Hôtel-Dieu hospital, Lyons, where he gave lectures on human anatomy, which was considered rather daring.

In August 1532, a Lyons publisher issued a collection of folk tales called *The Great and Inestimable Chronicles of the Huge Giant Gargantua,* a hero who had a boundless appetite and offered peasants a helping hand when they needed it. This book became a best-seller, and Rabelais decided to write a sequel. By December, he had produced *Les horribles et epouvantables faits et prouesses du très renommé Pantagruel, roy des Dipsodes (The Horrible and Terrifying Deeds and Words of the Reknowned Pantagruel, King of the Dipsodes).* This came to be known as Book II, about Gargantua's son, Pantagruel. One of the most notable parts of Book II is a letter Gargantua wrote to his son, urging a liberal education: the study of languages, history, mathematics, biology, philosophy, some law, and medicine. The work was written not in Latin, the language of church officials, lawyers, and scholars, but in the "vulgar" French language spoken by common people. Apparently fearing that the story and the language in which it was written would provoke the wrath of censors and jeopardize his medical career, Rabelais wrote under a pseudonym, Alcofribas Nasier.

He next decided to write *La vie inestimable du grand Gargantua (The Inestimable Life of the Great Gargantua),* which became known as Book I, about Gargantua himself. It seems to have been published in 1534. Rabelais's prologue declared that he wanted everybody to have a good time: "Most noble and illustrious drinkers, and you thrice precious pockified blades . . . do what lies in you to keep me always merry. Be frolic now, my lads, cheer up your hearts."

Gargantua, Rabelais explains, was born through his mother's left ear. His first cries reportedly were "Drink, drink, drink." He was so big that 17,913 cows were needed to supply him with enough milk. His clothing required a colossal amount of fabric: "To make him every shirt of his, were taken up nine hundred ells of Chateleraud linen, and two hundred for the gussets. . . . For his breeches, were taken up eleven hundred and five ells and a third of white broad cloth. . . . To wear about his neck he had a golden chain, weighing twenty-five thousand and sixty-three marks of gold." However one might translate these archaic measurements, Gargantua was clearly large, and he was brought up for drinking, eating, and sleeping. On one occasion, Gargantua ate six pilgrims who were hiding in a patch of cabbages and lettuce.

Much of Book I was an antiwar tract. For instance, Rabelais described a fight between bakers and shepherds. The bakers were carrying cakes to market, and the shepherds wanted some, but the bakers declined in a rather rude way, calling the shepherds "prating gablers, lickorous gluttons, freckled bittors, mangy rascals, shite-a-bed scoundrels, drunken roysters," and more. The bakers and shepherds went at one another, and the shepherds ended up buying several dozen cakes for cash plus over a hundred eggs and three baskets of mulberries. The bakers complained to King Picrochole, and he dispatched soldiers to ravage the countryside.

The good monk Frère Jean did much to help defend the shepherds, and Gargantua helped him by establishing a monastery, Theleme, which was a libertarian dream. Its motto was "DO WHAT THOU WILT." Here is how Rabelais described the place: "All their life was spent not in laws, statutes, or rules, but according to their own free will and pleasure. They rose out of the beds when they thought good; they did eat, drink, labour, sleep, when they had a mind to it, and were disposed for it. . . . By this liberty they entered into a very laudable emulation, to do all of them what they saw did please one." Albert Jay Nock remarked: "There was no discipline in the abbey but such as was self-imposed; every arrangement was based upon individual responsibility. . . . Nowhere, we believe, is there more elevated, convincing, and wholly sound conception of human nature's possibilities when invested with no more than mere freedom—only that—than in the fifty-seventh chapter, which expounds the discipline of the Thelemites."

Book I and Book II were reissued together and reportedly topped all other books in sales except the Bible and Thomas A Kempis's *The Imitation of Christ* (1426). In early 1543, the Sorbonne added both *Gargantua* and *Panagruel* to its list of books that good Catholics must not read. The Protestant John Calvin accused Rabelais of being an atheist, a serious charge in those days.

Rabelais produced *Tiers livre* (Book III) in 1546, this one under his name. The book is mainly about Pantagruel's spendthrift companion, Panurge, who was trying to decide whether to get married. Since he had no confidence in his own judgment, he sought advice from a clergyman, a doctor, a lawyer, and a philosopher, but they were not much help, so he set out on a journey to consult the Oracle of the Sacred Bottle. Book III went on to express more antiwar sentiments.

Rabelais seems to have settled in Paris, where he wrote eleven chapters of *Quart livre des faits et dits heroïques du noble Pantagruel* (*Book IV of the Heroic Deeds and Words of the Noble Pantagruel*); they appeared in 1547. It is believed to have been about a third of what Rabelais had contemplated. The book ended abruptly, leaving an episode incomplete. Jean Plattard speculated that Rabelais rushed it into print to raise money for a trip to Italy and to answer critics who were hounding him. Five years later, he revised and expanded Book IV, which continued Pantagruel's quest for the Holy Bottle. Reflecting the dreams of Europeans to find a Northwest Passage through America to China, Rabelais created an epic in the grand tradition of Homer and other chroniclers, abounding with storms, strange people, and places like the Cannibal Islands and the Pettifogging Islands (inhabited by clerks who spent their time issuing legal writs and summonses). Rabelais derided political fanatics, as in this passage by Homenas: "An end of all wars, plunderings, drudgeries, robbing, assassinates, unless it be to destroy these accursed rebels the heretics. Oh, then, rejoicing, cheerfulness, jollity, solace, sports, and delicious pleasures, over the face of the earth."

We know little about how Rabelais spent his last years. In 1552, there were rumors that he had been imprisoned, because friends could not find him. Then two years later came tributes apparently occasioned by his death. An eighteenth-century copy of parish records at St. Paul's Church in Paris reported that he had died on April 9, 1553. He would have been about fifty-nine. He was probably buried in Saint-Paul's Cemetery in Paris.

A work billed as *Cinquieme et dernier livre* (*Fifth and Last Book*) appeared with Rabelais' name in 1562, but scholars have doubted the authenticity of the work. As Jean Plattard explained, "The mere examination of the contents of this posthumous work and the circumstances of its publication lead us to doubt its genuineness as a whole. It may represent rough drafts or fragments cast aside by Rabelais, and preserved by him for various reasons, doubtless to be used later, and put together by another hand, probably a Huguenot [Protestant], who selected from these fragments the parts most easily adaptable to the passions of his co-religionaries." To be sure, the book often evoked the spirit of Rabelais, such as the call to "remove all manner of tyranny from the land."

Rabelais' work became widely read. "Few French books have been reprinted more often," according to Plattard. "There were ninety-eight editions of it in the 16th century, twenty in the 17th, twenty-six in the 18th, and about sixty in the 19th. . . . not only have they inspired story-tellers in prose and verse, pamphleteers, comic and satiric poets, but they have furnished scenarios for ballets, and comic operas, decorative motifs for fans or printed cloths. . . . A list of those famous in Literature, Art, Science and Politics, who delighted in reading Rabelais would be a long one."

Rabelais's writings remained intensely controversial. Both Protestant and Catholic writers denounced him as "the plague and gangrene of devotion," the author of "the most vicious book of the time," the purveyor of a "libertine's manual." When Voltaire was young, he considered Rabelais crude, but later he came to admire these writings, as many others did, for their learning, wisdom, and humor. Biographer Donald M. Frame reported that "translation of Rabelais into other languages was slow to start, but has become widespread."

Rabelais still strikes readers with his titanic energy, speaking against the barbaric cruelties of our time as he did in his time. Rabelais endures because of his great joy for life.

SPIRITUALITY OF INDIVIDUALISM

HENRY DAVID THOREAU was an individualist if ever there was one. As his friend the poet, essayist, and philosopher Ralph Waldo Emerson recalled, "He was bred to no profession; he never married; he lived alone; he never went to church; he never voted; he refused to pay a tax to the State; he ate no flesh, he drank no wine, he never knew the use of tobacco; and, though a naturalist, he used neither trap nor gun. He chose, wisely no doubt for himself, to be the bachelor of thought and Nature. He had no talent for wealth, and knew how to be poor without the least hint of squalor or inelegance." Emerson might have added that Thoreau denounced war and helped runaway slaves. The American poet Walt Whitman confided that "one thing about Thoreau keeps him very near to me: I refer to his lawlessness—his dissent—his going his absolute own road let hell blaze all if it chooses."

During Thoreau's short life, only two of his books were printed: *A Week on the Concord and Merrimack Rivers* (1849), which sold about three hundred copies, and *Walden* (1854), which sold fewer than two thousand. Yet as historian Samuel Eliot Morison wrote about one of Thoreau's posthumously published works, *"Civil Disobedience . . .* became the best-known work of American literature to the peoples of Asia and Africa struggling to be free, and has earned the honor of having its sale prohibited in Communist countries." His writings have been translated into Czech, Danish, Dutch, French, German, Hebrew, Japanese, Russian, Swedish, and Yiddish, among other languages. In *The Importance of Living,* philosopher Lin Yutang wrote, "Thoreau is the most Chinese of all American authors in his entire view of life. . . . I could translate passages of Thoreau into my own language and pass them off as original writing by a Chinese poet, without raising any suspicion."

Walter Harding, who was long the leading Thoreau scholar, observed in 1962 that "a hundred years ago Henry David Thoreau was looked upon as a minor disciple of Ralph Waldo Emerson. Fifty years ago he was thought of as an 'also-ran' who was rapidly and deservedly being forgotten. Yet today he is widely rated as one of the giants in the American pantheon and his fame is on an upward rather than a downward curve. It is universally agreed that he speaks more to our day than to his own."

He expressed important principles of individualism with extraordinary insight and passion and rejected claims that individuals owe an allegiance to collective authority. "I am more than usually jealous with respect to my freedom," he wrote. "I feel that my connection with and obligation to society are still very slight and transient." He believed there was a moral imperative to mind one's own business: "As for Doing-good, that is one of the professions which are full. Moreover, I have tried it fairly, and, strange as it may seem, am satisfied that it does not agree with my constitution." He did not suffer any illusions about government. "I saw that the State was half-witted," he reported, "and I lost all my remaining respect for it." He insisted that to achieve human dignity, people must take responsibility for their lives and maintain independence, which is undermined by government handouts. He displayed stubborn courage to persist in his maverick views despite being sometimes ridiculed as a crank. He seemed to speak for individualists everywhere when he wrote, "If a man does not keep pace with his companions, perhaps it is because he hears a different drummer. Let him step to the music which he hears, however measured or far away."

Thoreau was about five feet, seven inches tall and, said Emerson, "firmly built, of light complexion, with strong, serious blue eyes, and a grave aspect." Among other things, Emerson admired Thoreau as an outdoorsman: "He wore a straw hat, stout shoes, strong gray trousers, to brave scrub oaks and smilax and to climb a tree for a hawk's or a squirrel's nest. He waded into the pool for the water-plants, and his strong legs were no insignificant part of his armor." According to biographer Carlos Baker, Thoreau "had brown hair, fine-textured and abundant. . . . [His] arms were thickly matted with fur, like the pelt of an animal. . . . [His nose] curving out and down from the bridge with a pronounced hook, somewhat resembled the beak of a predatory bird. . . . [His eyes] often blazed with an icy grayish light."

HE WAS BORN David Henry Thoreau on July 12, 1817, in his widowed grandmother's house, on Virginia Road, in Concord, Massachusetts. He was the son of John Thoreau, a failed storekeeper, who became a pencil maker. His mother, Cynthia Dunbar, was the daughter of a Congregationalist minister.

Despite hard times, Thoreau's parents provided him with a good education. He went to Concord Academy, a private school considered better than the local public school, and entered Harvard College on August 9, 1833, when he was sixteen.

After he graduated, he called himself Henry David Thoreau and got a position teaching at Center School, an elementary school in Concord. Apparently there was some concern about discipline, and the local clergyman told him he must flog his students. But Thoreau decided that he could not abide flogging and quit. He and his brother John started a school in Parkman House on

Main Street, later the home of Concord's public library. The school thrived without flogging.

In late 1837, Thoreau met thirty-four-year-old Emerson. Biographer Ralph Rusk noted the "thinness of his body, accentuated by his nearly six feet of height . . . the narrow and sloping shoulders . . . his head gave the impression of firmness. His shock of brown hair . . . his short, unobtrusive side whiskers partly framed a face with rugged features and penetrating blue eyes." Born in Boston, May 3, 1803, the Harvard-educated Emerson developed the mystical philosophy of transcendentalism, explained in his first major essay, "Nature" (1836). His most enduring essays were "Self-Reliance" and "Compensation." Emerson's writing abounded with epigrams—for instance, "Whoso would be a man must be a nonconformist . . . Nothing can bring you peace but yourself . . . Character is higher than intellect . . . The only way to have a friend is to be one . . . Nothing great was ever achieved without enthusiasm . . . Self-reliance, the height and perfection of man . . . Make yourself necessary to somebody . . . The reward of a thing well done, is to have done it . . . Nothing astonishes men so much as common sense and plain dealing . . . The less government we have, the better . . . Great men are they who see that spiritual is stronger than any."

Thoreau showed Emerson his journal, which one of his Harvard professors, William Ellery Channing, had encouraged him to write. He had begun it in October 1837, and it became an important way to develop his views and practice expressing them. Apparently Emerson was impressed with Thoreau's gift for expression and invited him to literary gatherings, known as the Transcendental Club, at the Emerson's Concord home.

In 1839, Henry and John Thoreau went on a thirteen-day boat trip down the Concord River and up the Merrimack River, on experience that took on special meaning after John died from tetanus in 1842. Henry resolved to write a book about the good times he had with his brother but decided he could not work amid distractions at home. Accordingly, between July 4, 1845, and September 6, 1847, he lived on Emerson's property at Walden Pond, just south of Concord. Walden Pond was about three-quarters of a mile long and half a mile wide. With a borrowed ax, Thoreau built a cabin there. He certainly did not cut himself off from civilization as lore has it. He could see the Concord-Lincoln road from his field, the Fitchburg Railroad passed by on the other side of Walden Pond, his mother and sisters brought him pies and doughnuts, he continued to go out for dinners at the houses of his friends, he had frequent visitors, and on more than one occasion, his cabin was a station on the Underground Railroad, sheltering runaway slaves. Thoreau earned money by working as a carpenter, painter, and surveyor.

During his second year in the woods, he had more time for writing. He finished his first book, the tribute to his brother, *A Week on the Concord and*

Merrimack Rivers, but apparently was unable to interest a commercial publisher, because he had a printer produce one thousand copies in 1849. It took him several years to pay the bill, and unsold copies ended up in the attic of his parents' house.

People wanted to hear why a Harvard graduate would live alone in the woods, and on February 10, 1847, he gave a talk, "A History of Myself," at the Concord Lyceum. The audience loved it. Emerson wrote to Margaret Fuller that people came "to hear Henry's account of his housekeeping at Walden Pond, which he read as a lecture, and were charmed with the witty wisdom which ran through it all."

When he had enough of the woods, he went to live at Emerson's house. There he wrote *New York Tribune* editor Horace Greeley a long letter about his experiences and reflections at Walden, and Greeley published it in the May 25, 1848, edition of the newspaper. After two years at the Emersons', Thoreau helped his father with the family pencil factory and lived at his parents' house, which is where he turned the letter into *Walden.* It was issued in 1854 by the publisher Ticknor & Fields.

There is much of Emerson's epigrammatic style in *Walden.* The book contains diatribes against competitive enterprise, which had saved multitudes around the world from starvation, yet Thoreau's insistent individualism makes some beautiful music. Among his most memorable lines are there: "Love your life," "Let every man mind his own business, and endeavor to be what he was made," "If one advances confidently in the direction of his dreams, and endeavors to live the life which he has imagined, he will meet with a success," "I had three chairs in my house; one for solitude, two for friendship, three for society," and "If I knew for a certainty that a man was coming to my house with the conscious design of doing me good, I should run for my life."

Meanwhile, Thoreau had become a tax rebel. In 1840, somebody had added his name to the membership list of Concord's First Parish Church, and the town treasurer demanded that Thoreau pay a tithe. When he refused, officials threatened to jail him. Thoreau demanded that his name be removed from the church membership list. "I Henry Thoreau," he wrote, "do not wish to be regarded as a member of any incorporated society which I have not joined."

In 1845 and the following year, the United States annexed Texas, and President James K. Polk provoked war with Mexico. The war was especially popular in the South because Texas had land for growing cotton and sugar, which meant more proslavery territory.

Thoreau refused to pay his head tax since it meant collaborating with what he viewed an immoral government, and in July he was locked in the Concord jail on Mill Dam Road. Somebody (probably Thoreau's Aunt Maria) paid the tax, so he was in jail only for the night—he had hoped to stay longer as a protest against war and slavery. To explain his views on the tax, Thoreau wrote a paper, which he delivered at the Concord Lyceum on January 26, 1848. About a year later, Elizabeth Peabody asked permission to publish it in a new journal, *Aesthetic Papers*, appearing (for the first and last time) on May 14, 1849. Thoreau's piece, "Resistance to Civil Government," did not waste any time getting to the point in the opening lines: "I heartily accept the motto,—'The government is best which governs least,' and I should like to see it acted up to more rapidly and systematically. Carried out, it finally amounts to this, which I also believe,—'That government is best which governs not at all;' and when men are prepared for it, that will be the kind of government which they will have." "I think that we should be men first, and subjects afterward," he continued. "It is not desirable to cultivate a respect for the law, so much as for the right. . . . Law never made men a whit more just; and, by means of their respect for it, even the well-disposed are daily made the agents of injustice." He added: "I was not born to be forced. I will breathe after my own fashion. . . . There will never be a really free and enlightened State until the State comes to recognize the individual as a higher and independent power, from which all its own power and authority are derived, and treats him accordingly."

Outraged at how the Massachusetts state government had helped enforce the 1850 Fugitive Slave Act, Thoreau gave a talk at the Anti-Slavery Convention in Framingham, Massachusetts, on July 4, 1854, and it was published as "Slavery in Massachusetts" in William Lloyd Garrison's *Liberator* on July 21, 1854. The laws of the state," he asserted, "do not always say what is true; and they do not always mean what they say. . . . What is wanted is men . . . who recognize a higher law than the Constitution, or the decision of the majority. . . . Let the State dissolve her union with the slave-holder. . . . Let each inhabitant of the State dissolve his union with her, as long as she delays to do her duty."

Thoreau next spoke out after abolitionist firebrand John Brown convinced that slaves would be liberated only through armed rebellion, captured the federal arsenal at Harper's Ferry, Virginia, on October 16, 1859. Thoreau was disturbed by the violence but even more disturbed that none of the abolitionists defended Brown's intention to liberate slaves. On October 30, 1859, while Brown was still in jail, Thoreau appeared at Concord Town Hall, where he called Brown "the bravest and humanest man in all the country."

Walter Harding reported that "All his adult life Thoreau suffered on and off from tuberculosis. In December of 1860 he got bronchitis, which worsened the tuberculosis. He died around 9:00 P.M., May 6, 1862. He was just forty-four. His mother, sister, and Aunt Louisa were with him. The memorial service three days later at Concord's First Parish Church, was packed. Author Louisa May Alcott remarked, "Though he wasn't made much of while living, he was honored at his death." And for an author with nothing in print, Thoreau's death was widely reported. There were notices in the *Boston Daily Advertiser, Concord Monitor, Boston Transcript, Christian Register, Harvard Magazine, Liberator, Saturday Evening Post, New York Tribune, Harper's Monthly,* and *Atlantic Monthly,* among others.

Thoreau died obscure. "The world decided," wrote historian Perry Miller, "insofar as it bothered about him—that he would figure as a minor naturalist in a literature where the giants were Irving, Longfellow, Lowell, and Dr. Holmes. As for Thoreau's ideas, this same world assumed that the few he displayed were borrowed from Emerson and declared them reproduced in a clumsy awkwardness which, perhaps momentarily engaging, bespoke the bumpkin."

Thoreau left behind manuscripts running into the thousands of pages. His sister Sophia gathered essays into *Excursions* (1863), and worked with Ellery Channing to edit *The Maine Woods* (1864) and *Cape Cod* (1865). Emerson edited *Letters to Various Persons* (1865). *Yankee in Canada, with Anti-Slavery and Reform Papers,* appeared in 1866. Although these five volumes were incomplete and abounded with errors, they garnered at least thirty-six reviews and helped secure Thoreau's literary reputation. There was enough demand for his works that Houghton Mifflin issued the twenty-volume "Walden" edition in 1906.

Thoreau's paper "Resistance to Civil Government" is a story in itself. In 1866, four years after he died, it was retitled "On Civil Disobedience" and gathered into a book with his *Yankee in Canada, with Anti-Slavery and Reform Papers.* Few people outside the United States seemed to appreciate Thoreau's back-to-nature writings, but *Civil Disobedience* became a battle cry. The Russian novelist and philosopher Leo Tolstoy was impressed by it and cited Thoreau among authors who "specially influenced me." Tolstoy included many Thoreau selections in his anthology, *A Circle of Reading.*

Thoreau biographer Walter Harding found that "there has been a long-standing interest in Thoreau among the Jews. 'Civil Disobedience' was translated into Yiddish in New York in 1907 and again in Los Angeles in 1950. There have been frequent articles on Thoreau in Yiddish newspapers around the world."

When Mohandas Gandhi was studying law in England, he met Thoreau biographer Henry Salt. Around 1907, Gandhi campaigned in South Africa against laws that prevented Indians from traveling, trading, and living freely, and a friend gave him a copy of *Civil Disobedience,* which he read while imprisoned for three months in Pretoria. He acknowledged that Thoreau's "ideas influenced me greatly. I adopted some of them and recommended the study of Thoreau to all my friends who were helping me in the cause of Indian independence. Why, I actually took the name of my movement from Thoreau's essay, 'On the Duty of Civil Disobedience'. . . . Until I read that essay I never found a suitable English translation for my Indian word *Satyagraha*. . . . There is no doubt that Thoreau's ideas greatly influenced my movement in India." Harding reported that Gandhi "always carried a copy [of *Civil Disobedience*] with him during his many imprisonments." There was a New Delhi pamphlet, *Henry David Thoreau: The Man Who Moulded the Mahatma's Mind.*

Historian Perry Miller noted that *On Civil Disobedience* circulated "among resisters of the Nazi occupations in Europe, and it became a rallying tract." According to Harding, "leaders of the Danish resistance movement looked upon 'Civil Disobedience' as a manual of arms."

As Martin Luther King, Jr., was about to help launch the civil rights movement with nonviolent protests against government-enforced segregation in Montgomery, Alabama, he "began to think about Thoreau's *Essay on Civil Disobedience*. I remembered how, as a college student, I had been moved when I first read this work. I became convinced that what we were preparing to do in Montgomery was related to what Thoreau had expressed. We were simply saying to the white community, 'We can no longer lend our cooperation to an evil system.'"

In 1965, a group of scholars led by Walter Harding began work on *The Writings of Henry D. Thoreau,* the definitive collected works, and tracked down manuscripts at more than forty libraries; the major holdings are at Houghton Library (Harvard University), the Huntington Library (San Marino, California), the J. Pierpont Morgan Library (New York) and the New York Public Library. Then the manuscripts were laboriously transcribed. An editor noted, "Thoreau wrote with a heavy right slant. . . . Some of his letters look alike, especially r and s and z. To make matters worse, Thoreau often made mistakes in spelling or grammar. . . . He also ran words together, so it can be hard to tell where one word stops and another begins." Princeton University Press issued the first volume (*Walden*) in 1971; fourteen volumes have since followed, and the project continues.

Historian Miller observed that Thoreau, "has now become a god in modern literature. Wherever English is read, or can be translated, Thoreau is one of the major voices of the nineteenth century, who speaks to the twentieth in India, Japan, and West Africa as much as in the United States, with more and more resonance. . . . The disciple now shines a greater luminary than the master: Thoreau is more alive in popular estimation than Emerson, and Longfellow, Lowell, or Holmes have become hobbies for antiquarians."

The trend has been to emphasize Thoreau's nature writings above all else, undoubtedly a consequence of the environmentalist movement. The acclaimed Library of America series, for instance, issued a 1,114-page volume on Thoreau that did not include a single one of his political writings. Yet to people who cherish liberty, these writings place Thoreau among the immortals. He affirmed the imperative to judge laws according to moral principles and, when necessary, to stand alone against the state

CONSCIENCE AND WIT

NOBODY EXPRESSED RUGGED American individualism better than Samuel Langhorne Clemens—Mark Twain. This might seem surprising to those who think of him only as the author of children's classics like *The Adventures of Tom Sawyer, The Adventures of Huckleberry Finn, The Prince and the Pauper,* and *A Connecticut Yankee in King Arthur's Court.* But adults going back to those books are soon reminded how they affirm the moral worth of individual human beings.

Throughout much of Mark Twain's life, his opinions made news because he was the most famous living American. He was a friend of steel entrepreneur Andrew Carnegie. Helen Keller, amazingly cultured despite being blind and deaf, relished his company. Mark Twain introduced future English statesman Winston S. Churchill to an American audience. He published the hugely popular autobiography of General Ulysses S. Grant. English novelist Rudyard Kipling came calling at his upstate New York home. Mark Twain met scores of other illustrious people: oil entrepreneur John D. Rockefeller, Sr., biologist Charles Darwin, painter James McNeill Whistler, psychologist Dr. Sigmund Freud, waltz king Johann Strauss, violinist Fritz Kreisler, pianist Artur Schnabel, sculptor Auguste Rodin, philosophers Ralph Waldo Emerson and Herbert Spencer, playwright George Bernard Shaw, poets Lord Tennyson and Henry Wadsworth Longfellow, novelists Henry James and Ivan Turgenev, and inventors Nikola Tesla and Thomas Edison (who recorded the author's voice).

Although Mark Twain was not a systematic thinker, he was steadfast in his defense of liberty. He attacked slavery, supported black self-help, spoke out for immigrant Chinese laborers who were exploited by police and judges, acknowledged the miserable treatment of American Indians, denounced anti-Semitism, and favored women's suffrage. Defying powerful politicians like Theodore Roosevelt, he spearheaded the opposition to militarism. During his last decade, he served as vice president of the Anti-Imperialist League. "I am a moralist in disguise," he wrote, "it gets me into heaps of trouble."

He shared the capitalist dream. He speculated in mining stocks, and started a publishing company. Then he functioned as a venture capitalist, providing about $50,000 a year to inventors; he thought invention was perhaps the highest calling. He failed at all of these, though, and achieved financial success only as a writer and lecturer.

Mark Twain set a personal example for self-reliance. From the time he quit school at age twelve, he was on his own, working as a printer's assistant, typesetter, steamboat pilot, miner, editor, and publisher. He spent four years paying off his business debts rather than take advantage of limited liability laws. As a writer, he succeeded on his wits, without academic tenure or a government grant. He financed his extensive overseas travels by freelance writing and lecturing. During his lifetime, people bought more than a million copies of his books.

Mark Twain liked what he called "reasoned selfishness." As he put it, "A man's *first* duty is to his own conscience and honor—the party of the country comes second to that, and never first. . . . It is not *parties* that make or save countries or that build them to greatness—it is clean men, clean ordinary citizens."

A devilish wit, Mark Twain left memorable lines—for example, "What is the difference between a taxidermist and a tax collector? The taxidermist takes only your skin." "Public servant: Persons chosen by the people to distribute the graft." "There is no distinctly native American criminal class except Congress." "In the first place, God made idiots. This was for practice. Then He made School Boards." "In statesmanship, get the formalities right, never mind about the moralities."

Mark Twain was instantly recognizable. One scholar noted that "the young man from Missouri, with drooping moustache and flaming red hair, was unsually garbed in a starched, brown linen duster reaching to his ankles, and he talked and gesticulated so much that people who did not know him thought he was always drunk."

Audiences not only read his works; they saw him on lecture platforms in Europe, Asia, Africa, and Australia. "Mark Twain steals unobtrusively on to the platform," wrote one reporter in April 1896, "dressed in the regulation evening clothes, with the trouser-pockets cut high up, into which he occasionally dives both hands. He bows with a quiet dignity to the roaring cheers. . . . His long, shaggy, white hair surmounts a face full of intellectual fire. The eyes, arched with bushy brows, and which seem to be closed most of the time while he is speaking, flash out now and then from their deep sockets with a genial, kindly, pathetic look, and the face is deeply drawn with the furrows accumulated during an existence of sixty years. He talks in short sentences, with a peculiar smack of the lips at the end of each. His language is just that of his books, full of the quaintest Americanisms, and showing an utter disregard for the polished diction of most lecturers. . . . He speaks slowly, lazily, and wearily, as a man dropping off to sleep, rarely raising his voice above a conversational tone; but it has that characteristic nasal sound which penetrates to the back of the largest building. . . . To have read Mark Twain is a delight, but to have seen and heard him is a joy not readily to be forgotten."

SAMUEL LANGHORNE CLEMENS was born November 30, 1835, in Florida, Missouri. He was the fifth child of Jane Lampton, a plainspoken Kentucky woman from whom Sam reportedly acquired his compassion and sense of humor. His father, John, was a lanky, somber Tennessee lawyer-turned-grocer, who lost everything speculating in land and other ventures.

When Sam was four, the hapless family moved about thirty miles away to Hannibal, Missouri, a Mississippi River town, where they rented rooms above a drugstore. During his fourteen years in Hannibal, Clemens gained experiences that inspired his greatest classics: *The Adventures of Tom Sawyer*, *The Adventures of Huckleberry Finn*, and *Life on the Mississippi*. Although he attended several schools until he was about thirteen, his education really came from his mother, who taught him to learn on his own and respect the humanity of other people.

Soon after John Clemens died in 1847, Sam went to work as a printer's assistant and during the next decade worked for printers in St. Louis, New York, Philadelphia, and Cincinnati. Clemens, like Benjamin Franklin, educated himself by reading through printers' libraries. He loved history, and the more he read, the more he reacted against intolerance and tyranny.

Back in Hannibal, he got a job assisting steamboat pilot Horace Bixby who taught him how to navigate the roughly twelve hundred miles of the Mississippi River between New Orleans and St. Louis. During the next seventeen months, Clemens learned the shape of the river—the way it looked at night and in fog. But the Civil War disrupted commerce on the Mississippi, dashing his ambitions as a steamboat pilot. In 1861, he joined a company of Missouri volunteers known as the Marion Rangers, but when they shot an unarmed, innocent horseman, a disgusted Clemens quit.

Clemens then headed for the Nevada Territory where, after failing to strike it rich by finding silver, he wrote amusing articles about silver mining camps for Nevada's major newspaper, *Territorial Enterprise*, published in Virginia City, and landed a full-time job. Initially, his articles were unsigned. Then he decided that to become a literary success he must begin signing his articles. Pseudonyms were in vogue, so he reached back to his days as a Mississippi River pilot and thought of "Mark Twain," a term meaning two fathoms, or twelve feet—navigable water for a steamboat. His first signed article appeared February 2, 1863.

It was in Virginia City that Mark Twain met the popular humorist Artemus Ward who was on a lecture tour. His commercial success inspired Mark Twain to think about how he might make a career with his wit, and Ward urged him to break into the big New York market. Uncertain about his future, he wrote to his brother and sister in October 1865: "I never had but two powerful ambitions in my life. One was to be a pilot, & the other a preacher of the gospel. I accomplished the one & failed in the other, because I could not supply myself with the necessary stock in trade—i.e. religion. . . . I have had a 'call' to literature, of a low order—i.e. humorous. It is nothing to be proud of, but it is my strongest suit."

After silver mining stocks he had acquired became worthless, he resolved to make the best of humorous writing and contributed pieces to the *Californian,* a literary weekly edited by humorist Bret Harte. The following year, his story, "The Celebrated Jumping Frog of Calaveras County," was published in the *New York Saturday Press.* When many other publications reprinted it, suddenly he had a national reputation as "the wild humorist of the Pacific Slope." The *Sacramento Union* asked him to report on news in Hawaii, and he was off again, now writing four letters a month for $20 each. He got the idea of giving public lectures about his Hawaiian experiences and rented a San Francisco hall starting on October 2, 1866. Over the next three weeks he earned $1,500, which was far more than he had earned from writing.

Ever alert to opportunity, Mark Twain noticed an advertisement for the first transatlantic pleasure cruise, a seven-month excursion to the Holy Land, set to depart in June 1867. He spent most of his $1,250 lecture earnings on a ticket and earned money by reporting his experiences for the *San Francisco Daily Alta California*—fifty 2,000-word travel letters at $20 apiece. He also wrote travel letters for the *New York Tribune* and *New York Herald* about the voyage to Gibraltar and his adventures in Tangier, Paris, Genoa, Florence, Rome, Naples, Constantinople, the Black Sea, and Palestine.

Aboard the *Quaker City,* he met fellow passenger Charles Langdon, the eighteen-year-old son of an Elmira, New York, coal industry financier. Langdon showed Clemens a picture of his sister, Olivia (friends called her Livy). Clemens was taken by her, and soon after the ship returned to New York, Langdon introduced the two. On New Year's Eve 1867, Clemens joined Livy and the rest of her family to hear Charles Dickens read selections from his novels. That evening, Clemens remarked later, referring to Livy, he had discovered "the fortune of my life."

Then Mark Twain worked on *Innocents Abroad,* a book full of wry observations about the people he had met and the sights he had seen. He had this to say, for example, about Morocco: "When the Emperor or the Bashaw want money, they levy on some rich man, and he has to furnish the cash or go to prison. Therefore, few men in Morocco dare to be rich." *Innocents Abroad* became a best-seller, with over 100,000 copies in print within a year.

Mark Twain and Livy got married at Quarry Farm, her parents' estate, on February 2, 1870. She was the only woman he ever loved. They were an unlikely pair. A strict Victorian, she disapproved of alcohol, tobacco, and vulgar language—vices he enjoyed. (He promised only that he would not smoke more than one cigar at a time.) But she loved his tremendous enthusiasm and his refreshingly candid manner. She called him "Youth."

Livy became his most trusted editor, offering her judgment on the topics readers would be interested in and reading nearly every one of his drafts and suggesting changes. She provided advice about his lecture material too. "Mrs. Clemens," he remarked, "has kept a lot of things from getting into print that might have given me a reputation I wouldn't care to have, and that I wouldn't have known any better than to have published."

Roughing It (1872), a witty account of Mark Twain's travels throughout Nevada and northern California, buoyed his reputation. In it, among other things, he lavished praise on much-abused Chinese immigrants: they "are quiet, peaceable, tractable, free from drunkedness, and they are as industrious as the day is long. . . . All Chinamen can read, write and cipher with easy facility."

Meanwhile, in 1871 the family moved to Hartford, Connecticut, a New England commercial and cultural center about halfway between New York and Boston. They were in Hartford more than seventeen years, the period when Mark Twain wrote his most famous books. He collaborated with a neighbor, Charles Dudley Warner, to produce his first fictional work, *The Gilded Age* (1873). Among his contributions was this savvy passage: "If you are a member of Congress, (no offense,) and one of your constituents who doesn't know anything, and does not want to go into the bother of learning something, and has no money, and no employment, and can't earn a living, comes besieging you for help . . . you take him to . . . Washington, the grand old benevolent Asylum for the Helpless."

By 1874, Clemens had built an eclectic three-story, nineteen-room redbrick house in Hartford that reflected his success and individuality. Part of it looked like the pilot house of a Mississippi steamboat. Clemens spent most of his time there playing billiards and entertaining his daughters, Susy, Clara, and Jean (his son Langdon had died as an infant). "Father would start a story about the pictures on the wall," Clara recalled. "Passing from picture to picture, his power of invention led us into countries and among human figures that held us spellbound."

The family summered at Quarry Farm, and he focused on writing his books. Apparently the success of *Roughing It* suggested that he might do well drawing on other personal experiences, and he pondered his childhood days in

Hannibal, Missouri. His practice was to begin writing after breakfast and continue until dinner (he seldom ate lunch). Evenings, back in the main house, his family gathered around him, and he read aloud what he had written.

In 1875, when he was forty, he started his second novel, *The Adventures of Tom Sawyer,* about a poor orphan boy who gets in trouble and redeems himself by being resourceful, honest, and sometimes courageous. The book, which introduces Tom's friend Huckleberry Finn, is best remembered as a charming story of youthful good times in the summer.

Soon Mark Twain began writing his masterwork, *The Adventures of Huckleberry Finn,* which was not published until 1885. Unlike Tom Sawyer, this had the immediacy of a first-person story. In his distinctive colloquial manner, a poor and nearly illiterate fourteen-year-old son of the town drunkard told how he ran away and encountered an escaped slave, Jim. Together they floated down the Mississippi River on a raft and got into scrapes. Like other southerners, Huck had considered black slaves as subhuman, and he wrote Jim's owner a letter exposing the runaway. Then he thought about Jim's humanity. He finally decided he would rather go to hell than betray Jim. He tore up the letter.

Many people considered the book trashy. Many libraries banned it as racist; the word *nigger* occurs 189 times. But it became a classic for showing real people grappling with the issues of humanity and liberty. *Huckleberry Finn* went on to sell some 20 million copies.

Mark Twain tried public readings of his work, but initial results were a disappointment. "I supposed it would be only necessary to do like Dickens," he recalled, "get out on the platform and read from the book. I did that and made a botch of it. Written things are not for speech." He went on to develop his uniquely amusing conversational speaking style.

Clemens should have enjoyed financial peace of mind, but he invested his earnings as well as his wife's inheritance on inventions and other business ventures that never panned out. His investment in a new kind of typesetter turned into a $190,000 loss. Incredibly, he failed as the publisher of his own popular books. In 1894, his firm went bankrupt with $94,000 of debts owed to ninety-six creditors. He assumed personal responsibility instead of ducking behind limited liability laws and got invaluable help from a fan, John D. Rockefeller partner Henry Rogers, who from that time until his death in 1909 managed the author's financial affairs. Clemens resolved to repay his creditors by generating more lecture income. He, Livy, and their daughter Clara began a grueling cross-country tour. Lecture halls were packed. Then the family traveled to Australia, Tasmania, New Zealand, India, South Africa, and England, and everywhere he played to cheering crowds. "We lectured and robbed and raided for thirteen months," he recalled. By January 1898, he was debt free.

Mark Twain hailed individual enterprise and spoke out against injustice wherever he found it. He persuaded Rogers to help provide money so that Helen Keller could get an education commensurate with her extraordinary ability and presided at a large gathering to support Booker T. Washington and self-help among blacks. While Mark Twain was living in Vienna (1897–1900), he defied the anti-Semitic press and defended French captain Alfred Dreyfus whom French military courts had convicted of treason because he was Jewish.

When he was lecturing in England in 1894, his daughter Susy died of meningitis. Livy, his wife for thirty-four years, succumbed to a heart condition in 1904. "During those years after my wife's death," he recalled, "I was washing about on a forlorn sea of banquets and speech-making in high and holy causes, and these things furnished me intellectual cheer and entertainment; but they got at my heart for an evening only, then left it dry and dusty."

In this period, he significantly increased his output of political commentary. He attacked fashionable collectivist doctrines of "progressive" thinkers who called for more laws, bureaucrats, and military adventures. Like Lord Acton, Mark Twain demanded that the government class be held to the same moral standard as private individuals. Mark Twain's satirical "War Prayer" became an anthem for those who wanted to keep America out of foreign wars.

After the death of his daughter Jean in December 1909, the result of an epileptic seizure, Clemens tried to revive his spirits in Bermuda. But angina attacks, which had occurred during the previous year, intensified and became more frequent. Doctors administered morphine to relieve the pain, and he boarded a ship for his final trip home. He relaxed by reading *A History of England* by the libertarian Thomas Babington Macaulay. Clemens died at Stormfield, his Redding, Connecticut, house, on Thursday morning, April 21, 1910. Thousands of mourners took a last look at him, decked out in his white suit, at Brick Presbyterian Church in New York City. He was buried beside his wife in Elmira, New York.

At the time of his death, Mark Twain was quite out of tune with his times. Progressives and Marxists certainly did not like his individualism. His daughter Clara and his authorized biographer, Albert Bigelow Paine, blocked access to his papers. About the only defense came from literary critic H. L. Mencken, who called him "the first genuinely American artist of the blood royal."

The situation began to change in 1962 when respected University of Chicago English professor Walter Blair wrote *Mark Twain and Huck Finn*, which treated the author's Mississippi River epic as major league literature. Before Blair's book, *The Adventures of Huckleberry Finn* rarely appeared in a college curriculum. Now it is taught almost everywhere.

Also in 1962, Clara Clemens Samossaud died, and her Mark Twain papers—letters, speeches, original manuscripts, and unpublished works—became the property of the University of California at Berkeley. It encouraged writers to work with the material, and since then dozens of new books about Mark Twain have appeared. Moreover, editors at Berkeley launched an ambitious scholarly project to publish everything Mark Twain wrote, including papers held by other institutions and private individuals. Mark Twain project head Robert Hirst estimates the papers could eventually fill seventy-five robust volumes.

Mark Twain has been raked over by the politically correct crowd, but he endures as the most beloved champion of American individualism. Unlike so many of his contemporaries, he did not believe America was a European outpost. He cherished America as a distinct civilization and defended liberty and justice indivisible as he promoted peace. He portrayed rugged, resourceful free spirits who overcome daunting obstacles to fulfill their destiny. His personal charm and wicked wit still make people smile

STYLISH ELEGANCE

❧

AMERICAN INDIVIDUALISM HAD virtually died out by the time Mark Twain was buried in 1910. Intellectuals were promoting collectivism, while jurists hammered constitutional restraints as an inconvenient obstacle to expanding government power, touted as the cure for every social problem. Theodore Roosevelt glorified imperial conquest, and President Woodrow Wilson maneuvered America into a European war, jailed dissidents, and signed the income tax into law. Great individualists like Thomas Paine and Thomas Jefferson were ridiculed, if they were remembered at all.

Yet author Albert Jay Nock dared to declare that collectivism was evil. He denounced the use of force to impose one's will on others, believed the United States should stay out of foreign wars (because such participation inevitably subverts liberty), and insisted that individuals have the unalienable right to pursue happiness as long as they do not hurt anybody. Intellectual historian Murray N. Rothbard called Nock an "authentic American radical."

Although Nock did not contribute to mass circulation magazines, and his books had a limited audiences, he quietly affirmed that individualism was a living creed. Literary lion H. L. Mencken reportedly told Nock, "Nobody gives a damn *what* you write—it's *how* you write that interests everybody." Paul Palmer, who edited the *American Mercury* after Mencken and published a number of Nock's essays, remembered, "I suppose Nock was the greatest stylist among American writers. At least, no American ever wrote a purer prose."

Nock won respect too because he was a highly civilized man. Explained literary critic Van Wyck Brooks, "He was a formidable scholar and an amateur of music who remembered all the great singers of his day and could trace them through this part or that from Naples to St. Petersburg, London, Brussels and Vienna. He had known all the great orchestras from Turin to Chicago . . . and he had visited half the universities of Europe from Bonn to Bordeaux, Montpelier, Liege and Ghent. He could pick up at random, with a casual air, almost any point and trace it from Plato through Scaliger to Montaigne or Erasmus, and I can cite chapter and verse for saying that whether in Latin or Greek he could quote any author in reply to any question. I believe he knew as well the Old Testament in Hebrew." American historian Merrill D. Peterson called him "a finished scholar, a brilliant editor, and a connoisseur of taste and intellect."

Nock worked slowly, and with exceeding care. As his friend Ruth Robinson observed, "He wrote by hand with a fountain pen. His manuscripts rarely needed corrections or changes. His fine hand was considered difficult to read, but it was not, if you became accustomed to it."

Robinson recalled that "he was a finely constructed man, with small bones, hands, and feet. He was five-feet ten-inches tall, slight and quick in movement; he kept his excellent figure and carriage throughout life. The salient expressions of his strong face were conveyed through his brilliant blue eyes, which could change instantly, be impenetrable, mischievous, or express great kindliness and sympathy. He had fair skin and high color and during all the years I knew him wore a mustache. . . . Long before his hair turned white, an iron-grey band at the edge of his brown hair was an outstanding characteristic of his appearance."

Social philosopher Lewis Mumford, who knew Nock early in his career, described him "the very model of the old-fashioned gentleman, American style: quiet spoken, fond of good food, punctilious in little matters of courtesy, with a fund of good stories, many of them western; never speaking about himself, never revealing anything directly about himself." He was an intensely private man. People who worked with him for years had no idea that he had been a clergyman. "No one knew even where he lived," noted Van Wyck Brooks, "and a pleasantry in the office was that one could reach him by placing a letter under a certain rock in Central Park." Frank Chodorov recalled, "It was only after I was appointed administrator of his estate that I learned of the existence of two full-grown and well-educated sons." "Nock was an individualist," Chodorov continued, "and he got that way not as the result of study but by force of temperament. As he put it, the 'furniture' of his mind was so arranged because no other arrangement would quite fit his mind. A man thinks what he is, Nock would say, and no amount of education can make him think otherwise. . . . He was civilized; knowledgeable but never pedantic, reserved but companionable, cosmopolitan in his tastes and, above all, a gentleman to whom it never occurred to inflict hurt on any man."

ALBERT JAY NOCK was born October 13, 1870, in Scranton, Pennsylvania. He was the only child of Emma Sheldon Jay who descended from French Protestants. His father, Joseph Albert Nock, was a hot-tempered steelworker and Episcopal clergyman.

Nock grew up in a semirural Brooklyn, New York, neighborhood. According to his account, he learned the alphabet by puzzling over a newspaper and asking questions. He did not attend school until he was a teenager, but at home he was surrounded by books, which he explored. For quite a while, *Webster's Dictionary* was his favorite.

When Nock was ten, his father got a job on the upper shore of Lake Huron. There he observed "independence, self-respect, self-reliance, dignity, diligence. . . . Our life was singularly free; we were so little conscious of arbitrary restraint that we hardly knew government existed. . . . On the whole our society might have served pretty well as a standing advertisement for Mr. Jefferson's notion that the virtues which he regarded as distinctively American thrive best in the absence of government."

After attending a private preparatory school, Nock entered St. Stephen's College (later Bard College) in 1887. He relished ancient Greek and Latin literature. He reportedly went on to attend Berkeley Divinity School in Middletown, Connecticut, for about a year and was ordained in the Episcopal church in 1897. The following year, he began serving as assistant rector at St. James Church in Titusville, Pennsylvania. It was there that he met Agnes Grumbine; they were married on April 25, 1900. He was twenty-nine, and she was twenty-four. They had two sons: Samuel, born in 1901, and Francis, born in 1905. Nock left his wife soon thereafter. His sons became college teachers.

In 1909, Nock experienced a crisis of faith and quit the clergy to move to New York City and become an editor of *American Magazine,* a cauldron of radicalism where he worked four years. He befriended former Toledo mayor and aspiring scholar Brand Whitlock, who later wrote a biography of Lafayette. Nock spent time with muckraking journalists Lincoln Steffens and John Reed. He hung out at the Players Club, a fabled gathering place for people in the arts, established by actor Edwin Booth and author Mark Twain (a portrait of Mark Twain hangs over a fireplace and one of his pool cues is on display). Located at 16 Gramercy Park South, Manhattan, it's a Gothic Revival style five-story house that architect Stanford White transformed into the club in 1888. The Players Club has one of America's largest libraries on the theater and portrait paintings by Gilbert Stuart, John Singer Sargent, and Norman Rockwell. Nock liked to take mail, eat, and play pool at the club. His business card simply said: "Albert Jay Nock, Players Club, New York."

Nock had absorbed the ideas of German sociologist Franz Oppenheimer, whose radical book *Der Staat* was published in 1908. (An English translation, *The State,* appeared in 1915.) Oppenheimer had noted that there were only two fundamental ways of acquiring wealth—work and robbery, and he declared that government was based on robbery.

In 1914, Nock joined the staff of *The Nation* edited by Oswald Garrison Villard, grandson of abolitionist William Lloyd Garrison. He did not like the magazine's support for government interference with the economy, but admired its courageous opposition to President Woodrow Wilson who had maneuvered America into World War I. One of Nock's articles, on labor union agitator Samuel Gompers, provoked Wilson's censors to suppress *The Nation.*

Eventually *The Nation's* devotion to government interference became too much, and Nock resigned. Backed by Helen Swift Neilson, daughter of Gustavus Swift and heir to a meat-packing fortune, he became editor of a new magazine of opinion, the *Freeman*. The first weekly issue appeared March 17, 1920, with twenty-four pages of articles and letters about politics, literature, music, and other topics.

Nock's principal collaborator was Neilson's English husband, Francis, a former stage director at the London Royal Opera and radical Liberal member of Parliament who became a leading pacifist. Disgusted by England's entry in World War I, he moved to the United States and became a U.S. citizen. He stirred controversy with his book, *How Diplomats Make War*, published in 1915 by Benjamin W. Huebsch, who later was president of the *Freeman*.

Nock's policy was laissez-faire: hire talented people and let them run. According to biographer Michael Wreszin, "Members of the staff can remember no time when he attempted to revise their work. Copy, including his own, was subject to the managing editor's demands as to space—but that was the only limitation." Although the editorial staff included Suzanne La Follette, a rigorous opponent of government interference with private life, the *Freeman* was not consistently libertarian. Contributors included socialist literary critic Van Wyck Brooks, muckraker Lincoln Steffens, Lewis Mumford who believed technology was dehumanizing, and Thorstein Veblen who attacked competitive enterprise.

In his contributions, though, Nock discussed many issues involving liberty. He had this to say on Irish liberty in the October 26, 1921, *Freeman:* "We can see freedom in only one light; that is, as something not to be compromised with or watered down. . . . For us, freedom is freedom, absolutely and world without end. . . . We see Ireland demanding freedom from political domination by an alien race; and wherever freedom is demanded, be it political, social or economic, we are there unreservedly, and without asking any questions, to back that demand to the utmost of our slender abilities." World War I elicited these comments in the issue of September 19, 1923: "The war immensely fortified a universal faith in violence; it set in motion endless adventures in imperialism, endless nationalist ambitions. Every war does this to a degree roughly corresponding to its magnitude. The final settlement at Versailles, therefore, was a mere scramble for loot."

The *Freeman* never attracted more than about seven thousand subscribers, far from enough to become self-sustaining, and annual losses reportedly exceeded $80,000. The magazine ceased publication after the March 5, 1924, issue. Nock seems to have contributed 259 pieces. *Atlantic Monthly* editor Ellery Sedgwick remembered Nock's *Freeman* as "admirably written, diverting, original, and full of unpredictable quirks."

Nock became a good friend of H. L. Mencken who had edited *Smart Set* and then *American Mercury.* "There is no better companion in the world than Henry," Nock reported after one Manhattan dinner. He considered Mencken "immensely able, unselfconscious, sincere, erudite, simple-hearted, kindly, generous."

Soon Nock was writing for intellectual magazines like *American Mercury, Atlantic Monthly, Harper's, Saturday Review of Literature,* and *Scribner's. American Mercury,* for instance, published "On Doing the Right Thing," in which he wrote: "The practical reason for freedom, then, is that freedom seems to be the only condition under which any kind of substantial moral fibre can be developed. . . . We have tried law, compulsion and authoritarianism of various kinds, and the result is nothing to be proud of."

Three admirers from Philadelphia—Ellen Winsor, Rebecca Winsor Evans, and Edmund C. Evans—provided funds that enabled Nock to pursue projects of his choosing, and he turned to book-length biographical essays. The first was *Mr. Jefferson* (1926), which skipped the most famous events of the founder's life to focus on the development of his mind. H. L. Mencken wrote that Nock's essay "is accurate, it is shrewd, it is well ordered, and above all it is charming. I know of no other book on Jefferson that penetrates so persuasively to the essential substance of the man." Historian Merrill Peterson called *Mr. Jefferson* "the most captivating single volume in the Jefferson literature."

Nock loved the sixteenth-century French humanist scholar, extravagant satirist, and maverick individualist François Rabelais and in 1929 wrote a book about him, collaborating with scholar Catherine Rose Wilson. With her, he edited *The Works of François Rabelais* (two volumes, 1931), and he went on to write *A Journey into Rabelais's France* (1934).

Nock embraced ideas of Henry George. Nock explained: George's philosophy was the philosophy of human freedom. . . . He believed that all mankind are indefinitely improvable, and that the freer they are, the more they will improve. He saw also that they can never become politically or socially free until they have become economically free." Nock wrote a book-length essay on Henry George (1939).

Meanwhile, in 1930, backed by one Dr. Peter Fireman, Suzanne La Follette and Sheila Hibben had launched the *New Freeman,* but it lasted only about a year. Nock contributed fifty-four articles about art, literature and education, reprinted in *The Book of Journeyman* (1930).

Nock opposed every form of tyranny. He warned in July 1932, before Hitler came to power: "Things in Germany look bad at this distance. The new government, which is making use of Hitler, seems bent on a Napoleonic absolutism." Nock was decades ahead of most other intellectuals in recognizing the evil of all tyranny. "Refrain from using the word Bolshevism, or Fascism, Hitlerism, Marxism, Communism," he noted in November 1933, "and you have no trouble getting acceptance for the principle that underlies them all alike— the principle that the State is everything, and the individual nothing."

Nock became an implacable foe of Franklin D. Roosevelt's New Deal. In May 1934, he wrote: "Probably not many realize how the rapid centralization of government in America has fostered a kind of organized pauperism. The big industrial states contribute most of the Federal revenue, and the bureaucracy distributes it in the pauper states wherever it will do the most good in a political way. . . . All this is due to the iniquitous theory of taxation with which this country has been so thoroughly indoctrinated—that a man should be taxed according to his ability to pay, instead of according to the value of the privileges he obtains from the government."

Around 1934, Nock was invited to deliver a series of history lectures at Columbia University, and he focused on the struggle for liberty. He developed the lecture texts into his great radical polemic, *Our Enemy, the State*, drawing from the ideas of German sociologist Franz Oppenheimer who had written about the violent origins of the state. Nock championed the natural rights vision of Thomas Paine and Thomas Jefferson and the case for equal freedom articulated by Herbert Spencer. And he spoke kindly of the American Articles of Confederation (1781–1789), the association of states without a central government.

In *Our Enemy, the State*, which appeared in 1935, he wrote: "There are two methods, or means, and only two, whereby man's needs and desires can be satisfied. One is the production and exchange of wealth; this is the *economic means*. The other is the uncompensated appropriation of wealth produced by others; this is the *political means*. . . . The State invariably had its origin in conquest and confiscation. No primitive State known to history originated in any other manner. . . . The State, both in its genesis and by its primary intention, is purely anti-social. It is not based on the idea of natural rights, but on the idea that the individual has no rights except those that the State may provisionally grant him. It has always made justice costly and difficult of access, and has invariably held itself above justice and common morality whenever it could advantage itself by so doing."

In his June 1936 *Atlantic Monthly* article, "Isaiah's Job," Nock explained his view that the future of civilization depended on what he called "the Remnant": "They are obscure, unorganized, inarticulate, each one rubbing along as best they can. They need to be encouraged and braced up, because when everything has gone completely to the dogs, they are the ones who will come back and build up a new society, and meanwhile your preaching will reassure them and keep them hanging on. Your job is to take care of the Remnant."

Nock's last, most charming, and best-known book was *Memoirs of a Superfluous Man*. He worked at a house in Canaan, Connecticut. He remained as reticent as ever, omitting most personal details about his life, but he gracefully chronicled the development of his ideas. He assailed one of his favorite targets, compulsory government schooling that promoted "superstitious servile reverence for a sacrosanct State." He lamented, "The American people once had their liberties; they had them all; but apparently they could not rest o'nights until they had turned them over to a prehensile crew of professional politicians." *Harper's* published *Memoirs of a Superfluous Man* in 1943.

Nock seems to have had few friends during his last years. He corresponded with *Discovery of Freedom* author Rose Wilder Lane and former *American Mercury* editor Paul Palmer. He often lunched with Frank Chodorov who later recalled his times with Nock: "He would regale you with bits of history that threw light on a headline, or quote from the classics a passage currently applicable, or take all the glory out of a 'name' character with a pithy statement of fact. He was a library of knowledge and a fount of wisdom, and if you were a kindred spirit you could have your pick of both."

Maverick oilman William F. Buckley, Texas-born son of Irish immigrants, saw himself as part of "the Remnant" whom Nock cherished. Periodically he invited Nock to lunch at his family's Great Elm mansion in Sharon, Connecticut, despite Nock's well-known bohemian ways and hostility to the Catholic church. Buckley cherished Nock's individualism and his scholarship, and *Memoirs of a Superfluous Man* helped encourage his son, William F. Buckley, Jr., to defy the collectivist trends of the time.

Since no magazine would take Nock's writing, several friends set up the National Economic Council. Starting on May 15, 1943, it published the *Economic Council Review of Books,* which Nock edited for almost two years, until failing health led him to bow out.

In 1945, Nock developed lymphatic leukemia, and he gradually ran out of steam. He had told his son Francis: "If sometimes you begin to think the old man is pretty good, and you feel that maybe you ought to be a bit proud of him . . . realize that he ain't so much after all."

He moved in with his friend Ruth Robinson who lived in Wakefield, Rhode Island. He died there on August 19, 1945, at the age of seventy-four. A local Episcopal priest conducted a simple funeral service at Robinson's house, and he was buried nearby in Riverside Cemetery.

In his quiet way, Nock inspired others to carry on. Frank Chodorov championed his kind of individualism in his books *One Is a Crowd* (1952), *The Rise and Fall of Society* (1959), *Out of Step* (1962,) and *The Income Tax: Root of All Evil* (1963). Chodorov edited *analysis* (he didn't capitalize the first letter), a monthly four-page newsletter, and then became an editor of *Human Events,* a weekly newsletter. He started the Intercollegiate Society of Individualists which aimed to nurture individualism on American college campuses.

In 1950, Nock's former editorial associate Suzanne La Follette joined with *Life* editor John Chamberlain and *Newsweek* columnist Henry Hazlitt to launch another *Freeman*. There were editorial disagreements, and in 1955 *The Freeman* was acquired by Leonard Read's Foundation for Economic Education, which has published it ever since.

Albert Jay Nock's quiet voice has had an influence far beyond what anyone dared imagine a half-century ago. He showed that an intelligent person could embrace radical individualism, which was tremendously important for young people coming along amid a collectivist age. He set an inspiring example with his steadfast devotion, cosmopolitan scholarship, and elegant literary style. He helped win people's hearts for liberty, one by one.

FEISTY FREE SPIRIT

DURING THE FIRST half of the twentieth century, Henry Louis Mencken was the most outspoken defender of liberty in America. He spent thousands of dollars challenging restrictions on freedom of the press. He boldly denounced President Woodrow Wilson for whipping up patriotic fervor to enter World War I, which cost him his job as a newspaper columnist. And he denounced Franklin Delano Roosevelt for amassing dangerous political power and maneuvering to enter World War II. Amid the uproar, he ended up resigning his newspaper job. Moreover, the president ridiculed him by name. "The government I live under has been my enemy all my active life," Mencken declared. "When it has not been engaged in silencing me it has been engaged in robbing me. So far as I can recall I have never had any contact with it that was not an outrage on my dignity and an attack on my security."

Although he was intensely controversial, Mencken earned respect as one of America's foremost newspaperman and literary critics. He produced some thirty books, contributions to twenty more books, and thousands of newspaper columns. He wrote some 100,000 letters, or between 60 and 125 per working day. He hunt-and-pecked every word with his two forefingers—for years, he used a little Corona typewriter about the size of a cigar box.

Mencken had interesting things to say about politics, literature, food, health, religion, sports, and much more. No one else knew more about our American language. Influential pundits of the past like Walter Lippmann have faded considerably, but people still read Mencken's work, which goes back a century. In the 1990s, publishers issued almost a dozen books about him or by him, and biographer William Nolte reports that Mencken ranks among the most frequently quoted American authors.

Certainly Mencken was among the wittiest—for example: "Puritanism—the haunting fear that someone, somewhere may be happy," "Democracy is the theory that the common people know what they want, and deserve to get it good and hard," and "The New Deal began, like the Salvation Army, by promising to save humanity. It ended, again like the Salvation Army, by running flop-houses and disturbing the peace."

Mencken stood about five feet, eight inches tall and weighed around 175 pounds. He parted his slick brown hair in the middle. He liked to chew on a cigar. He dressed with a pair of suspenders and a rumpled suit. According to one chronicler, Mencken at his best looked "like a plumber got up for church."

Publisher Alfred Knopf had this to say about Mencken, a close friend for more than forty years: "His public side was visible to everyone: tough, cynical, amusing, and exasperating by turns. The private man was something else again: sentimental, generous, and unwavering—sometimes almost blind—in his devotion to people of whom he felt fond. . . . The most charming manners conceivable, manners I was to discover he always displayed in talking with women. . . . He spent a fantastic amount of his time getting friends to and from doctors' waiting rooms and hospitals, comforting them and keeping them company there."

Mencken inspired friends of freedom. He helped cheer up stylish individualist author Albert Jay Nock, a frequent contributor to Mencken's magazine, *American Mercury*, during Nock's declining years. He petitioned the U.S. State Department, unsuccessfully, to let his libertarian friend Emma Goldman be readmitted to the country after her deportation in 1919. When she had a stroke in Canada two decades later, he helped to pay her medical bills. Mencken's stalwart individualism awed the young Ayn Rand, who in 1934 called him "one whom I admire as the greatest representative of a philosophy to which I want to dedicate my whole life."

H. L. MENCKEN was born September 12, 1880, in Baltimore. His father, August Mencken, owned a cigar factory. His mother, Anna Abhau Mencken, like her husband, was a child of German immigrants. In 1883, the family moved to a three-story, red-brick row house with a backyard that went back about a hundred feet. He lived here until he got married, and he moved back about six years later, after his wife had died.

Mencken was a voracious reader from the start. At age nine, he discovered Mark Twain's *Huckleberry Finn,* which opened his eyes to rugged individualism and literary pleasures. This was, as he put it, "probably the most stupendous event in my whole life." He was thrilled: "What a man that Mark Twain was! How he stood above and apart from the world, like Rabelais come to life again, observing the human comedy, chuckling over the eternal fraudulence of man! What a sharp eye he had for the bogus, in religion, politics, art, literature, patriotism, virtue. . . . And seeing all this, he laughed at them, but not often with malice."

Mencken finished high school when he was fifteen and went to work in his father's cigar factory, work that he hated. Within a few days after his father died in January 1899, Mencken tried his hand as a newspaperman. The first story he ever sold, to the *Baltimore Herald,* was about a stolen horse; by June that year, he was a full-time reporter. Mencken proved to be unusually resourceful and industrious, and he rose to become drama critic, editor of the Sunday paper, and city editor of the morning paper.

Early on, Mencken displayed a tremendous zest for life. In 1904, for example, he began a musical group, which became known as the Saturday Night Club. Almost every week for forty-six years, as many as a dozen friends got together to play music of all sorts (Mencken played the piano). They most often played for a couple of hours in a violin-maker's shop and afterward went to the Hotel Rennert for beer. During the thirteen years of prohibition, they took turns hosting festivities in their homes. They enjoyed chamber music, marches, waltzes and operatic melodies. Mencken loved German romantics, Beethoven above all.

The *Baltimore Herald* went out of business in 1906, and Mencken eventually landed at the newspaper where he would write for more than forty years. One observer remarked: "The staid old *Baltimore Sun* has got itself a real Whangdoodle." The *Baltimore Evening Sun* was launched in 1910, and Mencken served as editor. From 1911 to 1915, he wrote a daily "Free Lance" column that covered politics, education, music, or whatever else interested him. (He also edited the adjacent letters-to-the-editor columns, and whenever a nasty letter came in attacking his work, he made sure it was printed.) He ridiculed hypocritical politicians, clergymen, and social reformers. For example, he called fundamentalist do-gooder William Jennings Bryan "the most sedulous flycatcher in American history . . . a charlatan, a mountebank, a zany without shame or dignity." He was accused of anti-Semitism because he gratuitously referred to so many people as "Jews," although he did not criticize Jews as much as others. He described Anglo-Saxons, for example, as "a wretchedly dirty, shiftless, stupid and rascally people . . . anthropoids." He lashed out at President Woodrow Wilson for maneuvering America into World War I. He insisted that the British government shared responsibility for the horrifying conflict and attacked the moral pretensions of British officials who pursued a naval blockade that punished innocent people as well as combatants in Germany. Mencken discontinued his column because of wartime hysteria.

Meanwhile he had established himself as a literary critic. Since 1908, he had reviewed books for *Smart Set*, a monthly literary magazine. He relentlessly attacked puritanical standards and hailed authors like Theodore Dreiser, Sherwood Anderson, and F. Scott Fitzgerald, whose fiction offered a realistic view of life.

Mencken turned increasingly to writing books. He had written eight on music, literature, and philosophy by 1919 when he published his most enduring work. It arose from his passion for American speech, which evolved spontaneously into something more dynamic than the English of England. No government planned it: the American language became more expressive as ordinary people went about their daily business, now and then contributing new words. The first edition of *The American Language* soon sold out, and

Mencken began work on the second of four editions. "All I ask," he wrote his publisher, Alfred Knopf, "is that you make *The American Language* good and thick. It is my secret ambition to be the author of a book weighing at least five pounds."

In 1920, with World War I a bad memory, the *Baltimore Sun* asked Mencken to resume writing a column. Thus began his memorable "Monday" articles, which appeared weekly for the next eighteen years. About two-thirds of them dealt with politics.

By 1923, Mencken decided he wanted a national forum for his political views. He resigned from *Smart Set* and with backing from Knopf, he and drama critic George Nathan launched the monthly *American Mercury*. The first issue, bearing a distinctive pea-green cover, appeared in January 1924. Nathan soon disagreed about which direction the magazine should go, and he left. Mencken offered his feisty commentary plus writing by many of America's most distinguished authors. There were articles by Emma Goldman, birth control advocate Margaret Sanger, W. E. B. Du Bois, Langston Hughes, James Weldon Johnson, and George Schuyler. Circulation grew for four years, peaking at around eighty-four thousand in 1928. Libertarian journalist John Chamberlain, a writer for *Fortune, Wall Street Journal,* and other publications, called Mencken's *American Mercury* "our anarchistic Bible."

Although Mencken was not known as a political philosopher, he made clear his commitment to individual liberty. "Every government," he wrote, "is a scoundrel. In its relations with other governments it resorts to frauds and barbarities that were prohibited to private men by the Common Law of civilization so long ago as the reign of Hammurabi, and in its dealings with its own people it not only steals and wastes their property and plays a brutal and witless game with their natural rights, but regularly gambles with their very lives. Wars are seldom caused by spontaneous hatreds between people, for peoples in general are too ignorant of one another to have grievances and too indifferent to what goes on beyond their borders to plan conquests. They must be urged to the slaughter by politicians who know how to alarm them."

As the leading champion of civil liberties, Mencken denounced President Wilson for imprisoning American socialist leader Eugene Debs, and he attacked Wilson's attorney general A. Mitchell Palmer who suppressed civil liberties in the name of catching bolsheviks.

Mencken played an important behind-the-scenes role in the notorious Scopes trial that he saw as a conflict between science and superstition. Dayton, Tennessee, biology teacher John Scopes offered to test the state law that banned Darwin's view of evolution from being taught in public schools. The prosecuting attorney was William Jennings Bryan. Mencken persuaded wily criminal lawyer Clarence Darrow to volunteer for the defense. Darrow agreed with Mencken that the best strategy was to make Bryan's dogmatic rejection of science the key issue, and he called Bryan to the witness stand. Nevertheless, Scopes was found guilty, although his punishment was only a fine. Mencken's caustic articles on the trial appeared in newspapers throughout the South, gaining him considerable notoriety.

He became more controversial as a result of the April 1926 *American Mercury*, which featured "Hatrack," an article about a religious prostitute in Farmington, Missouri. Although the article did not offer sexual titillation, it offended Rev. J. Franklin Chase, a Methodist preacher and secretary of the Boston Watch and Ward Society, which suppressed books. When it moved to ban *American Mercury*, Mencken decided to challenge the local law, selling a copy to Chase himself. Mencken was arrested on Boston Common and tried; he was acquitted. The case cost *American Mercury* more than $20,000, but the controversy confirmed Mencken's role as a bold defender of free speech.

Violence against blacks outraged Mencken. For example, he had this to say about a Maryland lynching: "Not a single bigwig came forward in the emergency, though the whole town knew what was afoot. Any one of a score of such bigwigs might have halted the crime, if only by threatening to denounce its perpetrators, but none spoke. So Williams was duly hanged, burned and mutilated."

As Hitler menaced Europe, Mencken attacked President Roosevelt for refusing to admit Jewish refugees into the United States: "There is only one way to help the fugitives, and that is to find places for them in a country in which they can really live. Why shouldn't the United States take in a couple hundred thousand of them, or even all of them?" Yet he was adamant that the United States not become entangled in another European war. He believed it would mean subverting civil liberties at home and incurring monstrous debts without ridding the world of tyranny. Better to keep America as a peaceful sanctuary for liberty, he thought. "I believe that liberty is the only genuinely valuable thing that men have invented," he wrote, "at least in the field of government, in a thousand years. I believe that it is better to be free than to be not free, even when the former is dangerous and the latter safe. I believe that the finest qualities of man can flourish only in free air—that progress made under the shadow of the policeman's club is false progress, and of no permanent value." Mencken added: "In any dispute between a citizen and the government, it is my instinct to side with the citizen. . . . I am against all efforts to make men virtuous by law."

As for economic liberty, Mencken declared that "we owe to it almost everything that passes under the general name of civilization today. The extraordinary progress of the world since the Middle Ages has not been due to the mere expenditure of human energy, nor even to the flights of human genius, for men had worked hard since the remotest times, and some of them had been of surpassing intellect. No, it has been due to the accumulation of capital. That accumulation permitted labor to be organized economically and on a large scale, and thus greatly enhanced its productiveness. It provided the machinery that gradually diminished human drudgery, and liberated the spirit of the worker, who had formerly been almost indistinguishable from a mule."

For a brief period, Mencken faced his ideological battles with a romantic partner. In May 1923, he delivered a talk about how to catch a husband at Baltimore's Goucher College. There he met a twenty-five-year-old, Alabama-born English teacher named Sara Haardt. He was taken by her good looks, radiant intelligence, and passion for literature; she saw a decent, joyous, civilized man. A lifelong bachelor who had lived with his mother until she died in 1925, Mencken at age forty-five was wary of marriage. Apparently Sara's worsening tuberculosis brought him to the altar. After her death on May 31, 1935, Mencken to wrote a friend: "When I married Sara, the doctors said she could not live more than three years. Actually, she lived five, so I had two more years of happiness than I had any right to expect."

Sara's death hit him especially hard, because he was already down. With the Great Depression everywhere blamed on capitalism, individualist Mencken seemed like a relic. He had seldom analyzed economic policy, so he was not intellectually equipped to explain how the federal government itself had triggered and prolonged the Great Depression. Circulation of *American Mercury* plunged, and Mencken had resigned as editor by December 1933, to be succeeded by economic journalist Henry Hazlitt. Three years after Sara died, Mencken attacked President Roosevelt for maneuvering America into another European war, but many people were upset, and he decided to discontinue writing his *Baltimore Sun* column. It did not help that Mencken's devotion to traditional German culture apparently led him to discount ominous news coming out of Hitler's Germany. He was an outcast.

Mencken did much to redeem himself as far as the public was concerned by affirming the joys of private life. He added two massive supplements to *The American Language*, acclaimed as a learned and entertaining masterwork about popular speech. He wrote his charming memoirs, which began as a series of *New Yorker* articles and then expanded into a trilogy: *Happy Days* (1940), *Newspaper Days* (1941), and *Heathen Days* (1943). They display a tolerant, enthusiastic view of life. He edited a generous collection of his newspaper articles into a book, *A Mencken Chrestomathy* (1949), still in print.

On November 28, 1948, Mencken went to pick up a manuscript from his secretary's apartment and suffered a stroke. Although he regained his physical capabilities, he lost the ability to read, and he had difficulty speaking. Most people forgot about him. He died in his sleep on Sunday, January 29, 1956. His ashes were buried near his parents and his wife at Loudon Park

Cemetery. Mencken's former *American Mercury* compatriot, *Newsweek* columnist Henry Hazlitt, called Mencken "a great liberating force. . . . In his political and economic opinions Mencken was from the beginning, to repeat, neither 'radical' nor 'conservative,' but libertarian. He championed the freedom and dignity of the individual."

Mencken still has legions of admirers. True, the 1989 publication of his candid diary brought renewed allegations of anti-Semitism, but long-time Jewish friends defended him. Unpublished manuscripts appeared, and new editions of his letters, newspaper columns, and other work have come out. Altogether, there are some thirty Mencken books in print.

Most of Mencken's chroniclers have opposed his political views—in particular, his hostility to the New Deal—but they have found him nevertheless appealing. Like everyone else, they have been drawn to his prodigious enterprise, vast learning, steadfast courage, good cheer, and free spirit.

BUOYANT OPTIMISM

DURING THE EARLY 1940s, tyrants oppressed or threatened people on every continent. Western intellectuals whitewashed mass murderers like Joseph Stalin, and Western governments expanded their power with Soviet-style central planning. Fifty million people were killed during the war that raged in Europe, Africa, and Asia. America, seemingly the last hope for liberty, was drawn into it.

Established American authors who defended liberty were a dying breed. Literary critic H. L. Mencken had turned away from bitter politics to write his memoirs, while others, like author Albert Jay Nock and journalist Garet Garrett, were mired in pessimism. Amid the worst of times, Rose Wilder Lane dared to declare collectivism evil. She stood up for natural rights, the only philosophy that provided a moral basis for opposing tyranny everywhere, and she celebrated old-fashioned rugged individualism. She envisioned a future when people could again be free, and expressed a buoyant optimism.

Lane was an outsider who came from territory that was not yet part of the United States and started her career before many women enjoyed equal rights. She made herself into one of the most successful freelance writers of her day. She traveled on assignment throughout Eastern Europe and at age seventy-eight became a war correspondent in Vietnam. Her work appeared in *American Mercury, Cosmopolitan, Country Gentleman, Good Housekeeping, Harper's, Ladies' Home Journal, McCall's, Redbook, Saturday Evening Post, Sunset, Woman's Day,* and other magazines. She produced scripts for radio broadcaster Lowell Thomas, whose specialty was exotic travel adventures, and wrote biographies of Charlie Chaplin, Henry Ford, and Jack London. Her novel *Let the Hurricane Roar* (1933) was a best-seller that remained in print for four decades and was dramatized on television as *Young Pioneers.* Her book *The Discovery of Freedom* (1943), still available, helped inspire the modern libertarian movement. She achieved her greatest impact when she turned her mother's story outlines into the beloved "Little House" books about individual responsibility, self-reliance, courtesy, courage and love. Many people consider this the greatest series of children's books ever written.

Referring to Lane and her compatriots, the journalist Isabel Paterson and novelist Ayn Rand, *Fortune* editor John Chamberlain wrote admiringly that "with scornful side glances at the male business community, they had decided to rekindle a faith in an older American philosophy. There wasn't an economist among them. And none of them was a Ph.D." Albert Jay Nock declared that "they make all of us male writers look like Confederate money. They don't fumble and fiddle around—every shot goes straight to the centre."

Biographer William Holtz noted that political philosophy was Lane's "consuming interest for over half of her adult life. She was an important figure in the transmission of that persistent strand of libertarian thought in our country, and many of those who respected and loved her were in fact a kind of comradeship of happy warriors against the state. . . . Largely self-educated, always a voracious and wide-ranging reader, and by temperament an independent thinker, she took little on faith and tested ideas instinctively against her own experience."

Lane once described herself as a "plump, Middle western, middle class, middle-aged woman, with white hair and simple tastes. I like buttered popcorn, salted peanuts, bread and milk." She had bad teeth, her marriage failed, she worked to support her aging parents, and at one point during the 1930s she was so hard up for cash that her electricity was cut off. Yet she soared with eloquence as she helped revive the libertarian principles of the American Revolution, and she inspired millions.

SHE WAS BORN Rose Wilder on December 5, 1886, near De Smet, Dakota Territory. Her father, Almanzo Wilder, and her mother, Laura Ingalls, were poor farmers, devastated by drought, hailstorms, and other calamities. For years, the family lived in a windowless cabin and missed many meals. They named their daughter after the wild roses that bloomed on the prairie.

"We did not like discipline," Rose recalled, "so we suffered until we disciplined ourselves. We saw many things and many opportunities that we ardently wanted and could not pay for, so we did not get them, or got them only after stupendous, heartbreaking effort and self-denial, for debt was much harder to bear than deprivations. We were honest, not because sinful human nature wanted to be, but because the consequences of dishonesty were excessively painful. It was clear that if your word were not as good as your bond, your bond was no good and you were worthless. . . . We learned that it is impossible to get something for nothing."

When Rose was four, the family gave up on Dakota and moved to Mansfield, Missouri, where they could grow apples. She attended a four-room, red-brick school that had two shelves of books, and she discovered the wonders of Charles Dickens, Jane Austen, and Edward Gibbon. Her mainstay was the famous *Readers* compiled by Cincinnati College president William Holmes McGuffey who imparted moral lessons as he taught the fundamentals of reading and exposed young minds to many great authors of Western civilization. But she quit school after the ninth grade and determined that somehow she would see the world beyond rural Missouri. She took a train to Kansas City and got a job as a Western Union telegraph clerk on the night shift. She spent most of her spare time reading. By 1908, she was off to San Francisco for another Western Union job. There was a romance with advertising salesman Gillette Lane whom she married in March 1909. She became pregnant but had either a miscarriage or stillbirth. It became impossible for her to conceive again.

By 1915, the marriage had broken up, but through Gillette's newspaper connections, Rose got her start as a journalist. For the *San Francisco Bulletin,* a radical labor paper, she began writing a women's column, then a series of daily fifteen-hundred-word personality profiles, and wrote an autobiographical novel serialized in *Sunset* magazine.

Somehow she became a Christian socialist and a fan of socialist Eugene Debs. Then the Bolshevik revolution captured her imagination, and she embraced communism. While staying in New York, where she hoped to launch a career as a freelance writer, she met communist promoter John Reed and communist author Max Eastman.

In March 1920, the Red Cross invited her to travel around Europe and report on their relief efforts, so that prospective donors—on whose support they depended—would know about the good they were doing. Based in Paris, she traveled to Vienna, Berlin, Prague, Warsaw, Budapest, Rome, Sarajevo, Dubrovnik, Tirana, Trieste, Athens, Cairo, Damascus, Baghdad, and Constantinople. Lane had imagined that Europe was the great hope for civilization, but instead she eluded bandits, encountered bureaucratic corruption, endured runaway inflation, and witnessed civil war horrors and the darkening shadows of ruthless tyranny.

When Lane visited the Soviet Union, the bolsheviks had been in power four years. She expected peasants to be rapturous about communism, but as she reported later, "My host astounded me by the force with which he said that he did not like the new government. . . . His complaint was government interference with village affairs. He protested against the growing bureaucracy that was taking more and more men from productive work. He predicted chaos and suffering from the centralizing of economic power in Moscow." "I came out of the Soviet Union no longer a communist," she continued, "because I believed in personal freedom. Like all Americans, I took for granted the individual liberty to which I had been born. It seemed as necessary and as inevitable as the air I breathed; it seemed the natural element in which human beings lived. The thought that I might lose it had never remotely occurred to me. And I could not conceive that multitudes of human beings would ever willingly live without it."

After returning to America in November 1923, her career blossomed as she wrote for popular magazines and published novels about pioneer life.

Famed actress Helen Hayes dramatized Lane's novel *Let the Hurricane Roar* on the radio. Nevertheless, Lane was financially devastated during the Great Depression. In 1931, she wailed, "I am forty-five. Owe $8,000. Have in bank $502.70. . . . Nothing that I have intended has ever been realized."

In 1936, Lane wrote "Credo," an article for the *Saturday Evening Post*. Three years later, Leonard Read, general manager of the Los Angeles Chamber of Commerce, helped establish a publishing firm he called Pamphleteers, which reprinted Lane's article as *Give Me Liberty*. "I began slowly to understand," she wrote, "that I am endowed by the Creator with inalienable liberty as I am endowed with life; that my freedom is inseparable from my life."

In 1942, an editor of the John Day Company asked Lane to write a book about liberty. She began work in a Texas trailer park during a tour of the Southwest and went through at least two drafts at her home in Danbury, Connecticut. *The Discovery of Freedom: Man's Struggle Against Authority*, published in January 1943, chronicled the epic struggle of ordinary people who defy rulers to raise their families, produce food, build industries, trade, and in countless ways improve human life. She was lyrical about the American Revolution, which helped secure liberty and unleashed phenomenal energy for human progress. "Why did men die of hunger, for six thousand years?" she asked. "Why did they walk, and carry goods and other men on their backs, for six thousand years, and suddenly, in one century, only on a sixth of this earth's surface, they make steamships, railroads, motors, airplanes, and now are flying around the earth in its utmost heights of air? Why did families live thousands of years in floorless hovels, without windows or chimneys, then, in eighty years and only in these United States, they are taking floors, chimneys, glass windows for granted, and regarding electric lights, porcelain toilets, and window screens as minimum necessities?"

She attributed these dramatic developments to liberty. She hailed constitutional protections "forbidding American Government to seize or search an American's person without due process of law; to imprison him without trial; to try him in secret or without letting him call witness in his defense; to try him twice on the same charge; to punish him for a crime that someone else committed; to refuse him a jury trial or to deny his right of appeal; to torture him; or to deny his right of assembly, or his right to petition the Government, or his right to bear arms, or his right to own property."

Lane was dissatisfied with the book and refused permission to reprint it. She never got around to completing another edition. Only a thousand copies of the book were printed during her lifetime. Nonetheless, *The Discovery of Freedom* had a big impact, circulating as an underground classic. It helped inspire the launching of several organizations to promote liberty during the 1940s and 1950s, among them, Leonard Read's Foundation for Economic

Education, F. A. Harper's Institute for Humane Studies, and Robert M. Lefevre's Freedom School.

Although *The Discovery of Freedom* was a founding document of the modern libertarian movement, Lane had perhaps a greater calling behind the scenes. In 1930, her mother, Laura Ingalls Wilder, gave her a manuscript about her early life from Wisconsin to Kansas and Dakota. Lane deleted the material about Wisconsin, then went through two drafts of the rest, fleshing out the story and characters. This became a hundred-page manuscript tentatively called *Pioneer Girl,* which she sent to her literary agent, Carl Brandt. The Wisconsin material became a twenty-page story, "When Grandma Was a Little Girl," a possible text for a children's picture book. One publisher suggested that the story be expanded to a book for younger readers.

Lane conveyed the news to her mother, and since the original manuscript had been rewritten beyond recognition, she explained, "It is your father's stories, taken out of the long PIONEER GIRL manuscript, and strung together, as you will see." Lane specified the kind of material she needed, adding, "If you find it easier to write in the first person, write that way. I will change it into the third person, later." Lane reassured her mother that the collaboration would remain a family secret: "I have said nothing about having run the manuscript through my own typewriter." By May 27, 1931, the book was done, and Lane sent it off to publishers. Harper Brothers issued it in 1932 as *Little House in the Big Woods,* and it became a landmark in children's literature.

In January 1933, Wilder gave Lane *Farmer Boy,* a manuscript about Almanzo's childhood recollections. Publishers had rejected it, presumably because it was mainly a chronicle of farm work. But Lane spent a month turning it into a flesh-and-blood story, and Harper Brothers bought it. The following year, Wilder gave Lane a manuscript about her life in Kansas, and she spent five weeks rewriting it into *Little House on the Prairie.*

The "Little House" books began generating significant income for the Wilders, a relief to Lane whose aim was to help provide their financial security. Wilder expanded part of *Pioneer Girl* into another manuscript and gave it to Lane in 1936. "I have written you the whys of the story as I wrote it," Wilder explained. "But you know your judgement is better than mine, so what you decide is the one that stands." Lane spent two months rewriting it and drafted a letter for their literary agent, asking better terms. This became *On the Banks of Plum Creek.* Lane spent most of 1939 rewriting the manuscript for *By the Shores of Silver Lake. The Long Winter* appeared in 1940, *Little Town on the Prairie* in 1941, and *These Happy Golden Years* in 1942.

The books portrayed a close family on the American frontier during the 1870s and 1880s: quietly courageous Pa (Charles Ingalls) who did stupendous amounts of work building homes, raising crops, tending farm animals, and helping neighbors; Ma (Caroline Ingalls) who took care of the children and maintained civilized life even in the most primitive conditions; and the children, Mary, Laura, Carrie, and Grace. The family endured one hardship after another: hungry wolves, brutal winters, hostile Indians, crops destroyed by locusts, ferocious prairie fires, scarlet fever, and disease that blinded Mary. The family never had much money, but they enjoyed a wonderful life together.

Pa was the great hero of the stories. *On the Banks of Plum Creek* told how, after locusts devoured the wheat and hay that he had grown in Minnesota, he twice walked more than two hundred miles east in his patched boots to earn money harvesting other people's crops. On another occasion, walking home from town, he was caught in a sudden blizzard and lost his way, but he survived three days in a hole until the blizzard was over. Again and again, Pa renewed everybody's spirits when he picked up his fiddle and filled their home with music.

Readers could behold the wonders of creative imagination: "First, someone had thought of a railroad. Then the surveyors had come out to that empty country, and they had marked and measured a railroad that was not there at all; it was only a railroad that someone had thought of. Then the plowmen came to tear up the prairie grass, and the scraper-men to dig up the dirt, and the teamsters with their wagons to haul it. And all of them said they were working on the railroad, but still the railroad wasn't there. Nothing was there yet but cuts through the prairie swells, pieces of the railroad grade that were really only narrow, short ridges of earth, all pointing westward across the enormous grassy land" (*By the Shores of Silver Lake*).

Individualism came across loud and clear: "Anybody knew that no two men were alike. You could measure cloth with a yardstick, or distance by miles, but you could not lump men together and measure them by any rule. Brains and character did not depend on anything but the man himself. Some men did not have the sense at sixty that some had at sixteen" (*The Long Winter*).

The books displayed the spirit of liberty: "The politicians are a-swarming in already, and ma'am, if'n there's any worst pest than grasshoppers it surely is politicians" (*The Long Winter*). In *Little Town on the Prairie*, Rose described her mother's thoughts this way: "Americans are free. That means they have to obey their own consciences. No king bosses Pa; he has to boss himself. Why (she thought), when I am a little older, Pa and Ma will stop telling me what to do, and there isn't anyone else who has a right to give me orders. I will have to make myself be good."

Intensely loyal to her mother, Lane wanted no credit for the "Little House" books, and her role was not documented until English professor William Holtz produced the biography, *The Ghost in the Little House* (1993). "In 1972," he recalled, "my wife and I began to read *Little House in the Big*

Woods to our daughters. The appeal of the book was immediate, and we went on to other books by Laura Ingalls Wilder. They were that rare accomplishment in children's literature, books for children that could at the same time hold an adult's interest; and we found vivid and persuasive their images of family devotion, disciplined hard work, and optimistic struggle against adversity. . . . As a literary scholar, I found myself more and more interested in the configuration of an entire set of circumstances. . . . [Laura was] in her sixties before her books appeared, and with no previous literary distinction before this sudden efflorescence, she struck the imagination as a literary Grandma Moses, an untutored talent springing to life after years of obscurity in the Missouri Ozarks. . . . The story told, of Laura Ingalls from childhood to marriage, was . . . presented for the most part with such a high degree of literary finish—in pacing, balance, structure, characterization, dialogue, dramatic impact, all within the confines of a deceptively simple style and point-of-view—as to achieve a portrait of a fictional character and a realized world of singular power. The impression of the author Laura Ingalls Wilder as a naive genius was very strong. . . .

"To appreciate Rose Wilder Lane's contribution to her mother's books, one must simply read her mother's fair-copy manuscripts in comparison with the final published versions. What Rose accomplished was nothing less than a line-by-line rewriting of labored and underdeveloped narratives." Holtz observed that a cheerful spirit pervades all the "Little House" books except the posthumously published *First Four Years* (1971), "the only book by Laura Ingalls Wilder that did not pass under the shaping hand of Rose Wilder Lane."

In 1974, NBC began adapting the books for *Little House on the Prairie*, a hugely popular television series that ran nine years. President Ronald Reagan remarked that *Little House* was his favorite television program. The programs have been seen in a hundred countries and syndication agreement ensured that the programs will be rerun again and again for at least the next quarter-century. Time-Life Video now markets the forty-eight most popular programs. Michael Landon wrote and directed many programs and starred as Laura's father Charles Ingalls.

Lane's last blast was *Woman's Day Book of American Needlework* (1963) that she turned into a hymn for liberty. "American needlework tells you," she wrote, "that Americans live in the only classless society. This republic is the only country that has no peasant needlework. . . . American women . . . discarded backgrounds, they discarded borders and frames. They made the details create the whole, and they set each detail in boundless space, alone, independent, complete. . . . Laces were in every home, no lower classes wore their lives away making laces for superior classes. Those Americans were free people, imaginative, creative, and daring; they liked swiftness and change.

American lace shows you that they were the people who would develop the clipper ships and the ocean steamers and the airplanes."

Talking about patchwork, she wrote: "Let us remember, too, that 'when Freedom from her mountain-height unfurled her standard to the air,' that standard was a patchwork pattern of thirteen stripes, red and white, and a blue patch that once held thirteen stars and now holds fifty. That standard was raised by poor and hungry people who had come, or been shipped like cattle, from all the lands of the Old World to live in the edge of a wilderness if they could. Let us remember that they found freedom here and fought to defend and preserve it, and that in freedom they made our country from nothing at all but bare hands and unconquerable spirit."

Although Lane remained active throughout her life—*Woman's Day* sent her to Vietnam as their correspondent in 1965—she cherished country living at her Danbury, Connecticut, home. On November 29, 1966, she baked several days' worth of bread and went upstairs to sleep. She never awoke. She was seventy-nine. Her close friend and literary heir, Roger MacBride, co-creator of the *Little House* television series, brought her ashes to Mansfield, Missouri, and had them buried next to her mother and father. Her simple gravestone was engraved with some words by Thomas Paine: "An army of principles will penetrate where an army of soldiers cannot. Neither the channel nor the Rhine will arrest its progress. It will march on the horizon of the world and it will conquer."

MacBride did much to preserve Lane's legacy. He authorized a new edition of *The Discovery of Freedom* in 1972. The following year, he edited *The Lady and the Tycoon: The Best of Letters Between Rose Wilder Lane and Jasper Crane.* For young adults, he brought out *Rose Wilder Lane, Her Story* (1977). Then in 1993: *Little House on Rocky Ridge*, the first of his stories about how she grew up, and very much in the style and spirit of the "Little House" books. They were followed by *Little Farm in the Ozarks* (1994) and *In the Land of the Big Red Apple* (1995). Miami-based MacBride suffered a fatal heart attack on March 5, 1995, at age sixty-five, but his daughter Abigail MacBride Allen has overseen the publication of her father's unpublished manuscripts, starting with *The Other Side of the Hill* (1995), *Little Town in the Ozarks* (1996), *New Dawn on Rocky Ridge* (1997), *On the Banks of the Bayou* (1998)., and *Bachelor Girl* (1999). The books take Rose up to age seventeen, when she is off to follow her dreams.

ECONOMIC LIBERTY

Intellectual freedom cannot exist without political freedom;
political freedom cannot exist without economic freedom;
a free mind and a free market are corollaries.
—AYN RAND (1961)

FOR MILLENNIA, GOVERNMENTS restricted the liberty of people to move freely, choose their work, keep their earnings, spend it, and pass it on as they wished. In medieval Europe, labor guilds blocked entry to trades and professions. Guilds, not customers, determined which firms would thrive and which would perish. In many places, there were road, bridge, river, and town tolls throttling trade. Defenders of economic restrictions claimed that if people were free to make their own choices, there would be chaos. But in the eighteenth century, French and Scottish thinkers realized that economic restrictions enrich special interests at the expense of everyone else. Millions would be better off if they were set free. Society as a whole would do just fine, because in free markets, people have plenty of incentives to seek each other's voluntary cooperation.

LAISSEZ-FAIRE

BY THE MID-EIGHTEENTH century, a number of authors had expressed the liberating vision that came to be known as laissez-faire. Anne Robert Jacques Turgot put it into action. As regional administrator and later comptroller-general of France, a nation with absolute monarchy, he took giant steps for liberty. He spoke out for religious toleration, granted freedom of expression, gave people freedom to pursue the work of their choice, cut government spending, opposed inflation and made a case for gold. He abolished obnoxious taxes, trade restrictions, monopoly privileges, and forced labor.

Turgot was respected by leading thinkers for liberty, including the baron de Montesquieu, the marquis de Condorcet, and Benjamin Franklin. Referring to Turgot, Adam Smith wrote, "I had the happiness of his acquaintance, and, I flattered myself, even of his friendship and esteem." After meeting Turgot in 1760, Voltaire told a friend, "I have scarcely ever seen a man more lovable or better informed." Jean-Baptiste Say, who inspired so many French libertarians during the nineteenth century, declared, "There are hardly any works which can yield to the journalist and to the statesman an ampler harvest of facts and of instruction than may be found in the writings of Turgot." Pierre-Samuel du Pont de Nemours, a French champion of laissez-faire and founder of the American industrial family, paid his friend Thomas Jefferson the supreme compliment by calling him "the American Turgot."

Turgot displayed fantastic vision. For instance, he predicted the American Revolution in 1750, more than two decades before George Washington and Benjamin Franklin saw it coming. "Colonies, like fruits," Turgot wrote, "are only held fast to the trees up to the time of their maturity. Having become ripe, they do that which Carthage did, and which America will one day do." In 1778, Turgot warned Americans that "slavery is incompatible with a good political constitution." He warned that Americans had more to fear from civil war than foreign enemies. He predicted that "Americans are bound to become great, not by war but by culture." Turgot warned French King Louis XVI that unless taxes and government spending were cut, there would be a revolution, which might cost him his head. Turgot warned too about the dangers of fiat paper money, and when it was resorted to during the French Revolution, the result was ruinous runaway inflation and a military coup. Turgot showed how people could make the transition from absolutism to self-government.

Although few of Turgot's writings were published in his lifetime, he was ablaze with important ideas. "Turgot was much too able a man to write anything insignificant," observed intellectual historian Joseph A. Schumpeter. Commenting on his most important work, a slim volume, Schumpeter noted that it contains "a theory of barter, price, and money that, so far as it goes, is almost faultless . . . comprehensive vision of all the essential facts and their interrelations plus excellence of formulation."

A bold champion of liberty, Turgot seems to have been shy around women. While studying at the Sorbonne, he met a charming aristocrat named Minette de Ligniville. They played badminton, and he fell in love. Historian Vincent Cronin explains that "although she was miles above him socially," Turgot proposed. She turned him down, and he never married.

Turgot was remembered by his friend du Pont de Nemours as "tall and well-proportioned; his face was beautiful. . . . His eyes were of a clear brown, and expressed perfectly the blending of firmness and suavity which made up his character. His forehead was dome-shaped, lofty, noble, and serene; his features well-pronounced. . . . His hair was brown, abundant, and very fine, and he retained it completely to the last; clad as magistrate, his locks scattered on his shoulders with a natural and negligent grace, he formed a striking picture."

ANNE ROBERT JACQUES Turgot was born in Paris on May 10, 1727, the third and youngest son of Michel Etienne Turgot and Madeleine Françoise Martineau. His father was a government official who helped build the Paris sewage system.

Early on, Turgot acquired a love for learning. He attended the Collège du Plessis where he discovered the theories of English physicist Isaac Newton. It was traditional for the youngest son to become a priest, and he studied for a clerical license at the Sorbonne. Turgot finished a Latin dissertation ("On the Successive Advances of the Human Mind") in which he expressed his excitement about America: "The soil, hitherto uncultivated, is made fruitful by industrious hands. Laws faithfully observed maintain henceforth tranquillity in these favoured regions. The ravages of war are there unknown . . . liberty, virtue and simplicity of manners." But by this time, Turgot had second thoughts about the priesthood, and he got his father's permission to pursue a law career. With his obvious intelligence and learning, he met many leading thinkers, including political philosopher Charles Louis de Secondat (baron de Montesquieu), philosopher Claude Adrien Helvetius, and mathematician Jean Le Rond d'Alembert.

Turgot's first published work, Le Conciliateur (1754), was a pamphlet protesting plans to renew religious persecution. As a Catholic addressing

Catholics, he wrote, "Men, for their opinions, demand only liberty; if you deprive them of it, you place arms in their hand. Give them liberty, they remain quiet. . . . It is then the very unity in religion we would enforce, and not the different opinions we tolerate, that produces trouble and civil wars."

Meanwhile, Turgot had become a good friend of Jacques Claude Marie Vincent, the marquis de Gournay, whom the intellectual historian Joseph A. Schumpeter called "one of the greatest teachers of economics who ever lived." Born in Saint-Malo, Gournay joined the family business and absorbed the ideas of Richard Cantillon, an Irishman who had moved to France, made a fortune, and wrote the *Essai sur la nature du Commerce en général* (about 1734) that offered perhaps the first comprehensive view of how a free market works. Turgot traveled with Gournay around France, inspecting businesses, and he embraced Gournay's free-trade principles. Gournay helped popularize the famous maxim *laissez-faire, laissez-passer* (generally meaning "let the goods pass"), originated by the seventeenth-century merchant Le Gendre, who protested government regulations under King Louis XIV.

The year Gournay died, Turgot wrote *Eloge de Gournay* (*Elegy for Gournay*) in which he explained why market competition best protects consumers by providing choices. Government regulations, he pointed out, impose significant costs on consumers while yielding dubious benefits.

Turgot defended economic liberty in "Fondations" ("Foundations") and "Foires et marchés" ("Fairs and Markets"), articles for Denis Diderot's seventeen-volume *Encyclopédie* (1751–1772), the great compendium of knowledge, which, featuring Voltaire, Montesquieu, Quesnay, and almost all the other important authors of the French Enlightenment, became an organ for promoting human progress. Some twenty-five thousand sets were sold before the French Revolution, half of them outside France.

Somewhere along the line, Turgot had become familiar with the views of the physiocrats, the name coined by du Pont de Nemours from the Greek words *physis* ("let nature") and *kratein* ("rule"). His book *Physiocratie* appeared in 1768. The brash, bold du Pont de Nemours became a close friend of Turgot, who was godfather to his third son and suggested the name of this boy—Euthère Irenée ("freedom and peace")—destined to launch the family colossus, E. I. du Pont de Nemours & Cie.

Physiocrat referred to ideas popularized by François Quesnay, a nobleman's son who made himself a surgeon and bought his post as physician to King Louis XV and his influential courtesan Madame de Pompadour. A friend of Gournay, Quesnay believed that human progress developed spontaneously, and people would do best when set free. He attacked taxes and trade restrictions in his articles for the *Encyclopédie* (1756), in his own book *Tableaux économique* (1758), and elsewhere. The political philosophy of the physiocrats was perhaps best expressed in the 1767 book *L'ordre naturel et essentiel des sociétés politiques* (*The Natural and Essential Order of Political Societies*) by Pierre-Paul Mercier de la Rivière. "Do you wish a society to attain the highest degree of wealth, population, and power?" he asked. "Trust, then, its interests to freedom, and let this be universal."

On August 8, 1761, Turgot was appointed an *intendant* (chief administrator) for the provinces of Angomois, Basse-Marche, and Limousin, a region in central France later known as Limoges. Almost all the approximately 500,000 people were peasants who lived on chestnuts, rye, and buckwheat, slept in mud huts, and dressed in rags. Historian Hippolyte Taine, who gathered a tremendous amount of material on living conditions, reported that many peasants used plows that were no better than those of ancient Rome.

Peasants in Limoges, as elsewhere, were crushed by taxes. Economic historian Florin Aftalion reported there were some sixteen hundred customs houses throughout France to collect *traites* as goods passed various points along roads and rivers. Moreover, there were the *gabelle* (a tax on salt), feudal duties, and church tithes. The *taille*, from which some 130,000 clergymen and 140,000 aristocrats were exempted, was based on a tax collector's estimate of a peasant's ability to pay. Overall, peasants got to keep about a fifth of their meager income.

Turgot focused on the most obnoxious taxes, starting with the *taille*. It was not within his power as a regional official to abolish the *taille*, but he did what he could. Traditionally, national government finance officials guessed how much money they were going to spend on wars, bureaucrats, the royal palace of Versailles, and other expenses, which determined the amount of tax revenue needed. Turgot got his district's tax quota cut by 190,000 livres. Year after year for the thirteen years that he was an *intendant* in Limoges, he pushed for tax cuts. He abolished the *corvée* (forced labor) in Limoges. Defended by Jean-Jacques Rousseau in *The Social Contract* (1762), the *corvée* was the most hated tax on peasants. It had originated as a feudal obligation and became a demand that peasants work as much as fourteen days a year without pay on the king's roads, breaking, carting, and shoveling stones. Turgot hired competent contractors to build and improve some 450 miles of roads in Limoges.

Turgot knew many friends of liberty. He dined with the Scottish moral philosopher Adam Smith who visited Paris in 1765, and later Turgot helped supply Smith with books for his work *The Wealth of Nations*. Like the physiocrats, both men believed in economic liberty, and unlike the physiocrats, they recognized the importance of commerce.

In 1766, Turgot wrote an eighty-page summary of his views for two Chinese students in Paris. This became *Réflexions sur la Formation et la Distribution des Richesses* (*Reflections on the Formation and Distribution of Riches*). It explained much about how free markets work and made a case for laissez-faire policy. Du Pont de Nemours published an edited version of *Réflexions* in the November and December 1769 issues of *Ephemerides du Citoyen,* the physiocratic journal.

Turgot made clear his opposition to slavery: "This abominable custom of slavery has once been universal, and is still spread over the greater part of the earth. . . . This brigandage and this trade still prevail in all their horror on the coasts of Guinea, where they are fomented by the Europeans who go thither to purchase negroes for the cultivation of the American colonies. The excessive labours to which avaricious masters drive their slaves cause many of them to perish." He also affirmed the importance of hard money (gold and silver) and opposed government interference with money markets. "It is," he wrote, "another mistake to suppose that the interest of money in commerce ought to be fixed by the laws of Princes."

During the famine of 1769–1772, Turgot mortgaged his estate to get money for famine relief and organized relief efforts financed almost entirely by voluntary contributions. He urged that France adopt free trade, so that people suffering from a crop failure would be able to avoid a famine by purchasing food from regions with grain surpluses.

Turgot further defended laissez-faire by writing *Lettres sur le commerce des grains,* seven letters opposing Comptroller-General Abbé Terray's policy that grain could be sold only in government-controlled marketplaces by licensed monopolists. In a related letter, *Sur la marque des fers (On the Mark of Iron),* Turgot wrote, "I know no other means of quickening any commerce whatever than by granting to it the greatest liberty and the freedom from all taxes."

Turgot opposed military conscription. "The repugnance to service in the militia was so widespread among the people," he wrote to the minister of war in January 1773, that it triggered "the greatest disorders throughout the country. . . . Loss of life and minor outrages were common. Depopulation of many of the parishes, with cultivation abandoned, often followed." Turgot let people voluntarily contribute cash to a pool for those conscripted, and many enlisted for the money. Moreover, instead of forcing local people to provide room and board for soldiers, Turgot rented some buildings as barracks and spread the cost among all taxpayers.

On May 10, 1774, King Louis XV died of smallpox and was succeeded by his awkward, timid nineteen-year-old grandson who became Louis XVI. His queen was the nineteen-year-old Marie Antoinette, a beautiful and frivolous daughter of the arrogant Austrian empress Maria Theresa. At the time, France had Western Europe's biggest government, and it was in desperate shape, having incurred massive debts during the Seven Years War (1756–1763) with Britain. The royal palace of Versailles was a big drain. On the payroll were 8 architects, 47 musicians, 56 hunters, 295 cooks, 886 nobles with their wives and children, plus secretaries, couriers, physicians, and chaplains, and some 10,000 soldiers who guarded the palace. Almost every week, two banquets, two balls, and three plays were held at Versailles. Marie Antoinette squandered large sums at card tables and lavished costly gifts on her court favorites. She spent staggering sums on dresses and jewelry.

To help bring the financial situation under control, Louis XVI named Turgot as comptroller-general in August 1774. Turgot's policy was big spending cuts, no new taxes, no new borrowing and no effort to dodge creditors via bankruptcy. One of his top priorities was to energize the economy by eliminating government restrictions on trade within France. For instance, he reported, "In the city of Rouen the trade in corn and flour is permitted exclusively to a Company of privileged merchants. . . . Their privileges extend not only to the right of being the sole sellers of grains in the market of the city and at their shops, but of being the sole purchasers of grains brought from the interior of the kingdom or from abroad." On September 13, 1774, Turgot began issuing edicts liberating the grain trade.

Although Turgot never challenged the legitimacy of a monarchy, he became convinced that people should prepare for self-government. Together with du Pont de Nemours, he outlined a plan for parish assemblies, village assemblies, district assemblies, provincial assemblies, and a General Assembly. This plan went nowhere.

Turgot conceived what became known as the six edicts. Two were of monumental importance. Turgot would abolish the *jurandes*—guilds—which monopolized various trades. Turgot would permit anyone, including foreigners, to enter virtually any trade. Turgot's second crucial edict would abolish the *corvée*, the practice of forcing peasants to work on roads without pay. He proposed that all property owners, the primary beneficiaries of road improvements, pay a tax which would provide money for hiring road contractors. Turgot thought of making these controversial proposals more acceptable by presenting them in a package with more popular proposals to abolish remaining restrictions on the grain trade, discharge officials who restricted Parisian markets, ports, and docks, abolish the tax on the cattle, and cut the suet tax. He issued another edict that would abolish myriad laws restricting the wine trade. In Bordeaux, for instance, it was illegal to sell and drink wine from another district. Wines from Languedoc could not be shipped down the Garonne River before St. Martin's Day. Amid all this, Turgot suffered an attack of gout, but when urged to go slow at age forty-eight, he replied, "The needs of the people are enormous, and in my family, we die of gout at fifty."

Over the objections of his brothers and almost all his advisers, Louis XVI endorsed the edicts, and on February 5, 1776, he presented them to the Parlement of Paris. The Parlement supported guilds because many members were lawyers who got fees from guilds. One notorious case between the guild of tailors and the guild of used clothes dealers had dragged on for more than 250 years. Lawyers, noblemen, monopolists, clergymen—every interest group—was against Turgot, and on May 12, 1776, he was dismissed. He reportedly warned Louis XVI, "Remember, sire, that it was weakness which brought the head of [England's King] Charles I to the block."

Turgot had probably achieved as much as anyone could without organizing popular support to buck special interests. His experience revealed how fragile were reforms that depended on the goodwill of a ruler. Edicts were no substitute for education of the people.

Turgot moved to Paris and studied science, literature, and music. For Benjamin Franklin, representing American interests in Paris, he wrote *Mémoire sur l'impôt* to explain his laissez-faire economic policy. In one of his last surviving writings, a controversial March 22, 1778 letter to English radical minister Dr. Richard Price, Turgot expressed his support for American independence. He urged that Americans "reduce to the smallest possible number the kinds of affairs of which the Government of each State should take charge." He declared that "the asylum which America affords to the oppressed of all nations will console the world."

Turgot suffered more attacks of gout and after 1778 could walk only with crutches. His situation worsened in early 1781, and he died at home around 11:00 P.M., on March 18. He was fifty-three. His friends Madame Blondel, the duchesse d'Enville, and du Pont de Nemours were with him.

Having rejected Turgot's peaceful reforms, the French monarchy collapsed. By 1788, military spending took a quarter of the budget, and half the budget was needed for payments on the national debt. There were tax riots. The king and queen were a pitiful sight as they handed over their silverware to the royal mint. Desperate for funds, the king agreed to summon the Estates General, an assembly of nobles, clergy, and taxpayers, which had not met for one and a half centuries. This became the National Assembly to which du Pont de Nemours had been elected. It abolished guilds, abolished some of the worst taxes, and confiscated church properties. Hatred boiled over, as Turgot had anticipated. On January 21, 1793, Louis XVI was led to a Paris guillotine and beheaded. Marie Antoinette, ridiculed as "Madam Deficit," followed him to the guillotine on October 16. The French people suffered through runaway inflation, the Reign of Terror, and the military takeover by Napoleon Bonaparte who pursued ruinous wars.

Turgot's steadfast friend du Pont de Nemours, who had been scheduled for the guillotine the very day the Reign of Terror ended, was rescued by Madame Germaine de Staël and emigrated to America. He edited the nine-volume *Oeuvres de Turgot* (*Works of Turgot*, 1808–1811). Another French edition of Turgot's works appeared in 1844. And there was G. Schelle's *Oeuvres de Turgot et documents le concernant* (1913–1923) with many documents from the Turgot family. A dozen books about Turgot were published during the nineteenth century.

Turgot inspired the economist Jean-Baptiste Say, who helped inspire the resurgence of libertarian writings in Europe. Leon Say, Jean-Baptiste's grandson, wrote an 1887 biography hailing Turgot's achievements. In recent years, Turgot's most ardent admirer has been Murray N. Rothbard who affirmed that "if we were to award a prize for 'brilliancy' in the history of economic thought, it would surely go to Anne Robert Jacques Turgot."

He had a liberating vision, told the truth, pursued justice, and was fearless in challenging special interests that capture government power. He showed why liberty is essential if the poorest among us are to improve their lives. He displayed the courage and compassion to help set people free

INVISIBLE HAND

BEFORE ADAM SMITH, most people seemed to believe government was necessary to make an economy work. In Britain and Europe, governments promoted economic self-sufficiency as a bulwark of national security. They subsidized "strategic" industries like mining and silk-making and helped protect apothecaries, bricklayers, woodmongers, playing-card makers, and a myriad of other workers against what they considered unfair competition. They protected overseas trading companies and restricted imports in the name of accumulating gold hoards, thought to be a secret of wealth and power. Life without considerable government intervention was unthinkable. Adam Smith defied all this with *The Wealth of Nations,* a clarion call for economic liberty. Although many specifics were not original with Smith, he created a bold vision that inspired people everywhere: the way to achieve peace and prosperity is to set individuals free. He attacked one type of government intervention after another, recommended liberating Britain's American colonies, and denounced slavery. Smith had an enormous impact on ideas, where change begins.

Smith was an unlikely revolutionary who came across as a serious, absent-minded, thoroughly likable man. He was a dedicated scholar, forming a personal library of some three thousand volumes, and was often so preoccupied with ideas that he forgot what he was doing. Once, reportedly, he was giving a tour of a Glasgow tannery, and he absent-mindedly fell right into the tannery pit, from which his friends extricated him. He seemed to make friends wherever people enjoyed playing cards or talking about current affairs, history, literature, philosophy, or government policy. Voltaire, the famed French defender of religious toleration, wrote admiringly about Smith: "We have nothing to compare with him, and I am embarrassed for my dear compatriots." Madame Riccoboni, a French novelist, gushed: "Scold me, beat me, kill me, but I like Mr. Smith, I like him greatly. I wish that the devil would carry off all of our own men of letters, all of our philosophers, and bring Mr. Smith to me. Superior men seek him out."

Smith never sat for a portrait, but James Tassie did a medallion in 1787 when Smith was sixty-four and ill. Medallions were typically modeled from wax, so this one is presumed to be accurate. As Royal Economic Society cataloger James Bonar described it, "The head, which appears turned in pure profile to the right of the spectator, shows a particularly full forehead, a full nose, slightly aquiline in its curve; a long thin upper lip and a lower lip that protrudes a little; and a firm, well-shaped chin and jaw. The eyebrow is strongly curved, the upper eyelid heavy and drooping, the eyeball particularly prominent; and beneath the lower eyelid the skin is loose and wrinkled. A wig is worn, tied behind in a bag with ribbons, showing small curls in front, and two large curls at the side which cover and conceal the ear." Smith admitted to a friend: "I am a beau in nothing but my books."

Writing was always difficult for Smith. The bookish bachelor wrote with a "schoolboy hand," laboriously forming and then connecting big, round letters. Composition was just as difficult. Smith wrestled with a few big ideas for decades and agonized over how to express himself. *The Wealth of Nations* was at least twenty-seven years in the making.

Biographer Ian Simpson Ross noted "his harsh voice with an almost stammering impediment, and a conversational style that amounted to lecturing. His friends understood this, and made allowances for his disposition. . . . What shines through all accounts of his character and characteristics, particularly as they were displayed in his relationships with young people, was his essential kindness."

IT IS NOT KNOWN exactly when Adam Smith was born, but he was baptized on June 5, 1723, in Kirkaldy, a small fishing village on Scotland's east coast. His house is no longer there, but some of the garden, which goes down to the sea, survives. Smith's father, a customs official also named Adam, died several months before he was born. The youngster was raised by his mother, Margaret Douglas, daughter of a landowner. All we know about his childhood was that at age four, he was briefly abducted by a band of gypsies. "He would have made, I fear, a poor gypsy," wrote biographer John Rae.

Smith entered Glasgow University at age fourteen, the customary age for enrollment. Glasgow, a town of twenty-five thousand, prospered largely as an entrepôt for American tobacco, and this commerce stimulated intellectual life; the Scottish Enlightenment was in full flower. Glasgow University was famed for its teaching. Professors were compensated directly by student fees and had an incentive to perform well. Smith studied with moral philosopher Francis Hutcheson, a forceful character who broke with the tradition and delivered his lectures in English instead of Latin. Hutcheson expressed a passion for reason, liberty, and free speech, inspiring Smith. It seems to have been Hutcheson who brought his bright student to the attention of the controversial rationalist philosopher David Hume; Smith and Hume were to become best friends. To be sure, Smith was his own man, disagreeing with Hutcheson on some key issues. Hutcheson, for example, believed that self-love was a bad thing and that only well-intended actions were virtuous. As

Smith wrote later, "The habits of economy, industry, discretion, attention and application of thought, are generally supposed to be cultivated from self-interested motives, and at the same time are apprehended to be very praise-worthy qualities which deserve the esteem and approbation of every body."

Smith was a remarkably perceptive person who spent years in a thriving commercial center and must have learned much from his own observations. Smith scholar Edwin Canaan thought that the Dutch doctor Bernard Mandeville probably influenced Smith's thinking, too, with his provocative satire, *The Fable of the Bees: or Private Vices, Public Benefits* (expanded edition, 1729), in which he scandalized high-minded folks by suggesting that self-interest is good because it leads people to serve each other and help society prosper.

Smith wanted to teach at a Scottish university, and the traditional method of seeking a professorship was to show what one could do: deliver some public lectures. If university officials were impressed and needed to fill an opening, he might be appointed. Accordingly, in 1748, in Edinburgh, Smith began delivering lectures about ethics, economics, and defense policy. He was to spend the rest of his life expanding this material into books.

As early as 1749—before major works of the French laissez-faire economists were published—Smith had concluded that the way to promote prosperity is for governments to leave people alone. Dugald Stewart, a student of his, reported that in a lecture that year, Smith declared, "Little else is required to carry a state to the highest degree of affluence from the lowest barbarism but peace, easy taxes, and a tolerable administration of justice; all the rest being brought about by the natural course of things. All governments which thwart this natural course, which force things into another channel, or which endeavor to arrest the progress of society at a particular point . . . are obliged to be oppressive and tyrannical."

Smith's lectures were well received, and by 1751, he was teaching logic at Glasgow University. A year later, he was asked to teach moral philosophy there. Five times a week at 7:30 A.M., he delivered an hour-long lecture. Three days a week at 11:00 A.M., he taught private classes. He seemed to have won the respect of students and faculty alike, because in 1758 he was named dean. Recalled one of his students, James Boswell, later a famous literary biographer: "Mr. Smith's sentiments are striking, profound and beautiful. He has nothing of that stiffness and pedantry which is too often found in professors."

Evenings, Smith played whist and chatted with some of Scotland's brightest minds. These included David Hume, steam engine inventor James Watt, and chemist Joseph Black. Smith also participated in a discussion club that was started in the 1740s by banker Andrew Cochrane and met weekly to talk about economic and political issues. Smith didn't have much luck with the ladies, however; he proposed marriage two or three times but was rejected.

Meanwhile, Smith spent four years transforming lecture material into his first book, *The Theory of Moral Sentiments,* which was about motivations other than self-interest that influenced human behavior. Published in London in 1759, it made him a literary celebrity, and he dined with all kinds of interesting people, including Benjamin Franklin.

In *The Theory of Moral Sentiments,* Smith announced his next project: "I shall in another discourse endeavour to give an account of the general principles of law and government, and of the different revolutions they have undergone in the different ages and periods of society, not only in what concerns justice, but in what concerns policy revenue and arms, and whatever else is the object of law." That project was *The Wealth of Nations.*

Hume sent a copy of *The Theory of Moral Sentiments* to the English statesman Charles Townshend, the colonial minister who earned notoriety for depriving the American colonies of cherished prerogatives and unintentionally provoking the revolutionary movement. Townshend wanted someone distinguished to tutor his stepson, Henry Scott, the duke of Buccleugh, and agreed to pay Smith about three times more than Smith got from the University of Glasgow for giving the duke a grand tour of Europe. Moreover, Smith got a generous annual pension for life. Smith met the duke in London in January 1764 and from there traveled to Toulouse, a resort town popular among the English. In Toulouse, Smith acquired another young charge, the duke's younger brother, Hew Campbell Scott.

Although Smith's tutoring deal might seem to have interrupted his studies, it offered him two unexpected opportunities. First, for anyone interested in liberty, France was an ideal destination at that time. Smith saw firsthand how the French were struggling with a much more costly interventionist government than he had experienced. He visited with leading intellectual rebels and then went to Geneva, where he met Voltaire, who reportedly declared, "This Smith is an excellent man!" Back in Paris, Smith visited François Quesnay, founder of the physiocratic school of laissez-faire economics, and got to know Jacques Turgot, who put laissez-faire principles into action. Smith remarked that the French laissez-faire philosophy, "with all its imperfections, is perhaps the nearest approximation to the truth that has yet been published upon the subject of political economy, and is, upon that account, well worth the consideration of every man who wishes to examine with attention the principles of that very important science."

While he was in Toulouse, Smith became bored and restless and resolved to pursue the project he had described five years earlier in *The Theory of Moral Sentiments.* On July 5, 1764, he wrote to Hume, "I have begun to write a book in order to pass away the time." Thus began his initial draft of *The Wealth of Nations.*

Smith's European stay ended abruptly after Hew Scott was murdered in Paris in October 1766. Smith and the duke returned to London, and Smith turned to revising *The Theory of Moral Sentiments*. Then he made his way back to Kirkaldy, where, living with his mother, he worked on *The Wealth of Nations*. "My business here is Study," he wrote. "My Amusements are long, solitary walks by the Sea side. . . . I feel myself, however, extremely happy, comfortable and contented. I never was, perhaps, more so in all my life."

By 1770, Smith had plunged into laborious revisions. During 1773, he added important material on rent, wages, and the American colonies. In April he moved to London so he could consult more research materials. He pored through documents at the British Museum and worked on revisions at the British Coffee-House, where many Scottish artists and intellectuals gathered. His weekly dining club at the coffee house, which included portrait painter Joshua Reynolds and architect Robert Adam, among others, discussed and criticized each new chapter. Smith's friend Adam Ferguson, in the fourth edition of his *History of Civil Society*, alerted readers to what was coming: "The public will probably soon be furnished (by Mr. Smith, author of *The Theory of Moral Sentiments*) with a theory of national economy equal to what has ever appeared on any subject of science whatever."

Finally, on March 9, 1776, *The Wealth of Nations* was published by the firm Strahan and Cadell. It was two nine- by twelve-inch volumes, and over a thousand pages. Smith was fifty-three. Biographer Ross reported that "publication . . . was timed to seize Parliament's attention, and influence members to support a peaceful resolution of the [American] conflict. America offered a major point of application for free-market theory, and if Smith could win supporters, there was some hope of ending the cycle of violence induced by efforts to preserve the old colonial system involving economic restraints and prohibitions."

Smith's painstaking revisions paid off, because the book reads as if he were speaking to his readers across a table, explaining clearly what makes an economy tick. "It is not from the benevolence of the butcher, the brewer, or the baker that we expect our dinner," he wrote, "but from their regard to their own interest. We address ourselves, not to their humanity but to their self-love, and never talk to them of our own necessities but of their advantages."

Again and again, Smith presented a stalwart defense of private individuals against rapacious politicians—for example: "It is the highest impertinence and presumption, therefore, in kings and ministers, to pretend to watch over the economy of private people, and to restrain their expense, either by sumptuary laws, or by prohibiting the importation of foreign luxuries. They are themselves, always, and without any exception, the greatest spendthrifts in the society. Let them look well after their own expense, and they may safely trust private people with theirs. If their own extravagance does not ruin the state, that of their subjects never will."

The Wealth of Nations conveyed a keen appreciation for the way a free society works best. Smith's most famous lines are these: "[A typical investor] intends only his own security; and by directing that industry in such a manner as its produce may be of the greatest value, he intends only his own gain, and he is in this, as in many other cases, led by an invisible hand to promote an end which was no part of his intention. Nor is it always the worse for the society that it was no part of it. By pursuing his own interest he frequently promotes that of the society more effectually than when he really intends to promote it. I have never known much good done by those who affect to trade for the public good."

The first reactions came from his friends who had seen the book evolve. David Hume, for example, wrote on April 1, 1776: "I am much pleas'd with your Performance." And historian Edward Gibbon wrote to Adam Ferguson: "What an excellent work is that with which our common friend Mr. Adam Smith has enriched the public! An extensive science in a single book, and the most profound ideas expressed in the most perspicuous language." Thomas Jefferson was enthusiastic, saying that on the subject of money and commerce, "Smith's Wealth of Nations is the best book to be read."

The first printing sold out in six months and made Smith a sensation. A German edition appeared in 1776, a Danish edition in 1779, an Italian edition in 1780, and a French edition in 1781. The Spanish Inquisition suppressed the book for what officials considered "the lowness of its style and the looseness of its morals."

Smith had no sooner finished the book than he began revising it. New English editions appeared in 1778, 1784, 1786, and 1789. Smith had time for little else. With a mischevious flash of humor, referring to his well-known absent-mindedness, he told his London publisher in 1780: "I had almost forgot that I was the author of the inquiry concerning the Wealth of Nations."

The duke of Buccleuch was thrilled with Smith's success and pulled strings to get his former tutor appointed commissioner of customs, a lucrative, though not very demanding, position, which Smith accepted. He also gathered material and made notes for a history of philosophy and a history of law and government, but he proceeded slowly, as he had with his other projects, and this work was doomed by his failing health. Smith died quietly at his Kirkaldy home on July 17, 1790, and was buried in the Cannongate cemetery. As he had asked, his executors Joseph Black and James Hutton burned almost all his papers, frustrating generations of biographers.

Smith's work lived on, and he became a guiding light whose love of liberty helped make the nineteenth century the most peaceful period in modern history. Now, some two hundred years after Smith's death, economists have identified technical errors in his work, yet his reputation still towers over seductive challengers like Karl Marx and John Maynard Keynes. Nobel laureate George Stigler dubbed Smith "the patron saint of free enterprise." H. L. Mencken declared, "There is no more engrossing book in the English language than Adam Smith's 'The Wealth of Nations.'" He is a major presence as liberty is being reborn at the dawn of the twenty-first century.

FREEDOM FROM PLUNDER

FRÉDÉRIC BASTIAT RANKS among the most spirited defenders of economic freedom and international peace. Nobel laureate F. A. Hayek called him "a publicist of genius." The great Austrian economist Ludwig von Mises saluted his "immortal contributions." Best-selling journalist Henry Hazlitt marveled at Bastiat's "uncanny clairvoyance." And intellectual historian Murray N. Rothbard noted that "Bastiat was indeed a lucid and superb writer, whose brilliant and witty essays and fables to this day are remarkable and devastating demolitions of protectionism and of all forms of government subsidy and control."

Bastiat explained the apparent miracle of free market prosperity: "Here are a million human beings who would all die in a few days if supplies of all sorts did not flow into [Paris]. . . . It staggers the imagination to try to comprehend the vast multiplicity of objects that must pass through its gates tomorrow, if its inhabitants are to be preserved from the horrors of famine, insurrection, and pillage. And yet all are sleeping peacefully at this moment, without being disturbed for a single instant by the idea of so frightful a prospect. . . . What, then, is the resourceful and secret power that governs the amazing regularity of such complicated movements, a regularity in which everyone has such implicit faith, although his prosperity and his very life depend upon it? That power is an *absolute principle*, the principle of free exchange. We put our faith in that inner light which Providence has placed in the hearts of all men, and to which has been entrusted the preservation and the unlimited improvement of our species, a light we term *self-interest*, which is so illuminating, so constant, and so penetrating, when it is left free of every hindrance."

Bastiat's work offers an enormous wealth of such insights. "The state is the great fictitious entity by which everyone seeks to live at the expense of everyone else," he wrote. "Nothing enters the public treasury for the benefit of a citizen or a class unless other citizens and other classes have been forced to put it there . . . Heavy government expenditures and liberty are incompatible. . . . To be free, on one's own responsibility, to think and to act, to speak and to write, to labor and to exchange, to teach and to learn—this alone is to be free." He helped keep alive a vision of natural rights, inspired his compatriots, and won new converts. He reached out to free trade crusader Richard Cobden in England, and he inspired John Prince Smith who launched the free trade movement in Germany. His influence extended into Belgium, Italy, Spain, and Sweden as well.

"With his long hair, his small hat, his large frock coat and his family umbrella," his friend Gustave de Molinari recalled in 1845, he could have been easily mistaken for an honest peasant who had come to Paris for the first time to see the sights of the city." Another friend, Louis Reybaud, added, "There was a natural dignity of deportment and flashes of a keen intelligence, and one quickly discovered an honest heart and a generous soul. His eyes, especially, were lighted up with singular brightness and fire."

Biographer George Roche noted that "the Bastiat of 1848 was far more cosmopolitan, arriving dressed in the styles of the time. More important, though his emaciated face and hollow voice betrayed the ravages of disease within him, there was something about the glitter of his dark eyes which made immediately clear to all his associates that Bastiat now possessed both the worldly experience of Parisian society and a strong sense of mission."

CLAUDE FRÉDÉRIC BASTIAT was born on June 30, 1801, in Bayonne, a seaport in the Landes in southwestern France. His father, Pierre, worked with the family banking and export firm, which did business in Spain and Portugal. His mother, Marie-Julie Frechou, died when he was seven. After his father died two years later, he lived with his aunt Justine Bastiat and paternal grandfather Pierre Bastiat. They sent him to schools in Bayonne, and then to the Benedictine college of Soreze, which attracted students throughout Europe and America, contributed to his cosmopolitan outlook. While there, he learned English, Italian, and Spanish. He left at age seventeen to join his uncle Henry de Monclar in the family business, where he observed the civilizing influence of commerce and the many ways that laws hurt people. He noted, for instance, that the 1816 French tariff throttled trade, resulting in empty warehouses and idle docks.

Bastiat explored books about political economy, as economics was called then. "I have read the *Traite d'Economie Politique* by Jean Baptiste Say, an excellent and methodical study," he wrote a friend. Say had read Adam Smith's *Wealth of Nations* while working for a Paris insurance company. The book thrilled him, and he resolved to learn more about how an economy works. His own first literary work was a 1789 pamphlet defending freedom of the press. Then he cofounded a republican periodical, *La Décade philosophique,* and it published many of his articles about economic liberty.

The *Traite d'Economie Politique,* Say's major work, appeared in 1803 and reintroduced free market views to France and Europe generally. Before the French Revolution, Jacques Turgot and the other intellectuals known as physiocrats had done much to promote economic liberty—and made the phrase *laissez-faire* a battle cry—but these intellectuals accepted royal absolutism. Moreover, they believed land was the primary source of wealth, which seemed to mean support for the landholding aristocracy. These were major reasons that free market views fell out of fashion after the French Revolution. As a republican, Say was in a position to help convince future generations about the importance of economic liberty. "He held that the most productive economy must rest on private property, private enterprise, and private initiatives," noted historian Robert R. Palmer in his recent intellectual biography of Say.

Say discarded Smith's labor theory of value, insisting that value was determined by customers and recognizing the creative role of entrepreneurs. He also rejected the dark pessimism of English economist Robert Malthus who feared that population growth would outstrip the capacity of private food producers. Say believed free markets could achieve unlimited progress. He viewed taxation as theft and condemned wild government spending, military conscription, and slavery ("the most shameful traffic in which human beings have ever engaged"). After Say's book was censored, he started a cotton spinning mill that eventually employed more than four hundred people. Later, he became a professor at the Collège de France, and Thomas Jefferson reportedly hoped he would teach at the University of Virginia. English philosopher and economist John Stuart Mill, who met Say in Paris, called him "the ideal type of French republican." From Say, Bastiat learned that economic liberty works better than government interference with the economy. Say's experience also suggested to Bastiat that he might do good by popularizing fundamental principles.

In 1824, Bastiat dreamed of going to Paris and somehow making a difference, but his ailing grandfather persuaded him to live on the 617-acre family property near the small town of Mugron. When his grandfather died the following year, he inherited the property. Bastiat spent most of his time with books. He came across a copy of *Poor Richard's Almanack* in 1827 and wrote to a friend, "I have discovered a real treasure—a small volume of the moral and political philosophy of Franklin. I am so enthusiastic about his style that I intend to adopt it as my own."

Around 1830, Bastiat decided "I would like a wife." He married one Marie Hiard, but, as biographer Louis Baudin noted, "he left the bride at the church after the wedding and continued to live as a bachelor." Nevertheless, a son was born, though his wife continued to live with her parents.

While going through some London newspapers, Bastiat was thrilled to read that textile entrepreneurs Richard Cobden and John Bright had led the Anti-Corn-Law League, a crusade for free trade. Bastiat began gathering material for a book on the league and started corresponding with Cobden. In

July, he crossed the English Channel to visit Cobden and Bright. According to biographer John Morley, Bastiat's "admiration for Cobden as a public leader grew into hearty affection for him as a private friend, and this friendship became one of the chief delights of the few busy years of life that remained to him."

Bastiat's book *Cobden et la Ligue* (1845) scooped all other French journalists. He was the first Frenchman to talk about Cobden and Bright, who persuaded Parliament to abolish grain tariffs unilaterally without demanding "concessions" from any nation, including France, which had fought England through many bitter wars. Cobden and Bright had presented a compelling case that free trade would benefit England, especially poor people who needed access to cheap food, even if other nations kept their trade restrictions. Moreover, they maintained, unilateral free trade would contribute to international peace by taking politics out of trade, reducing the risk that economic disputes might escalate into military conflicts.

Bastiat wrote a series of articles for *Journal des économistes*, attacking the fallacies of protectionism (tariffs) and explaining how free trade raises living standards and promotes peace and national security. He gathered twenty-two of his lucid, dramatic, insightful, and often amusing essays in a book, *Sophismes économiques* (*Economic Sophisms*), which appeared in late 1845. A second volume of seventeen essays appeared three years later. Both were translated into English and Italian.

Bastiat's most famous piece was "A Petition" (1845), a satire in which candlemakers appealed to the French Chamber of Deputies for protection: "We are suffering from the ruinous competition of a foreign rival who apparently works under conditions so far superior to our own for the production of light that he is flooding the domestic market with it at an incredibly low price; for the moment he appears, our sales cease, all the consumers turn to him." The rival was the sun, and the petition pleaded for "a law requiring the closing of all windows, dormers, skylights, inside and outside shutters, curtains, casements, bull's eyes, deadlights, and blinds . . . through which the light of the sun is wont to enter houses."

Mindful that the English free trade movement had been launched in a regional city, Manchester, Bastiat helped form the Association bordelaise pour la liberté des échanges (Bordeaux Association for Free Trade) on February 23, 1846. Cobden had gone national after a regional free trade association was under way, and Bastiat adopted the same strategy. He went to Paris and launched the Association pour la liberté des échanges (Free Trade Association) on May 10, 1846, with Michel Chevalier, Charles Dunoyer, Gustave de Molinari, and Jean Baptiste Say's son, Horace. On August 18, they kicked off their campaign with a dinner featuring Cobden and held a succession of public meetings at Montesquieu Hall in Paris.

On November 29, Bastiat began publishing *Le Libre-Echange*, a four- to eight-page weekly free trade newspaper. He wrote, "We demand for all of our fellow citizens, not only freedom to work but also freedom to exchange the fruits of their work." In 1847, French protectionists defeated a bill that would have abolished about half of French tariffs, and free traders never recovered. *Le Libre Echange* ceased publication after the April 16, 1848, issue.

Bastiat nevertheless was an inspiration for people who organized free trade associations in Belgium, Italy, and Spain, and he had an impact on intellectuals in Germany too. The Englishman John Prince Smith, who had gone to Prussia and become a citizen, was influenced by Bastiat and launched the German free trade movement. As historian Ralph Raico noted, Prince Smith worked at "disseminating good translations of the works of Frédéric Bastiat and in gathering about him a circle of like-minded enthusiasts."

By this time, reform of the corrupt French government had become the hottest political issue, and the situation reached a climax on February 21, 1848, when National Guards shot about twenty republican demonstrators in Paris. The city exploded into revolution, the king abdicated three days later, and the Chamber of Deputies proclaimed France a republic. Ten republican leaders, including the socialist Louis Blanc, headed a provisional government, which demanded nationalization of industry and other schemes. Amid the upheaval, Bastiat published about a dozen issues of *La République française*, a two-page periodical defending libertarian principles, and produced articles for a dozen newspapers and journals about the fallacies of socialism. He ridiculed claims that government could increase the number of productive jobs: "The state opens a road, builds a palace, repairs a street, digs a canal; with these projects it gives jobs to certain workers. *That is what is seen.* But it deprives certain other laborers of employment. *That is what is not seen.* . . . Do millions of francs descend miraculously on a moonbeam into the coffers of [politicians]? For the process to be complete, does not the state have to organize the collection of funds as well as their expenditure? Does it not have to get its tax collectors into the country and its taxpayers to make their contributions?"

When, in the name of compassion, socialists demanded more powerful government, Bastiat fired away with tough questions: "Is there in the heart of man only what the legislator has put there? Did fraternity have to make its appearance on earth by way of the ballot box? Are we to believe that women will cease to be self-sacrificing and that pity will no longer find a place in their hearts because self-sacrifice and pity will not be commanded by the law?" And he warned that socialism must mean slavery because the state "will be the arbiter, the master, of all destinies. It will take a great deal; hence, a great deal will remain for itself. It will multiply the number of its agents; it will enlarge the scope of its prerogatives; it will end by acquiring overwhelming proportions."

Even before it had finished drafting a new constitution, the Constituent Assembly decided that France must have a strong president. Their choice in December 1848 was Louis Napoleon Bonaparte, who mainly traded on his name as conqueror Napoleon Bonaparte's nephew. The Constituent Assembly concluded its business in May 1849 and was succeeded by the Legislative Assembly. Bastiat was elected a deputy. He urged lower government spending, lower taxes, and free trade and again and again voted to defend civil liberties.

In June 1850, Bastiat returned to Mugron and produced his most beloved work, *The Law*, which affirmed natural rights philosophy, the most powerful intellectual defense of liberty. "It is not because men have passed laws that personality, liberty, and property exist," he declared. "On the contrary, it is because personality, liberty, and property already exist that men make laws. . . . Each of us certainly gets from Nature, from God, the right to defend his person, his liberty, and his property." Bastiat went on to attack what he called "legal plunder"—laws that exploit some people to benefit powerful interest groups. Once again Bastiat demonstrated vivid understanding of what socialism was all about: "Socialists consider mankind as raw material to be fitted into various social molds . . . inert matter, receiving from the power of the government life, organization, morality and wealth." In *The Law*, Bastiat celebrated "liberty, whose name alone has the power to stir all hearts and set the world to shaking . . . freedom of conscience, of education, of association, of the press, of movement, of labor, of exchange; in other words, the freedom of everyone to use all his faculties in a peaceful way."

Bastiat plunged into his next work, *Les Harmonies économiques (Economic Harmonies)*. He expanded on a cherished theme: that free people cooperate peacefully and gain the benefits of voluntary exchange. "Men's interests," he wrote, "left to themselves, tend to form harmonious combinations and to work together for progress and the general good." Yet he was pessimistic:"We see plunder usurping the citizens' liberty in order the more readily to exploit their wealth, and draining off their substance the better to conquer their liberty. . . . A stupid and vexatious bureaucracy swarms over the land." The first volume of *Harmonies économiques* was published in late 1850. He never finished the work.

By August 1850, Bastiat's tuberculosis worsened. He wrote to Cobden lamenting "these unfortunate lungs, which are to me very capricious servants." Doctors soon ordered Bastiat to Rome, where they heard someone had a cure. On December 24, 1850, Bastiat was fading. He uttered two words, *la verité* ("the truth"), and took his last breath a few minutes after five in the afternoon. His cousin, the priest Eugène de Monclar, was at his side. He was only forty-nine. Two days later, there was a funeral service at Rome's Saint-Louis des Français church, and he was buried in its cemetery.

Michel Chevalier gained influence in the French government and used it to promote free trade. In 1859, he and Cobden began negotiating a significant trade liberalization treaty between their respective countries that abolished all French import prohibitions and cut many tariffs. France went on to liberalize trade with Austria-Hungary, German states, Italy, Norway, Portugal, Spain, Sweden, and Switzerland.

Bastiat's seven-volume *Oeuvres complètes* (*Complete Works*) appeared between 1861 and 1864. There continued to be French interest in classical liberalism, as evidenced by a succession of books about Bastiat: A. B. Belle's *Bastiat et le Libre-Echange* (*Bastiat and Free Trade*, 1878), Edouard Bondurand's *Frédéric Bastiat* (1879), Alphonse Courtois' *Journal des Economistes* (1888), A. D. Fouville's *Frédéric Bastiat* (1888), C. H. Brunel's *Bastiat et la réaction contre le pessimisme économique* (*Bastiat and the Reaction Against Pessimistic Economics*, 1901), and G. de Nouvion's *Frédéric Bastiat, Sa Vie, Ses Oeuvres, Ses Doctrines* (*Frederic Bastiat, His Life, Work and Doctrines*, 1905). The glorious French laissez-faire tradition passed into history with the death of Bastiat's friend Gustave de Molinari on January 28, 1912, although he influenced American individualists like Benjamin Tucker whose radical ideas persist to this day.

Most twentieth-century academics banished Bastiat's name from serious discussion. Intellectual historian Joseph Schumpeter, for instance, wrote, "I do not hold that Bastiat was a bad theorist, I hold that he was no theorist." In their *History of Economic Doctrines*, Charles Gide and Charles Rist remarked that "it is easy to laugh . . . and to show that such supposed harmony of interests between men does not exist."

A few scholars nevertheless acknowledged Bastiat's contributions. Economist John A. Hobson called him "the most brilliant exponent of the sheer logic of Free Trade in this or any other country," and respected economic historian John H. Clapham hailed Bastiat for "the best series of popular free trade arguments ever written." The scholarly eleventh edition of the *Encyclopedia Britannica* (1913) offered these stirring words: "He alone fought socialism hand to hand, body to body, as it were . . . taking it as actually presented by its most popular representatives, considering patiently their proposals and arguments, and proving conclusively that they proceeded on false principles. . . . Nowhere will reason find a richer armoury of weapons available against socialism than in the pamphlets published by Bastiat."

Leonard E. Read, who established the Foundation for Economic Education in 1946, resolved to make Bastiat's work better known and persuaded scholar Dean Russell to prepare a new translation of *The Law*. Over the years, it has reportedly sold several hundred thousand copies. Russell went on to earn his Ph.D. under free market economist Wilhelm Röpke at the University of Geneva, writing his dissertation on Bastiat. Russell adapted this into *Frédéric Bastiat: Ideas and Influence* (1965).

Meanwhile, *New York Times* editorial writer Henry Hazlitt produced the million-copy best-seller *Economics in One Lesson* (1946). "My greatest debt," Hazlitt acknowledged, "is Frédéric Bastiat's essay, 'What Is Seen and What Is Not Seen,' now nearly a century old. The present work may, in fact, be regarded as a modernization, extension and generalization of the approach found in Bastiat's pamphlet."

That frail Frenchman, whose public career spanned just six years, belittled as a mere popularizer and dismissed as an ideologue, turns out to have seen our future. Even before Karl Marx began scribbling *The Communist Manifesto* in December 1847, Bastiat knew that socialism is doomed. Marx called for a vast expansion of government power to seize privately owned land, banks, railroads, and schools, but Bastiat correctly warned that government power is a mortal enemy. Prosperity everywhere, he declared, is the work of free people. He was right. He maintained that the only meaningful way to secure peace is to secure human liberty. Bastiat took the lead. He stood alone when he had to, displayed a generous spirit, shared epic insights, gave wings to ideas, and committed his life for liberty.

A FREE CIVILIZATION

THOMAS BABINGTON MACAULAY ranks among the most eloquent of all authors on liberty. In terms of the sheer quantity and range of eloquence, perhaps only Thomas Jefferson soared to such breathtaking heights.

Macaulay's essays and *History of England* had an enormous sale during the nineteenth century. When English emigrants left for far corners of the world, they invariably brought with them three essentials of civilization: the Bible, Shakespeare, and Macaulay. His work was even more popular in America than England, and it was translated into nine languages. Nobel laureate F. A. Hayek observed that "it is doubtful whether any historical work of our time has had a circulation or direct influence comparable with, say, Macaulay's *History of England.*"

Throughout his life, Macaulay expressed a sincere, exuberant, unwavering love for liberty. He called for the abolition of slavery, advocated repeal of laws against Jews, defended freedom of the press, spoke out for free trade and the free movement of people, celebrated the achievements of free markets, and rejected government excuses for suspending civil liberties. He wrote "There is only one cure for the evils which newly acquired freedom produces; and that cure is freedom." Macaulay believed women should be able to have property in their own name, and he insisted liberty is impossible without secure private property—"that great institution to which we owe all knowledge, all commerce, all industry, all civilization."

Macaulay recognized evil much more clearly than did sophisticated philosophers of his century and ours. He thundered against "profuse expenditures, heavy taxation, absurd commercial restrictions, corrupt tribunals, disastrous wars, seditions, persecutions." He recognized the twisted logic of those who claimed that more government interference in the economy would make life better: "The calamities arising from the collection of wealth in the hands of a few capitalists are to be remedied by collecting it in the hands of one great capitalist, who has no conceivable motive to use it better than other capitalists, the all-devouring state."

Back when historians focused on political history (mainly the story of rulers), Macaulay pioneered economic history and social history (the story of ordinary people). He inspired generations of historians to chronicle struggles for liberty.

It has long been fashionable to sneer at him as a superficial materialist, but that line is just a smokescreen. Socialists, Marxists, and other critics certainly did not consider living standards unimportant. Rather, they claimed that liberty led to people being exploited in wretched factories and that government intervention was needed to set things right. What critics couldn't bear was Macaulay's confidence that free markets were a blessing for millions who would have starved in rural squalor without privately owned businesses.

Macaulay has been derided as a shill for Whig aristocrats, yet he had commoner origins and earned a livelihood from his pen. At one point, he was so strapped for cash that he sold a gold medal he had won at Cambridge. After his father's business went broke, he helped pay off the creditors and provided support for his younger siblings and aging parents. He paid all bills within twenty-four hours. "I think that prompt payment is a moral duty," he remarked, "knowing, as I do, how painful it is to have such things deferred." When Macaulay had little money, he resigned political office rather than compromise his principles.

Macaulay's most severe critics were the enemies of civilization. Karl Marx dismissed him as a "Scottish sycophant." Thomas Carlyle called him an author without "the slightest tincture of greatness." This was the Carlyle who attacked another author as "a slimy and greasy Jew" and derided abolitionists as "Nigger-Philanthropists." Historian A. J. P. Taylor observed that "those who criticize Macaulay either do not care about liberty, or they think it can take care of itself. Macaulay was a good deal more sensible. Not only did he regard liberty as supremely important; he knew that it needs ceaseless defending."

Macaulay was an inviting target because of his popularity as one of the supreme masters of the English language. He was lucid and clear, and he told a compelling story, portraying unforgettable characters and offering striking illustrations drawn from his vast knowledge of history and literature. Taylor observed, "Start off on any page, in the middle of a paragraph, and it is impossible not to read on. . . . [Macaulay] remains the most readable of all historians." Lord Acton considered him "very nearly the greatest of English writers."

Winston Churchill was among those inspired by Macaulay. At age thirteen, Churchill memorized the twelve hundred lines of Macaulay's heroic poem, *Lays of Ancient Rome*. A little later, he was thrilled when a friend read to him aloud from Macaulay's *History of England*. At age twenty-three, Churchill read Macaulay's *History* and essays for himself—twelve volumes—and declared triumphantly; "Macaulay crisp and forcible." Churchill acknowledged that in his own writing, "I affected a combination of the style of Macaulay and Gibbon."

Macaulay was devoted to books and to his family, especially younger sisters Hannah and Margaret. When he was in his mid-thirties, he despaired that "I never formed any serious attachment—any attachment which could possibly end in marriage." Following Margaret's death at twenty-two from scarlet fever, Macaulay spent considerable time with Hannah, her husband, Charles Trevelyan, and their son, George Otto Trevelyan. In 1876, George repaid his uncle's affection by writing an impassioned biography of him.

Macaulay spoke rapidly in a loud voice without much variety of intonation, yet his considerable knowledge and elegant phrases caused a stir in Parliament. "It was little wonder," reported biographer Richmond Beatty, "that, almost from his first speech in the House, something resembling a rush from the smoking rooms to the benches took place whenever it was whispered that Mr. Macaulay was on his legs."

Apparently Macaulay was not much to look at—short, stout, large gray eyes, sandy hair, an expansive forehead, and a wide mouth. Charles Fulke Greville, a Tory diarist, recalled his astonishment: "The ugliness and ungainless of his appearance; not a ray of intellect beams from his countenance; a lump of more ordinary clay never enclosed a powerful mind and lively imagination. . . . It was MACAULAY, the man I had been so long most curious to see and to hear, whose genius, eloquence, astonishing knowledge, and diversified talents have excited my wonder and admiration for such a length of time."

THOMAS BABINGTON MACAULAY was born at his uncle's mansion, Rothley Temple, in Leicestershire, England, on October 25, 1800. He was the eldest of nine children. His mother, Selina Mills, was the daughter of a Quaker bookseller. His father, Zachary Macaulay, was a stern evangelical crusader against slavery.

Tom was a precocious child. With little encouragement, he began reading widely at around age three. At seven, he wrote a "Compendium of World History" in which, among other things, he called Puritan dictator Oliver Cromwell "an unjust and wicked man." In October 1818 he enrolled at Trinity College, Cambridge University, where he deepened his knowledge of the classics and apparently studied law. He became an eager debater in the Cambridge Union, on such issues as free trade, Catholic emancipation, and Greek independence and he wrote essays and poems for *Knight's Quarterly.* In his November 1824 review of William Mitford's *History of Greece,* he first expressed his view that historians should focus not just on rulers but on the lives of ordinary people and factors that contribute to "the strength, the wisdom, the freedom, and the glory, of the western world."

In June 1824, Macaulay first caused a stir as a public speaker by appearing before the annual meeting of the London Anti-Slavery Society. Among those attending were William Wilberforce, who had led the English antislavery movement for nearly three decades; Henry Brougham, a leading Whig reformer; and Daniel O'Connell, the Irish patriot. Published excerpts suggest

Macaulay's trademark eloquence: "The peasant of the Antilles will no longer crawl in listless and trembling dejection round a plantation from whose fruits he must derive no advantage, and a hut whose door yields him no protection; but when his cheerful and voluntary labour is performed, he will return with the firm step and erect brow of a British citizen from the field which is his freehold to the cottage which is his castle."

Meanwhile, Francis Jeffrey, editor of the pro-liberty *Edinburgh Review*, England's leading journal of political opinion, invited Macaulay to write for him. In his first article, "The West Indies," published in January 1825, Macaulay attacked slavery and ridiculed the view that a colony could be a source of wealth, since they are costly to administer. A little-known essay that later was attributed to him was "Social and Industrial Capacities of Negroes," published in an 1827 *Edinburgh Review*. He attacked one Major Thomas Moody who had issued a British Colonial Office report claiming that blacks were inferior to whites. Macaulay explained that economics, not genetics, accounted for the apparent laziness of blacks, and he denounced the major's view that compulsion was needed to get work done.

In 1824, Utilitarians had started the *Westminster Review* to promote their views and challenge the influence of the *Edinburgh Review*. Jeffrey asked Macaulay to mount a counterattack, and his opening salvo appeared in the March 1929 issue. Two more essays followed, in the June 1829 and October 1829 *Edinburgh Review*. He attacked James Mill's "Essay on Government," written for the *Encyclopedia Britannica*, which claimed that a philosophy of government could be deduced from axioms about human nature. Macaulay expressed an empirical view that one must see what actually works.

Macaulay's most important political essay was "Southey's Colloquies" (January 1830), in which he emerged as perhaps the first and still the most eloquent defender of the Industrial Revolution. It had begun in England, which offered entrepreneurs a bigger free trade area, lower taxes, and more secure private property rights than countries in continental Europe. By creating factory jobs for poor people who did not have their own tools, the Industrial Revolution saved millions from starvation, especially children. But aristocrats were horrified as the people who worked their lands migrated to cities for factory work, so it was not surprising that Tories were the original critics of the Industrial Revolution. They promoted the dogma that the Industrial Revolution exploited people and harped on the alleged evils of children working in factories—as if children had not been working even longer hours on the farms. Often the alternative to factory work was starvation. The Tory dogma was later picked up by socialists.

Macaulay wrote, "People live longer because they are better fed, better lodged, better clothed, and better attended in sickness, and. . . . These improvements are, owing to that increase of national wealth which the manufacturing system has produced. . . . We see in almost every part of the annals of mankind how the industry of individuals, struggling up against wars, taxes, famines, conflagrations, mischievous prohibitions, and more mischievous protections, creates faster than any governments can squander, and repairs whatever invaders can destroy. We see the wealth of nations increasing, and all the arts of life approaching nearer and nearer to perfection, in spite of the grossest corruption and the wildest profusion on the part of rulers."

"It is not by the intermeddling of Mr. Southey's idol, the omniscient and omnipotent State," Macaulay insisted, "but by the prudence and energy of the people, that England has hitherto been carried forward in civilization; and it is to the same prudence and the same energy that we now look with comfort and good hope. Our rulers will best promote the improvement of the nation by strictly confining themselves to their own legitimate duties, by leaving capital to find its most lucrative course, commodities their fair price, industry and intelligence their natural reward, idleness and folly their natural punishment, by maintaining peace, by defending property, by diminishing the price of law, and by observing strict economy in every department of the state. Let the Government do this: the People will assuredly do the rest."

Altogether Macaulay wrote thirty-nine essays for the *Edinburgh Review*, the last appearing in 1844. "Macaulay," noted biographer and essayist John Morley, "had an intimate acquaintance both with imaginative literature and the history of Greece and Rome, with the literature and the history of modern Italy, of France, and of England. Whatever his special subject, he contrives to pour into it with singular dexterity a stream of rich, diversified sources. Figures from history, ancient and modern, sacred and secular; characters from plays and novels from Plautus down to Walter Scott and Jane Austen; images and similes from poets of every age and every nation. . . . All throng Macaulay's pages with the bustle and variety and animation of some glittering masque and cosmoramic revel of great books and heroical men. . . . His essays are as good as a library." Commenting on Macaulay's essays, historian John Clive referred to "the sheer pleasure of being a spectator at a literary fireworks display." Historian G. P. Gooch said that "if Macaulay did not invent the historical essay, he found it of brick and left it of marble."

The *Edinburgh Review* essays, especially Macaulay's attacks on Utilitarianism, enabled him to fulfill one of his ambitions; a seat in Parliament. The essays impressed the moderate Whig Lord Lansdowne who offered him a "pocket borough" he controlled in Calne. Macaulay, who accepted the seat in February 1830, played a key part promoting the Reform Act of 1832, which abolished pocket boroughs and extended the franchise to the middle class.

In Parliament, Macaulay contributed many of the most eloquent words ever spoken. For instance, on April 17, 1833, he spoke out for a bill to abolish laws against Jews. "Let us do justice to them," he pleaded. "Let us open to them every career in which ability and energy can be displayed. Till we have done this, let us not presume to say that there is no genius among the countrymen of Isaiah . . . [the] religion which first taught the human race the great lesson of universal charity."

Meanwhile, Parliament passed a law to reform the administration of India, and Macaulay was asked to take the lead. He sailed there with his sister Hannah in February 1834. At the time, the Indian Penal Code encompassed Hindu and Muslim law, variously interpreted in different regions of the country, overlaid with British East India Company regulations. Macaulay applied "the principle of suppressing crime with the smallest amount of suffering, and the principle of ascertaining the truth at the smallest possible cost of time and money." He established a rule of law for all races—that foreigners and natives alike were subject to the same rules—and he moved to eliminate what remained of slavery in India. He abolished laws censoring the press, limited the death penalty to treason and murder, and provided that women could own property. His Indian Penal Code was adopted in 1837, and its fundamentals endure in Indian law today.

By the time Macaulay returned to England in January 1838, he had decided to write a history of England from ancient times to the death of King William IV in 1837. "It will be my endeavor," he wrote, "to relate the history of the people as well as the history of the government, to trace the progress of the useful and ornamental arts, to describe the rise of religious sects and the changes in literary taste, to portray the manners of successive generations." Macaulay did a prodigious amount of research. He pored through archives in England and Holland, acquired a vast collection of document transcriptions from France, Spain, and the Papacy, and examined transcriptions of French diplomatic dispatches collected by Charles James Fox who had contemplated a history of late seventeenth-century England. Macaulay read diaries, pamphlets, broadsheets, ballads, and newspapers of the period. Novelist William Makepeace Thackeray marveled that he "reads twenty books to write a sentence; he travels a hundred miles to make a line of description."

He began writing on March 9, 1839, working in a suite of rooms on the second floor of the Albany, a building between Vigo Street and Picadilly, London, every room overflowed with books. He went through many drafts, struggling to achieve greater clarity and interest. "The great object is that, after all this trouble, they may read as if they had been spoken off, and may seem to flow as easily as table talk," Macaulay noted in his diary. "How little the art of making meaning pellucid is studied now. Hardly any popular writer, except myself, thinks of it. Many seem to aim at being obscure. Indeed they may be right enough in one sense; for many readers give credit for profundity to whatever is obscure, and call all that is perspicuous shallow."

Macaulay was not always fair in his judgments of people, but he soared to heights rarely seen in historical literature before or since. He explained that "the authority of law and the security of property were found to be compatible with a liberty of discussion and of individual action never before known; how, from the auspicious union of order and freedom, sprang a prosperity of which the annals of human affairs had furnished no example. . . . The history of our country during the last hundred and sixty years is eminently the history of physical, of moral, and of intellectual improvement. . . . We rejoice that we live in a merciful age, in an age in which cruelty is abhorred. . . . Every class doubtless has gained largely by this great moral change: but the class which has gained most is the poorest, the most dependent, and the most defenseless."

Macaulay's first two volumes were published on December 1, 1848, and they were an immediate hit. Within four months, some 13,000 copies were sold in Britain and about 100,000 in the United States. Two more volumes appeared on December 17, 1855. The *History* was translated into Bohemian, Danish, Dutch, French, German, Hungarian, Italian, Polish, and Spanish. After the third and fourth volumes sold 26,500 copies in ten weeks, Macaulay's publisher wrote him a check so large that it became a landmark in literary history.

As Macaulay focused more intently on his *History* and tired more easily because of a heart condition, he withdrew from London society, living with a butler at Holly Lodge, a villa between Palace Gardens and the Fox family's Holland House, in Campden Hill, London. In 1857, Prime Minister Henry Palmerston named him a peer—Baron Macaulay of Rothley.

On Wednesday morning, December 28, 1859, Macaulay dictated a letter accompanying a contribution to a poor clergyman. Sometime after seven that evening, he suffered a fatal heart attack while reading a book in his library easy chair. He was buried in Poets' Corner, Westminster Abbey.

A posthumously published fifth volume brought his *History* only up to the death of William III, in 1702. This work is a towering fragment that offers a glimpse of what might have been had Macaulay lived longer, but what he did do was awesome. His story of liberty, peace, and progress inspired readers for generations.

Intellectual trends ran against Macaulay as collectivism engulfed Europe, and his work was relentlessly attacked. Biographer Richmond Croom Beatty even blamed World War I on the libertarian philosophy that Macaulay expressed. Yet his influence persisted, and in 1931 Professor Herbert Butterfield issued a famous attack, *The Whig Interpretation of History*. Belittling tyranny, Butterfield denounced the Whig "division of mankind into good and evil."

Debate raged for decades about whether free markets promote human progress, and today Macaulay stands vindicated. Among the works that affirm his view are John H. Clapham's *An Economic History of Modern Britain* (1926), T. S. Ashton's *The Industrial Revolution* (1948), John U. Nef's *War and Human Progress* (1950), F. A. Hayek's *Capitalism and the Historians* (1954), William H. McNeill's *The Rise of the West* (1963), David S. Landes's *The Unbound Prometheus* (1969), Douglass North and Robert Thomas's *The Rise of the Western World* (1973), Fernand Braudel's *Civilization and Capitalism* (1979), Julian L. Simon's *The Ultimate Resource* (1981), Asa Briggs's *A Social History of England* (1983), J. M. Roberts's *The Triumph of the West* (1985), Nathan Rosenberg and L. E. Birdzell's *How the West Grew Rich* (1986), Rondo Cameron's *A Concise Economic History of the World* (1989), Joel Mokyr's *The Lever of Riches* (1990), and David S. Landes's *The Wealth and Poverty of Nations* (1998).

Macaulay was correct to insist that people thrive when they are free. He insisted that government intervention would make millions miserable—and it has. He believed that by telling a simple, stirring story in bold colors, he could help win the hearts of people—and he did. Long after the most fashionable pundits are forgotten, readers are still thrilled by Thomas Babington Macaulay's extraordinary eloquence for liberty.

SPONTANEOUS PROGRESS

FABLED STEEL ENTREPRENEUR Andrew Carnegie hungered to know the secret of human progress. During the early 1880s, he found out, after he joined a Manhattan discussion group. There he heard about British philosopher Herbert Spencer who had written volumes on the subject. Spencer explained that free markets—without government intervention—provide powerful incentives for people to improve life continuously.

Apparently Carnegie was overwhelmed to realize that his daily work served a larger purpose. He adopted as his motto, "All is well since all grows better." The more Carnegie read by Spencer, the more he wanted to meet the philosopher. "Few men have wished to know another man more strongly than I to know Herbert Spencer," Carnegie recalled. Through a mutual acquaintance, the British libertarian John Morley, he got a letter of introduction and traveled with Spencer on a steamship from Liverpool to New York.

Spencer, then in his sixties, was about five feet, ten inches tall and reasonably thin. Although his hairline had receded, his hair remained brown, and it fluffed out at the sides. He complained about his difficulty sleeping and suffered from nervous ailments. He was quick to criticize the work of others, and although he was sensitive to criticism himself, he remained honest enough to acknowledge his errors. He seemed unhappy living alone, as he lamented, "One who devotes himself to grave literature must be content to remain celibate; unless, indeed, he obtains a wife having adequate means for both. . . . Even then, family cares and troubles are likely to prove fatal to his undertakings."

In June 1891, Carnegie surprised Spencer by delivering a token of his appreciation. Spencer wrote to Carnegie, "I was alike astonished and perplexed on entering my room yesterday evening to see placed against the wall a magnificent grand piano. . . . I have all along sympathised in your view respecting the uses of wealth, but it never occurred to me that I should benefit by the carrying of your view into practice."

Carnegie was among the millions, then and now, inspired by Spencer. He revived the revolutionary battle cry for natural rights that had been trashed by British philosopher Jeremy Bentham and his followers, the Utilitarians. Spencer showed why the theory of evolution, which naturalist Charles Darwin documented, meant that human progress occurs spontaneously as long as people are free and governments stay out of the way. He stood as the most passionate defender of liberty when socialism and militarism gathered momentum throughout Europe.

Spencer was a prolific writer, producing books and articles on biology, education, ethics, psychology, sociology and government policy, among other subjects. He had a gifted pen—coining, for example, the phrase "survival of the fittest." From the 1860s until his death on December 8, 1903, authorized editions of Spencer's books reportedly sold 368,755 copies in the United States alone, a remarkable number for a serious author. Supreme Court Justice Oliver Wendell Holmes doubted that "any writer of English except Darwin has done so much to affect our whole way of thinking about the universe."

HERBERT SPENCER WAS born in Derby, England, on April 27, 1820. His father, George Spencer, struggled for years to develop a career. He repeatedly tried manufacturing lace, then fashionable, but failed and earned a little money teaching school. Friends suggested that he work at a tannery or become a clergyman. Spencer's mother, Harriet Holmes, did not have it any easier; although she gave birth to five boys and four girls, only Herbert survived beyond age two.

Spencer gained a fiercely independent mind from his parents, who were Quakers. "Individuality was pronounced in all members of the family," he recalled, "and pronounced individuality is necessarily more or less at variance with authority. A self-dependent and self-asserting nature resists all such government as is not expressive of equitable restraint." His formal education was quite limited. He spent three years in one elementary school and then, for an unknown (probably brief) time, he attended his uncle William's school and was intermittently tutored by his uncle Thomas, a clergyman. By age eleven, he seemed to be on his own, reportedly attending a science lecture. When his father was teaching physics and chemistry, the lad helped prepare experiments. He taught himself about plants and animals and became accomplished at sketching. He learned much by listening when friends of his parents visited to talk about politics, religion, science, and right and wrong. His father belonged to the Derby Philosophical Society, which had a modest library of science books and periodicals, and he browsed through those.

When Spencer was fifteen, his first article, about boats, was published in a little magazine. "I found *my article* looking very pretty," he noted at the time. "I began shouting and capering about the room. . . . And now that I have started I intend to go on writing things."

Meanwhile, Spencer needed steady pay. A railroad building boom was underway, and in November 1837, he secured a job producing engineering drawings for the London and Birmingham Railway. Ever resourceful, he invented several railroad-related measuring devices and wrote seven articles for *Civil Engineer's and Architect's Journal.* After four years, he had saved some money and decided to take time off to pursue a writing career. He attended meetings of free trade, antislavery, and antistate church groups, and wrote a dozen articles about political philosophy for the *Nonconformist,* a radical journal. These were subsequently reprinted as a pamphlet, *On the Proper Sphere of Government* (1843), a work of tremendous insight. Spencer attacked welfare by demonstrating that taxes needed to pay for it are regressive, and he demolished the assumption "that public charity proceeds from the stores of the rich, when, as has been shown, the greater portion of it comes from the toils of the labouring classes. The very parties for whose benefit the fund is raised, are, in virtue of their productive industry, chiefly instrumental in raising it." Thus he anticipated the soak-the-rich appeal, which would be made for communism, socialism, and the welfare state during the twentieth century.

Spencer nevertheless was still a long way from being able to earn a livelihood writing, so he returned to railroad work as a draftsman for three years. He continued to read all kinds of books and keep himself informed about public affairs, and in November 1848, he was offered an editorial position at the *Economist,* the free trade journal where he worked for five years. One of the editors was Thomas Hodgskin, a philosophical anarchist who might have influenced him.

Spencer used spare time to write his first book, *Social Statics* (1851). It presented an inspiring moral and practical case for individual rights, which he called "equal freedom." Everyone should be free to do what they wish, he insisted, as long as they do not infringe on somebody else's equal freedom. Accordingly, he advocated abolishing all trade restrictions, taxpayer church subsidies, overseas colonies, medical licensing, legal tender laws, central banks, government schooling, government welfare, government postal monopolies, and so-called public works. He showed how self-interest leads people not only to achieve prosperity, as Adam Smith had explained, but to improve life in countless ways. For example, he had this to say about sanitation: "Although everyone knows that the rate of mortality has been gradually decreasing and that the value of life is higher in England than elsewhere— although everyone knows that the cleanliness of our towns is greater now than ever before and that our spontaneously grown sanitary arrangements are far better than those existing on the Continent, where the stinks of Cologne, the uncovered drains of Paris, the water tubs of Berlin, and the miserable footways of the German towns show what state management effects—although everyone knows these things, yet it is perversely assumed that by state management only can the remaining impediments to public health be removed."

Anticipating the revelations of public choice economics, which developed in the late twentieth century and netted James M. Buchanan a Nobel Prize, Spencer made clear how government relentlessly pursues its own self-interest at the expense of ordinary people. He explored how governments in Greece, Rome, China, Russia, Austria, France, and Britain used control over education to secure their own power. Government schools, he observed, "have an instinct of self-preservation growing out of the selfishness of those connected with them." He added that the self-interest of these schools resists innovation, writing, "They are among the last places to which anyone looks for improvement in the art of teaching."

The most famous chapter was entitled "The Right to Ignore the State." Even during the heyday of classical liberalism, it was bold for Spencer to declare that "if every man has freedom to do all that he wills, provided he infringes not the equal freedom of any other man, then he is free to drop connection with the state—to relinquish protection and to refuse paying toward its support. It is self-evident that in so behaving he in no way trenches upon the liberty of others, for his position is a passive one, and while passive he cannot become an aggressor."

Social Statics established Spencer as a rising star, and by July 1853, he had resigned from the *Economist,* determined to make a living as an independent author. He sold articles to the *Westminster Review, Edinburgh Review, Fortnightly Review, British Quarterly,* and other influential publications, and he applied his ideas to science as well as ethics and government policy. This work introduced him to leading lights of the era: philosopher-economist John Stuart Mill, free trade crusader John Bright, Liberal statesman William Ewart Gladstone, and zoologist Thomas H. Huxley, among others. In November 1858, Charles Darwin, who was writing *The Origin of Species,* acknowledged the importance of Spencer's writings about evolution: "Your argument could not have been improved on, and might have been quoted by me with great advantage."

Financially, Spencer was hard-pressed and for a while pursued a government job that would allow him time to write, although he never became a bureaucrat. A proud man, he declined John Stuart Mill's generous offer to cover his expenses and resolved to earn his living in the marketplace. By 1860, Spencer conceived the idea of integrating ethics, biology, psychology, and sociology into a multivolume work on philosophy and making the venture pay by soliciting subscribers, who would pay a half-crown for each installment, several times a year. He asked his famous friends to offer testimonials, and some 450 people became subscribers, among them respected American intellectuals like newspaperman Horace Greeley, historian George Bancroft, clergyman Henry Ward Beecher, botanist Asa Gray, political scientist Francis

Lieber, and abolitionist Charles Sumner. Spencer began working on *First Principles*, a book about the development of life.

Alas, Spencer experienced subscriber attrition like everyone else in the publishing business. When he no longer had enough income from the project, he announced he would discontinue it. But in 1865, Dr. Edward Youmans, a lecturer and founder of *Popular Science* magazine, who had become a big fan of Spencer, helped raise enough money from American friends for Spencer to continue. He produced so many installments of different works during the 1860s and 1870s that it is hard to keep track of them all, plus revised editions he issued along the way. He became a major name. John Stuart Mill wrote to Spencer: "I have seldom been more thoroughly impressed by any scientific treatise than by your *Biology;* that it has greatly enhanced my sense of the importance of your philosophical enterprise as a whole."

Again and again, Spencer emphasized that extraordinary human progress develops naturally when people are free. "The turning of the land into a food-producing surface," he wrote in *Principles of Sociology* "cleared, fenced, drained, and covered with farming appliances, has been achieved by men working for individual profit not by legislative direction. . . . villages, towns, cities, have insensibly grown up under the desires of men to satisfy their wants . . . by spontaneous cooperation of citizens have been formed canals, railways, telegraphs, and other means of communication and distribution. . . . Knowledge developing into science, which has become so vast in mass that no one can grasp a tithe of it and which now guides productive activities at large, has resulted from the workings of individuals prompted not by the ruling agency but by their own inclinations. . . . And supplementing these come the innumerable companies, associations, unions, societies, clubs, subserving enterprise, philanthropy, culture, art, amusement; as well as the multitudinous institutions annually receiving millions by endowments and subscriptions; all of them arising from the unforced cooperations of citizens. And yet so hypnotized are nearly all by fixedly contemplating the doings of ministers and parliaments, that they have no eyes for this marvellous organization which has been growing for thousands of years without governmental help—nay, indeed, in spite of governmental hindrances." Spencer anticipated the work of Nobel laureate F. A. Hayek who explained how the essential institutions of a free society are the result of spontaneous human action.

Spencer had his greatest impact in the United States, By 1864, *Atlantic Monthly* reported, "Mr. Herbert Spencer . . . represents the scientific spirit of the age." His principles, the magazine concluded, "will become the recognized basis of an improved society." Yale sociologist William Graham Sumner emerged as the best-known advocate of Spencer's ideas.

Despite his heroics, public opinion increasingly favored government inter-ference during the late nineteenth century. Perhaps this was because govern-ment had been cut back so much that it no longer seemed like a public menace. More people imagined government could do good. Spencer responded by writing four powerful articles that affirmed the bedrock princi-ples of laissez-faire and attacked government intervention, published in the *Contemporary Review* in 1884. They unleashed what he called "a hornet's nest about my ears in the shape of criticisms from the liberal journals." In July 1884, the articles were issued as a book, *The Man Versus the State.* It was a magnifi-cent performance as Spencer hammered his adversaries—socialists espe-cially—with dramatic facts to show why laws tend to backfire. He explained how government-enforced interest rate ceilings, supposedly enacted to help people, made it more difficult to borrow money, how price controls turned regional crop failures into general famines, and how well-meaning London officials demolished homes for twenty-one thousand people but built new homes for only 12,000, leaving nine thousand homeless (the same kind of thing that U.S. urban renewal programs did more than a century later). Journalist Henry Hazlitt called this "one of the most powerful and influential arguments for limited government, *laissez faire* and individualism ever written."

Spencer was apparently depressed by accusations that he was superficial and heartless, and in 1892 he approved a revised edition of *Social Statics* without the original chapter 19, "The Right to Ignore the State." This com-promise hardly satisfied critics. Justice Oliver Wendell Holmes, defending government regulation (of working hours), thought it necessary to denounce him by name: "The Fourteenth Amendment does not enact Mr. Herbert Spencer's *Social Statics."*

Spencer's health declined for years. He died in his sleep around 4:40 in the morning, Tuesday December 8, 1903, at his home No. 5 Percival Ter-race in Brighton. He was eighty-three. His ashes were buried at Highgate Cemetery.

The twentieth century, bloodiest in history, has shown Spencer to be a phe-nomenal prophet who called the shots. More loudly and clearly than anyone else during his lifetime, he warned that socialism must lead to slavery. He condemned militarism long before a European arms race exploded into World War I; anticipated the evils of welfare state policies that undermine incentives for poor people to achieve independence; predicted the colossal failure of public schools; and affirmed that private individuals are responsible for human progress. He would be thrilled by the worldwide resurgence of market economies today, vindicating his conviction that there will be decency and improvement in the lives of ordinary people.

MARKETS UNLIMITED

ECONOMIST MURRAY N. ROTHBARD mounted the most comprehensive intellectual challenge ever attempted against the legitimacy of government. During a career that spanned more than forty years, he explained why private individuals, private companies, and other voluntary associations can do whatever needs to be done. He insisted that individuals should be free to go about their business peacefully without interference from anybody, including government. He objected to robbery, whether committed by a private criminal or a tax collector. And he acknowledged that there are plenty of problems affecting the private sector, but historically government has made things worse by throttling enterprise and oppressing people. Governments, he noted, are driven to expand their power, not to serve people. That is why, regardless of which political party is in power, governments tend to get bigger, enact more laws, and tax and spend more of what hard-working people produce.

Rothbard wrote a dozen major books and several hundred articles about ethics, philosophy, economics, American history, and the history of ideas. His work appeared in the *New York Times, Wall Street Journal, Washington Post, Los Angeles Times, Christian Science Monitor, Fortune,* and other major publications, and he was interviewed in *Penthouse.* He contributed to such scholarly journals as *American Economic Review, Quarterly Journal of Economics, Journal of Economic History, Columbia Journal of World Business, Journal of the History of Ideas,* and the *Journal of Libertarian Studies.* He contributed to just about every publication in the libertarian movement, including *Reason* and *Liberty.* For a number of years, he published his own newsletters, *Left and Right* and the *Libertarian Forum.* His work has been translated into Chinese, Czech, French, German, Italian, Japanese, Polish, Portuguese, Romanian, Russian, and Spanish. He gave talks and participated in conferences across the United States at Harvard Law School, Yale University, Princeton University, Stanford University, and elsewhere. For a long time, he was involved with the Libertarian party after it was established in 1972. He worked with the Cato Institute (started in 1977) during its early days and later became a key player at the Ludwig von Mises Institute, which he served for the rest of his life. In 1994, Rothbard received the Richard M. Weaver Award for Scholarly Letters from the Illinois-based Ingersoll Foundation (previous winners included distinguished American historians Shelby Foote and Forrest McDonald). The *New York Times* featured Rothbard among the most important contemporary thinkers about liberty.

Rothbard was about five feet, six inches tall. He gained weight over the years in New York City (he would have been horrified at the idea of jogging) but slimmed down later when he began teaching at the University of Nevada. He kept his curly hair short. He always wore a conservative suit and bow tie. Although slightly rumpled, he looked good.

Until his late forties, Rothbard had a travel phobia and did not like tunnels, bridges, trains, planes, or, for that matter, elevators, but he overcame his phobia and went around the world. When he spoke at a dinner atop Manhattan's 110-story World Trade Center, he opened by saying, "Greetings from earth!"

He was an incurable night owl. Entrepreneur Robert D. Kephart remembered "the Handel's *Messiah* singalong which the Rothbards had in their living room every Christmas season, with friends visiting all through night to join in snatches of the chorus. Here you would find Murray engaged in simultaneous conversations with a half-dozen people until his wife Joey would shush him. A chastened Murray would return to the chorus, squeaky and off key, until he could restrain himself no more and stop singing to pick up the conversations.

"And there was the evening I introduced him to Victor Niederhoffer, then reigning world squash champion. Vic had long admired Murray, and over dinner the two hit it off very well. Murray was awed to be in the company of a famous athlete, and he began asking Vic about the game. On the walk home, Vic asked if we would like to stop in at the Harvard Club to see the courts where Vic had done so much training. Murray took off his shoes, and we walked onto the court, Murray peppering Vic with questions. Then Vic suggested that Murray take a racket and hit a few balls. Murray, perhaps the least athletic person in Manhattan, was soon slashing away at shots lobbed to him by a world champion, the walls shaking with Murray's laughter."

MURRAY NEWTON ROTHBARD was born in the Bronx, New York, on March 2, 1926. He was the only child of Ray Babushkin Rothbard, who had emigrated from Russia, reportedly Minsk. Murray's father, David Rothbard, born in a little village near Warsaw, Poland, became chief chemist of Tidewater Oil Company in Bayonne, New Jersey. A believer in reason and liberty, David Rothbard honored the great mathematician and physicist Isaac Newton with his son's middle name, and he encouraged Murray philosophically.

Rothbard enrolled at Columbia University in 1942, where he majored in economics and mathematics, graduating Phi Beta Kappa three years later. He earned his M.A. in economics there the following year and began working on his Ph.D. under economic historian Joseph Dorfman whom Rothbard later called "my first mentor in the field of American history." Rothbard received his Ph.D. in 1956.

According to Rothbard's longtime friend Leonard Liggio, in 1946 Rothbard had taken a class from George J. Stigler at Columbia soon after Stigler had collaborated with Milton Friedman on a pamphlet *Roofs or Ceilings,* an attack on rent control published by the Foundation for Economic Education (FEE) in Irvington-on-Hudson, about thirty miles north of New York City. Stigler suggested that Rothbard might be interested in visiting the place. At FEE Rothbard learned about libertarian journalists like H. L. Mencken, Albert Jay Nock, Frank Chodorov, Garet Garrett, and John T. Flynn, who were opposed to militarism and conscription as well as big government. "All this rapidly converted me from a free-market economist to a pure libertarian," Rothbard recalled.

He heard about the great Austrian economist Ludwig von Mises in the spring of 1949, probably from economist F. A. "Baldy" Harper who worked at FEE. Three decades earlier, Mises had correctly predicted that socialism would impoverish millions. He had fled from the Nazis to America, and Harper seems to have told Rothbard that Mises would be conducting a weekly seminar at New York University, 100 Trinity Place. He attended the first seminar and continued attending for years.

Rothbard broke into print by writing book reviews for *analysis,* a libertarian newsletter started in November 1944 by Frank Chodorov, the New York–born son of a Russian Jewish immigrant peddler whose essay "Taxation Is Robbery" had an impact on his thinking. Rothbard first reviewed *A Mencken Chrestomathy,* a collection of writings by H. L. Mencken that appeared in August 1949. Between March 1950 and December 1956, Rothbard contributed thirteen articles to the libertarian monthly *Faith and Freedom* on topics that included inflation, price controls, and Thomas Jefferson.

At Columbia, while continuing his Ph.D. studies, Rothbard met and became charmed by JoAnn Beatrice Schumacher, a Presbyterian who had earned her B.A. degree at Columbia and her M.A. degree at New York University. Born in Chicago, she grew up in Virginia. They were married on January 16, 1953. He was twenty-seven, and she was twenty-five. They moved into apartment 2E, 215 West 88th Street, New York City, which remained their primary residence for the rest of his life. His New Year's resolution for 1954, which Joey had him sign, was to be in bed every night by 5:00 A.M. and to arise no later than 1:30 P.M.

Perhaps in 1954, Rothbard met Russian-born Ayn Rand, who was working on her philosophical novel *Atlas Shrugged.* Later he was among those invited to her apartment where completed portions of the novel were read. Rand was horrified that Rothbard was married to a religious woman and in 1958 urged that the Rothbards get divorced. In response, Rothbard quit Rand's circle.

He struggled to do scholarly work and pay bills. Since January 1952, his principal income had been an annual grant from the William Volker Fund, established by a Kansas City furniture wholesaler, to help him write a primer on free market economics. Rothbard's project expanded until it became a nineteen-hundred-page manuscript tentatively titled *Man, the Economy and the State.* The Volker Fund grant ran out on June 30, 1956, and he finished the manuscript in 1957. Several publishers rejected it. Next, Rothbard wanted to write a book explaining why the Great Depression was the result not of free market excesses but of government credit, trade, and tax policies. In April 1956, he was awarded a one-year grant from the Earhart Foundation.

By this time the Volker Fund had supported about a dozen professors who wrote manuscripts about liberty, but all remained unpublished. During the late 1950s, it was probably the Volker Fund's Herbert Cornuelle who arranged with D. Van Nostrand company to publish the manuscripts. Among them was Rothbard's *Man, Economy and State: A Treatise on Economic Principles.* It was cut by seven hundred pages, and Rothbard wrote a new ending. The book, which nevertheless filled two volumes, appeared in 1962.

Rothbard explained how market incentives spur the development of a complex, successful social order. He emphasized that markets and market prices are ultimately determined not by businesses but by consumers. Monopolies tend to persist, he showed, only when they are supported by government. Rothbard affirmed Mises's view that government causes inflation by artificially expanding money and credit and that depression is a consequence of prior inflation. He concluded, "There can be no business cycle in the purely free market."

Rothbard insisted that politicians and bureaucrats cannot fix whatever problems there might be in free markets, because they are imperfect human beings with limited knowledge, driven by their own self-interest—and possessing the power to disrupt the entire economy, something even the mightiest corporate executives are incapable of doing. Manuel S. Klausner, a Ford Foundation fellow in comparative law at New York University, wrote in *New York University Law Review* that there was "no more readable treatise and no more forthright case for freedom and free enterprise."

Van Nostrand published Rothbard's *America's Great Depression* in 1963. He maintained that the depression was the consequence of the government's prior credit expansion and that stepped-up government interference with the economy prolonged it. Rothbard discussed government blunders, including the Smoot-Hawley tariff and the steep hike in income, corporate, excise, and stock transfer taxes. Rothbard influenced historian Paul Johnson's view of the Great Depression, explained in his 6-million-copy-seller *Modern Times* (1983). Johnson called the book "an intellectual tour de force . . . presented with relentless logic, abundant illustration, and great eloquence."

In September 1966, Rothbard secured a steady job teaching at the Brooklyn Polytechnic Institute, which trained engineers (not what he hoped for but he was thankful for a steady paycheck). He plunged into his next project: to make a book out of the material cut from *Man, Economy, and State*. He was determined to present a thorough case that people would be better off if there were no government interference with their lives. Rothbard wrote that private, competitive judiciaries had played an important role in Western history and expressed the view that in the absence of government judges, insurance companies would have strong incentives to provide courts. He explained how private defense agencies could work and answered objections to this concept. F. A. Harper, who by this time had started the Institute for Humane Studies in Burlingame, California, published *Power and Market* in 1970.

The Vietnam War had intensified while Rothbard was producing scholarly work, and neither Democrats nor Republicans offered much hope for peace. Rothbard tried to forge an alliance with the New Left, which organized protests against the war and conscription. Rothbard and his friend Leonard P. Liggio, a historian, started *Left and Right: A Journal of Libertarian Thought*, in the spring of 1965. Further cultivating the New Left, Rothbard wrote an article for *Ramparts* magazine in June 1968.

After reading the article, journalist and political speechwriter Karl Hess contacted Rothbard, and they met at his New York apartment. "It was a classical salon," Hess recalled, "a roomful of a dozen or so extraordinarily bright and witty men and women united by enthusiasm for liberty. There was only one difficulty. They never slept, at least not at night. . . . [Here] I learned, with great excitement, about a grand tradition in this country . . . laissez-faire capitalism and human association based on voluntary agreement and absolute individual responsibility." Hess wrote for Rothbard's newsletter the *Libertarian*, then joined Rothbard as coeditor of the bimonthly *Libertarian Forum*. Hess aired his libertarian views with "The Death of Politics," an article in the March 1969 issue of *Playboy*. Rothbard, Liggio, and Hess deserve credit for reaching out, but they did not prevail. The New Left split into factions, some of which turned to violence.

On February 9, 1971, the *New York Times* published Rothbard's op-ed article, "The New Libertarian Creed," which reported on the growing numbers of young people who were rebelling against the Vietnam War, military conscription, skyrocketing taxes, and government intrusion into personal life. He attracted the attention of Tom Mandel, an editor at Macmillan, and soon Rothbard had his first commercial book contract. The result was *For a New*

Liberty, the Libertarian Manifesto (1973), a sturdy natural rights defense of liberty, beginning with the principle of self-ownership and private property. Rothbard debunked the conventional view that government, the principal agency of coercion and violence, could be counted on to do good. He critiqued welfare, government schools, compulsory unionism, urban renewal, farm subsidies and other government programs that benefit powerful interest groups at the expense of everyone else. Nicholas von Hoffman praised the book in the *Washington Post*. The *Los Angeles Herald Examiner* wrote, "Overall, *For a New Liberty* presents an articulate, well-reasoned and mostly well-documented argument for the truly radical changes advocated by members of the Libertarian Movement."

Kenneth Templeton, who had been with the William Volker Fund and later moved to the Institute for Humane Studies, encouraged Rothbard to write a book affirming that the American Revolution was about liberty. He was able to concentrate on this project when the Lilly Endowment provided a five-year grant. Kansas oilman Charles Koch and Washington, D.C., publisher Robert D. Kephart also provided financial support. Scholar Leonard Liggio collaborated with Rothbard on the project.

Volume 1 of *Conceived in Liberty* (*The American Colonies in the Seventeenth Century*) and volume 2 (*"Salutary Neglect": The American Colonies in the First Half of the 18th Century*) appeared in 1975, volume 3 (*Advance to Revolution, 1760–1775*) in 1976, and volume 4 (*The Revolutionary War, 1775–1784*) in 1979. Rothbard discussed the development of libertarian ideas and celebrated great libertarians like Roger Williams, Anne Hutchinson, Thomas Paine, and Thomas Jefferson. He regaled readers with outrageous, sometimes amusing stories about the ways government officials interfered with people's lives. Rothbard dictated much of a fifth volume that would have brought the story through the Constitution, but the publisher got into financial trouble, and the dictating machine belts were damaged.

While *Conceived in Liberty* was being published, Kansas entrepreneur Charles Koch arranged financial support so that Rothbard could take a year off from teaching to write a book presenting his political philosophy. The result was *The Ethics of Liberty*, published by Humanities Press in 1982. He explained why government, based on coercion, is inherently immoral and developed a sophisticated case for ethics grounded on natural rights. This has turned out to be one of his most enduring works.

Rothbard's next project was inspired by one of Rothbard's admirers, Florida-based investment adviser Mark Skousen. In September 1981, he proposed that Rothbard write a popular survey of economics suitable for college courses. He offered a advance—half on signing and the balance on completion, supposedly within a year. The project expanded in Rothbard's mind, and years passed.

In 1982, Llewellyn H. Rockwell Jr., who had worked for Arlington House Publishers, founded the Ludwig von Mises Institute (now affiliated with Auburn University, Alabama) and persuaded Rothbard to become vice president for academic affairs. He provided Rothbard with research support, and Rothbard led Mises Institute seminars. Rothbard also edited the *Review of Austrian Economics*, the first journal to focus on Austrian economics, and he wrote for the Mises Institute's *Free Market* newsletter. In 1985 he was appointed the S. J. Hall Distinguished Professor of Economics at the University of Nevada, Las Vegas (Las Vegas did not have great library resources, but the city was open all night). He continued his work with the Mises Institute. Then in April 1991 came the *Rothbard-Rockwell Report,* a monthly twelve-page newsletter with commentary about the libertarian movement and world news. When the cold war ended, conservatives no longer focused on anti-communism, and the newsletter urged an alliance between libertarians and conservatives.

During the summer of 1994, Rothbard had trouble sleeping because of fluid in his lungs. On January 7, 1995, Murray and Joey went to a late afternoon appointment at an optometrist's office. While Joey was in another room, Murray asked a technician to have his glasses tightened. Then he collapsed, unconscious, on the floor. Paramedics took him to Roosevelt Hospital, where he died of congestive heart failure. He was sixty-eight. His ashes were buried in Joey's family plot at Oakwood Cemetery, Unionville, Virginia.

At a memorial service at Madison Avenue Presbyterian Church, which Joey had attended for years, historian Ralph Raico remarked, "Murray was totally inner-directed, in every way his own man, guided always by values that were an inseparable part of him—above all, his love of liberty and of human excellence." Historian Ronald Hamowy said, "I'm not a religious man and I have no right to ask for a place in heaven. But I hope that when I die God will choose to let me in, because it sure would be nice to see Murray again."

Soon after Rothbard's death, the project started by Mark Skousen appeared as the two-volume *An Austrian Perspective on the History of Economic Thought.* Volume 1 was titled *Economic Thought Before Adam Smith* and volume 2, *Classical Economics.* Rothbard traced the intellectual history of natural rights and economic liberty from ancient China to early nineteenth-century Europe. His favorite thinkers included Lao-Tzu, Chrysippus, Marcus Tullius Cicero, Francisco Suarez, Jacques Turgot, Jean-Baptiste Say, and Frédéric Bastiat.

Rothbard's papers were shipped to the Mises Institute. There scholar Jeff Tucker reported the discovery of several unpublished manuscripts. The Mises Institute issued *Making Economic Sense,* 112 of his topical essays from *Free Market,* in 1995. Then came *The Logic of Action* (1997), with forty-three of Rothbard's major essays about economics; *Education: Free and*

Compulsory (1999); and a reissue of *America's Great Depression* (1999), with a new introduction by Paul Johnson.

Joey Rothbard suffered a stroke in January 1999 and was transferred to Virginia where her relatives lived. She died October 29.

Murray Rothbard did more than anyone else to show that society generally does just fine without government interference. He helped inspire confidence in the unlimited potential of free people.

THE SPIRIT OF LIBERTY

Eternal spirit of the chainless mind,
Brightest in dungeons, Liberty! thou art.
—LORD BYRON (1816)

MANY OF THE GREATEST artists, composers, poets, dramatists, and
novelists have celebrated liberty, one of the most enduring and electrifying themes. People have risked their lives to smuggle works about liberty behind closed borders because they help inspire resistance to tyranny.
Novels about liberty have sold tens of millions of copies and continue to
sell without any advertising. Many have been made into hit movies. Liberty has been the theme of some of the most beloved television series. The
world's most popular musical, seen by an estimated 41 million people, is
Les Misérables, about a good man's struggle with police. After the Berlin
Wall came down, Beethoven's Ninth Symphony was performed in Berlin;
the choral movement became the ode to freedom, and it was broadcast to
every continent.

HEROIC VISION

FRIEDRICH SCHILLER WAS one of the world's greatest poets and dramatists for liberty. Nobel laureate F. A. Hayek ranked him among the "leading political thinkers." Schiller's work abounds with gems about liberty. For example: "Man must have his freedom to be ready for morality," "Surely the man is great who has shaped and created himself," "It's safest to rely upon oneself," "Whoever subjects us to compulsion, denies us nothing less than our humanity," "The state as at present constituted has been the cause of evil," "Warfare is a raging horror," and "We stand here joyously upon the ruins of tyranny." Schiller celebrated "everlasting rights, which still abide on high, inalienable and indestructible as are the stars."

German philosopher Immanuel Kant, Schiller's contemporary, has traditionally been considered a much more important thinker, but Kant opposed the right of revolution against tyranny, while Schiller affirmed that right. His most beloved play, *Wilhelm Tell*, celebrated a legendary freedom fighter. It inspired Gioacchino Rossini's opera *Guillaume Tell* whose famous overture became the theme of *The Lone Ranger*, the popular television series in the 1950s about the pursuit of liberty and justice.

Schiller recognized that political power was the most persistent and serious threat to liberty. "Every one of the figures of power in his dramas is profoundly flawed, and in most cases the flaws are not so much nobly tragic as contemptible," noted German literature professor Jeffrey L. Sammons. "Schiller was immune to nationalistic feeling; for him the invader was always in the wrong."

Schiller had a tolerant, cosmopolitan vision. He wrote one play about liberating the Swiss (*Wilhelm Tell*), another about liberating the Dutch (*Don Carlos*), and yet another about liberating the French (*The Maid of Orleans*). He wrote historical epics because stories about contemporary rebellion would have been banned by censors. In his unfinished poem *German Greatness*, he urged his compatriots to renounce politics and war.

Schiller was widely revered. The American author Washington Irving was a fan, as were the English novelist Walter Scott and the English poet Samuel Taylor Coleridge. The French political thinker Benjamin Constant cherished Schiller's company. After visiting his home, the French novelist Germaine de Staël remarked, "I found him so modest and so unconcerned about his own successes, so ardent and animated in the defense of what he believed was true, that I vowed him from that moment a friendship full of admiration." Political thinker Wilhelm von Humboldt called Schiller, "the greatest and finest person I have ever known." Poet and dramatist Johann Wolfgang von Goethe told Schiller; "You have given me a second youth, made me a poet again." And it was to Schiller that Ludwig van Beethoven turned when he needed inspiring words for the climactic fourth movement of his Ninth Symphony.

F. A. Hayek observed that Schiller "did probably as much as any man to spread liberal ideas in Germany." Austrian economist Ludwig von Mises called him "the preferred poet of the nation; in his enthusiastic devotion to liberty the Germans found their political ideal." That is why Schiller's work was banned by both Napoleon and Hitler.

The eloquence that Schiller achieved was phenomenal. "No other writer except Martin Luther," reported professor Sammons, "has had so enduring an impact on the German language in its common usage. A well-known compendium of . . . familiar quotations, even in a current edition lists some three hundred lines and phrases from Schiller."

Nobel Laureate Thomas Mann: "He invented a theatrical idiom of his own. Its intonations, gestures, and melodies are unmistakable, instantly recognizable as his; and it is the most brilliant, rhetorically stirring idiom that was ever created in Germany, perhaps in the world. . . . It is not easy to stop, once I have begun to speak of Schiller's special greatness—a generous, lofty, flaming, inspiring grandeur such as we do not find even in Goethe's wiser, more natural and elementary majesty. . . . Schiller's mighty talent . . . his libertarian sentiments . . . he is a poet who knows how to bring tears to our eyes while at the same time rousing us to indignation against despotism."

Best-selling novelist and philosopher Ayn Rand, who began her career as a screenwriter, declared; "He is the only classical dramatist in whom I sensed an enormous hero worship."

Schiller displayed heroics in his personal life, creating his greatest work despite severe asthma, tuberculosis, and liver and heart disease. The last nine years of his life, when he was virtually an invalid, were his most productive. A visitor reported in 1796; "His mind, accustomed to never-resting activity, is spurred to still greater efforts by physical suffering."

Biographer H. B. Garland noted that Schiller "was tall and upright, though with thin, weedy legs and arms, and a tendency to be knock-kneed. His hair, which he always wore long and brushed back from his forehead, was reddish, his eyes blue, his nose thin and slightly hooked, his lips full and well-shaped. He dressed in plain colours, usually grey or dark blue, and normally wore an open-necked shirt. . . . His salient characteristic, remarked by all observers, was his gentleness . . . warm-hearted kindness." Schiller, added Sammons, "drew to himself some of the best and most worthwhile friends and sincere admirers any man has ever had; at times they virtually saved his life. What may seem to a modern sensibility forbidding and moralistic in him must have struck a temper of the late eighteenth century differently, must have met a yearning for a higher and firmer ground beyond that age's frivolity, cruelty, and injustice. In Schiller, contemporaries encountered a man of high visionary purpose and, though not guileless in personal and business relations, basically incorruptible integrity, free of compromise with evil or petty selfishness. For various reasons such virtues have paled in modern times; but they were significant and magnetic then and continued to inspire subsequent generations, with greater or lesser understanding, for more than a century afterward."

JOHANN CHRISTOPH FRIEDRICH Schiller was born on November 10, 1759, in Marbach, duchy of Wurtemberg. He was the son of Johann Kaspar Schiller, a military officer serving the petty tyrant Duke Karl Eugen of Wurtemberg. Schiller's mother was Elisabetha Dorothea Kodweis, an innkeeper's daughter. In December 1776, at the duke of Wurtemberg's palace, young Schiller saw opulent productions of Italian operas, kindling his love for the theater. But the duke ordered the boy to study law at the Herzogliche Militr-Akademie (Ducal Military Academy). Schiller endured regimentation from age thirteen to twenty-one without being permitted to see his father, mother, or sister. His graduation was held up a year, until December 1780, because his first dissertation was rejected for being critical of authorities. Outraged, Schiller wrote a poem, *The Conqueror*, which scorned a tyrant like the duke.

Schiller moved to Stuttgart and finished his first play, *Die Rauber (The Robbers)*, about the futility of violence. After it was performed in Mannheim on January 13, 1782, the duke warned Schiller that he would be imprisoned if he wrote more plays. Schiller fled to Mannheim, bringing with him a nearly finished manuscript for his next play, *Die Verschwörung des Fiesco zu Genua (Fiesco's Conspiracy at Genoa)*, about the rise and fall of a man who tried to be a dictator. It opened in Mannheim on January 11, 1784.

For a while Schiller stayed in the Bauerbach home of Henriette von Wolzogen, whose sons had been his classmates. He worked on *Kabale und Liebe (Cabal and Love)*, a tragedy about Ferdinand von Walter who struggles against authority to live his own life. This play, which opened April 15, 1784, was a hit.

Next the young playwright moved to Leipzig, where a wealthy admirer named Chrstian Gottfried Korner provided financial support for two years. In November 1785, he wrote *An die Freude (Ode to Joy)*, the first of his poems to find a popular audience. In its original version, noted music historian Irving Kolodin, this was *An Die Freiheit (Ode to Freedom)*.

In *Don Carlos,* Schiller transformed the unhappy son of Spain's mighty King Philip II into a champion of liberty who courageously opposes his father's repression in the Netherlands. Schiller portrays the Marquis de Posa as even bolder, demanding freedom of speech. That such things never could have occurred under Philip II hardly seemed to matter, because after the play opened on August 29, 1787, in Hamburg, audiences were swept away by this stirring story about a struggle for liberty.

Schiller began work on *Die Geschichte des Abfalls der vereinigten Nieder- lande von der spanischen Regierung (The History of the Secession of the United Netherlands from Spanish Rule).* He exulted that "a vigorous resis- tance can strike down the upraised arm of the despot." Although he was able to cover only the period 1560 to 1567, the work, published in 1788, was among his most commercially successful.

On a trip to visit Frau von Wolzogen, he stopped in Rudolstadt, where her relatives, the Lengefeld family, lived. He and young Lotte von Lengefeld became enchanted with each other, and they got married in Wenigenjena on February 22, 1790. They had four children.

The specter of a war arising from the French Revolution evoked the hor- rors of the Thirty Years War (1618–1648), which had devastated Germany, and Schiller started a history of it. The first part of *Die Geschichte des dreis- sigjahrigen Krieges,* covering the story up to 1631, was published in 1790 and sold out the press run of seven thousand copies.

On January 3, 1791, Schiller suffered a fever and chest pains, and he coughed up blood; he had tuberculosis and needed prolonged rest. He and his wife moved to Rudolstadt, where better air might help relieve his symp- toms, but he soon started suffering from asthmatic breathing spasms too. By December, he had improved somewhat, and he got heartening news: two Danish noblemen, Prince Friedrich Christian von Augustenburg and Count Schimmelmann, offered him a pension for three years, providing some finan- cial security.

Schiller wrote a series of essays on aesthetics that included comments about achieving inner freedom. The best known are *Uber Anmut und Wurde (On Grace and Dignity,* 1793), *Briefe über die asthetische Erziehung des Menschen (On the Aesthetic Education of Man,* 1794), and *Über naive und sentimental- isch Dichtung (On Naive and Sentimental Poetry,* 1796). As Jeffrey L. Sam- mons observed, "Ultimately their principal object is not the nature of art, nor even the definition of beauty, but the achievement of human freedom."

In Jena, Schiller got to know the man of letters and political thinker Wil- helm von Humboldt who had just written *Ideen zu einem Versuch die Gren- zen der Wirkamkeit des Staats zu bestimmen (The Limits of State Action),* a book that influenced John Stuart Mill's *On Liberty* (1859). A friend of Hum- boldt reported he was "regularly with Schiller every evening from eight till ten. . . . He lives only in his ideas, in a continual intellectual activity. Thinking and writing are all he needs; everything else he respects or likes only in so far as it is connected with this, his real life. Humboldt is therefore very valuable to him. These hours Schiller regards as his hours of recreation and he talks of everything. . . . With Schiller he is without any strain and is just as funny as we have ever seen him."

Thomas Mann called the blossoming of Schiller's relationship with Goethe "the most famous of intellectual alliances." The two had met at Schiller's in-laws' house on September 7, 1788, when Schiller was twenty-eight and Goethe thirty-nine. They shared a passion for literature and believed they were defenders of civilization against ignorance. They wrote each other more than a thousand letters. Goethe invited Schiller to his house in Weimar, and Goethe regularly visited Schiller and his family in Jena.

Schiller described Goethe as "of middle height, and carries himself rather stiffly. . . . He has a very expressive and lively look, and it is a great pleasure to look into his eyes. . . . His voice is exceedingly pleasing and his conversation flowing, lively and amusing." Born in Frankfurt on August 28, 1749, Goethe was the reigning genius of German literature who had written a number of widely regarded poems and dramas before *Die Leiden des jungen Werther* (*The Sorrows of Young Werther*) captivated German readers in 1774. Goethe went on to write satires about Jean-Jacques Rousseau, among other subjects, and wrote some serene nature poems. He embraced classical ideals of beauty. His *Egmont* (1788) is about a man who led a Dutch revolt against Spanish tyranny. Some scholars believe Goethe became more productive—and, among other things, finished *Faust*, Part I—because Schiller spurred him on.

"When Goethe wishes to apply his full powers, I do not measure myself against him," Schiller wrote. "He has a far greater wealth of knowledge, a surer sensuousness, and with all this an artistic sense refined and purified by acquaintance with all types of art. This I lack to a degree that amounts to sheer ignorance. If I did not have a few other talents, and if I had not been clever enough to apply these talents and abilities to the field of the drama, I would have made no showing at all beside him in this profession." Goethe remarked, "The Germans are always bickering about who is greater. They ought to be glad they have two such boys to bicker with."

As Napoleon menaced Europe, Schiller remarked that the general "is completely repugnant to me." In 1797, he made notes for a poem, *Deutsche Grosse* (*German Greatness*), asserting that individual improvement, not political power, is the key to making the world better.

As Schiller focused on producing more plays, it became clear he must join Weimar's theatrical community, and he moved there in 1799. He worked on *Wallenstein*, a ten-act tragedy about the general who played a major role in the Thirty Years War. Schiller showed how power corrupts the mighty and how war devastates ordinary people. The first part of his new play, *Wallensteins Lager (Wallenstein's Camp)*, opened on October 12, 1798, in the Weimar Court Theatre; the second part, *Die Piccolomini (The Piccolomini)*, on January 30, 1799; and the third part, *Wallensteins Tod (Wallenstein's Death)*, on April 20, 1799.

While studying history, Schiller became fascinated with the exploits of Joan of Arc who, near the climax of the Hundred Years War, helped drive the English out of Orléans and Rheims. She was wounded in the struggle for Paris and burned by the English on May 30, 1431. Schiller determined to rescue Joan of Arc from Voltaire who had ridiculed her as a religious fanatic. His *Jungfrau von Orleans (The Maid of Orleans)* is a hymn for independence. If some people objected to Schiller's departure from historical fact (he had Joan die gloriously in battle), the play was a hit with the public after it opened on September 11, 1801.

In December 1803, Schiller welcomed the French novelist and friend of liberty Germaine de Staël who had eluded the guillotine during the French Revolution. She was a whirlwind. "She wants to explain everything, apprehend everything, measure everything," Schiller remarked. They spoke in French, since she did not know German, and she wrote of him, "I was much struck by this simplicity of character." The conversations figured in her book, *De l'Allemagne (On Germany)*, which helped put German ideas before French readers.

After Goethe dropped the idea of doing an epic poem about Wilhelm Tell, Schiller began reading Swiss history and vowed that "if the gods are kind to me and let me carry out what I have in my head, it will be a mighty work which will shake the theatres of Germany. . . . My *Tell*, I think, is going to warm people's blood again." He presented Wilhelm Tell as a man whose plain talk sparkled with aphorisms about individualism—for example, "A real hunter helps himself," "Whoever wants to make his way through life must be prepared," "The strong man will be strongest when alone," "I am free and master of my strength," "No one shall go uncomforted from Tell," "I do what's right and fear no enemy," "The weak are also furnished with a sting," and "This house of freedom God himself created."

The play opens after a Swiss countryman named Baumgarten has killed the Habsburg emperor's bailiff, who had threatened his wife. To elude the emperor's soldiers who were rushing to avenge the killing, Baumgarten had to get away across Lake Lucerne, and Wilhelm Tell offered to take him. Tell ran afoul of authorities by refusing to bow before a hat mounted on a pole, symbolizing the tyrannical Governor Gessler. The outraged governor forced Tell to try shooting an arrow off his son's head. Tell hit the apple, of course, but he did not forgive Gessler for putting his son's life at risk and later assassinated the tyrant. This enabled Swiss patriots to overrun their oppressors and secure their liberty. *Wilhelm Tell* opened on March 17, 1804, and it was more popular than anything else he had done.

The winter of 1804 and 1805 was the worst he had experienced, and Schiller could not get beyond the second act of his next play, *Demetrius*, about a struggle for power in seventeenth-century Russia. "If only I can reach my fiftieth year with unimpaired intellectual powers," he wrote, "I hope to be able to save enough so that my children will be independent."

He suffered high fevers and pain and on April 29, 1805, chatted with Goethe for the last time. As his condition worsened, his wife brought in their nine-month-old daughter, Emilie, and Schiller seemed to realize he would never see her again. He died on Monday, May 9, 1805, his wife holding his hand. He was just forty-five. He had requested the simplest possible observance, and his coffin was carried to the St. James Church cemetery. There was a memorial service the following day.

When Napoleon marched through central Europe after 1805, he banned Schiller's *Jungfrau von Orléans*, which was seen as a patriotic battle cry against any foreign invader. Goethe, always aloof from politics, expressed the view that the French might be a civilizing influence. German-speaking people turned their back on Goethe and revered Schiller.

One of Schiller's ardent admirers was composer Ludwig van Beethoven who as early as 1793 thought about doing something with the poem *An die Freude* (1785). Nothing came of this at the time, but Beethoven continued to read Schiller's writings. In a journal, he wrote down some words from Schiller's *Don Carlos*. Beethoven swore "to love liberty above all else, never to deny the truth, even before the throne." In May 1817, Beethoven honored a friend who had died by setting to music some passages from *Wilhelm Tell*. In mid-1823, Beethoven decided to finish his D-Minor Symphony with a choral movement and to draw the words from Schiller's *An die Freude*. As the deaf composer wrote in his notebook to associate Anton Schindler, *"Lass uns das Lied des unsterblichen Schiller singen"* ("Let us sing the song of the immortal Schiller").

Schiller's ideal of liberty inspired the greatest composers of Italian opera. Gioacchino Rossini based his last opera, *Guillaume Tell* (1829), on Schiller's last play. It opened in Paris and played five hundred performances there. Then it played to audiences in Brussels, Frankfurt, London, New Orleans, and New York (in English, French, German, and Italian). "In Italy," reported Rossini biographer Francis Toye, "there was trouble with the Austrian censorship. . . . All references to patriotism, liberty, or tyranny were suppressed, and the scene of the apple was omitted altogether. In Rome the Papal censorship . . . thought it well to sprinkle the opera with pious references to God, heaven, and the saints."

Inspired by Schiller's story of Tell, Giuseppe Verdi went to see "William Tell's Chapel and the house where he lived, the place where he killed Gessler, the man who oppressed the Swiss." Verdi drew on Schiller's *Die Jungfrau von Orléans* for *Giovanna d'Arco,* which opened on February 15, 1845; he drew on *Die Rauber* for *I Masnadieri,* which opened on July 22, 1847; on *Kabale und Liebe* for his opera *Luisa Miller,* which opened on December 8, 1849; and on *Don Carlos* for *Don Carlo,* which opened on March 11, 1867. According to Sammons, two dozen more operas were based on Schiller's plays.

The English writer Thomas Carlyle helped popularize Schiller in the English-speaking world by writing a biography (1824). Goethe helped get it translated into German and wrote an introduction for it. According to biographer John Morley, philosopher and economist John Stuart Mill "greatly prefers Schiller in all respects; turning to him from Goethe is like going into the fresh air from a hothouse."

The hundredth anniversary of Schiller's birth, in November 1859, inspired what Ludwig von Mises described as "the most impressive political demonstration that ever took place in Germany. . . . The German nation was united in its adherence to the ideas of Schiller, to the liberal ideas." Although churches banned the use of their property for Schiller celebrations and government schools banned his writings, there were readings, performances, and torchlight parades in just about every German city. Some sixteen hundred speeches were given on Schiller, and about three hundred subsequently were published in commemorative volumes. The centennial was celebrated around the world. Eighty-nine celebrations were reported in twenty-three of the thirty-three United States. In New York, festivities went on for four days. There were celebrations in St. Petersburg, Moscow, and other capitals as well. More celebrations were held on the 150th anniversary of Schiller's birth in 1909. At Harvard Stadium, a performance of Schiller's *The Maid of Orleans* had some fifteen hundred actors on stage and fifteen thousand people in the audience.

Schiller remained a great name in German literature until after World War I. Then he was rejected by writers like the Marxist Bertold Brecht, who wrote a Schiller parody, *St. Joan of the Stockyards.* But Thomas Mann recalled, "I saw *Love and Intrigue* in Munich after the First World War . . . the performance was mediocre. And yet the fire of the play threw this . . . audience into a kind of revolutionary frenzy. The audience became Schiller fanatics, like every audience that has ever witnessed his plays."

When Adolf Hitler heard that Schiller's *Wilhelm Tell* justified the toppling of tyrants, he banned the work. From Schiller's *Don Carlos,* Nazi censors cut the famous line, "Give freedom of thought!" which always inspired a burst of applause from the audience. But on subsequent performances, as the action got to that point in the play, audiences applauded the missing line, and further performances were banned. In 1946, the defeat of the Nazis was celebrated by twenty-six theatrical companies that produced *Don Carlos* throughout Germany.

People yearned to rediscover what was decent in German culture, especially Goethe and Schiller. Scholar John Bednall remarked that "without Schiller, German letters, poetry, historical and aesthetic thought, and, above all, the living theatre in the German-speaking countries would be disastrously impoverished." On the bicentennial of Schiller's birth in 1959, Thomas Mann wrote, "let divided Germany feel united in his name. . . . May it stand under the sign of universal sympathy, true to the spirit of his own noble-minded greatness. . . . May something of his heroic will enter into us through this celebration of his interment and resurrection, some small part of his will to achieve beauty, truth, and goodness, moral excellence, inner freedom, art, love, peace."

There have been few performances of Schiller's plays in the United States since World War I when jingoism banished German culture. Knowledge of his work has been limited to students of German literature. For most people, Schiller remains one of the greatest treasures yet to be rediscovered.

JOYOUS AFFIRMATION

LUDWIG VAN BEETHOVEN inspired the world with his titanic liberating spirit. "His emotions at their highest level were almost godlike," declared critic H. L. Mencken, "he gave music a sort of Alpine grandeur." A bold maverick, Beethoven broke free of conventional forms so music could plumb the depths of despair, express heroic struggles, and reach astonishing peaks of joy. Beethoven scholar Robert Haven Schauffler wrote, "Whenever the spirit moved him he could squeeze blood out of bricks. And he made rubies of the blood, and platinum out of the residue of the bricks, and organized these products into miracles of design."

Beethoven took orchestral music out of aristocratic salons and into packed concert halls. After 1815, he composed mostly for publishers rather than patrons. He was proud to have pioneered a commercial market where composers earned a livelihood from the rights to their work. "What I am," he wrote, "I am through myself."

Beethoven was an outspoken republican amid a continent of kings. He was outraged after Napoleon, who long claimed to uphold republican principles of the French Revolution, had himself crowned emperor. Beethoven admired England for its House of Commons, and he followed parliamentary debates reported in the German-language newspapers. "The sum of his message was freedom," observed critic Paul Bekker, "artistic freedom, political freedom, personal freedom of will, of art, of faith, freedom of the individual in all aspects of life."

Beethoven was tormented by demons. He endured a rude upbringing and chronic health problems, especially deafness, and his personal life was a mess. He neglected his appearance so badly that he was once mistaken as a tramp and arrested. His apartments (he moved dozens of times) were strewn with decaying food and dirty clothing. His handwriting was virtually illegible. He could not keep track of money. Longing for domestic happiness, he courted a succession of women but was rejected by all of them. He never married. He was impossible for most people to deal with. He was a suspicious person who often accused friends of cheating him, and by the end of his life there were few left. He had a volatile temper. Lost in his thoughts, he sometimes seemed like a wild man. Once he waved his arms as he walked across a field, scaring a pair of oxen, and they took off down a steep hill, pulling a panicked peasant behind. Beethoven got custody of his nephew Karl, and his overbearing presence provoked the boy to attempt suicide.

Yet these personal failings are dwarfed by his music, which expressed a love of liberty in ways millions could understand. He gave the world the most glorious affirmations for life. Contemporaries commented on the extraordinary intensity of the man. "Everything about his appearance," observed Dr. W. Christian Muller in 1820, "is powerful, much of it coarse, like the raw-boned structure of his face, with a high, broad forehead, a short, angular nose, with hair standing up and divided into thick locks. But he is blessed with a delicate mouth and with beautiful, eloquent eyes which reflect at every moment his quickly changing ideas and feelings."

LUDWIG VAN BEETHOVEN was born on December 16, 1770, in Bonn. (He had Dutch-Flemish ancestors, which is why *van* rather than the German spelling *von* is used.) He was the eldest surviving child of Maria Magdalena, a maid. Four of his six siblings died in infancy. His father, Johann Beethoven, was a tenor in the choir of Maximilian Friedrich, elector of Cologne.

Early on, Beethoven displayed musical talent and, hoping to strike it rich, his father pushed him hard. The young Beethoven took piano lessons from the time he was four years old. He devoted most of his waking hours to the piano, often practicing till midnight to improve his technique and try new variations. At eight, he gave an impressive public performance. Six years later, he was playing the harpsichord, viola, and organ in the elector's orchestra. The elector paid expenses to have Beethoven visit Vienna, Europe's musical capital.

There, probably in April 1787, sixteen-year-old Beethoven met the thirty-one-year-old reigning musical genius, Wolfgang Amadeus Mozart. After hearing the young man's facility for improvisation, Mozart declared, "Keep your eyes on him; someday he will give the world something to talk about." Beethoven seems to have taken a few lessons from Mozart, but their visits were cut short when both got bad news about their families. Mozart's father, Leopold, had died on May 28, 1787. Beethoven's mother suffered from tuberculosis, and he returned home to see her die on July 17, 1787. "She was such a good loving mother, my best friend!" he wrote.

Although Beethoven's formal education ended at age eleven, he attended some classes at the University of Bonn. A highlight were lectures on literature, ethics, and law by the anticlerical republican Eulogius Schneider. Beethoven frequented the Zehrgarten, a tavern and bookshop where radical intellectuals gathered. Like so many other German artists and thinkers of that period, Beethoven believed passionately in individual liberty.

In 1790, the influential composer Franz Joseph Haydn, then fifty-eight years old, stopped in Bonn on his way back to Vienna. Beethoven played him a cantata he had composed, and Haydn offered enough encouragement that Elector Maximilian Friedrich provided funds so Beethoven could study with Haydn in Vienna. He arrived on November 10, 1792, and never looked back. Still, he became restless with Haydn's musical formulas and insisted on charting his own course. He took violin lessons from Ignaz Schuppanzigh; went to Antonio Salieri, director of the Vienna Opera, for lessons on composing for the voice; and learned counterpoint from Johann Georg Albrechtsberger, Vienna's most famous teacher of composition and author of an internationally respected book on the subject.

By the mid-1790s Beethoven ranked as Vienna's most popular pianist, with a powerful style, and he excelled at improvisation. Ferdinand Ries, who studied with both Haydn and Beethoven, recalled, "No artist that I ever heard came at all near the height which Beethoven attained in this branch of playing. The wealth of ideas which forced themselves on him, the caprices to which he surrendered himself, the variety of treatment, the difficulties, were inexhaustible."

The French Revolution (before the Terror) had inspired musicians to pursue serious themes instead of light entertainment. Among Beethoven's early efforts were the First Symphony (1800), C Minor Piano Concerto no. 3 (1800), and the C-sharp piano sonata ("Moonlight," 1801). He said this about what it was like for him to compose: "From the focus of enthusiasm, I must discharge melody in all directions; I pursue it, capture it again passionately; I see it flying away and disappearing in the mass of varied agitations; now I seize upon it again with renewed passion; I cannot tear myself from it; I am impelled with hurried modulations to multiply it, and, at length I conquer it: behold, a symphony!"

He was extraordinarily resourceful. "It would be hard to think of a composer, even of the fourth rate," observed H. L. Mencken, "who worked with thematic material of less intrinsic merit. He borrowed tunes wherever he found them; he made them up out of snatches of country jigs; when he lacked one altogether he contented himself with a simple phrase, a few banal notes. All such things he viewed simply as raw materials; his interest was concentrated upon their use. To that use of them he brought the appalling powers of his unrivaled genius."

After about 1800, Beethoven was clearly departing from Haydn and Mozart, and some influential critics objected. A critic for the *Allgemeine Musikalische Zeitung* wrote, "Herr von Beethoven goes his own gait; but what a bizarre and singular gait it is! . . . a heaping up of difficulties on difficulties till one loses all patience and enjoyment."

While Beethoven had exulted in the republican ideals of the French Revolution, he was shocked by both its violence and the severity of the reaction against it. The Austro-Hungarian emperor jailed republican activists. "The soldiers are heavily armed," Beethoven warned a friend. "You must not speak too loud here or the police will give you lodgings for the night."

Beethoven's first great work, the Third Symphony ("Eroica," 1803), seems to have been inspired by struggles against tyranny. He used combinations of instruments and harmonies that had not been heard before. Whether he originally dedicated this symphony to Napoleon, as legend has it, he was disgusted when Napoleon brazenly betrayed republican principles and became an emperor.

In 1805, Beethoven experienced tyranny firsthand as Napoleon unleashed the full fury of his Grand Army across the European continent. On November 13, fifteen thousand French soldiers entered Vienna, occupying private homes and seizing food and any valuables they could. Napoleon demanded that the Viennese pay tribute of 2 million francs and cover the cost of maintaining several thousand French soldiers in the city. Beethoven suffered from inflation, food shortages, and military rule like everyone else. Furthermore, he was distracted by poor health. Since 1799, he had suffered from chronic stomach trouble and diarrhea. Then came ominous signs of hearing trouble. "My ears hum and buzz all the time, day and night," he wrote. "I can truly say my life is miserable, for two years I have avoided almost all social gatherings because I can't possibly say to people 'I am deaf.' . . . In the theater, if I am a little way off I don't hear the high notes of the instruments or singers." By 1812, he could hear people only when they shouted at him. Four years later, he would endure silence.

The loss of hearing made clear that Beethoven's future would have to be as a composer, not a performer, and between 1803 and 1812, he created one astounding masterpiece after another. Besides the "Eroica," Beethoven composed the Fifth Symphony (1808), which music critic Irving Kolodin described as the most frequently performed of all orchestral works. During this period, Beethoven also produced his Fifth Piano Concerto (1809). Historians Will and Ariel Durant commented, "Of all his works, this is the most lovable, the most enduringly beautiful, the one of which we never tire; however often we have heard it, we are moved beyond words by its sparkling vivacity, its gay inventiveness, its inexhaustible fountains of feeling and delight." Beethoven created so much more at this time, including his G Major Piano Concerto no. 4 (1806), Violin Concerto (1806), F Minor piano sonata ("Appassionata") (1806), F Major Symphony no. 6 (1808), A Major Symphony no. 7 (1812), and F Major Symphony no. 8 (1812).

Beethoven often worked and reworked his ideas until he was satisfied. His most arduous creation was the opera *Fidelio*. In 1803, he was commissioned to write an opera that would be performed at Vienna's Theater an der Wien. Rather than do the fashionable light entertainment about the sexual escapades of aristocrats, he chose a serious subject: the liberty of ordinary people. He turned to a libretto by Josef Sonnleithner, based on *Leonore, or l'Amour conjugal,* a story by J. N. Bouilly based on actual events during the French Revolution's Reign of Terror. To protect the living, the story was discreetly set in Spain. It involves Florestan, imprisoned for telling the truth about the corrupt tyrant Pizarro. He decides that Florestan must be murdered, but Florestan's wife, Leonore, gets a job in the prison, stops the murder attempt, and helps expose Pizarro.

Beethoven lacked dramatic experience, and although there was much inspiring music, the work wasn't coherent, and the first performance, on November 20, 1805, was not well received. Several months later, Beethoven met with his principal patron, Prince Karl Lichnowsky, who persuaded the composer to make a number of cuts. Beethoven rewrote the overture, producing Leonore Overture no. 2, and then the more ambitious Leonore Overture no. 3 which introduced the next performance on March 29, 1806. It was still a long way from satisfactory.

In 1814, three Viennese artists suggested that they perform *Fidelio* as a benefit for him. This stimulated him to try resolving problems with the work again. He had more experience and perspective on it. He enlisted a collaborator, Georg Friedrich Treitschke, a Viennese playwright who significantly strengthened the story and dialogue. Beethoven did a tremendous amount of rewriting; a single aria of Florestan's went through eighteen revisions. The new *Fidelio* opened on July 18, 1814, and this time it was a hit. French composer Hector Berlioz declared, "That music sets your insides on fire. I feel as if I'd swallowed fifteen glasses of brandy." Music critic Kolodin attributes some of the appeal to Beethoven's "enkindling response to human distress, his abhorrence of injustice, his compelling belief that rank is an accident of birth and superiority a condition of the person who demonstrates it."

Beethoven's most famous work, his D Minor Ninth Symphony, marked a return to his heroic style after exploring more intimate themes. He drew on ideas going back more than thirty years. Musical lines in the chorale, for instance, originally appeared in the Joseph cantata of 1790. He had wanted to write music for Friedrich Schiller's poem "An die Freude" ("Ode to Joy") since he had read it soon after publication in 1785. In 1812, he noted some ideas for the chorale movement of a D minor symphony. In 1822, Beethoven was commissioned by the Philharmonic Society of London to write a symphony, and began work in D minor. At about the same time, he started sketching a D minor "sinfonie allemande" with a chorale finale, probably with Schiller's "Ode to Joy." The projects merged somewhere along the line. During the first half of 1823, Beethoven struggled with the first movement, based on a melody he had sketched about six years before. Then he tackled the second and third movements simultaneously. By about August, he finished the second movement. After many revisions, the slow third movement was done in mid-October.

Meanwhile, perhaps in July, he had sketched a melody identified as "Finale instromentale." Scholars do not know when he set it aside (he later adapted the melody for the finale of his A minor Quartet op. 132), but he resolved that the fourth movement would reach a choral climax with Schiller's "Ode to Joy." He edited the poem, cutting lines that made it sound a bit like a drinking song. The result was a simpler, more powerful affirmation of life. Integrating the chorale into the symphony proved to be Beethoven's toughest challenge. All the sketching was done by year end, and the score was written out in February 1824.

The first performance was set for May 7, 1824, at the Karnthnerhor Theater, a double-billing with his new *Missa Solemnis*. Around 12:30 P.M., Beethoven lifted his baton. Violinist Joseph Bohm recalled that the composer "stood in front of the conductor's stand and threw himself back and forth like a madman. At one moment he stretched to his full height, at the next he crouched down to the floor, he flailed about with his hands and feet as though he wanted to play all the instruments and sing all the chorus parts." The performance was interrupted by applause many times. Afterward, Beethoven was preoccupied with his score, and mezzo-soprano Caroline Unger tugged on his sleeve, indicating that he should turn around to acknowledge the cheers. "The Ninth Symphony," noted Irving Kolodin, "possesses a cachet, an aura, an identity not commanded by any other work in the orchestral literature. It stands taller, strides longer, reaches higher toward the Infinite than any work even remotely like it." As historian Paul Johnson observed, "There was a new faith, and Beethoven was its prophet. It was no accident that, about this time, new concert halls were being given temple-type facades, thus exalting the moral and cultural status of the symphony and chamber music."

In December 1826, Beethoven began suffering from a severe cough. Soon he was enveloped by pain, and his feet became swollen. On March 26, 1827, he went into a coma. There was a violent thunderstorm, and for a moment Beethoven opened his eyes, raised his right hand, and clenched his fist defiantly toward the heavens. Then he collapsed forever. Three days later, an estimated twenty thousand people lined the streets as eight musicians carried his coffin to Trinity Church of the Minorities, and afterward four horses took it to the cemetery at Wahring. The grave was marked by a pyramid inscribed with a single word: "Beethoven."

More than a century and a half later, after restless Germans rebelled against communist tyranny and pulled down the Berlin Wall, conductor Leonard Bernstein gathered musicians from East and West Germany for a performance of Beethoven's Ninth Symphony. He changed the word *Freude* ("joy") to *Freiheit* ("freedom") throughout the chorale, because Beethoven's work resonated with the spirit of freedom, and it was past time to make this explicit. Declared Bernstein, "If not now, when?" From Berlin on Christmas Day 1989, the climactic "Ode to Freedom" was heard around the world. A joyous celebration of freedom goes on wherever people can hear Beethoven.

MAJESTIC COMPASSION

LITERARY LION VICTOR Hugo inspired an outpouring of generous sympathy for wretched people oppressed by government. He chronicled the evils of police power, spoke out against capital punishment, denounced taxes and tyrants, opposed war, and expressed confidence in the ability of free people to achieve unlimited progress.

He was a leading light for liberty during the nineteenth century because of his prodigious and often lyrical output: nine novels, ten plays, and about twenty volumes of poetry, plus essays and speeches. He broke away from the suffocating formality of classical French literature and achieved the immediacy of plain talk. He wrote with high moral purpose about dramatic events and created great heroes of world literature. He enjoyed unprecedented popular acclaim.

Hugo's most beloved work, *Les Misérables*, nails government as a chronic oppressor. He shows poor people being helped not by government but by the charitable works of a private individual. He tells why a resourceful entrepreneur is an engine of human progress. And he celebrates revolution against tyranny while making clear why egalitarian policies backfire. His hero, Jean Valjean, does good voluntarily, and peacefully.

Hugo fan Ayn Rand, whose novels about heroic individualism have sold more than 20 million copies, told biographer Barbara Branden, "*Les Misérables* was *the* big experience. Everything about it became important to me, holy, everything that reminded me of it was a souvenir of my love. It was my first view of how one should see life, wider than any concretes of the story. I didn't approve of the ideas about the poor and the disinherited, except that Hugo set them up in a way that I could sympathize with; they were the victims of government, of the aristocracy, or established authority. The personal inspiration for me was that I wanted to match the grandeur, the heroic scale, the plot inventiveness, and those eloquent dramatic touches."

Hugo courageously backed his convictions with action. In 1822, when he was twenty, he defended Vicomte François-René de Chateaubriand, a famed French author who fell out of favor with the government. A childhood friend named Delon was hunted by police, presumably for his republican politics, and Hugo offered his house as a sanctuary. During the Revolution of 1848, Hugo ducked gunfire as he went from place to place, urging an end to violence.

Hugo committed himself to the cause of liberty late in life, when he had the most to lose. As a youth, he had supported the French monarchy, and later he admired Napoleon Bonaparte for supposedly upholding the principles of liberty and equality. When Hugo was forty-nine, he publicly defied tyrannical Emperor Napoleon III. As a consequence, he lost his luxurious homes, his vast antiques collection, and his splendid library of ten thousand books, but he emerged as an eloquent exile who championed liberty for people everywhere.

Like Jean Valjean in *Les Misérables,* Hugo helped the poor by going into his own pocket. He started at home, providing for his estranged wife and his sons, who did not earn much money on their own. He instructed his cook to feed beggars who showed up at his front door. Every other Sunday for about fourteen years, he served "poor children's dinners" to about fifty hungry youngsters in his neighborhood. His diaries abound with examples of personal charity. According to biographer André Maurois, personal charity accounted for about a third of Hugo's household expenses during his peak earning years.

Hugo was such an idol that his portrait engraving was sold at practically every bookstall in Paris. An athletic figure, he stood about five feet, seven inches tall. His trademarks were a vast forehead and intense light brown eyes. Early in his career, his long brown hair was brushed back in waves. In later years, his hair turned white; he had it cropped short and grew a moustache with a neatly trimmed beard.

He abounded with contradictions. As biographer Graham Robb put it, "Hugo was not just a real person with several masks but a limited liability company of egos, each one feeding off the other and maintained by an army of commentators. . . . Familiarity with Hugo did nothing to dispel the rumors that he was not entirely human. He could eat half an ox at a single sitting, fast for three days, and work non-stop for a week. He went out in the worst weather and walked the unlit streets after dark, armed only with his housekey."

If Hugo was not an original thinker, he brought intense commitment and self-confidence to the cause of liberty. Literary critic Charles-Augustin Sainte-Beuve observed that when Hugo "grabs an idea, all his energy pushes at it and concentrates on it, and you hear arriving from afar the heavy cavalry of his wit and the artillery of his metaphors." As Hugo himself declared, "Nothing is so powerful as an idea whose time has come."

VICTOR HUGO WAS born February 26, 1802, in Besançon, France, the third child of Sophie Trebuchet, a sea captain's daughter. An admirer of Voltaire, the witty eighteenth-century French critic of religious intolerance, she apparently never had Victor baptized. His father, Joseph-Leopold-Sigisbert Hugo, had quit school to enlist in the army of the French Revolution, where he displayed unusual ability and became a major general under Emperor Napoleon Bonaparte.

Hugo dreamed of a literary career, but in 1821 his mother died. She left large debts, and his father disapproved of an ambition that was likely to mean tough times. "I shall prove to him," Victor told his older brother, Abel, "that a poet can earn sums far larger than the wages of an Imperial general."

Hugo struggled to live on two francs a day as he worked in an austere room with plain rugs, plain draperies, and no wall decorations. He stood while writing at a polished wood desk secured to a wall. He started work soon after 8:00 A.M. and continued until 2:00 P.M. After a big lunch, he wrote from 4:00 to 8:00 P.M. and then did work-related reading for three more hours. By 11:00 P.M., he was ready for a light meal with his wife and friends. "My colleagues spend their days visiting each other, sitting and posing in cafés, and talking about writing," he remarked. "But I am not like them. I write. That is my secret. What I achieve is done by hard work, not through miracles."

Hugo's first collection of poems was published as *Odes et poésies diverses* (1822). Then came a succession of poetic works that put Hugo in the forefront of the romantic movement, exploring emotions with melodrama and exuberant style. He ventured into politics with a poem saluting young French revolutionaries who had toppled tyrannical King Charles X in July 1830.

He found himself repeatedly clashing with the government. Censors interpreted his first play, *Marion de Lorme*, as a slap at Charles X, and the production was shut down. Hugo responded by writing *Hernani,* discreetly set in sixteenth-century Spain, about a heroic rebel. It opened at the Comédie Française theater on February 25, 1830, and reportedly enjoyed the most enthusiastic reception since the acclaimed plays of Voltaire a century earlier. Government censors feared that closing it down would provoke an uproar. Two years later, censors did shut down Hugo's next hit play, *Le Roi s'amuse,* which included an unflattering portrayal of François I, among the most famous French kings. Giuseppe Verdi, Italy's outstanding opera composer, who turned *Hernani* into an opera (*Ernani*), called *Le Roi s'amuse* "the greatest drama of modern times," and it became the basis for his popular opera *Rigoletto.*

Hugo had already set his sights on writing fiction. His first novel, *Bug-Jargal* (1826), was a melodrama about blacks rebelling in Santo Domingo, and though critics considered it trash, the public loved it. Then came a medieval epic, the antiroyalist *Notre-Dame de Paris* (1831) about the hunchback Quasimodo who falls in love with the gypsy heroine Esmeralda. The intensity of feeling and vividness of language captivated readers throughout the Western world.

Meanwhile, Hugo's wife, Adèle (they had been married in 1822) was bored, and by 1831, she had begun an affair with literary critic Sainte-Beuve. She refused to continue relations with Hugo, and he launched an extraordinary succession of affairs. Most were short-lived, but one—with actress Juliette Drouet—began in February 1833 and endured until her death a half-century later. Four years younger than Hugo, she had long black hair, violet eyes, a slim figure, and considerable knowledge of French literature. He paid her debts, and she copied his manuscripts.

He plunged into political controversies. He had already written *Le Dernier jour d'un condamné* (*Last Day of a Condemned Man*), a polemic against capital punishment. King Louis-Philippe named Hugo a peer, which meant he became member of the French Senate and could participate in political deliberations. The French Revolution of 1848 overthrew Louis-Philippe, and in December there was to be an election for president of France. Hugo and a newspaper he edited, *L'Evénement,* backed Louis-Napoléon, who won—and then conspired for absolute power. Government thugs smashed printing presses and newspaper offices. Hugo recognized the evil of political power and became the leading voice of opposition to Louis-Napoléon, whom ridiculed as "Napoléon le Petit" ("Napoléon the Little.") In response, Louis-Napoléon imprisoned Hugo's sons, Charles and François-Victor. In December 1851, Louis-Napoléon disregarded a law limiting the president to one term and declared himself Emperor Napoléon III. Hugo formed a Committee of Resistance, but the emperor's soldiers crushed all opposition and went hunting for Hugo.

Juliette Drouet arranged a safe house, disguised him as a shabby laborer, provided a passport for a new identity, and on December 11 got him aboard a night train for Brussels. She followed two days later. By becoming a political exile, Hugo forfeited virtually all his assets; moreover, his royalty income had exceeded 60,000 francs a year, and it was illegal for French publishers to continue sending him checks. He soon proved too controversial for the Belgians who were trying to maintain good relations with Napoléon III. Hugo and his entourage settled on the Channel Isle of Guernsey, and that became his home for the next fourteen years.

Hugo earned a good living from his political writings. *Les chatiments* (*Castigations*), a six-thousand-line poem, garnered him 75,000 francs, so he was able to buy Hauteville House, a magnificent four-story manor. He resumed his rigorous work routine in the solarium with unbleached linen curtains, a plain rug, and a slab of wood hinged to the wall for his standing desk. Hugo was in the tradition of literary exiles like Rabelais and Voltaire.

After a morning of intense work, Hugo had a "light meal" consisting of pâté, omelet or fish, then roast beef, lamb, pork, or veal with potatoes and several other vegetables, salad, English puddings, several kinds of cheese, and a different wine with each course. He did his serious eating at dinner, which included a dozen or two oysters, hearty soup, fish, perhaps roast chicken, then a rich meat dish like Beef Wellington, salad, and a rich dessert such as chocolate mousse, followed by perhaps a half-dozen oranges. He nevertheless remained in reasonable shape because every day, regardless of weather, he spent a couple of hours hiking along Guernsey's rugged coast.

From Guernsey came one literary triumph after another. In 1859, Hugo published *La Legende des siècles* (*Legend of the Centuries*), an epic poem about the struggle for liberty and human progress. He denounced French King Louis XIV as a tyrant, celebrated the English defeat of the Spanish Armada, and portrayed Napoléon III as a frog.

Napoléon III made a public appeal for French exiles to return, but Hugo replied, "I swore that I would remain in exile until the end, either my own or that of Napoléon *le Petit*." The *Times* of London declared, "We are proud that Victor Hugo elects to live on British soil, which is enriched and nourished by his presence." The *New York Tribune* added, "His voice is that of free men everywhere."

Hugo began speaking out more about liberty. He denounced the December 1859 execution of John Brown who tried to stir slave revolts in Virginia, and encouraged the efforts of Giuseppe Garibaldi to establish a liberal democracy in Italy. "Liberty," Hugo told a thousand people gathered on the Isle of Jersey, "is the most precious possession of all mankind. Food and water are nothing; clothing and shelter are luxuries. He who is free stands with his head held high, even if hungry, naked and homeless. I dedicate my own life, whatever may be left of it, to the cause of liberty—liberty for all!"

Hugo turned to a project long simmering in his mind—a novel tentatively titled *Misères*, for which he started making notes in 1840. From 1845 until work was interrupted by another French revolution on February 21, 1848, he pushed ahead with it, changed the tentative title to *Jean Trejean*, and put aside the manuscript. On April 26, 1860, he went to the tin trunk where he had stored the manuscript and resumed work. "I have spent almost seven months in thinking over and clarifying in my mind the whole work as I first conceived it," he noted, "so that there might be complete unity in what I wrote twelve years ago and what I am going to write now. He suspended his twice-a-day feasts, and his pen was ablaze. He wrote about two-thirds of the book in 1861 and finished *Les Misérables* on May 19, 1862.

The book chronicles the saga of Jean Valjean, a peasant who escaped from prison after serving nineteen years for stealing a loaf of bread. He adopts a new identity, and redeems himself through peaceful commerce, creating a successful manufacturing business that helps an entire region prosper. He builds schools and distributes a substantial part of his wealth to the poor. He rescues Cosette, an impoverished girl, from a monstrously abusive foster father and raises her himself. Despite abundant good works, Valjean is trailed by ruthless police inspector Javert, who is intent on returning him to prison. He flees with Cosette, the business closes, and the region plunges into depression. When Valjean finds himself in a position to kill Javert, he lets the inspector go free. Meanwhile, Cosette falls in love with Marius, a revolutionary republican who becomes severely wounded amid the failed Paris uprising of 1832. Valjean saves him from police by carrying him through the only available escape route: the dangerous sewers of Paris. Marius marries Cosette, Valjean confesses to Marius that he is an old convict, and the horrified Marius banishes him from the household, which brings on his final illness. But just before Valjean dies, everyone is reconciled as Marius learns the full story about the man's saintly deeds.

While *Les Misérables* exudes generous sympathy for the most wretched among us, Hugo stood apart from the socialist trend of his time. He seemed to be countering the Marxist dogma of class warfare when he wrote, "There has been an attempt, an erroneous one, to make a special class of the bourgeoisie. The bourgeoisie is simply the contented portion of the people. The bourgeois is the man who has now time to sit down. A chair is not a caste." Hugo pressed his attack: "Communism and agrarian law think they have solved the second problem [distribution of income]. They are mistaken. Their distribution kills production. Equal partition abolishes emulation. And consequently labour. It is a distribution made by the butcher, who kills what he divides. It is therefore impossible to stop at these professed solutions. To kill wealth is not to distribute it." He expressed confidence that private enterprise and peace would alleviate poverty: "All progress is tending toward the solution. Some day we shall be astounded. The human race rising, the lower strata will quite naturally come out from the zone of distress. The abolition of misery will be brought about by a simple elevation of level."

Hugo decided to have *Les Misérables* brought out by Albert Lacroix, a Brussels publisher whom he considered a good businessman. The contract called for Hugo to receive a million francs: one-third upon signing, one-third in six years, and one-third in 12 years. The book was perhaps the first international publishing event, going on sale simultaneously in Amsterdam, Leipzig, London, Madrid, New York, Paris, Turin, and St. Petersburg. Within a decade, it was published in some forty countries. In 1874, full rights reverted to Hugo, and he authorized inexpensive editions. Altogether, some 7 million copies of the book sold during the nineteenth century. With *Les Misérables*, Hugo earned more money than any author before him.

He continued to focus on novels. In 1866, he produced *Les Traveilleurs de la mer* (*Toilers of the Sea*), about a heroic fisherman who struggles against the elements, and in 1869, *L'Homme qui rit* (*The Man Who Laughs*), a historical romance about a kidnapped English boy reared by gypsies, who exposes the failure of ruling elites.

Hugo spoke out anew as Napoléon III intervened in the affairs of other countries. His military adventure in Mexico backfired. He got into a war with Prussia, and Prussian soldiers advanced toward Paris. Napoléon III abdicated on September 4, 1870. Hugo gathered together his family and arrived in Paris the following day. He had gained some weight since he went into exile, there were circles around his eyes, and he sported a white beard, but his spirit was unmistakable. Thousands of people lined the streets as Hugo's carriage made its way to his new residence. There were shouts of "Vive la République!" and "Vive Victor Hugo!" Vendors openly sold his polemical poetry, and popular actresses like Sarah Bernhardt held public readings of it, donating the proceeds to help defend France against the Prussian onslaught. Hugo wrote a prophetic letter to the Germans, which urged that they make peace and warned that humiliation of France would trigger venomous hatred and ultimate defeat of Germany. Germany's "Iron Chancellor" Otto von Bismarck disregarded Hugo's appeal, Paris surrendered on January 29, 1871, and a half-century later embittered Frenchmen got even by demanding huge reparations from Germany after World War I.

Hugo continued his disciplined writing. His most notable work in France—and his last novel—was *Quatrevingt-treize (Ninety-Three)* whose hero, Gauvain, was a liberal republican courageously opposing the French Reign of Terror. Ayn Rand wrote an enthusiastic introduction to a reprint, because the book was about individuals' committing themselves to moral values, and Hugo inspired much of her own work.

During his last years, Hugo was depressed by the death of his sons, but in other respects he had a grand time. He continued to arise at dawn and write until midday. *L'Art d'être grand-père (The Art of Being a Grandfather,* 1877), a collection of sentimental poems, enhanced his popularity. Hugo had more romantic adventures. His personal fortune surpassed $1.4 million, an enormous sum in those days, and he entertained as many as thirty dinner guests nearly every night. As Hugo began his eightieth year on February 26, 1881, he was honored with a national festival, a celebration the likes of which had never been seen for a private individual. Some 600,000 admirers paraded by his opulent residence, in the Champs-Elysées quarter, leaving huge mounds of flowers.

Nothing, however, could restore his spirits after the death of his beloved Juliette of cancer on May 11, 1883. She was seventy-seven. Then on May 15, 1885, Hugo got what seemed like a bad cold, but it turned out to be pneumonia. Wracked with fever and struggling to breathe, he died around 1:30 in the afternoon, May 22, at the age of eighty-three. He was placed in a pauper's coffin, as he had requested, and set beneath the Arc de Triomphe. An estimated 2 million people watched as a mule cart carried him to his resting place at the Pantheon where he was buried beside Voltaire.

Few biographers have addressed all of his complex, contradictory character. His wife wrote a memoir. Edmond Bire attacked Hugo with three volumes published during the 1890s. Some recent biographers have focused on Hugo's early years. The most authoritative biography is Graham Robb's, published in 1997, although it is hard to follow the story of Les Misérables among the details.

Since Hugo's time, his reputation outside France has endured with one novel, with nearly all his other novels, plays, and poems forgotten. But that one novel, Les Misérables, has touched more hearts than ever. In 1978, French composer Claude Michel-Schonberg and lyricist Alain Boublil began work on a musical production of Les Misérables, which opened in London on October 8, 1985. Two years later, on March 12, 1987, it came to Broadway. "A thrilling musical experience," declared Time magazine. Les Misérables has played in twenty-two countries, and some 41 million people have seen this inspiring story of liberty and justice for all, Victor Hugo's most precious gift to the world.

SONG AND DANCE

FEW OTHER PEOPLE earned as much popular acclaim for challenging authority as William S. Gilbert, and he did it while making everybody smile. For two decades after he had emerged as England's premier dramatist, with thirty-eight plays to his credit, Gilbert joined composer Arthur Sullivan and created comic operas that joyfully ridiculed the establishment. Interviewed by a reporter, maverick Mark Twain "spoke particularly in favor of Gilbert. . . . He referred to it being marvellous that a man should have the gift of saying not only the wittiest of things, but saying them in verse, and said he had been struck dumb with astonishment when reading Gilbert's operas."

Individualist H. L. Mencken wrote, "The great quality of Gilbert's humor was its undying freshness, an apparent spontaneity which familiarity could not stale. . . . Here, indeed, was wit that Aristophanes might have fathered; here was humor that Rabelais might have been proud to own . . . humor which made him, even above Mark Twain, the merrymaker of his generation."

Author Isaac Asimov said: "There are a great many composers who might have done nearly as well as Sullivan where the music was concerned, but no one, either before Gilbert or after him, even came close to the humor of the dialogue or the cleverest of his lyrics. No one, Cole Porter may be second— he studied Gilbert carefully—but he is a distant second."

Gilbert entertained people as he made serious points. This comes from *H.M.S. Pinafore* (1878): "I always voted at my party's call, And I never thought of thinking for myself at all." This from *Princess Ida* (1884): "I know everybody's income and what everybody earns; And I carefully compare it with the income tax returns." And this from *The Pirates of Penzance* (1879): "Go ye heroes, go to glory, Though you die in combat gory, Ye shall live in song and story. Go to immortality!"

Critic Clement Scott wrote in *Theatre*, in May 1880, "The style of humour . . . has been called topsy-turvy, deformed, exaggerated, caricature, grotesque; it has been compared to the effect of a man looking at his face in a spoon. . . . Mr. Gilbert makes his conscience . . . a friendly jester." Scholar Alan Jefferson wrote, "The situations are . . . based on timeless themes, thwarted love, highborn-lowborn transference, mistaken identity, curses. The libretti have none of the superficial sophistication of the French and Viennese operettas, but Gilbert's alternatives in wit and topsy-turvydom make infinitely more absorbing entertainment."

Gilbert himself explained in an 1895 interview, "I am not ambitious to write up to the epicurean tastes, but contented to write down to everybody's comprehension. For instance, when I am writing, I imagine it is for one particularly dull individual not quick to grasp an idea; so I make nothing long and explanatory, but short, sharp, and clear." Gilbert did most of his work between 11 P.M. and 3 A.M. "Then you have absolute peace," he reflected. "The postman has done his worst, and no one can interrupt you unless it be a burglar."

Until Gilbert came along, English theater was dominated by actors and stage managers who did what they liked with a dramatist's work. Gilbert wrote high-quality librettos and insisted that they be performed as written. One exasperated actor snapped, "I will not be bullied. I know my lines!" Gilbert replied: "That may be, but you don't know mine!"

Gilbert and Sullivan were a striking pair. A *New York Herald Tribune* reporter wrote in 1879: "Mr. Gilbert is a fine, well-made, robust man, apparently forty-five, above the medium stature, with the brightest and rosiest of faces, an auburn moustache, and short 'mutton chop' whiskers, tipped only slightly with grey, large and clear blue eyes, and a forehead of high, massive and intellectual cast. His voice has a hearty, deep ring, and his utterance is quick and jerky. . . . Mr. Sullivan is quite different. . . . He is short, round and plump, with a very fleshy neck, and as dark as his 'collaborator' is fair, with a face of wonderful mobility and sensitiveness. . . . With all this Mr. Sullivan, who keeps a monocle dangling over one eye while the other twinkles merrily at you and whose dark whiskers and hair have an ambrosial curl, is also something of a polished man of fashion."

WILLIAM SCHWENCK GILBERT was born at his grandfather's house, 17 Southampton Street, Strand, London on November 18, 1836. His mother, Anne Mary Bye Morris, was Scottish. His father, Dr. William Gilbert, was a retired naval surgeon and author of *Memoirs of a Cynic.*

Gilbert spent much of his youth traveling around Europe with his parents. When he was two years old—and known as "Bab"—his family was vacationing in Naples, and a couple of thieves snatched him from his nurse. His father bought him back. As an actor at London's Great Ealing School, he portrayed rebel Guy Fawkes who had tried to blow up the king and Parliament in 1605. Perhaps because his parents were always squabbling, observed biographer Hesketh Pearson, Gilbert lightened his life with "visits to the theatre, practical jokes, writing verses, drawing cartoons, and flirting with girls who took his fancy." He enrolled at King's College, University of London, in March 1853 and graduated three years later.

In 1861, Gilbert sold a satirical article and caricature drawing to *Fun,* a weekly humor magazine, and for a decade produced weekly poems, puzzles, puns, and caricatures. His best-known work for *Fun* was the *Bab Ballads* that often satirized the establishment, including the navy, the army, and the Church of England.

Gilbert began to write comedies. His first, *An Old Score*, appeared in 1869. The first with his byline was *Dulcamara!, or The Little Duck and the Great Quack*. Gilbert's quack, Dr. Dulcamara, says: "I amass my patients' wealth, by telling them that they're all in ailing health." The play opened December 29, 1866, and ran for about three months. In *The Wedding March* (1873), Gilbert hit on the approach that he would later use in his work with Sullivan. As biographer Jane W. Stedman explained, "The success of the piece depends principally on the absence of exaggeration in dress and 'make-up' . . . the most improbable things being done in the most earnest manner by persons of every-day life."

Perhaps confident that his career was under way, the thirty-one-year-old Gilbert married nineteen-year-old Lucy Agnes Blois Turner on August 6, 1867. Her family had served in India, and she had known Gilbert for about three years. "She was," according to Stedman, "small and delicate, 'dainty' as contemporaries described her. Even in middle age, her arms and skin would still be lovely and youthful. . . . Her voice was gentle and quiet." Although they never had children, they enjoyed a long and happy life together.

In November 1869, Gilbert was introduced to Arthur Sullivan by composer Frederic Clay after a break in the rehearsal of their musical comedy *Ages Ago* at the Royal Gallery of Illustration, Lower Regent Street. Gilbert was thirty-three. Sullivan, twenty-seven years old, was England's best-known composer. Born on May 13, 1842, in Lambeth, London, he grew up in modest circumstances; his father, Thomas Sullivan, was bandmaster at the Royal Military College, Sandhurst. Arthur won the first Mendelssohn Scholarship at the Royal Academy of Music and studied at the Leipzig conservatory started by Felix Mendelssohn. He wrote music for comic operas (*Cox and Box* and *The Contrabandista*) as well as a symphony, oratorio, ballet, overtures, marches, and hymns like "Onward, Christian Soldiers." He traveled to Paris with Charles Dickens and visited Italian composer Gioacchino Rossini.

It was in Paris that Sullivan met Fanny Ronalds, an American-born socialite who, though separated from her husband, never got a divorce—presumably because that would have scandalized their friends. She and Sullivan were together for twenty-seven years, until he died.

Gilbert and Sullivan's first collaboration was *Thespis, or the Gods Grown Old*, Gilbert's thirty-ninth play. A company of actors go up to Mount Olympus, encounter the dissolute gods, and encourage them to regain their influence by mixing with ordinary folks. It opened December 23, 1871, and ran for sixty-four performances—a financial failure. The score was not saved, but Sullivan adapted much of it for later operettas.

The thirty-one-year-old impresario Richard D'Oyly Carte (born Richard Doyle McCarthy) was convinced another Gilbert & Sullivan collaboration could be a hit. He was managing the Royalty Theatre in Soho, which struggled to fill seats with *La Périchole,* a comic opera by the French composer Jacques Levy Offenbach. Carte asked Gilbert for a curtain raiser, and he replied that seven years earlier he had written a ballad for *Fun* called *Trial by Jury.* He adapted it as a one-act musical comedy, and Carte suggested working with Sullivan. "Gilbert came to my rooms," recalled Sullivan, "and read it through to me in a perturbed sort of a way with a gradual crescendo of indignation, in the manner of a man considerably disappointed with what he had written. As soon as he had come to the last word he closed up the manuscript violently, apparently unconscious of the fact that he had achieved his purpose, inasmuch as I was screaming with laughter the whole time. The words and music were written, and all the rehearsals completed within the space of three weeks time."

Trial by Jury opened March 25, 1875, and ran 175 performances. It was the first really new English comic opera since John Gay's *The Beggar's Opera* (1728). Both draw from English characters, English institutions, and English tunes. *Trial by Jury* tells the story of a breach-of-promise suit filed by a lady whose fiancé wanted to call off the wedding. The judge resolves the dispute by agreeing to marry her himself.

Buoyed by success, Carte established the Comedy Opera Company. Gilbert and Sullivan helped select not magnificent operatic voices but singers who could articulate words. They would perform at the Opera Comique.

In 1876, Gilbert read the short story "An Elixir of Love" and turned it into a three-act libretto for *The Sorcerer.* The lead character, John Wellington Wells, gives a love potion to everybody in a village, and each one falls in love with the wrong person. *The Sorcerer* opened November 17, 1877, and ran 178 performances.

Gilbert turned to a new libretto that satirized politics and the British Navy: *H.M.S. Pinafore, or the Lass That Loved a Sailor. H.M.S. Pinafore* opened May 25, 1878. A heat wave kept people away from theaters, and many people were offended at the idea of satirizing the British Navy. Conservative Benjamin Disraeli, the prime minister best known for promoting British imperialism, wrote that he "had never seen anything so bad as *Pinafore.*" But Sullivan popularized *Pinafore* by playing tunes from it during promenade concerts which he conducted at Covent Garden Opera House. By September, the Comedy Opera Company was selling out every night, and music shops sold as many as ten thousand copies of the piano score every day. *H.M.S. Pinafore* played for over 700 performances. Sullivan replenished his bank account, which he had spent at the Monte Carlo gaming tables, and Gilbert bought his first yacht, *Druidess.*

Unauthorized productions attracted big audiences in America. There were eight unauthorized productions going in New York City alone. Philadelphia had a production with an all-black cast, and a Boston production featured "fifty voices from various Catholic churches."

Carte, Gilbert, and Sullivan formed a partnership and agreed the only hope for stopping unauthorized productions of their work in the United States was to have the next operetta, *The Pirates of Penzance*, debut in the United States so it could be copyrighted there. It opened December 31, 1879, in New York, but the strategy did not work. The story is about a gang of English pirates who are having a hard time making piracy pay. They have one rule—never to hurt an orphan—and everybody they capture claims to be an orphan. Despite all the unauthorized productions, Gilbert, Sullivan, and Carte made a lot of money. During the first six weeks alone, the New York show generated over $4,000 of royalties per week. *The Pirates of Penzance* opened in London on April 2, 1880, and had a run of 363 performances.

Next, Gilbert ridiculed pretentious intellectuals and macho militarists in *Patience, or Bunthorne's Bride*, which opened on April 23, 1881. Partway through the run of 578 performances, the show was moved to the new 1,292-seat Savoy, the first theater with electric lighting, specially designed for D'Oyly Carte. Thereafter, Gilbert & Sullivan operettas were often referred to as "Savoy operas" and the performers as "Savoyards."

Gilbert wrote *Iolanthe, or the Peer and the Peri* (a descendant of fallen angels). Based on one of his Bab ballads, the story is about a conflict between fairies and politicians. The show opened November 25, 1882, the day Sullivan learned that his stock portfolio was wiped out. He coolly conducted on opening night, and *Iolanthe* ran for 398 performances.

Then Gilbert turned Alfred Tennyson's poem "Princess" into *Princess Ida, or Castle Adamant*, with barbs aimed at feminists, macho men, and militarists. *Princess Ida* opened on January 5, 1884, and ran 256 performances. Prime Minister William Ewart Gladstone loved it.

On May 22, 1883, Queen Victoria knighted Sullivan for his "serious" music, not his work with Gilbert. This looked like a snub at Gilbert, because as far as the general public was concerned, Sullivan was known for his work with Gilbert.

When a Japanese executioner's sword fell off Gilbert's wall and crashed to the floor while he was trying to come up with a new story, he was reminded that Japanese culture had captured people's imagination. He produced a libretto for *The Mikado, or the Town or Titipu*, about the folly of a ruler (the Mikado) who interferes with private life. A law provided the death penalty for anybody caught flirting, but the Lord High Executioner had already been convicted of flirting, so he was obliged to cut off his own head before he cut off anybody else's head—something he seemed unable to do. *The Mikado* opened March 14, 1885, and there were 672 performances. It has become the most popular operetta in the Gilbert & Sullivan repertoire.

Gilbert decided to rework his 1869 play *Ages Ago* into a satire of melodrama: *Ruddygore, or the Witch's Curse* (the name later modified to *Ruddigore*). Set in the early nineteenth century, it explored popular views of morality. *Ruddygore* opened January 22, 1887, and ran for 288 performances. Gilbert reported that *Ruddigore* earned him £7,000.

Walking through a train station, Gilbert noticed an advertisement showing a picture of one of the Beefeaters who guard the Tower of London. Gilbert saw comic possibilities in a story about the Tower, even though so many people had been executed there. Sullivan suggested the title, *The Yeomen of the Guard, or the Merryman and His Maid.* The show opened on October 3, 1888, and Gilbert's sure touch was evident throughout. There were 423 performances.

Gilbert wrote *The Gondoliers; or the King of Barataria.* Set in Venice, it is a brilliant satire of egalitarians like Karl Marx who claimed that a more powerful government would make life better. The showed opened December 7, 1889, and ran for 559 performances.

In April 1890, when Gilbert returned from vacation in India, he found his royalty payments to be less than anticipated. He accused Carte of charging Sullivan and him to get new carpets for the Savoy Theatre. A weary Sullivan sided with Carte in the "carpet quarrel." Gilbert sued and won, but the working relationships soured.

Sullivan told Gilbert he wanted to focus on a grand opera, and Carte would build the Royal English Opera House to showcase it. Gilbert pointed out that "the more reckless and irresponsible the libretto has been, the better the piece has succeeded." Sullivan's grand opera *Ivanhoe* opened July 31, 1891, and it bombed at the box office. Carte had to cut his losses and sell the opera house to a vaudeville syndicate. Ironically, when Queen Victoria honored Sullivan by requesting a command performance at Windsor Castle, she chose not Sullivan's *Ivanhoe* but *The Gondoliers,* his work with Gilbert whom she had snubbed.

Gilbert indulged and bought Grim's Dyke, an 1875 Tudor-style mansion in Harrow Weald, just north of London. Recalled actress Nancy McIntosh: "He had a varied collection of lemurs, pigeons, cats, cranes, dogs, but they had one characteristic in common—a great love of being in the library. . . . A wide French window opened to the south through which the animals could come and go as they liked. The pigeons came in search of cigar ash, the lemurs wandered in at teatime to beg fruit, and on one occasion when a family of a dozen half-grown turkeys made their escape from the farmyard even they came straight to the library, where Mr. Gilbert found them . . . all holding a most animated discussion apparently about the manuscript on the desk."

Gilbert went to work on *Utopia Limited, or the Flowers of Progress,* about a tropical paradise where two wise men are obliged to blow up a king if he violates the laws. The show opened October 7, 1893, and although it has many fine points, it was a disappointment after *The Gondoliers,* and ran for only 245 performances.

Finally, Gilbert wrote the libretto for *The Grand Duke, or the Statutory Duel.* This involves a scheme to overthrow the grand duke: the parties draw cards. The loser dies, but the winner must adopt the loser's poor relations. The show opened March 7, 1896, and had only 123 performances, closing on July 10—the shortest run since *Thespis* almost a quarter-century before.

Gilbert was away when Sullivan died of pneumonia around six in the morning on November 22, 1900, at his Queen Anne's Mansion's residence. He was fifty-eight. He was buried in the crypt of St. Paul's Cathedral. His nephew Herbert Sullivan asked Gilbert to suggest some lines for his uncle's bust, to be erected in Embankment Gardens, and he chose from *The Yeomen of the Guard.*

Gilbert was in ill health too. "I had gout all my life," he reflected, "until 1900 when rheumatoid arthritis came along. They eloped together—the only scandal I ever had in the family." Gilbert was knighted at last by King Edward VII in July 1907.

On May 29, 1911, Gilbert took two friends, Isabel Emery and Ruby Preece, for a swim in the lake on his estate. Preece got over her head and screamed that she was drowning. Gilbert rushed out to save her. "Put your hands on my shoulders," he told her. Then he suffered a fatal heart attack and sank. He was seventy-four. The two women survived. Gilbert's ashes were buried in the parish cemetery at St. John the Evangelist Church, Stanmore, near his mansion.

Reflecting soon after Gilbert's death, H. L. Mencken wrote, "*The Mikado* was given in Baltimore last year without the change of a line. . . . After a quarter of a century, how delightfully brisk and breezy it seemed. . . . *Pinafore* made a hit in New York the other night—for the twentieth or thirtieth time in 33 years. . . . No other comic opera ever written—no other stage play, indeed, of any sort—was ever so popular . . . from Moscow to Buenos Aires, from Cape Town to Shanghai; in Madrid, Ottawa and Melbourne; even in Paris, Rome, Vienna and Berlin." Gilbert and Sullivan, Mencken continued, "left the world merrier than they found it. They were men whose lives were rich with honest striving and high achievement and useful service."

Over the years, there have been dozens of books about Gilbert and Sullivan, several biographies of Sullivan, a little literary criticism, and only three biographies of Gilbert: Edith Browne's *W. S. Gilbert* (1907), which drew on her interviews with him; Sidney Dark and Rowland Grey's *W. S. Gilbert, His Life and Letters* (1923), which gathered a lot of entertaining correspondence and anecdotes; and Jane W. Stedman's *W. S. Gilbert, A Classic Victo-*

rian and His Theatre (1996), the first book to chronicle his prolific career before Sullivan.

New York producer Joseph Papp showed how to attract new generations with his 1980 Central Park performance of *The Pirates of Penzance*, which featured synthesizers, rock stars, and a couple of songs from other Gilbert and Sullivan operettas. "Audiences loved it and even traditionalists like me had to concede that it made very good entertainment and in a strange way preserved the spirit of the original," wrote British Broadcasting Corporation commentator Ian Bradley.

The D'Oyly Carte Opera Company went out of business in 1982, apparently because it insisted on offering period pieces rather than living interpretations, but interest in Gilbert & Sullivan productions remained strong. Six years later, D'Oyly Carte reformed with an updated style and staging, and they were enormously popular.

Gilbert and Sullivan Lexicon compiler Harry Benford reports that in the United States alone, there are some 150 theatrical companies that produce at least one Gilbert & Sullivan operetta a year. According to the BBC's Bradley, their work is "performed more often than those of anyone else except the Beatles. . . . In terms of the number of both amateur and professional performances they are well ahead of more recent musical partnerships like Rodgers and Hammerstein or Rice and Lloyd Webber." Gilbert & Sullivan videos are popular. Internet sites attract enthusiasts around the world. Gilbert's free spirit is soaring into the new millennium

WHITE HATS, BLACK HATS

THE WESTERN NOVEL has long been the most popular expression of American individualism. In its classic form, it is a morality tale with a dramatic struggle between good and evil. If the hero is not always a cowboy, he or she is an individual who came up the hard way, overcame obstacles, and fought for what was right.

Nobody has dominated westerns like Louis L'Amour. Over 260 million copies of his 105 books have been sold, more than any other master of the genre. His work has been translated into Chinese, Danish, Dutch, Finnish, French, German, Greek, Italian, Japanese, Norwegian, Polynesian, Portuguese, Serbo-Croatian, Spanish, and Swedish. More than thirty of his stories and books have been made into movies.

The spirit of individualism runs through L'Amour's work in lines like these: "I had found no luck and opportunity except that I made" (*Sackett's Land*); "A name is only what a person makes it" (*Lonely on the Mountain*), "A man who travels alone must look out for himself" (*Lando*), "It is the willingness to accept responsibility, I think, that is the measure of a man . . . We in America always believe we have only to pass a law and everything will be changed" (*Bendigo Shafter*), "You are your own best teacher . . . When one has lost his freedom it is always a long walk back" (*The Walking Drum*).

L'Amour portrayed individualism as a civilizing influence: "The lawlessness in Western communities has been much over-rated because of its dramatic aspects," he wrote. "The stories of outlaws and badmen are exciting, and Western men themselves still love to relate them. However, over most of the West schools and churches had come with the first settlers. . . . The gunfighters and cardsharks were on the wrong side of the tracks, most of them unknown to the general run of the population."

L'Amour did not achieve his amazing record by being the most productive western writer; Frederic Faust, who wrote westerns under the pseudonym Max Brand, holds the record with over three hundred, about triple the number of L'Amour titles. Nor did he become the top seller with brilliant craftsmanship. Irwyn Applebaum, who edited L'Amour's books for years, remarked, "You may find writers who produce a better book in terms of pure literary quality, but I don't think you'll ever find a better storyteller."

He created memorable characters embroiled in dramatic conflicts, starting the action on the first line of the first page. He was famous for his research, which enabled him to produce a vivid narrative. He got crucial details by reading historic diaries, letters, and newspapers. He learned about weapons and Indians; and made it his business to know the land where events took place. Most of his books were set in the American West during the 1860s, 1870s, and 1880s.

Robert Weinberg, author of *The Louis L'Amour Companion* (1994), reflected, "In L'Amour's books, I found a mythic quality that seemed to define the Old West. Most prominent in *Flint,* my choice for L'Amour's best novel, it appears throughout all of his stories, elevating many of them (including most of the Sackett novels, *Bendigo Shafter,* and *The Lonesome Gods*) out of the realm of genre fiction."

A school dropout because of the need to earn money, L'Amour took charge of his education and was an omnivorous reader throughout his life. "Obviously, there are advantages to programmed reading that cannot be secured in any other way," recalled former librarian of Congress Daniel J. Boorstin. "Louis, by force of circumstances and from a passion for books, sought and found other advantages. He enjoyed and was stirred by countless unprogrammed juxtapositions—the fate of the Incas and of the Roman Empire, Shakespeare's sonnets, Jack London's tales and Plato's dialogues. He could quote Robert W. Service and William Butler Yeats, Rudyard Kipling and Percy Bysshe Shelley and Oscar Wilde in the same breath."

After a youth spent wandering around the world, L'Amour settled into a highly disciplined work schedule, which he maintained during his last four decades: arising around 5:30 A.M. and writing for six hours at his typewriter (later two electric typewriters). Then he would go for a workout, have lunch, and return to work. "I work all the time," he told interviewer Harold Keith. "I love it and can't stay away from it. I am a man intoxicated with my country and its people. If I had a thousand years, I could not tell the stories, nor put into words half of what I feel."

Buoyed by his success, L'Amour moved into a palatial Los Angeles home, where his widow still lives. The home, according to biographer Robert L. Gale, "is a rambling, Spanish-style adobe hacienda located on a quarter-block off Sunset Boulevard, and it is complete with shaded patios and colorful gardens, a covered pool, a huge living room with fireplace, hallway, and study wing. This area includes a workroom with a high ceiling lighted by a rosette window. Interiors are decorated with Indian rugs and paintings and dolls, mounted longhorns, original paintings first used as covers for many L'Amour best-sellers, a portrait of the author, and hinged double shelves for thousands of books, and even an adjacent gymnasium."

Beau L'Amour reported, "The room where Dad worked is roughly 25 by 15, and its twelve-foot walls are lined with book cases which, mounted on huge hinges, swing out to reveal even more books. His desk—a handcarved wooden table as big as a double bed, a coffee table, the hearth of the fire-place, and most of the floor were covered with precariously balanced piles of paper, magazines (Dad subscribed to more than twenty), reference books and artifacts. . . . It was a magnificent mess."

L'Amour was an impressive-looking man, six feet, one inch tall. "Still ruggedly handsome in his late 70s," noted a reporter for *Smithsonian,* "broad-shouldered with eyebrows that peak in gray-brown arrowheads. He wears Western style shirts and string ties and cowboy boots, and speaks in a mea-sured, confident baritone. His manner is sober, self-contained and unaffect-edly modest."

LOUIS DEARBORN LAMOORE was born in Jamestown, North Dakota on March 22, 1908. He was the youngest of six children of Emily Dearborn. His father, Louis Charles LaMoore, was a veterinarian, chief of police, and Sun-day school teacher.

Young Louis went to school for six years, but he became increasingly rest-less. He quit school at age fifteen and embarked on the most amazing adventures. He worked as an elephant handler for a circus that toured Ari-zona and Texas. He was a ranch hand in West Texas. Because he needed the money, he did the smelliest job: working for three dollars a day to skin over nine hundred dead cattle, salvaging the hides. He worked part-time for an undertaker, cleaning the bodies of people who had died in fights. He cut hay, bailed hay, and picked fruit in New Mexico. He was a lumberjack in Oregon. He moved carts of ore at a Nevada mine. He was a professional boxer. He hopped the freight trains as a hobo looking for work. He became a seaman aboard freighters bound for the Far East, and he fought off pirates in Indonesia. His ports-of-call included Singapore, Borneo, Java, Sumatra, Singapore, Yokohama, Kobe, and Nagasaki. He described his experiences living among bandits in western China and Tibet. He witnessed the beheading of Chinese criminals. "In short," reported journalist Harold R. Hinds, Jr., "he was a jack-of-all-trades, and self-reliant man who could survive on any frontier."

L'Amour reflected, "Often, when people hear of my career and the many jobs at which I worked, they believe I did this for writing experience. That's nonsense. I worked at those many jobs because work was hard to get and one took what was available at the time. During the Depression years and imme-diately before, jobs were scarce and a man had to keep hustling to keep work-ing. A job might last for an hour or two, or perhaps for several days, and often weeks went by with no work at all."

Wherever L'Amour went, he brought books or read the books he found, especially those of great storytellers like Honoré de Balzac, Charles Dickens, Feodor Dostoevsky, Alexandre Dumas, Zane Grey, O. Henry, Victor Hugo, Jack London, Edgar Allan Poe, Walter Scott, William Shakespeare, Robert Louis Stevenson, Leo Tolstoy, and Anthony Trollope. "Often I hear people say they do not have time to read," he remarked. "In the one year during which I kept that kind of record, I read twenty-five books while waiting for people. In offices, applying for jobs, waiting to see a dentist, waiting in a restaurant for friends, many such places. . . . If one really wants to learn, one has to decide what is important. Spending an evening on the town? Attending a ball game? Or learning something that can be with you your life long?"

He wrote stories and sent them to magazines, but all he got were rejection slips. "My secret," he remarked, "was that no sooner did I put something in the mail than I wrote something else and sent it off. Each rejection was cushioned by my expectations for the other manuscripts."

He broke into print in October 1935 with "Anything for a Pal," a story published by *True Gang Life*, a pulp magazine that offered cheap entertainment. He was paid $6.54. Over the years he sold to such pulps as *Thrilling Adventures, Story Magazine, Detective Short Stories, Rob Wagner's Script, New Western, Thrilling Sports, Sky Fighters, Popular Sports, Dime Western, Popular Western, Texas Rangers, Thrilling Ranch Stories,* and *Ace-High Western*. The best of the pulps offered about a penny a word, and they paid on acceptance rather than on publication. Along the way—it is not clear why—he changed his name to the French-sounding "L'Amour."

Drafted into the army in 1942, he was assigned to a Michigan training school, which showed recruits how to survive bitter-cold winters. Two years later, he was sent to France, where he served in a tank-destroyer corps. When he returned from the war, he lived in New York City and called on Leo Margulies, editor in chief of Standard Publications, which had been a major market for him before the war. Margulies offered this suggestion: "You know about the West. So why don't you write me some Western stories?" At the time, they were the most popular type of American fiction.

In 1946, L'Amour moved to Los Angeles, the center of moviemaking, especially westerns. Short stories, which he wrote through the 1950s, were collected in a number of volumes, including *War Party* (1975), *The Strong Shall Live* (1980), *Buckskin Run* (1980), *Bowdrie* (1983), and *Law of the Desert* (1983).

L'Amour's first western novel was *Westward the Tide* (1950), which, published in Britain of all places, apparently did not do well. Between 1950 and 1952, he wrote four Hopalong Cassidy books under the Tex Burns pseudonym, which belonged to the publisher Doubleday. Hopalong Cassidy was an immensely popular cowboy hero in movies and television. Although L'Amour later disavowed this work, it got him started writing book-length stories for a major publisher. Then he wrote *Yellow Butte* (1953) and *Utah Blaine* (1954) under the pseudonym Jim Mayo.

During the early 1950s, pulp magazines faded away as millions turned to television for entertainment, but L'Amour began selling to better-paying slick-magazine markets like the *Saturday Evening Post* and *Collier's*. His big breakthrough was "Gift of Cochise," which *Collier's* published in its July 5, 1952, issue. This was so well received that he turned it into the novel *Hondo*, set in Arizona in 1874. Scout Hondo Lane saved Angie Lowe, a ranch woman whose husband Ed abandoned her and her six-year-old son, Johnny. Hondo endured torture by Apache Indians and won Angie's hand.

For readers during the 1950s, the successors to pulp magazines were novels that appeared as paperback originals. Saul David, then with Fawcett Books, remembered getting a telephone call in 1953: "'This is Louis L'Amour. You've never heard of me but I want to see you right now.' He came up with an envelope, made a pitch and told me to read his samples. He said he was going to be the next great Western writer and we'd do well to take him on. I read it, while he waited. It was *Hondo,* and it knocked me out. I signed him to a contract on the spot." David added that his skeptical associates thought a L'Amour byline seemed like "a Western written in lipstick."

Hondo was L'Amour's sixth novel, the first published in the United States under his own name. It soon sold over 300,000 copies. "In *Hondo*," wrote critic Scott A. Carp, "L'Amour created those basic Western characters who continued throughout his novels. . . . The straight-shooting, fair-playing, self-reliant hero and the strong-minded, hard-working, loyal, and dedicated woman who stood by her man and never regretted the life she might have had." Hollywood star John Wayne called *Hondo* "the best Western novel I have ever read," and he starred in the movie *Hondo* along with Geraldine Page, Ward Bond, and James Arness. L'Amour received only $4,000 for the movie rights.

Until this time, publishers let an author's books go out of print, especially westerns, which were considered a minor art form, but Bantam offered to keep all of L'Amour's books in print, so in 1955 he went with Bantam. The result was that the success of a new book generated interest in his backlist.

Meanwhile, there was romance. L'Amour married actress Katherine Elizabeth Adams on February 19, 1956, at the Beverly Hilton in Los Angeles. He was forty-eight, and she was twenty-two. They spent their honeymoon in the West Indies and northern South America. Their son, Beau Dearborn L'Amour, was born in 1961 and their daughter, Angelique Gabrielle L'Amour, in 1964.

In 1957 he wrote *Last Stand at Papago Wells,* about Logan Cates who encountered a dozen wayward characters at Papago Wells, a water hole in the Arizona desert. Apache-Yaquis Indians attacked, but Cates showed the whites how to overcome fear, and he won the heart of a woman named Jennifer.

L'Amour's more ambitious novel *Sitka* appeared the same year. It told the story of adventurer Jean LaBarge in the rugged Alaska Territory. He read Homer and the Bible, captained a schooner, traded furs, and tangled with Russian Baron Paul Zinnovy who monopolized the Alaska fur trade. LaBarge was sent to Siberia but gained his liberty and joined the Russian beauty Helena.

The Daybreakers (February 1960) introduced Tyrel Sackett, who with his brother Orrin left Tennessee and headed west in 1870. Although worried about Indians, rustlers, and murderers, they were determined to build a community where decent people could raise children. The success of this book led to sixteen more that chronicled the Sackett family from about 1600 until about 1879.

Flint was published in November 1960, and the Western Writers of America voted it among the twenty-five best Westerns ever written. Gunman Flint taught an orphan named James T. Kettleman about survival in New Mexico. Kettleman moved to New York where he became a successful businessman. When he was diagnosed with cancer, he returned to New Mexico, only to find an evil swindler and notorious assassin plotting to steal a ranch from a woman named Nancy Kerrigan. Kettleman used his wits, his money, and his gun to save the ranch.

In 1963, L'Amour made a novel out of James R. Webb's script for *How the West Was Won.* This was a successful movie with an all-star cast that included James Stewart, Debbie Reynolds, Karl Malden, George Peppard, and Agnes Moorehead. The result was an epic about the courageous men and women who endured harsh conditions and cruel enemies as they ventured West.

Bendigo Shafter (1979) is about a French-Canadian adventurer who worked as a homesteader, trail boss, hunter, writer, and peacemaker. There are a bewildering number of characters—more than eighty—but this is quite a story about the struggle to build a community in the Wyoming wilderness despite blizzards, hostile Indians, and devious rustlers. One of L'Amour's finest works.

In 1980, when his reported sales hit 100 million, L'Amour boarded the Louis L'Amour Overland Express, a 1972 Luxury Custom Silver Eagle bus in which he spent three weeks touring the West and the Southwest to do interviews, sign books, and generally promote his writings. This was the kind of fanfare usually associated with country and western singers.

L'Amour was at his peak of popularity. His books began appearing as hardcover originals, and they hit national best-seller lists. Sales of each new book reached a million within eighteen months after publication. L'Amour was awarded the Congressional Medal of Honor, which President Ronald Reagan presented on September 24, 1983. The following year, he received the Presidential Medal of Freedom.

In *Comstock Lode* (1981), Val Trevallian, a man with a violent past, and Grita Redaway, a beautiful actress, meet in Nevada's silver mining camps. He becomes a successful mine operator and faces the men who murdered his parents—and are intent on murdering him too.

The Lonesome Gods (1983) told how Johannes Verne, abandoned by his grandfather, Don Isidro, was saved by desperados and raised by Indians. He learned to handle wild horses, to fight, to love, and to make something of himself.

L'Amour tried something different with *The Walking Drum* (1984). Set in the twelfth century, it is a sprawling epic about Mathurin Kerbouchard, the son of a murdered mother and missing father, who became a linguist, horseman, swordsman, archer, acrobat, and lover venturing from Britanny to Spain, the Black Sea, Constantinople, and Persia. He avenged the murder of his mother and rescued his father who was held captive.

Jubal Sackett (1985) was the seventeenth novel about the Sackett family, whose exploits L'Amour had chronicled during the past quarter century. There were some 30 million copies of the Sackett novels in print, and many readers considered this to be the most satisfying. Jubal Sackett was a restless explorer who endured great hardships to cross the American continent. He lived and fought among the Indians, and he fell in love with a Nanchez Indian princess.

Last of the Breed (1986) is a twentieth-century adventure. U.S. Air Force Major Joseph "Joe Mack" Makotozi, flying an experimental aircraft over the Bering Sea, is forced down by Soviets. He is sent to a remote prison camp but makes a dramatic escape into the Siberian wilderness and survives bitter cold weather without food, shelter, or guns. Along the way, he finds a free spirit named Natalya.

In *The Haunted Mesa* (1987), L'Amour combines elements of a western and science-fiction. Investigator Mike Ragland, who wants to know why the cliff-dwelling Anasazi disappeared, enters a realm of the supernatural.

L'Amour approached the end of the trail. Although he never smoked, he was diagnosed with lung cancer. He spent his last hours proofreading *The Education of a Wandering Man*, the memoir about his love of reading and his knock-about years. He died at home on June 13, 1988. He was eighty. There was a private funeral service.

There has been an outpouring of previously unpublished work, new editions, and collections, which seem likely to continue for years. Almost 100 million copies of his books have sold since he died.

With prodigious industry, Louis L'Amour dramatically expanded the audience for western stories and novels. He gave western movies and television shows a second wind. He began to gain a respectable hearing from mainstream critics. He was a wondrous gift to all who cherish personal responsibility, individualism, liberty, and justice.

OUT OF THIS WORLD

A PIONEERING MASTER of speculative fiction, Robert Heinlein captured the imagination of millions for liberty. Five of his novels chronicle rebellion against tyranny, other novels are about different struggles for liberty, and his writings abound with declarations on liberty.

Heinlein is the world's most celebrated science-fiction author. In June 1969, as *Apollo 11* astronaut Neil A. Armstrong set foot on the moon, Heinlein was a guest commentator with CBS-TV anchorman Walter Cronkite, speaking to millions around the world. "When the Science Fiction Writers of America began to hand out their Grand Master Awards in 1975, Heinlein received the first by general acclamation," noted Isaac Asimov, himself the respected author of more than three hundred books, including much science fiction. Heinlein is the only author to have won four Hugo awards for best science-fiction novel—for *Double Star* (1956), *Starship Troopers* (1959), *Stranger in a Strange Land* (1961), and *The Moon Is a Harsh Mistress* (1966). He was the first science-fiction author to make the *New York Times* best-seller list (*Stranger in a Strange Land*), and his last five books made it too.

Heinlein's work—fifty-six short stories and thirty novels—has been translated into Bulgarian, Croatian, Czech, Dutch, Farsi, Finnish, French, German, Greek, Hebrew, Hungarian, Italian, Japanese, Lithuanian, Portuguese, Rumanian, Russian, Spanish, and Swedish. His books have sold over 30 million copies in the United States and 100 million worldwide.

Isaac Asimov, whose astonishing career began at the same time as Heinlein's got under way, disagreed with many of Heinlein's views but declared: "From the moment his first story appeared, an awed science fiction world accepted him as the best science fiction writer in existence, and he held that post throughout his life." Best-selling fantasy writer Stephen King wrote that "following World War II, Robert A. Heinlein emerged as not only America's premier writer of speculative fiction, but the greatest writer of such fiction in the world. He remains today as a sort of trademark for all that is finest in American imaginative fiction."

The *New York Times Book Review* hailed Heinlein as "one of the most influential writers in American literature." Gene Roddenberry, creator, writer, and producer of the hugely popular *Star Trek* TV series, acknowledged that Heinlein was among the few authors "at whose feet I'd gladly sit." Robert Silverberg, author of over a hundred science-fiction books, explained that Heinlein's "belief that a story had to make sense, and the irresistible vitality of his storytelling, delighted the readership of *Astounding,* who called for more and even more of his material. [Editor] John Campbell had found the writer who best embodied his own ideals of science fiction. In one flabbergasting two-year outpouring of material for a single magazine Heinlein had completely reconstructed the nature of science fiction, just as in the field of general modern fiction Ernest Hemingway, in the 1920s, had redefined the modern novel. No one who has written fiction since 1927 or so can fail to take into account Hemingway's theory and practice without seeming archaic or impossibly naive; no one since 1941 has written first-rate science fiction without a comprehension of the theoretical and practical example set by Heinlein." Added best-selling thriller writer Tom Clancy: "What makes Mr. Heinlein part of the American literary tradition is that his characters do prevail. His work reflects the fundamental American optimism that still surprises our friends around the world. As Mr. Heinlein taught us, the individual can and will succeed. The first step in the individual's success is the perception that success is possible. It is often the writer's task to let people know what is possible and what is not, for as writing is a product of imagination, so is all human progress."

Heinlein holds a special place in the hearts of millions who discovered him during their teenage years. Before he emerged as a best-selling author of adult books, he had established his reputation with more than a dozen classic books for young people: *Rocket Ship Galileo* (1947), *Space Cadet* (1948), *Red Planet* (1949), *Farmer in the Sky* (1950), *Between Planets* (1951), *The Rolling Stones* (1952), *Starman Jones* (1953), *Star Beast* (1954), *Tunnel in the Sky* (1955), *Time for the Stars* (1956), *Citizen of the Galaxy* (1957), *Have Space Suit—Will Travel* (1958), and *Starship Troopers* (1959). Author J. Neil Schulman spoke for many when he confided that "if Robert Heinlein hadn't written the books he wrote, and I hadn't read them, I doubt very much that I would have had the intellectual background necessary to climb out of the hole I was in between the ages of fifteen and eighteen. He wrote about futures that were worth living for. He wrote about talented people who felt life was worth living and made it worth living, no matter what the breaks that fell their way. His characters never had an easy time of it, but they persevered."

Heinlein's work has inspired readers around the world. For instance scholar Tetsu Yano said, "I had lost all my books during the war and had little money then to buy new ones. I wanted to and had to read something. Despite my lack of proper education in English, I found science fiction magazines quite readable. I became particularly inspired by the stories written by Robert Heinlein and Anson McDonald [one of Heinlein's pseudonyms]. His exhilarating tales gave me the will, hope and courage to go on living in the devastations of the postwar Japan. Robert Heinlein was my teacher and benefactor. I learned English reading his stories and became a translator. It has been an honor to translate many of Heinlein's books into Japanese."

Science-fiction critic Alexei Panshin described Heinlein as "about five feet eleven inches tall, with brown hair and brown eyes. He is solidly built and carries himself with an erect, almost military bearing. He has worn a trim moustache for years and is reputedly the sort of man who would always dress for dinner, even in the jungle. . . . His voice is a strong, very even, somewhat nasal baritone with a good bit of Missouri left in it." As Isaac Asimov remembered, "In some ways, my most important friendship was with Robert Anson Heinlein . . . a very handsome man . . . with a gentle smile, and a courtly way about him that always made me feel particularly gauche when I was with him. I played the peasant to his aristocrat."

Robert Silverberg recalled Heinlein as "a delightful human being, courtly, dignified, with an unexpected sly sense of humor. I met him first . . . at the 1961 World Science Fiction Convention in Seattle, where he was Guest of Honor. He amazed everyone there by holding an open-house party in his suite and inviting the entire convention to attend. That would be unthinkable today, when five or six thousand people go to such conventions. The attendance in 1961 was only about two hundred, but it was still a remarkable gesture: Heinlein in his bathrobe, graciously greeting every goggle-eyed fan (and a few goggle-eyed writers) who filed into the room. . . . I remember telling him that I had already published seven million words of fiction . . . to which he replied, 'There aren't that many words in the language. You must have sold several of them more than once.'"

ROBERT ANSON HEINLEIN was born on July 7, 1907, in a two-story frame house at 805 North Fulton Street, Butler, Missouri, about sixty-five miles south of Kansas City. His father, Rex Ivar, the son of a plow salesman, was a clerk and bookkeeper. His mother, Bam Lyle, was a doctor's daughter.

In 1910, his ten-year-old brother Lawrence took him to see Halley's comet streak across the sky, and it was a sight he would never forget. He became fascinated with astronomy and built himself a small telescope. He became an avid reader of adventure stories, science fiction in particular and relished work by Mark Twain, Rudyard Kipling, Jules Verne, H. G. Wells, Edgar Rice Burroughs, and H. Rider Haggard.

He spent a year at the University of Missouri, then transferred to the U.S. Naval Academy where he became a champion swordsman. He graduated in June 1929 as a mechanical engineer. Soon afterward, he married Leslyn McDonald. Not much is known about her. He served on destroyers and aircraft carriers until he contracted tuberculosis and was discharged from the Navy in 1934 as a lieutenant junior grade. He enrolled at the University of

California at Los Angeles, for graduate study in physics and mathematics, but frail health forced him to drop out.

"The beginning of 1939 found me flat broke," Heinlein recalled. "About then THRILLING WONDER STORIES ran a house ad reading (more or less): GIANT PRIZE CONTEST—Amateur Writers!!!!! First prize $50 Fifty Dollars $50. In 1939 one could fill three station wagons with fifty dollars worth of groceries. . . . So I wrote the story LIFE-LINE. It took me four days—I am a slow typist. But I did not send it to *Thrilling Wonder*. I sent it to *Astounding*, figuring they would not be so swamped with amateur short stories." His story was about the inventor of a machine that told people how long they would live. Editor John W. Campbell, Jr., bought it for seventy dollars and published it in the August 1939 issue. "There was never a chance that I would ever again look for honest work," Heinlein quipped.

In the late 1930s, science fiction was bursting into the modern era. The month before Heinlein's debut, *Astounding Science Fiction* had published its first story by an emerging star named A. E. Van Vogt, and the following month it published the first story by Theodore Sturgeon, another emerging star. Earlier that year, *Thrilling Wonder Stories* published the first story by Alfred Bester, and *Amazing Stories* magazine had introduced the world to Isaac Asimov.

Heinlein's second published story was "Misfit," in the November 1939 *Astounding Science Fiction*. His first work, aimed at young readers, this was about a teenage troublemaker who, relocated by the government to an asteroid, saves a spaceship.

One story after another affirmed Heinlein's belief in liberty. In January 1940, *Astounding Science Fiction* published "Requiem." The hero, an entrepreneur named Delos D. Harriman, develops communities on the moon. He fights "damn persnickety regulations" and fulfills his dream. "If This Goes On—" (*Astounding Science Fiction*, February, March 1940) is the story of the Second American Revolution, against twenty-first-century tyranny. "Coventry" (*Astounding Science Fiction*, July 1940) shows how a reasonably free society might be based on a voluntary social contract called the "Covenant." In "Sixth Column" (*Astounding Science Fiction*, January–March 1941), resourceful scientists develop a secret weapon, which helps repel conquerors. Jefferson Thomas is a hero. "Logic of Empire" (*Astounding Science Fiction*, March 1941) tells how Sam Houston Jones fights slavery on Venus. "Methuselah's Children" (*Astounding Science Fiction*, July–September 1941) chronicles the adventures of Americans who interbreed to achieve longevity three times greater than average, and, persecuted by envious people, find a place where they can be free. "Beyond This Horizon" (*Astounding Science Fiction*, April and May 1942) offers a vision of a libertarian society where private individuals do just about everything that needs to be done.

Discharged by the Navy because of his nearsightedness and prior tuberculosis, Heinlein spent the war years as an engineer at the Naval Air Experimental Station's Materials Laboratory in Philadelphia. Meanwhile, he thought about ways to expand his horizons as an author. He began working with literary agent Lurton Blassingame who helped him sell "Green Hills of Earth" to the weekly *Saturday Evening Post,* which paid the highest rates for fiction. Famous for its Normal Rockwell covers, it was the premier market for short stories as well as serialized novels.

In 1946, Heinlein decided to write a book for young readers. The result was *Rocket Ship Galileo,* about three boys who cobble together a rocket, fly to the moon, and encounter a nest of Nazis determined to win back the earth. This was published by Scribner's, which had published work by mainstream novelists like Ernest Hemingway, F. Scott Fitzgerald, and Thomas Wolfe.

Heinlein got divorced in 1947, and the following year, on October 21, he married Virginia Doris Gerstenfeld, whom he had met in Philadelphia. "My wife Ticky is an anarchist-individualist," he exulted. She was, explained science-fiction author Poul Anderson, "his full partner, as strong and intelligent in every way as himself. He remarked once with a grin that during World War II, when they were both in naval service, she was his superior officer." The Heinleins honeymooned in the Colorado Rockies and decided they'd like to live there. They bought property between 1700 and 1800 Mesa Drive, Colorado Springs, and picked the address they wanted: 1776. Out front they had a brass house sign which evoked the famous Archibald Willard painting *Spirit of '76:* three marchers—a man playing a fife and a man and a boy with drums. The Heinleins were to live in Colorado Springs for the next seventeen years. Among their friends was Freedom School founder Robert M. Lefevre.

Heinlein turned to motion pictures. In 1948, he adapted *Rocket Ship Galileo* into a script for a movie, *Destination Moon.* It showed how private entrepreneurs might arrange the first trip to the moon and handle all the things that might go wrong. *Destination Moon* was the first modern science-fiction movie, and it was reasonably successful.

Heinlein continued to turn out books for young readers. For instance, *Space Cadet* (1948) is the story of boys who train for the most important mission in the solar system, "to keep the peace . . . and protect the liberties of the peoples." *Red Planet* (1949) is about people on Mars who resent being exploited by absentee rulers on Earth. There's a revolution, beginning with a Proclamation of Autonomy modeled on the Declaration of Independence. In *Between Planets* (1951), teenager Donald Harvey becomes embroiled in a struggle for independence. He lands on Venus, a colony controlled by the Earth-based federation dictatorship, and joins freedom fighters rebelling against the federation. *Citizen of the Galaxy* (1957), perhaps Heinlein's most outstanding juvenile, is about a ragged boy named Thorby who is brought in chains to Sargon, and is sold as a slave. He gets free and struggles to stop the slave trade. In *Starship Troopers* (1959), Juan Rico volunteers for the Terran Federation's Mobile Infantry, which defends freedom against collectivists. Rico reflects on the teachings of Lieutenant-Colonel Jean Dubois, his revered high school instructor who denounces the "turgid, tortured, confused, neurotic, unscientific, illogical, pompous fraud Karl Marx."

Fellow science-fiction author Jack Williamson marveled that "juvenile science fiction, as a labeled category, begins with Heinlein. . . . The Heinlein series was a pioneer effort, quickly imitated. . . . Heinlein never writes down. His main characters are young, the plots move fast, and the style is limpidly clear." Heinlein reflected, "I've taken great pride in these juveniles. It seemed to me a worthwhile accomplishment to write wholesome stories which were able to compete with the lurid excitements of comic books."

Besides juveniles, Heinlein wrote *The Puppet Masters* (1951), which tells how the earth is invaded by flying saucers loaded with collectivist slugs. They get on people's backs and gain control of their bodies and minds, wiping out their individuality. In the name of fighting these slugs, the government assumes enormous power to monitor the population. Fortunately, a way is found for people to regain their liberty. In *Double Star* (1956), Lorenzo Smythe discovers the principles of natural rights and helps the native populations of Venus and Mars to enjoy the same liberties as earthlings. "If there were ethical basics that transcended time and place," he reflected, "they were true on any planet."

Stranger in a Strange Land affirmed Heinlein's capacity to extend the frontiers of science fiction. It is the story of Valentine Michael Smith, an earthling who was brought up by Martians and returns to Earth. He establishes a religion that involves "grokking" (empathizing with others) and free love. *Stranger in a Strange Land* (1961) made national bestseller lists and sold some 2 million copies. Heinlein won his third Hugo Award for the book.

Glory Road (1963) is a "sword-and-sorcery" adventure. The hero, "Oscar" Gordon, denies that government had any moral justification for taxing people. "What had Uncle Sugar done for me? He had clobbered my father's life with two wars. . . . the privilege of staying alive is subject to tax—and delinquents are killed out of hand by the Department of Eternal Revenue."

By 1965, Virginia Heinlein had begun to suffer the effects of high altitude in Colorado Springs, and they moved to Bonny Doon, a lovely rural area about sixteen miles north of Santa Cruz, California. He described their place to interviewer J. Neil Schulman: "It's circular because Mrs. Heinlein wanted a circular house . . . Got a big atrium in the middle of it—twelve feet across, open to the sky—which has a tree and flowers. And it has all sorts of things I put in to make housekeeping easier."

There he wrote *The Moon is a Harsh Mistress* (1966), which offered his most well-developed libertarian vision. The moon, referred to as Luna, is a colony of the Earth, used to keep convicts and political dissidents, who cherish individual initiative and enterprise. They tolerate other people's lifestyle choices and mind their own business. They resolve to take charge of their own destiny and declare independence on July 4, 2076. The conspirators recruit Mycroft Holmes, or Mike, the computer, who runs Luna, to help the revolution. Wyoming Knott, an individualist feminist, says: "Here in Luna, we're rich. Three million hardworking, smart, skilled people, enough water, plenty of everything, endless power, endless cubic. *But . . . what we don't have is a free market. We must get rid of the Authority!*" And Professor Bernardo de la Paz ("Prof"), the revolutionary philosopher, replies: "You are right that the Authority must go. It is ridiculous—pestilential, not to be borne—that we should be ruled by an irresponsible dictator in all our essential economy! It strikes at the most basic human right, the right to bargain in a free marketplace." Prof adds, "In terms of morals, *there is no such thing as 'state.'* Just men. Individuals. Each responsible for his own acts."

The Moon Is a Harsh Mistress sounds one of Heinlein's favorite philosophical themes: "'tanstaafl.' Means 'There ain't no such thing as a free lunch' . . . anything free costs twice as much in long run or turns out worthless. . . . One way or other, what you get, you pay for." *The Moon Is a Harsh Mistress* depicts a free society where private individuals, not government, provide education, insurance, security, and conflict resolution. The book has sold almost a million copies.

I Will Fear No Evil (1970) is the story of a terminally ill ninety-four-year-old multibillionaire named Johann Sebastian Bach Smith who's determined to survive a dictatorship rife with violence. He arranges an operation to transplant his brain into the first healthy young body available, which turns out to be that of his black female secretary. He maintains free will and explores the meaning of sexuality.

That year, Heinlein nearly died of peritonitis, his life saved by blood donations. He was especially appreciative because he had a rare blood type (A2 negative), and he urged people to donate blood. He promoted donation at science-fiction conventions.

In *Time Enough for Love* (1974) Lazarus Long becomes his own ancestor. The book includes his many wise sayings—for instance: "The human race divides politically into those who want people to be controlled and those who have no such desire . . . The greatest productive force is human selfishness . . . Of all the strange 'crimes' that human beings have legislated out of nothing, 'blasphemy' is the most amazing . . . Throughout history, poverty is the normal condition of man. Advances which permit this norm to be exceeded—here and there, now and then—are the work of an extremely small minority, frequently despised, often condemned, and almost always opposed by all right-thinking people."

Heinlein, approaching seventy, continued to travel as he and his wife had for years. "We went around the world four times," recalled Virginia. In late 1978, while travelling near Tahiti, Heinlein experienced double vision and had trouble walking—warning signs of a stroke. Back in the United States, he had an operation to relieve blockage of the carotid artery to the brain.

In *The Number of the Beast* (1980), Zeb and Deety, Jake and Hilda fight alien Black Hats out to vaporize them. The book features individualist Grandpa Zach, who "hated government, hated lawyers, hated civil servants . . . public schools . . . supported female suffrage . . . split his time between Europe and America, immune to inflation and the confiscatory laws."

Friday (1982) is the story of heroic courier Friday who carries out dangerous missions throughout North America, a tangle of oppressive states. She says, "There is a moral obligation on each free person to fight back wherever possible—keep underground railways open, keep shades drawn, give misinformation to computers."

In *Job: A Comedy of Justice* (1984), Heinlein explores the shocks of moving suddenly from one era to another. Among other things, he talks about money. "I had figured out," the narrator says, "that while paper money was never any good after a world change, hard money, gold and silver, would somehow be negotiable."

In *The Cat Who Walks Through Walls* (1985), philosopher-rogue Colonel Colin Campbell embarks on whirlwind adventures and among other things explores the free enterprise zones of the moon. One dreary character is described like this: "Bill has the socialist disease in its worst form; he thinks the world owes him a living."

Heinlein's farewell work was *To Sail Beyond the Sunset* (1987), which tells how the father of narrator Maureen Johnson loved Mark Twain's work and corresponded with him. She affirms the principles of personal responsibility and individualism.

During the fall of 1987, Heinlein's frail health forced him and Virginia to move away from Bonny Doon to be closer to a major hospital; twice in 1987 he suffered hemorrhages and was rushed to San Francisco. They bought a home at 3555 Edgefield Place, in the hills above Carmel, with a spectacular view of the Pacific. Heinlein radiated optimism even as his health declined. "I believe in my whole race," he declared. "Yellow, white, black, red, brown. In the honesty, courage, intelligence, durability, and goodness of the overwhelming majority of my brothers and sisters everywhere on this planet. . . . I believe that . . . we always make it just by the skin of our teeth, but that we will make it."

Overwhelmed by heart ailments and emphysema, Heinlein died of heart failure, in his sleep at home, on May 8, 1988. About ten days later, Virginia Heinlein boarded a U.S. Navy ship in Monterey, sailed into the Pacific, and committed his ashes to eternity.

Tributes came from all over. Isaac Asimov: "He had kept his position as greatest science fiction writer unshaken to the end"; Tom Clancy: "We proceed down a path marked by his ideas"; science-fiction author Arthur C. Clarke: "Goodbye, Bob, and thank you for the influence you had on my life and career. And thank you too, Ginny, for looking after him so well and so long"; long-time friend Catherine Crook de Camp: "The last telephone call I made to Robert Heinlein was about a month before he died, while he was at home between two hospital stays. His voice seemed resonant and almost young that evening as we recalled the many happy times we'd shared. He described the splendid vistas from the windows of his new home as he looked towards his beloved sea. Finally, Bob and I said how much we'd always loved each other and always would. It was a heart-to-heart recap of forty-six years of tender friendship. And when there was nothing left to say, I sat beside the silent phone and wept."

Today Robert Heinlein inspires young people much as he inspired their parents and grandparents. His books continue to sell over 100,000 copies a year. *Tunnel in the Sky* is a popular CD-ROM game. In 1994, Disney released the movie *Puppet Masters*. Then came the movie *Starship Troopers*. Major studios currently have movie options on *Glory Road, The Moon Is a Harsh Mistress, Orphans of the Sky,* and *Stranger in a Strange Land.* Robert Heinlein, now and forever—a great spirit for liberty

DANGERS TO LIBERTY

Power tends to corrupt, and absolute power corrupts absolutely.
— LORD ACTON (1887)

POLITICAL POWER HAS been the biggest threat to liberty everywhere. Throughout history, governments have killed more than 300 million people. During the twentieth century alone, governments killed some 170 million people. Only about 38 million were battle deaths. The great bulk of the deaths resulted from mass murder in the name of political, ethnic, racial, or religious doctrines. These crimes were anticipated by some of the most astute political thinkers, who deserve to be better known.

CENTRALIZED POWER

ALEXIS DE TOCQUEVILLE was a gentleman-scholar who emerged as one of the world's great prophets. More than a century and a half ago, when most people were ruled by kings, he declared that the future belonged to democracy. He explained what was needed for democracy to work and how it could help protect human liberty. At the same time, he warned that a welfare state could seduce people into servitude. He saw why socialism must lead to slavery.

Tocqueville staked his life on liberty. "I have a passionate love for liberty, law, and respect for rights," he wrote. "I am neither of the revolutionary party nor of the conservative. . . . Liberty is my foremost passion."

Reflecting on Tocqueville's famous book, *Democracy in America*, historian Daniel J. Boorstin observed; "The most interesting question for the new-comer to Tocqueville is why this book, of all the myriad travel accounts of the United States, should have become a classic—the standard source for generalizing about America. From Tocqueville's era, two best-selling books on the United States—Mrs Trollope's *Domestic Manners of the Americans* (1832) and Charles Dickens' *American Notes* (1842)—by more clever stylists and more acute observers than Tocqueville, survive only as scholarly footnotes. They tell us about those curious earlier Americans, but Tocqueville tells us about ourselves. He speaks to us every day."

Tocqueville was a good listener with a keen memory. He had a remarkable mind capable of discerning trends that almost all his contemporaries missed and drew shrewd lessons from experience. He envisioned the insidious long-term consequences of government intervention.

To be sure, as a member of the landed gentry who earned most of his income from tenant farmers, Tocqueville shared the usual aristocratic prejudices against business enterprise. He hardly uttered a word about the Industrial Revolution, which enabled millions to avoid starvation.

He worked long hours completing important books despite health problems that plagued him: migraine headaches, neuralgia, and stomach cramps lasting a week at a time. Undoubtedly these afflictions were a major reason for his irritability. In his books, Tocqueville seems like a realist, yet his letters suggest he was a romantic who dreamed of great adventures and endured bouts of depression. At age nineteen, he wrote to a friend that he wished "to roam about for the rest of time." When he was nearly thirty, after *Democracy in America* became a hit, he lamented: "Oh! How I wish that Providence would present me with an opportunity to use, in order to accomplish good and grand things . . . this internal flame I feel within me that does not know where to find what feeds it." And at forty-one; "Perhaps a moment will come in which the action we will undertake can be glorious."

Tocqueville, according to historian George Wilson Pierson, was "almost diminuitive in stature; a dignified, reserved, shy little gentleman, delicate of feature and restrained in gesture. Proud, dark, troubled eyes arrested the glance and fitfully illuminated his pale and serious face. A sensitive mouth and lightly cleft chin, below a strong aquiline nose, betrayed his breeding and bespoke a more than ordinary determination. The finely shaped head was darkly framed in his long black hair, which he wore falling in locks to his shoulders, in the proud fashion of the day. When receiving, or conversing, he waved his narrow hands with grace and distinction. . . . When he spoke, a resonant and moving voice, surprising so in small and frail a body, made his listeners forget all but the intense conviction and innate sincerity of the man."

ALEXIS-CHARLES-HENRI Clerel de Tocqueville was born the youngest of three boys on July 29, 1805, in Paris. His father, Hervé-Louis-François-Jean-Bonaventure Clerel, was a landed aristocrat descended from Norman nobles. His mother was Louise-Madeleine Le Peletier Rosanbo. Both were imprisoned during the French Revolution and maintained their royalist ties throughout the Napoleonic era; after the restoration of the Bourbon dynasty in 1815, Hervé served as a regional government administrator. Alexis was tutored by Abbé Lesueur, a priest who taught devotion to the Catholic church and the French monarchy.

At age sixteen, Alexis began exploring his father's library, which included such provocative French Enlightenment authors as Montesquieu and Voltaire. "When I was prey to an insatiable curiousity whose only available satisfaction was a large library of books," he recalled, "I heaped pell-mell into my mind all sorts of notions and ideas which belong more properly to a more mature age. Until that time, my life had passed enveloped in a faith that hadn't even allowed doubt to penetrate into my soul. Then doubt entered, or rather hurtled in with an incredible violence, not only doubt about one thing or another in particular, but an all-embracing doubt. All of a sudden I experienced the sensation people talk about who have been through an earthquake."

Rather than become an officer in the French army like his two brothers, Alexis preferred the intellectual career for aristocrats: law. He studied law from 1823 to 1826, then traveled in Italy with his brother Edouard. As he saw how war and despotism had ravaged the land, he pondered how once-mighty civilizations could perish.

In 1827, his father got him appointed as a judge at Versailles, serving the Bourbon monarchy, but he was uncomfortable. "I had spent the best years of my youth," he wrote later, "in a society that seemed to be regaining prosperity and grandeur as it regained freedom; I had conceived the idea of a regulated and orderly freedom, controlled by religious belief, mores and laws; I was touched by the joys of such a freedom, and it had become my whole life's passion."

On July 25, 1830, the people rebelled and drove the Bourbon king, Charles X, into exile. The new king was Louis-Philippe, from the house of Orléans, which Tocqueville figured was better than chaos, so he took a new loyalty oath, like many other judges, outraging his friends and relatives. But the king didn't trust holdovers and demoted Tocqueville to a post without pay. His warm and easy-going friend Gustave de Beaumont, a fellow judge at Versailles, was in a similar situation. Since the Chamber of Deputies talked about reforming the criminal code, Tocqueville and Beaumont secured official permission to study America's prison system. Their families would pay expenses. The two men canvassed friends and relatives about possible contacts in America, they read American literature, and read some of the travel books that Europeans had written about America. Tocqueville spent forty francs on a leather trunk to carry two pairs of boots, a silk hat, hose, and other fashionable apparel, plus note paper and a copy of *Cours d'économique politique* by French laissez-faire economist Jean-Baptiste Say.

On April 2, 1831, Tocqueville and Beaumont boarded the American ship *Le Havre*, which carried 163 passengers and a cargo of silk from Lyon. After four days of seasickness, Tocqueville and Beaumont adopted a schedule that they continued throughout their trip: up around 5:30 A.M., work until breakfast at 9, then work from 11 to 3 P.M. when they had dinner, and work until bedtime. They didn't join other passengers for supper. In thirty-eight days, they reached New York.

During the next nine months, they inspected many prisons and toured cities: New York, Albany, Boston, Philadelphia, Washington, Montreal, and Quebec. They passed through Buffalo, Cincinnati, Detroit, Knoxville, Louisville, Mobile, Montgomery, Nashville, Memphis, New Orleans, and Pittsburgh. They ventured into the hinterlands as far west as Lake Michigan and took a boat trip down the Mississippi River. They visited Niagara Falls, traveled along the Hudson River Valley, and saw the Mohawk River Valley, the setting of James Fenimore Cooper's best-selling novel, *The Last of the Mohicans*. They met many notable Americans, including Unitarian William Ellery Channing, historian Jared Sparks, Senator Daniel Webster, former president John Quincy Adams, Texas adventurer Sam Houston, lawyer Salmon Chase who was to become Supreme Court chief justice, and Charles Carroll, last surviving signer of the Declaration of Independence.

Soon after they left America on February 20, 1832, they began to write the promised book on America's penal system, with Beaumont doing most of the writing. The book, published in January 1833 as *Du système pénitentiaire aux Etats-Unis et de son application en France,* set out their belief that many prisoners could be reformed through isolation and work, but they insisted the primary purpose of imprisonment must be to punish wrongdoers. The work was a critical success, and the Académie française awarded them the prestigious Montyon Prize.

Although they had talked about collaborating on a book about America, their interests diverged. Beaumont, most concerned about slavery, wrote a novel, *Marie, ou l'esclavage aux Etats-Unis.* For his part Tocqueville was fascinated with American social and political life because of the difficulties his own country had in developing institutions favorable to liberty. He attributed French political problems to centralized government—"Most of those people in France who speak against centralization do not really wish to see it abolished; some because they hold power, others because they expect to hold it"—and observed that liberty makes for a peaceful social order. "Picture to yourself," he wrote a friend, "a society which comprises all the nations of the world—English, French, German: people differing from one another in language, in beliefs, in opinions; in a word a society possessing no roots, no memories, no prejudices, no routine, no common ideas, no national character, yet with a happiness a hundred times greater than our own . . . . How are they welded into one people? By community of interests. That is the secret!"

Tocqueville decided that before he could write about liberty and democracy, he had to visit England. After his trip in 1833; he wrote that it was "the land of decentralization. We have a central government, but not a central administration. Each county, each borough, each district looks after its own interests. Industry is left to itself. . . . It is not in the nature of things that a central government should be able to supervise all the wants of a great nation. Decentralization is the chief cause of England's material progress."

In an attic room of his parents' Paris house at 49 rue de Verneuil, he spent almost a year writing the first two volumes of *De la Démocratie en Amérique.* In mid-September 1833, he wrote to Beaumont: "Upon arriving here, I threw myself on America in a sort of frenzy. The frenzy is still going on, though now and then it seems to die down. I think my work will benefit more than my health, which suffers a little from the extreme exertion of my mind; for I hardly think of anything else as I fire away. . . . From morning until dinner time my life is altogether a life of the mind and in the evening I go to see Mary." He was referring to Mary Mottley, an English commoner he had met while a judge at Versailles. They got married October 26, 1835. She had a calming influence but couldn't keep up with his interests. "In our hearts we understand each other," he told a friend, "but we cannot in our minds. Our natures are too different. Her slow and gradual way of experiencing things is completely foreign to me."

Publisher Gosselin reportedly hadn't read the manuscript and agreed to issue only five hundred copies. But Tocqueville publicized the book, which came out on January 23, 1835, when he was twenty-nine, in newspaper advertisements, and an ideological adversary unintentionally drew attention to the book by attacking it in a newspaper article. An immediate hit, the book won another Montyon Prize, which brought a 12,000-franc award, and it was reprinted eight times before the third and fourth volumes appeared in April 1840. They were less successful commercially than the first two, but critics considered them more important, and they helped buoy Tocqueville's reputation.

Henry Reeve, a twenty-two-year-old editor of the influential *Edinburgh Review,* began translating the book into English, and a revised version remains the most popular translation. In the October 1835 *London and Westminster Review,* English thinker John Stuart Mill called *Democracy in America* "among the most remarkable productions of our time." Mill gave the third and fourth volumes an even bigger boost in the October 1840 *Edinburgh Review:* "The first philosophical book ever written on Democracy, as it manifests itself in modern society; a book, the essential doctrines of which it is not likely that any future speculations will subvert, to whatever degree thay may modify them." Mill asked Tocqueville to write an article for the *London and Westminster Review,* widening his exposure in the English-speaking world. The book was also translated into Danish, German, Italian, Russian, Serbian, and Spanish.

This book has had a lasting impact because Tocqueville offered a broad vision rather than a journalistic chronicle, which would become dated. He was interested in the workings of democracy and illustrated general principles with his observations about America, the largest country to try democracy. He was concerned about what America meant for liberty in France and elsewhere.

Tocqueville was the man who discovered American individualism. Although he described it somewhat negatively in one place, he talked approvingly about self-help, a hallmark of American individualism. For example: "The citizen of the United States is taught from infancy to rely upon his own exertions in order to resist the evils and the difficulties of life; he looks upon the social authority with an eye of mistrust and anxiety, and he claims its assistance only when he is unable to do without it."

Tocqueville explained the American dream: "There is no man who cannot reasonably expect to attain the amenities of life, for each knows that, given love of work, his future is certain. . . . No one is fully contented with his present fortune, all are perpetually striving, in a thousand ways, to improve it.

Consider one of them at any period of his life and he will be found engaged with some new project for the purpose of increasing what he has."

The peaceful influence of free enterprise received his approval: "I know of nothing more opposite to revolutionary attitudes than commercial ones. Commerce is naturally adverse to all the violent passions; it loves to temporize, takes delight in compromise, and studiously avoids irritation. It is patient, insinuating, flexible, and never has recourse to extreme measures until obliged by the most absolute necessity. Commerce renders men independent of one another, gives them a lofty notion of their personal importance, leads them to seek to conduct their own affairs, and teaches how to conduct them well; it therefore prepares men for freedom, but preserves them from revolutions."

Tocqueville observed that liberty and the need for social cooperation give people incentives to be virtuous. "I have often seen Americans make great and real sacrifices to the public welfare; and I have noticed a hundred instances in which they hardly ever failed to lend faithful support to one another. The free institutions which the inhabitants of the United States possess, and the political rights of which they make so much use, remind every citizen, and in a thousand ways, that he lives in society. They every instant impress upon his mind the notion that it is the duty as well as the interest of men to make themselves useful to their fellow creatures; and as he sees no particular ground of animosity to them, since he is never either their master or their slave, his heart readily leans to the side of kindness."

Tocqueville denounced American slavery, saying that "the laws of humanity have been totally perverted." He anticipated civil war and he predicted that blacks and whites would have a tough time getting along after the abolition of slavery, but he expressed confidence that blacks could do fine if truly liberated: "As long as the Negro remains a slave, he may be kept in a condition not far removed from that of the brutes; but with his liberty he cannot but acquire a degree of instruction that will enable him to appreciate his misfortunes and to discern a remedy for them."

Tocqueville warned against war and violent revolution: "It is chiefly in war that nations desire, and frequently need, to increase the powers of the central government. All men of military genius are fond of centralization, which increases their strength; and all men of centralizing genius are fond of war. . . . A people is never so disposed to increase the functions of central government as at the close of a long and bloody revolution. . . . The love of public tranquillity becomes at such times an indiscriminate passion, and the members of the community are apt to conceive a most inordinate devotion to order."

With phenomenal foresight, Tocqueville predicted that the welfare state would become a curse: "Above this race of men stands an immense and tutelary power, which takes upon itself alone to secure their gratifications and to watch over their fate. That power is absolute, minute, regular, provident, and mild. It would be like the authority of a parent if, like that authority, its object was to prepare men for manhood; but it seeks, on the contrary, to keep them in perpetual childhood; it is well content that the people should rejoice, provided they think of nothing but rejoicing. For their happiness such a government willingly labors, but it chooses to be the sole agent and the only arbiter of that happiness; it provides for their security, foresees and supplies their necessities, facilitates their pleasures, manages their principal concerns, directs their industry, regulates the descent of property, and subdivides their inheritances; what remains, but to spare them all the care of thinking and all the trouble of living?"

"Our contemporaries," he continued, "combine the principle of centralization and that of popular sovereignty; this gives them a respite: they console themselves for being in tutelage by the reflection that they have chosen their own guardians."

Like some other nineteenth-century gentleman-scholars such as Thomas Macaulay, Tocqueville hoped to shape public policy and spent a dozen frustrating years as an elected representative in the Chamber of Deputies and Constituent Assembly, where he focused on such controversies as abolishing slavery in French colonies. For five months, he served as finance minister. But he had little influence on François Guizot (pro-business) or Louis Adolph Thiers (moderate opposition), who utterly dominated French politics during this era.

During the Revolution of 1848, which toppled King Louis-Philippe, when socialism reared its head, Tocqueville was far ahead of his time in seeing why it must mean slavery. He told fellow representatives: "Democracy extends the sphere of individual freedom, socialism restricts it. Democracy attaches all possible value to each man; socialism makes each man a mere agent, a mere number. Democracy and socialism have nothing in common but one word: equality. But notice the difference: while democracy seeks equality in liberty, socialism seeks equality in restraint and servitude."

Since Tocqueville believed individuals should be judged on their own merits, he rejected the racist theories of Arthur de Gobineau, who wrote *The Inequality of Human Races* (1855). Tocqueville told Beaumont that Gobineau "has just sent me a thick book, full of research and talent, in which he endeavors to prove that everything that takes place in the world may be explained by differences of race. I do not believe a word of it." To Gobineau, he wrote, "What purpose does it serve to persuade lesser peoples living in abject conditions of barbarism or slavery that, such being their racial nature, they can do nothing to better themselves, to change their habits, or to ameliorate their status?"

Tocqueville's last great work, *L'Ancien Régime et la Révolution* (1856), interpreted the French Revolution, which ignited war throughout Europe. Once again, he confronted the demon of centralized government: "The object of the French Revolution was not only to change an ancient form of government, but also to abolish an ancient state of society. . . . clear away the ruins, and you behold an immense central power, which has attracted and absorbed into unity all the fractions of authority and influence which had formerly been dispersed amongst a host of secondary powers, orders, classes, professions, families and individuals, and which were disseminated throughout the whole fabric of society."

Tocqueville's health had always been delicate, but it took a turn for the worse in March 1850 when he developed tuberculosis. It went into remission for several years and then became more serious. He could talk only in a low voice. Advised to spend time in a sunny climate, he and Mary went to Cannes in January 1859. Lord Broughham, an English friend who lived there, made available his luxurious library so Tocqueville could relieve the boredom of illness. But he suffered agonizing pain in his stomach and bladder, and on March 4, 1859, he wrote to Beaumont: "I know nothing that has ever grieved me so much as what I am going to say to you . . . COME. COME, as fast as you can . . . I embrace you from the depth of my soul." Beaumont hurried to be with Tocqueville who lost consciousness and died on April 16. He was buried in Tocqueville, Normandy, his family's birthplace. The following year Beaumont, steadfast for more than thirty years, published his friend's works and correspondence.

Tocqueville fell out of fashion during the late nineteenth century, perhaps because Germany, not America, seemed to have caught the wave of the future. German chancellor Otto von Bismarck embraced socialism and established the first modern welfare state, and people everywhere looked to Germany for leadership. But socialist centralization led to communism, fascism, national socialism, and other brutal tyrannies. The welfare state shackled hundreds of millions more with taxes and regulations. Then after World War II, America emerged as the world's brightest hope. Tocqueville predicted it all. Now he's hailed as a prophet. Recent decades have brought the most comprehensive biography of him (1988) and new editions of his complete works, the latest beginning in 1991. Today everyone can see for themselves the wonder of this troubled man who peered into the mists of time, warned against the horrors of collectivism, and boldly proclaimed redemption through liberty.

POWER CORRUPTS

DURING THE TWENTIETH century, people tried everything they could think of to make governments do good. The voting franchise was extended, so governments would better reflect the will of a majority. In many places, each nationality got its own government. Political parties searched for rulers with compassion who sought to do justice. Bureaucracies were filled with trained technicians, enabling governments to plan for a better future, and they commanded vast resources. Yet everywhere the results were horrifying: majorities oppressed minorities; supposedly virtuous politicians turned out to be as brutal as the scoundrels they replaced; nationality attacked nationality; taxes soared.

Few recognized the dangers of political power as clearly as Lord Acton. He understood that rulers put their own interests above all others and will do just about anything to stay in power. They routinely lie, smear their competitors, seize private assets, destroy property, and sometimes assassinate people, even mark multitudes for slaughter. In his essays and lectures, Acton declared that political power was a source of evil, not redemption. He called socialism "the worst enemy freedom has ever had to encounter."

Acton sometimes rose to commanding eloquence when he affirmed that individual liberty is the moral standard by which governments must be judged. He believed "that liberty occupies the final summit. . . . It is almost, if not altogether, the sign, and the prize, and the motive in the onward and upward advance of the race. . . . A people adverse to the institution of private property is without the first element of freedom. . . . Liberty is not a means to a higher political end. It is itself the highest political end."

Although Acton increasingly stood alone, he was admired for his extraordinary knowledge of history. He transmitted to the English-speaking world the rigor of studying history as much as possible from original sources, pioneered by nineteenth-century German scholars. His estate at Cannes (France) had more than three thousand books and manuscripts; his estate at Tegernsee (Bavaria), some four thousand; and Aldenham (Shropshire, England), almost sixty thousand. He marked thousands of passages he considered important. He was awarded an honorary doctor of philosophy from the University of Munich (1873), honorary doctor of laws from Cambridge University (1889), and honorary doctor of civil law from Oxford University (1890)—yet he never earned an academic degree in his life, not even a high school diploma.

To be sure, Acton had some big blind spots. For example, science didn't interest him, and although he expressed concern for the poor, he spurned as materialistic the Manchester Liberals who cared about raising living standards. He knew little about economic history, which tells how ordinary people are faring.

Published photoraphs generally show Action with a long beard. He had piercing blue eyes and a high forehead. "He was of middle height and as he grew older he developed a full figure," added biographer David Matthew. "He was reknowned as a conversationalist, but his talk was on the German model, full of facts and references. . . . He enjoyed walking, traversing the lower slopes of the Bavarian mountains or wandering on the lip of the Alpes Maritimes, where they fall towards the sea."

Acton conveyed tremendous passion. "There was a magnetic quality in the tones of his voice," recalled one student who heard his Cambridge lectures. "Never before had a young man come into the presence of such intensity of conviction as was shown by every word Lord Acton spoke. It took possession of the whole being, and seemed to enfold it in its own burning flame. And the fires below on which it fed were, at least for those present, immeasurable. More than all else, it was perhaps this conviction that gave to Lord Acton's Lectures their amazing force and vivacity. He pronounced each sentence as if he were feeling it, poising it lightly, and uttering it with measured deliberation. His feeling passed to the audience, which sat enthralled."

JOHN EMERICH EDWARD Dalberg-Acton was born on January 10, 1834, in Naples. His mother, Marie Pelline de Dalberg, was from a Bavarian Catholic family with roots in the French aristocracy. His father, Ferdinand Richard Edward Acton, was an English aristocrat. Acton's father died when he was three years old, and by the time he was six, his mother had remarried Lord Leveson, who later served as foreign minister in the Liberal cabinet of Prime Minister William Ewart Gladstone.

Acton was mainly educated as a Catholic at Saint Nicholas (France), St. Mary's, Oscott (England), the University of Edinburgh (Scotland) where he studied for two years, and the University of Munich (Bavaria) where he went after being refused admission to Cambridge and Oxford because of his Catholicism.

Soon after he arrived in Munich in June 1850, he began his apprenticeship to become an historian. "I breakfast at 8," he wrote his stepfather, "then two hours of German—an hour of Plutarch and an hour of Tacitus. This proportion was recommended by the professor. We dine a little before 2—I see him then for the first time in the day. At 3 my German master comes. From 4 till 7 I am out—I read modern history for an hour—having had an hour's ancient history just before dinner. I have some tea at 8 and study English literature and composition till 10—when the curtain falls."

Johann Ignaz von Dollinger, among Europe's most distinguished historians, was Acton's most important teacher. The two traveled in Austria, England, Germany, Italy, and Switzerland, visiting libraries and bookstores, and they analyzed manuscripts and met with poets, historians, scientists, and statesmen. While with Dollinger, Acton attended lectures by the great German historian Leopold von Ranke who stressed that the role of a historian is to explain the past, not judge it.

Those familiar with Acton's famous blasts against tyranny will be startled at his early conservatism. Unlike Manchester Liberals such as Richard Cobden and John Bright, but along with most other Englishmen, Acton sided with the South during the American Civil War. "It is as impossible to sympathize on religious grounds with the categorical prohibition of slavery as, on political grounds, with the opinions of the abolitionists," he wrote in his essay "The Political Causes of the American Revolution" (1861). Five years later, in a lecture about the Civil War, Acton remarked that slavery "has been a mighty instrument not for evil only, but for good in the providential order of the world . . . by awakening the spirit of sacrifice on the one hand, and the spirit of charity on the other."

In "The Protestant Theory of Persecution," (1862) he refused to condemn persecution across the board and seemed to defend Catholic rulers who claimed that persecution was the only way of keeping society together. He suggested that Protestants like John Calvin were worse because they persecuted people just to suppress dissident views. In private, Acton was more outspoken: "To say that persecution is wrong, nakedly, seems to me first of all untrue."

Yet Dollinger and Acton became outspoken critics of Catholic intolerance. Their contemporary targets were the ultramontanes who sought to suppress freedom of thought. Dollinger and Acton took issue with Vatican policy, especially after Pope Pius IX issued his notorious Syllabus of Errors (1864), which condemned alleged heresies including the scandalous idea that "the Roman Pontiff can and ought to reconcile himself to, and agree with, progress, liberalism and recent civilization."

Acton contributed to a succession of Catholic journals whose mission was to help liberalize the church: the bimonthly *Rambler* (1858–1862), the quarterly *Home and Foreign Review* (1862–1864), and the weekly *Chronicle* (1867–1868). These efforts were defeated in 1870 when the Vatican Council declared that the pope was an infallible authority on church dogma. Because Dollinger was a priest, his refusal to submit resulted in excommunication. Acton, a layman, wasn't required to acknowledge the Vatican Council decrees officially, and he remained within the church. It was during this period that

Acton wrote one of his most prophetic essays, "Nationality" (1862), which offered an early warning about totalitarianism: "Whenever a single definite object is made the supreme end of the State, be it the advantage of a class, the safety or the power of a country, the greatest happiness of the greatest number, or the support of any speculative idea, the State becomes for the time inevitably absolute. Liberty alone demands for its realisation the limitation of the public authority, for liberty is the only object which benefits all alike, and provokes no sincere opposition."

In 1865, Acton, at age thirty-one, had married a cousin, Countess Marie Anna Ludomilla Euphrosyne Arco-Valley, the twenty-four-year-old daughter of Count Johann Maximilian Arco-Valley who had introduced Dollinger to Acton, so they had known each other since he began his studies in Bavaria. She seems to have shared his interests in religion and history. They had six children, four of whom survived into adulthood. At meals, Acton spoke German with his wife, Italian with his mother-in-law, French with his sister-in-law, English with his children, and perhaps another European language with a visitor.

Religion was always on Acton's mind, and he came around to the view, shared with the eloquent historian Thomas Babington Macaulay, that historians must expose evil. In February 1879, he split with Dollinger after the professor had taken the view that historians should remain silent about terrible crimes. "The papacy contrived murder and massacred on the largest and also on the most cruel and inhuman scale," he wrote, referring to the Inquisition. "They were not only wholesale assassins, but they made the principle of assassination a law of the Christian Church and a condition of salvation. Acton, the devout Catholic, went so far as to say that unbelievers deserved credit for combating the "appalling edifice of intolerance, tyranny, cruelty" that the Christian church had become.

Acton faced not only intellectual shocks but hard times during the 1870s. Much of his livelihood came from his inherited agricultural land, but farm income declined. He sold some properties in 1883 and sublet his Aldenham estate. He sought a respectable salaried position.

Thanks to Acton's stepfather, he had served as a member of Parliament for a half-dozen years. It was there he met Gladstone, who was to become prime minister. In 1869, after Acton lost a bid for reelection, Gladstone named him a baron, and he sat in the House of Lords, but during all the years he was in Parliament, he never participated in a debate. He quietly supported Gladstone whom he viewed as a great moral leader and with whom he shared a passion for discussing history and religion.

In critical reviews, Acton faulted Anglican priest Mandell Creighton, author of *History of the Papacy During the Period of the Reformation*, for not condemning the medieval papacy that promoted the Inquisition. But Acton and Creighton had a cordial correspondence that led to Acton's most unforgettable lines, written on April 5, 1887: "I cannot accept your canon that we are to judge Pope and King unlike other men, with a favourable presumption that they did no wrong. If there is any presumption it is the other way against holders of power, increasing as power increases. Historic responsibility has to make up for the want of legal responsibility. Power tends to corrupt and absolute power corrupts absolutely."

Acton pursued one book idea after the other, only to drop it: a history of the popes, a history of books banned by the Catholic church, a history of England's King James II, and a history of the U.S. Constitution. He then contemplated a kind of universal history, with the theme of human liberty. This became his dream for a history of liberty.

Author James Bryce wrote that Acton "spoke like a man inspired, seeming as if, from some mountain summit high in the air, he saw beneath him the far winding path of human progress from dim Cimmerian shores of prehistoric shadow into the fuller yet broken and fitful light of the modern time. The eloquence was splendid, but greater than the eloquence was the penetrating vision which discerned through all events and in all ages the play of those moral forces, now creating, now destroying, always transmuting, which had moulded and remoulded institutions, and had given to the human spirit its ceaselessly-changing forms of energy. It was as if the whole landscape of history had been suddenly lit up by a burst of sunlight."

Acton covered part of his beloved subject in two lectures, "The History of Freedom in Antiquity" (1877) and "The History of Freedom in Christianity" (1877), as well as his lengthy review of Sir Erskine May's *Democracy in Europe* (1878). He traced liberty's origins to the ancient Hebrew doctrine of a higher law that applies to everyone, even rulers. He explained how, uniquely in the West, competing religions prevent any religion from maintaining a monopoly, and as a result individuals gained religious liberty. He explored other themes: how democracy emerged from commercial towns, the radical doctrine that individuals may rebel when rulers usurp illegitimate power, and epic struggles against tyrants. These essays abound with memorable observations—for example: "[Liberty] is the delicate fruit of a mature civilization . . . In every age its progress has been beset by its natural enemies, by ignorance and superstition, by lust of conquest and by love of ease, by the strong man's craving for power, and the poor man's craving for food . . . At all times sincere friends of freedom have been rare, and its triumphs have been due to minorities, that have prevailed by associating themselves with auxiliaries whose objects often differed from their own; and this association, which is always dangerous, has been sometimes disastrous . . . The most certain test by which we judge whether a country is really free is the amount of security enjoyed by minorities."

In explaining why liberty had become more secure in America than almost anywhere else, Acton wrote to Gladstone's daughter Mary that "liberty depends on the division of power. Democracy tends to the unity of power. . . . Federalism is the one possible check upon concentration and centralism."

Acton, unfortunately, lacked the single-minded focus for a big project. His voluminous papers don't even include an outline for a history of liberty. Indeed, he never started it. All he left were some five hundred black boxes and notebooks mainly filled with disorganized extracts from various works— much of it about abstract ideas rather than historical events. Later, historian E. L. Woodward remarked that Acton's history of liberty was probably "the greatest book that never was written."

In 1895 Cambridge historian John Seeley died, and it was Prime Minister Rosebery's responsibility to name a new Regius Professor of Modern History. Although Acton hadn't taught a class in his life, he was recommended because of his learning, his loyalty to the Liberal cause, and his need for a salary. And so Acton, rejected when he tried to enter Cambridge as an undergraduate, received the prestigious appointment. In his famous inaugural lecture, he insisted that politicians should be judged like ordinary people: "I exhort you never to debase the moral currency or to lower the standard of rectitude, but to try others by the final maxim that governs your own lives, and to suffer no man and no cause to escape the undying penalty which history has the power to inflict on wrong. . . . History does teach that right and wrong are real distinctions. Opinions alter, manners change, creeds rise and fall, but the moral law is written on the tablets of eternity. . . . The principles of true politics are those of morality enlarged; and I neither now do, nor ever will admit of any other."

During his last years at Cambridge, Acton delivered only two series of lectures—on modern history and on the French Revolution—but colleagues viewed him with awe. Historian George Macaulay Trevelyan recalled, "His knowledge, his experience and his outlook were European of the Continent, though English Liberalism was an important part of his philosophy. . . . Dons of all subjects crowded to his oracular lectures, which were sometimes puzzling but always impressive. He had the brow of Plato, and the bearing of a sage who was also a man of the great world. His ideas included many of our own, but were drawn from other sources and from wider experience. What he said was always interesting, but sometimes strange. I remember, for instance, his saying to me that States based on the unity of a single race, like modern Italy and Germany, would prove a danger to liberty; I did not see what he meant at the time, but I do now!" Acton, Trevelyan continued, generously shared his vast knowledge: "He sat at his desk, hidden away behind a labyrinth of tall shelves which he had put up to hold his history books, each volume with slips of paper sticking out from its pages to mark passages of importance. . . . I remember a walk we had together, and the place on the Madingley road where he told me never to believe people when they depreciated my great-uncle [Thomas Babington Macaulay], because for all his faults he was on the whole the greatest of all historians."

Since Acton came to recognize he would never write a history of liberty, he agreed to edit a series of books that would gather contributions from many respected authorities. Thus was born the *Cambridge Modern History,* a mundane series that squandered his last energies.

Acton suffered from high blood pressure, and in April 1901, after having edited the first two volumes, he suffered a paralytic stroke. He retired to his home in Tegernsee, Bavaria, and a little over a year later, on June 19, 1902, at age sixty-eight, he died while a priest administered last rites. He was buried in a nearby churchyard.

After Acton's death, his sixty-thousand-volume Aldenham library, his principal collection on liberty, was purchased by American steel entrepreneur Andrew Carnegie and given to John Morley, among the last English libertarians. Morley presented the books to Cambridge University, so they would always be kept together.

During the next several years, Cambridge lecturers John Neville Figgis and Reginald Vere Lawrence gathered Acton's most important works, and they appeared as *Lectures on Modern History* (1906), *The History of Freedom and Other Essays* (1907), *Historical Essays and Studies* (1908), and *Lectures on the French Revolution* (1910), followed by *Selections from the Correspondence of the First Lord Acton* (1917).

Amid the monstrous bloodshed of the twentieth century, some people began to remember Acton's warnings about the evils of political power and his call to cherish human liberty. "It appears that we are privileged to understand him as his contemporaries never did," observed historian Gertrude Himmelfarb. "He is of this age, more than of his. He is one of our great contemporaries."

PLANNED CHAOS

❧

THE UNPRECEDENTED SLAUGHTER of the twentieth century was primarily carried out in the name of socialism, the doctrine that government must control everything. Socialism's most outspoken adversary was the Austrian economist Ludwig von Mises who wrote twenty-nine books in German and English, which were translated into Chinese, Czech, Dutch, French, Greek, Italian, Japanese, Korean, Lithuanian, Polish, Portuguese, Russian, Spanish, and Swedish.

Mises displayed extraordinary foresight. In 1920, just three years after the socialist coup in Russia, he boldly predicted that socialist economies would be a mess. He warned that civil liberties were impossible under socialism. In 1927, he sounded an alarm: "Whoever does not deliberately close his eyes to the facts must recognize everywhere the signs of an approaching catastrophe in world economy . . . a general collapse of civilization." "In exclusively controlling all the factors of production," he explained, "a socialist regime controls also every individual's whole life. The government assigns to everybody a definite job. It determines what books and papers ought to be printed and read, who should enjoy the opportunity to embark on writing, who should be entitled to use public assembly halls, to broadcast and to use all other communication facilities. This means those in charge of the supreme conduct of government affairs ultimately determine which ideas, teachings, and doctrines can be propagated and which not. Whatever a written and promulgated constitution may say about the freedom of conscience, thought, speech, and the press and about neutrality in religious matters must in a socialist country remain a dead letter if the government does not provide the material means for the exercise of these rights."

Mises described a comprehensive vision of economic liberty: "There is private property in the means of production. The working of the market is not hampered by government interference. There are no trade barriers; men can live and work where they want. Frontiers are drawn on the maps but they do not hinder the migration of men and shipping of commodities. Natives do not enjoy rights that are denied to aliens. Governments and their servants restrict their activities to the protection of life, health, and property against fraudulent or violent aggression. They do not discriminate against foreigners. The courts are independent and effectively protect everybody against the encroachments of officialdom. . . . Education is not subject to government interference. . . . Everyone is permitted to say, to write, and to print what he likes."

Mises persisted in expressing these radical views even though it meant being treated as an outcast. He was a highly respected economist in Austria, but the University of Vienna four times refused to make him a paid professor, and for fourteen years he conducted a prestigious Vienna seminar without a salary. For most of the quarter-century that he conducted a seminar in New York, his salary was paid by private individuals. Future Nobel laureate F. A. Hayek told Mises: "You have shown a relentless consistency and persistence in your thought even when it led to unpopularity and isolation. You have shown an undaunted courage even when you stood alone." Economist Murray N. Rothbard said, "Never would Mises compromise his principles. As a scholar, as an economist, and as a person, Ludwig von Mises was a joy and an inspiration, an exemplar for us all."

Mises was about five feet, eight inches tall and had sparkling blue eyes. "He held himself straight and erect and walked with a firm step," recalled Bettina Bien Greaves, the world's leading Mises scholar. "He wore a suit, usually gray, and even in the hottest weather he insisted on keeping his jacket on. His grey hair and moustache were always neatly brushed. He was serious, no frivolity. Asked if he played tennis, he replied 'No, because I'm not interested in the fate of the ball.' But he loved to walk, and during his summers in Austria, Switzerland and the United States, he went hiking through the moun tains. As a bachelor until the age of 57, he enjoyed giving tea parties. Later, he and his wife Margit often went to the theater, even when their finances were tight. He was a man of remarkable grace, charm and culture."

LUDWIG EDLER VON MISES was born on September 29, 1881, in Lemberg, then part of the Austro-Hungarian Empire, about 350 miles east of Vienna. (It is now known as Lviv in the Ukraine.) He was the oldest of three boys of Adele Landau, who did charity work for a Jewish orphanage. His father was Arthur Edler von Mises, a railroad engineer.

It was at the University of Vienna, around Christmas 1903, that Mises read a book that inspired him to become an economist and steered him toward free markets: *Grundsatze der Volkswirtschaftslehre* (*Principles of Economics*), by Carl Menger. An economics professor at the University of Vienna for three decades, he explained that prices reflect what customers are willing to pay in free markets. Menger's subjective value theory was a break with the prevailing labor theory of value—that labor costs determine prices. The greatest champion of his ideas was Eugen von Bohm-Bawerk, whose masterwork, *Kapital und Kapitalzins* (*Capital and Interest*), was published in 1884. Mises attended Böhm-Bawerk's University of Vienna seminar until he began teaching in 1913. Meanwhile, on February 20, 1906, he earned a degree as doctor of laws and social sciences. Then he began working for the Vienna Chamber of Commerce, which advised government officials about laws affecting business.

Mises started his first book, *Theorie des Geldes und der Umlaufsmittel* (*The Theory of Money and Credit*). Published in 1912, it attacked the popular view that government officials could dictate the value of money. On the contrary, Mises showed that the value of money was determined by the users and suppliers of money in free markets. Mises insisted that inflating the money supply is futile, because people will bid up prices. The beneficiaries will be those who, starting with government itself, spend new currency before prices go up. The losers will be the last ones to get new currency after prices have risen, and the currency has depreciated in the marketplace.

After World War I, England and France demanded war reparations, which put pressure on Germany and Austria to inflate their currencies. Socialist welfare state spending made things worse. The German inflation climaxed in 1923 as average prices soared over 300 percent a month and wiped out millions. Austrian inflation wasn't this bad, but it was bad enough—average prices up almost 50 percent a month. Mises seems to have persuaded Austrian chancellor Ignaz Seipel and Austrian National Bank president Richard Reisch that the money printing must be stopped.

Socialism too had become a serious problem. Socialism had been put into practice on a large scale for the first time as World War I governments dramatically expanded their bureaucracies, enacted confiscatory taxes, seized private businesses, fixed prices, suppressed markets, dictated production, conscripted labor, and suppressed dissent. Many intellectuals claimed that peacetime socialism could achieve paradise on earth. Mises bristled with defiance. Far from achieving a rational order, he explained in *Nation, Staat und Wirtschaft* (*Nation, State, and Economy*, 1919) that socialism caused chaos. He cited "the stupidities of the economic policy of the Central Powers during the war. At one time, for example, the word was given to reduce the livestock by increased slaughtering because of a shortage of fodder; then prohibitions of slaughtering were issued and measures taken to promote the raising of livestock. . . . Measures and countermeasures crossed each other until the whole structure of economic activity was in ruins."

In 1920, Mises determined why chaos is inevitable under socialism and explained his epic insight in a paper, "Wirtschaftsrechnung im sozialistischen Gemeinwesen" ("Economic Calculation in the Socialist Commonwealth"), before the Economic Society. Under socialism, there were no markets where people reveal their preferences by bidding for things, so central planners, even if they cared, wouldn't know specifically what consumers wanted. And without market prices for the myriad factors of production, it would be impossible to calculate the cost of alternatives and organize production efficiently. "There is only groping in the dark," Mises wrote.

Mises decided to write a book exposing all the errors of socialism. He declared, "If history could prove and teach us anything, it would be that private ownership of the means of production is a necessary requisite of civilization and material well-being. All civilizations have up to now been based on private property. Only nations committed to the principle of private property have risen above penury and produced science, art and literature."

F. A. Hayek remembered, "When *Socialism* first appeared in 1922, its impact was profound. It gradually but fundamentally altered the outlook of many of the young idealists returning to their university studies after World War I. I know, for I was one of them. . . . We were determined to build a better world, and it was this desire to reconstruct society that led many of us to the study of economics. Socialism promised to fulfill our hopes for a more rational, more just world. And then came this book. Our hopes were dashed. *Socialism* told us that we had been looking for improvement in the wrong direction."

Mises sparked a debate that raged for years. The Polish socialist Oskar Lange and others claimed that "market socialism" could somehow have market-like prices without actually having markets. Socialist intellectuals claimed that Lange had won the debate, although Lange's theoretical model was never tried anywhere.

Mises was denied a teaching position for which he was obviously qualified, in part because European universities were government owned, and only those who belonged to one of the favored political parties could become a professor. Hayek added, "For a Jew to get a professorship he had to have the support of his Jewish fellows. . . . But the Jews who were teaching were all socialists, and Mises was an anti-socialist, so he could not get the support of his own fellows. . . . The Vienna of the 1920s and 1930s is not intelligible without the Jewish problem."

Mises became a *privatdozent,* granted permission to teach and be called a professor, but without pay. Beginning in 1920, October through June, he explained, "A number of young people gathered around me once every two weeks. My office in the Chamber of Commerce was spacious enough to accommodate twenty to twenty-five persons. We usually met at seven in the evening and adjourned at ten-thirty. In these meetings we informally discussed all important problems of economics, social philosophy, sociology, logic, and the epistemology of the sciences of human action. . . . All who belonged to this circle came voluntarily, guided only by their thirst for knowledge." Hayek described the seminar as "the most important center of economic discussion in Vienna."

One of Mises most accessible and appealing works, *Liberalismus (Liberalism,* 1927), presented his case for liberty and peace. He explained that free markets dramatically raise living standards and promote social harmony, and he made clear why government interference tends to impoverish people and provoke conflict. Rejecting nationalism, he wrote, "The liberal abhors war, not, like the humanitarian, in spite of the fact that it has beneficial consequences, but because it has only harmful ones."

Everywhere the Great Depression was blamed on free markets, but Mises countered with *Die Ursachen der Wirtschaftskrise: Ein Vortrag* (*The Causes of the Economic Crisis*, 1931). He maintained that recession and depression were the results of prior inflation caused by governments' expansion of money and credit. When inflation slows, or the volume of money and credit contract, many businesses stimulated by inflation are likely to collapse. Mises believed unemployment wouldn't fall until sellers accepted lower prices and workers accepted lower wages, reflecting the reality of what buyers and employers can pay. He warned that chronic unemployment would be the consequence of policies that artificially prop up wages in a depression, and he was right: over 11 million Americans were unemployed in 1940, almost as many as when the New Deal began in 1933. English economist John Maynard Keynes, however, was acclaimed because he told politicians to interfere with the economy and spend other people's money—what they wanted to do anyway.

Invited by William E. Rappard to join the Graduate Institute of International Studies at the University of Geneva, Mises departed for Geneva on October 3, 1934. He left a lot of personal possessions, including thousands of books he didn't need for his current work, in the Vienna apartment where he had lived with his mother since 1911. He remained in Geneva six years, conducting a seminar in French on Saturday mornings.

About a year after his mother died, Mises surprised his friends by getting married on July 6, 1938, in a Swiss civil ceremony that required five lawyers to execute nineteen documents. Mises's wife was Margit Herzfeld, an actress who had performed in plays by Johann Wolfgang von Goethe, Henrik Ibsen, Friedrich Schiller, William Shakespeare, and Leo Tolstoy, among others. They had known each other for thirteen years, and she had had two children, Guido and Gitta, with her late husband. Born on July 6, 1890, she was, according to Bettina Bien Greaves, "a glamorous woman about five feet six inches tall. She was a bit vain and something of a snob, but she was always a gracious host. Mises cautioned her, 'I write about money, but I'm never going to have much.'"

Mises next focused on writing a big book, which became the 756-page *Nationaloekonomie, Theorie des Handelns und Wirtschaftens* (*Economics: Theory of Action and Exchange*), published in 1940. Reasoning from fundamental axioms about human action, he developed a comprehensive case for free markets and attacked every type of government interference with the economy. It was an act of courage to go public with such a book while totalitarian regimes were gaining power. The book was published in Geneva by Editions Union.

After the fall of France, the Miseses decided to leave Europe. On July 4, 1940, they boarded a bus for Cerberes, France, near the Spanish border, often changing routes to avoid the Nazis. Three times they were turned back as they tried to enter Spain. Finally, they made it to Lisbon, and after almost two weeks of constant effort Margit von Mises secured steamship tickets to New York. They arrived on August 2, 1940, and settled in a small apartment at 777 West End Avenue that they would occupy for the rest of their lives.

Mises was deeply depressed that his efforts to fight socialism and achieve some economic security had come to naught. He didn't have any prospects for a steady job, and although he had some funds in England, he couldn't transfer them to the United States because of exchange controls. Hayek helped by using Mises' funds to purchase rare books (like a first edition *Wealth of Nations*) and send them to him, which was legal.

Within a month after he arrived in America, Mises gave *New York Times* financial editor, Henry Hazlitt, a call. Hazlitt had first encountered Mises' name when he was reading *The Value of Money* (1917) by Benjamin Anderson, and he had reviewed the English edition of *Socialism* in the *New York Times* (January 9, 1938), calling it "the most devastating analysis of socialism yet penned." Hazlitt helped get Margit von Mises' thirteen-year-old daughter, Gitta out of Nazi-occupied Paris by using his *New York Times* connection with a State Department official. He also encouraged Mises to write nine articles about the European situation, and they were published in the *New York Times*. The articles led to a connection with the National Association of Manufacturers (NAM), a leading opponent of government interference with the economy. He contributed to a two-volume NAM-sponsored study, *The Nature and Evolution of the Free Enterprise System*, and met many of America's leading industrialists. Meanwhile, on December 24, 1940, Mises was notified that the Rockefeller Foundation had made a grant to the National Bureau of Economic Research, enabling him to write *Omnipotent Government* and *Bureaucracy*, his first books in English. Hazlitt brought these books to the attention of Yale University Press editor Eugene Davidson, who agreed to publish them.

Bureaucracy explained that private businesses are far more dynamic than government bureaucracies because managers can use their imagination and try new things, their performance easily monitored by profit and loss. The performance of bureaucrats cannot be easily monitored. Giving them a lot of discretion results in corruption and arbitrary power. Hence, Mises pointed to the need for rigid regulations in order to prevent a socialist economy from adapting in a changing world.

In *Omnipotent Government,* Mises linked Nazism (National Socialism) and communism, which fashionable intellectuals claimed were two utterly different phenomena. Mises countered that "the Nazis have not only imitated the Bolshevist tactics of seizing power. They have copied much more. They have imported from Russia the one-party system and the privileged role of this party and its members in public life; the paramount position of the secret police . . . execution and imprisonment of political adversaries; concentration camps."

Hazlitt encouraged Eugene Davidson to consider publishing Mises' *Nationaloekonomie,* translated and adapted for American readers. Mises wrote to Davidson that his aim "was to provide a comprehensive theory of economic behavior which would include not only the economics of a market economy (free-enterprise system) but no less the economics of any other thinkable system of social cooperation, viz., socialism, interventionism, corporativism and so on. Furthermore I deemed it necessary to deal with all those objections which from various points of view—for instance: of ethics, psychology, history, anthropology, ethnography, biology—have been raised against the soundness of economic reasoning and the validity of the methods hitherto applied by the economists of all schools and lines of thought."

When *Human Action* was published in September 1949, it was respectfully reviewed in many publications, including the *New York Herald Tribune, New York Journal American, New York World-Telegram, Wall Street Journal, Commentary, Saturday Review of Literature* and *American Economic Review.* In the *New York Times,* socialist John Kenneth Galbraith credited Mises as "a learned man and a famous teacher." Friends of liberty were ecstatic. Henry Hazlitt, who had left the *New York Times* and begun writing the weekly "Business Tides" column for *Newsweek,* said in the September 19, 1949, issue, "*Human Action* is . . . at once the most uncompromising and the most rigorously reasoned statement of the case for capitalism that has yet appeared." *Discovery of Freedom* author Rose Wilder Lane called *Human Action* "the most powerful product of the human mind in our time." Austrian economist Murray N. Rothbard hailed it as "the economic Bible for the civilized man."

Human Action described free markets as "a democracy in which every penny gives a right to cast a ballot. . . . In the political democracy only the votes cast for the majority candidate or the majority plan are effective in shaping the course of affairs. The votes polled by the minority do not directly influence policies. But on the market no vote is cast in vain. Every penny spent has the power to work upon the production processes. The publishers cater not only to the majority by publishing detective stories, but also to the minority reading lyrical poetry and philosophical tracts. The bakeries bake bread not only for healthy people, but also for the sick on special diets. . . . It is true, in the market the various consumers have not the same voting right. The rich cast more votes than the poorer citizens. But this inequality is itself the outcome of a previous voting process. To be rich, in a pure market economy, is the outcome of success in filling best the demands of consumers."

An alternate selection of Book-of-the-Month Club (America's biggest book seller), *Human Action* was translated into French, Italian, Japanese, and Spanish. Yale published a new edition of *Socialism* (1951), a new edition of *The Theory of Money and Credit* (1953), and *Theory and History: An Interpretation of Social and Economic Evolution* (1957). Van Nostrand published Mises' *The Anti-Capitalistic Mentality* (1957) that told how free markets enrich culture. Yale's 1963 second edition of *Human Action*, however, was one of the worst publishing fiascos ever seen; there were pages missing, pages printed in boldface, pages printed in light type, and other problems. Chicago-based Henry Regnery Co. soon brought out a cleaned-up third edition, and San Francisco publisher Fox & Wilkes introduced a paperback.

Meanwhile, Mises spoke out for free markets wherever he could, and along the way, he met Leonard E. Read, general manager of the Los Angeles Chamber of Commerce. Two years later, Read established the Foundation for Economic Education (FEE) and retained Mises as an author and lecturer for $6,000 a year. Mises was among those invited by F. A. Hayek to form the Mont Pelerin Society, an international group of libertarian scholars formed in 1947.

Mises had agreed in 1945 to give a Monday evening lecture course on socialism at the New York University Graduate School of Business, 100 Trinity Place. He would be paid $1,000 per semester, and in 1948, Mises began a Thursday evening seminar on government controls. When New York University announced it wouldn't pay him anymore, Harold Luhnow of the Kansas City-based William Volker Charities Fund came through with $8,500 a year. After it dissolved in 1962, Leonard E. Read, Henry Hazlitt and advertising man Lawrence Fertig raised money for Mises' salary, initially $11,700. The Monday seminar continued until 1964. The Thursday seminar, until 1969. Between 1960 and 1964, the Thursday seminar was held in Room 32, Gallatin House, 6 Washington Square North.

According to Barbara Branden, biographer of bestselling novelist and philosopher Ayn Rand, "Beginning in the late fifties and continuing for more than ten years, Ayn began a concerted campaign to have his [Mises'] work read and appreciated: she published reviews, she cited him in articles and in public speeches, she attended some of his seminars at New York University, she recommended him to admirers of her philosophy."

After Mises' ninetieth birthday, he suffered from painful bowel obstructions. On September 7, 1973, he went to St. Vincent's Hospital at 11th Street and 7th Avenue. He died there on October 10 around 8:30 in the morning. He was ninety-two. The funeral service three days later was attended by twenty-nine friends at Ferncliff Cemetery, Hartsdale, New York. There was a memorial service at Universal Chapel, 1976 Madison Avenue, New York, on October 16.

Mises was dramatically vindicated by the 1991 collapse of the Soviet empire. In *The New Yorker*, influential socialist author Robert L. Heilbroner recalled that Mises had long maintained "that no Central Planning Board could ever gather the enormous amount of information needed to create a workable economic system." Heilbroner confessed: "Mises was right."

Journalist-editor Llewellyn H. Rockwell, Jr., founded the Ludwig von Mises Institute to nuture scholarship on Austrian free market economics. Margit von Mises was chair. Murray N. Rothbard observed that "Margit . . . dug up unpublished manuscripts of Lu's, had them translated and edited, and supervised their publication. She also supervised reprints and translations of Mises' published work." She died in their New York apartment on June 25, 1993, at age 102. The Mises Institute published a magnificent scholars edition of *Human Action*.

In the fall of 1996, Professor Richard M. Ebeling and his Russian-born wife, Anna, tracked down about ten thousand documents Mises had left in his Vienna apartment. These had been confiscated by the Gestapo and after the war were seized by the Soviets, taken to Moscow, and declassified following the Soviet collapse. Ebeling reported, "Ludwig von Mises is shown to be more influential and important than even his strongest admirers had imagined." Ebeling is writing one biography, and German scholar Guido Hulsmann is completing another.

Long after Karl Marx and John Maynard Keynes are forgotten, Ludwig von Mises will be known as a man who told the truth about government power which blighted the twentieth century. He showed with blazing clarity that free markets relieve misery, liberate the human spirit, and make it possible for people everywhere to breathe free.

THE WORST ON TOP

SOCIALISM APPEALED TO the idealism of intellectuals, yet it brought the most hideous tyrannies. Just from the standpoint of human liberty, socialism was a total catastrophe. More than anyone else, Nobel laureate Friedrich Hayek showed why socialism undermines human liberty and, if pursued far enough, must result in tyranny. He told why thugs dominate so many socialist regimes and explained how institutions of a free society develop without central planning.

"Over the years," Nobel laureate Milton Friedman remarked, "I have again and again asked fellow believers in a free society how they managed to escape the contagion of their collectivist intellectual environment. No name has been mentioned more often as the source of enlightenment and understanding than Friedrich Hayek's. . . . I, like the others, owe him a great debt. . . . His powerful mind . . . his lucid and always principled exposition have helped to broaden and deepen my understanding of the meaning and the requisites of a free society." Former British Prime Minister Margaret Thatcher wrote that "the most powerful critique of socialist planning and the socialist state which I read at this time [the late 1940s], and to which I have returned so often since [is] F. A. Hayek's The Road to Serfdom." Futurist Peter F. Drucker called him "our time's preeminent social philosopher." And Pulitzer Prize–winning journalist Daniel Yergin reported in The Commanding Heights (1998), written with Joseph Stanislaw, "Concepts and notions that were decidedly outside the mainstream have now moved, with some rapidity, to center stage and are reshaping economies in every corner of the world. . . . Hayek, the fierce advocate of free markets . . . is preeminent."

A thin, distinguished-looking man who stood an inch or two over six feet, Hayek had a small gray moustache and, in his later years, neatly combed white hair. He spoke in a slow, thoughtful manner with a thick Austrian accent. He was an ardent hiker, spending as many summers as he could in the Alps. He collected rare books on economics, philosophy, and history, and he assembled three formidable libraries during his lifetime.

While some students found his lectures hard to follow, others were enthralled. Majorie Grice-Hutchinson, for instance, who saw him at the London School of Economics during the 1940s, described his lecturing style: "He generally strolled up and down while lecturing, and he talked in a conversational tone, without emphasis or pedantry. His excellent memory and wide humanistic background allowed him to present attractively the ideas of philosophers, jurists, politicians and businessmen of many countries and every period, and he had no difficulty in holding the attention of the large numbers of students who always filled his classroom."

Although Hayek defended controversial views for decades, he usually managed to maintain the goodwill of his adversaries. He developed a warm relationship with the English economist John Maynard Keynes whose advocacy of government intervention in the economy he emphatically disagreed with. As a gesture of goodwill, Hayek dedicated his best-known work, *The Road to Serfdom* (1944), to "socialists of all parties." Nobel laureate George J. Stigler observed that "Hayek has always been both a gentleman and a scholar."

FRIEDRICH AUGUST VON HAYEK was born on May 8, 1899, in Vienna, one of Europe's great intellectual capitals. He was the oldest of three boys born to Felicitas Juraschek and Dr. August von Hayek, a botany professor at the University of Vienna.

Early on, he enjoyed reading widely, and it was during World War I, when he was in the Austrian army, that he read Carl Menger's *Grundsatze der Volkswirtschaftslehre (Principles of Economics)*, about how markets work. Hayek was fascinated and after the war, in 1918, enrolled at the University of Vienna where he earned degrees in law (1921) and political science (1923).

In October 1921, Hayek met Ludwig von Mises, a financial adviser at the Vienna Chamber of Commerce. Mises' 1912 book, *The Theory of Money and Credit,* had made him a respected economist, who explained how government expansion of money and credit caused the runaway inflation that was front page news. Mises found Hayek a job with an initial salary of 5,000 old kronen per month. In an effort to maintain purchasing power amid Austria's postwar inflation, the salary was tripled within thirty days, and nine months later the salary was about 1 million old kronen per month.

Mises had an enormous impact on Hayek's career. Mises' 1922 book, *Die Gemeinwirtschaft (Socialism)*, convinced Hayek that a government-run economy would be a mess. Thanks to Mises' efforts Hayek was awarded a Rockefeller Foundation grant, which enabled European intellectuals to visit the United States. From March 1923 to June 1924, he attended classes at New York University, Columbia University, and the New School, which helped him learn English. He broke into print in English with a letter about runaway inflation, published in the August 19, 1923, *New York Times*. At the New York Public Library, he read news accounts of World War I and was astonished that they differed so dramatically from the Austrian government's war reports. This discrepancy made him profoundly skeptical of government.

Back in Vienna, Hayek began attending Mises' twice-monthly private seminar on free market economics, meeting in Mises' office at the Chamber of Commerce. In January 1927, Hayek, with Mises' help, established Oster-reichische Konjunkturforschunginstitut (Austrian Institute for Business Cycle Research). Two years later, Hayek became a *privatdozent* at the University of Vienna, which meant he could teach students there—without pay.

Hayek had fallen in love with his cousin, Helene Bitterlich, but he never got around to asking her to marry him before he left for America, and when he came back fourteen months later, she was involved with another man, whom she married. Hayek met Berta Maria von Fritsch, known as Hella, whom he married in the summer of 1926. They had two children: Christina Maria Felicitas (1929) and Lorenz (Laurence) Josef Heinrich (1934).

Impressed by Hayek's work on the causes of economic depressions, economics professor Lionel Robbins invited him to deliver guest lectures at the London School of Economics and later to become a full professor there. Hayek introduced English-speaking economists to the Austrian view that a depression was the consequence of a prior inflation of money and credit. When ruinous inflation is stopped, many businesses collapse because they had become dependent on ever-rising prices. Hayek became a British citizen and taught at the London School until 1949.

Hayek's seminars had a broad influence. Future Nobel laureate Ronald H. Coase, for example, remembered Hayek for "encouraging rigour in our thinking and in enlarging our vision." Hayek had Austrian-born philosopher Karl R. Popper speak at a seminar, and Popper expanded his talk into his most controversial book, *The Open Society and Its Enemies* (1945), a passionate attack on collectivists Plato and Karl Marx. Hayek helped find a publisher and persuaded colleagues at the London School of Economics to give Popper a teaching position.

During the 1930s, Hayek's influence was dwarfed by Cambridge-based John Maynard Keynes whose book *The General Theory of Employment, Interest and Money* (1936) told politicians to try curing depression with inflation. It didn't work, but the politicians wanted to spend money, so that's what they did, and Keynes was hailed as a genius. Despite their disagreements, Hayek and Keynes became good friends.

Hayek's focus on central planning captured the imagination of intellectuals and politicians almost everywhere. He realized that decisive critiques of central planning, published in German, were virtually unknown among English-speaking readers. Accordingly, he gathered English translations of essays by Ludwig von Mises, N. G. Pierson, and Georg Halm into a book, *Collectivist Economic Planning* (1935). Without free market prices, they showed, an economy won't work efficiently.

In 1936, Hayek gave a talk, "Economics and Knowledge," at the London Economic Club, and *Economica* reprinted it. Prosperity, he explained, depends on tapping vast amounts of information about what people want and how best to supply it. The information is dispersed among millions of people and constantly changing, which dooms central planning to failure.

Meanwhile, Hayek emphatically disagreed with intellectuals who claimed the Nazis were "a sort of capitalist reaction to the socialist tendencies of the immediate postwar period," as he put it. He believed socialism leads to tyranny, and that the Nazis were a variety of socialist tyranny. The May 1940 issue of *Economica* published Hayek's article, "Socialist Calculation: The Competitive 'Solution,'" in which he wrote that in a government-controlled economy, "all economic questions become political questions, because it is no longer a question of reconciling as far as possible individual views and desires, but one of imposing a single scale of values."

In September 1940, Hayek began turning this idea into a book, which wasn't completed for almost four years. After the Germans started bombing London, the London School of Economics moved to Cambridge, and Keynes found rooms for Hayek's family at King's College, Cambridge. The rooms were cold, so they moved to a semi-converted barn nearby, and that's where he finished his book.

Called *The Road to Serfdom*—after Alexis de Tocqueville's phrase "the road to servitude"—Hayek's book was published in England on March 10, 1944. He noted in it that there is general agreement about a few functions of government, such as providing national defense and punishing violent criminals, but as government expands beyond the realm of general agreement, it must enforce conformity. Central economic planning, Hayek explained, means more and more coercion as officials gain power to decide what work people must do; which kinds of cars, pens, apples, and everything else must be produced; and who should get them. He observed that power attracts those who don't have scruples about imprisoning or even executing people. That's why "the worst get on top." The book provoked controversy, and the two-thousand-copy press run sold out. To secure an American publisher, Hayek sought help from Fritz Machlup, an economist who had attended Mises' Vienna seminar, emigrated to the United States, and worked in Washington, D.C. Machlup couldn't interest any publisher in the book, but he showed English page proofs to Aaron Director, Milton Friedman's brother-in-law. Apparently he sent them to Professor Frank Knight in the University of Chicago's economics department. Knight recommended the book to William Couch, editor of the University of Chicago Press, and it was accepted. They had 2,000 copies printed.

Then came libertarian journalist Henry Hazlitt's fifteen-hundred-word review on the front page of *New York Times Book Review*, on September 24,

1944. He declared that "Friedrich Hayek has written one of the most important books of our generation." The University of Chicago Press ordered another 10,000 copies, and there were requests for rights to translate the book into German, Spanish, and Dutch. *Reader's Digest* editor-in-chief DeWitt Wallace devoted the first twenty pages of the April 1945 issue to a condensation of *The Road to Serfdom*. At the time, *Reader's Digest* had a circulation of around 8 million. Moreover, Harry Scherman's Book-of-the-Month Club, America's biggest book seller, distributed some 600,000 copies of the condensation. Since the book appeared, it has sold over 80,000 hardcover copies and 175,000 paperback copies in the United States, plus authorized editions in almost twenty languages and unauthorized editions in Eastern European languages.

The book struck a responsive chord with at least some of Hayek's intellectual adversaries. Keynes wrote Hayek: "In my opinion it is a grand book. . . . morally and philosophically, I find myself in agreement with virtually the whole of it; and not only in agreement with it, but in a deeply moved agreement." George Orwell, the socialist who attacked totalitarianism in his novels *Animal Farm* and *1984*, acknowledged that Hayek's thesis contains "a great deal of truth. . . . Collectivism is not inherently democratic, but, on the contrary, gives to a tyrannical minority such powers as the Spanish Inquisitor never dreamed of."

The University of Chicago Press rushed Hayek onto the lecture circuit, a new experience for him. He told an interviewer, "When I was picked up at my hotel [in New York] . . . I asked, 'What sort of audience do you expect?' They said, 'The hall holds 3,000 but there's an overflow meeting.' Dear God, I hadn't an idea what I was going to say. 'How have you announced it?' 'Oh, we have called it 'The Rule of Law in International Affairs.' My God, I had never thought about that problem in my life. . . . I asked the chairman if three-quarters of an hour would be enough. 'Oh, no, it must be exactly an hour. . . . You are on the radio." Hayek was a hit.

During the 1945 parliamentary elections, Winston Churchill drew a campaign theme from Hayek's book. On June 4, he warned that a Labour government wouldn't "allow free, sharp or violently worded expressions of public discontent. . . . They would have to fall back on some form of Gestapo." Laborite Clement Attlee derided this speech as a "second-hand version of the academic views of an Austrian professor, Friedrich August von Hayek." The Labour party won the election, Attlee became the next prime minister, and by the fall of 1947, they enacted peacetime forced labor. Economist John Jewkes explained, "The Minister of Labour had the power to direct workers changing their jobs to the employment he considered best in the national interest." Fortunately, the Labour party was defeated in the 1950 elections.

Meanwhile, in 1947 Hayek called a meeting of scholars, journalists, and others who were concerned about liberty. "After the publication of *The Road to Serfdom*," Hayek recalled, "I was invited to give many lectures. During my travels in Europe as well as in the United States, nearly everywhere I went I met someone who told me that he fully agreed with me, but that at the same time he felt totally isolated in his views and had nobody with whom he could even talk about them. This gave me the idea of bringing these people, each of whom was living in great solitude, together in one place. And by a stroke of luck I was able to raise the money to accomplish this." Thirty-six participants from ten countries gathered at the Hotel du Parc, Mont Pelerin, near Vevey, Switzerland, between April 1 and April 10, 1947. They exchanged views and formed the Mont Pelerin Society. Four of the original members went on to win Nobel Prizes.

The *University of Chicago Law Review* published Hayek's essay "The Intellectuals and Socialism" in 1949. He wrote, "The main lesson which the true liberal must learn from the success of the socialists," he wrote, "is that it was their courage to be Utopian which gained them the support of the intellectuals and therefore an influence on public opinion which is daily making possible what only recently seemed utterly remote." Thousands of copies of this essay were distributed over the years, and Hayek inspired efforts in many countries to influence intellectuals and ultimately public policy for liberty.

While visiting Austria to see family members who had survived the war, Hayek learned that his first love, Helene Bitterlich, had become a widow and was free to marry him. He and his wife, Hella, separated in December 1949, to the dismay of friends. Soon after the divorce in July 1950, Hayek married Bitterlich, and they were together for the rest of his life.

Hayek had to get away from England, and the best bet was the United States. The University of Chicago was a possibility because of *The Road to Serfdom*, but the economics department didn't want him. Princeton and Stanford turned him down too. After he taught for a year at the University of Arkansas, John U. Nef, chairman of the University of Chicago's Committee on Social Thought, invited him to be professor of social and moral science. The University of Chicago wouldn't pay him a salary, but the William Volker Fund's Harold W. Luhnow agreed to cover it. Hayek's office was Room 506 of the Social Sciences building on 59th Street. One of his students, Shirley Robin Letwin, remembered that "on Wednesdays, after dinner, a large assortment of the wise and callow, coming from all disciplines and all nations, assembled around a massive oval oak table in a mock Gothic chamber to talk about topics proposed by Hayek . . . philosophy, history, social science, and knowledge generally. . . . Hayek presided over this remarkable company with a gentle rectitude that made his seminar an exercise in the liberal virtues. . . . The general subject was [market] liberalism. . . . The only obligation was to enter into the thoughts of others with fidelity and to accept questions and dissent gracefully."

Since views about history influence current policies, Hayek edited *Capitalism and the Historians* (1954) with contributions by economic historians T. S. Ashton and Louis Hacker and economists W. H. Hutt and Bertrand de Jouvenal. They rejected the widely held view that free markets made people worse off and that government regulation was needed. The book told how people voluntarily migrated from poor rural areas to factories because tough as factory work might have been, it made possible a better and longer life.

When Hayek was invited in 1956 to deliver some lectures for the National Bank of Egypt, he chose as his subject "The Political Ideal of the Rule of Law." He surveyed the history of efforts to limit government power by achieving a rule of law—meaning laws that apply equally to everybody and are predictable so that people can plan their lives accordingly. Hayek developed these ideas more fully in *The Constitution of Liberty*. Like John Milton and John Stuart Mill, he went on to say that because one never knows where discoveries might come from, it's essential that people be free to pursue the truth. He wrote, "The chief reason why we should be held wholly responsible for our decisions is that this will direct our attention to those causes of events that depend on our actions. . . . The recognition of property is clearly the first step in the delimitation of the private sphere which protects us against coercion. We are rarely in a position to carry out a coherent plan of action unless we are certain of our exclusive control of some material objects."

Hayek summarized a legal framework for liberty. First, laws should be rules rather than commands dictating specifically what people must do. "The rationale for securing to each individual a known range within which he can decide on his actions is to enable him to make the fullest use of his knowledge," Hayek noted. Moreover, laws should be general, applying to government as well as the people. This won't prevent all bad laws from being passed, but if lawmakers know that laws apply with full force to them, they'll be less prone to mischief. Hayek pointed out that "today the conception of the rule of law is sometimes confused with the requirement of mere legality in all government action. The rule of law, of course, presupposes complete legality, but this is not enough: if a law gave the government unlimited power to act as it pleased, all its actions would be legal, but it would certainly not be under the rule of law. The rule of law, therefore, is also more than constitutionalism: it requires that all laws conform to certain principles. . . . The rule of law is therefore not a rule of the law, but a rule concerning what the law ought to be."

Hayek had high hopes for *The Constitution of Liberty*, published on February 9, 1960, which he seems to have considered his best work. Although he did get reviewed in friendly publications, like the *Wall Street Journal*,

Chicago Tribune, Fortune, and Henry Hazlitt's *Newsweek* column, the book was generally ignored, and he became depressed.

In April 1962, the Volker Fund was dissolved, and Hayek feared that meant no more income at the University of Chicago. Consequently, when he received an offer to teach at the University of Freiburg in southwestern Germany, he took it. Hayek pushed his thinking beyond *The Constitution of Liberty,* but suffered ill health and didn't write much. In 1969, he became a visiting professor at the University of Salzburg, Austria, because it was closer to his wife's family in Vienna, and the law faculty bought his library while letting him continue to use it.

Five years later, those on the Nobel Prize nominating committee wanted to honor Swedish socialist Gunnar Myrdal, but they decided to share the award with somebody holding contrary views. They settled on Hayek. The Nobel Prize lifted his spirits, and as Daniel Yergin and Joseph Stanislaw observed in *The Commanding Heights* (1998), "documented the beginning of a great shift in the intellectual center of gravity of the economics profession toward a restoration of confidence in markets, indeed a renewed belief in the superiority of markets over other ways of organizing economic activity."

Hayek completed his long-dormant trilogy *Law, Legislation and Liberty,* consisting of *Rules and Order* (1973), *The Mirage of Social Justice* (1976), and *The Political Order of a Free People* (1979). He attributed much of the decline of liberty to the mistaken belief "that democratic control of government made unnecessary any other safeguards against the arbitrary use of power." He attacked "social justice" as a vague idea aimed to justify the endless expansion of government power during the twentieth century. The most disastrous consequences, he said, occurred in countries that adopted parliamentary government and lacked a constitutional tradition limiting, at least to some degree, what government could inflict on people.

In 1976, Hayek produced *The Denationalization of Money,* a report for the Institute of Economic Affairs (London), which challenged what he called "the source and root of all monetary evil, the government monopoly of the issue and control of money." He made a case that private institutions would do a better job of avoiding inflation or depression because they'd be watched by competitors, currency exchanges, and the financial press.

Hayek's writings inspired Ronald Reagan in the United States and Margaret Thatcher in Great Britain. He was revered by people who suffered from socialist tyranny in Eastern Europe, the Soviet Union, and China. Hayek's last work was *The Fatal Conceit: The Errors of Socialism* (1988), substantially edited by William Bartley III whom he had picked to write a biography and assemble his collected works. Bartley died in 1990, the biography unwritten, but Bartley's associate, Stephen Kresge, has ably directed the publication of Hayek's collected works.

Although Hayek was lucid almost to the end, he couldn't do any writing after about 1985. Besides the infirmities of old age, he suffered a bout of pneumonia and seldom ventured out of the third-floor apartment in a big stucco house in Freiburg, West Germany, next to the Black Forest, where he had moved in 1977. Biographer Alan Ebenstein reported, "His library contained perhaps 4,000 volumes across a number of disciplines, including economics, psychology, anthropology, and political philosophy. The furniture was not new, nor the interior recently painted. . . . He had on his desk a picture of his second wife as a beautiful young woman in Vienna many years before."

He died on March 23, 1992, in the apartment at age ninety-two. About a hundred people attended a funeral service on April 4, conducted by Father Johannes Schasching. Hayek was buried in the hilly Neustift am Wald cemetery, overlooking the Vienna Woods.

Hayek had lived just long enough to see the Union of Soviet Socialist Republics disappear from the map. He had insisted, as Mises had before him, that socialism would impoverish multitudes, and he was vindicated. He correctly warned that socialism ultimately means oppression, slavery, and mass murder. He did perhaps more than anyone else to show that free people, not government planners, are the key to a flourishing civilization.

As John Cassidy wrote in the February 7, 2000, *New Yorker*: "If there are two things most people can agree on these days, they are that free-market capitalism is the only practical way to organize a modern society and that the key to economic growth is knowledge. So prevalent are these beliefs that their origins are rarely examined, which is somewhat surprising, since both statements can be traced back, in large part, to one man, Friedrich August von Hayek." His moral courage and dazzling insights made clear that ideas shape our destiny.

REGULATIONS BACKFIRE

UNTIL THE EARLY 1960s, almost everybody seemed to assume government regulations did what they were supposed to: protect consumers from being exploited by business. Then, six-foot three-inch University of Chicago economist George J. Stigler realized that nobody had ever tried to measure the actual effects of laws and regulations. He began measuring, and he either couldn't find any effects of a regulation or the effects were the opposite of what was intended. Stigler went on to make a revolutionary case that government regulations were lobbied for by interest groups to restrict competition, raise prices, and in other ways gain a privileged position not available in an open market.

Stigler spurred economists across the United States to measure one regulation after another, and his analysis was confirmed. By the 1970s, there was a substantial consensus in the economics profession that many regulations were counterproductive, and the movement to deregulate the economy gained momentum. The principal targets were economic regulations. The Interstate Commerce Commission and the Civil Aeronautics Board were abolished. Deregulation gained momentum around the world.

Stigler wrote or edited twenty-three books, all distinctive work, but he exerted his main influence through articles in academic journals, and the most important of these appeared when he was past fifty years old. The next most important article appeared when he was over sixty. He kept producing noteworthy articles until the day he died. "What Stigler really taught," recalled prolific author and columnist Thomas Sowell, who wrote his Ph.D. dissertation under Stigler, "was intellectual integrity, analytical rigor, respect for evidence—and skepticism toward the fashions and enthusiasms that come and go."

Serious scholar though he was, Stigler was a source of mirth. He identified himself as an intellectual "because I am a professor, and buy more books than golf clubs." Friedman recalled, "One day George came into the office nursing his elbow after slipping on the ice. I examined it carefully and solemnly pronounced it a minor sprain. George subsequently had it X-rayed and learned that he had fractured a bone. He never let me live that episode down. Ever after, when any medical topic came up, I was 'Dr. Friedman.'" While in London, Stigler complained about the food and exulted that he was being paid for some lectures. As he put it, "Here I am losing weight and gaining pounds." A reporter noted that Stigler had written a hundred articles, far fewer than a colleague who had written about five hundred articles. Stigler replied, "Mine are all different!" When a student complained that he didn't deserve an F, Stigler agreed but lamented that an F was the lowest grade the University of Chicago let him give out. Mainstream economist Paul Samuelson preceded Stigler on a panel discussion, declaring, "I know what George Stigler is going to say, and he's all wrong." Stigler got up and declared, "2 plus 2 equals 4," then returned to his seat.

Stigler's son Stephen observed that "the number of hours he gave to friends, students, family would have exhausted two ordinary lifetimes. He built furniture, ran errands, washed dishes, painted houses, built wharves, replanked boats, sawed down forests, came close to moving mountains. To his friends in academia, he offered criticism, debate, suggestions, references, redirection. And with all of this, his dedication to his friends was without bounds. Whether it was a golf match in Florida, a wedding in Canada, a ninetieth birthday party in California, he was off to the plane without a second thought, eagerly."

Nobel laureate Gary S. Becker wrote, "To Stigler's inner circle he was a warm and dear friend, generous with both his time and his wallet. He was always bringing up articles, reviews, and other materials that were relevant to our work. He read without much delay but with great insight drafts of essays and monographs. One always knew his true opinions, for he expressed them in no uncertain terms. But he gave many valuable suggestions on how to improve both the analysis and presentation. I benefited from his comments on virtually everything I wrote during the 20 years while we were colleagues at Chicago."

"George would pretend that he never did any work," said Milton Friedman. "You wouldn't hear him talking about work. He always had plenty of time to go play golf or tennis or bridge, yet somehow or other, a series of path-breaking articles kept coming from his pen. We used to kid him and say he must be staying up at night writing in the dark when nobody could see he was working. But of course, part of it was that he wrote so easily and fluently and well—because he thought so easily and fluently and well. . . . As a stylist, John Maynard Keynes was George's only peer among modern economists. I say modern because George would have insisted that Adam Smith topped them all. . . . There was no one from whom you could learn more by exchanging ideas, no one who would criticize your articles with the same incisiveness and sympathy."

GEORGE JOSEPH STIGLER was born in Renton, Washington, on January 17, 1911. His father, Joseph, had immigrated from Bavaria and married Elizabeth Hungler, who had come from Hungary. Although Joseph was in a family of farmers, he became a brewer until Prohibition put him out of business, and he went to work as a longshoreman.

The family earned money by buying run-down houses and fixing them up. "By the time I was sixteen," Stigler wrote in his *Memoirs of an Unregulated Economist,* "I had lived in sixteen different places in Seattle. But my family had a comfortable if nomadic existence, and my father acquired an astonishing knowledge of Seattle real estate."

After graduating from the University of Washington in 1931, he was unable to find a job, but he did get a fellowship at Northwestern University, and there he went for a master's degree. Following that, he recalled, "My destination was the University of Chicago, and without knowing it, I was trying out for the major leagues. I chose Chicago because my Washington teachers told me (correctly, it transpired) that Frank Knight and Jacob Viner were good economists." He entered the University of Chicago in 1933.

Every bit as important as the professors were the students. Stigler's best friends were fellow students Milton Friedman and W. Allen Wallis who, because of their zeal, were referred to as the "three musketeers" of the Chicago school. Stigler, Friedman, Wallis, and Homer Jones edited a collection of Knight's essays, which appeared as *The Ethics of Competition* (1935).

It was at Chicago that Stigler met anthropology graduate student Margaret Mack, who was known to everybody as "Chick," a nickname given her by her older sister. She came from Indiana, Pennsylvania, where her father was a lawyer. She was a friend of future Hollywood star Jimmy Stewart who grew up a block away, and she went on to Mount Holyoke College. She was a lively personality with a mischievous sense of humor. Stigler and Mack were married in her home town on December 26, 1936. They had three sons: Stephen (1941), now a University of Chicago statistics professor; David (1943), an attorney; and Joseph (1946), in computer services.

Stigler's Ph.D. thesis was about the history of economic thought, a subject he returned to again and again throughout his life. His favorite economic thinker by far was Adam Smith who, Stigler wrote, contributed "the crucial argument for unfettered individual choice in public policy . . . the efficiency property of competition: the manufacturer or farmer or laborer or shipper who was seeking to maximize his own income would in the very process be putting resources where they were most productive to the nation." His thesis, plus an additional chapter, was published as *Production and Distribution Theories* (1941).

In 1936, Stigler's career got off to a modest start with a post at Iowa State College and then the University of Minnesota. In 1942, he took a leave of absence and went to the National Bureau of Economic Research, where he worked with Friedman and others, analyzing statistics on U.S. output, productivity, and employment. He left to join Friedman and Wallis at the Statistical Research Group, which applied statistical analysis to military weapons systems. After the war, he returned to the University of Minnesota and had Friedman join him for a year. Stigler was turned down for a professorship at the University of Chicago (the president considered him too empirical), and Friedman got the job. Stigler went to Brown University. In 1946, Stigler and Friedman collaborated on a booklet, *Roofs or Ceilings?* which made a case that rent controls brought on shortages. The following year, Stigler accepted F. A. Hayek's offer to gather with Friedman and several dozen other friends of liberty who were launching what came be known as the Mont Pelerin Society.

In 1957, Wallis, dean of the University of Chicago Business School, invited Stigler to become the Charles R. Walgreen Distinguished Service Professor of American Institutions. Stigler accepted, and the family moved to the Chicago suburb of Flossmoor, 2621 Brassie Avenue. Stigler settled into his offices at Haskell Hall, Room 119.

For a number of years, Stigler had pursued research to determine the prevalence of monopolies. Gradually he was persuaded by Harvard economics professor Joseph Schumpeter, Milton Friedman's brother-in-law Aaron Director, and his own findings that it didn't take many competitors to drive down consumer prices significantly. As he remarked, "More and more economists have come to believe that competition is a tough weed, not a delicate flower." Stigler initially had favored breaking up monopolies—including monopoly unions—but later realized this policy tends to reflect the influence of lobbyists, who gain from busting up their competitors. He observed "that antitrust policy has often, even increasingly, been bent to such perverse ends, protecting rather than challenging sheltered and inefficient enterprises. Indeed, the antitrust laws have become a hunting license for lawyers, with the tripling of damages the reward for successful suits."

In 1962, Stigler's reflective mind focused on government regulations. "The literature of public regulation," he observed, "is so vast that it must touch on everything, but it touches seldom and lightly on the most basic question one can ask about regulation: does it make a difference in the behavior of an industry?" He continued, "The innumerable regulatory actions are conclusive proof, not of effective regulation, but of the desire to regulate. . . . The question of the influence of regulation can never be answered by an enumeration of regulatory policies. A thousand statutes forbid us to do things that we would not dream of doing even if the statutes were repealed: we would not slay our neighbor, or starve our children, or burn our house for the insurance, or erect an abattoir in the back yard. Whether the statutes really have an appreciative effect on actual behavior can only be determined by examining the behavior of people not subject to the statutes."

Stigler and his research associate Claire Friedland figured that a good test case would be the electrical power industry. Since these tended to be local private monopolies, and private monopolies were thought to exploit consumers unless restrained by regulators, people in localities without regulation ought to pay higher rates for electricity. Stigler and Friedland found that while electricity rates were often lower in states with regulation than states without regulation, the lower rates prevailed before there was any regulation! Stigler and Friedland couldn't find much difference between the level of rates or the rate structures of unregulated compared with regulated electrical utilities. Nor was there evidence that investors in unregulated electrical utilities fared any better than investors in regulated utilities. They were unable "to find any significant effects of the regulation of electrical utilities."

How could this be? Stigler and Friedland explained in the October 1962 *Journal of Law and Economics,* "The individual utility system is not possessed of any large amount of long run monopoly power. It faces the competition of other energy sources in a large proportion of its product's uses, and it faces the competition of other utility systems, to which in the long run its industrial (and hence many of its domestic) users may move." Subsequent studies by other researchers found that regulated utilities charged *higher* rates than unregulated utilities.

Economist Sam Peltzman noted, "the effect of the Stigler-Friedland article on the profession owed as much to this then startling result as to the methodological innovation of estimating the effect of regulation from an explicit statistical model. Had the result merely confirmed the conventional wisdom, economists might have been less eager to pursue the effects of regulation."

Two years after their breakthrough analysis of electrical utilities, Stigler and Friedland addressed Securities and Exchange Commission regulation of the securities industry. What attracted their attention was an official report, which, they noted in the April 1964 *Journal of Business of the University of Chicago,* justified SEC regulation by pointing to abuses by inexperienced stockbrokers at new firms. Stigler and Friedland suggested that the investigators should have analyzed "the experience of customers of a randomly chosen set of account men with diverse amounts of training and experience: Have differences in experience or training had any effect on the profits of their customers?"

The SEC has had its greatest impact on new stock issues, since investors have the least amount of information about these; there's abundant information about seasoned issues. Stigler proposed a simple test: "How did investors fare before and after the SEC was given control over the registration of new issues? We take all the new issues of industrial stocks with a value exceeding $2.5 million in 1923–27, and exceeding $5 million in 1949–55, and measure the values of these issues (compared to their offering price) in five subsequent years. It is obviously improper to credit or blame the SEC for the absolute differences between the two periods in investors' fortunes, but if we measure stock prices relative to the market average, we shall have eliminated most of the effects of general market conditions." He concluded that "investors in common stocks in the 1950s did little better than in the 1920s, indeed clearly no better if they held the securities only one or two years. In fact the differences between the averages in the two periods are not statistically significant in any year. . . . These studies suggest that the SEC registration requirements had no important effect on the quality of new securities sold to the public. . . . Grave doubts exist whether if account is taken of costs of regulation, the SEC has saved the purchasers of new issues one dollar."

Stigler maintained that investors benefit far more from efficient capital markets than from SEC regulations. A serious drag on capital markets, he observed, was SEC-sanctioned collusion among Wall Street firms to fix brokerage commissions. Stigler attacked the New York Stock Exchange practice, sanctioned by the SEC, of suspending trading during volatile market conditions. "To prevent a trade is no function of the exchange," he wrote, "and any defense must lie in a desire to avoid 'unnecessary' price fluctuations. . . . This suspension of trading means that the exchange officials know the correct price change when there is a flood of buy or sell orders. We need not pause to inquire where they get this clairvoyance; it is enough to notice that the correct way to iron out the unnecessary wrinkles in the price chart is to speculate: to buy or sell against the unnecessary movement."

After these articles appeared, an increasing number of economists tested the effects of regulations, and their findings were more radical than those of Stigler and Friedland: that the effects of regulation were the opposite of what policymakers had intended. In response, Stigler wrote "The Theory of Economic Regulation," an enormously influential article that appeared in the Spring 1971 *Bell Journal of Economics and Management Science.* He expressed an insight that catapulted him into the major leagues of economic thinkers: "As a rule, regulation is acquired by the industry and is designed and operated primarily for its benefit." He explained that the actual purpose of regulations is to provide special privileges for powerful interest groups that want to restrict competition and raise prices, so regulations hurt the public. Because members of an interest group know who they are—they invariably belong to an industry association—they're in a position to organize lobbying and pool resources. Their livelihoods are at stake, and they have a strong incentive to spend plenty. Moreover, when regulators need expertise about an industry, they turn to people in the industry, and the advice the regulators get tends to reflect the views of the industry. By contrast, customers who suffer from regulations are dispersed, they can't easily get in touch with one another, and individually they have less at stake in regulations than the manufacturers and labor unions do.

While many interest groups lobby for government subsidies, Stigler pointed out that success in gaining subsidies encourages other interest groups, including rivals, to seek subsidies too. Consequently, the preferred benefit is not a subsidy but a regulatory barrier that restricts competition. For example, as Stigler observed, "The Civil Aeronautics Board has not allowed a single new trunk line to be launched since it was created in 1938. The power to insure new banks has been used by the Federal Deposit Insurance Corporation to reduce the rate of entry into commercial banking by 60 percent. . . . We propose a general hypothesis: every industry or occupation that has enough political power to utilize the state will seek to control entry."

Finally, regulatory processes themselves contribute to higher consumer costs. Stigler cited economist Robert Gerwig who "found the price of gas sold in interstate commerce to be 5 to 6 percent higher than in intrastate commerce because of the administrative costs (including delay) of Federal Power Commission reviews."

Stigler was devastated when his wife, Chick, suffered a fatal heart attack on August 22, 1970, at Rothesay, where the family had summered for more than two decades. It was a one-story white cottage on Lake Rosseau, about 130 miles north of Toronto. Chick's ashes were scattered on the property.

In 1972, Stigler accepted a position at the Hoover Institution for War, Revolution and Peace, in Stanford, California, and began spending winters there. He won his Nobel Prize in 1982. Asked how he felt about waiting several years longer than Friedman, who had won his Nobel Prize in 1976, Stigler quipped that during those years, the cash award had been increased, so he was better off because of the delay. He was retired from the University of Chicago because of his age in 1982, but soon afterward, presumably because of the Nobel Prize, he was asked to resume conducting workshops in industrial organization and teaching classes in industrial organization and the history of economic thought. Meanwhile, he continued serving as an editor of The *Journal of Political Economy,* which he had done since 1974.

In early November 1991, Stigler entered the University of Chicago Hospital with respiratory complaints, apparently due to pneumonia. He seemed to be recovering when he suffered a fatal heart attack on December 1. He was eighty. There was a service for the family at the University of Chicago and a public memorial service at the university's Rockefeller Chapel on March 14. The speakers were Stephen Stigler, Milton Friedman, W. Allen Wallis, Gary Becker, business executive J. Irwin Miller, University of Chicago president Hanna Gray, and former University of Chicago president Edward H. Levi. Stigler's ashes were scattered at the family's summer place in Canada.

"Despite deep sadness at George's death," wrote Milton Friedman, "I cannot recall him without a smile rising to my lips. He was as quick of wit as of mind. He brought a sense of joy and excitement to any company he joined. Hardly a day goes by that we are not reminded of something he said that was both witty and pertinent."

Friends remembered the game Stigler had invented for children. He offered them a million dollars if they could answer three questions. First: "Who was buried in Grant's Tomb?" Second: "Whose head is on the Lincoln penny?" Children anticipated great riches. Then their hopes were dashed when Stigler asked the third question: "Who was Adam Smith's best friend?" He had in mind a contemporary of Smith, but on one occasion a boy responded: "Who was Adam Smith's best friend? Why, you are, Uncle George!" And so he was.

INFLATION AND DEPRESSION

THE GREAT DEPRESSION of the 1930s was blamed on free markets and brought a vast expansion of government interference with the economy. Anybody who favored rolling back the power of government inevitably faced the question, "What about the Great Depression?" Without all the laws from that era, it was feared, there would again be high unemployment, chronic monopolies, and gross inequality.

Nobel laureate Milton Friedman did more than anyone else to change thinking on these issues. He gathered massive documentary evidence that the Great Depression occurred primarily because the money supply contracted by one-third between 1929 and 1933, although a central bank (the Federal Reserve) had been granted the power to prevent just such a catastrophe. The Great Depression was a government failure. Moreover, Friedman showed that "inflation is always and everywhere a monetary phenomenon." He made a formidable case that government "fine-tuning" is more likely to backfire: by the time central bankers realize the economy is slipping into a recession or depression and they inflate the money supply, the effects are likely to be felt after the economy has already recovered, worsening the subsequent inflation. Conversely, by the time central bankers realize inflation is a problem and they contract the money supply, the effects are likely to be felt after the economy has slowed down, worsening the next recession or depression. Government, Friedman made clear, is the biggest source of instability in the economy.

While champions of liberty have generally done well to achieve significant impact on a single area of public policy, Friedman has had an impact on many public policies. He helped usher in the era of free foreign exchange markets. He campaigned for ballot initiatives to limit government spending and taxes; he inspired the movement for educational choice using tuition vouchers that would enable poor people to opt out of public schools; he courageously spoke out against drug prohibition; and he helped fight President Clinton's effort to seize an eighth of the U.S. economy in his plan for government-run health care. Friedman is proudest of helping to end military conscription in the United States.

Friedman has gained influence through his scholarly achievements, his teaching at the University of Chicago for thirty years, the *Newsweek* column that he wrote for eighteen years, popular books that sold over a million copies, dozens of articles in *the Wall Street Journal, Reader's Digest, Harper's, New York Times Magazine,* and other publications, as well as countless speeches, debates, and TV interviews. Milton and his wife Rose showed how to tell the story of liberty on television, reaching millions around the world with their ten-part documentary *Free to Choose.*

Although Friedman has welcomed opportunities to urge that politicians pursue free market policies, he has had no interest in public office. Controversy dogged him, though, after it was reported that University of Chicago–trained Chilean economists advised Chilean dictator Augusto Pinochet. His military regime followed the catastrophic runaway inflation of Marxist Salvador Allende, as military regimes have followed runaway inflation elsewhere, and the Chilean free market economists urged a policy of economic liberty, including spending cuts, tax cuts, free trade, and privatization. These policies brought prosperity and generated pressure for political liberty, which ended the military regime. Ironically, when Friedman offered free market advice during his 1980 and 1988 visits to Communist China, nobody complained.

Friedman has displayed buoyant energy throughout his life. He rebounded from a 1972 open heart operation to campaign for a spending limit by the state of California, wrote two books as well as resumed tennis after his 1984 heart attack and open heart operation, and was past eighty when he enjoyed skateboarding with his grandson Patri. As *Playboy* wrote when the magazine published an interview with him, "It is testimony to Milton Friedman's tireless, good-natured efforts and the vigor of his arguments that economic ideas once regarded as hopelessly out of date are now being seriously discussed again." The *New York Times* gushed that "in economics, he is certainly the most irrepressible, outspoken, audacious, provocative and inventive thinker in the United States—and even at 5 foot 3, he may stand taller than all his colleagues in the profession."

Friedman's friend and colleague George Stigler reflected, "He has an extraordinarily lucid mind. His ability to think very fast and to conduct himself with complete propriety in the heat of debate makes him an extremely formidable debater in person as well as on paper. He is a marvelous empirical worker, prepared to isolate what he believes are the essential elements of a problem, and to bring the analysis to bear most ingeniously upon empirical data. Finally, he is quite talented in outraging his intellectual opponents, who have accordingly devoted much energy and knowledge to advertising his work."

MILTON FRIEDMAN WAS born on July 31, 1912, at 502 Barbey Street, Brooklyn, New York. He was the fourth child and only son of Jeno Saul Friedman and Sarah Ethel Landau, both from Beregszasz, Carpatho-Ruthenia, which was part of the Austro-Hungarian empire and now is part of Ukraine. Sarah worked as a seamstress in a sweatshop. With thirteen-month-old Milton, the family moved to Rahway, New Jersey, about twenty miles from New York, where his father started a clothing factory. "The one thing I know," Friedman recalled, "is that he never made much money." He died at age forty-nine because of heart problems.

Milton entered Rutgers University in 1928. "I originally intended to major in mathematics," he explained in his autobiography, *Two Lucky People* (written with his wife). "The only paying occupation I had heard about that used mathematics was actuarial work, so I had informed myself about that and planned to become an actuary." He switched his major from mathematics to economics because of two teachers: Arthur F. Burns, who was completing his Ph.D. dissertation at Columbia University, and Homer Jones, who was completing his Ph.D. dissertation at the University of Chicago. Burns, recalled Friedman, "instilled a passion for scientific integrity and for accuracy and care that has had a major effect on my scientific work."

Jones steered Friedman toward the University of Chicago after his 1932 graduation from Rutgers because he got a $300 scholarship. In Jacob Viner's price theory class, students were seated alphabetically, and Friedman found himself next to petite and lively Rose Director. She had been born the last week of December 1911, the youngest of five children, in Charterisk, a Russian village now part of Ukraine. She grew up in a home without electricity or running water. Her father, a grain miller, had sisters and cousins who had emigrated to America, and he traveled there to establish himself. He began as a peddler, opened a general store, and earned enough money to have his family join him and most of their relatives in Portland, Oregon. They fortunately arrived just before World War I began; emigration might have been impossible afterward. Rose's older brother, Aaron, went to Yale University and then the University of Chicago for graduate work. Rose stayed closer to home, commuting to Reed College, but after two years she transferred to the University of Chicago.

She decided to pursue a Ph.D. in economics and worked as an assistant to Frank Knight, while Milton worked as an assistant for another economics professor, Henry Schultz. Milton's first published article was a by-product of his work with Schultz, a critique of "Professor Pigou's Method for Measuring Elasticities of Demand from Budgetary Data." Since A. C. Pigou, among the most respected economists of his day, was at Cambridge University, Milton submitted it to the *Economic Journal* published there, and received a rejection from the editor, John Maynard Keynes. The article was subsequently published by Harvard University's *Quarterly Journal of Economics* in November 1934. Friedman was twenty-two.

Another Chicago economist, Henry Simons, had a big impact on Friedman. In 1934, Simons wrote *A Positive Program for Laissez Faire*, a pamphlet distributed by the University of Chicago Press in which he emphasized that people generally share common goals, such as promoting prosperity, and the major differences of opinion are about the most effective ways to achieve the goals. Friedman won over millions by embracing this approach and making a practical case that private individuals in competitive markets are much better at solving problems than bureaucrats are. Simons warned that "political liberty can survive only within an effective competitive economic system," and this became a major theme of Friedman. Simons believed a monetary contraction was primarily responsible for bringing on the Great Depression, and Friedman documented this thesis. Simons, however, supported nationalization of railroads, a graduated income tax, and other policies that Friedman opposed.

When Columbia University offered Friedman a much larger fellowship (tuition plus living expenses) than his Chicago scholarship, that's where he decided to do his Ph.D.

In September 1937, future Nobel laureate Simon Kuznets invited Friedman to work at the National Bureau of Economic Research, where he studied independent professionals: lawyers, accountants, engineers, dentists, and doctors. This work became the basis for Friedman's doctoral dissertation and first book, *Income from Independent Professional Practice*, coauthored by Kuznets. Although the manuscript was finished in 1941, publication was delayed four years because of controversy about the book's contention that barriers to entry into the medical profession, enforced by the government, artificially raised the incomes of physicians.

Meanwhile, Milton and Rose got married in New York, where they planned to live, on June 25, 1938. Their daughter, Janet, was born in 1943 and their son, David, two years later.

From 1941 to 1943, Friedman worked in the Treasury Department's Division of Tax Research, when government spending soared because of World War II. Until then, people calculated tax due and paid it in quarterly installments the following year. Friedman analyzed proposals that employers withhold taxes from paychecks, and that system began in 1943. He regretted that withholding was one of those "temporary" wartime measures that became permanent.

In September 1946, Friedman began teaching at the University of Chicago where he was to be based for three decades. His most widely quoted essay, "The Methodology of Positive Economics," published in 1953, maintained that when one makes statements about phenomena, they ought to be verified by some kind of observation. The primary test of economic analysis is the correctness of predictions.

In *A Theory of the Consumption Function* (1957), Friedman explained that people decide how much to spend and save according to their expected earnings, not the amount of government spending. Friedman's work, together with data developed by Simon Kuznets and others, overthrew a key Keynesian claim that government spending was essential for prosperity. His most important single work on economics was *A Monetary History of the United States, 1867–1960* (1963), coauthored with Anna Jacobson Schwartz. They amassed overwhelming evidence to show that changes in the money supply best explain the boom and bust cycle. In particular, prevailing opinion was that the 1929 stock crash caused the Great Depression, but Friedman and Schwartz showed that it occurred because the Federal Reserve System failed to prevent the money supply from contracting one-third between 1929 and 1933.

Writing in *The Journal of Monetary Economics*, Nobel laureate Robert Lucas reflected on the book after thirty years: "It told a coherent story of important events, and it told it well. . . . Its beautiful time series on the money supply and its components, extended back to 1867, painstakingly documented and conveniently presented. . . . Such a gift to the profession merits a long life, perhaps even immortality." As for the main contention that monetary fluctuations explain major economic events, Lucas added, "I will say that I find the argument of *A Monetary History* wholly convincing. . . . I find their diagnosis of the 1929–33 downturn persuasive and indeed uncontested by serious alternative diagnoses, and remain deeply impressed with their success in explaining the remarkable events of these four years."

F. A. Hayek, whose book *The Road to Serfdom* appeared in 1944, did much to stimulate Friedman's desire to influence public opinion for liberty. Friedman's first popular work on public policy, *Roofs or Ceilings?*, which he wrote with George Stigler, was a booklet attacking rent controls, published by the Foundation for Economic Education (FEE) in 1946. Friedman was an original member of the Mont Pelerin Society, which Hayek launched in April 1947. "Here I was," Friedman recalled, "a young, naive provincial American, meeting people from all over the world, all dedicated to the same liberal principles as we were; all beleaguered in their own countries, yet among them scholars, some already internationally famous, others destined to be; making friendships which have enriched our lives, and participating in founding a society that has played a major role in preserving and strengthening liberal ideas."

In 1956, the William Volker Charities Fund arranged for Friedman to deliver a series of lectures about general principles and major public policy issues such as unemployment, monopolies, racial discrimination, social security, and international trade. Rose Friedman edited the lectures into a book, *Capitalism and Freedom*, which the University of Chicago Press published in

1962. Friedman recommended abolishing farm subsidies, tariffs, import quotas, rent controls, minimum wage laws, subsidized housing, occupational licensing, social security, the U.S. postal monopoly, military conscription, and many regulatory agencies. The book went on to sell some 500,000 copies. "We have been told that it was smuggled into the Soviet Union and served as the basis for an underground edition," the Friedmans reported. "We know that an underground Polish version was published sometime in the early eighties. Since the fall of the Berlin Wall, the book has been translated into Serbo-Croatian, Chinese, Polish, and Estonian, and still other translations are pending."

In 1962 and 1963, the Friedmans traveled around the world, visiting twenty-one countries altogether. He reported in *Harper's*, "Wherever we found any large element of individual freedom, some beauty in the ordinary life of the ordinary man, some measure of real progress in the material comforts at his disposal, and a live hope of further progress in the future—there we also found that the private market was the main device being used to organize economic activity. Wherever the private market was largely suppressed and the state undertook to control in detail the economic activity of its citizens . . . there the ordinary man was in political fetters, had a low standard of living, and was largely bereft of any conception of controlling his own destiny."

The Friedmans decided they wanted to spend their summers in Vermont and in 1965 bought about 120 acres overlooking Lake Fairlee. They built a hexagonal house with a fireplace in the center, the design inspired by Robert Lefevre's Freedom School in Colorado Springs, Colorado, where Friedman had taught a couple of years before. They named the house Capitaf, after *Capitalism and Freedom* (they hoped royalties would pay for it). That's where Friedman did much of his work until 1980 when they began living full time in California.

In 1966, *Newsweek's* editors decided to drop the "Business Tides" column, which libertarian journalist Henry Hazlitt had written for two decades, and decided to try rotating three economists: Friedman, "liberal" Paul Samuelson, and mainstreamer Henry Wallich. The limited column space forced Friedman to express his views more simply and concisely than ever before. "My writing style improved not only in the columns but everything else I wrote, and so did my coherence in stating a position," he reflected. There were three collections of his *Newsweek* columns: *An Economist's Protest* (1972), *There's No Such Thing as a Free Lunch* (1975), and *Bright Promises, Dismal Performance* (1983). Friedman's output of popular articles continued after *Newsweek*: eighty-two op-eds and letters to the editor for the *Wall Street Journal, New York Times, Washington Post, San Francisco Chronicle*, and other publications.

Being awarded the Nobel Prize in 1976 was a highlight of Friedman's career, but what Rose Friedman called "the most exciting venture of our lives" was suggested by Robert J. Chitester, president of Erie, Pennsylvania, public TV station WQLN. A "liberal" Democrat, Chitester had been given a copy of *Capitalism and Freedom* and found it persuasive. He proposed that Friedman consider doing a lecture series on topics that could be developed into a TV documentary and companion book. On July 26, 1977, Friedman agreed to pursue the project.

Chitester raised about $2.8 million for production and promotion of a ten-part documentary, a remarkable achievement because corporate executives generally didn't want to sponsor a show about political issues, even economic liberty. Moreover, he had to assure potential backers that if the show were produced, it would be broadcast. Although PBS executives and producers were openly hostile to Friedman's views, they had been criticized for broadcasting socialist John Kenneth Galbraith's documentary *Age of Uncertainty* and decided to provide some balance by broadcasting the proposed Friedman documentary.

Documentaries of the highest technical quality were done in Britain, and Ralph Harris, director of the Institute of Economic Affairs, London, recommended Anthony Jay who had broken away from the British Broadcasting Corporation bureaucracy and become a partner at the TV production company Video Arts. Jay proposed that each program should consist of a thirty-minute documentary and a thirty-minute discussion, since this would be much less expensive than filming an hour-long documentary with footage from around the world. "Who Protects the Consumer?" was the pilot program for working out production problems and providing a sample for raising money. It was filmed in San Francisco, Sacramento, and Washington, D.C. Friedman spoke his own words without a script. The suggested title of the pilot program was "Free to Choose," and the Friedmans thought this would be an apt title for the series.

In one of the most memorable scenes, Friedman talks while walking behind stacks of the *Federal Register* (listing new federal regulations) arranged in chronological order. There are only one or two volumes per year from the 1930s, so viewers can see his full figure. Then during the 1940s came increasing numbers of regulations, and each year's stack of volumes blocks the view of his legs. The 1960s brought an explosion of regulations, and the stacks of volumes are so high that Friedman can no longer be seen.

The first part of *Free to Choose* was broadcast January 1980 over 196 PBS stations (72 percent of all PBS stations). *Free to Choose* reportedly attracted a bigger audience than *Masterpiece Theater*, one of the most popular PBS programs. The series was subsequently broadcast in more than a dozen countries with and without subtitles; reportedly it was smuggled into Communist

China and the Soviet Union, among other places. Encyclopedia Britannica distributed 16-mm prints of the series and sold them for $3,000 apiece. In 1987, the Friedmans bought the rights for $25,000 and arranged distribution of the video at $110.

"The book *Free to Choose,*" Friedman recalled, "which we wrote to accompany the video, is . . . the only book [of ours] that is based almost entirely on spoken rather than written English. Partly for that reason, it has sold many more copies than any other book that we have written." When *Free to Choose* reached bookstores in December 1979, it soared to become the top-selling nonfiction book in 1980. More than 400,000 hardcover copies were sold, and the paperback edition brought total sales over million. The book was translated into seventeen languages.

Over the years, Friedman helped many campaigns for liberty. In 1969, President Nixon, who had long supported conscription, appointed Friedman to the fifteen-member Advisory Commission on an All-Volunteer Armed Force. Friedman helped achieve a unanimous recommendation for an all-volunteer military, and conscription ended on January 27, 1973.

In 1971, after the U.S. government abandoned efforts to dictate currency exchange rates, Friedman advised Chicago Mercantile Exchange chairman Leo Malamed that the era of free exchange rates had arrived. In June 1972 the Chicago Mercantile Exchange opened the International Monetary Market, which dramatically expanded global currency trading.

Friedman launched the movement for educational choice. As long ago as 1955, he had written "The Role of Government in Education," an article that became the basis for chapter 6 of *Capitalism and Freedom.* Only parents who could afford to pay tuition twice—school taxes plus private tuition—had any real choice, he said, and proposed that "parents who choose to send their children to private schools would be paid a sum equal to the estimated costs of educating a child in a public school." They established the Milton and Rose D. Friedman Foundation to promote the privatization of public schools.

In his American Economic Association presidential address (1967) and elsewhere, Friedman challenged the Keynesian doctrine that inflation cured unemployment. He was vindicated during the 1970s when many countries suffered through stagflation—high inflation and high unemployment simultaneously. Friedman put pressure on governments to stop inflating the money supply, and those following his advice set the stage for extraordinary prosperity without inflation.

Friedman promoted ballot initiatives to limit government spending and taxes, starting in 1973 when he went on a speaking tour with California governor Ronald Reagan. He helped Reagan assistant Lewis K. Uhler establish the National Tax Limitation Committee, which has campaigned for a constitutional amendment limiting government spending. In recent years, ballot initiatives have proved to be the most effective strategy for limiting government power.

Friedman ranks as the greatest champion of liberty during the twentieth century. He worked in more media on more issues than anyone else, for more than fifty years. His influence extended around the world. He could never forget that Jews and other persecuted minorities found refuge in free markets. He was grateful his parents and his wife's family got to America. He appreciated that because there was reasonably secure private property, an independent university could hire individuals like himself with unorthodox views—and he could speak and write freely. He inspired millions to help carry the torch of liberty on its next lap.

INVOLUNTARY COMMITMENT

IN THE UNITED STATES, government has exercised more direct control over mental patients than it ever had over American Indians or black slaves. Mental patients have had whatever independence they possessed obliterated by the administration of drugs, electroshock, insulin shock, lobotomies, and other so-called treatments. Supposedly, these people suffer from "mental illness," which has been the rationale for husbands' committing unwanted wives into mental institutions, families' dumping embarrassing relatives, and communities' putting away social deviants. While the number of people in mental hospitals has declined in the United States during the past four decades, the number of people in other government-funded and insurance-funded programs has increased. These programs involve Veterans Administration hospitals, general hospitals, nursing homes, alcohol and drug rehabilitation centers, forensic psychiatric facilities, government housing projects, single-room-occupancy hotels, boardinghouses, and shelters, as well as prisons and jails. The number of people in all these places is estimated around 1 million.

More than anyone else in recent times, psychiatrist Thomas S. Szasz has expressed opposition to involuntary commitment, and his writings inspired the movement to restore the civil liberties of patients. "In a free society," he declared, "I don't believe anybody should be deprived of his liberty on any ground other than accusation, trial and being found guilty of a criminal charge . . . Mental patients in the United States . . . suffer widespread and grievous violations of their constitutional rights. I believe that today these people, more than members of particular racial or religious groups, are the principal scapegoats of our society." He added: "State hospitals have been notorious for their neglect, and indeed abuse, of the mental patient. There is evidence that incarceration in a mental hospital may be more harmful for the personality than incarceration in a prison."

Szasz denounced the psychiatric theory that "decisions are somehow secreted by the brain just as sugar is secreted by the kidney when you have diabetes. It's not a decision. It comes out. Well, I believe in free will. I believe that what people do cannot be the proper subject matter of some kind of deterministic investigation. People can make choices and ought to be held responsible in various ways for what they do in life."

Szasz was widely blamed when government mental hospitals began de-institutionalization—suddenly releasing large numbers of patients. Rael Jean

Isaac and Virginia C. Armat, in *Madness in the Streets: How Psychiatry and the Law Abandoned the Mentally Ill* (1990), claimed, "It is Szasz's ideology that is truly inhumane." Harvard Law School professor Alan Dershowitz remarked that "you can't believe Szasz's arguments." Journalist Pete Hammill, writing in the *New York Times Magazine,* called Szasz a "crackpot." But deinstitutionalization had begun in about 1955, eight years before Szasz's first major attack on involuntary commitment. Deinstitutionalization was mainly the consequence of financial pressure on state budgets. Many deinstitutionalized patients fared poorly, their spirit of independence crushed by prolonged deprivation of liberty, isolation from family members and work, and the effects of gruesome psychiatric "treatments."

Szasz has spoken out for everyone persecuted because of peaceful deviant behavior. This has included reading forbidden books, having unorthodox sex, and ingesting substances that authorities disapproved of. "To the extent that people have characteristics that set them apart from others," he insisted, "the truly liberal and humane attitude toward these differences can only be one of acceptance."

Szasz's work has become known around the world, translated into Czech, Dutch, French, German, Greek, Hungarian, Italian, Japanese, Serbo-Croatian and Swedish. He has lectured at Harvard, Yale, Princeton, Columbia, University of Michigan, University of California (Berkeley, Los Angeles, Sacramento), and other campuses across the United States. In addition, he has given lectures in more than a dozen countries. Among the awards he was received are the Mencken Award and the Patient's Rights Advocate Award. San Francisco's Center for Independent Thought established the annual Thomas S. Szasz Award for Contributions to the Cause of Civil Liberties.

Irving Louis Horowitz, Hannah Arendt Distinguished Professor of Sociology and Political Science, Rutgers University, observed, "Ultimately, the achievement of Szasz is the unique ability to bring into a discipline which, ostensibly at least, has come to pride itself on its indifference to moral claims, precisely a sense of morality—an ethic of responsibility. . . . When everyone from the street pusher to the university president can claim a victim status, it is precisely this sense of ethical responsibility that vanishes behind a cloud of psychiatric smoke."

Szasz is a wiry man, five-feet, eight-inches tall who likes to dress well. He has led a vigorous life, hiking, playing tennis, and swimming almost every day. A *Philadelphia Inquirer* reporter was impressed by Szasz's "emotional intensity and intellectual vitality." *Cosmopolitan* called Szasz "a witty and moving speaker, whose unusual views—and verbal gymnastics—attract large audiences."

Donald Oken, former chair of psychiatry at the Upstate Medical Center in Syracuse, New York, told the *New York Times:* "When people hear I was head of the department Tom Szasz is in, they can't wait to hear what wild fantastic stories I have to tell. You'd have to know Tom personally to realize how ridiculous that idea is. He sounds polemical in his writing, but he's nothing like that. He's a warm, personable guy—there's absolutely nothing flamboyant about him. He wears a dark gray flannel suit to work every day. He's a conservative person basically."

Historian Ralph Raico wrote, "Against the current of a culture that would deny it, Szasz restores the human world of purpose and choice, of right and wrong. For friends of liberty, he is one of the most important intellectuals alive today."

THOMAS STEPHEN SZASZ was born in Budapest, on April 15, 1920. His mother was Lily Wellisch, the daughter of a grain trader. His father, Julius Szasz, was trained as a lawyer and owned some buildings in Budapest. Julius was an atheist, but his passport indicated he was Jewish (Hungarian passports specified the bearer's religion or ancestry). Thomas had an older brother, George.

There was a partnership between Jews and non-Jews, as Columbia University historian Istvan Deak explained: "From the 1840s to the onset of the First World War, the Hungarian gentry and the Jewish social elite had quietly worked together to modernize Hungary. The Jews had taken charge of economic development, and the aristocracy and gentry had governed the country." Jews still had to be wary. The ruler of Hungary was Miklos Horthy, who promoted "Christian nationalism," which meant anti-Semitism. The gentile middle class began lobbying for preferential treatment against Jews, and Horthy's legislature enacted quotas effectively limiting the number of Jews who could be admitted to universities.

Szasz attended fine schools, where he studied Latin, French, German, mathematics, physics, history, and Hungarian literature for eight years. In his German classes, he loved reading works by Friedrich Schiller, the great German dramatist who championed liberty. Szasz read works by Leo Tolstoy, the Russian author whose work expressed a spirit of individualism. "I was very much influenced by Mark Twain," he added. "I loved *Tom Sawyer* and *Huckleberry Finn*. I wanted to become a writer."

His uncle Otto was a theoretical mathematician who emigrated to Frankfurt, Germany, where he taught university courses. After Hitler seized power in 1933 and Jewish professors were fired, Otto Szasz emigrated to the United States and became a research professor at the University of Cincinnati. When he visited his family in Budapest once a year, he always talked about America, which was clearly the place to be. Finally, in 1938, the family prepared to leave Hungary. Because of government restrictions severely limiting mobility, they had to do it in steps. Julius Szasz obtained a visa for France, where he had relatives. Once in Paris, he obtained a visa for Holland, and there he applied for a visa to the United States. At that time, the United States assigned immigration quotas based on where an individual was born. Julius was from a town north of Bratislava in what became Czechoslovakia. The quota for Czechoslovakia was small, but very few people applied for it, and he was able to obtain a visa. After arriving in America, he requested preference visas for his wife and children. Then Thomas and George followed the same route. Their mother came a little later, after taking care of business in Budapest.

Thomas and George arrived in the United States on October 25, 1938, not knowing a word of English. They were met by their mother's sister, who helped them proceed to Cincinnati, where the plan was to see Otto. They couldn't stay with him, since he rented a single room, but he arranged for Thomas to audit classes at the University of Cincinnati, so he could begin learning English. Thomas did odd jobs like working as a chauffeur.

Otto arranged for Thomas to enroll at the university. He went on to medical school there, graduating first in his class and becoming an American citizen. During these years, about the only book he read relating to liberty was John Stuart Mill's *On Liberty*. He did a one-year internship at Boston City Hospital, then became a medical resident at the University of Chicago Clinics, and was trained in psychoanalysis at the prestigious Chicago Institute for Psychoanalysis.

Meanwhile, he met and fell in love with Rosine Loshkajian, an Armenian-Lebanese social worker in Chicago. Married on December 19, 1951, they had two daughters. Margot, born in 1953, became a dermatologist at the Mayo Clinic. Susan, born in 1955, became a reference librarian at Cornell University. Thomas and Rosine Szasz were married nineteen years until their divorce in 1970.

His first scholarly journal article appeared in September 1947 (on congestive heart failure), and for a number of years he contributed articles to respected medical journals like *Archives of Internal Medicine* and *American Journal of Psychiatry*. In 1956, he was appointed a professor of psychiatry at the State University of New York Health Science Center in Syracuse, where he has remained. That year, he began writing articles that anticipated his later themes. Szasz's first book, *Pain and Pleasure* (1957), offered gentle criticism of the psychiatric (medical) view that all pain has some kind of physical basis for which medication is appropriate. A year after he was awarded tenure, he published his first big book, *The Myth of Mental Illness* (1961). He saw it as flowing naturally from *Pain and Pleasure,* but it shocked the psychiatric profession. In *The Myth of Mental Illiness,* he maintained that while psychiatrists label certain forms of behavior as mental illness, it isn't in any way comparable to an illness caused by something like a virus or bacteria. These, Szasz explained, could cause a disease of the brain, but not "mental illness."

The doctrine of "mental illness" had serious consequences. First, labeling behavior as mental illness meant no longer holding people responsible for their actions. Murderers, for instance, could avoid being convicted by pleading insanity—after having been pronounced "insane" by a psychiatrist. Second, psychiatrists gained the power to commit people involuntarily into mental institutions. Far from being the agent of a patient to help treat a physical disease, psychiatrists were often agents of the state.

After *The Myth of Mental Illness* appeared, Szasz testified in the defense of John Chomentowski, an Onondaga County, New York, man who fired warning shots at "goons" sent by a real estate developer who wanted to take over his property before the agreed-on date. Police arrested him, government psychiatrists claimed he was mentally incompetent, and he was committed to Matteawan State Hospital for the Criminally Insane. "Szasz testified at a habeas corpus hearing in which Chomentowski was suing to gain his freedom from confinement," recalled psychiatrist Ronald Leifer. "The trial, which I attended, was a highly anticipated event in psychiatric circles, since for the first time Szasz was in an adversarial confrontation with conventional psychiatrists in a public forum. . . . He believed that mental hospitals are prisons and that, in effect, Mr. Chomentowski had been imprisoned without having been convicted of a crime. He translated the state hospital psychiatrists' psychobabble testimony into ordinary language with devastating effect."

The county commissioner of mental health, Abraham Halpern, filed a protest with New York State commissioner of mental hygiene, Paul Hoch, who ordered Szasz to stop teaching at Syracuse Psychiatric Hospital. The *Psychiatric Quarterly* published an attack, "Szasz for the Gander." Two of Szasz's compatriots were fired, but Szasz held onto his teaching job because he fought back, and he had tenure.

Szasz expanded his attack on mental illness in *Law, Liberty and Psychiatry* (1963): "The notion of mental illness derives its main support from such phenomena as syphilis of the brain or delirious conditions—intoxication, for instance—in which persons may manifest certain disorders of thinking and behavior. Correctly speaking, however, these are diseases of the brain, not of the mind. According to one school of thought, all so-called mental illness is of this type. The assumption is made that some neurological defect, perhaps a very subtle one, will ultimately be found to explain all the disorders of thinking and behavior. Many contemporary psychiatrists, physicians and other scientists hold this view, which implies that people's troubles cannot be caused by conflicting personal needs, opinions, social aspirations, values, and so forth. These difficulties—which I think we may simply call problems in living—are thus attributed to physiochemical processes which in due time will be discovered (and no doubt corrected) by medical research . . . [but] a person's belief—whether it be in Christianity, in Communism, or the idea that his internal organs are rotting and that his body is already dead—cannot be explained by a defect or disease of the nervous system."

Involuntary commitment is worse than going to prison, Szasz pointed out, because prisoners are released after serving their sentence, if not before, whereas individuals in a mental hospital are doomed to remain there indefinitely, at the discretion of psychiatrists. "Neither internists nor obstetricians nor surgeons operate special institutions for involuntary patients, nor are they authorized by law to subject people to treatments they do not want," Szasz wrote. "The mental patient enters the hospital in one of two ways: voluntarily or involuntarily. It must be emphasized that in neither case does he have a true contractual relationship with the hospital. Irrespective of the method of entry, the patient finds himself in a committed status. . . . If a patient enters a mental hospital voluntarily, and with the understanding that he may leave at will, the psychiatrists may nevertheless refuse to release him. . . . Voluntary admission is in fact voluntary commitment. Or to put it another way, the voluntary mental patient's role is a cross between the role of medical patient and prisoner."

What about the view that individuals ought to be committed if they're a danger to themselves or society? "In my opinion," Szasz wrote, "whether or not a person is dangerous is not the real issue. It is rather who he is, and in what way he is dangerous. Some persons are allowed to be dangerous to others with impunity. Also, most of us are allowed to be dangerous in some ways, but not in others. Drunken drivers are dangerous both to themselves and to others. They injure and kill many more people than, for example, persons with paranoid delusions of persecution. Yet people labeled paranoid are readily committable, while drunken drivers are not. Some types of dangerous behavior are even rewarded. Race-car drivers, trapeze artists, and astronauts receive admiration and applause. . . . Thus, it is not dangerousness in general that is the issue here, but rather the manner or style in which one is dangerous."

Szasz dismissed the claim that mental hospitals have any ability to make patients better: "The damaging effects of mental hospitalization on the personality of the inmate are most convincingly demonstrated by the fact that so-called chronic patients rarely try to escape. Persons confined in mental institutions for an appreciable length of time lose whatever social skills they had for getting along on the outside."

Psychiatrists throttled individual responsibility not only by committing people to mental institutions against their will, but also by certifying criminal defendants as insane. The vague, easily expanded rationale of mental illness has meant that all kinds of people have committed terrible crimes without being held accountable.

Law, Liberty and Psychiatry made Szasz a controversial figure, and he began writing for popular publications including *New York Times Magazine,*

New York Times Book Review, Boston Sunday Herald, Atlantic Monthly, Harper's, National Review, New Republic, and *Science Digest.* Psychiatrists were outraged. Manfred Gutmacher, a psychiatrist who earned money testifying in criminal cases, snarled: "A bird that fouls its nest courts criticism."

Psychiatrists got a boost when Thorazine and other tranquilizers became readily available. Then came antipsychotic and antidepressant drugs. "As new generations of drugs were developed," Ronald Leifer explained, "the pharmacological treatment of mental illness appeared to be more cost effective and became more popular. Made more confident by drugs, psychiatrists have purged Szasz. His papers were unwelcome at psychiatric journals. It would be virtually impossible for anybody who shared his views on 'mental illness' to obtain a full-time academic position teaching psychiatric residents."

Yet psychiatrists have failed to prove that every human behavior has a physical cause that can be effectively treated with medication. *New York Times* science writer Natalie Angier reported: "Every time they think they have unearthed a real, analyzable gene to explain a mental disorder like manic depression or alcoholism, the finding dissolves on closer inspection or is cast into doubt." David Cohen, associate professor at the University of Montreal School of Social Work, observed that "after four decades of clinical use of neuroleptics [antipsychotic drugs], the following facts emerge from any gleaning of the contemporary psychiatric literature: clinicians do not agree on what constitutes rational use of these drugs; the optimal dose of any neuroleptic is unknown; for one-half of patients, the symptoms are not suppressed by the drugs or are made worse; drug effects are confused with psychiatric symptoms; despite a lack of data on long term therapeutic or toxic effects . . . the treatment of psychosis with neuroleptic drugs is, on a theoretical and practical level, in a state of confusion."

Amid all this controversy, Szasz wrote fifteen books. The most notable include *The Manufacture of Madness, A Comparative Study of the Inquisition and the Mental Health Movement* (1970); *The Age of Madness, A History of Involuntary Mental Hospitalization Presented in Selected Text* (1973); and *The Therapeutic State, Psychiatry in the Mirror of Current Events* (1984).

Szasz became even more controversial when he defied the conventional wisdom by denouncing the war on drugs. In his 1974 book *Ceremonial Chemistry,* Szasz discussed seven thousand years of history to show that there have always been drugs, and there have always been some "abusers," but when individuals are held responsible for any harm done to others, drug-taking (and other harmful behavior) is kept in check.

Drug prohibition has revealed the blazing contradictions of government interference with private life, Szasz pointed out. People die from the impurities in illegal drugs, something that is virtually unknown when drugs are legal and drug manufacturers can be held liable. People die in fights among drug distributors who, because they are engaged in illegal activity, cannot litigate their claims. Innocent people are burglarized, robbed, and killed as drug users seek money for their habit because it's much more costly than it would be in an open market.

Szasz rejected the view that individuals are helplessly addicted by drugs and that the solution for addiction is to undermine the responsibility of individuals for their actions. He noted that all habits can be hard to break, but people are endowed with free will and have the capacity for change. He warned that having an entire population addicted to government is far more dangerous than having some people addicted to drugs. He expanded his case in *Our Right to Drugs* (1992).

Throughout his life, Thomas Szasz has displayed the courage to stand alone. He defied a powerful profession and was banished from influential journals; high government officials did their best to ruin his career. But he spoke out for the most vulnerable among us. He defended the equal rights of people who have no voice because they're locked away in mental institutions or languish in prisons for the "crime" of being different. He affirmed the compassion of liberty.

PROTECTING LIBERTY

*A good constitution is infinitely
better than the best despot.*
—Thomas Babington Macaulay (1825)

Throughout history, limiting coercive political power has been the key to protecting liberty. Major insights came from thinkers in England, France, and America. Their ideas and struggles led to the most important protections for liberty.

AN INDEPENDENT JUDICIARY

ONE IMPORTANT REASON that civil liberties were first secured in England was the development of common law principles and precedents independent of a ruler. Edward Coke (pronounced "Cook") was more responsible for this than anybody else. Intellectual historian Murray N. Rothbard called him a "great early seventeenth century liberal." Winston S. Churchill observed that "his knowledge of the Common Law was unique." Historian George Macaulay Trevelyan considered him "one of the most important champions of our liberties." Nobel laureate F. A. Hayek referred to him as "the great fountain of Whig principles."

Coke had a gift for expressing ideas in unforgettable ways. "The common law," he wrote, "is the best and most common birth-right that the subject hath for the safeguard and defense, not merely of his goods, lands and revenues, but of his wife and children, his body, fame and life. . . . No man ecclesiastical or temporal shall be examined upon secret thoughts of his heart. . . . The house of an Englishman is to him as his castle."

Trevelyan credited Coke with "ferocious power of self-assertion, working through the medium of a legal learning, memory and intellect. . . . At a dangerous period in the development of the constitutional struggle, it was he who first revived the theory that the law was not the instrument but the boundary of royal prerogative, and that the Judges were not, as his rival [Francis] Bacon declared: 'lions under the throne,' but umpires between King and subject."

As a lawyer and judge, Coke worked with arguments based on precedents, which one might think would mean that if he couldn't cite precedents, he didn't have a case. But he was the best at discovering precedents for liberty. If at times he claimed precedents went back further and proved more than they actually did, he was almost always right about basic principles.

His *Reports* and *Institutes* did much to give the English a coherent constitution. Even Bacon conceded; "Had it not been for Sir Edward Coke's reports . . . law by this time had been almost like a ship without ballast; for that the cases of modern experience are fled from those that are judged and ruled in former times."

Although Coke embraced conventional religious beliefs, he promoted religious toleration. As chief justice of common law courts, he worked to keep many cases out of ecclesiastical courts that sentenced religious dissenters to be tortured, imprisoned or burned. He appointed Puritan ministers to the churches he owned. He hired an independent-minded secretary named Roger Williams, who went on to establish Rhode Island as a sanctuary for religious toleration.

More than a jurist, Coke deserves much credit for the emergence of representative government. Under Elizabeth I, Parliament was a cipher for the monarch. Members of Parliament lacked the ideological vision as well as practical experience to provide effective opposition or leadership. In 1621, 1624, 1625, and 1628, Parliament demanded that government ministers be accountable for their actions. Parliament articulated constitutional principles and took initiative in formulating policy. Coke framed the issues, served on more committees, and delivered more committee reports and speeches than anybody else. "Coke's great influence both in the Commons and in Parliament as a whole is easily explained," according to historian Stephen D. White. "His extensive governmental experience both in and out of Parliament and his formidable legal reputation naturally brought him respect from other members. He had held many high offices in both central and local government. . . . He had participated in every meeting of Parliament since 1589, had served as Speaker of the Commons in 1593, and was an expert on parliamentary precedents and procedure. And his published writings and his years as a judge and legal officer of the crown had established his reputation as the most eminent legal authority of the era."

Coke has had an enormous influence in the United States. "The men of the American Revolution were nurtured upon Coke's writings," observed constitutional historian Bernard Schwartz. "To them, Coke was the contemporary colossus of the law." Coke's principal gifts to America were the independence of the judiciary and the principle that judges may overturn statutes that are contrary to the Constitution.

Biographer Catherine Drinker Bowen noted that "Coke stood out above a crowd, a noticeably handsome man, tall, big-boned, inclined to spareness. His face was oval and a trifle long; between mustache and pointed short beard the lower lip showed full and red. Dark hair, cut even with the ears, had as yet no trace of gray but had begun to recede at the temples, accentuating the height of his forehead. Coke's eyebrows were heavy and smooth, his complexion somewhat swarthy; there were few lines to his face. His eyes, large, dark, and brilliant, bore the watchful look of a man ambitious and self-contained."

Coke, to be sure, was often difficult. Historian Thomas Babington Macaulay wrote, "He behaved with gross rudeness to his juniors at the bar, and with execrable cruelty to prisoners on trial for their lives. But he stood up manfully against the King and the King's favourites. No man of that age appeared to so little advantage when he was opposed to an inferior, and was in the wrong. But, on the other hand . . . no man of that age made so creditable a figure when he was opposed to a superior, and happened to be in the right."

EDWARD COKE WAS born with law in his blood on February 1, 1552, in Mileham, Norfolk, England. His father, Robert Coke, was a lawyer practicing in London and Norfolk. His mother, Winifred Knightley, was the daughter of an attorney.

Coke graduated from Trinity College, Cambridge. Destined for a legal career, he began studying at Clifford's Inn in 1571 and the next year transferred to Inner Temple. These were guilds where young men went to acquire knowledge of common law for professional practice. Common law was the law that applied to everyone. It encompassed Saxon legal customs, standard commercial practices for resolving disputes, parliamentary statutes, judicial decisions, and some royal decrees. In addition, there were treatises going back several hundred years, written by respected judges. Judicial decisions were not systematically based on precedents, because it was difficult to determine what the precedents were. "Argument from decided cases, though frequent and persuasive," noted English constitutional law scholar Charles M. Gray, "did not dominate courtroom dialogue. Prior decisions were sometimes followed by judges who professed not to agree with them, but they were sometimes rejected for reason or simply ignored." Students of the common law had to learn "law French," the language of common law pleadings, and Latin, the language in which medieval court records were kept.

Coke started practicing law in 1578. He spent a lot of time in Coventry, Essex, Norwich, and London, and he always had a notebook, which he filled with his observations about courtroom proceedings. He was to continue recording his observations for more than four decades, and they became the basis of the published works that secured his reputation.

When Coke was thirty, he married seventeen-year-old Bridget Paston, who descended from a wealthy Suffolk family and came with a sizable dowry. He developed ties with Lord Burghley, a councilor to Queen Elizabeth, and held a number of official positions before the queen appointed him solicitor general in 1592. She named him Speaker of the House of Commons the following year and then chose him over Francis Bacon to be attorney general.

The two men were to be rivals for nearly three decades. Bacon, nine years younger than Coke, was the son of an Elizabethan courtier, the Lord Keeper of the Great Seal. Bacon, according to biographer Bowen, "was spare, quick, of middle height and decently proportioned figure. . . . The hazel eye, neither green nor brown, had a darting quality. . . . None could deny his brilliance." Bacon learned law, pulled strings, and got into Parliament. One of his secretaries was Thomas Hobbes who later distinguished himself as a theoretician for political absolutism. In his lucid *Essays* (first edition, 1597), Bacon expressed admiration for Machiavelli's political writings and made clear his distrust of Parliament and his belief in government power.

When Queen Elizabeth died on March 24, 1603, she was succeeded by thirty-seven-year-old James VI of Scotland, who became James I of Great Britain. A monarch was supposed to pay the cost of his palace and retainers with hereditary income, while Parliament financed national defense and wars, but James asked Parliament—the taxpayers—to help cover his royal household expenses. "Clothes became richer and more extravagant," reported historian Maurice Lee, Jr., "because both James and Anne liked to cover themselves with jewels. . . . A feast for the court employed one hundred cooks for eight days, involved sixteen hundred dishes." Moreover, wrote historian Paul Johnson, "James was a loutish savage. When hunting, he liked to plunge his bandy legs into the stag's bowels. . . . He delighted in getting the young court ladies drunk, and seeing them collapse in vomit at his feet."

He was determined to assert his power. "The state of monarchy," James maintained, "is the supremest thing upon earth. For Kings are not only God's lieutenants upon earth and sit upon God's throne, but even by God himself they are called Gods." As Trevelyan wrote, "He knew nothing of the peculiar laws and liberties of England. . . . His dogma of the divine right of Kings was gleaned from the new theory of State now in favour among the monarchies of the continent."

Attorney General Coke emerged as a formidable man when he handled some sensational trials, and he soon challenged the king. The Court of the Exchequer ruled that tariff policy was the king's jurisdiction, not Parliament's. But Coke insisted that Parliament's approval was required since tariffs were for revenue. Biographers Hastings Lyon and Herman Block noted Coke's crucial insight that if James controlled more revenue, he "would have a nearly complete system of extra-Parliamentary taxation, and Parliament would soon become an unnecessary assembly, with a consequent corruption of the State into tyranny." Indeed, representative institutions were dying out in France and Spain as the monarchies there gained exclusive control of public finance.

In June 1606, Coke was appointed chief justice of the Court of Common Pleas, which primarily handled private actions between citizens. When James issued a writ ordering people in England's seaports to equip his fleet, Coke protested that the writ violated principles of liberty, which he called the "birthright and inheritance of the subjects of England." James warned, "It is sedition in Subjects to dispute what a King may do."

Meanwhile, Coke labored to share his knowledge of common law. He had begun issuing an annual *Report* on cases in 1600, and he continued until 1616. "Anything that could be gleaned in Westminster, London Guildhall or the circuit courts in the counties he set down in his own form and fashion, adding comment, aside, comparison," noted biographer Bowen. "No law reports had hitherto been half so comprehensive; Coke must have lived and walked and sat and talked with notebook in hand. At once the books became—as Blackstone indicated in 1765—an intrinsic authority in the courts of justice."

Coke objected to the king's men trying to influence a judge when neither a defendant nor defense counsel was present for cross-examination. This became an issue in the case of Edmund Peacham, a Puritan minister summoned before the High Commission for criticizing a bishop. As Bacon reported to the king, "Peacham was examined before torture, in torture, between torture, and after torture . . . he still persisting in his obstinate and inexcusable denials and former answers." Peacham died in prison.

In *Bonham's Case* (1610), Coke ruled that the common law stood above Parliament. Dr. Thomas Bonham had been imprisoned for practicing medicine without a certificate from the Royal College of Physicians. Coke ruled that "when an Act of Parliament is against common right and reason, or repugnant, or impossible to be performed, the common law will control it and adjudge such Act to be void." This was his most controversial decision.

In September 1610, Coke appeared before the Privy Council, which had the responsibility of advising the king on executive, judicial, and financial business, and he dared to declare that the king's proclamations didn't have the force of law. The Privy Council upheld his view.

Coke issued prohibitions to curb the power of ecclesiastical courts, especially the High Commission, which imprisoned individuals for preaching nonconformist doctrines. A prohibition ordered an ecclesiastical court not to proceed with a case if it might belong in a common law court.

James needed money, so he summoned Parliament in 1610, but reluctant members drew up a petition of grievances. Coke declared, "I must fly to Magna Carta and entreat explanation of his Majesty. Magna Carta is called . . . The Charter of Liberty because it maketh freeman. When the King says he cannot allow our liberties of right, this strikes at the root." James fumed against Parliament, saying, "I am surprised that my ancestors should ever have permitted such an institution to come into existence."

In 1613, Bacon persuaded James to try taming Coke by naming him chief justice of the King's Bench, which handled civil as well as criminal actions, and by promising him a seat on the twelve-member Privy Council. "Coke will thereupon turn obsequious," Bacon assured James. But after James granted income properties to the bishop of Coventry, two men protested that the properties were theirs and not for the king to give away. In this *Case of Commendams,* Coke insisted that plaintiffs were entitled to a hearing despite the king's objections. He was dismissed.

"Coke had not striven in vain," noted historian George Macaulay Trevelyan. "He had enlisted the professional pride of the students of the common law against the rival systems of law specially favoured by the Crown in the Star Chamber, the admiralty and the Ecclesiastical Courts. He had turned the minds of the young gentlemen of the Inns of Court, who watched him from afar with fear and reverence, to contemplate a new idea of the constitutional function and of the political affinities of their profession."

Coke was so desperate to regain a high position that he pressured his fourteen-year-old daughter, Frances, to marry John Villiers, the impotent older brother of James's most influential advisor, George Villiers (later the duke of Buckingham). This was the low point of Coke's career. Although he didn't get back his judgeship, he regained his position on the Privy Council.

James summoned Parliament, which met on January 13, 1621, for the first time in seven years. He needed money, but members were determined to pursue corruption, in particular, concerning Bacon, who had been appointed lord high chancellor, the top-ranking position outside of the royal family. On March 17, Coke, who had emerged as the leading prosecutor, used the fateful word *bribe* and warned that "a corrupt judge is the grievance of grievances." The list of Bacon's loot included a diamond ring, gold buttons, furniture, and wine as well as cash. Bacon was impeached, dismissed as lord high chancellor, fined, imprisoned in the Tower of London, and banished from London and the law courts. Historian Lord Acton later remarked, "The Commons, guided by the most famous English lawyer, Coke, struck down Bacon, and deprived the Stuarts of the ablest counsellor they ever had. Impeachment and responsibility of ministers remained."

On December 18, James dissolved Parliament and got even by having his tormentor imprisoned. Coke endured a damp, bitter cold, urine-soaked cell in the Tower of London. Denied access to books, he wrote Latin verses with pieces of coal. After seven months, officials admitted they couldn't find any evidence of wrongdoing, and he was released.

Coke led the attack on government-granted monopolies of wool, brick making, glass making, salmon fishing, and the transcribing of wills. "Generally," he contended, "all monopolies are against the great Charter, because they are against the liberty and freedom of the subject, and against the law of the land."

James died on March 27, 1625. He had achieved a long period of peace, which enabled the English to prosper, but he left an enormous debt. His twenty-four-year-old son became King Charles I and immediately began spending money at a reckless pace. He borrowed £60,000 to finance the most spectacular funeral ever seen in England. To help secure an ally against Spain, he married the fifteen-year-old French Catholic princess, Henriette

Marie, and this cost him a great deal of treasures even though she came with a big dowry.

Charles summoned Parliament in May 1625 because he wanted money for military adventures. When Parliament wouldn't give him as much as he wanted, he dissolved it and resorted to conscription. The government rounded up as many able-bodied men as they could find around the port towns and forced private individuals to feed and house the conscripts. This provoked unrest and resulted in martial law. Charles summoned Parliament again, and again demanded money, but the House of Commons began impeachment proceedings against his adviser who had promoted military adventures. On June 12, 1627, Charles dissolved Parliament.

"At the back of the Parliamentary movement in all its expressions lay a deep fear," explained Winston S. Churchill. "Everywhere in Europe they saw the monarchies becoming more autocratic. The States-General, which had met in Paris in 1614, had not been summoned again; it was not indeed to be summoned until the clash of 1789. The rise of standing armies, composed of men drilled in firearms and supported by trains of artillery, had stripped alike the nobles and the common people of their means of independent resistance."

Charles ordered that tariff revenue go into royal coffers, without parliamentary approval. When he resorted to forced loans, seventy-six men refused to comply. They were denied the right to a trial and imprisoned. But Charles wanted even more money, and on March 27, 1628, he summoned Parliament for the third time. Coke presented a bill that specified no one could be imprisoned more than three months without being brought to trial. The House of Commons approved resolutions saying that nobody should be imprisoned unless the government specified the charges, and the writ of habeas corpus must not be denied. When the House of Lords defended prerogatives claimed by the king, Coke warned that the prerogatives had no basis in English law. Yet the king continued to make demands, and on May 8 Coke proposed that Parliament adopt a petition of right on "1. The personal liberty of the subject. 2. His propriety in his goods. 3. Unbilletting of soldiers. And 4. Silencing of martial law in time of peace." Charles insisted on his prerogatives, but Coke remained defiant. On June 8, Charles met both Houses of Parliament in the afternoon. He capitulated and accepted the petition of right as law.

"We reach here," wrote Churchill, "amid much confusion, the main foundation of English freedom. The right of the Executive Government to imprison a man, high or low, for reasons of State was denied; and that denial, made good in painful struggles, constitutes the charter of every self-respecting man at any time in any land. Trial by jury of equals, only for offenses known to the law, if maintained, makes the difference between bond and free."

Coke retired to Stoke House in Stoke Poges, Buckinghamshire, just west of London, where he completed his life work. This place was a splendid manor with diamonded windows, formal Italian gardens, and a thousand acres of woodland. He prepared commentaries on Thomas Littleton's *Treatise on Tenures,* one of the most important English law books.

While his health declined in 1634, the Privy Council issued a warrant to search his house, and police seized manuscripts for his *Institutes* as well as two unpublished volumes of *Reports.* Coke died at Stoke House on September 3, 1634. A month later, he was buried in the church graveyard at Tittleshall, about six miles southwest of Fakenham, Norfolk, next to his first wife.

Charles disregarded the Petition of Right and refused to call another Parliament for eleven years, but Coke's principles inspired John Lilburne and other English freedom fighters. When Parliament met in 1640, it arranged for publication of the *Institutes* because they "contain many monuments of the subject's liberties." The second part of the *Institutes* appeared in 1642, a commentary on Magna Carta and almost forty other charters and statutes. The third part of the *Institutes* (1644) discussed many more laws. The fourth part (1644) covered Parliament.

By the time of the Glorious Revolution in 1688, long-standing English grievances had been resolved, the monarchy had a Protestant succession, and there was a considerable degree of religious toleration. People were protected from arbitrary search and seizure and couldn't be held in prison unless formal charges were filed, alleging violation of a law. Above all, the power of the monarch was limited by Parliament, which had achieved supremacy. Ironically, this meant judges couldn't overturn an act of Parliament. They could only rule that the government exceeded the powers granted by a statute.

In America, Rhode Island's founder Roger Williams wrote, "His [Coke's] example, instruction, and encouragement have spurred me on to a more than ordinary, industrious, and patient course in my whole course hitherto." Thomas Jefferson remarked that "Coke Lyttleton was the universal elementary book of law students and a sounder Whig never wrote nor of profounder learning in the orthodox doctrines of British liberties." Patrick Henry, John Adams, John Quincy Adams, John Jay, Daniel Webster, and many other influential Americans read Coke. Historian Bernard Schwartz observed that "the influence of Coke may be seen at all of the key stages in the development of the conflict between the Colonies and the mother country."

Although judicial review had disappeared from England, it took hold in America. "The institution that best embodies this idea," wrote Schwartz, "is the United States Supreme Court." New judges naturally tended to reflect the views of the politicians who appointed them, but those politicians didn't have the power to fire judges they disagreed with.

Although judges have made plenty of bad decisions, they have the power to strike down unconstitutional statutes, and sometimes they do. This is a big advance from the era when judges were everywhere intimidated into doing what a ruler wanted—eloquent testimony to the vision and courage of Edward Coke.

POPULAR SOVEREIGNTY

ONE OF THE MOST important checks on government power has been the principle of popular sovereignty: people should be able to choose their rulers and throw them out when they become scoundrels.

The influential English agitator and thinker Algernon Sidney championed popular sovereignty back when kings ruled the earth. For years, he stirred opposition to the English king, Charles II, for which he was hunted by assassins. He spoke out against slavery in the British West Indies. There were two attempts on his life, and he suffered the ultimate tragedy: beheading. He became the most famous English martyr for liberty.

His major work, *Discourses Concerning Government*, appeared in 1698, fifteen years after his execution, and it did much to develop the case for liberty that was to inspire Americans and sweep the world. For instance, he wrote: "No man is to be entrusted with an absolute Power . . . in all controversies concerning the power of magistrates, we are not to examine which conduces to their profit or glory, but what is good for the publick . . . the right of magistrates do essentially depend upon the consent of those who govern . . . Laws therefore they are not, which publick consent hath not made so . . . The Liberties of Nations are from God and Nature, not from Kings . . . [human beings] have by the law of nature a right to their liberties, lands, goods . . ."

Sidney was revered by all who cherished liberty. He knew English natural rights philosopher John Locke, and he worked with Quaker William Penn to bring libertarian ideas into Parliament. Thomas Jefferson considered Sidney to be one of the most important thinkers on liberty and called the *Discourses* "a rich treasure of republican principles . . . probably the best elementary book of the principles of government, as founded on natural right which has ever been published in any language." John Adams, John Dickinson, Benjamin Franklin, James Otis, and other American writers of the Revolutionary era hailed Sidney.

Historian Thomas G. West called Sidney "precocious, energetic, and honorable." He was tall and thin, and in his youth he had red hair. A portrait was painted when he was a forty-year-old exile, and as historian John Carswell noted, it "shows him in the breastplate of a soldier and a leader, and it could be engraved and circulated for propaganda purposes: the picture of a leader in the cause for the restoration of the English republic." By his fifties, Sidney was in France, and Carswell described him as "spare, graying now, he is as active as ever, shooting, writing, riding. In the voluminous correspondence of his lifetime, with its litany of complaints about circumstances and other people, there is hardly a syllable about not feeling well."

He was an unforgettable character. "There is the solitary Sidney who spent much of his time alone and in exile," explained historian Jonathan Scott. "There is the familial Sidney, who never produced a family of his own to supplant that under whose troubled shadow he remained. There is the 'retired' Sidney, in Augsburg, Nerac and Rome. There is Sidney the scholar, and never far behind him, the man of action . . . [pursuing] 'that liberty in which God created us.'"

ALGERNON SIDNEY WAS born around January 15, 1623. The exact day isn't known, but on that date a midwife was paid for attending his mother, Dorothy, Lady Lisle, who descended from the powerful Percy family. Algernon's father was Robert Lisle, heir to the earldom of Leicester and the 4,000-acre Penshurst mansion in Kent, where Algernon was born. He was the fourth surviving child and second son.

His father enrolled him at Gray's Inn when he was ten. He seems to have absorbed his father's philosophical views, reportedly believing that Grotius's *Law of War and Peace* was the most important work on political philosophy.

Sidney participated in the rebellion against King Charles I who had ruled arbitrarily without a Parliament from 1629 until the need for money forced him to call it back in 1640. Six years later, Sidney was elected to what became known as the Long Parliament. He was named a commissioner for the trial of the king and called the 1649 execution "the justest and bravest action that ever was done in England, or anywhere."

On April 20, 1653, Oliver Cromwell shut down Parliament and began his military dictatorship known as the Protectorate. Sidney went to The Hague where he seems to have served as an agent for English constitutionalists opposed to Cromwell.

Richard Cromwell assumed power following his father's death on September 3, 1658, and Sidney was somehow appointed ambassador to Denmark and Sweden. The two countries had fought each other for a decade, and another war loomed. Sidney helped negotiate a peace settlement, signed on May 27, 1660, that has lasted more than three hundred years. It ensured international access to the Baltic.

After Richard Cromwell was overthrown by the army in April 1659, Parliament invited the son of Charles I to become King Charles II. He ordered the hanging of those who had played a key role in the execution of his father, and Sidney thought it prudent to go abroad. Historian Trevelyan wrote, "The gallows and butchery were set up in Charing Cross, in sight of the place before Whitehall where the scaffold had been dressed for Charles; as the hangman cut the king-killers to pieces, their heads and hearts were shown reeking to the people, whose shouts testified that on this occasion they felt neither pity nor respect. Hugh Peters had scarcely the strength to face so terrible a scene, and came staggering on to the scaffold. But Cook the lawyer, Harrison and the other soldiers and politicians proved worthy of their cause and of that hour. And none died better than Sir Harry Vane (1662), proclaiming the principles of liberty to the last."

Sidney stayed in Europe, trying to elude the assassins Charles II dispatched to kidnap or kill his political enemies. He visited Copenhagen University and signed the guest book with these explosive words: *"Manus haec inimica tyrannis, Ense petit placidam sub liberate quietem"* ("This hand, enemy to tyrants, By the word seeks calm peacefulness with liberty"). Sidney's friends were so shocked that they offered to remove the page, but he insisted it remain. His words caused a sensation in Europe and England. His father wrote to him, "No man will open his mouth for you."

Little is known of his underground life, including the sources of funds that enabled him to live and travel without any visible means of support. Undoubtedly they were in England. "The nature of the evidence about him changes," noted biographer Carswell, "and we can no longer look for letters. Though he must have written many, their recipients prudently did not keep them, and only five survive that can with certainty be assigned to the next fourteen years. News of him is traced in intelligence reports, official communications, diplomatic memoirs, by those concerned to watch him."

Sidney headed south, stopping in Hamburg, Frankfurt, Augsburg, and Venice and he lived in Rome until it became thick with spies and assassins. He headed for Bern, Switzerland, where many English exiles had found sanctuary, but even Bern wasn't safe; one of the exiles, John Lisle, was assassinated on his way to church. Sidney left for Augsburg, then Brussels. Apparently while Sidney was in Holland, three exiles were seized, taken to England, and executed.

Among the most steadfast Dutch supporters was Quaker merchant Benjamin Furley who assisted William Penn's struggle for religious toleration and provided lodging for John Locke when he became an exile in Holland. Furley evidently helped get money for Sidney, and he copied Sidney's manuscripts and kept them safe. Furley, according to biographer John Carswell, was "a plumpish, rather clumsy-looking man with a round, ugly, but highly intelligent face under a thatch of dark hair . . . genuinely likeable and warm-hearted man, with a talent for making friends. . . . For many years he lent them money, gave them house-room, handled their business affairs, and with his international contacts acted as their banker. He was the repository of their secrets, their trusted advisor, a solid resource in their shifting and uncertain world."

At this time, Sidney's principal manuscript, *Court Maxims*, attacked Charles II and encouraged the Dutch to support the republican struggle against him. *Court Maxims* consists of fifteen dialogues between the republican Euonomius and the royal courtier Philalethes, who discuss maxims of political absolutism, such as "monarchy is the best form of government" and "monarchy ought to be absolute and hereditary." Sidney (Euonomius) affirmed the doctrine of a "higher law" that had been championed by Cicero, and he insisted that if rulers subvert the interests of the people, they "ought no longer to be looked upon as fathers or shepherds, which are titles of love and sweetness, but thieves, wolves, tyrants, the worst of enemies." He continued, "The essence of the law consists solely in the justice of it: if it be not just, it is no law. . . . The law that should be for our defense is a snare . . . what law soever is made prejudicial to those of that society, perverting justice, destroys the end for which it ought to be established, is therefore in the highest degree unjust and utterly invalid. . . . The most important temporal interests of all honest men are: to preserve life, liberty, and estate."

By 1677 Charles II, feeling more confident about his power, issued a pass that enabled Sidney to return, supposedly to visit his frail father, now more than eighty years old. But his family was mired in financial problems, and he was immediately imprisoned for debt. Somehow Sidney emerged as a major figure among English dissidents. In a bid to influence British politics in his favor, the wily Louis XIV channeled subsidies to dissidents including Sidney and provided a large subsidy to Charles II. Louis leaked news about the subsidy to Charles II, and it triggered outrage against him. Later, when news came out about the French money Sidney had received, people turned against him too.

Charles II claimed more and more power, provoking a debate about the most fundamental issues of government. Lawyer Robert Filmer published *Patriarcha: A Defense of the Natural Power of Kings Against the Unnatural Power of the People*, which he had written forty-two years earlier when Charles I was losing his grip on the throne. Filmer denied that human beings have natural rights and insisted that even a bad ruler must be obeyed because he was, in effect, the head of a family. The doctrine of political absolutism seemed to be gaining support, and it became the universal creed, a monarch could not be safely opposed.

Some of the greatest minds of the era began refuting Filmer. John Locke, secretary and medical adviser to radical Anthony Ashley Cooper, the earl of Shaftesbury, began defending natural rights in two treatises; being a cautious man, he kept them out of circulation until 1689, after the Stuarts had been overthrown—and even then the books were published anonymously. Locke's long-time friend and assistant James Tyrrell was more daring: he wrote *Patriarcha non Monarchia,* published in 1681.

Sidney, too, worked on a massive point-by-point refutation of Filmer. He might well have seen Filmer's manuscript years earlier, when the two men were neighbors. In any case, Sidney refined his thinking and gathered more material for an intellectual attack on monarchy. "He wrote rapidly and in a passion of self-expression, hardly pausing, one feels, to check or improve," noted biographer Carswell. The work displayed Sidney's vast learning. He drew extensively on English and European history, ancient Greek history, Roman history, and the Old Testament. But he never finished, and the original manuscript was lost. Fortunately a copy was located and the work appeared in print fifteen years after Sidney's death. The book was called *Discourses Concerning Government.*

Sidney wrote, "The whole fabrick of tyranny will be much weakened, if we prove, that nations have a right to make their own laws, constitute their own magistrates; and that such as are so constituted owe an account of their actions to those by whom, and for whom they are appointed." Sidney warned, "All governments are subject to corruption and decay. . . . Absolute power to which [Filmer] would exalt the chief magistrate, would be burdensome, and desperately dangerous, if he had it."

Kings, he continued, must be "under the law, and the law is not under them; their letters or commands are not to be regarded: In the administration of justice, the question is not what pleases them, but what the law declares to be right, which must have its course, whether the king be busy or at leisure, whether he will or not. . . . Kings not being fathers of their People, nor excelling all others in Virtue, can have no other just Power than what the Laws give; nor any title to the privileges of the Lord's Annointed. . . . nothing can be more absurd than to say, that one man has an absolute power above law to govern according to his will, for the people's good, and the preservation of their liberty: For no liberty can subsist where there is such a power." Sidney added: "The Legislative Power . . . [is] not to be trusted in the hands of any who are not bound to obey the Laws they make."

Sidney affirmed the natural right of people to rebel against unjust rulers: "Every man has a right of resisting some way or other that which ought not to be done to him. . . . No People can be obliged to suffer from their King what they have not a right to do. . . . Unjust Commands are not to be obey'd; and no man is obliged to suffer for not obeying such as are against Law. . . . It would be madness to think, that any nation can be obliged to bear whatsoever their own magistrates think fit to do against them."

Sidney joined the underground opposition to Charles II and his Catholic heir James, the duke of York. He was involved with the Rye House Plot to assassinate both Charles II and the duke of York when they passed the Rye House in Herfordshire, between Newmarket and London. But somebody leaked details about the plot. The earl of Shaftesbury, who had conceived it, fled to Holland, and was soon followed by John Locke. On June 26, 1683, Sidney was arrested while eating lunch at his home in London. His personal papers were seized, and he was charged with treason. This was the first big case for Judge George Jeffreys, and he hoped it would be his ticket to the top. The prosecution used "Col. Sydney's paper," the manuscript for *Discourses* that had been found at his house, as evidence. Jeffreys denounced the work for "fixing power in the people." Sidney was found guilty and sentenced to death.

In a brief final piece, *Apology in the Day of His Death*, Sidney wrote; "I had from my youth endeavored to uphold the common rights of mankind, the laws of this land, and the true Protestant religion, against corrupt principles, arbitrary power, and Popery, and I do now willingly lay down my life for the same." His execution was set for December 7, 1683. "When he came to the scaffold," one witness recalled, "instead of a speech, he told them only that he had made his peace with God, that he came not thither to talk, but to die; put a paper into the sheriff's hand, and another into a friend's, said one prayer as short as a grace, laid down his neck, and bid the executioner do his office." Sidney was sixty-one. He was buried at Penshurst.

Charles II died, and his Catholic brother was crowned James II. People rebelled against him in 1688, and the Protestant prince of Orange became King William III. Sidney was soon hailed as a martyr for liberty. The *Discourses* was initially published in 1698, and at least eight editions appeared during the eighteenth century.

Sidney's reputation declined in England, though, when details emerged about his receiving French money. The English generally wanted even less to do with him after he was embraced by rebellious Americans, but he was defended by Charles James Fox, the great orator who opposed policies of King George III. There were two German translations of the *Discourses* and two French translations. In France, Sidney's greatest fans included the political philosophers Montesquieu and Condorcet.

Sidney was especially admired in America. Historian Alan Craig Houston observed, "To the colonists, the single most important fact about Sidney's life was the manner of his death. By his unselfish devotion to liberty, Sidney set a standard against which men repeatedly measured themselves; by his martyrdom, he graphically demonstrated the evils of unchecked power. Colonial Americans also read the *Discourses Concerning Government* with care and precision. They cited Sidney on a wide range of issues, from the corruption of men to the rule of law, and from the representative nature of government to the right of revolution." "Sidney's martyrdom," he continued, "was the most powerful piece of evidence that could have been given to verify the truth of his writings. As the latter preached, so the former graphically demonstrated the consequence of permitting one man to enjoy the arbitrary and unlimited power. Had Sidney not been a martyr, it is unlikely the *Discourses* would have been as widely read in eighteenth-century America; had he not written the *Discourses,* on the other hand, it is unlikely his death would have received the attention it did."

Referring to American writers of the Revolutionary era, historian Bernard Bailyn observed that "above all, they [the American colonists] referred to the doctrines of Algernon Sidney." In 1775, Massachusetts took its motto from Sidney's words in the Copenhagen guest book ("This hand, enemy to tyrants, By the word seeks calm peacefulness with liberty").

After the Revolution, Americans thought they had less of need for Sidney's teachings, but there was a revival during the movement to abolish slavery. William Lloyd Garrison called Sidney "the father of modern Abolitionism" and "an uncompromising enemy of slavery." Garrison praised the *Discourses* as an "exhaustless treasury of free thoughts." Wendell Phillips, the greatest antislavery orator, considered the *Discourses* an "immortal book." When Senator William H. Seward fought the Compromise of 1850, which, among other things, made it easier to capture runaway slaves, he recalled Sidney's words: "The liberty of one man cannot be limited or diminished by one or any number of men, and none can give away the right of another." In 1866, Radical Republican Senator Charles Sumner cited Sidney and Locke when he delivered a speech affirming the political rights of liberated slaves.

Nonetheless, as historian Thomas G. West reported, "Sidney fell out of fashion during the nineteenth century. The educated began to favor statesmen like Cromwell and Napoleon, who relished the exercise of unrestrained power for grand projects in the service of mankind."

Yet another Sidney revival has been stirring. In 1988 Jonathan Scott produced the first new biography in a century, *Algernon Sidney and the English Republic, 1623–1677,* followed by *Algernon Sidney and Restoration Crisis, 1677–1683* (1991). John Carswell wrote *The Porcupine: The Life of Algernon Sidney* (1989). In 1990, Liberty Fund brought out the first new edition of Sidney's *Discourses* in 185 years. Then Princeton University Press published Alan Craig Houston's *Algernon Sidney and the Republican Heritage in England and America.* In 1996, Cambridge University Press issued Sidney's unpublished *Court Maxims,* the lost manuscript of which turned up in Warwick Castle during the 1970s. Sidney truly died that his bold ideas could live.

A SEPARATION OF POWERS

DISPERSING POLITICAL POWER has proved to be crucial for protecting people against tyranny. The pioneering thinker on the subject was the eighteenth-century Frenchman, Charles-Louis Secondat, baron de Montesquieu. As a political philosopher, he towered above his contemporaries, including Voltaire and other celebrated French *philosophes* who favored centralizing political power and pursuing reform through "enlightened despotism."

Montesquieu inspired some of the greatest French thinkers on liberty. Benjamin Constant cited him frequently in his writings about the dangers of centralized political power. *Democracy in America* author Alexis de Tocqueville acknowledged, "I spend a little time each day" reading Montesquieu. James Madison reflected that Montesquieu "lifted the veil from the venerable errors which enslaved opinion, and pointed the way to those luminous truths of which he had but a glimpse himself." Madison referred to Montesquieu as "the oracle who is always consulted and cited" about the separation of powers.

Historians have long recognized the importance of Montesquieu in America. Wrote legal historian Henry Maine in 1897, "It may be confidently laid down, that neither the institution of the Supreme Court, nor the entire structure of the Constitution of the United States, were the least likely to occur to anybody's mind before the publication of [Montesquieu's principal work] *Esprit des Lois.*"

English observer James Bryce wrote in 1898, "Montesquieu, contrasting the private as well as public liberties of Englishmen with the despotism of Continental Europe, had taken the Constitution of England as his model system, and had ascribed its merits to the division of legislative, executive, and judicial functions which he discovered in it, and to the system of checks and balances whereby its equilibrium seemed to be preserved. No general principle of politics laid such hold on the constitution-makers and statesmen of America as the dogma that the separation of these three functions is essential to freedom. It had already been the groundwork of several State constitutions. It is always reappearing in their writings; it was never absent from their thoughts."

Harvard University historian Bernard Bailyn reported that Montesquieu was among the thinkers "quoted everywhere in the colonies, by everyone who claimed a broad awareness. . . . The pervasiveness of such citations is at times astonishing." Montesquieu was quoted "on the character of British liberty and on the institutional requirements for its attainment."

Historians Will and Ariel Durant rated Montesquieu's major work *De l'esprit des lois (Spirit of the Laws)* as "the greatest intellectual production of the age." Historian Peter Gay called him "the most influential writer of the eighteenth century." He added, "I make this assertion after due consideration for the claims of potential rivals."

Montesquieu made many keen observations about liberty—for instance: "Commerce cures destructive prejudices, and it is an almost general rule that everywhere there are gentle mores, there is commerce and that everywhere there is commerce, there are gentle mores. . . . [Slavery] is not good by its nature. It is useful neither to the master nor to the slave; not to the slave, because he can do nothing from virtue; not to the master, because he contracts all sorts of bad habits from his slaves, because he imperceptibly grows accustomed to failing in all the moral virtues, because he grows proud, curt, harsh, angry, voluptuous, and cruel."

Biographer Judith N. Shklar noted that "we know very little about Montesquieu's personal life. His surviving correspondence is completely unrevealing. . . . He was the least confessional of writers. On the two occasions when he tried his hand at autobiography, he began by declaring that it was a silly thing to do" There are, nonetheless, clues about what Montesquieu was like. Biographer Robert Shackleton noted that "geniality, affability, generosity and simplicity, as well as his absent-mindedness, are the subjects of unnumbered stories."

Shackleton continued, "He was short, thin, and fair." Around 1749, "His appearance, which is surprisingly old for a man who was barely fifty, is one of placid dignity. His face is elongated with a pointed chin. His jaw is firm. His eyes are blue. His nose, though he is not shown in profile, is prominent, and there is a swelling to the right of the left eye. It is a formal portrait with all the shortcomings that implies. It tells more about the full-dress costume of a parliamentary magistrate than about the character of Montesquieu." The Swiss medallist Jacques-Antoine Dassier produced the best-known image, a medal that, as Shackleton wrote, "shows a left profile of of Montesquieu. He has a thin neck, firm chin, elongated but sensitive nose, and fearless, with thick and disarranged hair: it is a magnificent Roman head. . . . His eyes, to the last, gave him trouble. And though he faced the threat of blindness with courage and adaptability . . . this affliction was a great impediment in social life as well as in his researches. . . . Montesquieu has been absent-minded in his early days. In his old age this characteristic was intensified, partly by the deterioration of his sight, and was the subject of anecdotes both during and after his life."

Montesquieu was a devoted scholar. "Study has been for me," he reflected, "the sovereign remedy against all the disappointments of life. I have never known any trouble that an hour's reading would not dissipate."

CHARLES-LOUIS DE SECONDAT was born on January 19, 1689, in the castle of La Brede, southwest of Bordeaux, which had been inherited by his mother, Marie-Françoise de Pestel. After she died in childbirth when he was seven, he became the baron de La Brede. His father, Jacques de Secondat, was a soldier.

Charles-Louis spent his first three years nursing with a local miller. He was tutored at home until he was eleven, then sent to a school in Juilly. "The instruction itself was thorough," according to biographer Shackleton. "Latin and French were the languages mainly studied, Greek being at all times subordinate; and although it was deemed necessary to be proficient in the speaking of Latin, the actual language of instruction was French. Geography, history, and mathematics were in the time-table, and instruction was given also in such subjects as drawing, music, riding, fencing, and dancing."

Charles-Louis entered the University of Bordeaux, where he studied law, and after he received his degree in 1708, he moved to Paris for further legal studies. He seems to have become acquainted with mathematicians and scientists. As the eldest son, he inherited the family estates when his father died in 1713, at age fifty-eight. After the death of his uncle, Charles-Louis inherited his uncle's post as *président à mortier* of the Bordeaux *parlement* (there were nine officials with this title), a hereditary institution that functioned as a law court.

As Montesquieu approached his twenty-fifth birthday, he decided to get married, and on March 11, 1715, he signed a contract with Jeanne de Lartique, the daughter of a wealthy Huguenot merchant. There didn't seem to be much love in the marriage, but the couple had a son and two daughters born between 1717 and 1727.

Meanwhile, he had begun writing a novel, *The Persian Letters*, about two Persian men, Usbeck and Rica, who visited France between 1711 and 1720, writing letters to their friends, lovers, and each other about their observations. The novel was published anonymously in Amsterdam in 1721 and subsequently smuggled into France. This work made him a major name in French literature, and he was elected to the prestigious Académie française. One of the letters (no. 85), defended toleration: "It is noticed that members of tolerated religions usually render more service to their country than do those of the dominant religion because, cut off from customary honors, they can distinguish themselves only by an opulence and wealth acquired by their labor alone, and often in the most difficult professions." In letter no. 122, Montesquieu observed the link between liberty and prosperity: "Nothing attracts foreigners more than liberty and the wealth which always follows from it. The one is sought for itself, and our needs direct us to countries where we may find the other." And letter no. 83 seemed to recall a vision of "higher law": "justice is eternal and independent of human conventions. . . . Justice is the proper relationship actually existing between two things. This relationship is always the same whoever contemplates it, whether God, or angel, or, finally, man."

During the 1720s, Montesquieu traveled to Austria, Germany, Holland, Hungary, and Italy and spent eighteen eye-opening months in England. He attended parliamentary debates and studied the journals of parliamentary leaders in order better to understand England's constitutional system, which provided more liberty than anyplace else in Europe. Montesquieu was in England during the heyday of Robert Walpole who helped pioneer the cabinet system. This was, historian George Macaulay Trevelyan explained, "a group of Ministers dependent on the favour of the House of Commons and all having seats in Parliament, who must agree on a common policy and who are responsible for one another's action and for the government of the country as a whole. Neither Prime Minister nor Cabinet system was contemplated in the Revolution Settlement [1689]. . . . It was Sir Robert Walpole, the Whig peace Minister from 1721 to 1742, who did most to evolve the principle of the common responsibility of the Cabinet, and the supremacy of the Prime Minister as the leading man at once in the Cabinet and in the Commons."

Montesquieu conceived of the separation of powers principle while observing the English constitutional system, but the English didn't actually go very far with the principle. As historian Peter Gay wrote, "The executive met and mingled with the legislature in the House of Commons; the peers exercised judicial as well as legislative functions; and there were other mutual invasions of presumably reserved territory that compromised the neatness of Montesquieu's model."

Voltaire's experience showed that an author had to proceed with caution. It was against French law to praise Isaac Newton, William Shakespeare, and other things English, and there were about seventy censors who enforced such restrictions. "Not all censors were lax or corrupt," remarked Peter Gay, "some were devoted to their repressive task. Besides, there was less risk in erring on the side of severity than on the side of leniency: one never knew what allusion might seem offensive to a bishop, a minister, or a royal mistress. Therefore censors often held up manuscripts for months and engaged publishers in tedious, exhausting negotiations." In 1733, the government ordered the burning of Voltaire's irreverent *Lettres philosophiques* (*Philosophical Letters*), which expressed his enthusiasm for England and made fun of French royal absolutism. Voltaire had not said much about England's political system. He noted that aristocrats paid taxes—a dramatic contrast with France—and that taxes were set by Parliament. He admired the lower level of taxes in England and talked about power divided between the House of Commons and the House of Lords.

There was much more to be covered, and Montesquieu resolved to do it. He began work on De l'esprit des lois around 1729, when he was about forty. For fifteen years, he persisted with the project, and nearly went blind doing the research. Toward the end of the project, he had become dependent on secretaries and copyists. Because he was afraid of French government censorship, he arranged for the book to be published anonymously by the Geneva publisher Barrillot. When it appeared in October 1748, it caused a sensation. Within a year, there were twenty-two editions. On November 29, 1751, church officials added it to the Index of books that Catholics were forbidden to read.

A weary Montesquieu told a friend about his work: "I can say that I have worked on it my whole life; I was given some law books when I left my collège; I sought their spirit, I worked, but I did nothing worthwhile. I discovered my principles twenty years ago; they are quite simple; anyone else working as hard as I did would have done better. But I swear this book nearly killed me; I am going to rest now; I shall work no more."

The book is a hodgepodge, with some chapters only a few lines long. But it abounds with important ideas. For instance, Montesquieu recognized that power tends to corrupt. "A monarchy is ruined," he wrote, "when the prince, referring everything to himself exclusively, reduces the state to its capital, and the capital to the court, and the court to his person alone."

Montesquieu maintained that for liberty to be secure, the executive, legislative, and judicial powers must be separated. He wrote, "So that one cannot abuse power, power must check power by the arrangement of things. A constitution can be such that no one will be constrained to do the things the law does not oblige him to do or be kept from doing the things the law permits him to do. . . . One must combine powers, regulate them, temper them, make them act; one must give one power a ballast, so to speak, to put it in a position to resist another; this is a masterpiece of legislation that chance rarely produces and prudence is rarely allowed to produce."

He affirmed the crucial importance of a rule of law and believed punishment must fit the crime. "It is a triumph of liberty," he wrote, "when criminal laws draw each penalty from the particular nature of the crime. All arbitrariness ends; the penalty does not ensue from the legislator's capriciousness but from the nature of the thing, and man does not do violence to man." Montesquieu described the principle of just compensation, which became part of the U.S. Fifth Amendment: "If the political magistrate wants to build some public edifice, some new road, he must pay compensation; in this regard the public is like an individual who deals with another individual." He spoke out against religious intolerance. "Penal laws must be avoided in the matter of religion," he wrote. "History teaches us well enough that the penal laws have never had any effect other than destruction."

Montesquieu recognized the civilizing influence of commerce. As he wrote, "Commerce has spread knowledge of the mores of all nations everywhere; they have been compared to each other, and good things have resulted from this. The spirit of commerce produces in men a certain feeling for exact justice, opposed on the one hand to banditry and on the other to those moral virtues that make it so that one does not always discuss one's own interests alone and that one can neglect them for those of others."

Voltaire, who took many swipes at *De l'esprit des lois,* offered this salute: "Montesquieu . . . was almost always right against the fanatics and the promoters of slavery. Europe owes him eternal gratitude. . . . Humanity had lost its title deeds [to liberty], and Montesquieu recovered them."

In 1755, some kind of fever swept through Paris, and Montesquieu caught it. Doctors bled him, making his condition worse. Wishing to make peace with the world, he called for a parish priest, and a Jesuit named Bernard Routh grilled him about his views on church dogma, then demanded access to his papers. He was interrupted by one of Montesquieu's friends, the duchesse d'Aiguillon. Routh did authorize a priest to administer last rites. Montesquieu died on February 10, 1755. The next day he was interred at the Sainte-Geneviève chapel, the church of Saint-Sulpice.

Montesquieu had an enormous influence, especially outside France. The shrewd English observer Horace Walpole called *De l'esprit des lois* "the best book that ever was written—at least I never learned half so much from all I ever read." Historian Edward Gibbon, who chronicled Rome's decline, wrote, "In the forty years since the publication of *The Spirit of the Laws,* no work has been more read and criticized, and the spirit of inquiry which it has excited is not the least of our obligations to the author."

According to historian Peter Gay, "The men of the Scottish Enlightenment studied *De l'esprit des lois* with great care and great profit. The book was read, clandestinely, in Vienna and, more openly, in the Italian states, where Genovesi, Beccaria, Filangieri, and other *illuminati* confessed themselves the disciples of 'the immortal Montesquieu.' In the Germanies, Lessing and the Göttingen historical school admired and imitated Montesquieu's cultural relativism while political thinkers absorbed his views on the British Constitution. . . . And it is instructive to see Catherine of Russia, who was, after all, relatively untouched by his comprehensive liberality, finding it useful to borrow Montesquieu's prestige by proclaiming herself his devoted follower. . . . *De l'esprit des lois* was the common coin of learned discussion."

In America, Montesquieu's books were widely advertised, they were made available through library companies and circulating libraries, and they were in the libraries at Harvard, Princeton, Brown, and other colleges. Not many library catalogs survive from colonial America, but Montesquieu's works were known to be in the personal collections of John Adams, Benjamin Franklin, Thomas Jefferson, James Madison, James Wilson, and John Marshall, among others.

Although Jefferson didn't like Montesquieu because of his attachment to monarchy, especially the British monarchy, he did concede that Montesquieu's works were "generally recommended." Samuel Adams studied Montesquieu. John Adams was a fan, and so was James Otis who was credited with originating the phrase, "No taxation without representation." Richard Henry Lee ranked Montesquieu among "the greatest geniuses." George Mason often quoted Montesquieu in his writings. And in *The Federalist* Number 47, James Madison, who memorized large parts of *De l'esprit des lois,* wrote, "The oracle who is always consulted and cited on this subject [separation of powers] is the celebrated Montesquieu. If he be not the author of this invaluable precept in the science of politics, he has the merit at least of displaying and recommending it most effectually to the attention of mankind."

Montesquieu was popularized in American newspapers. "Although no tabulation has been kept," reported historian Paul Merrill Spurlin, "an attentive reading of hundreds of newspapers has given the present writer some rather definite impressions. Looking back to 1760 and confining the estimates solely to the press, he has not much hesitancy in affirming that Montesquieu, line for line, was quoted more extensively than any other French writer. This statement is made on the basis that the author of the matter quoted was acknowledged. At the same time it must be admitted that often Montesquieu was quoted without acknowledgement. As regards comparison with English writers, one does not expect to find his name mentioned in the press as often, for example, as Locke's or Blackstone's. It is this investigator's impression, however, that in actual inches quoted, when sources were named, Montesquieu surpassed Locke and compared favorably with Blackstone."

Montesquieu's ideas fell out of favor as the French Revolution spun out of control and turned into the Reign of Terror, because there was no separation of powers. Maximilien Robespierre controlled the Committee on Public Safety, which ordered executions at will.

Reflecting on totalitarian power during the French Revolution and the Napoleonic era, political thinker Benjamin Constant wrote: "All the constitutions that have been given to France guaranteed individual liberty, yet under each of them individual liberty was constantly violated. The reason is that a mere declaration is not enough; positive safeguards are needed." And so he turned to Montesquieu who had written about institutions that help protect liberty. He cited Montesquieu in his major work, *De l'esprit de conquête* (1814).

Two decades later, Alexis de Tocqueville pondered the future of liberty in France and drew inspiration from Montesquieu. Tocqueville's monumental *Democracy in America* (1835, 1840) described institutions that helped protect liberty. A friend of Tocqueville's called him "a direct heir of Montesquieu."

By the late nineteenth century, Montesquieu had become a forgotten man. Subsequent decades proved to be the bloodiest in human history as regimes around the world amassed awesome political power and slaughtered tens of millions. Montesquieu had it right: liberty is virtually impossible to protect unless there is a separation of powers.

A WRITTEN CONSTITUTION

❦

JAMES MADISON DIDN'T originate the idea of checks and balances for limiting government power, but he helped push it further than anyone else. Previous political thinkers, citing British experience, had talked about checks and balances with a monarch in the mix, but Madison helped apply the principle to a republic. Contrary to such respected thinkers as baron de Montesquieu, Madison insisted that checks and balances could help protect liberty in a large republic.

If one must endure a central government, it seems hard to improve on the checks and balances provided in the U.S. Constitution, which reflects a good deal of Madison's handiwork. Stalwart republican Thomas Jefferson embraced it. He told Madison, his best friend, "I like much the general idea of framing a government which should go on of itself peaceably, without needing continual recurrence to the state legislatures. I like the organization of the government into Legislative, Judiciary and Executive. I like the power given the Legislature to levy taxes; and for that reason solely approve of the greater house being chosen by the people directly . . . preserving inviolate the fundamental principle that the people are not to be taxed but by representatives chosen immediately by themselves. I am captivated by the compromise of the opposite claims of the great and little states, of the latter to equal, and the former to proportional influence. . . . I like the negative given to the Executive with a third of either house"

Madison didn't have as grand a vision of liberty as Jefferson did, but he acquired practical insights about how to protect liberty. Madison, recalled William Pierce, a Georgia delegate to the Constitutional Convention, "blends together the profound politician, with the Scholar. In the management of every great question he evidently took the lead in the Convention, and tho' he cannot be called an Orator, he is a most agreable eloquent, and convincing Speaker. From a spirit of industry and application, which he possesses in a most imminent degree, he always comes forward the best informed Man of any point in debate . . . a Gentleman of great modesty—with a remarkably sweet temper."

Like his compatriots from Virginia, Madison's record was stained by slavery, an inheritance he could never escape. He tried several business ventures aimed at generating adequate income without slaves, but none worked. Ultimately he didn't even liberate his slaves upon his death, as George Washington had done.

Madison, a shy man, was perhaps the least imposing founder. He stood less than five feet, six inches tall. He had a sharp nose and receding hairline. He suffered a variety of chronic ailments including fevers, diarrhea, and seizures. "I am too dull and infirm now," he wrote at age twenty-one, "to look out for any extraordinary things in this world for I think my sensations for many months past have intimated to me not to expect a long or healthy life." The most distracting ailment, Madison recalled much later, was "a constitutional liability to sudden attacks, somewhat resembling Epilepsy, and suspending the intellectual functions."

But he blossomed when, at age forty-three, he met a twenty-six-year-old black-haired, blue-eyed widow, Dolley Payne Todd. One of her friends reported: "At Night he Dreams of you & Starts in his Sleep a Calling on you to relieve his Flame for he Burns to such an excess that he will be shortly consumed." They were married on September 15, 1794, and for the next four decades were the "first couple" of republican politics, keepers of the Jeffersonian flame.

JAMES MADISON WAS born on March 16, 1751, at his step-grandfather's plantation on the Rappahannock River, King George County, Virginia. He was the eldest child of Nelly Conway, a tobacco merchant's daughter. His father, James Madison, Sr., was a tobacco farmer.

Biographer Ralph Ketcham described Madison as "a sandy-haired, bright-eyed, rather mischievous youth." He had private tutors who taught him Latin, arithmetic, algebra, geometry, history, and literature. Although most Virginians considering college would have chosen William and Mary, it had a reputation as a "drinking school," and in 1769, Madison left home for the College of New Jersey (later, Princeton University). Its library was well stocked with books by Scottish Enlightenment authors like Adam Smith and Adam Ferguson, as well as influential works on natural rights by John Locke and *Cato's Letters* coauthors John Trenchard and Thomas Gordon. Madison was drawn to current affairs, devoured newspapers, and read books about liberty, such as Josiah Tucker's *Tracts,* Philip Furneaux's *Essay on Toleration,* Joseph Priestley's *First Principles on Government,* and Thomas Paine's pamphlet *Common Sense.* He graduated in September 1771.

On April 25, 1776, twenty-five-year-old Madison was elected a legislator to help draft a state constitution for Virginia. His first contribution to liberty was a measure that affirmed that "all men are equally entitled to enjoy the free exercise of religion according to the dictates of conscience, unpunished and unrestrained by the magistrate, Unless the preservation of equal liberty and the existence of the State are manifestly endangered."

Madison worked with Thomas Jefferson who shared his passion for religious liberty, and the two men began meeting frequently after Jefferson was elected governor of Virginia. They both loved books, ideas, and liberty, and they were best friends for a half-century.

In 1784, Madison persuaded the Virginia legislature to enact Jefferson's Bill for Establishing Religious Freedom. He defeated Patrick Henry's proposal that the state subsidize the Anglican church. Christianity, Madison noted, "flourished, not only without the support of human laws, but in spite of every opposition to them." During these debates on religious Freedom, Madison got a key idea for protecting individual rights: "Freedom arises from that multiplicity of sects which pervades America, and which is the best and only security for religious liberty in any society."

Meanwhile, in December 1779, Madison had been appointed to the Continental Congress, which, meeting in Philadelphia, performed legislative, executive, and judicial functions during the Revolutionary War. The government was broke and financed the war effort with vast issues of paper money known as continentals, which triggered ruinous runaway inflation. Madison became the most articulate advocate of an alliance with France, and he supported Benjamin Franklin who was lobbying King Louis XVI for help.

Madison served in Congress under the Articles of Confederation, which were ratified on March 1, 1781. The Articles set up an association of states, with Congress dependent on voluntary contributions, not taxes. If people in a particular state didn't approve what Congress was doing, they kept their money. Although states squabbled with each other, they were bit players in world politics, unlikely to became entangled with foreign wars. Because the general rules people lived by couldn't be upset easily, amending the Articles required unanimous consent. Voluntary cooperation worked well enough that the states defeated Britain, the world's mightiest naval power, and they negotiated tremendous territorial concessions.

Madison, however, was frustrated at what he considered the irresponsible behavior of states. He objected to their trade wars and continued paper money inflation, a result of Revolutionary War costs. Devious New Englanders tried to arrange a monopoly on codfish sales to Spain in exchange for giving up American rights on the Mississippi River, which would have devastated people in the Kentucky territory. Madison believed things would be better if Congress could function as a central government. Just twelve days after ratification of the Articles, he conceived the dubious doctrine of implied power: if a government agency were assigned a particular responsibility, it could assume power it considered necessary to fulfill that responsibility even if the power wasn't enumerated in a constitution.

On February 21, 1787, Madison and Alexander Hamilton, Washington's former assistant, who believed passionately in a powerful central government, persuaded Congress to name delegates who would revise the Articles of Confederation. Madison persuaded George Washington to attend the national convention, and he served as presiding officer. This meant serious business would be done, convincing distinguished citizens that they too should attend. Benjamin Franklin would be present as well, lending his international prestige to the gathering.

Madison arrived in Philadelphia on May 3, 1787, one of fifty-five delegates from twelve states (Rhode Island refused to send delegates)—attorneys, merchants, physicians, and plantation owners. Thirty-nine delegates had served in the Continental Congress, and they were inclined to seek more power than was permitted by the Articles of Confederation.

A quorum of seven states was present by May 25, and proceedings began on the first floor of the Pennsylvania State House. During the next four months, delegates met six days a week, from late morning until early evening. The details of what went on were kept secret at the time. "I chose a seat in front of the presiding member, with the other members on my right & left," Madison recalled. "In this favorable position for hearing all that passed . . . I was not absent a single day, nor more than a casual fraction of an hour in any day, so that I could not have lost a single speech, unless a very short one." Madison was a major influence, rising to speak 161 times through the convention.

Defying explicit instructions to revise the Articles of Confederation, Madison launched the debates by helping to draft the Virginia Plan, which called for a new constitution. It described a two-branch national legislature, with the House elected directly by the people and the Senate by the House. Seats would be proportionate to population, and there would be a national executive and a national judiciary, both chosen by the legislature. Madison insisted the proposed national government must be the supreme power with a "negative" over state legislatures. Large states supported this plan, but small states rallied to the New Jersey Plan, which aimed to revise the Articles of Confederation with a single legislative body, with each state having equal representation. The New Jersey Plan accepted the principle that all acts of Congress "shall be the supreme law of the respective States." There was a "great compromise": each state would have equal representation in the Senate, the House would be apportioned by population, and money bills would originate in the House.

Madison hadn't worked out his ideas for the executive before the convention. The Committee on Detail recommended an executive who would be called "president," would be elected by the legislature, would serve a single seven-year term, and would function as commander-in-chief of armed forces. Once delegates decided that each state would have an equal number of senators, Madison became convinced that the executive should be elected independently of the legislature and helped draft the final proposal to have the president selected by electors whom the people choose—the "electoral college."

Madison's collaborator, Alexander Hamilton, was the most outspoken critic of democracy at the convention. His proposal was to "let one branch of the Legislature hold their places for life or at least during good behavior. Let the Executive also be for life."

Slavery was an explosive issue. If the Constitution had prohibited it, southern states would have surely bolted the convention. Madison successfully pressed for a clause calling for the slave trade to end in twenty years (1808), and he kept direct support for slavery out of the Constitution. The Constitution provided that the census count slaves ("other persons") as three-fifths of a person, thereby reducing southern representation in the House.

The final draft of the Constitution, about 5,000 words, was signed by thirty-eight delegates on September 17, 1787. Sixteen delegates had quit the convention or refused to sign it at the end. It was sent to Congress where it was referred to the states for ratification by conventions of elected delegates. The Constitution would be adopted upon ratification in nine states.

By eliminating state tariffs, the Constitution created a large free trade area—eventually the world's largest—that helped make possible America's phenomenal peacetime prosperity. Entrepreneurs could travel freely without the myriad tolls, tariffs, and other obstacles that plagued business enterprise in Europe.

Madison conceived a limited government. "The powers delegated by the proposed Constitution to the federal government," he explained, "are few and defined. Those . . . will be exercised principally on external aspects, as war, peace, negotiation and foreign commerce." The Constitution did attempt to limit the power of central government through a separation of powers: those who make laws, enforce laws, and interpret laws should be substantially independent and capable of limiting each other's power. The two houses of Congress provide a check on each other. The president can veto legislation but can be overruled by a two-thirds majority in both houses. Judges can strike down laws considered unconstitutional. Proposed amendments become part of the Constitution when approved by two-thirds of Congress and by legislatures in three-quarters of the states.

The Constitution established unprecedented government power in America. It authorized federal taxes, which never existed before, and gave the federal government power to overrule elected state and local officials who were closer to the people. Control over larger territory increased the temptation for U.S. presidents to become entangled in foreign wars, which had the consequence of further expanding federal power. (There's some irony here: Many people supported the Constitution because of their dissatisfaction with high inflation, high taxes, and other economic consequences of the Revolutionary War.)

Madison accepted Alexander Hamilton's invitation to help promote ratification in New York State. Between October 1787 and March 1788, Madison wrote twenty-nine essays, which, with fifty-six more essays by Hamilton and lawyer John Jay, appeared in New York newspapers. The essays, which became known as *The Federalist Papers*, were signed "Publius," after the Roman lawmaker Publius Valerius Publicola who helped defend the Roman republic. In July 1788, the essays were published as a two-volume book. Madison seems to have recognized that by setting up a central government, the Constitution conflicted with ideals of liberty. Not until August 1788 did he finally tell Jefferson about his collaboration: "Col. Carrington tells me he has sent you the first volume of the *Federalist*, and adds the 2nd. by this conveyance. I believe I never have yet mentioned to you that publication."

Because the Constitution proposed to expand government power, there was substantial opposition, spearheaded by the so-called Antifederalists, who included New York governor George Clinton, Revolutionary War organizer Samuel Adams, and Virginians George Mason and Patrick Henry. Respected pro-Constitution historians Samuel Eliot Morison, Henry Steele Commager, and William E. Leuchtenburg acknowledged, "There is little doubt that the Antifederalists would have won a Gallup poll."

The Antifederalists presented a wide range of views about the Constitution. Most important, they felt, was the lack of a Bill of Rights. Madison, however, considered bills of rights to be mere "parchment barriers" that an oppressive majority could easily ignore. He was convinced that liberty would be best protected in a large republic with many competing interests, where it would be difficult for a single one to oppress the others.

Jefferson stood with the Antifederalists as far as a bill rights was concerned. On December 20, 1787, he told Madison he objected to "the omission of a bill of rights providing clearly and without the aid of sophisms for freedom of religion, freedom of the press, protection against standing armies, restriction against monopolies, the eternal and unremitting force of the habeas corpus laws, and trials by jury." Jefferson added that a bill of rights is "what the people are entitled to against every government on earth, general or particular, and what no just government should refuse, or rest on inference."

The Constitution was ratified in Delaware (December 7, 1787), Pennsylvania (December 12), New Jersey (December 18), Georgia (January 2, 1788), Connecticut (January 9), Massachusetts (February 7), Maryland (April 28), South Carolina (May 23), New Hampshire (June 21), Virginia (June 25), and New York (July 26), but the Antifederalists threatened to campaign for a second constitutional convention, which Madison didn't want. He realized that to gain needed support, the Constitution had to have a bill of rights, and after his election to the House, he did more than anyone else to maneuver a bill of rights through Congress. The House voted for what became the Bill of Rights on September 24, 1789, and the Senate followed the next day. State legislatures ratified the Bill of Rights on December 15, 1791.

Madison was shocked at how fast the Federalists, led by President Washington's treasury secretary, Alexander Hamilton, expanded central government power beyond the limits he helped set up. As early as November 1789, Madison opposed Hamilton's recommendation that the self-interest of wealthy investors should be linked to the central government by issuing bonds—running up a big national debt. Hamilton convinced President Washington to approve the establishment of a central bank as a convenience for the government, and Madison opposed it because such a bank meant exceeding powers enumerated in the Constitution. Indeed, the Constitutional Convention had specifically rejected a proposal that the federal government charter corporations such as a bank. Madison rejected the doctrine of implied powers, which he had previously advocated during his campaign for the central government. Implied powers, he realized, would undermine constitutional restraints on government power.

Madison became nearly as libertarian as Jefferson. Both men praised Thomas Paine's *The Rights of Man* (1791), a clarion call for liberty that alarmed the Federalists. Hamilton unleashed nasty attacks against Jefferson in Philadelphia newspapers, and Madison, together with James Monroe, wrote counterattacks. Madison denounced Hamilton's view that the president should have vast discretionary power to conduct foreign policy. In 1793, Madison spoke out against the military buildup that the Federalists sought. Three years later, Federalists wanted to suppress American societies sympathetic to the French Revolution, but Madison insisted they were innocent until proved guilty of some crime. Federalists warned that aliens posed grave dangers, but Madison nevertheless introduced a bill that made it easier for aliens to become American citizens. Madison resisted Federalist demands for higher taxes and denounced the Alien and Sedition Acts (1798) that empowered the government to silence, even deport, critics. His was a crucial, courageous voice during the Federalist assault on liberty.

Jefferson won the 1800 presidential election, turning the Federalists out, and Madison became secretary of state for two terms. Then Madison won the presidency twice himself. These years were marked by frustration as he was unable to stop the warring British and French from seizing American merchant ships. He stumbled into the War of 1812, and the British torched Washington, D.C. Demands of wartime finance spurred Madison to ask for higher taxes and advocate a central bank, which he had once opposed. Madison was vindicated on one point, though: he relied on volunteers, not conscripts, and it was American privateers who ravaged the British coastline, forcing the British government to negotiate peace. London merchants couldn't even get maritime insurance between Britain and Ireland.

Madison outlived all the other founders and continued expressing the ideals of republican liberty. As Jefferson wrote in his most poignant letter, on February 17, 1826: "The friendship which has subsisted between us, now half a century, and the harmony of our political principles and pursuits, have been sources of constant happiness to me. . . . It has also been a great solace to me, to believe that you are engaged in vindicating to posterity the course we have pursued for preserving to them, in all their purity, the blessings of self-government. . . . To myself you have been a pillar of support through life. Take care of me when dead, and be assured that I shall leave with you my last affections."

In early 1836, Madison began suffering from chronic fevers, fatigue, and shortness of breath. On June 27, he wrote his final words, about his friendship with Jefferson. During breakfast the next day, he slumped over and died. He was buried in the family plot a half-mile south of his house.

For all their flaws, constitutional checks and balances endure as the most effective means ever devised for limiting government—a tribute to the insight, industry, and devotion of James Madison

TAXING LIMITS, SPENDING
LIMITS, TERM LIMITS

For MORE THAN a century, especially since the triumph of democracy in the Western world, the tendency has been to view government as a benevolent institution seeking the public good. Elections seemed to be the only necessary restraint on government power. When reform was needed, it involved defeating bad politicians and electing good politicians. Yet good people, once they become politicians, frequently turn into scoundrels. Economist James Buchanan observed that this is the general rule because people in government pursue their self-interest just as private individuals do. They aren't magically transformed into altruistic beings when they gain political power. They pursue more power, bigger budgets, and bigger bureaucracies, and they do everything to maintain their grip on power.

During the late 1940s, when Buchanan started his career, it was still fashionable for economists to compare actual markets with ideal government and then call for government intervention to remedy "market failures." Buchanan insisted on comparing actual governments with actual markets. He observed that voters have little impact on the power-maximizing behavior of governments. Whatever politicians might promise during an election campaign, they proceed to expand their power, their budgets, and their bureaucrats after they get into office. Major party politicians have a common interest against the people. Buchanan maintained that constitutional restraints, the general rules within which politicians operate, were the only way to limit government power. He provided inspiration for popular ballot initiatives on spending limits, tax limits, and term limits. He became the most distinguished modern thinker on constitutional issues, and he won a Nobel Prize in 1986.

George Mason University economist David M. Levy, a friend of Buchanan for almost twenty years, called him "the most intellectually honest person I have ever met. If you provide good reasons to believe he is mistaken about a particular position, he'll check things out, and if he becomes convinced of error, he'll change his mind and never look back. You don't see that very much in the academic world."

Buchanan has always been exceptionally industrious. "Ever since anyone can remember, he went to his office and began work at 7:00 A.M., and he put in a full day's work," recalled Thomas J. DiLorenzo of Loyola College in Baltimore. "He expected others to work as hard as he did, and he didn't think much of those who took a leisurely approach to life."

Buchanan's *vita* lists thirty-seven books and twenty-two monographs, published in Catalan, Chinese, German, Hungarian, Italian, Japanese, Korean, Portuguese, Romanian, Slovak, Swedish, and Spanish as well as English. In addition, he has contributed essays to over 350 books and monographs. He has written over 250 journal articles and 75 book reviews, which have been translated into a number of languages, including French and Turkish.

Buchanan never gave up his roots as a country boy. For years, he and his wife have spent a few days each week at their farm in hilly Blacksburg, in southwestern Virginia. He tends his garden, chops wood, and takes care of other chores of a gentleman farmer—and does more work on books and articles.

Charles Goetz, who earned his Ph.D. under Buchanan at the University of Virginia and later became a law professor there, remarked, "I guess I've known a hundred—if not hundreds—of more polished classroom performers than James Buchanan. Yet, I have on numerous occasions acknowledged that he is, by a very wide margin, the finest teacher I have ever encountered. . . . Each week he assigned a question to be answered in about 4 or 5 typewritten pages. The answers were usually not so hard; it was figuring out what the question was really about that was difficult."

Buchanan stands ramrod straight, about five feet, eleven inches tall. He combs his hair back and has a pencil-thin moustache. "When I was taking classes with him," recalled DiLorenzo, "he reminded me of a jazz band bass player. He came to classes wearing a rather baggy dark suit. But he was an inspiring teacher. He was always thoroughly prepared. Speaking with a soft Southern drawl, he delivered an organized presentation, and he handled questions gracefully."

JAMES MCGILL BUCHANAN, JR., was born on October 3, 1919, on a farm near Murfreesboro, in middle Tennessee. Buchanan recalled that his father "was a jack-of-all-trades—farmer, sometime carpenter, veterinarian, insulator, and equipment operator." Buchanan's mother, Lila Scott, was from a family of deputy sheriffs and Presbyterian preachers.

Buchanan's parents struggled with a run-down farm. "My early times," he wrote in his autobiographical *Better Than Plowing* (1992), "were times without indoor plumbing, electricity, radio, television, or air travel. . . . Water was drawn from a well in a covered wellhouse near the back porch of the big house. . . . Bodily functions were carried out, expeditiously in winter months, in a privy removed some fifty yards from the house. . . . Heat was supplied by open fireplaces. . . . I slept in a nonheated bedroom far removed from any fireplace. And winters in Tennessee can be very cold. . . . Light was supplied by kerosene lamps"

Buchanan's mother taught him how to read, write, and do arithmetic. He thrived on western novels, murder mysteries, and populist pamphlets. "This motley assortment," he noted, "accomplished a purpose that a forced diet of the classics might have thwarted. I learned to enjoy reading, as such, and I became 'bookish' early. . . . From my earliest recollection, books were more important than toys."

Buchanan graduated from Middle Tennessee State Teachers College in 1940. His options were to teach school for $65 per month, work at a Nashville bank for $75 a month or pursue a $50 per month fellowship at the University of Tennessee. He went to the University of Tennessee, earning an M.A. the following year.

With war approaching, Buchanan enlisted in the navy and served on the staff of Admiral Chester W. Nimitz, commander in chief of the U.S. Pacific Fleet. Buchanan remembered that "observing quite ordinary persons making decisions critical to so many lives gave me a sense of the relative importance of things that I have never lost." On October 5, 1943, he married Ann Bakke who had been working for the Army Air Force in Oahu.

A University of Tennessee professor, Carlton C. Sims, had earned his Ph.D. in economics at the University of Chicago and told Buchanan that Chicago was an intellectually exciting place. Buchanan enrolled there in 1945. "Those of us who entered graduate school in the immediate postwar years were all socialists," Buchanan recalled. But economics professor Frank H. Knight did more than anyone else to set him straight. Buchanan learned from economic historian Earl J. Hamilton whose "most important influence on my career came after 1948, during his tenure as editor of the *Journal of Political Economy*. First of all, he forced me to follow up on his recommendation about language skills by sending me French, German, and Italian books for review. Secondly, he handled my early submissions of articles with tolerance, understanding, and encouragement rather than with brutal or carping rejections that might, in my case, have proved fatal to further effort." The most famous member of the Chicago school was Milton Friedman. Buchanan remembered, "A relatively obscure scholar, Cecil G. Phipps, of the University of Florida, located and exposed a logical error in one of Friedman's papers, an error that Friedman graciously acknowledged. To this day, I have never told Milton how this simple event contributed so massively to my self-confidence."

Buchanan began his teaching career at the University of Tennessee in 1948. Two years later he went to Florida State University and in 1954 was named the chairman of the economics department. In 1955, he left for Rome, where he spent eleven months studying classical Italian works on public finance, which dealt with notorious political corruption and instability. Buchanan concluded it was foolish to assume that government policy is driven by good intentions. He became familiar with a number of Italian thinkers, including Amilcare Puviani. To Puviani, Buchanan explained, "the State represents an agency through which one group of persons, those possessed with power, exerts its will upon persons in another group, those who are dominated. This is essentially a force theory of politics, a 'ruling class' model."

Buchanan next accepted an offer to head the economics department at the University of Virginia in 1956. With G. Warren Nutter, another University of Chicago Ph.D. appointed to a professorship the same year, Buchanan helped establish the Thomas Jefferson Center for Studies in Political Economy. A colleague described Nutter as "a rather dashing figure, a rough-cut Humphrey Bogart type of a man." Buchanan and Nutter were joined by other brilliant economists, including future Nobel laureate Ronald Coase, a very proper Englishman who had taught at the London School of Economics during the 1940s when Hayek was there.

Buchanan was a maverick in public finance, a field where economists traditionally advised governments about the most efficient ways to extract more money from the population. His early books, including *Public Principles of Public Debt* (1958) and *The Public Finances* (1960), touched on themes that became his hallmarks. For instance, in *The Public Finances* he countered the English economist John Maynard Keynes's advocacy of government deficits by defending the balanced budget rule: "Representative government being as it is, the legislator, regardless of his personal integrity, is constantly under pressure from two opposing forces. . . . Voters want tax reductions and federal expenditure projects (veterans' hospitals, Air Force installations, river basin developments, and so on) in their local areas. Unless some central control feature exists to keep these two opposing forces in rough equality with each other, the limited rationality that seems to be present in legislative decisions will be still further reduced."

Buchanan began a great collaboration with Gordon Tullock, a restless genius who had earned a law degree at the University of Chicago (1947), practiced law, worked for the U.S. State Department in China before and after the communist takeover, went into the import-export business, and then entered the academic world. He had taken just one economics course at Chicago (with professor Henry Simons) and never earned a Ph.D. in economics, but he was to make himself a distinguished economist. "I first encountered Gordon Tullock in 1958," Buchanan recalled, "when he came to the University of Virginia as a postdoctoral research fellow. I was impressed by his imagination and originality, and by his ability to recognize easily the elements of my own criticism of public debt orthodoxy. Tullock insisted not only that analysis be reduced to individual choice and that individuals be modeled always as maximizers of self-interest, a step that I had sometimes been unwilling to take, despite my exposure to the Italians. . . . We decided to collaborate on a book that would examine . . . the individual's choice among alternative political rules for reaching political decisions." The book was *The Calculus of Consent: Logical Foundations of Constitutional Democracy* (1965).

It's not easy to read, but the insights are profound. Among other things, the authors aimed to determine how minorities might be protected from exploitation by majorities. Buchanan and Tullock rejected the common view that blames bad politicians. They make clear that different constitutional rules affect incentives for political practices and policies and observed that it was a normal part of government, not an aberration, to have interest groups scrambling for special favors. Accordingly, they stripped away the romantic view of government as a high-minded, selfless pursuit of the public good. They maintained that modifying constitutional rules would change the incentives influencing politicians, and government exploitation could be limited.

After *The Calculus of Consent* was published, Buchanan and Tullock obtained a National Science Foundation grant for a gathering of thinkers who worked along similar lines. About twenty met in Charlottesville and formed what they called the Committee for the Study of Non-Market Decision Making. Tullock edited *Papers on Non-Market Decision Making*. They began looking around for a better name to describe what they were doing, and somebody suggested "public choice." This had its drawbacks, too, but it caught on. Buchanan and Tullock formed the Public Choice Society. Tullock edited its journal, *Public Choice*.

Buchanan's book *Public Finances in Democratic Process* (1967) explored the nature of political institutions and their impact on fiscal policy. He observed, for instance, that voters have imperfect knowledge about what government does. He cited surveys showing that fewer than half the people have a reasonably accurate idea about their total tax burden: income taxes, social security taxes, property taxes, excise taxes, sales taxes, telephone taxes, and the myriad of taxes absorbed in the price of consumer products. He went on to show how different tax and spending policies affect the incentives of participants in the political process.

Buchanan and Tullock's compatriots at the University of Virginia helped put its economics department on the map. Coase wrote an article, "The Problem of Social Cost," which appeared in the *Journal of Law and Economics* (October 1960) and became the most widely cited article in the entire economics literature. The article told how undesirable effects of private activity, such as pollution, could be efficiently resolved through private negotiation without government intervention. The article helped spawn a new research program, law and economics, which analyzed the economic consequences of laws. Nutter's contribution, *The Growth of Industrial Production in the Soviet Union* (1962), defied conventional wisdom that the Soviet communism was an industrial wonder and showed that the Russian economy had done better under the czars. He was later vindicated by the collapse of the Soviet Union.

Intellectual adversaries became hysterical; some reportedly suggested these men might be fascists. Around 1961, Kermit Gordon, who headed the Ford Foundation's economics funding program, told University of Virginia president Edgar F. Shannon, Jr., that continued Ford Foundation support for the economics department was jeopardized by the "Nineteenth century Ultra-Conservatism" of Buchanan, Tullock, Coase, and Nutter. The economics department was secretly evaluated, and the ensuing report recommended that "additions should be made to the staff of full professional members of different 'modern' outlook" and that "care should be taken in making or renewing non-tenure appointments, as well as those of higher rank, to avoid recruitment from the Chicago School." Accordingly, Shannon ordered a purge. Coase left for the University of Chicago. Three times the university refused to name Tullock a full professor, and after the third refusal, in 1967, he accepted a professorship at Rice University, Houston. The following year, Buchanan went to the University of California at Los Angeles. Nutter left to become assistant secretary of defense for international affairs. Many of the students these men attracted went elsewhere. Thus, the University of Virginia forced out two future Nobel laureates and a lot more talent as well.

By 1969, Buchanan and Tullock were together again at Virginia Polytechnic Institute in Blacksburg. Together with Charles Goetz, a Ph.D. student of Buchanan from the University of Virginia, and a more sympathetic administration, they established the Public Choice Center. It was located in a two-story house on a hill overlooking campus, a house that the university's president had abandoned for more secure quarters following student riots in the 1960s. Distinguished free market economists from around the world came as visiting lecturers.

The 1970s were plagued with chronic federal budget deficits, high inflation, high unemployment, and slow economic growth, which leading Keynesian economists certainly hadn't predicted. Prevailing opinion blamed the Vietnam War and Watergate for everything, but Buchanan wasn't convinced. John Maynard Keynes's theories had called for more government power over the economy, assuming this power would be used as he intended. Keynes never considered what real governments might do with his theories.

Accordingly, Buchanan and his colleague Richard E. Wagner collaborated on *Democracy in Deficit: The Political Legacy of Lord Keynes* (1977). They explained why politicians are much less accountable than individuals in the private sector: "Market competition is continuous; at each instance of purchase, a buyer is able to select among alternative, competing sellers. Political competition is intermittent; a decision is binding for a fixed period, usually two, four, or six years. Market competition allows several competitors to survive simultaneously; the capture by one seller of a majority of the market does not deny the ability of the minority to choose its preferred supplier. By contrast, political competition has an all-or-none feature; the capture of a majority of the market gives the entire market to a single supplier. In market competition, the buyer can be reasonably certain as to just what it is he will receive from his act of purchase. This is not true with political competition, for there the buyer is, in a sense, purchasing the services of an agent, but it is an agent whom he cannot bind in matters of specific compliance, and to whom he is forced to grant wide latitude in the use of discretionary judgment. Politicians are simply not held liable for their promises and pledges in the same manner that private sellers are."

In *The Power to Tax: Analytical Foundations of a Fiscal Constitution* (1980), written with Geoffrey Brennan, Buchanan presented his strongest case for constitutional reform. The book portrayed government as a leviathan that pursues its self-interest by taking as much taxpayer money as it can get away with. Since there isn't much difference between taxation and outright theft of assets, Buchanan and Brennan insisted that taxation must be subject to constraints. "Perhaps at one period in history it might have seemed reasonable to rely on the operation of majority rule in legislatures to hold governmental fiscal activities in bounds," they wrote. "However, confronted with public sectors of modern scope and bureaucracies that demonstrably possess power quite apart from specifically legislated authority, the democratic-limits model of governmental fiscal restraint becomes increasingly naive."

Many intellectuals focused on procedural reforms, but Buchanan and Brennan pointed out that procedural reforms don't prevent undesirable outcomes. For instance, a bill to expropriate the assets of an unpopular minority would satisfy procedural reforms if it gains the support of a majority of legislators, is signed by the executive, and is upheld by judges. By contrast, a constitutional restraint means that a particular policy is illegitimate because of what it does to people, regardless of who approved it. Buchanan and Brennan discussed a wide range of constitutional measures, including spending limits, taxing limits, borrowing limits, lending limits, and a rule to limit the discretion of monetary authorities.

In 1983, differences with the new head of the economics department led Buchanan, Tullock, and their colleagues to accept an offer from George Mason University, Fairfax, Virginia, and they took the Center for Study of Public Choice with them.

Since his influential collaboration with Buchanan, Tullock had done much to push the frontiers of public choice. He spent five years at George Mason

University, then accepted an endowed chair at the University of Arizona. In mid-1999, he rejoined Buchanan at George Mason University. Tullock's books include *The Politics of Bureaucracy* (1965), *The Logic of the Law* (1971), *Economics of Income Redistribution* (1985), *The Economics of Wealth and Poverty* (1986), and *The Economics of Special Privilege and Rent-Seeking* (1989).

Without missing a step, Buchanan and Brennan followed up *The Power to Tax* with *The Reason of Rules—Constitutional Political Economy* (1985). Among other things, they showed why incentives for short-term thinking are stronger in government than in the free markets. This is why taxes and inflation tend to increase, even though such increases do long-term damage to an economy. Buchanan and Brennan explained that constitutional constraints, including spending and taxing limits, are needed to help assure a long-term perspective in public policy.

Buchanan's Nobel Prize in 1986 turned out to be contentious. Lehman College socialist professor Robert Lekachman, for instance, dismissed the award as more of a "testimonial to the fashionable popularity of conservative politics in the United States and elsewhere than a tribute to Mr. Buchanan's rather modest achievements." But the humiliating collapse of the Soviet Union and the chronic failures of socialist regimes everywhere have confirmed Buchanan's view about the government problem.

Now approaching his eightieth year, Buchanan continues his work at what is now known as the James M. Buchanan Center for Political Economy, in a refurbished farmhouse on the edge of the George Mason University campus. He leads seminars on constitutional economics and philosophy, and he delivers lectures across the United States and abroad. The world still has a lot to learn from this remarkably insightful man.

PRIVATIZATION

AROUND THE WORLD during the twentieth century, government got into the business of providing goods and services, often by nationalizing private companies. The rationale was that bureaucrats would be more efficient and just than money-grubbing private entrepreneurs. Bureaucrats were assumed to be all-knowing and all-caring, somehow capable of doing everything that needs to be done. But government enterprises were a bust everywhere. In Britain, for instance, Alan N. Miller reported in the *Columbia Journal of World Business,* "the performance of nationalized industries was below that of the private sector. . . . [Nationalized] industries' total return on capital was close to zero. . . . Customer satisfaction with the services and products of nationalized industries was often low. . . . employment costs per employee in the large nationalized industries increased faster than the national average, without equivalent increases in productivity. . . . Nationalized industries were characterized by high costs, high prices, low productivity and inefficient use of resources."

Then Margaret Thatcher became Britain's prime minister in 1979 and began selling off government-owned enterprises. At the time, it was an unthinkable thing to do. But privatization, as the process came to be called, was a huge hit, and since then more than a hundred countries have sold over $500 billion worth of government-owned enterprises. While Thatcher was a strong believer in individual liberty and saw privatization as a way to expand it, privatization has been embraced by financially strapped socialist governments that were mainly in it for the money. They realized they could raise money by selling the enterprises, they could get the enterprises' losses off their books, and since privatized enterprises tend to become profitable, they end up paying taxes rather than consuming subsidies.

Although Thatcher wasn't the first to privatize government enterprises, she made privatization a battle cry. She wanted as many people as possible to become stockholders and thereby have a greater stake in defending a free society. Her aim, she explained, was "to change Britain from a dependent to a self-reliant society; from a give-it-to-me to a do-it-yourself nation; a get-up-and-go instead of a sit-back-and-wait Britain. . . . A man's right to work as he will, to spend what he earns, to own property, to have the state as servant and not as master; these are the British inheritance. . . . What I am desperately trying to do is create one nation with everyone being a man of property or having the opportunity to be a man of property. . . . That is what capitalism is: a system that brings wealth to the many, not just to the few."

Thatcher turned privatization into a big, sophisticated program. Her ministers and staff pioneered a wide range of privatization methods. Thatcher's experience proved that obstacles could be overcome, and privatization would help millions. "If any economic policy could lay claim to popularity, it would certainly be privatization," observed Harvey B. Feigenbaum and Jeffrey R. Henig in the *Journal of International Affairs*.

Privatization nevertheless provoked fierce opposition and tested Thatcher's strength of will. Privatization meant undoing what the Labour party saw as their most glorious achievements: the seizing of private property. Bureaucrats who ran government-owned enterprises feared losing their sinecures, so they protested that privatization wouldn't work, and many workers feared layoffs. After a privatization was done, Thatcher was criticized for pricing the shares too low or substituting a private monopoly for a government monopoly.

It's true that pain came before gain. There were huge layoffs as some of the big government-owned enterprises went private, but this only meant the end of concealed unemployment. These people had been receiving a lot of money for producing very little that anybody wanted. As far as productivity was concerned, they were already unemployed. Layoffs began the long-overdue process of fixing enterprises and getting unproductive people to search for places where they could contribute. Privatized enterprises soon prospered and created new jobs—real jobs—for millions.

Daniel Yergin and Joseph Stanislaw reported in their book, *The Commanding Heights* (1998), that Thatcher "recast attitudes toward state and market, withdrew government from business, and dimmed the confidence in government knowledge. Thatcherism shifted the emphasis from state responsibility to individual responsibility, and sought to give first priority to initiative, incentives, and wealth generation rather than redistribution and equality. It celebrated entrepreneurship. Privatization became commonplace." About 90 percent of British employees purchased shares in the privatized companies they worked for; almost half of shareholders owned stock in more than one company, and about 20 percent of shareholders owned stock in more than four companies. The Labour party bowed to the obvious, abandoning its pledge to nationalize the economy, and when Labourite Tony Blair became prime minister in 1997, he too pursued privatization.

Many people found Thatcher overbearing (she was sometimes derided as "Attila the Hen"), but even her critics conceded her stunning achievements, which went beyond privatization. The *New Republic*, for instance, wrote: "She cut the top rate of income tax from 83 percent to 40 percent. . . . the basic rate from 33 percent to 25 percent, removed the burden of income tax from millions of low-paid workers altogether, and ran a budget surplus at the same time. She quadrupled the number of British shareholders, presided over a doubling of British productivity, and privatized two thirds of state-owned companies. . . . Britain's unemployment rate went from the worst of the European economies to the best. The 1980s growth rate was almost double West Germany's. . . . Her empowerment of the British middle class against the snobbery of the elites and the thuggery of the old trade unions was a thoroughly liberal reform. She was also, odd though it is to recall it, a woman. In a ruthlessly sexist society, she not only made it to the top but flourished there. (She was, incidentally, pro-choice, and also reformed British tax laws to give women greater fiscal independence from their husbands.)"

Thatcher was the first woman to be Britain's prime minister. She served longer than any other twentieth-century British prime minister—eleven and a half years—and won an unprecedented three consecutive terms. She prevailed despite ferocious opposition because she had a dynamic vision of liberty and the strength and perseverance to put it into action.

Thatcher was noted for her loyalty. She told President Ronald Reagan, "When you look for friends, we will be there"—and she was, a number of times when it counted. Biographer Chris Ogden wrote, "They don't make allies any more loyal than Thatcher. She has backed colleagues accused of shoplifting and homosexual cruising. She has consistently helped pals in trouble."

MARGARET HILDA ROBERTS was the second of two daughters born in the apartment above her father Alfred's Old North Parade Road grocery store on October 13, 1925, in Grantham, Lincolnshire, England. Margaret's mother, Beatrice Stephenson, was a seamstress.

Alfred was determined that his daughters—especially Margaret, the more academically inclined—get a proper education. They made frequent visits to the local library, and she attended Kesteven and Grantham Girls School, at the far end of town, because it was considered better than the school nearby. Margaret entered Somerville College, Oxford University, in 1943. Oxford was a pathway to power; about half of Britain's prime ministers were educated at Oxford or Cambridge. She majored in chemistry and became an early riser, getting up at 6:30 A.M. and studying or working in a laboratory until late at night. The Oxford Union, where most of the student debates took place, wouldn't admit women, so Margaret joined the Oxford University Conservative Association. She met all the influential Conservatives when they visited Oxford.

After graduation, Margaret worked for three years as a research chemist at one company that made plastic for eyeglass frames and at another company that tested the quality of ice cream and cake fillings. Then she ran for Parliament three times—and lost. She decided to improve her political prospects by studying at the Council for Legal Education and passed her bar exams in December 1953. During the next five years, she practiced law while keeping a hand in the Conservative political scene.

It was through her membership in the Young Conservatives that she met Denis Thatcher, chief executive of the Atlas Preservative Company, a business started by his grandfather that produced paints and weed killers. Denis was ten years older than Margaret. They were married on December 13, 1951, in London. Two years later, twins Mark and Carol were born. Later, the family business was sold for a large sum, and Denis was the biggest booster of his wife's political career.

In 1958, at age thirty-two, Thatcher won election to Parliament from Finchley, a district near Westminster. She served in Conservative governments and worked diligently on a variety of issues. During the 1970s, Conservatives as well as Labour party socialists failed to deal with rising inflation and labor union violence. Thatcher spoke out decisively for free market reforms, and on February 4, 1975, Conservatives made her their leader.

Then came the winter of 1978–1979, with the worst episode of strikes and violence since Britian's general strike of 1926. Government employees— teachers, doctors, nurses, ambulance drivers, gravediggers, garbage collectors, and railway workers—staged a series of crippling strikes. There were plant closings and shortages and some school closings, which forced a reported 500,000 children to stay home. Huge mounds of uncollected trash attracted swarms of rats, and corpses filled cold-storage facilities. Unions demanded pay hikes five times higher than the Labour government's wage guidelines. Meanwhile, Labour Prime Minister James Callaghan relaxed in sunny Guadeloupe.

In the May 3, 1979, election, Conservatives won a 45-seat majority of the 635 seats in Parliament, and Thatcher became prime minister. She began weeding out bureaucrats (there were about 732,000) whose cost and meddling were a burden on hard-working taxpayers. Her first budget cut government spending by $10 billion (a significant number), corporate welfare by $500 million, and income tax rates (the top rate would drop from 83 percent to 60 percent). However, the value-added tax, concealed in the prices consumers pay for goods, rose from 8 percent to 15 percent. About $2.4 billion of privatizations were planned.

Thatcher began to reform unjust laws that enabled labor union bosses to intimidate employees and employers alike. Parliament repealed the legal support of a closed shop (compulsory union membership), and political strikes were outlawed; union members could strike only their employer. Union elections were to be by secret ballot.

Thatcher ended exchange controls, which disrupted the flow of capital, and stopped inflating the money supply. Consumer prices fell from 18 percent in 1980 to 3 percent by 1986. Getting rid of the inflation-caused distortions in the economy took time, and powerful interest groups demanded that Thatcher instead raise taxes and spending. She quipped: "The lady's not for turning." She got a lift when she defeated Argentina's president, General Leopoldo Fortunato Galtieri, whose forces had invaded the Falkland Islands in the South Atlantic, presumably to distract the Argentines from 130 percent inflation. The Falklands were inhabited by only 1,800 people, 750,000 sheep, and several million penguins, but the conflict showed Thatcher's decisive character. In the June 10, 1983, election, the Labour party had its worst defeat in sixty-five years.

Thatcher approved plans to cut 70,000 unproductive jobs from British Steel. Then came plans to cut 20,000 unproductive jobs at the nationalized coal mines, whose losses cost British taxpayers over $1 billion a year. Marxist Arthur Scargill, head of the National Union of Mineworkers, ordered a strike, and there was much union violence. Lost production exceeded $2 billion, and the budget deficit surged, putting downward pressure on the pound. After about fifty one weeks, in March 1985, the strike fell apart as union members returned to work. Government unions in the post office, railways, and bureaucracies had contemplated strikes, but abandoned these plans. It was clear Thatcher could not be intimidated, and union bosses virtually gave up trying. Private-sector executives stood up to union bosses; companies began to streamline, boost productivity, and regain their competitiveness in global markets

Breaking the monopoly power of union bosses made it possible to accelerate privatization that was needed, in part, because nationalized enterprises lost enormous amounts of money, which burdened taxpayers. Nationalized factories, airplanes, and other facilities were run-down, and service was terrible. Privatization aimed to get losses off the government books, tap private investment capital for rebuilding infrastructure, and improve customer service. Although inevitably there would be be payroll cuts (because payrolls had become bloated), privatized enterprises had incentives to achieve efficiency, expand business, and create more real jobs. Finally, as the number of shareholders increased, so would the number of people who would lose from any future nationalization. Privatization was a key strategy for preventing the return of socialism.

Thatcher faced opposition to privatization, as she did everything else. Former Prime Minister Harold Macmillan (a Conservative) complained that privatization meant selling "the family jewels." Executives of government-owned enterprises feared being booted out and did as much as they could to stop privatization. And Labourites were horrified at the thought of government's reducing its control over people's lives.

The most important early privatization involved government housing, known as "council houses," which had been built because rent controls made it unprofitable for private developers to build apartments. Government housing, as the *Economist* reported, turned out to be "flats in big, ill-designed blocks on big, ill-planned city estates." Thatcher offered these flats to residents at big discounts. Within two years, some 350,000 flats were in private hands. By 1990, the privatized total had risen to more than 1.25 million flats—about a quarter of government housing.

Privatization of industries began with Keith Joseph who, as minister of the Department of Energy, had hired David Young to be his principal adviser on privatization. Nigel Lawson, the first financial secretary, handled important responsibility for privatization, as did his successor, Norman Lamont. For several years, their efforts were low-key, and government holdings were sold to the employees of an enterprise, its management, or private industrial bidders. The deals weren't promoted to the general public because nobody had any idea what the potential might be.

Bigger sales almost certainly meant public offerings. In some cases, the government's holding was sold right away. In other cases, new managers were brought in to try streamlining operations to make the enterprises more attractive before they went on the market. No one knew how much demand there might be for shares of privatized companies, so it was prudent to have stock offerings proceed in stages and thereby reduce the risk of oversupplying the market. There were a number of government enterprises in such difficulty that they were given away to get their losses off the government's books.

The first privatization offering was a November 1979 sale of 5 percent of British Petroleum, which brought the government's stake under 50 percent and aroused some controversy. Then came successive issues in 1983 and 1987. Starting in December 1979, the government sold major components of the National Enterprise Board, a bureaucracy that Thatcher's Labour predecessors had set up to take over and bail out money-losing companies. February 1981 brought the sale of 51 percent of British Aerospace. The government sold 49 percent of Cable & Wireless, 100 percent of Amersham International, and 51.5 percent of Associated British Ports. Thatcher's men chipped away at some of the biggest government enterprises by selling British Rail's hotels and British Airways' International Aeradio. In these and subsequent privatizations, employees received preferential offers of stock, and blocks of stock were added to employee pension funds.

Britoil involved the first privatization offering over £500 million (for 51 percent of the enterprise), and it illustrated the problems. The government had set the price of the early privatizations low, so they'd be sure of selling. This brought criticism that the government was giving away its assets. So with Britoil, the government asked for tender offers from potential bidders. Subsequently, the OPEC cartel cut its oil price, and this reduced the value of Britoil, which would probably be forced to cut its price too if it wanted to sell oil. A number of investors dropped out of the bidding, and the government didn't sell all the shares. Another tender offering, for Enterprise Oil (a new entity which acquired oil interests of British Gas), fell short of expectations because both oil prices and stock prices fell before the deal closed.

The 1984 British Telecom offering put privatization on the map. Daniel Yergin and Joseph Stanislaw noted that "relatively few people actually paid attention to the oil and gas privatizations; almost everybody knew that something dramatic was going to happen to the phones. The telephone system, part of the post office until separated by Keith Joseph, embodied many of the worst traits of state-owned companies. Bureaucratic state control repressed innovation. The customer did not count. It took months to get a new telephone. There were only two choices—the design offered or nothing. The only way to get a phone fixed in any reasonable time was to pay a repairman, who freelanced after hours, under the table."

Thatcher wanted as many people as possible to become shareholders. Shares were offered through post offices; purchases were tied to phone bills; people could pay on the installment plan. There were applications for four times more stock than was available. More than 2 million people bought stock, half of whom were investors for the first time. The offering raised £3.9 billion, the biggest equity offering of any kind, for 51 percent of the enterprise and seven times more than was raised by the next-biggest privatization. It was later topped by the privatization offers for British Gas (1986) and British Petroleum (1987).

By 1986 the government had sold all its holdings of British Aerospace, Britoil, Cable & Wireless, British Shipbuilders Warship Yards, and BA Helicopters. That year, it sold National Bus Company and deregulated the bus industry. In 1987 came privatizations of British Airways, Rolls-Royce, and BAA, and the government sold the rest of its holdings in British Petroleum. British Steel was privatized in 1988. Even such traditional government monopolies as water and electricity were broken up and sold.

Many programs run out of steam as time goes on, but Thatcher's privatization program actually gained momentum. During her first term (1979–1983), twelve government-owned enterprises were partially or fully privatized, realizing £1.625 billion. In her second term (1983–1987), there were twenty-four part or full privatizations, realizing £10.983 billion. In her third term (1987–1990), there were forty part or full privatizations, realizing £22.514 billion.

Thatcher called an election on June 11, 1987, and won her third term with a majority of 101 seats, about double what many observers had predicted. Since World War II, the only parliamentary majority larger than this was the majority she won in 1983. People didn't necessarily love her, but they certainly respected her strength of character in turning Britain around.

Thatcher tried to stop runaway spending by local government councils, which taxed some people to benefit others. She believed there would be discipline if everybody had a stake in what the councils did, and she proposed to achieve this through equality of taxation: a "community charge" of about $300 per person annually, with rebates for the poor. The councils responded by hiking spending and forcing the community charge higher than anticipated. Voters blamed Thatcher rather than their councils, and on November 22, 1990, she announced her resignation.

John Major, her chancellor of the exchequer, became prime minister and abandoned the community charge in March 1991. He went back to property-based rates supplemented by a higher (hidden) value-added tax. He privatized British Rail, British Coal, and several port facilities, as well as the government's last 21 percent holding in British Telecom. Net proceeds from Major's privatizations exceeded £21 billion.

Thatcher could be immensely proud of her achievements. Daniel Yergin and Joseph Stanislaw reported in *The Commanding Heights* (1998), "Some two-thirds of state-owned industries had moved into the private sector. Altogether, 46 major businesses, with 900,000 employees, had been privatized, and the government's take was well over $30 billion. What was once a massive drain on the public purse had turned into a major source of tax revenue. . . . The most important consequence of privatization was that, together with labor union reform, it changed the basic institutional relationships that had defined Britain since 1945—and that had brought the country to a standstill in 1979. In that year, 1,274 working days were lost to strikes for every thousand people working. By 1990, that figure was down to 108—less than one tenth. The political and economic culture in Britain had been permanently altered."

Meanwhile, privatization has advanced rapidly around the world. It has played a key role as people in Eastern Europe and the former Soviet Union have struggled to achieve a freer society. Although Argentina was humiliated during the Falklands War, it has embraced Thatcher-style privatization. Privatization has penetrated the farthest reaches of civilization, including Mongolia—all because a grocer's daughter decided to run with a great idea about liberty.

EDUCATING PEOPLE

❧

SOCIALISM DIDN'T ENGULF the world because it was right or inevitable. During the late nineteenth century, some determined individuals developed a strategy for promoting socialism in Western countries. They aimed at converting intellectuals, who, in turn, would swing politicians around to their views.

Since World War II, some resourceful individuals have launched campaigns for liberty, and three stand out: Leonard E. Read from Hubbardston, Michigan; Antony Fisher from London; and Edward H. Crane III from Los Angeles, California. They didn't begin with much money. Two lost their fathers at an early age. One never went to college. But these men achieved an enormous influence promoting liberty worldwide.

READ, FOUNDER OF the Foundation for Economic Education, was about six feet, one inch tall, a trim man with a disarming personal manner who made friends easily. He knew how to dramatize abstract principles and say things in plain language. He excelled as a public speaker and fund raiser.

Read worked with just about everybody who was anybody in the modern libertarian movement. When novelist-philosopher Ayn Rand couldn't find a U.S. publisher for her book *Anthem* (1937), he arranged to publish it. Two years later, he arranged for the reprinting of Rose Wilder Lane's inspiring *Saturday Evening Post* article "Credo" as the popular pamphlet *Give Me Liberty.* In 1946, he published *Roofs or Ceilings?* the first popular work on public policy by Milton Friedman and George J. Stigler, both of whom went on to win a Nobel Prize. Read provided financial support for the great Austrian free market economist Ludwig von Mises. In 1947, he became a founding member of the Mont Pelerin Society, which brought together pro-liberty professors, journalists, and entrepreneurs from around the world. Seven years later, he acquired *The Freeman*, which published articles by leading libertarian thinkers.

Leonard Edward Read was born on September 26, 1898, on an eighty-acre farm outside Hubbardston, Michigan, the son of Orville Baker Read and Ada Sturgis Read. When he was in the fifth grade, his father died from blood poisoning. His mother sold the farm and bought a building in town, which she turned into a boarding house.

In 1917, Leonard graduated from the Ferris Institute, a Big Rapids, Michigan, college preparatory school for poor boys who had to combine a job with class work. By this time, the United States had entered World War I, and Read helped assemble fighter planes in France. Afterward he met Gladys "Aggie" Cobb, whose mother owned the boarding house where he lived in Ann Arbor, Michigan. On July 15, 1920, they were married. They had two sons, Leonard, Jr. (1921), and James (1924), and remained together for fifty-four years, until her death.

Read moved his family to California and helped turn around the financially troubled Burlingame Chamber of Commerce, near San Francisco. He had supported President Franklin Roosevelt's New Deal until, in 1933, Southern California Edison executive vice president William Mullendore explained that government can't create prosperity because money it gives away to some people comes from taxing other people who are made worse off than they were before.

In 1946, B. F. Goodrich chairman David Goodrich encouraged Read, then general manager of the Los Angeles Chamber of Commerce, to establish an institute for promoting economic liberty. The Foundation for Economic Education (FEE) was incorporated on March 16. Read raised $40,000 to purchase a shuttered 1889 mansion on 6.88 acres in Irvington-on-Hudson, New York, where FEE moved on July 5, 1946, and remains today.

Read provided a forum where the great Austrian economist Ludwig von Mises could speak. FEE distributed Mises' books. When New York University wasn't willing to pay Mises a salary for teaching there, Read helped persuade the William Volker Fund to pay him, and he raised money for Mises after the Volker Fund disbanded in the 1960s.

Henry Hazlitt was an important FEE trustee. Although his father died when he was an infant and he couldn't afford college, he taught himself how to write well. He worked for the *Wall Street Journal* and the *New York Post* and wrote editorials on economics for the *New York Times*. His front-page *New York Times Book Review* write-up on F. A. Hayek's *The Road to Serfdom* (1944) helped propel it onto the best-seller list. He helped find a publisher for Mises' books *Omnipotent Government* (1944), *Bureaucracy* (1944), and *Human Action* (1949). Hazlitt's first major book, *Economics in One Lesson* (1946), became a best-seller. As a *Newsweek* columnist from 1946 to 1966, he became America's best-known champion of libertarian views. Altogether, he produced eighteen books and some ten thousand editorials, articles, and columns.

In 1951, recognizing that most politicians start out as high school debaters, FEE began a program to help educate these debaters. Bettina Bien Greaves, who directed this program for more than two decades, produced *Free Market*

Economics: A Syllabus (1975) and *Mises: An Annotated Bibliography* (1993), and she edited a half-dozen books.

FEE had some big hits. Staffer Dean Russell translated *The Law*, a pamphlet written in 1850 by Frédéric Bastiat, the eloquent French champion of laissez-faire principles, and FEE reportedly distributed some 500,000 copies. When Rose Wilder Lane's *The Discovery of Freedom* (1943) went out of print, she refused to authorize a new edition because she never got around to revising it, but General Motors customer researcher Henry Grady Weaver obtained Lane's permission to adapt her inspiring story as *The Mainspring of Human Progress* (1947, 1953), and FEE issued more than 400,000 copies. In 1959, FEE reprinted *Fiat Money Inflation in France* (1876), the best brief account about how inflation gets out of control and devastates people, written by Andrew Dickson White, the cofounder of Cornell University. Several hundred thousand copies were distributed.

Of Read's own books, the most popular was *Anything That's Peaceful* (1964), with his famous story "I, Pencil." He explained that there isn't a single person on earth who could do everything needed to make such a seemingly simple item as a pencil, and it illustrates the wonders of voluntary cooperation. He talked about equipment needed to cut down trees, move logs, process them into properly shaped pieces, mine the graphite, and make the paint, the brass ferrule, and the eraser used to finish a pencil. Components come from many countries, and people cooperate without any government telling them what to do. Milton Friedman adapted the story in his 1980 TV documentary and book *Free to Choose*.

In 1955, Read acquired *The Freeman*, a biweekly magazine launched in 1950 by Henry Hazlitt, *Fortune* writer John Chamberlain, *analysis* editor Frank Chodorov, and Suzanne LaFollette, who had worked with the American individualist author Albert Jay Nock on his magazine *The Freeman* (1920–1924). Under Read, *The Freeman* achieved distribution in several dozen countries.

FEE began holding seminars on liberty in 1959. Missouri entrepreneur Ethelmae Humphreys remembered Read's most dramatic talk, which was given countless times over the years: "He would turn off the overhead lights, then turn on an electric candle at the podium. That by itself was dramatic because you couldn't take your eyes off it. He would say that all the darkness couldn't snuff out the light of a single candle. He said a candle enabled you to read a book—and maybe write one. Then he talked about how, by better understanding liberty, you can develop 'circles of influence,' and he increased the brightness of the candlelight until it filled the room."

Read died in his sleep on May 14, 1983, at his home adjacent to FEE's headquarters. He was eighty-four years old. Three days later, more than a hundred people attended a memorial service at Irvington Presbyterian Church. His ashes were scattered on the wooded slope behind his home.

Nobel laureate F. A. Hayek wrote that Read was "a profound and original thinker who disguised the profundity of his conclusions by putting them into homely everyday language, and those of us who for a time, and perhaps somewhat condescendingly, had seen in him mainly a popularizer, found that they had a great deal to learn from him."

BACK WHEN LEONARD Read had been thinking what he could do in America, Antony Fisher was searching for an opportunity to make a difference in Britain. A tall, slim, good-looking man, he developed a bold new strategy for promoting liberty, generously supported his cause, and shared expertise with people around the world.

His daughter Linda Whetstone reminisced, "He was very charming. Always immaculately dressed. He had a marvelous sense of humor. He had an inner tranquility. And of course, he was utterly devoted to the cause of human liberty. Whatever the occasion, sooner or later conversation with the person next to him would turn to liberty." Fisher's longtime associate Ralph Harris recalled, "Antony was the most uncomplicated, honest and upright man I have ever known. Perhaps his most endearing hallmark was modesty. . . . It owed everything to his private devotion to Christian Science, his awe for God's creation, and his simple instinctive belief in freedom."

Born in London on June 28, 1915, Antony George Anson Fisher was the son of George and Janet Anson Fisher. When Antony was twenty-six months old, his father was killed by a Turkish sniper at Gallipoli during World War I. At the time, his mother was pregnant with his brother, Basil. She had grown up in New Zealand and was a strong character who brought up the boys despite her multiple sclerosis.

Fisher studied engineering at Trinity College in Cambridge University. In 1936, he pioneered Britain's rent-a-car business. Three years later, he married Eve Lilian Naylor, and they had four children: Mark (1941), Linda (1942), Michael (1945), and Lucy (1948).

During World War II, both Antony and his brother flew in Hurricane Squadron 111. On August 15, 1940, Antony was shocked to see Basil shot down over Selsey, along England's southeastern coast. Determined to help more pilots survive, Fisher invented a device that showed pilots how, when firing their machine guns, they could anticipate where enemy planes would be. He was awarded the Air Force Cross.

Socialists came to power after the war, and Prime Minister Clement Attlee's government began seizing private property and introduced forced labor. Fisher, who by this time worked for a London bank, read the April 1945 *Reader's Digest*, which excerpted twenty pages from F. A. Hayek's *The Road to Serfdom* (1944). Hayek warned that although the Nazis had been defeated, liberty was doomed if collectivist trends continued to gain momentum in the West. Fisher visited Hayek at the London School of Economics. As Fisher recalled, "My central question was what, if anything, could he advise me to do to help get discussion and policy on the right lines. . . . Hayek first warned against wasting time—as I was then tempted—by taking up a political career. He explained his view that the decisive influence in the battle of ideas and policy was wielded by intellectuals whom he characterized as the 'second-hand dealers in ideas'. . . . His counsel was that I should join with others in forming a scholarly research organization to supply intellectuals in universities, schools, journalism and broadcasting with authoritative studies of the economic theory of markets and its application to practical affairs."

Fisher's pamphlet *The Case for Freedom* (1948) critiqued government interference with the economy. Copies of the pamphlet reached Henry Hazlitt and Leonard E. Read in the United States, and the result was an invitation for him to join the Mont Pelerin Society, which they, together with Hayek and about thirty other pro-liberty thinkers, had established in April 1947.

Meanwhile, at a dairy farm that Fisher had bought in Framfield, Sussex, foot-and-mouth disease struck his herd of shorthorn cows, and they all had to be destroyed. In 1952, he visited the United States for ideas about what he might do with his farm. At the same time, he wanted to find out if there was a libertarian institute that might be a model for Britain. He went to Read's Foundation for Economic Education.

There he talked with staff economist F. A. Harper who had taught at Cornell University until he was forced out for assigning *The Road to Serfdom* to his students. It was through Harper that Fisher saw factory farming of chickens. Fisher turned his dairy farm into the Buxted Chicken Company, which soon employed some two hundred people and produced more than 800,000 chickens per week, driving down the price of chickens about 85 percent. He did more than any politician to put a chicken in every pot.

Fisher used some of his chicken profits to fund the Institute of Economic Affairs. Fisher, libertarian activist Oliver Smedley, and Smedley's friend J. S. Harding signed the IEA trust deed in November 1955. Each of the trustees contributed £100. For several years after that, Fisher contributed £250, and during the 1960s he upped this to £12,000 annually. On January 1, 1957, the IEA began in a room within Smedley's suite near the London Stock Exchange. Since Smedley had as much work as he could handle, Fisher tracked down Ralph Harris, a journalist who had impressed him a half-dozen years earlier. Harris became the first general director of the IEA.

A friend recommended Arthur Seldon to take charge of the program. Seldon, a cobbler's son who was orphaned and grew up in London's East End, had studied at the London School of Economics (1934–1937). There he learned the importance of economic liberty from Hayek. The single most important influence was *Collectivist Economic Planning* (1935), Hayek's book that exposed fatal flaws of socialism. During World War II, Seldon saw the chaos of government planning.

Historian Richard Cockett, author of *Thinking the Unthinkable: Think-Tanks and the Intellectual Counter-Revolution*, observed that "the central partnership within the IEA was that between Harris and Seldon. . . . They were both working-class in origin fighting against the intellectual creed, collectivism, which was supposed to have done the most to improve the conditions of their class. Both Harris and Seldon could call on their own experience when arguing with high-minded middle-class defenders of Keynesian orthodoxy who claimed to be acting on behalf of the less well-off in society. . . . Seldon and Harris formed such an effective partnership because they were very different people, and so complemented each other perfectly. Harris was the convivial, witty and extrovert 'front-man' of the IEA. . . . Seldon, by contrast, was the more scholastic and thoughtful of the two, with none of Harris's flair as a genial and persuasive public speaker; he concentrated on maintaining the IEA's scholastic reputation and publishing output through a meticulous attention to detail as the editorial director. . . . Seldon once described the team as 'The Gilbert and Sullivan combination of producer and projector respectively of the case for liberal capitalism.'"

The IEA's basic strategy was to document problems caused by government interference with the economy and make a case for market alternatives. It published paperbound reports that were long enough to cover a substantial amount of material yet short enough to be inexpensively produced and distributed to professors, journalists, and broadcasters. The IEA stayed out of party politics.

By the late 1960s, Fisher had a couple of setbacks. He and his wife, Eve, who was never interested in his business ventures or his libertarian crusade, got divorced. After he and his partners sold Buxted Chicken Company in August 1969, he invested a substantial chunk of his proceeds into creating a Cayman Islands operation to farm green sea turtles, because they offered low-cholesterol meat, and almost every part of a turtle could be used. But in 1973 the United States banned the importation of green sea turtles, whether farmed or caught. The business closed, and Fisher paid the $600,000 in debts. He was sixty, an age when few men are able to rebuild.

It became clear, though, that his avocation, the IEA, was beginning to swing British opinion away from socialism. Among many influential visitors were members of Parliament Keith Joseph, Geoffrey Howe, and Margaret Thatcher.

In 1975, Fisher was invited to help the newly established Fraser Institute (Vancouver, Canada) gain influence like the IEA, and he stayed on until a qualified Canadian could be recruited. Economist Michael Walker became the key man who made Fraser successful. In 1977, Fisher was asked to help launch the International Center for Economic Policy Studies (New York), which, renamed the Manhattan Institute, became the leading think tank in New York.

Fisher's life got an unexpected lift when he met Dorian Crocker during the September 1975 Mont Pelerin Society regional meeting at Hillsdale College. She had been married to the late George N. Crocker, a lawyer and *San Francisco Examiner* columnist. Antony and Dorian were married on October 8, 1977, in Monterey, California. They moved into her 3,600-square-foot co-op atop Russian Hill, 1750 Taylor Street, the same building where their friends Milton and Rose Friedman were to live. "Dorian enjoyed everything my father did and became part of it," remembered Linda Whetstone.

Fisher no longer had much money of his own, but he had a big idea: that libertarian views would gain credibility more quickly if there were many voices. Accordingly, people gave him money to launch pro-liberty institutes around the world. In the United States, he helped establish the Pacific Research Institute (San Francisco) and the National Center for Policy Analysis (Dallas), as well as the Manhattan Institute. He helped the Adam Smith Institute in Britain and helped establish several dozen pro-liberty institutes in Australia, Brazil, Chile, Hong Kong, Iceland, Italy, Mexico, Peru, Venezuela, and elsewhere. He and Dorian traveled from one continent to another, offering advice and dispensing funds—probably over $2 million altogether. Fisher set up the Atlas Economic Research Foundation in 1981 and brought in the IEA's John Blundell to handle much of this work.

In late 1987, Fisher learned he had bone cancer that had metastasized. "In his final year of painful illnesses, stoically borne," recalled Ralph Harris, "Antony was able to rejoice in the multiplying tributes to the success of his treasured IEA. The crowning knighthood came just in time, as a wonderful surprise and a bonus for work which had been its own reward." Fisher died of a heart attack on July 9, 1988, at San Francisco's St. Francis Memorial Hospital, where he had been transferred a couple of days before. He was seventy-three years old.

Ten days later, about a dozen family members and friends boarded the sixty-foot yacht *Naiad*, sailed into the Pacific, and scattered his ashes and flowers while a Christian Science practitioner prayed. There was a memorial service at St. Lawrence Jewry-Next-Guildhall, a church in the City of London. The *Times* of London observed, "For someone who was not academic, and was not generally known, his indirect influence on the intellectual climate was remarkable."

❉   ❉   ❉

MEANWHILE, IN THE United States dramatic steps were being taken to achieve direct influence for libertarian ideas. The principal intellectual entrepreneur was six foot, two inch, solidly built, wise-cracking Ed Crane, cofounder of the Washington-based Cato Institute, now the world's largest pro-liberty institute. Some thirty thousand people a year attend Cato programs, which cover the complete range of public policy issues, mainly at the federal level. With analyses prepared by the world's leading libertarian thinkers, Cato backs specific alternatives such as social security privatization, term limits, tax reform, school choice, medical savings accounts, free trade, deregulation, and drug legalization. It favors staying out of other people's wars, which has meant opposing both George Bush's 1991 Gulf War and Bill Clinton's 1999 Balkan War.

With his bold vision, wry wit, forceful salesmanship, and organizational ability, Crane emerged as the greatest fund raiser the libertarian movement has ever seen. Cato gets almost two-thirds of its financial support from private individuals and the rest from companies and foundations. He recruited to Cato's board global heavyweights like investment banker Theodore Forstmann, media billionaire Rupert Murdoch, cable TV billionaire John Malone, and Federal Express founder and chairman Fred Smith, among others. He showed that libertarians could play in the big leagues.

The *Washington Post* called Cato "the hot policy shop." The *Boston Globe* rated Cato as "Washington's hottest think tank." *Atlantic Monthly* noted that "the Cato Institute is in the vanguard of market thinking." Said *Newsweek,* "Cato has helped change the terms of debate." And the *Wall Street Journal* wrote that "Cato's intellectual guns now roar throughout the capital."

Edward Harrison Crane III was born on August 15, 1944, in Los Angeles. He was the second of three children of Mary Barbara Greene Crane and ophthalmologist Edward H. Crane, Jr.

At the University of California at Berkeley, he ran for student senate, promising to abolish student government. He was soundly defeated by Bettina Aptheker. "She pulled out her Communist Party card which was a sure means to victory," he quipped.

He earned an M.B.A. at the University of Southern California and joined the investment firm Scudder, Stevens & Clark, where he soon assumed responsibility for institutional clients. By the time Crane was twenty-five, he managed over $250 million. Alliance Capital Management lured him away, and he worked in their San Francisco office.

In 1972, during the Libertarian party's first election campaign, he helped vice presidential candidate Toni Nathan, an Oregon radio and TV producer who had been a Democrat. By 1976, he quit his job to work full-time for the Libertarian party. He proved to be a formidable organizer, achieving higher vote totals in the 1976 and 1980 presidential campaigns. Although the party afforded splendid opportunities to publicize libertarian ideas, he concluded that laws were stacked against third parties.

Through 1976 Libertarian presidential candidate Roger MacBride, an attorney and friend of *Discovery of Freedom* author Rose Wilder Lane, Crane met Charles Koch, the soft-spoken chairman and chief executive of Wichita-based Koch Industries. His father, Fred, had been a Texas poor boy who graduated from the Massachusetts Institute of Technology and helped develop a better process for refining crude oil, which made him a millionaire before he was forty. MIT graduate Charles took over Koch Industries following Fred's death in 1967 and made it America's #2 privately held company.

Koch didn't think the prospects were very good for promoting liberty through political action. He favored an institute aimed at changing the terms of policy debates. Crane established the Cato Institute, named after *Cato's Letters*, the radical libertarian tract that influenced the American Revolution. "Cato began business," Crane recalled, "the first work-day of January 1977 in small offices on San Francisco's Kearny Street, while we awaited the build-out of our first real home at 550 Bay Street, near Coit Tower." Crane brought in Kentucky-born editor David Boaz to take charge of publications, and Boaz recruited hundreds of libertarian scholars who produced thoughtful analyses of current and proposed laws. His books *Libertarianism* and *The Libertarian Reader* appeared in 1997.

Because Cato focused on national policy, it moved in 1982 to Washington, D.C. Crane recruited former member of the president's Council of Economic Advisors William Niskanen as Cato chairman. College economics teacher Jim Dorn came on board to edit the scholarly *Cato Journal*. University of Chicago–trained legal scholar Roger Pilon worked to get more libertarian Supreme Court decisions. Journalist Doug Bandow emerged as one of America's most prolific writers of op-ed newspaper articles.

Crane continued to help the Libertarian party, and it was through this activity that he met Kristina Knall Herbert. They were married in China, where Cato was holding a conference. They had three children: Geoffrey, who was born in 1986, Kathleen in 1989, and Mary in 1991.

Crane persuaded Harvard Ph.D. José Pinera to help direct Cato's Project on Social Security Privatization, launched on August 14, 1985. He had previously led the hugely successful privatization of Chile's government-run pension system. It is set up so that retirement accounts are each individual's private property that can't be raided by politicians. People choose among prudent investments and at any time can see how much they have. Pinera established the International Center for Pension Reform, which helps privatize troubled government-run pension systems around the world. Cato created a web site, www.socialsecurity.org, with a calculator enabling people to see how their average yield from a private retirement account would compare with social security.

If there was ever a defining moment for Cato, it came in 1991. When President George Bush went to war against Iraq's brutal dictator, Saddam Hussein. Cato senior policy staff, led by foreign policy specialist Ted Galen Carpenter, made dozens of media appearances rebutting the claim that America's vital interests were at stake. Cato stood its ground even though some wealthy backers withdrew their support.

Cato helped stop President Clinton from seizing America's health care industry. It published John Goodman and Gerald Musgrave's 671-page book *Patient Power* that introduced the idea of medical savings accounts, a market solution for the health care crisis. Cato distributed 300,000 copies of a condensed 134-page *Patient Power.*

A sign that Cato was playing in the big leagues, its $14 million headquarters went up at 1000 Massachusetts Avenue in Washington, D.C. Five and a half years after the May 1993 opening, all debt was paid, and Cato's annual budget had nearly tripled to $12 million. A *Washington Post* reporter wrote that Cato won respect "for not compromising its core beliefs even when they get in the way of practical politics."

THUS DID LEONARD E. Read, Antony Fisher, and Edward Crane win friends, recruit talent, raise money, develop strategies, build organizations, and turn ideas into a political movement that is influencing the world.

COURAGE FOR LIBERTY

*We are not to expect to be transported
from despotism to liberty in a featherbed.*
—THOMAS JEFFERSON (1790)

LIBERTY DEVELOPED where people were willing and able to fight for it. Ideas counted most when put into action, as people rebelled against their oppressors, pushed for peaceful reform, or started over in a new land. Often the struggle for liberty has required extraordinary persistence. The U.S. civil rights movement developed for almost a decade before achieving a national consensus on equal rights. The successful campaign for free trade in England had gathered momentum for a quarter-century. The American abolitionist movement continued for about three decades until slaves were emancipated. In 1920, all American women had the vote—forty-two years after the first suffrage amendment was introduced into the U.S. Congress and seventy-two years after the first call for woman suffrage. Perhaps the most colossal courage has been shown by lone individuals who dared to go behind enemy lines and rescue people from totalitarian executioners.

SPARK OF REVOLUTION

SAMUEL ADAMS WAS more effective than anyone else at popularizing ideas that inspired the American Revolution. He had a clear understanding about the perennial threat to liberty: "That ambition and lust of power above the law are . . . predominant passions in the breasts of most men . . . in all nations combined the worst passions of the human heart and the worst projects of the human mind in league against the *liberties* of mankind." Political power, he declared, is "known to be intoxicating in its nature . . . too intoxicating and liable to abuse."

Historian Thomas Fleming observed that "without Boston's Samuel Adams, there might never have been an American Revolution. His skill at combining agitation and propaganda put the British constantly on the defensive. He created committees of correspondence to link the colonies and was the chief organizer of the Boston Tea Party." The British governor of Massachusetts, Francis Bernard, snarled, "Every tip of his pen stung like a horned snake." Thomas Hutchinson, British-appointed chief justice, snapped that there wasn't "a greater incendiary in the King's dominion, or a man of greater malignity of heart who has less scruples any measure however criminal to accomplish his purposes."

But Adams was revered by American colonists. Thomas Jefferson called him "my very dear and ancient friend." John Adams described Sam, his older second cousin, as "cool, abstemious, polished, and refined. . . . When his deeper feelings were excited, he erected himself, or rather nature seemed to erect him, without the smallest symptoms of affectation, into an upright dignity of figure and gesture, and gave a harmony to his voice which made a strong impression . . . the more lasting for the purity, correctness and nervous elegance of his style."

Historian Samuel Eliot Morison acknowledged that "he was no orator—he had a quavering voice and a shaky hand; so he let other Sons of Liberty like Joseph Warren and the firebrand [James] Otis make the speeches, while he wrote provocative articles for the newspapers and pulled political strings." Biographer Cass Canfield added, "Nor was Sam at his best as a writer, though he wrote voluminously. He had a clear style based on the classics, but the intensity of his conviction sometimes made him narrow. It was as a . . . manager of men that he starred; the world has seldom seen a man so able in his methods of swaying a meeting. His sense of timing—when to advocate controversial action—was extraordinary, and Adams, though emotional and passionate by nature, knew just when it was necessary to conciliate rather than press."

When he led successful resistance to the Stamp Act in 1765, reported Canfield, he "was a middle-aged fellow, already stricken with palsy, wearing clothes rusty from the years. . . . [He] lived frugally and took pride in his poverty." Historian Page Smith described him as "mild as milk, quiet, prudent, with a strange delicacy of manner, a soft persuasiveness, had the keenest grasp of the temper and character of the people."

SAM ADAMS WAS born in his family's Purchase Street home fronting Boston Harbor, September 16, 1722. His mother, Mary Fifield, was reported to be an intensely religious woman. His father, Samuel Adams, Sr., was deacon of the Congregational church and a merchant who prepared barley for brewing into beer.

After attending Boston's Latin School, young Sam studied natural law philosophers John Locke and Samuel Pufendorf at Harvard. In a debate, he defended the affirmative view of the question "whether it be lawful to resist the Supreme Magistrate, if the Commonwealth cannot be otherwise preserved." His father lost his savings in a bad investment, and Sam had to pay his expenses by working as a waiter in Harvard's dining hall. Following graduation (1740), he worked at his father's brewery.

Adams married twenty-four-year-old Elizabeth Checkley, a clergyman's daughter, on October 17, 1749. After seven years and five pregnancies, she died, leaving a son, Samuel, and a daughter, Hannah. Sam Adams married again: Elizabeth Wells, age twenty-four, on December 6, 1764. She didn't have much money, but she helped stretch his meager income and provided moral support.

He tried his hand at politics and 1756 was elected a tax collector. As Cass Canfield noted, "His easygoing attitude was popular with the taxpayers, to whom he listened sympathetically when they pleaded for delay, but he failed to collect what was due. . . . The citizens of the town liked Sam so much that they enthusiastically re-elected him."

Meanwhile, England had concluded a succession of wars with France, the last being the Seven Years War (1756–1763), known in the American colonies, as the French and Indian War. Britain, though victorious, ended up with a debt that strained its taxing capacity. According to some modern estimates, British taxes per capita were the highest in the world. British politicians demanded that American colonists help pay a portion of war costs. Hence, new or higher tariffs were levied on imported cloth, coffee, indigo, and various wines. Rum was banned unless it came from British-controlled islands in the West Indies, and the list of colonial exports that must go only to Britain was expanded to include hides and potash. Adams, James Otis, and others staged protests against the new taxes. Then came the Stamp Act (1765), which imposed taxes on all newspapers, pamphlets, almanacs, college diplomas, licenses, bonds, playing cards, and dice.

Adams formed a group of tax resisters known as Sons of Liberty. According to biographer John C. Miller, they "met in a counting room on the second floor of Chase and Speakman's distillery. This building stood in Hanover Square near the Tree of Liberty—a huge oak that had been planted, it was significantly pointed out, in 1646, three years before the execution of [British king] Charles I."

Adams became the most exciting publicist for liberty. Biographer Miller reported his "journalism was so lively that the *Gazette* became practically the only newspaper read outside of Boston. Although it was packed with sedition and libel, it could not be suppressed by the Crown officers; when Hutchinson attempted to induce the Suffolk Grand Jury to indict the author of a particularly 'blasphemous Abuse of Kingly Government,' Sam Adams brought so much pressure to bear upon the jury that the indictment was promptly quashed." Adams was elected to the Massachusetts House of Representatives and helped pass the Massachusetts Resolves against the Stamp Act.

On August 14, Adams led the Sons of Liberty in hanging Massachusetts Bay stamp tax collector Andrew Oliver in effigy from the Liberty Tree. Then they hauled down the effigy, and an estimated five thousand people, about a third of Boston's population, marched to Oliver's Fort Hill house, chanted "Liberty, property and no stamps," and beheaded the effigy. They burned a new building intended as a headquarters for Stamp Act tax collection. Thanks to Adams's efforts, the Stamp Act was ignored, and goods came into Boston tax free. Parliament repealed the Stamp Act.

As he aggressively sought new recruits, Adams talked with shipyard workers and artisans in North Boston and visited shops, taverns, lodges, and volunteer fire companies. "He could explain political science to an illiterate sailor without condescending," explained historian A. J. Langguth. He sought out influential people, too, like thirty one-year-old John Hancock, the Boston smuggler who employed a thousand people around Boston. With money and connections, Hancock became the leading angel of the American cause, providing free rum for rallies and paying the bills for banners and publications. He named his smuggling ship *Liberty*.

Sam encouraged John Adams to join the political struggle. Biographer Page Smith reported that "from his cousin Samuel he had already learned to evaluate a man in terms of future dependability, to measure his orthodoxy and assess his firmness. How might he be useful? What were his loyalties, his talents, his attachments, his vanities and foibles? Resistance to authority was not work for boys or mobs."

The principal villain was King George III, the most powerful monarch in Europe, who presided over England, Wales, Scotland, Ireland, India, the Duchy of Hanover (Germany), and colonies in Africa, the West Indies, and North America. England at that time had the world's largest navy. Although Parliament dominated the government when George III ascended to the throne in 1760, he achieved dominance over Parliament through his shrewd political manipulation and distribution of favors.

Colonial resolve was tested in 1767 when Parliament enacted the Townshend Acts, another attempt to extract revenue from the colonies—this time by taxing imported glass, lead, paint, paper, and tea. Adams helped persuade members of the Massachusetts House of Representatives to adopt a circular letter that condemned the Townshend Acts.

At an October 1868 Faneuil Hall gathering, Sam Adams declared that British soldiers must go. John Adams remembered the occasion: "With a self-recollection, a self-possession, a self-command, a presence of mind that was admired by every person present, S.A. arose with an air of dignity and majesty, of which he was sometimes capable, stretched forth his arm, though even quivering with palsy, and with an harmonious voice and decisive tone said, 'If the Lt. Gov. or Col. Darymple, or both together, have authority to remove one regiment, they have authority to remove two, and nothing short of the total evacuation of the town by all regular troops will satisfy the public mind or preserve the peace of the province. These few words thrilled through the views of every man in the audience, and produced the great result. After very little awkward hesitation, it was agreed that the town should be evacuated. . . . These troops were called with humor and sarcasm 'Sam Adams' regiments.'"

On March 5, 1770, some British soldiers fired into a hostile crowd of about sixty people gathered in front of the State House, killing five civilians. An outraged Adams resolved, "Where there is a spark of patriotic fire, we will enkindle it." Accordingly, he wrote more than forty articles for the *Boston Gazette* between August 1770 and December 1772, many reprinted in New York and Philadelphia newspapers and even some in England, where they provided arguments for members of Parliament opposed to the government's get-tough colonial policy.

Sam Adams formed the Boston Committee of Correspondence for establishing a network of communications throughout the colonies. Twenty-one people attended the first meeting, held on November 3, 1772. They prepared a declaration of the rights of colonists, a list of grievances against England, and a letter encouraging other towns to form similar committees, which would keep in touch with one another. One British official singled out

Adams, calling him "the foulest, subtlest and most venomous serpent ever issued from the egg of sedition."

Meanwhile, colonists were aggravated that the British government had moved to bail out the financially troubled British East India Company by enforcing its monopoly of the American market. Colonists boycotted its tea and made their own less savory "Liberty Tea" from sage, currant, or plantain leaves. In the fall of 1773, British East India Company ships sailed for Boston, New York, Philadelphia, and Charleston, the biggest colonial ports. In New York and Charleston, public pressure led tea agents to quit.

The Boston tea agent, however, insisted on accepting the shipments, which arrived in the ships *Dartmouth, Eleanor,* and *Beaver.* Adams called a meeting at the Old South Church, and some eight thousands people showed up. He thundered, "Fellow countrymen, we cannot afford to give a single inch! If we retreat now, everything we have done becomes useless!" As many as 150 colonists dressed up as Mohawk Indians, went to Griffin's Wharf, boarded the tea ships, and dumped 342 chests of tea into Boston Harbor. British outrage transformed the Boston Tea Party into a pivotal event. Lord North, the British prime minister, proposed a series of harsh measures against Massachusetts.

New York Sons of Liberty supported the idea that Adams had suggested in the *Boston Gazette:* "That a Congress of American States be assembled as soon as possible; to draw up a Bill of Rights, and publish it to the world; choose an Ambassador to dwell at the British Court to act for the united Colonies." The Virginia House of Burgesses embraced the idea. A Boston meeting elected Samuel Adams, John Adams, James Bowdoin, Thomas Cushing, and Robert Treat Paine as their representatives at the First Continental Congress, called to express grievances against the British. The congress included representatives from every colony except Georgia, and they gathered in Carpenter's Hall, Philadelphia, from September 5 to October 26, 1774. They approved the formation of a continental association to help maintain a boycott of British goods.

On April 19, 1775, General Thomas Gage dispatched several hundred British soldiers to Concord, twenty-one miles away, where they planned to capture American gunpowder and arrest Adams and Hancock. Dr. Joseph Warren, who took charge of colonial resistance in Boston when Adams was away, asked silversmith Paul Revere to alert as many people as he could. He reached Lexington in time, and Adams and Hancock escaped.

The American Revolution began as sixteen-year-old William Diamond rolled his drums, and Captain John Parker assembled about seventy Minutemen in Concord village to face British soldiers marching toward them. The skirmish left eight dead Minutemen and ten wounded versus only one wounded British soldier. Hundreds of colonists were inspired to join the fight, and during subsequent encounters around Concord, Minutemen adopted guerrilla tactics and fired at marching British soldiers from behind rocks and trees. The British retreated as quickly as they could to Boston.

The Second Continental Congress began meeting May 10, 1775, to decide what should be done next, and Adams was there. Biographer Canfield noted that Adams "normally wore shabby clothes, stained as well. For this occasion, however, his friends had put up money to outfit him properly. So he looked resplendent in new suit, wig and cocked hat, and a gold-headed cane." He anticipated that a high priority for the British must be to cut off New England from the other colonies, and that would likely be done by having an army march to Lake Champlain, then down the Hudson River into New York City. Accordingly, two boats with eighty-three militiamen stormed Fort Ticonderoga, a base of British operations, and captured it.

The Second Continental Congress authorized the creation of a colonial army. John Adams persuaded his compatriots to name forty-three-year-old Colonel George Washington as commander in chief. Washington, who headed the Virginia militia, could help win southern support for the Revolution. Sam Adams seconded the nomination, and it was approved.

More Americans realized that it wasn't enough to rebel against England. The issues of arbitrary power made it clear that a new form of government was needed—one that better controlled political power. Sam Adams was among those who signed the Declaration of Independence on August 2, 1776.

Historian Pauline Maier commented that "he was fifty-four in 1776 . . . ten years the senior of George Washington, thirteen of John Adams; he was twenty-years older than Thomas Jefferson, twenty-nine than James Madison, thirty-three than Alexander Hamilton. Yet he served tirelessly on committees of the Continental Congress from its outset until 1781, a period in which the administrative as well as legislative burden of the new nation was borne by a handful of hard-worked delegates."

Sam Adams emerged as a legendary figure. When, in 1778, John Adams reached France as the American representative, people asked if he was "the famous Adams"—meaning Sam. "All that I could say or do," he wrote in his diary, "would not convince any Body, but that I was the fameux Adams." Eventually the French accepted his denials, but then he lamented that he had become "a Man whom Nobody had ever heard before."

Sam Adams helped draft the Articles of Confederation, a great experiment with limited government that collapsed amid the crises caused by Revolutionary War debts and inflation. When the Constitution was debated in 1788, Adams spoke out as an Antifederalist who demanded a bill of rights. He was a delegate to the Massachusetts ratifying convention. He was elected lieutenant governor of Massachusetts in 1789 and following the death of Governor John Hancock was elected governor, serving for three terms.

During his last years, he was by turns conservative and radical. He seemed to be conservative when he denounced the Shays' Rebellion against unjust taxes. But he also defended the ideals of the French Revolution and criticized Federalists who favored repression to curb revolutionary zeal. His influence was waning, though, and he failed in his bid to prevent John Adams, who had become a staunch Federalist, from being elected president in 1796. Sam watched helplessly as President Adams signed the Alien and Sedition Acts (1798), which were intended to crush Jefferson's Republican party by, among other things, empowering the federal government to suppress dissent.

Sam lived to see Jefferson win the 1800 presidential election and stop the Federalists from undermining civil liberties further. Reflecting on the tumultuous election campaign and on their friendship, Jefferson wrote to him in March 1801: "There exists not in the heart of man a more faithful esteem than mine to you, and that I shall ever bear you the most affectionate veneration and respect." Adams replied, "The storm is over, and we are now in port. . . . May Heaven grant the principles of liberty and virtue, truth and justice, may pervade the whole earth."

By 1803, Sam Adams was feeling his years; he had trouble taking more than a few steps, and his mind seemed to wander. He slipped away peacefully on October 2, 1803, in the humble house where he and his wife lived in Boston. He was eighty-one years old. Church bells tolled for a half-hour. Four days later, reported biographer William V. Wells, friends and dignitaries formed a funeral procession which "passed up Winter Street, down West and through Washington, around the old State House, and thence by Court and Tremont Streets to the Granary Burying-ground, where the body was placed in the family tomb."

John Adams did as much as anyone else to uphold Sam's reputation. "You say Mr. S. Adams 'had too much sternness and pious bigotry,'" he told one critic. "A man in his situation and circumstances must possess a large fund of sternness of stuff, or he soon will be annihilated."

Sam Adams was long neglected and then increasingly disparaged. The first major biography of him didn't appear until 1865 when a descendant, William V. Wells, produced three substantial volumes. Two decades later, James K. Hosmer's *Samuel Adams* still treated Adams as a hero while expressing regret that he "stooped now and then to a piece of sharp practice." But Abraham Lincoln had fought the Civil War because he believed rebellion was illegitimate, and this view hardened during the "progressive" era. Ralph Volney Harlow's *Samuel Adams: Promoter of the American Revolution* (1923) portrayed Adams's rebellion as irrational, unjustified by any acts of the British, and driven by Adams's "tiresome mental problems." John C. Miller's *Sam Adams: Pioneer in Propaganda* (1936) similarly belittled the idea that the American Revolution was a struggle for liberty by presenting Adams as a Machiavellian manipulator. The low point occurred when Clifford Shipton poured out forty-five pages of abuse in *Sibley's Harvard Graduates* (1958); among other things, Shipton asserted, Adams "preached hate to a degree without rival."

Adams began to get better treatment in Stuart Beach's biography, *Samuel Adams: The Fateful Years, 1764–1776* (1965). Murray N. Rothbard's *Conceived in Liberty, Advance to Revolution, 1760–1775* (1976) hailed Adams as "the great popular leader of the Massachusetts liberals . . . [who rebelled] on constitutional and libertarian principles." Historian Thomas Fleming, in his 150,000-copy seller *Liberty!* (1997), a lavishly produced companion to the popular TV documentary, affirmed that the American Revolution was a struggle for liberty and that Sam Adams played a key role in it. Now, hopefully, he will be able to rest in peace.

VALIANT VOICE

❧

WARTIME PROVIDES THE severest test for defenders of liberty. That's when governments everywhere tend to censor, jail, and even execute opponents. Charles James Fox became a legend for defending liberty during two major wars. Uniquely among great British political figures, he spent almost his entire parliamentary career—thirty-eight years—in the opposition. King George III viewed Fox as perhaps his most dangerous adversary, calling him "as contemptible as he is odious." Literary lion Samuel Johnson wondered "whether the nation should be ruled by the sceptre of George III or the tongue of Fox."

John Russell, one of Fox's intellectual successors, noted that it was his mission "to vindicate, with partial success, but with brilliant ability, the cause of freedom and the interests of mankind. He resisted the mad perseverance of Lord North in the project of subduing America. He opposed the war undertaken by Mr. Pitt against France, as unnecessary and unjust. He proved himself at all times the friend of religious liberty, and endeavoured to free both the Protestant and Roman Catholic dissenter from disabilities on account of their religious faith. He denounced the slave trade. He supported at all times a reform of the House of Commons."

Thomas Babington Macaulay, the most passionate chronicler of English liberty, referred to Fox as "the great man whose mighty efforts in the cause of peace, of truth, and of liberty, have made that name immortal." Macaulay called Fox quite simply "the greatest parliamentary defender of civil and religious liberty."

Fox gained influence in part because he made friends easily. He was cheerful, affectionate, generous, and kind. "I have passed two evenings with him," wrote Tory wit George Selwyn, "and never was anybody so agreeable, and the more so from his having no pretensions to it." Edward Gibbon, famed historian of ancient Rome's decline, remarked, "Perhaps no human being was ever more perfectly exempt from the taint of malevolence, vanity, or falsehood."

More than most other men of his time, Fox was generous toward women. Biographer George Otto Trevelyan explained, "His notion of true gallantry was to treat women as beings who stood on the same intellectual tableland as himself; to give them the very best of his thoughts and his knowledge, as well as of his humour and his eloquence; to invite, and weigh, their advice in seasons of difficulty; and if ever they urged him to steps which his judgment or

his conscience disapproved, not to elude them with half-contemptuous ban-
ter, but to convince them by plain-spoken and serious remonstrance. . . .
There have been few better husbands than Fox, and probably none so
delightful; for no man ever devoted such power of pleasing to the single end
of making a wife happy."

If it weren't for his wild ways, Fox might well have headed a ministry and
had more direct influence on events rather than spend so many years in
opposition. During his early manhood, Fox consumed a lot of alcohol and
reportedly even pawned his gold watch for a beer. He didn't get drunk much,
though, because he wanted to stay sober enough for gambling. He became a
skilled handicapper at the race tracks. The problem was that he lost even
more money at cards and borrowed money from friends and from money-
lenders. His losses exceeded £140,000, an astounding sum, and at one point,
creditors seized his furniture.

Fox was among the most famous—and frequently caricatured—English
faces of his generation. "It was impossible to contemplate the lineaments of
his countenance," recalled one observer, "without instantly perceiving the
marks of genius. His features in themselves dark, harsh and saturnine . . .
derived a sort of majesty from the addition of two black and shaggy eyebrows
which sometimes concealed but more frequently developed the workings of
his mind. Even these features, however, did not readily assume the expressions of anger or enmity. They frequently and naturally relaxed into a smile,
the effect of which became irresistible because it appeared to be the index of
a benevolent and complacent disposition. His figure, broad, heavy and
inclined to corpulence, appeared destitute of elegance or grace, except the
portion conferred on it by the emanations of intellect, which at times diffused over his whole person, when he was speaking, the most impassionated
animation."

Many of Fox's speeches have been lost to posterity, but they inspired raves
aplenty. For instance, Herr Moritz, a German pastor visiting Parliament,
recalled: "It is impossible for me to describe with what fire and persuasive
eloquence he spoke, and how the Speaker in the chair incessantly nodded
approbation from beneath his solemn wig; and innumerable voices incessantly called out, hear him! hear him! and when there was the least sign that
he intended to leave off speaking, they no less vociferously exclaimed, go on;
and so he continued to speak in this manner for nearly two hours."

It's hard to believe every superlative showered on Fox, but they surely suggest that he had a remarkable ability to touch people's hearts. Henry
Brougham, who joined Fox's crusade against slavery, considered him "if not
the greatest orator, certainly the most accomplished debater, that ever
appeared upon the theatre of public affairs in any age of the world." And

Macaulay gushed that Fox was "the most brilliant and powerful debater who ever lived."

CHARLES JAMES FOX was born at 9 Conduit Street, Westminister, London on January 24, 1749. He was the third son of courageous and corrupt Henry Fox, who enriched himself as paymaster-general, quite possibly the most lucrative post in the British government. Charles's mother was an aristocrat, Georgiana Caroline Lennox.

Fox entered Hertford College, Oxford, in October 1764. During his two years there, he acquired a love of reading classic literature that was to refresh him untill his dying days. After Oxford, Fox spent two years traveling through Europe. On the way back, he stopped in Geneva to visit Voltaire who recommended some books.

Concerned about his son's directionless drifting, Henry Fox arranged for him to get elected a member of Parliament from Midhurst, one of many pocket boroughs controlled by a few aristocrats (Parliament was very much an exclusive club with 558 members intent on protecting their privileges). Charles took his seat in November 1768.

In July 1774, his father and mother died; his older brother Stephen died in November. Charles was left with an annual income and an inheritance, which he soon lost at the gaming tables.

Resisting both King George III and the patronage-driven Whigs in Parliament, Fox embraced libertarian principles. This made him a compatriot of reformer Charles Wentworth, Lord Rockingham. Fox was inspired by Lord Rockingham's Dublin-born private secretary, Edmund Burke, a tall man who spoke with an Irish accent, who was two decades his senior. Burke's father was a Protestant attorney, his mother was Catholic, and his best teacher was a Quaker. Burke wasn't a great orator; indeed, his speeches, which were sometimes three hours long, emptied the seats in Parliament. But he had acquired a deep knowledge of history, which gave him a valuable perspective, and he developed a passionate pen. He urged religious toleration for Irish Catholics, supported freer trade, favored ending the secrecy of parliamentary proceedings, expressed his outrage when a mob murdered two men convicted of homosexual contact, and defended the right of Middlesex voters who had four times chosen the maverick printer John Wilkes to be their representative in Parliament.

Then came the epic debate about how to pay off the debts from the Seven Years War (1756–1763). The purpose of this war had been to defend the American colonies from the French, but the colonists—about 2 million of them at the time—saw proposed taxes as tribute to the British empire, whose major feature was the aggravating mercantilist system in which British merchants reserved the colonies as their exclusive territory. If somebody in Rhode Island wanted to buy, say, hats from Virginia, he had to go through British merchants. The result of such restrictions was widespread smuggling. In addition, each colony had its own elected assembly and did not accept the supremacy of Parliament over its affairs.

Burke opposed schemes to tax the American colonists because he believed the proposed taxes were unjust. They would yield little revenue and trigger rebellion. After the schemes were enacted, Burke called for repeal. Chancellor of the Exchequer George Grenville's stamp duty (1765)—some fifty taxes on newspapers and legal documents—had provoked such a storm of protest that it was repealed in a year. Then in 1767 came Chancellor of the Exchequer Charles Townshend's taxes on tea and other articles, provoking the Boston Tea Party, which led to the British blockade of Boston, opposed by Burke.

Fox worked to become the most effective orator and debater in the House of Commons. He refined his skills by speaking at least once every day and rejected the traditional style of speaking with flowery metaphors, extensive quotations, and allusions to ancient Greece and Rome, a style practiced by William Pitt who had been an influential member of Parliament for three decades. Fox was spontaneous, direct, and passionate. Again and again, he hammered the ministry of Lord North. In 1775, he denounced the suspension of habeas corpus, a bulwark of civil liberties. On February 2, 1777, he warned that Britain would lose the war and that sending over more troops could leave Britain defenseless against France. After the British surrender at Yorktown, Fox insisted that recognition of American independence must be given unconditionally, not made a price of peace.

Dressed in a blue frock coat and a yellow waistcoat—colors later adopted by the Whig party as well as the Whig journal *Edinburgh Review*—Fox championed liberal reform during the 1780s. For example, he advocated complete religious toleration. This meant expanding the Toleration Act (1689), which required that to serve legally as a clergyman, a religious dissenter must acknowledge the divinity of Christ, a measure specifically aimed at Unitarians. Fox also favored abolishing religious tests to exclude dissenters from political office.

Although Fox seemed to support the Church of England, he opposed using coercion to support it. As he declared in 1787: "It was an irreverent and impious opinion to maintain, that the church must depend for support as an engine or ally of the state, and not on the evidence of its doctrines, to be found by searching the scriptures, and the moral effects which it produced on the minds of those whom it was the duty to instruct."

Fox supported the campaign of fellow member William Wilberforce to abolish the slave trade and opposed proposals that it be continued under government regulation. According to one summary of the debate in Parliament in May 1789, "He knew of no such thing as a regulation of robbery or a restriction of murder. There was no medium; the legislature must either abolish the trade or avow their own criminality."

Fox's leading adversary was William Pitt the Younger who served as prime minister from 1784 to 1802. Pitt was a tall, slim man whose face was often wracked by anxiety and whose hair turned nearly white during his last years. Loyal to the king, he displayed more integrity than most other politicians, declining easy opportunities to enrich himself in government. He was self-disciplined, utterly devoted to his work, stiffly formal, and cool amid a crisis—and he seldom forgot grudges, including disagreements with Fox. They presented a dramatic contrast as they debated in the House of Commons. "Fox, with his harsh, thrilling voice and rapid delivery," reported biographer Edward Lascelles, "poured out his arguments in an impetuous torrent of urgency, while Pitt presented his case with faultless precision and complete self-possession." As an observer recalled, "Mr. Pitt conceives his sentences before he utters them. Mr. Fox throws himself into the middle of his, and leaves it to God Almighty to get him out again."

Meanwhile, Fox had fallen in love with a tall, elegant woman two years younger than he. She called herself "Mrs. Armistead," although there never seems to have been a Mr. Armistead. She was reportedly linked to a "notorious establishment" in London and later became the mistress of a duke. During the early 1770s, she and Fox settled down to contented domesticity and were secretly married on September 28, 1795. They lived on her thirty-acre estate, St. Anne's Hill near London.

Political constellations began to move after July 14, 1789, when angry mobs stormed the Bastille, launching the French Revolution. In January 1790, Burke rose in the House of Commons to hurl his first salvos against "the excesses of an irrational, unprincipled, proscribing, confiscating, plundering, ferocious, bloody, and tyrannical democracy." He denounced the Declaration of the Rights of Man and the Citizen as a "digest of anarchy." Fox responded discreetly, hoping to avoid a painful break with Burke. He affirmed that he had "learnt more from his right honourable friend than from all the men with whom he had ever conversed." He went on to emphasize he was "the enemy of all absolute forms of government, whether an absolute monarchy, an absolute aristocracy, or an absolute democracy."

Then came Burke's explosive pamphlet, *Reflections on the Revolution in France,* published in November 1790. He declared that before the Revolution, the corrupt French government "had the elements of a constitution very nearly as good as could be wished." Burke began calling for war against France to stop the contagion of revolution. At first, few Englishmen were interested, although Prime Minister Pitt was contemplating war to stop Russia from expanding in Turkey.

The two men had moved far apart. Fox was for reforming Parliament; Burke was against. Fox revived a proposal to end the requirement that candidates for political office swear allegiance to the Church of England; Burke was against (many Protestant dissenters were "men of factious and dangerous principles," he warned). In 1791, Fox praised the new French Constitution, in which staunch defenders of liberty like Lafayette and Condorcet had a hand. Burke complained that Fox "had ripped up the whole course and tenour of his private and public life, with a considerable degree of asperity." Fox was in tears, shocked that Burke would suddenly and publicly renounce their friendship that had endured for a quarter-century. Fox expressed regret at his own "rash and imprudent words" and offered to "keep out of his right honourable friend's way." Fox attempted a reconciliation when Burke lay dying in July 1797, but Burke had his wife turn him away.

While Burke promoted hysteria, Fox fought for liberty. He had long been concerned about freedom of speech, especially restrictions imposed by libel law. The burden of proof was on the defendant. Judges, not juries, had the power to decide whether a libel had occurred, and since judges were connected with government and the established church, they generally considered attacks on either to be libelous. Fox believed the burden of proof should be on government, so he wanted to make it more difficult to win a conviction for libel. Accordingly, in May 1791, he introduced his libel bill, which would give juries the power to decide not only the facts about whether something had been published but also whether a libel had occurred. Fox's libel bill was passed and signed by the king after June 1, 1792. Determined to silence dissidents, though, the government filed more libel cases in the two years following passage of Fox's libel bill than had been filed during the entire eighteenth century. Juries saved many defendants from the gallows or banishment to Australia.

Fox's generous hopes for France came crashing down as the Revolution spun out of control. By September 1792, the French central government was controlled by the Convention, an assembly that operated without effective checks or balances. Its Jacobin leaders started a European war. This accelerated the trend toward unlimited centralization in France, climaxing with the Reign of Terror, in which an estimated forty thousand people were murdered.

Despite Burke's dire warnings, there wasn't much evidence of revolutionary unrest in Britain, but war hysteria led Pitt to make a major assault on civil liberties. In 1794, Parliament passed the Act Suspending Habeas Corpus, empowering "his majesty to secure and detain such persons as his majesty shall suspect are conspiring against his person and government." The next year, Parliament passed the Treasonable and Seditious Practices Act that among other things made it unlawful to "declare any words or sentences to excite or stir up the people to hatred or contempt to the person of his majesty, his heirs, or successors, or the government." Finally, Parliament passed the Seditious Assemblies Act that effectively banned meetings of more than fifty people who wanted to petition the government "on the pretext of deliberating upon any grievance in church or state." Fox led the opposition to these measures every step of the way. He warned that "either your Bills must remain waste-paper, or they must be carried into execution with circumstances of the greatest oppression."

Supposedly to protect Britain against oppression from abroad, the government pursued oppression at home. It shut down publications and prosecuted editors, harassed nonconformist Protestant preachers, and imprisoned protesters. The proper policy, Fox declared, was less government interference with life, not more. "I would instantly repeal the Test and Corporation Acts, and take from [dissenters], by such a step, all cause of complaint. If there were any persons tinctured with a republican spirit, because they thought that the representative government was more perfect in a republic, I would endeavor to amend the representation of the Commons, and to show that the House of Commons, though not chosen by all, should have no other interest than to prove itself the representative of all. If there were men dissatisfied in Scotland or Ireland, or elsewhere, on account of disabilities and exemptions, or unjust prejudices, and of cruel restrictions, I would repeal the penal statutes, which are a disgrace to our law books."

By May 1797, support for Pitt's war policies had become overwhelming. Fox's supporters in Parliament had dwindled to about twenty-five, compared with about fifty-five in 1794 and ninety during the 1780s. Fox stopped going to Parliament and spent time mainly at St. Anne's Hill, reading and gardening. Nevertheless, he looked back with pride: "It is a great comfort to me to reflect how steadily I have opposed this war, for the miseries it seems likely to produce are without end."

Fox returned to Parliament long enough for a blaze of glory. After the death of William Pitt on January 23, 1806, Fox was the leading political figure of the era, and he could no longer be excluded from a ministry. He accepted the post of secretary of state. Working with Wilberforce and others, Fox introduced a bill that would make it illegal for a British citizen to trade in slaves under a foreign flag or to fit a foreign slave ship in a British port. Enacted in the spring of 1806, this measure had the potential of wiping out three-quarters of the British slave trade. Next, Fox sought a parliamentary commitment for total abolition. On June 10, 1806, he offered his resolution: "This House, conceiving the African slave trade to be contrary to the principles of justice, humanity, and sound policy, will, with all practicable expedition, proceed to take effectual measures for abolishing the said trade." The House of Commons voted 114 to 15 in favor, and the House of Lords assented on June 25. "If, during the almost forty years that I have now had the honour of a seat in Parliament," Fox remarked, "I had been so fortunate as to accomplish that, and that only, I should think I had done enough, and could retire from public life with comfort, and conscious satisfaction, that I had done my duty."

The next step would have been to introduce an abolition bill, but Fox's health deteriorated during the summer of 1806, and others had to carry on the fight. His arms and legs swelled up, and he suffered chronic exhaustion. He was persuaded to let doctors do a couple painful "taps," presumably efforts to drain the excess fluids. For days, at his home in London, he lay listlessly in a lounge chair as his wife read aloud from Virgil, John Dryden, Jonathan Swift, and other favorite authors. On September 13, 1806, he got out a few puzzling words to his wife, "It don't signify, my dearest, dearest Liz," and died that afternoon. He was buried on October 10 next to William Pitt in Westminster Abbey.

As the valiant voice of the opposition nearly all his career, Fox saw few of his dreams come true, yet he struck mighty blows for liberty. He kept the spirit of liberty alive when government was determined to crush it, and he won important victories. He inspired the Whig and Liberal parties, which did much to make the nineteenth century the freest, most peaceful period in human history. He affirmed that people who stubbornly speak out against oppression can be free.

GENEROUS HEART

THE FREEDOM FIGHTER marquis de Lafayette changed history. He helped defeat the British at Yorktown, winning American Independence, and in France, he helped topple two kings and an emperor. Jean-Antoine Houdon, the great eighteenth-century sculptor who created busts of many great heroes, dubbed Lafayette "the apostle and defender of liberty in the two worlds."

Cornell University historian Stanley Idzerda remarked, "Lafayette knew only one cause during his long lifetime: human liberty. As a young man he risked his life in war and revolution for that cause. In middle age, living under the barely concealed dictatorship of Napoleon, a regime he detested, he recalled how he had been wounded, denounced, condemned to death, despised, imprisoned, beggared, and exiled—all in the service of human liberty. Poor, powerless, and with no prospects at that time, Lafayette asked, 'How have I loved liberty? With the enthusiasm of religion, with the rapture of love, with the conviction of geometry: that is how I have always loved liberty.'"

Lafayette was a tireless champion of natural rights and the principal author of the Declaration of the Rights of Man and of the Citizen. "There exist certain natural rights inherent in every society of which not only one nation but all the nations together could not justly deprive an individual," he insisted. He maintained these rights aren't "subject to the condition of nationality," and they include "freedom of conscience and opinions, judicial guarantees, the right to come and go." He promoted free trade and fought for religious toleration and freedom of the press. When the French government harassed immigrants, he sheltered many in his own house, and he spent a lot of his own money to help free slaves in French colonies.

He did more than anybody else to link friends of liberty everywhere. He was in touch with Thomas Jefferson, Thomas Paine, George Washington, Benjamin Franklin, James Madison, James Monroe, John Quincy Adams, Daniel Webster, Andrew Jackson, and James Fenimore Cooper, among other Americans. He was a friend of Pierre-Samuel du Pont de Nemours, Germaine de Staël, Benjamin Constant, and Horace Say in France. He corresponded with Charles James Fox in Britain and Simón Bolívar, who helped secure the independence of Venezuela, Colombia, Ecuador, Peru, and Bolivia. Lafayette encouraged Italian liberals, Spanish consitutionalists, and Greek and Polish freedom fighters. Respected Lafayette scholar Louis

Gottschalk wrote that "for most of the last fifty years of his long life, he was the outstanding champion in Europe of freedom—freedom for all men, everywhere."

Lafayette certainly stood out in a crowd. He was tall and bony with green eyes. "Pale, lanky, red-haired, with a pointed nose and receding forehead," added biographer Vincent Cronin, "he looked less like an officer than a wading bird. Nor was he a shining courtier, being slow to speak and awkward."

Washington saluted Lafayette's abilities as a strategist and commander: "He possesses uncommon military talents, is of quick and sound judgment, persevering, and enterprizing without rashness, and besides these, he is of a very conciliating temper and perfectly sober, which are qualities that rarely combine in the same person." Jefferson told Lafayette, "According to the ideas of our country, we do not permit ourselves to speak even truths, when they may have the air of flattery. I content myself, therefore, with saying once and for all, that I love you, your wife and children."

MARIE JOSEPH PAUL Yvres Roche Gilbert du Motier was born on September 6, 1757, in Château de Chavaniac, Auvergne, in south-central France. His father was Michel Louis Christophe Roche Gilbert du Motier, marquis de La Fayette, colonel of the French Grenadiers. He descended from a long line of warrior-aristocrats, one of whom fought with Joan of Arc against the English. La Fayette's mother was Marie-Louise-Julie de la Rivière, whose family was wealthy.

When he was two, his father was killed by a British cannon ball at the battle of Minden (about forty miles west of Hanover, Germany) during the Seven Years War, and he became the marquis de La Fayette (as he spelled it before the French Revolution). One of his early heroes was Vercingetorix who had defended Gaul against Julius Caesar. His mother died in April 1770, and his grandfather, the marquis de la Rivière, died soon afterward, leaving La Fayette an inheritance that assured him a princely annual income.

At fifteen, he met fourteen-year-old Marie Adrienne Françoise de Noailles (known as Adrienne) and fell in love. They married about a year later, on April 11, 1774. According to biographer André Maurois, she had "large, brooding eyes and an air of alert intelligence."

La Fayette heard that insurgent Americans were looking for French recruits, and he sailed for America on April 20, 1777. In July, he met General George Washington during a dinner at Philadelphia's City Tavern. Washington had only about eleven thousand men in his army. They were poorly equipped, and they were being pursued by the British. La Fayette joined American forces as they evaded an attack by British General Charles Cornwallis. They were overrun at Brandywine, Pennsylvania, and La Fayette was wounded in the leg. La Fayette, who shared the hardships at Valley Forge in 1777–1778, became Washington's information officer.

He decided to try soliciting French assistance for the Americans, sailing from Boston in January 1779. King Louis XVI authorized a mission headed by Jean Baptiste Donatien, comte de Rochambeau, a veteran of the Seven Years War. On March 11 the following year, La Fayette sailed back to America on the *Hermione,* to bring news that six French battleships and six thousand soldiers were coming.

Washington asked La Fayette to take about two thousand men to Virginia, so they could limit damage by the British and keep an eye on them. La Fayette borrowed money from Baltimore merchants so he could make sure all his men had shoes and clothing. La Fayette proved himself adept at harassing and escaping from the British.

In June 1781, British general Charles Cornwallis was ordered to establish a defensive position in Virginia and send some of his forces to New York. La Fayette monitored Cornwallis's movements as he occupied the Yorktown peninsula facing Chesapeake Bay, a potential staging area for attacks on Philadelphia. On July 31, Washington, who was camped at West Point, New York, ordered La Fayette to build his forces as fast as possible, so he could keep Cornwallis bottled up at Yorktown. Admiral François-Joseph-Paul, comte de Grasse, was sailing to Yorktown from French possessions in the Caribbean, and Washington and Rochambeau were on the way.

On August 30, Admiral de Grasse's fleet—six frigates and twenty-eight battleships, with 15,000 sailors and 3,100 marines on board—reached Yorktown. These ships prevented Cornwallis from escaping by water and helped bring more American and French soldiers to the scene quickly. Soon La Fayette commanded over fifty-five hundred regular troops and another three thousand militia men. Cornwallis's eighty-eight hundred British, Hessian, and provincial troops were outnumbered by the time Washington and Rochambeau arrived on September 9. "If Cornwallis now faced the prospect of surrender," wrote historian Louis Gottschalk, "it was in large part because Lafayette had persisted where others might have given up or had been cautious where others, yielding to an alluring temptation, might have proved too bold." The siege of Yorktown began on October 6, and La Fayette helped lead the capture of British positions. Cornwallis surrendered on October 19, 1781. Historian Gottschalk observed, "No other person (except perhaps De Grasse) had contributed so much or so directly to the capture of one of England's finest armies as had the young general fresh from the 'Society' of Paris."

Washington urged La Fayette to "come with Madame La Fayette and view me in my domestic walks. . . . No man could receive you in them with more friendship and affection than I should do." La Fayette visited Washington for eleven days in August 1784. After they said their final farewells, they never saw each other again.

La Fayette worked tirelessly for liberty. He promoted freer trade between France and the United States, became a charter member of the Society of the Friends of the Blacks, and was an honorary member of the New York Manumission Society and the British Committee for the Abolition of the Slave Trade. In 1785, he and his wife bought two plantations in French Guiana and liberated the forty-eight black slaves who worked there, giving them some land with which to start providing their own livelihood. The aim was to show how emancipation could be handled successfully.

The slavery issue was soon overtaken by revolution. The French government had incurred enormous debts during the Seven Years War with Britain (1756–1763), and the situation worsened when the government gave substantial aid to the American struggle against Britain. To get new taxes, Louis XVI agreed to summon the Estates General, an assembly of clergy, nobles, and taxpayers that hadn't met in a century and a half. Lafayette called for a truly national assembly, and Louis XVI finally agreed. Representatives were elected, and the Estates General convened at Versailles in May 1789.

By this time, to make clear the proper aims of policy, La Fayette had drafted the Declaration of the Rights of Man and of the Citizen. He was inspired by the Virginia Declaration of Rights, and his draft reflected his view that the primary threat to liberty was royal absolutism. He gave this draft to Jefferson, who praised it and sent along a copy to James Madison, then contemplating a bill of rights for America. The National Assembly began debating on July 11. Three days later, the Bastille, a medieval prison, had been seized by some eight hundred angry people, and the French Revolution was underway. Members of the National Assembly became convinced that the primary threat to liberty was mob violence, and they insisted that the Declaration be modified. The final version offered a more fully developed vision of liberty than the American Declaration of Independence. As for specific constitutional arrangements, La Fayette believed there should be a separation of powers, but he was defeated when the National Assembly voted 490 to 89 for a legislature with a single chamber. As a gesture for Republican ideals he changed the spelling of his name to Lafayette.

Citizen militias that formed throughout France came together as the National Guard, which served the National Assembly. Lafayette, appointed commander of the Paris National Guard, saved people from being murdered by mobs. He rescued the king and queen from angry mobs at Versailles and escorted the royal family to the Tuileries Palace in Paris. During the night of June 20, 1791, Louis XVI secretly made his "flight to Varennes," near the Belgian frontier, an attempt at rallying royalists. Lafayette awakened his houseguest, *Rights of Man* author Thomas Paine, and exclaimed: "The birds have flown away!" Outraged, since he had assured people that the king would stay put, Lafayette signed the first order in French history for the arrest of a king, and he brought the royal family back to Paris.

The Jacobins wanted blood, and they gained more of a following every day. Named after the hall where they first met, which had belonged to Jacobin monks, they were egalitarian admirers of Jean-Jacques Rousseau. Among them were Paul Marat, Jacques René Hebert, Pierre Brissot, and Maximilien Robespierre. They thought Lafayette should be executed as a traitor, so he headed for the Belgian border, on his way to Holland. He was detained in Rochefort, Belgium, which was controlled by the Austrian emperor François II. Considered a dangerous revolutionary, he was sent to one dungeon after another and endured swarms of mosquitoes, the stench of open sewers, and the bitter cold of winter. He was stripped of virtually all possessions except a few books, including a copy of Thomas Paine's *Common Sense*. He wrote a friend: "Liberty is the constant subject of my solitary meditations. . . . It is what one of my friends once called my 'holy madness.'"

Meanwhile, during the Reign of Terror in 1793 and 1794, when Robespierre ordered some sixty executions a day, Adrienne Lafayette's mother, grandmother, and sister were guillotined, and Adrienne was imprisoned in Paris. She was eventually released, thanks, in part, to efforts by American diplomat James Monroe who had also helped free Thomas Paine from a French prison. She arranged for fourteen-year-old George Washington Lafayette to find a safe haven in America. He brought her letter to George Washington, saying, "I send you my son."

François II let her and daughters Anastasie and Virginie join Lafayette in prison. As Lafayette descendant and scholar René de Chambrun explained, "Lafayette had not spoken to a human being and had been completely isolated from the outside world for nearly one year when suddenly, on October 15, 1795, the door of his narrow cell was thrown open. Into the dim room entered a woman and two children. This was the most dramatic instant of his life."

Lafayette's friends, including George Washington, the influential Frenchwoman Germaine de Staël, and the Englishman Charles James Fox tried to get them out of prison. Finally, after Napoleon's armies swept east into Austrian territory in 1797, they were released and journeyed to Holstein, a province of Denmark that wasn't likely to become embroiled in war.

Most of Lafayette's properties had been confiscated and sold during the French Revolution. The family was left with La Grange, an abandoned fifteenth-century castle about thirty-five miles east of Paris. They cleaned out a few rooms where they might live. President Thomas Jefferson had the government reimburse Lafayette for some of the supplies he had bought his soldiers during the American Revolution, and this made it possible to fix the roof. Jefferson pleaded with Lafayette to make America his home, offering land from the Louisiana Purchase.

In October 1807, Adrienne developed a fever and went into a delirium. Her family gathered around. On Christmas Eve, she put her arm around Lafayette's neck and whispered, "Je suis toute à vous" ("I am all yours"). She groped for his fingers, squeezed them, and was gone. Lafayette wrote to Jefferson, "Who better than you can sympathize for the loss of a beloved wife?"

René le Chambrun reported that every day at La Grange, Lafayette awoke at five in the morning and "remained in bed for two hours writing friends of liberty all over the world: Poles, Hungarians, Greeks, Spaniards and Portuguese, North and South Americans . . . and, alone on his knees, holding in his hand a small portrait of Adrienne and a lock of her hair, he would spend a quarter of an hour in meditative devotion."

Although Napoleon was defeated at Waterloo in 1815, he remained the most feared military commander in Europe and tried to hold onto his power. Lafayette, who had been elected to the new Chamber of Deputies, expressed outrage that Napoleon's wars had cost the lives of 3 million Frenchmen and demanded that Napoleon abdicate. Napoleon was soon exiled, but fanatical royalists took over and assassinated many opponents. Lafayette started a group, Friends of Liberty of the Press, and pleaded for toleration.

In 1823, Lafayette accepted President James Monroe's invitation for a farewell tour of America. When he arrived in New York on August 15, 1824, he was greeted by some thirty thousand people. An estimated fifty thousand cheered Lafayette and threw flowers at him as he rode a wagon drawn by four white horses to New York's City Hall. Mothers brought their children for his blessing, and some six thousand people attended a ball in his honor. As he began a thirteen-month tour through all twenty-four states, he commended Americans for what they had accomplished: "In the United States the sovereignty of the people, reacquired by a glorious and spotless Revolution, universally acknowledged, guaranteed not only by a constitution . . . but by legal procedures which are always within the scope of the public will. It is also exercised by free, general, and frequent elections. . . . Ten million people, without a monarchy, without a court, without an aristocracy, without trade-guilds, without unnecessary or unpopular taxes, without a state police, a constabulary, or any disorder, have acquired the highest degree of freedom, security, prosperity, and happiness, which human civilization could have imagined. . . . In France, on the contrary, there are no longer any municipal or administrative elections nor any other popular elections, no freedom of the press, no jury . . . nor any representation of the heart of the people."

At Bunker Hill, Massachusetts, the orator Daniel Webster declared: "Heaven saw fit to ordain, that the electric spark of liberty should be conducted through you, from the New World to the Old." Lafayette entered Philadelphia, escorted by four wagons carrying about 160 Revolutionary War veterans. He stopped at the Brandywine battlefield where he had been wounded and returned to a Yorktown that was still in ruins. He was welcomed by big crowds everywhere: ten thousand people in Newburgh (New York), fifty thousand in Baltimore, and seventy thousand in Boston. He was cheered in Richmond, Columbia, Charleston, Savannah, Augusta, Montgomery, Mobile, New Orleans, Natchez, St. Louis, Nashville, Lexington, Cincinnati, Pittsburgh, Buffalo, and Albany. He appeared at Catholic churches, Protestant churches, and Masonic lodge gatherings. He attended receptions open to everybody, and publicly welcomed all blacks and Indians who came. Lafayette descended to the vault of George Washington's tomb at Mount Vernon. There was a reception at the University of Virginia. He saw John Adams in Quincy, Massachusetts, and James Madison in Montpelier, Virginia.

And Lafayette reached Monticello. "The Marquis got out of his barouche and limped as fast as he could toward the house," explained biographer Brand Whitlock. "Between the white columns of the portico appeared a tall, spare figure of a man stooped with age, wearing the swallow-tailcoat, the long waistcoat and the high stock of another epoch; he had cut off his queue, and his thin white locks hung about his hollow temples and lean cheeks; he tottered down the steps, and came towards him.

"'Ah, Jefferson!' cried Lafayette.

"The two old men broke into a shuffling run.

"'Ah, Lafayette!' cried Jefferson.

"No need for eloquence now! They burst into tears and fell into each other's arms."

Sometime later, Lafayette's secretary Auguste Levasseur described an awesome sight in Charlottesville: "The Nation's Guest, seated at the patriotic banquet between Jefferson and Madison." On September 7, Lafayette went down the Potomac River on the steamboat *Mount Vernon,* boarded the frigate *Brandywine,* and sailed back to France.

Lafayette began spending the winter months in Paris and there held Tuesday evening receptions that attracted liberals from America and Europe. The American author James Fenimore Cooper reported that the gatherings "are exceedingly well attended." Benjamin Constant and Alexander von Humboldt attended, as did members of the Chamber of Deputies. Historian Lloyd Kramer noted that "Lafayette's soirées in Paris, like his long conversations with guests at La Grange, thus facilitated contact between different generations in much the same way as they contributed to new connections between politicians and writers or between his French friends and foreigners."

Meanwhile, in 1824, Charles X had become king of France and reasserted the power of church and throne. The Catholic church regained control over French schools, and anyone convicted of committing a sacrilege in a church building could be put to death. On July 26, 1830, the king issued decrees that dissolved the Chamber of Deputies, suppressed freedom of the press, and restricted the voting franchise. Paris erupted in revolt. "Make a revolution," the seventy-three-year-old Lafayette urged. "Without it, we shall have made nothing but a riot." He played a key role in deposing Charles X and picking his successor, Louis-Philippe, a monarch subject to a constitution, which provided some protection for individual liberty.

Lafayette continued to be a champion of liberty. He defended individuals jailed for political offenses, opposed capital punishment, denounced slavery, and supported insurgents in Belgium. He supported Polish freedom, and—defying French laws on refugees—hid Polish patriots like Antoine Ostrowski and Joachim Lelewell at his estate.

In early February 1834, Lafayette reported pain and fatigue, perhaps triggered by prolonged exposure to bitter cold air. He had pneumonia. On May 20, 1834, his children with him, Lafayette pressed to his lips a medallion with a picture of Adrienne and took his last breath. He was seventy-seven. The funeral service was at the Church of the Assumption in Paris. Tens of thousands of people turned out to see three thousand National Guards accompany Lafayette's coffin to the humble Picpus cemetery, where he would join Adrienne and so many guillotined victims of the French Revolution. Lafayette was laid to rest in American soil he had brought back on the *Brandywine*.

Lafayette was idolized during the nineteenth century, especially in the United States. His portrait hung everywhere. American Friends of Lafayette has over a thousand historic portraits of Lafayette. Dozens of American towns, counties, and schools were named after him. "Pronounce him one of the first men of his age," John Quincy Adams proclaimed in his tribute, "and you have not done him justice."

Lafayette's grandson inherited La Grange, and he married a British woman (a Tory), who consigned Lafayette's books, papers, and other personal possessions to the third-floor attic of the northwest tower, a space that Lafayette had called the *couloir des polonais* ("hiding place of free Poles"). Most twentieth-century historians belittled Lafayette as a vain, doctrinaire simpleton.

Happily, there has come a renewed appreciation for Lafayette. René le Chambrun, descended from Lafayette's daughter, Virginie, acquired La Grange in 1955 and explored the northwest tower attic. He and his wife discovered a treasure trove, surviving thanks to the absence of humidity and vermin. Lafayette's three thousand-volume library was there, as were some twenty-five thousand letters to people like Jefferson, Washington, and Madison. The only book drawing on this material is a 1961 biography of Adrienne by le Chambrun's friend André Maurois. The papers have been microfilmed on sixty-four reels and are housed in the Library of Congress.

Historian Lloyd Kramer recalled the revelation he experienced when he helped edit Cornell University's vast collection of Lafayette letters, gathered from Lafayette's birthplace at the Château de Chavaniac: "I soon came to realize the historical value of reading 'primary sources' and to believe that Lafayette's life had been far more varied and complex than the ironic, historical narratives suggested. Reading and discussing Lafayette's mail with my fellow editors gradually made me wonder how the simple mediocrity who appeared in modern history books could be the same man whom his contemporaries sought out in a wide variety of political, personal, and revolutionary crises from the 1770s to the 1830s."

Even a tart-tongued biographer like Olivier Bernier acknowledged that "whatever his limitations, it is to Lafayette's glory that the one idea he seized on was that of liberty. Nothing can replace the right to speak, think, organize, and govern freely: from this all benefits derive. With his vanity, his obstinacy, his self-satisfaction, his thirst for popularity, Lafayette never lost sight of that all-desirable principle. For that, he deserved the gratitude of his contemporaries and the esteem of later generations. In a world where liberty is in very short supply, there are worse heroes than a man who never stopped worshipping freedom." The one thing Lafayette's critics concede is the most important of all: he is still the great hero of two worlds.

PASSIONATE ORATORY

IN 1695, BRITAIN began enacting a series of Penal Laws on Ireland. They denied Irish people the liberty to own land, attend school, learn a trade, bear arms, hold public office, travel abroad, or practice their religion without interference. Moreover, to support the Church of England, the government taxed Irish peasants who shivered in windowless one-room mud huts, slept on straw, and subsisted on potatoes and water. Britain ruled Ireland primarily through a viceroy appointed by the king, although an Irish Parliament—consisting of Protestant landlords—was summoned from time to time. In 1800, the Irish Parliament, bribed by the promise of favors, voted to abolish itself and embrace the Union, which meant Irish affairs would be governed from London by the British Parliament.

Then came Daniel O'Connell who became the great champion of Irish emancipation and Ireland's major political leader for a half-century. He declared, "My political creed is short and simple. It consists in believing that all men are entitled as of right and justice to religious and civil liberty. . . . I have taken care to require it only on that principle which would emancipate the Catholics in Ireland, would protect the Protestants in France and Italy, and destroy the Inquisition, together with inquisitors, in Spain. Religion is debased and degraded by human interference; and surely the worship of the Deity cannot but be contaminated by the admixture of worldly ambition or human force."

O'Connell, who recognized that violence brings out the worst in everyone, insisted on pursuing liberty with nonviolent methods, and he led the first nonviolent mass movement in European history. He was farsighted enough to see that even if Irish violence fulfilled immediate aims, it would poison future relations. His cherished goals were liberty and peace. "He was the leader of a nation," wrote four-time Liberal prime minister William Ewart Gladstone, "and this nation, weak, outnumbered, and despised, he led, not always unsuccessfully, in its controversy with another nation, the strongest perhaps and the proudest in Europe."

O'Connell displayed extraordinary devotion. "For more than twenty years before Emancipation," he recalled, "the burden of the cause was thrown upon me. I had to arrange the meetings, to prepare the resolutions, to furnish replies to the correspondence, to examine the case of each person complaining of practical grievances, to rouse the torpid, to animate the lukewarm, to control the violent and inflammatory, to avoid the shoals and breakers of the law, to guard against multiplied treachery, and at all times to oppose at every peril the powerful and multitudinous enemies of the cause. . . . There was no day that I did not devote from one to two hours, often much more, to the working out of the Catholic cause, and that without receiving or allowing the offer of any remuneration, even for the personal expenditure incurred in the agitation of the cause itself."

Besides specifically helping Ireland, O'Connell supported an expansion of the voting franchise, which became the Reform Bill of 1832. He spoke out for eliminating civil disabilities against Jews, favored the repeal of usury laws (which fixed interest rates), opposed capital punishment, and advocated free trade. An outspoken foe of slavery, he shared the podium with the American antislavery orator Frederick Douglass. The methods he used to rally Irish multitudes were adapted by Richard Cobden and John Bright when they led their great campaign to abolish trade restrictions that prevented hungry people from buying cheap imported food.

"It was really the example of America, rather than France, that determined his early political outlook," wrote historian T. Desmond Williams. "He inherited much from the doctrines of the American Revolution." Biographer Raymond Moley observed: "There is an amazing parallel between O'Connell and Jefferson. The Irish leader, in his student days in London and Dublin, was reading the same books which had been so influential with Jefferson earlier. Their political and philosophical conclusions were almost identical. Both were children of the French Enlightenment and English liberalism. Both, influenced by the anti-clerical literature of the times, embraced Deism— O'Connell for a very few years, Jefferson permanently."

O'Connell was unforgettable. According to Moley, "even before he could be called a Liberator—a magnificent presence, a face beneath those curly locks which never lost its charm. Tall, powerfully built, and with the poise of an actor, he had a sharp memory and a mind like a finely articulated mechanism. . . . One account places his height at slightly below six feet. His shoulders were broad and his chest was massive. His posture was erect and commanding. He had dark curly hair and blue eyes. . . . Shining eyes and delicate features suggest nothing more appropriate than 'feminine sweetness."

Biographer Charles Chenevix Trench wrote that "in his forties, O'Connell was still a fine figure of a man. He was chested like a bull, and not without a magisterial protuberance lower down, about which he was very sensitive. . . . His clothes, every stitch of Irish cloth, seemed to make him larger than life— a high, wide-brimmed top hat, or a fur hat in cold weather, a coat with padded shoulders, and over it a long, sweeping cloak. His face was like a Roman Emperor's—one of the strong Emperors—square, heavy-jowled, with a broad nose and big eyes, rather pale from much work indoors. His hair was blacker, thicker, curlier and glossier than ever, being, in fact, a wig. This, when quizzed, he turned to his advantage, boasting that he had gone bald in the service of his country."

O'Connell was one of the greatest orators. "Such tenderness, such pathos, such world-embracing love," recalled Frederick Douglass, "and, on the other hand, such indignation, such fiery and thunderous denunciation, such wit and humor, I never heard surpassed, if equaled, at home or abroad." His voice, reported Trench, "was wonderfully flexible, changing from an angry or challenging roar to a confidential near-whisper which in some extraordinary way he projected effortlessly to the most distant man in a crowd." Scholar Arthur Houston, too, marveled at O'Connell's voice—"powerful. . . . sonorous, melodious, penetrating, capable of expressing every shade of human feeling. But a voice is nothing without a command of words, and words are nothing where ideas are lacking. O'Connell had an abundance of both. Poetic fancy and homely wit, delicate humor and deep pathos, subtle flattery and bitter sarcasm, persuasion and denunciation, each, as the occasion required, flowed in an inexhaustible stream to charm or dismay. Nor was it the masses alone that fell under the spell of his eloquence. Judges and juries bowed to his influence, and this wonder at his eloquence was affirmed later by those who heard him in the House of Commons."

DANIEL O'CONNELL WAS born on August 6, 1775, on Carhen, a farm owned by Morgan O'Connell, near Caherciveen. His mother was Catherine O'Mullane from County Cork. The family, which included older brother Maurice, lived in a stone house over a general store. Daniel was sent to nurse with a peasant family in the Iveragh Mountains, and he lived there four years.

Young Daniel hardly saw his parents because, soon after he returned from the peasant family, he was sent to live with an uncle, Hunting Cap, at Derrynane where he remained for a decade. While English Penal Laws suppressed Irish schools, perpetuating widespread illiteracy, "hedge" schools provided underground education, and this is how Daniel gained much of his early education. "The schoolmasters or teachers operated not only outside the law, but in direct violation of the law," reported biographer Raymond Moley. "Any householder was subject to severe penalties if he harbored one of these schoolmasters—who consequently lived and taught his pupils, when the weather permitted, out of doors. He would select a remote spot on the sunny side of a ledge or hill, use rocks for desks and seats, with pupils scattered on the ground before him. In winter the schoolmaster moved from place to place, sheltered always by peasants in their miserable huts. In bad weather he would usually acquire an abandoned cabin, more often without windows and heated by sods of peat brought by the pupils. Much of the instruction was in

Gaelic, but the English language, Latin, and occasionally Greek were taught. Reading, writing, and 'cyphering' were also included." All this shows, Moley added, "the insatiable instinct of even the most illiterate peasants for the schooling of their children."

After spending time at schools in France, O'Connell decided to train as a lawyer in London. He entered Lincoln's Inn, a private association where people studied English law (as opposed to Roman law studied at Oxford and Cambridge). O'Connell's journal shows that he read Edward Coke's *Commentary on Littleton's Treatise on Land Tenures* (1644) and William Blackstone's *Commentaries on the Laws of England* (1765–1769). O'Connell also absorbed many recent writings on liberty, including Adam Smith's *Wealth of Nations* (1776), marquis de Condorcet's *Life of Turgot* (1786), and Mary Wollstonecraft's *A Vindication of the Rights of Woman* (1792). Thomas Paine's *Age of Reason* (1794) moved him.

In January 1800, O'Connell delivered his first political speech, an attack on the Union with Britain. The Union occurred when the British bribed members of the Irish Parliament to abolish it and have minority representation in the British Parliament. The aim was to secure more British control over Ireland.

Uncle Hunting Cap pressured him to marry a Cork woman who anticipated a substantial inheritance, but O'Connell had fallen in love with Mary O'Connell, a distant cousin, and they were secretly married. Hunting Cap cut O'Connell's inheritance anyway. As an Irishman, O'Connell wasn't permitted to handle the most important and lucrative cases, but he became Ireland's foremost lawyer by handling small cases.

O'Connell petitioned Parliament to repeal anti-Catholic laws. In a Dublin speech in 1807, O'Connell championed religious liberty, which applied not only to Irish Catholics but also to "Protestants in Spain and Portugal, and the Christian in [Muslim] Constantinople." Prime Minister William Pitt, however, refused to present Irish petitions in the House of Commons because of resistance by King George III. Member of Parliament Charles James Fox, who had opposed British efforts to subdue Americans during the Revolutionary War and had championed the liberation of slaves, agreed to present the petitions in 1806, but they were voted down.

Then in 1812, twenty-four-year-old Tory Robert Peel was named Irish secretary in the British cabinet. Determined to stop political agitation among the Irish, he started libel proceedings against *Dublin Evening Post* editor John Magee for attacking a high-ranking British official in Ireland. O'Connell agreed to defend Magee, and the case came before the King's Bench on July 20, 1813. The prosecutor was anti-Catholic, and the jury was packed with Protestants, so O'Connell knew he didn't have a chance of winning the case. Instead, he used it as an opportunity for protest. He attacked the prosecutor as "an infamous and profligate liar." Then O'Connell declared that "no judge ought to dictate to a jury, no jury ought to allow itself to be dictated to." The jury found Magee guilty, and he was sentenced to a fine and two years in prison, but all the Irish newspapers reported O'Connell's presentation. About 100,000 copies of it were believed to have been sold in Ireland. O'Connell's presentation was translated into French, and copies were distributed in Spain where liberals were attempting to limit government power.

In early 1823, O'Connell, then forty-eight, recruited thirty-two-year-old lawyer Richard Lalor Sheil to help energize the movement. Short and sloppy looking, he didn't seem impressive, but he was devoted to the Irish cause and he was a spellbinding orator. Sheil reflected, "The monster abuses of the Church Establishment, the frightful evils of political monopoly, the hideous anomaly of the whole structure of our civil institutions, the unnatural ascendancy of a handful of men over an immense and powerful population—all these, and the other just and legitimate cause of public exasperation, were gradually dropping out of the national memory. . . . We sat down like galley slaves in a calm."

O'Connell envisioned an association that would involve the entire Irish population—about 7 million people—for the peaceful pursuit of liberty. Since Irish society consisted of peasants, priests, and a minuscule number of business and professional people, O'Connell thought the officers of this association should be the priests who were in weekly contact with everybody. On May 12, 1823, O'Connell and Sheil established the Catholic Association. They decided to try financing the association by selling subscription memberships for a penny a month and toured the country promoting the cause and seeking members.

Home Secretary Robert Peel prosecuted him for his remark that continued British refusal to grant Catholic emancipation would bring forth "another Bolívar," a reference to the champion of South American independence from Spain. But a jury refused to indict O'Connell.

O'Connell and Sheil went to London, greeted along the way by big crowds, to testify about Irish grievances in the House of Lords. Someone suggested that the movement would have an even greater impact if the leaders wore distinctive uniforms. O'Connell and Sheil, reported Moley, had "a blue coat with a velvet collar, a yellow waistcoat and white pantaloons. For O'Connell, as a symbol of leadership, there was a gold button on the shoulder."

Events came to a head in September 1828 when O'Connell campaigned to represent Clare, Ireland, in Parliament. Elected by a substantial majority, he told a crowd in County Tipperary, "We will plant in our Native Land the Constitutional Tree of Liberty. That noble tree will prosper and flourish in our Green and Fertile Country. It will extend its protecting branches all over this lovely island. Beneath its sweet and sacred shade, the universal People of Ireland, Catholics and Protestants, and Presbyterians, and Dissenters of every Class, will sit in peace and unison and tranquility. Commerce and Trade will flourish; Industry will be rewarded; and the People, contented and happy, will see Old Ireland what she ought to be, Great, Glorious and FREE, First Flower of the Earth, first gem of the Sea."

Amid the seething anger and likely violence in Ireland, Parliament approved the emancipation bill by April 10, 1829, and King George IV gave his assent three days later. Tories got even by citing a technicality that forced O'Connell to stand for election again, and they upheld laws that continued to exclude him from the Inner Bar and the biggest law cases. "In these two petty acts of spite against the man who had defeated them," wrote Raymond Moley, "the Tory party, the King, and undoubtedly Peel himself, lost any moral credit for Emancipation. . . . The government admitted that it yielded, not because of considerations of justice, but only because of fear and under coercion."

O'Connell remained Ireland's best lawyer. In one of his most dramatic cases, in October 1829, he was called to save men convicted and sentenced to death after the prosecutor resorted to devious methods. Biographer Moley wote that O'Connell "made the first stage of the journey on horseback since there was no road for the first twenty miles of the way from Derrynane to Cork. After that he was able to travel in a carriage in which he studied the briefs. He continued at a furious pace through the night, and arrived in Cork in the morning to find the court already in session. With no rest or refreshment but a sandwich and a bowl of milk, which he consumed in court while the state prosecutor was summing up, O'Connell plunged into the proceedings. By means of a brilliant cross-examination he succeeded in exposing the witnesses as perjurers, and obtained an acquittal for all his clients. The government then commuted the death sentences passed on the first batch of prisoners."

O'Connell challenged municipal corporations that, run by appointed Protestants, controlled governments in the towns and cities throughout Ireland, influenced the selection of juries, and pocketed tax revenue without providing much in return. Parliament enacted a bill that abolished most of the municipal corporations. The remaining corporations were to be elected, their powers limited. After this bill took effect, O'Connell was elected lord mayor of Dublin.

O'Connell generated pressure for repealing the Union. He helped recruit political candidates, raised money for them, generated publicity, and spoke in their behalf. He had as many as thirty candidates in Parliament at one time. His efforts to build an Irish political organization provoked bitter criticism from British newspapers; the *London Times* alone published over three hundred editorials attacking him.

He launched the Repeal Association to make repeal of the Union a top priority, but the Irish members of Parliament were generally unwilling to risk their gains by pushing a policy that faced certain defeat. Protestant landlords, who had supported O'Connell during his campaign for religious liberty, wanted nothing to do with repealing the Union. Irish people who had emigrated to America sent contributions for the Repeal Association, but O'Connell made clear his opposition to slavery, and those contributions dried up because many Irish immigrants had become slave owners.

O'Connell began a series of "Monster Meetings." At Kilkenny, for instance, he addressed an audience estimated around 300,000 and reportedly drew about that many people at Mallow. The crowd was believed to be much bigger at Tara, outside Dublin. Robert Peel, who had become prime minister, tried to stop his old rival by ordering the cancellation of what was to have been the biggest "Monster Meeting" at Clontarf and arranging for artillery aimed at the meeting ground. O'Connell was arrested, charged with conspiracy, found guilty, and sentenced to a year in prison and a large fine. O'Connell's lawyers appealed, and after he had been in prison three months, law lords voted three (Whigs) to two (Tories) that he should be released because of irregularities in the proceedings against him. He mounted a huge chariot that was drawn through cheering crowds. "The chariot was halted when it reached College Green," reported biographer Moley, "and O'Connell, always ready to seize the dramatic moment, stood upright and pointed in silence to the Bank of Ireland, until 1800 the seat of the Irish Parliament." O'Connell resumed his meetings, attracting as many as several hundred thousand people in Cork, Dublin, Dundalk, Navan, and Tara.

Then he returned home to Derrynane for some rest, and probably in September 1845 he heard news of the potato blight, *Phytophthora infestans*. Throughout Ireland, this blight turned potatoes soft, black, and smelly. The potato crop failed again the following year, the first time anybody could remember two Irish crop failures in a row. Desperate Irish peasants pawned their clothes and fishing gear. Many fell behind in their rent, which meant eviction and beggary. Some ate sorrel and nettles, which had a few nutrients but hardly any calories. Many peasants developed scurvy; their gums became swollen, their teeth fell out, their skin developed black sores, and in many cases they died from gangrene. Altogether, about a million people died during the famine. There was a coffin shortage, and coffins with a hinged bottom came into use, so a body could slide into the grave, making it possible to reuse the coffin. About the only good that came out of the famine was the June 25, 1846, repeal of the Corn Laws (grain tariffs) that enabled hungry people to import cheaper food.

Meanwhile, radicals who called themselves the Young Irelanders became O'Connell's adversaries. They demanded political independence, whereas

O'Connell had sought legislative independence. He denounced slavery, while one of his harshest critics, John Mitchel, emigrated to America and supported slavery. Young Irelanders talked about violence, and O'Connell was utterly opposed to violence.

O'Connell's colossal energy faded away. Biographer Charles Chenevix Trench speculated that he seems to have suffered from a brain tumor. Doctors suggested that a trip abroad might help revive O'Connell's spirits. Accordingly, on March 22, 1847, he sailed from Folkstone, Ireland, to Boulogne, France, accompanied by one Father Miley. They traveled south, hoping for warmer weather, and got as far as Genoa when O'Connell took a turn for the worse. He died there on May 17, at age seventy-one. As he had requested, his heart was buried in Rome, at the Irish College. His body was buried in Glasnevin Cemetery, Dublin.

William Ewart Gladstone, who served four times as Britain's prime minister, was a great admirer of O'Connell. In an 1889 article for *Nineteenth Century*, he wrote: "As an advocate, it may, I apprehend, be asked, without creating surprise, whether the entire century has produced any one more eminent. . . . As an orator of the platform, he may challenge all the world; for who ever in the same degree as O'Connell trained and disciplined, stirred and soothed, a people? . . . [He had energy] for whatever tended, within the political sphere, to advance human happiness and freedom."

Violent nationalism gathered momentum during the twentieth century, and O'Connell's reputation declined. University College Dublin historian Donal McCartney reported, "Supporters of the Gaelic Revival, Sinn Feiners, Socialists and Republicans were inclined to accept the. . . . view that it were better for Ireland had O'Connell never been born. The men of the Gaelic Revival argued that because O'Connell was a political giant he had done more than any other man to kill the language."

By the 1960s, though, more sympathetic biographies of O'Connell began to appear, the most important being Angus Macintyre's *The Liberator: Daniel O'Connell and the Irish Party 1830–1847* (1965), Lawrence J. McCaffrey's *Daniel O'Connell and the Repeal Year* (1965), Raymond Moley's *Daniel O'Connell: Nationalism Without Violence* (1974), and Charles Chenevix Trench's *The Great Dan: A Biography of Daniel O'Connell* (1984). Although Trench provided a sober portrait of O'Connell as a practical political leader, he was lyrical: "The reputation of this greatest of Irishmen deserves to rest not on what he might have done, not on what he failed to do, but on his wonderful achievement in 1828 which raised his people's heads and straightened their backs after generations of subjection and failure." Amen!

EYEWITNESS TESTIMONY

❦

FREDERICK DOUGLASS MADE himself the most compelling witness to the evils of slavery and prejudice. He suffered as his master broke up his family and he endured whippings and beatings. Although it was illegal to teach slaves how to read and write, Douglass learned anyway, and he secretly educated other slaves. After he escaped to freedom, he tirelessly addressed antislavery meetings throughout the North and the British Isles for more than two decades. When it became clear that the Civil War was only a bloody benchmark in the struggle, he spearheaded the protest against northern prejudice and southern states that subverted the newly won civil liberties of blacks.

Douglass embraced the ideal of equal freedom. He supported woman suffrage, saying "we hold woman to be justly entitled to all we claim for man," and urged toleration for persecuted Chinese immigrants: "I know of no rights of race superior to the rights of humanity." Overseas, he joined the great Daniel O'Connell in demanding Irish freedom, and he shared lecture platforms with Richard Cobden and John Bright, speaking out for free trade.

Douglass believed that private property, competitive enterprise, and self-help are essential for human progress. "Property," he wrote, "will produce for us the only condition upon which any people can rise to the dignity of genuine manhood. . . . Knowledge, wisdom, culture, refinement, manners, are all founded on work and the wealth which work brings. . . . Without money, there's no leisure, without leisure no thought, without thought no progress."

Critics considered Douglass stubborn, arrogant, and overly sensitive to slights, but he earned respect from friends of freedom. For years he appeared on lecture platforms with William Lloyd Garrison and Wendell Phillips, leading lights of the antislavery movement. *Uncle Tom's Cabin* author Harriet Beecher Stowe praised Douglass, and essayist Ralph Waldo Emerson declared, "Here is Man; and if you have man, black or white is an insignificance." Mark Twain was proud to count Douglass as a friend. John Bright contributed money to help buy his freedom. "He saw it all, lived it all, and overcame it all," exulted black self-help pioneer Booker T. Washington.

The personal costs of Douglass's antislavery campaign were high. He spent hardly any time at home. He missed seeing his five children growing up, and his wife, Anna, resented being left alone to tend the children and earn extra money.

Ottilia Assing, a German friend, described Douglass as a "rather light mulatto of unusually large, slender and powerful build. His features were marked by a distinctly vaulted forehead and with a singularly deep indentation at the base of the nose. The nose itself is arched, the lips are small and nicely formed, revealing more the influence of the white man than of his black origins. His thick hair is mixed here and there with grey and is curly though not woolly." An American observer recalled Douglass's presence as a speaker: "He was more than six feet in height, and his majestic form, as he rose to speak, straight as an arrow, muscular, yet lithe and graceful, his flashing eye, and more than all, his voice, that rivaled Webster's in its richness, and in the depth and sonorousness of its cadences, made up such an ideal of an orator as the listeners never forgot."

Individualist feminist Elizabeth Cady Stanton saw how, at a Boston antislavery meeting, "with wit, satire, and indignation [Douglass] graphically described the bitterness of slavery and the humiliation of subjection to those who, in all human virtues and powers, were inferior to himself. . . . Around him sat the great antislavery orators of the day, earnestly watching the effect of his eloquence on that immense audience, that laughed and wept by turns, completely carried away by the wondrous gifts of his pathos and humor. . . . All the other speakers seemed tame after Frederick Douglass. . . . [He] stood there like an African prince, majestic in his wrath."

FREDERICK DOUGLASS WAS born Frederick Augustus Washington Bailey sometime in February 1818 (slave births weren't recorded) on a plantation along Maryland's Eastern Shore, near Easton. He didn't know who his father was. His mother, Harriet Bailey, was a slave, and consequently all her children were condemned to be slaves. "I never saw my mother, to know her as such, more than four or five times in my life," he recalled, "and each of these times was very short in duration, and at night." She died when he was seven.

Bailey was brought to the mansion of Edward Lloyd, a former Maryland governor and U.S. senator and among the richest men in the South. Lloyd owned a number of farms, and Bailey remembered how one overseer, Austin Gore, was whipping a slave named Denby. When Denby tried to escape into a stream, Gore shot him dead—and got away with it. "Killing a slave, or any colored person, in Talbot County, Maryland," Bailey explained, "is not treated as a crime."

In November 1826, Bailey was assigned to Thomas Auld who sent him to his brother Hugh in Baltimore. Hugh's wife, Sophia, read to him from the Bible, and he noticed the connection between marks on the page and the words she spoke. She began teaching him the alphabet. Bailey recalled that

Hugh Auld snarled, "If you learn him how to read, he'll want to know how to write; and this accomplished, he'll be running away with himself."

Bailey learned more on the streets of Baltimore: "When I met with any boy who I knew could write, I would tell him I could write as well as he. The next word would be, 'I don't believe you. Let me see you try it.' I would then make the letters which I had been so fortunate as to learn, and ask him to beat that. In this way I got a good many lessons in writing, which it is quite possible I should never have gotten in any other way."

When Bailey was twelve, he heard his friends read from a collection of great speeches that had been assigned in school. He took fifty cents that he had hoarded, went to Knight's Bookstore, and bought his own copy of *The Columbian Orator.* Compiled by Caleb Bingham, it first appeared in 1797 and went through many editions. "Alone, behind the shipyard wall," reported biographer William McFeely, "Frederick Bailey read aloud. Laboriously, studiously, at first, then fluently, melodically, he recited great speeches. With *The Columbian Orator* in his hand, with the words of great speakers coming from his mouth, he was rehearsing. He was readying the sounds—and meanings—of words of his own that he would one day write. He had the whole world before him. He was Cato before the Roman senate, [William] Pitt [the Elder] before Parliament defending American liberty, [Richard Brinsley] Sheridan arguing for Catholic emancipation, Washington bidding his officers farewell." The book included a "Dialogue between Master and Slave" in which the Slave tells the Master he wants not kindness but liberty. There was also a short play, "Slave in Barbary," where the ruler Hamet declares: "Let it be remembered, there is no luxury so exquisite as the exercise of humanity, and no post so honourable as his, who defends THE RIGHTS OF MAN."

Bailey recalled, "The silver trump of freedom had roused my soul to eternal wakefulness. Freedom now appeared, to disappear no more. . . . It was heard in every sound, and seen in every thing. It was ever present to torment me with a sense of my wretched condition. I saw nothing without seeing it, I heard nothing without hearing it, and felt nothing without feeling it. It looked from every star, it smiled in every calm, breathed in every wind, and moved in every storm."

In March 1832, Thomas Auld decided he needed Bailey, and he returned to Auld's place in St. Michaels, Maryland. Auld discovered that the taste of freedom in Baltimore had had a pernicious effect on Bailey and that harsh discipline was called for. Accordingly, in January 1833, he was hired out as a field hand to Edward Covey, a small tenant farmer known as a "nigger-breaker." Bailey was brutally whipped once; when Covey tried again, Bailey successfully defended himself with his powerful arms and indomitable spirit. "I was *nothing* before," Bailey wrote later. "I WAS A MAN NOW."

He resolved to be free and did what he could to nourish the spirit of freedom in others. At the house of a free black man, he educated some forty slaves with his *Columbian Orator* and a copy of *Webster's Spelling Book,* which he apparently had acquired from a friend. "These dear souls came not to Sabbath school because it was popular to do so, nor did I teach them because it was reputable to be thus engaged," he wrote. "Every moment they spent in that school, they were liable to be taken up, and given thirty-nine lashes. They came because they wished to learn. Their minds had been starved by their cruel masters. . . . The work of instructing my dear fellow-slaves was the sweetest engagement with which I was ever blessed."

In April 1836, Bailey and four other slaves plotted their escape, but they were betrayed. They were dragged behind horses some fifteen miles to the Easton jail. Bailey was considered a dangerous influence on a plantation, and Thomas Auld decided that he should be returned to his brother Hugh in Baltimore. Bailey got a job in Gardiner's shipyard as an apprentice caulker. In the spring of 1838, he proposed a deal to Hugh Auld: let him be free to hire himself out. He would buy his own tools, pay his own room and board, and would remit three dollars per week. Auld figured that if he said no, Bailey would probably run away, so he agreed. Bailey joined the East Baltimore Mental Improvement Society, an association of free black caulkers who gathered to debate issues and learn more about living on one's own.

Meanwhile, he met Anna Murray, a free black woman whose parents reportedly had been freed before her birth. She was about five years older than he and worked as a domestic servant in Baltimore. Although she was illiterate, she was probably the one who encouraged him to play the violin. This became a favorite pastime, and he especially loved Handel, Haydn, and Mozart.

Anna reportedly raised money for Bailey's escape by selling her featherbed. Since he had worked around the Baltimore docks, he could talk like a sailor, and he decided to escape dressed like a sailor, wearing a red shirt, a flat-topped sailor's hat, and a handkerchief around his neck. On September 3, 1838, he boarded a crowded northbound train, and when the conductor asked for his "free papers," certifying that he wasn't a slave, he presented seaman's papers (used by American sailors when traveling overseas) that he had borrowed from a retired free black sailor. The conductor didn't notice that the papers described somebody else. He eluded several people who recognized him and made his way to New York where he joined Anna and got married. Then they headed for New Bedford, Massachusetts, a shipbuilding boom town where they would be safer from slave hunters and he could probably find a job as a caulker. New Bedford had some twelve thousand people, a black community, and a significant contingent of antislavery Quakers.

Bailey marveled at the prosperity in New Bedford: "I had very strangely supposed, while in slavery, that few of the comforts, and scarcely any of the luxuries, of life were enjoyed at the north, compared with what were enjoyed by slaveholders of the south. I probably came to this conclusion from the fact that northern people owned no slaves. I supposed that they were about upon a level with the non-slaveholding population of the south. I knew *they* were exceedingly poor, and I had been accustomed to regard their poverty as the necessary consequence of their being non-slaveholders. I had somehow imbibed the opinion that, in the absence of slaves, there could be no wealth, and very little refinement. . . .

"Here I found myself surrounded with the strongest proofs of wealth. Lying at the wharves, and riding in the stream, I saw many ships of the finest model, in the best order, and of the largest size. Upon the right and left, I was walled in by granite warehouses of the widest dimensions, stowed to their utmost capacity with the necessaries and comforts of life. Added to this, almost every body seemed to be at work, but noiselessly so, compared with what I had been accustomed to in Baltimore. . . . I heard no deep oaths or horrid curses on the laborer. I saw no whipping of men; but all seemed to go smoothly on. Every man appeared to understand his work, and went at it with a sober yet cheerful earnestness, which betokened the deep interest which he felt in what he was doing, as well as a sense of his own dignity as a man. To me this looked exceedingly strange. From the wharves I strolled around and over the town, gazing with wonder and admiration at the splendid churches, beautiful dwellings, and finely-cultivated gardens; evincing an amount of wealth, comfort, taste, and refinement, such as I had never seen in any part of slaveholding Maryland."

Until the couple found their own lodgings, they stayed with black caterers Mary and Nathan Johnson. Bailey reported that Nathan read "more newspapers, better understood the moral, religious, and political character of the nation—than nine-tenths of the slaveholders in Talbot County, Maryland. Yet Mr. Johnson was a working man. His hands were hardened by toil, and not his alone, but those also of Mrs. Johnson. I found the colored people much more spirited than I had supposed they would be. I found among them a determination to protect each other from the blood-thirsty kidnapper, at all hazards." Nathan suggested that Bailey adopt a distinctive free name—like Douglas, the name of a Scottish lord in Walter Scott's poem *The Lady of the Lake*. He did, adding an extra "s" for individuality.

He landed a steady job at a Quaker-owned whale oil refinery, and he and Anna attended the African Methodist Episcopal Zion church. The minister, Thomas James, was active in the antislavery movement and editor of a twice-monthly publication, called *Rights of Man*. On March 12, 1839, Douglass rose at a church meeting and delivered a speech denouncing proposals that blacks be shipped back to Africa. He wanted to stay in America. His remarks were stirring enough to be mentioned in the *Liberator*, the radical antislavery newspaper that William Lloyd Garrison had published weekly since January

1831. He was invited to speak at an August 10 Nantucket gathering of the Massachusetts Anti-Slavery Society. Garrison and his compatriot Wendell Phillips would be there.

In Nantucket, Garrison recalled, Douglass "came forward to the platform with a hesitancy and embarrassment. After apologizing for his ignorance, and reminding the audience that slavery was a poor school for the human intellect and heart, he proceeded to narrate some of the facts in his own history as a slave, and in the course of his speech gave utterance to many noble thoughts and thrilling reflections. As soon as he had taken his seat, filled with hope and admiration, I rose, and declared that PATRICK HENRY, of revolutionary fame, never made a speech more eloquent in the cause of liberty."

Douglass was asked to become a salaried speaker for the Massachusetts Anti-Slavery Society. He joined Garrison, Phillips, Stephen S. Foster, and Charles Lenox Remond, speaking wherever a couple of dozen people could be gathered. Douglass delivered over a hundred speeches a year in Massachusetts, New Hampshire, and Rhode Island, and he became a valued contributor to the *Liberator.* But he was heckled and beaten a number of times.

His first autobiography, *Narrative of the Life of Frederick Douglass* (June 1845), helped secure his fame. It was written as an antislavery tract, with details of his escape left out to protect others. Published by the Anti-Slavery Office, Boston, the book included a letter by Phillips and a preface by Garrison. There were three European editions, and total sales reportedly reached thirty thousand within five years.

Douglass seemed like a natural to help turn Europeans against the South and isolate it in the international community. In fall 1845, he and Garrison addressed audiences in Scotland, England, and Wales. They dramatized the evils of American slavery, attacked clergymen who supported slavery, called on people to cut off ties with the slaveholding South, and asked for contributions. In Ireland, Douglass was horrified to see worse poverty than anything he had experienced. At a gathering of some twenty thousand people, he shared the lecture platform with six-foot, red-haired Daniel O'Connell, and he was moved when the Irishman dubbed him the "Black O'Connell of the United States." After the failure of the potato crop and the resulting famine-devastated Ireland, Douglass joined the lean, dark-haired, cool-headed free trade agitator Richard Cobden and his stockier compatriot, John Bright, a passionate orator. The three traveled from town to town, urging immediate repeal of the Corn Laws (grain tariffs), so hungry people could buy cheap food. Douglass was welcomed at London's Free-Trade Club, and he cherished his times as "a welcome guest at the house of Mr. Bright in Rochdale . . . treated as a friend and brother among his brothers and sisters."

Meanwhile, he learned that Hugh Auld was determined to have him captured when he returned to the United States. Since he had become a key player in the abolitionist movement, Douglass's friends thought it best to purchase his freedom. Douglass was legally free on December 12, 1845, and sailed for the United States on April 4, 1847.

Douglass played a role in the Underground Railroad. Reportedly, a slave could travel from a border state to Canada within forty-eight hours. Many runaway slaves showed up at Douglass's three-story Rochester, New York, home, and his family took care of them until they could go the seven miles to Charlotte and catch a steamer across Lake Ontario to Canada. Most escapes occurred during the winter when there was less supervision on plantations, and Douglass tirelessly raised money to provide the destitute runaway slaves with warm clothing and food.

Douglass cherished his independence. He believed in pursuing all peaceful methods against slavery, including political action, while Garrison opposed political action. Douglass started his own antislavery newspaper, an idea opposed by Garrison's supporters, who noted that the *Liberator* lost money. On December 3, 1847, with $4,000 raised from a speaking tour, Douglass published the first issue of *North Star.* He was to keep it going for seventeen years.

On July 19 and 20, 1848, he spoke at the Seneca Falls Convention, organized by housewife Elizabeth Cady Stanton to promote women's rights. Douglass was the only man who supported Stanton's proposal for woman suffrage. He agreed that wives should be able to earn their own money; that widows, like widowers, should be able to serve as legal guardians of their children; and that women, like men, should be able to own property, inherit property and administer estates.

On March 6, 1857, Supreme Court Chief Justice Roger B. Taney ruled in the notorious *Dred Scott* case that neither a slave, nor a former slave, nor a descendant of slaves could become a U.S. citizen. Outraged, Douglass was willing to hear any ideas that might help the fight against slavery. In 1858, abolitionist John Brown was at Douglass's Rochester home, working on his idea for stirring a slave insurrection and forming a black state in the Appalachians. Police sought Douglass after Brown's October 16, 1859, raid on the federal arsenal at Harpers Ferry, Virginia, and he fled to England for several months.

After the April 1861 firing on Fort Sumter, which marked the beginning of the Civil War, Lincoln made clear this was a struggle to preserve the Union, not abolish slavery. Lincoln's policy was that runaway slaves must be returned to their masters. Douglass nevertheless demanded "the unrestricted and complete Emancipation of every slave in the United States whether claimed by loyal or disloyal masters." On January 1, 1863, Lincoln issued the Emancipation Proclamation saying that slaves were liberated in rebellious states, which he obviously didn't control. The proclamation didn't free slaves in the North, but it did make abolition a war aim. While Douglass certainly admired

Lincoln, he was mindful of all the ways Lincoln was willing to compromise with slavery.

After slavery was abolished, Douglass set his sights on getting blacks the vote so they could establish a political presence (blacks were denied the vote in Connecticut, New Jersey, Pennsylvania, and several western states), but it became politically impossible to push for giving both blacks and women the vote at the same time. Immediately after the March 30, 1870, adoption of the Fifteenth Amendment, granting blacks the right to vote, Douglass supported the campaign for woman suffrage.

Douglass hitched himself to the Republican party during the long sunset of his career, but his political connections did little good. Terrorist groups like the Pale Faces, Knights of the White Camelia, and the Ku Klux Klan murdered blacks and burned black homes, schools, and churches, and neither state nor federal governments did much.

Douglass encouraged self-help. He encouraged black parents, "Educate your sons and daughters, send them to school. . . . Wherever a man may be thrown by misfortune, if he have in his hands a useful trade, he is useful to his fellow-men, and will be esteemed accordingly."

In 1881, he published *The Life and Times of Frederick Douglass*, which provided more details about his experience as a slave, revealed (for the first time) how he escaped, and discussed subsequent struggles. An expanded edition appeared eleven years later.

Douglass's wife, Anna, died on August 4, 1882. When he married a white abolitionist, Helen Pitts, both blacks and whites were horrified. Arsonists torched his beloved Rochester home, and the couple moved to a twenty-room white frame house on twenty-three acres across the Anacostia River from Washington, D.C. The place had once been owned by Robert E. Lee. Called Cedar Hill, it included a library, and a music room where Douglass could play his violin.

On February 20, 1895, he attended a Washington, D.C., rally for women's rights. When he finished dinner that night, he rose from his chair, then collapsed and died. There was a private funeral service at his home, and the casket was moved to the Metropolitan African Methodist Episcopal Church, where tremendous crowds paid their respects. After another service at Rochester's Central Church, he was buried in Mount Home Cemetery near his first wife and daughter.

More than anyone else, Douglass put a human face on the horrors of American slavery. He helped convince millions that it must be abolished, courageously spoke out against the subversion of civil rights, and expressed generous sympathy for all who were oppressed. He urged people to help themselves and fulfill their destiny and longed for the day when men and women, blacks and whites, and everyone else could live in peace.

STEADFAST DEVOTION

ABIGAIL ADAMS REPORTEDLY cautioned her husband, John Adams, before he signed the Declaration of Independence: "If particular care and attention is not paid to the Ladies, we are determined to foment a Rebellion, and we will not hold ourselves bound by any Laws in which we have no voice, or Representation." For decades, little happened.

Then Elizabeth Cady Stanton launched the movement for women's rights and helped establish four organizations to promote it. She set the agenda: equal property rights, including the right to make and terminate contracts, the right to hold property, and the right to inherit property; the right to share in the custody of children; and woman suffrage, to help secure these rights.

Impressed with her determination, the Quaker abolitionist Lucretia Mott told Stanton, "Thou art so wedded to this cause that thou must expect to act as a pioneer in the work." Abolitionist editor William Lloyd Garrison declared, "Mrs. Stanton is a fearless woman and goes for women's rights with all her soul." Abolitionist orator Frederick Douglass recalled how Stanton, "by that logic of which she is master, successfully endeavored to convince me of the wisdom and truth of the then new gospel of woman's rights."

Susan B. Anthony, whom Stanton had converted to the cause of women's rights, wrote, "Always I have felt that I must have Mrs. Stanton's opinion of things before I knew where I stood myself." Stanton worked with Anthony for more than a half-century in one of the greatest partnerships in the history of liberty. Anthony became the principal organizer for women's rights, while Stanton expressed the ideology for women's rights, developed the strategy, and wrote many of Anthony's speeches, proclamations, and eulogies. Again and again, Anthony pleaded for material: "Mrs. Stanton . . . I beg you . . . set yourself about the work. . . . Don't say No, nor don't delay it a moment; for I must have it all done and almost commited to memory. . . . Now will you load my gun, leaving me to pull the trigger and let fly the powder and ball?"

Even Wendell Phillips, the greatest abolitionist orator, appreciated help from Stanton's fiery pen. "If you'll forgive and forget," he wrote her, "and ask me to breakfast, dinner, or tea, I will snap my fingers at audiences and eat as many of your good things as I did before, and steal for speeches as many of your good things that can't be eaten."

Stanton learned from many of the greatest thinkers on liberty. She read the writings of Mary Wollstonecraft, who first applied natural rights principles to women; she met John Bright, who crusaded for free trade, peace, and a broader suffrage; and John Greenleaf Whittier, the most celebrated poet of the abolitionist movement. She praised Herbert Spencer, the champion of laissez-faire, for his "grand philosophy of life." She read books by moralist Leo Tolstoy and enjoyed individualist Mark Twain "whose fun is only equaled by his morals." She wrote to philosopher John Stuart Mill, author of *The Subjection of Women*, "I lay the book down with a peace and joy I never felt before."

This is how biographer Elizabeth Griffith characterized her in the 1870s, when she was a popular lecturer: "Mrs. Stanton was skilled at pleasing crowds. Her platform style was engaging, her voice was low and soothing, her manner was gracious and feminine. One observer recalled that she was a 'powerful, uplifting' speaker, whose natural wit made her audiences laugh. Despite the gravity of her subject matter, the San Francisco *Chronicle* found Mrs. Stanton simply 'jolly.' Another onlooker described her as 'plump as a partridge.' With her rosy complexion, 'unstuffy' white hair, and generous figure, 'she would anywhere be taken for the mother of a governor or a president,' wrote one male admirer. Stanton's appearance began to be compared to that of Queen Victoria or George Washington's mother. She was perceived as maternal, dignified, and eminently respectable."

Scholar Ellen Carol DuBois marveled that Stanton lived "in nearly perfect health, mental as well as physical. She was brilliant and learned, and she was also sensuous, defending her own weight (175 pounds in 1860, over 240 when she was an old woman), her propensity to take frequent naps, and the sexuality of all women when none of these things was considered respectable. She had a powerful wit that she used to demolish her enemies and keep her friends at a respectful distance. Above all, she was committed to unearthing and understanding the long history of women's oppression, and to leading women to revolt against it. Her strength of character, intelligence, and vitality were so great, her anger at the oppression of women so profound, that coming to know her now . . . is still as inspiring an experience as it must have been when she was in her prime."

ELIZABETH CADY WAS born on November 12, 1815, in Johnstown, New York. She was the seventh child and second daughter of Margaret Livingston who had eleven children altogether. Elizabeth's father, Daniel Cady, was a self-made man who apprenticed as a shoemaker and took up law. Cady longed for a son and was depressed by the deaths of all five boys, as well as one of his daughters. Elizabeth was anguished when her father said, "I wish you were a boy!'"

She attended the Troy, New York, Seminary for women run by Emma Willard who embraced the vision of natural rights and believed that education must help form good character, essential for the advancement of women. Willard taught classical literature, science, and philosophy.

In October 1839, Elizabeth met Henry Stanton who recruited members and raised money for the American Anti-Slavery Society. "He was," noted biographer Griffith, "handsome, intelligent, engaging, eloquent, dominant, masculine, demanding, charming, and a good dancer. . . . And he was either not aware of or not alarmed by her strengths." They were married in Johnstown on May 1, 1840.

The Stantons sailed to London for the World Anti-Slavery Convention. They met several women from Philadelphia, notably the Quaker Lucretia Mott, who in 1833 had established the Philadelphia Female Anti-Slavery Society and, four years later, the Anti-Slavery Convention of American Women. "Mrs. Mott," recalled Stanton, "was to me an entire new revelation of womanhood. I sought every opportunity to be at her side, and continually plied her with questions. . . . She told me . . . of Mary Wollstonecraft, her social theories, and her demands of equality for women."

The London convention began amid controversy on June 12, 1840 at Freemason's Hall, Great Queen Street. Some clergymen contended that women shouldn't be present. There was a compromise: women could participate, but they had to sit up in the gallery. *Liberator* editor William Lloyd Garrison joined the women, and Stanton and Mott resolved that when they returned to America, they would do something. Thus, the women's rights movement was born.

Stanton was inspired by Daniel O'Connell. "He paid a beautiful tribute to woman," she recalled. "One could almost tell what he said from the play of his expressive features, his wonderful gestures, and the pose of his whole body." The Irish Liberator told Stanton that in her quest for women's rights she must aim high, and she did.

In June 1847, the Stantons moved into a house on 32 Washington Street, Seneca Falls, New York. The following year, Elizabeth Cady Stanton was invited to visit Lucretia Mott and three Quaker friends in Waterloo, about six miles north of Seneca Falls. They resolved to hold a meeting about women's rights on July 19 and 20, 1848.

They needed some kind of statement to focus their efforts. Stanton drafted *A Declaration of Rights and Sentiments*, which embraced the natural rights philosophy of the Declaration of Independence. She wrote, in part, "Resolved, That all laws which prevent woman from occupying such a station in society as her conscience shall dictate, or which place her in a position inferior to that of man, are contrary to the great precept of nature, and therefore of no force or authority." She included a suffrage clause: "Resolved, That it is the duty of the women of this country to secure themselves their sacred right to the elective franchise." She declared, "The right is ours. Have it we must. Use it we will." Frederick Douglass affirmed that "the power to choose rulers and make laws was the right by which all others could be secured." On July 19, *The Declaration of Rights and Sentiments* was signed by fifty-eight women and thirty-two men.

In March 1851, Stanton met Susan Brownell Anthony who was staying with Amelia Bloomer (the designer of loose trousers that made it far easier for women to work in than the hoop skirts in style then). "How well I remember the day!" Stanton wrote later. "There she stood, with her good earnest face and genial smile, dressed in gray delaine, hat and all the same color, relieved with pale blue ribbons, the perfection of neatness and sobriety. I liked her thoroughly."

Anthony was born on February 15, 1820, the daughter of Daniel Anthony, an Adams, Massachusetts, Quaker cotton mill entrepreneur and abolitionist. His marriage to the Baptist Lucy Read scandalized the Quaker community. When his business was wiped out during the Panic of 1837, he started farming near Rochester, and Susan became a school teacher. The farm was a local center of abolitionist activity, and Frederick Douglass was among the many visitors. Anthony was active in the Daughters of Temperance and left the organization in 1852 to help form the New York State Temperance Society. Temperance was a big issue because there was a lot of drunkenness. Since a husband held a wife's assets in his name, she had no recourse if he squandered everything. Discouraging alcohol consumption appeared to be a good way to help women. Anthony was a single woman with time to help organize the women's movement.

A partnership began to blossom. At her dining room table, Stanton developed strategy and wrote speeches, and she offered Anthony advice about how to improve her delivery and handle hecklers. "Susan presented a solid factual argument, dazzling and stimulating to the mind," noted biographer Rheta Childe Dorr, "but sometimes over the heads of people who listened only with their emotions." Anthony delivered Stanton's speeches, gathered petition signatures, arranged meetings, and raised money.

Stanton often did more than write speeches. In February 1854, she addressed the New York State Senate, declaring that a marriage contract should be treated like any other contract, with mutual privileges and obligations. Women, she insisted, should be able to own property, since many men lost their wives' assets as well as their own. William Lloyd Garrison had her speak at an American Anti-Slavery gathering, and she wrote articles for Horace Greeley's *New York Tribune*.

The Civil War brought a crisis for the women's movement. Stanton welcomed the prospect of crushing slavery, and she accepted setting aside women's issues for the duration of the war, but after the war, many leading abolitionists feared demands for woman suffrage would undermine efforts to secure fundamental rights for former slaves. Scholar Ellen Carol DuBois observed, "Black suffrage helped to destroy whatever doubts remained among feminists that the suffrage was the key to the legal position of women as well."

Stanton and her husband drifted apart, and she became more active in the women's rights movement. She was elected first vice president of the American Equal Rights Association. Stanton and Anthony campaigned for two Kansas ballot initiatives about voting. She recalled, "We spoke in log cabins, in depots, unfinished school houses, churches, hotels, barns, and in the open air." Stanton began editing the weekly *Revolution*, but it lost money, and Anthony paid the debt. Stanton formed the Woman Suffrage Association of America.

In May 1869, Stanton was elected president of the National Woman Suffrage Association, which addressed a wide range of women's issues. Lucy Stone established the rival American Woman Suffrage Association, drawing on New England women who were abolitionists first and feminists second. Stone was a respectable New Englander and viewed the West as uncivilized. Stanton enjoyed campaigning out West where a lot of people accepted women as individuals.

Stanton soon had enough of organizational battles and became a professional lecturer. For about a decade during the 1870s, she was in demand as a speaker and a celebrity. Starting every January, she went on a five-month lecture tour. She spent summers with her children, and once they were off to school again, she returned to the lecture circuit for another three months.

On November 5, 1872, sixteen Rochester women, including Anthony, voted, risking a large fine and three years in jail. Anthony had persuaded officials to register her by reading from the Fourteenth Amendment (ratified in 1868) and the Fifteenth Amendment (ratified in 1870), which supposedly protected the right to vote. Officials subsequently decided her vote was illegal, and on November 18 Anthony was arrested her at home. She refused to pay the fine, but the judge closed the case without imprisoning her, avoiding further controversy.

With women's rights going nowhere in the courts, the American Woman Suffrage Association focused on state legislatures, and the National Woman Suffrage Association launched a campaign for a woman suffrage constitutional amendment. In 1878, California Senator A. A. Sargent introduced this: "The right of citizens of the United States to vote shall not be denied or abridged by the United States or by any state on account of sex." Proposed again and again during the next four decades, it was later referred to as the Anthony amendment.

Inspired by Lucretia Mott, who died in November 1880, Elizabeth Cady Stanton began to write a history of women suffrage. She worked with Anthony and Matilda Joslyn Gage, a *Revolution* contributor, to gather documents. Stanton did most of the writing; Anthony did most of the research and published the work. The three volumes, published between 1881 and 1886, were offered free to libraries, but many, including Harvard, declined to accept them.

In 1890, leading suffragists decided to heal the split in the movement, and the National Woman Suffrage Association merged with the American Woman Suffrage Association, thereafter becoming known as the National-American. Stanton was elected the first president. Her retirement in 1892 marked the end of her career as an organizational leader.

Stanton raised the standard of self reliance in her farewell speech, "The Solitude of Self," delivered at the 1892 convention. "Nothing strengthens the judgment and quickens the conscience like individual responsibility," she said. "Nothing adds such dignity to character as the recognition of one's self-sovereignty . . . a place earned by personal merit, not an artificial attainment by inheritance, wealth, family and position. Conceding, then, that the responsibilities of life rest equally on man and woman, that their destiny is the same, they need the same preparation for time and eternity . . . each soul must depend wholly on itself." She delivered this speech again before the House Committee on the Judiciary and the Senate Committee on Woman Suffrage. Some ten thousand copies of the speech were distributed.

Increasingly, because of her hefty weight and her frailty, Stanton was confined to the eight-room penthouse apartment in New York City that she shared with her daughter Margaret and her son Robert. But Anthony continued asking her to write speeches, letters, resolutions and eulogies.

Stanton's eightieth birthday was celebrated at the Metropolitan Opera. Her name was spelled out in a banner of carnations, and she sat in a chair surrounded by roses. She was too frail to do more than salute "the great idea I represent—the enfranchisement of women."

Stanton led a committee of seven scholars who worked on *The Woman's Bible.* "When, in the early part of the Nineteenth century," she explained, "women began to protest against their civil and political degradation, they were referred to the Bible for an answer. When they protested against their unequal position in the church, they were referred to the Bible." *The Woman's Bible* appeared in 1895; it was reprinted seven times within six months, and there were several translations. It provoked so much anger that the National-American debated a motion to censure their first president, but Anthony offered a stalwart defense.

Stanton produced her autobiography, *Eighty Years and More* (1898), to affirm her reputation as an intelligent, kindly, and self-reliant champion of women's rights. It's a remarkable work, although some details of her life conflict with earlier accounts. The autobiography, observed Ann D. Gordon, "gives us a very strong individual whose sense of her power and leadership rarely falters. Although internally the story reminds readers time and again that the author is not yet free and awaits her equality, it avoids the suggestion that in their lack of freedom women are victims. . . . it depicts enormous change wrought by women."

Meanwhile, the women's movement had stalled. Wyoming, the first U.S. territory with woman suffrage, had become the first state with woman suffrage on March 28, 1890, but the only other states to embrace suffrage were Colorado (1893), Idaho (1896), and Utah (1896). No eastern states showed any interest. Since 1893, neither the U.S. Senate nor the House of Representatives had acted on the proposed suffrage amendment.

In June 1902, Anthony visited Stanton, whose health was failing. Anthony embraced her and cried, "Shall I see you again?" Stanton replied, "Oh yes, if not here, then in the hereafter, if there is one, and if there isn't we shall never know it." Anthony wrote her last and most poignant letter to Stanton, reminiscing that "in age as in all else I follow you closely. It is fifty-one years since first we met and we have been busy through every one of them, stirring up the world to recognize the rights of women. . . . We little dreamed when we began this contest, optimistic with the hope and buoyancy of youth, that half a century later we would be compelled to leave the finish of the battle to another generation of women. But our hearts are filled with joy to know that they enter upon this task equipped with a college education, with business experience, with the fully admitted right to speak in public—all of which were denied to women fifty years ago. They have practically one point to gain—the suffrage; we had all. These strong, courageous, capable young women will take our place and complete our work. There is an army of them where we were but a handful. Ancient prejudice has become so softened, public sentiment so liberalized and women have so thoroughly demonstrated their ability as to leave not a shadow of doubt that they will carry our cause to victory."

Elizabeth Cady Stanton died on October 26, 1902, at age eighty-six, with all six of her surviving children with her. There was a private memorial service in her New York City apartment. The table on which she had written the Seneca Falls *Declaration of Rights and Sentiments* was by her casket, bearing a set of *The History of Woman Suffrage*. Phebe Hanaford, who had contributed to *The Woman's Bible*, conducted a burial service at Woodlawn Cemetery.

Anthony carried on for about three more years. In January 1906, she got a cold, which turned into pneumonia. Anna H. Shaw, president of the National-American, stayed with her and recalled: "On the last afternoon of her life, when she had lain quiet for hours, she suddenly began to utter the names of the women who had worked with her, as if in a final roll call." Anthony died at her Rochester home, 17 Madison Street, on Tuesday, March 13, 1906, at age eighty-six. She wore a jeweled pin of an American flag with four diamond stars, the only stars, for the suffrage states. An estimated ten thousand people paid their respects at Rochester's Central Presbyterian Church. She left all her assets to the National-American.

The women's movement regained momentum in 1910 when suffragists gathered 404,000 signatures on their petitions, and the state of Washington enacted woman suffrage. The following year, California granted woman suffrage. The House of Representatives supported the suffrage amendment on January 10, 1918, and on June 4, 1919, the Senate approved it. On August 26, 1920, Tennessee was the thirty-sixth state to ratify; the suffrage amendment became the Nineteenth Amendment, and 26 million American women could vote. The Supreme Court upheld the Nineteenth Amendment in February 1922.

It had been an astonishing journey. In fifty-two years, recalled Carrie Chapman Catt, suffragists conducted "fifty-six campaigns of referenda to male voters; 480 campaigns to get Legislatures to submit suffrage amendments to voters; 47 campaigns to get State constitutional conventions to write woman suffrage into state constitutions; 277 campaigns to get State party conventions to include woman suffrage planks; 30 campaigns to get presidential party conventions to adopt woman suffrage planks in party platforms, and 19 campaigns with 19 successive Congresses."

Anthony was considered the greatest heroine for woman suffrage, and a number of biographies appeared. The U.S. Mint paid tribute to Anthony alone when it issued a new dollar coin in 1979. But since then, historians have taken another look at Stanton. Little, Brown published *Elizabeth Cady Stanton: A Radical for Woman's Rights* by Lois Banner (1980). Oxford University Press issued Elizabeth Griffith's *In Her Own Right: The Life of Elizabeth Cady Stanton* in 1984. Ellen Carol DuBois emphasized the great partnership in *The Elizabeth Cady Stanton–Susan B. Anthony Reader* (1981). At Rutgers University, scholars began a search of archives, newspapers and private collections for material on Stanton and Anthony. "Documents were located and copied in two hundred libraries and archives in the United States, Canada, New Zealand, England, the Netherlands, France, and Germany and in nearly seven hundred different newspapers and periodicals," reported Ann D. Gordon. The first volume appeared in 1997.

Elizabeth Cady Stanton was right to stay focused on the ultimate issue, human liberty, and not just the vote. She displayed bold vision when she insisted that natural rights principles, expressed in the Declaration of Independence, are a key to liberating people everywhere. She understood the lifeblood of self-ownership, private property, freedom of contract, and freedom of movement. She gave her heart and soul for women's rights. Nobody had a more eloquent pen. She was an awesome champion.

COLOSSAL COURAGE

❧

How CAN A SINGLE individual fight tyranny? What can be done for liberty against overwhelming odds? There are few other stories as stirring as that of Raoul Wallenberg who defied the evil forces of Adolf Hitler and Joseph Stalin, two of history's worst mass murderers, and confronted racists, torturers, assassins, and even Hitler's chief executioner, Adolf Eichmann, while saving almost 100,000 lives. More astounding, he saved lives inside enemy territory, since escape was impossible. He was armed only with a pistol, which he never used.

Working in Nazi-controlled Hungary, Wallenberg liberated thousands of Jews from boxcars bound for the gas chambers. He pulled Jews out of the death marches and saved Jews from being shot and dumped into the Danube. He single-handedly thwarted Nazi plans to massacre seventy thousand Jews remaining in the Budapest central ghetto. After the Red Army captured Budapest, Wallenberg was taken away by Stalin's NKVD secret police. Apparently they tortured him and tried to turn him into a Soviet spy, but he remained defiant.

Wallenberg, the greatest libertarian hero of the twentieth century, vanished into the gulag. For people around the world, he is the angel of rescue, and the mere mention of his name can bring tears.

Wallenberg certainly didn't look like the stuff that heroes are made of. He was medium height with brown eyes, a large nose, a small chin, and receding curly brown hair. Tibor Baranski, an associate, described Wallenberg as "a thin man, rather shy and virtually fearless. He dressed elegantly and was always clean-shaven." He looks like an ordinary person on the 1998 commemorative stamp issued by the U.S. Postal Service.

Björn Burckhardt, who had met Wallenberg in South Africa, described him this way: "Raoul did not do things in a normal manner. His way of thinking was so winding and involuted. But his intellect impressed everyone. And he could outtalk anyone. Perhaps his greatest asset was his charm, which influenced people to respect him." Wallenberg, recalled Swedish diplomat Per Anger, "was not a superman type. We met in Stockholm some years before he came on his mission to Budapest in 1944, and we became very good friends. . . . He spoke with a soft voice and sometimes looked like a dreamer. At heart he was no doubt a great idealist and a warm human being. It did not take long, however, till you discovered that he had a remarkable inner strength, a core of fighting spirit. Furthermore, he was a clever negotiator and organizer, unconventional and extraordinarily inventive. I became convinced that no one was better qualified for the assignment to Budapest than Raoul."

RAOUL GUSTAF WALLENBERG was born on August 4, 1912, in his maternal grandparents' summer home on Kapptsta, an island near Stockholm. He descended from a long line of Lutheran entrepreneurs who built banks, factories, ships, and railroads—some fifty businesses altogether. His father, Raoul Wallenberg, Sr., a twenty-three-year-old naval officer, died of abdominal cancer three months before he was born. His mother, Maj Wising, was the great-granddaughter of a German Jewish jeweler. Raoul's paternal grandfather, Gustaf Wallenberg, Swedish ambassador to Turkey, became his mentor. Gustaf was an individualist, an entrepreneur, and a free trader who believed people should be bound together by peaceful commercial relations rather than military alliances.

When Raoul was eleven, Gustaf arranged for him to broaden his vision by spending summers in France and Germany, and he learned those languages as well as English. To understand America, he enrolled at the University of Michigan (avoiding elitist schools), where he earned an architecture degree in 1935. He became an intern with a Dutch business in Haifa, Palestine, where he heard European refugees tell horrifying stories of Nazi barbarism.

Wallenberg heard about a job with Kalman Lauer, a short, stout Hungarian Jew whose Stockholm-based company, Mellaneuropeiska Handelsaktiebolaget (Middle European Trading Company, or Meropa as it was called), mainly shipped grain, chickens, and goose liver pâté from Hungary to Sweden. Since Hungary had allied itself with Hitler in 1941, Lauer couldn't safely travel through Europe; he needed a gentile fluent in the major European languages and adept at negotiation. Wallenberg went to work. He became skilled at dealing with Nazis and got to know the Budapest Jewish community.

On January 20, 1942, in a villa at Wannsee, a town outside Berlin, Adolf Hitler met with high-ranking officers of the SS, his elite secret police. Among those present were General Reinhard Heydrich and SS Lieutenant Colonel Adolf Eichmann. They agreed it wasn't practical to rid Europe of Jews through emigration; the Jews had to be deported east and exterminated. In his conference notes, Eichmann described this as "the final solution." The killing agent would be Zyklon B, a compound of hydrogen and cyanide developed to kill rodents. Orders went out to build gigantic gas chambers.

By 1944, the only European Jewish community that hadn't been eliminated was in Hungary, an Axis power that nevertheless retained some independence from Germany. Following German losses on the eastern front, Hungarian diplomats started sounding out the Allies for an armistice. This would have cut off Germany from its Axis allies, Rumania and Bulgaria—and from vital oil supplies—so Hitler ordered his soldiers to occupy Hungary on March 19. Among the arrivals was Eichmann who came with a mile-long column of his special forces. He had a sharp nose, thin lips, and a contorted mouth; his black SS uniform had a death's head insignia on the epaulets. Eichmann headed the Gestapo's Section IV B4 (Jewish affairs) and organized the extermination of Jews in Germany, Austria, and Czechoslovakia. It was only because of Nazi infighting that he didn't exterminate Jews in Poland too. He had developed a four-step killing process: mark Jews by requiring them to wear a yellow Star of David patch on their outer garments; collect Jews from their scattered residences, commonly in the middle of the night; isolate Jews in ghettos; and deport them to the death camps.

Eichmann didn't want Jews to panic and disrupt his plans before he was ready, so he ordered leading members of the Budapest Jewish community to form a "Jewish Council." He told them, "I will visit your museum soon, because I am interested in Jewish cultural affairs. You can trust me and talk freely to me—as you see, I am quite frank with you. If the Jews behave quietly and work, you will be able to keep all of your community institutions."

On May 15, death trains began rolling to Auschwitz. There were as many as five trains a day, each with about ten thousand Jews. By June 13, 147 trains had taken 437,000 Jews. "It went like a dream," Eichmann bragged.

At last, the Allies stirred. The American Air Force and Britain's Royal Air Force bombed Budapest, but this didn't work. It was decided that the United States would support an effort to save some Jews by working within Hungary. Funding would be provided through the War Refugee Board whose representative in Sweden, Iver Olsen, was assigned the task of finding somebody from a neutral country. This person had to be a gentile, fluent in European languages, capable of dealing successfully with the Nazis and unimaginably courageous. Olsen heard thirty-one-year-old Wallenberg's name mentioned in the elevator of the eight-story building on Strandvagen Street where American diplomatic offices were located. He heard it from Kálmán Lauer whose import-export company's offices were in the same building. Olsen met Wallenberg for dinner at Saltsjobaden, a summer resort built by grandfather Gustaf.

Wallenberg spelled out his terms. He must have diplomatic status, and so he was named second secretary of the Swedish legation. He could send his own messages by diplomatic courier. If funds provided by the U.S. War Refugee Board and the American-Jewish Joint Distribution Committee were inadequate, he could raise funds by other means. He could contact anyone, including the ruler of the country and the anti-Nazi underground. He could use whatever means he considered necessary, including bribery. He could provide asylum to persecuted people with Swedish documents.

On July 6, 1944, Wallenberg flew from Stockholm to Berlin, and two days later was on a train for Budapest. His train probably passed the twenty-nine-boxcar train carrying the last of Hungary's rural Jews to Auschwitz. Eichmann boasted that it was "a deportation surpassing every preceding deportation in magnitude."

According to Nazi statistics, about 230,000 Jews were left in Budapest. Eichmann relished the prospect of shipping them out in a few days, but Hungary's seventy-five-year-old regent Miklos Horthy still retained nominal independence from Germany, and he suspended the deportations. Although he was certainly anti-Semitic (he had approved laws persecuting Jews), he feared his own execution as a war criminal by the Russians who were advancing in the East, or the Americans and English, who had landed in Normandy.

Wallenberg arrived in Budapest on July 9. The city had representatives from five neutral nations—Portugal, Spain, Switzerland, Turkey, and Sweden—and representatives from the International Red Cross and the pope. Some had already made limited efforts to save Jews. Wallenberg spent a couple of weeks finding recruits and building an organization. Budapest Jews were so demoralized, and Wallenberg looked so unfit for the task, with his fresh face and clean-cut dark blue suit, that he had considerable difficulty persuading people they could help themselves.

Wallenberg recognized there were several ways he could appeal to those in power. First, Horthy's puppet regime wanted the legitimacy that comes with international acceptance. Second, Swedish representatives handled Hungarian and German business in several countries. Third, many in the puppet regime feared possible execution by the Allies after the war. Finally, there were many others whose cooperation could be bought with food or cash bribes.

Wallenberg took immediate steps to make his mission look impressive. He designed a *Schutz-Pass* certificate with official-looking triple crown of the Royal Swedish government. He had it printed in Sweden's colors, yellow, and blue, and embellished it with seals, stamps, and signatures. These passes suggested the holder had a connection to Sweden and intended to leave Hungary for Sweden. Until that could happen, the holder was under the protection of the Royal Swedish Legation. Although these had no standing in international law, Wallenberg had thousands produced, and they worked. One of Wallenberg's drivers noted that he "understood the German mentality. He knew that Germans reacted to formal documents and authority." It's likely, too, that the Nazis tolerated the passes as long as they affected a minority of the Jews. The Nazis probably figured they could disregard the passes whenever they wished, but Wallenberg's strategy was delay. With the Allies winning the war, he believed that the longer people could be maintained under Swedish protection, the more survivors there would be.

But Jews couldn't leave Budapest, and their situation became ever more desperate. Wallenberg stockpiled food, clothing, and medicine. He built a staff of around four hundred people, with shifts working around the clock, and they established nurseries, food distribution points, and hospitals that served two hundred patients at a time. He tried to get as many Jews as possible under international protection. He needed housing, which meant dealing with Eichmann who controlled properties taken from Jews. Eichmann spent evenings at Budapest's mirror-lined Arizona nightclub, and Wallenberg observed him closely there—twice bribing headwaiters to seat him at a table next to Eichmann who proposed a get-acquainted discussion. Wallenberg explained he wanted about forty Budapest buildings for his operations, and he offered the equivalent of $200,000 in Swedish kroner. Eichmann was willing to talk because he figured he would get the Jews wherever they lived. Wallenberg rented thirty-two Budapest buildings, each displaying the Swedish flag. They became the core of the "international ghetto," which eventually accommodated some fifty-thousand Jews. Usually Jews were moved in under the cover of night, so they would be less vulnerable to attack, and the government wouldn't be aware how many Jews were sheltered

Wallenberg then hit on a brazen strategy that saved more and more Jews from the death trains. As one of his drivers explained: "Raoul usually had with him a book with names of passport holders. Sometimes the book had all blank pages. When he arrived at the train, he then made up Jewish names and began calling out. Three or four usually had passports. For those who didn't, I stood behind Raoul with another fifty or more unfilled passports. It only took me ten seconds to write in their names. We handed them out calmly and said, 'Oh, I'm terribly sorry you couldn't get to the legation to pick it up. Here it is. We brought it to you.' The passport holder showed it to the SS and was free."

On October 15, Horthy announced that his government was negotiating with the Russians for an armistice, news that triggered a Nazi coup. Horthy was out, and fanatical Arrow Cross (Hungarian fascist party) head Otto Skorzeny was in command. When he ordered that the deportations of Jews be resumed, Wallenberg's whole campaign was in jeopardy.

"I was forced out of one of the Swedish safe houses and taken to a brick factory yard," Ferenc Friedman remembered. "It would be only minutes before we boarded the death trains. Suddenly two cars drove up. There was Wallenberg in the first one, with Hungarian officials and German officers in the second car. He jumped out, shouting that all those with Swedish papers were under his protection. I was one of 150 saved that day. None of the others ever came back."

Wallenberg's driver Sandor Ardai told biographer Harvey Rosenfeld, "We had come to a station where a train full of Jews was on the point of leaving for Germany and the death camps. The officer of the guard did not want to let us enter. Raoul Wallenberg then climbed up on the roof of the train and handed in many protective passports through the windows. The Arrow Cross men fired their guns and cried to him to go away, but he continued calmly to hand out passports to the hands which reached for them. But I believe that the men with the guns were impressed by his courage and on purpose aimed above him. Afterwards, he managed to get all Jews with passports out from the train."

In early November, Nyilas, as Arrow Cross goons were called, held several hundred Jews at Dohany Synagogue. Joseph Kovacs recalled that "on November 4, Wallenberg burst into the temple and stood himself in front of the altar and made this announcement: 'All those who have Swedish protective passes should stand up.' That same night a few hundred Jews were freed, and they returned to their houses under the protection of Hungarian policemen.

"People often ask me," Kovacs continued, " 'Why did Raoul Wallenberg succeed?' The way I saw it, Raoul Wallenberg was forceful, determined, and never hesitated in saying what he had to say and doing what he had to do."

Jonny Moser, one of Wallenberg's assistants, "remembered when we were told . . . that 800 Jews were to be transported away. The deportations had started on foot to Mauthausen. Wallenberg caught up with them at the frontier. 'Who of you has a Swedish protective passport? Raise your hand!' he cried. On his order I ran between the columns and told the people to raise their hand, whether they had a passport or not. He then took command of all who had raised their hand, and his attitude was such that nobody of the guards opposed it, so extraordinary was the convincing force of his attitude."

Tibor Vayda, another assistant, recalled: Every morning about six or seven of us met with Wallenberg and then left to aid those Jews who had trouble at the hands of the SS or Nyilas. One day at the end of November, I left at 5 A.M., accompanied by a fellow worker. We headed for a trouble spot on Jokai Street. Wallenberg told us he would be there before 8 A.M. We waited and waited, and there was still no Wallenberg. Some three hundred people were being lined up for deportation to Jozefvaros. We were ready to leave. Frankly, we were afraid that we might be in trouble, to. Out of nowhere came a black car with Wallenberg, at one minute to eight."

But Eichmann faced serious obstacles. Since the Red Army was advancing from the east and south, roads to the Polish death camps were blocked. The German military needed all available railroad capacity for moving war material. The only way out of Hungary was to Austria, so Eichmann decided Jews would walk; thus began the death march to Hegyeshalom, 125 miles away, near the Austrian border. Between mid-November and mid-December, some 40,000 Jews were ordered to march in frigid weather. A quarter of them died.

Often Eichmann himself was at Hegyeshalom. According to Per Anger, "The persecuted Jews' only hope was Wallenberg. Like a rescuing angel he often appeared at the very last moment. Just when a deportation was about to start—some people were actually also sent by train—he used to arrive at the station with a written—false or genuine—permission to separate and set free all Jews with Swedish protection passports. If his protégés had already been brought out of the city, he hurried after them and conducted back as many as he could on hastily procured trucks. His movable and always accompanying chancellery manufactured all kinds of identification and protection documents on an endless scale. Uncountable were those Jews who during the march toward Vienna had given up all hope, when suddenly they received from one of Wallenberg's 'flying squadrons' a Swedish protection document, like their ancestors once upon a time during their long journey were rescued by manna from Heaven."

Susan Tabor remembered: "My mother, my husband, and I had been two nights without food. Then we heard words, human words, the first we had heard in what seemed like an eternity. It was Raoul Wallenberg. He gave us that needed sense that we were still human beings. We had been among thousands taken to stay at a brick factory outside Budapest. We were without food, without water, without sanitation facilities. Wallenberg told us he would try and return with safety passes. He also said that he would try to get medical attention and sanitary facilities. And true to his word, soon afterward some doctors and nurses came from the Jewish hospital. But what stands out most about Raoul Wallenberg is that he came himself. He talked to us, and, most important, he showed that there was a human being who cared about us."

Wallenberg even tried to influence Eichmann. Shortly before Christmas, he invited the Nazi to dinner. "The war is over," Wallenberg told Eichmann. "Why don't you go while you still can and let the living live?" Eichmann replied, "I have my job to do." Swedish diplomat Lars Berg reported that "Wallenberg fearlessly tore Nazi doctrines to shreds and predicted that Nazism and its leaders would meet a speedy and complete destruction. I must say that these were rather unusual, caustic words from a Swede who was far away from his country and totally at the mercy of the powerful German antagonist Eichmann and his henchmen."

Stunned by Wallenberg's bold attack, Eichmann reportedly replied: "I admit that you are right, Mr. Wallenberg. I actually never believed in Nazism as such, but it has given me power and wealth. I know this pleasant life will soon be over. My planes will no longer bring me women and wines from Paris nor any other delicacies from the Orient. My horses, my dogs, my palace here in Budapest will soon be taken over by the Russians, and I myself, an SS officer, will be shot on the spot. But for me there is no rescue any more. If I obey my orders from Berlin and exercise my power ruthlessly enough here in Budapest, I shall be able to prolong my days of grace." Eichmann added, "I warn you, Herr Legationsekretar. I shall do my very utmost to defeat you. And your Swedish diplomatic passport will not help you. . . . Even a neutral diplomat might meet with accidents." Several days later, a big German truck smashed into Wallenberg's car. Wallenberg wasn't inside, and Eichmann vowed, "I will try again."

The Red Army began its siege of Budapest on December 8. That day, Wallenberg wrote his last letter to his mother: "I really thought I would be with you for Christmas. . . . I hope the peace so longed for is no longer so far away."

Wallenberg's people were increasingly at risk. Tibor Vayda recalled, "There were more than three hundred men and women at our office, which was also a Swedish protected house at 4 Üllöi Street. The Nyilas stormed in and shouted, 'Wallenberg is not here. Everybody, get out. Swedish protection means nothing. Protective passes mean nothing.' People wanted to take their luggage, but the Nyilas sneered. 'You don't need luggage because you will be dead soon.' About noon we were marched to SS headquarters. We expected to be shot after being thrown into the Danube. Somehow—and I still do not know how—a message was gotten to Wallenberg. At 2:00 in the afternoon his car roared through the courtyard. Not one of the three hundred was lost. He simply put it straight to the SS commando: 'You save these men, and I promise your safety after the Russians win the war.'"

Eichmann fled Budapest on December 23, but the crisis for the Jews got worse. Wallenberg moved to Pest, east of the Danube, where seventy thousand Jews had been forced into the central ghetto without diplomatic protection. On Christmas Day, Arrow Cross goons seized some of Wallenberg's staffers from a hospital. Dr. Stephen I. Lazarovitz, whom Wallenberg had already rescued from a similar episode on October 28, described what happened: "They planned to take us to the Danube, where thousands of people had been executed. One of us was able to get in touch with Wallenberg who arrived within ten minutes with his aides and the books of the embassy. He argued with the Arrow Cross people with calm and determination, showing them official papers. Finally, the Nazis left. Wallenberg had saved the life of my parents, and had saved my life—for the second time!"

Paula Auer, who had sought refuge in a Swedish house said that "when the Russians reached the gates of Budapest, the Nazis broke into this and other Swedish homes and like crazed beasts shot all the Jews they saw. Then they threw the bodies into the Danube. Somehow I escaped the Nazis' search and got word to the Swedish legation. Wallenberg and his assistants arrived in time to prevent the massacre of the remaining 160 Jews in the home."

The Nazi frenzy against Jews intensified as Russian guns pounded Budapest. Nyilas pulled children out of an International Red Cross children's home and a Jewish orphanage, and many were shot. The Institute of Forensic Medicine in Budapest reported, "In the most brutal manner, the Nyilas made short work of their victims. A few were simply shot, but the majority were mercilessly tortured. . . . Shooting out of eyes, scalping, deliberate breaking of bones, and abdominal knife wounds were Nyilas specialties."

Wallenberg organized a new campaign to help save Jewish children. Working with the International Red Cross and the Swedish Red Cross, he provided food, shelter, and medical care for some seven thousand children.

Finally, just days before the Russians entered Budapest, Wallenberg learned that about five-hundred SS and Arrow Cross soldiers were preparing to murder all seventy thousand people in the central ghetto, "this being the particular wish of Hitler and Himmler," according to the German general of police. Wallenberg contacted German general August Schmidthuber, an SS commander, and demanded that he stop the planned massacre, warning that he would make sure the general got hanged as a war criminal if the bloodbath occurred. Apparently frightened at that prospect, Schmidthuber ordered the conspirators to desist. This was Wallenberg's crowning achievement—a single negotiation that saved the lives of seventy thousand people.

"It is of the utmost importance," wrote the Hungarian author Jeno Levai, "that the Nazis and Arrow Crossmen were not able to ravage unhindered— they were compelled to see that every step they took was being watched and followed by the young Swedish diplomat. From Wallenberg they could keep no secrets. The Arrow Crossmen could not trick him. They could not operate freely. . . . Wallenberg was the 'world's observing eye,' the one who continually called the criminals to account."

Wallenberg looked forward to better times following the defeat of the Nazis. "Now the bad dream will soon be over," he told his driver Sandor Ardai. "Now we will soon be able to sleep." But the Russians came in the tradition of conquerors, not liberators. They considered the local population an enemy and seized thousands of Budapest civilians for forced labor, many never to return. Accustomed to the misery of Stalin's socialist paradise, Russian soldiers went wild, robbing people everywhere. They broke into apartments; "bourgois" janitors' apartments were especially vulnerable, since they were invariably on the first floor. Most Budapest women had horrifying stories to tell about brutal rape by Russian soldiers.

On January 13, 1945, Russian soldiers banged on the door of the Benczur Street cellar apartment where Wallenberg was sleeping. He showed his papers and asked to see the division's commanding officer; he hoped to discuss plans for relieving the Jewish population. Asked why he was staying in Pest instead of Buda, where all other diplomats were located, Wallenberg replied that he wanted to be near the Jewish quarters. Mystified, the Russians drove him to Russian quarters on Erzebet Kiralyno (Queen Elizabeth) Street. They indicated that he would be taken to see General Rodion Malinovsky. Colorblind, Wallenberg probably didn't notice red tabs on the shoulders of his new escorts, identifying them as officers of the Soviet secret police, NKVD. Their mission was to turn Hungary into a Soviet puppet regime, which meant suppressing any potential dissidents or independent leaders. Wallenberg was someone to reckon with, since thousands of documents circulated around Budapest with his signature. The Soviets considered him a capitalist adversary because of his well-known entrepreneurial family and his education in the United States, and they were convinced he must be a spy. Reportedly it was the future Soviet boss Leonid Brezhnev who issued the direct order for Wallenberg's arrest.

On January 17, 1945, Wallenberg was taken to Budapest's Eastern Rail Road Station and a train bound for Moscow. Then he was driven to Lubyanka Square where a five-story hotel had been converted into NKVD headquarters and dungeons for political prisoners. He was taken to Cell 123. The NKVD tortured and interrogated Wallenberg. By April 1945, he was transferred to Leftortovo Prison.

Soviet officials refused to answer inquiries about him. Osten Unden, the Marxist foreign minister in Sweden's socialist government, defended Stalin by saying that if Wallenberg hadn't done anything wrong, then the Soviets couldn't have imprisoned him. In August 1947, Soviet foreign minister Andrei Vyshinsky, who had served as prosecutor during Stalin's purge "trials," told the United Nations, "There is no Raoul Wallenberg in any Soviet prison." But many former political prisoners in the Soviet Union reported having had contact with Wallenberg, and on February 6, 1957, Soviet Deputy Foreign Minister Andrei Gromyko admitted that Wallenberg had been in Lubyanka Prison but claimed he died of a heart attack in July 1947 when he would have been thirty-five. Nobody ever produced witnesses, a body, or a death certificate.

Spurred by reports that he might still be alive in the 1970s, Wallenberg Committees were formed around the world. The Raoul Wallenberg Committee of the United States organized an exhibition that traveled across the country. Schools, hospitals, parks, and streets were named after him. Soviet dissident Andrei Sakharov demanded that the government turn over its Wallenberg files to independent investigators. President Ronald Reagan pushed the Soviets for answers and urged Congress to pass a bill naming Wallenberg an honorary U.S. citizen, signed into law on October 5, 1981. A bust of Wallenberg by Israeli sculptor Miri Margolin was placed in the U.S. Capitol. In 1984, Wallenberg was the first person named an honorary citizen of Israel. The following year, NBC broadcast a two-part, four-hour miniseries, *Wallenberg: A Hero's Story*, starring Richard Chamberlain.

Wallenberg's half-brother, Guy von Dardel, and and half-sister, Nina Lagergren, got no new information when they visited the Soviet Union in October 1989, although they were given Wallenberg's diplomatic passport, diary, address book, cigarette case, and some foreign currency. President Reagan discussed Wallenberg with Mikhail Gorbachev when Gorbachev visited the United States in December 1989, but again nothing new was learned. Nor has the collapse of the Soviet Union brought any news. Observers like the former *New York Times* editor Abe Rosenthal believe the Soviets murdered him, and confessing would be too embarrassing because "they were all involved." Guy von Dardel says human rights activists continue to pore through archives seeking an answers.

Raoul Wallenberg long ago joined the ranks of immortals. People will continue to be inspired by his heroism, which saved so many human beings from hideous evil. Wherever this beloved man is now, he will endure as the great angel of rescue who redeemed hope for humanity and liberty.

MILITANT NONVIOLENCE

DR. MARTIN LUTHER KING, Jr., provided crucial moral leadership for eradicating government-enforced racial segregation in the United States. Inspired by American individualist Henry David Thoreau and Indian nonviolent crusader Mohandas Gandhi, King established militant nonviolent political action as the principal strategy for attacking segregationist laws. This required considerable courage, since he was jailed fourteen times, was the target of countless death threats, was stoned, was stabbed, his home was blasted by a shotgun, his home was bombed, and a motel room where he stayed was bombed, too, before he was assassinated.

Dr. King exposed the outrageous corruption of southern sheriffs, mayors, and governors, who approved of police attacking peaceful demonstrators with cattle prods, unleashing ferocious police dogs, and aiming high-pressure water hoses at children. They did nothing while the Ku Klux Klan beat up black bus riders and let southern racists get away with murder.

Dr. King's most fundamental principles harked back to the natural law tradition: there are moral standards for judging the legitimacy of laws. They aren't legitimate just because government officials say they are. "A man-made code that squares with the moral law, or the law of God, is a just law," he explained. "But a man-made code that is inharmonious with the moral law is an unjust law. . . . Let us not forget, in the memories of six million who died, that everything Adolph Hitler did in Germany was 'legal,' and that everything the Freedom Fighters in Hungary did was 'illegal.'"

King didn't push his thinking nearly as far as philosophers of natural law did, but he said this: "An unjust law is a code that the majority inflicts on the minority that is not binding on itself. . . . Another thing that we can say is that an unjust law is a code which the majority inflicts upon the minority, which that minority had no part in enacting or creating, because that minority had no right to vote. . . . Our conscience tells us that the law is wrong and we must resist, but we have a moral obligation to accept the penalty. . . . We've made no gains without pressure, and I hope that pressure will always be moral, legal and peaceful."

Court decisions, he said, could be as bad as laws: "Though the rights of the First Amendment guarantee that any citizen or group of citizens may engage in peaceable assembly, the South has seized upon the device of invoking injunctions to block our direct-action civil rights demonstrations. When you get set to stage a nonviolent demonstration, the city simply secures an injunction to cease and desist. Southern courts are well known for 'sitting on' this type of case; conceivably a two or three-year delay could be incurred. . . . In Birmingham, we felt that we had to take a stand and disobey a court injunction against demonstrations, knowing the consequences and being prepared to meet them—or the unjust law would break our movement."

King aroused controversy throughout his tumultuous public career. Conservatives opposed him for challenging "states' rights." So-called liberals like President John F. Kennedy were concerned that he would provoke disorder, and Attorney General Robert F. Kennedy approved FBI bugging of King's home, office, and hotel rooms across the country. FBI director J. Edgar Hoover warned that King was consorting with communists.

FBI bugging failed to provide any evidence that King was involved with a communist conspiracy, but it did reveal his extensive womanizing. This has deeply embarrassed civil rights leaders. Many people were further scandalized by the revelation that phrases, sentences, and some paragraphs in his book *Stride Toward Freedom* (1958) had been lifted from *Basic Christian Ethics* by Paul Ramsay and *Agape and Eros* by Anders Nygren. King, it seems, had flaws, like many other people. Moreover, he had some muddled ideas. Exasperated by the intransigence of state and local governments, he pleaded for federal intervention to enforce equal rights, and apparently he came to believe that federal power could cure poverty. One biographer claimed he was a closet socialist.

Yet he protested many laws. Some laws denied blacks access to government services for which they were forced to pay taxes. There were state and local laws mandating private sector segregation. Municipal buses were government-protected monopolies, making it illegal for entrepreneurs to operate competitive, integrated buses. When King helped lead a bus boycott, the boycotters were hit with penalties provided by antiboycott laws. Carpools were organized to help boycotters get to work, and they were prosecuted for violating laws requiring that carpool vehicles be licensed as taxis and that riders be charged government-mandated minimum fares. Dr. King tangled with police and tax collectors and considered military conscription a form of slavery.

Dr. King, who was awarded the Nobel Peace Prize in 1964, always insisted on nonviolence: "As you press on with justice, be sure to move with dignity and discipline using only the weapon of love. . . . Always avoid violence. If you succumb to the temptation of using violence in your struggle, unborn generations will be the recipients of a long and desolate night of bitterness, and your chief legacy to the future will be an endless reign of meaningless chaos. . . . In your struggle for justice, let your oppressor know that you are not attempting to defeat or humiliate him. . . . You are merely seeking justice for him as well as yourself."

MARTIN LUTHER KING, JR., was born in Atlanta on January 15, 1929, the second child of Martin Luther King, Sr., pastor at the Ebenezer Baptist Church, and Alberta Williams, a preacher's daughter. Young Martin's maternal grandmother, "Mama" Williams, lived with the family, helping to raise him and his two siblings.

At age twelve, he entered an oratorical contest sponsored by the black Elks, he delivering his talk, "The Negro and the Constitution," without text or notes. Martin followed his father by attending Morehouse College, a popular institution of higher education for middle-class blacks. He decided on the ministry at around the age of nineteen, entering Crozer Theological Seminary, Chester, Pennsylvania, for a three-year program. A talk by Howard University president Mordecai Johnson aroused his interest in the nonviolent methods used by Mohandas K. Gandhi. After graduating from Crozier with distinction, he pursued doctoral studies at Boston University's School of Theology. There he embraced a religious version of individualism known as personalism. Biographer David J. Garrow reported this meant "the human personality, i.e. all individual persons, was the ultimate intrinsic value in the world. Some of King's own strong attraction to that philosophy was rooted in one of its major corollaries: if the dignity and worth of all human personalities was *the* ultimate value in the world, racial segregation and discrimination were among the ultimate evils."

While he was in Boston, he was introduced to Alabama-born Coretta Scott who had graduated from Ohio's Antioch College and gone on to the New England Conservatory of Music. "This little man, who was so short," she reflected, "I looked at him and thought to myself, 'He doesn't look like much.'" Daddy King presided at their wedding in, June 1953 in her parents' Perry County, Alabama, home. The couple returned to Boston, and he earned his Ph.D. in June 1955.

Daddy King wanted his son to become co-pastor at Atlanta's Ebenezer Baptist Church, but King cherished his independence and instead accepted a position at Montgomery, Alabama's, Dexter Avenue Baptist Church. In August 1955, he spoke at a meeting of the National Association for the Advancement of Colored People and subsequently was asked to serve on its their executive committee.

Meanwhile, trouble was brewing over government-enforced racial segregation. The laws had been passed during the early twentieth century, despite the objections of private businesses that such laws would raise their costs and alienate customers. As Hoover Institution scholar Thomas Sowell noted,

"*Laws* were necessary to get racial prejudice translated into pervasive discrimination, because the forces of the marketplace operated in the opposite direction. Prejudice is free but discrimination has costs."

Down South, explained historian Stephan Thernstrom and Manhattan Institute fellow Abigail Thernstrom in their book *America in Black and White* (1997), "The races were strictly separated by law on streetcars, buses, and railroads; in schools; in waiting rooms, restaurants, hotels, boarding houses, theaters, cemeteries, parks, courtrooms, public toilets, drinking fountains, and every other public space. The mania for separation went to such lengths that Oklahoma required separate telephone booths for the two races. . . . Macon County, Georgia, took the prize for absurdity by seriously debating a proposal that the county maintain two separate sets of public roads, one for each race, and rejecting the idea only because of the prohibitive cost."

A Montgomery ordinance required that blacks give up their seats when whites needed seats. In many cases, blacks, and especially women, were told to pay their fare at the front of the bus, then leave the bus and reenter at the back door, only to see the bus drive away.

On December 1, 1955, forty-two-year-old Rosa Parks, who worked as a tailor's assistant and helped out at the NAACP Youth Council, boarded a bus at Court Square, Montgomery. Driver J. F. Blake ordered blacks to the back of the bus, but Parks refused. She was tired. Blake stopped the bus, went to a telephone, and called the police, who escorted Parks to jail. A woman on the bus got word to E. D. Nixon of the NAACP, who, accompanied by white attorney Clifford Dorr, signed bond papers and secured Parks's release

Nixon lined up the support of black ministers. They formed the Montgomery Improvement Association and chose King as the first president because his education and public speaking ability would appeal to sophisticated blacks as well as ordinary folks. King explained, "We are not advocating violence. . . . The great glory of American democracy is the right to protest for right." He was surprisingly moderate in his demands: "We are not asking for an end to segregation. That's a matter for the legislature and the courts. . . . All we are seeking is justice and fair treatment in riding the buses."

Montgomery mayor W. A. Gayle blamed the boycott on "Negro radicals" and wouldn't make any concessions. The Montgomery Improvement Association set up a volunteer carpool for getting boycotters to work. City officials threatened to arrest drivers if they charged bus boycotters less than the government-mandated minimum forty-five-cent taxi fare. State judge Eugene W. Carter issued an injunction barring the MIA's carpool as an infringement of the government-granted bus monopoly franchise, and the resourceful MIA organized a share-a-ride program. A grand jury indicted more than ninety MIA members for violating the state antiboycott law. King, the first of the boycotters on trial, was ordered to pay $1,000. A bomb exploded in front of the parsonage where King's family lived, shattering windows and filling their home with smoke. In weekly mass meetings, King referred to Gandhi's long-term strategy of nonviolence.

In June 1956, a federal court voted two to one to strike down the Montgomery bus segregation ordinance, and later that year the U.S. Supreme Court upheld this decision. On December 21, 1956, at 5:55 A.M., the first bus of the day stopped near King's home. He was the first one on board, accompanied by Ralph Abernathy, E. D. Nixon, Rosa Parks, and Glenn Smiley, a white supporter from Texas. Things seemed to go well until December 23, when a shotgun blasted through King's front door. Five days later, snipers shot at three desegregated buses, wounding one black rider. On January 27, 1957, twelve sticks of dynamite with a burned-out fuse were found on the porch of Dr. King's home. Eight months later, he was in Harlem's Blumstein's department store, promoting his book *Stride Toward Freedom,* the story of the Montgomery bus boycott, when a deranged black woman pulled out a letter opener and plunged it into his chest. It missed his heart by a fraction of an inch.

To promote a broader civil rights movement, King helped organize a May 17 "Washington Pilgrimage," which climaxed with an estimated fifteen thousand people gathering at the Lincoln Memorial. *Ebony* magazine rated King "the No. 1 Negro leader of men." He helped form the Southern Christian Leadership Conference (SCLC), an Atlanta-based organization whose primary mission was to register black voters. On Labor Day 1957, King and Abernathy attended the Highlander Folk School in Tennessee and heard banjo-playing Pete Seeger sing "We Shall Overcome," which became the anthem of the civil rights movement.

The next phase of the civil rights movement began in February 1960 when four black students at North Carolina A&M College tried to get served at a Greensboro F. W. Woolworth whites-only lunch counter. Denied service, the students refused to leave. Dozens more students showed up, and the lunch counter closed. Soon there were sit-in protests throughout North Carolina. Then sit-ins spread to South Carolina, Virginia, Florida, and Tennessee. Sit-ins became the specialty of the Student Non-Violent Coordinating Committee (SNCC). King, who by this time had resigned from Dexter and become co-pastor with Daddy King at Ebenezer Baptist Church, addressed a rally of sit-in demonstrators in Durham, North Carolina.

Then two sheriffs arrested him and sought his extradiction to Alabama, where he faced charges of perjury and felony for his Alabama state tax returns. Tax collectors claimed that in 1956 and 1958, he had earned $27,000 more than the roughly $5,000 in pastor's salary and $4,100 in speaking fees he had reported. A conviction would ruin his reputation. Five lawyers considered King's prospects bleak, but analysis of his financial records showed he earned only $368 more than reported. On May 28, a jury of twelve white men returned a not-guilty verdict. Many observers thought he had been singled out for harassment.

On October 12, 1960, Dr. King joined sit-ins at Rich's department store in Atlanta, and he was arrested for violating an antitrespass law. Because he had previously been ticketed for driving a borrowed car with expired plates and for failing to get a Georgia license within ninety days after having moved into the state (he still had an Alabama license), he was sentenced to four months in a Georgia state prison.

A man punched Dr. King in the face while he was addressing SCLC's September 1962 convention in Birmingham. King remained at the podium, and the man hit him again and again. Rather than turn away, King spoke calmly to the man, who turned out to be Roy James, a twenty-four-year-old member of the American Nazi party. Police arrived, but Dr. King declined to press charges. The episode, noted biographer David J. Garrow, "left most onlookers stunned and impressed by Dr. King's lack of fear when confronted by direct physical violence."

King next turned his attention to Birmingham, one of the most staunchly segregationist cities. For years, black homes had been dynamited, and police had never solved the cases. One black neighborhood, in fact, was referred to as "Dynamite Hill." Although there weren't enough registered black voters to have an impact, black customers were important to local businesses. King's principal objectives in Birmingham were to desegregate facilities in stores, such as bathrooms and changing rooms; establish color-blind hiring practices by the stores as well as the government; and reopen taxpayer-financed recreation facilities.

State Supreme Court Judge William A. Jenkins, Jr., issued an injunction against marches, so when King led a Good Friday march toward city hall, he was jailed. Wyatt Walker, a minister working with King, recruited hundreds of black high school students to march toward city hall, and they too were jailed. Public safety commissioner "Bull" Connor had high-pressure water hoses turned on the marchers and bystanders. Police dogs went on the attack, and police chased demonstrators with clubs. When a settlement was finally reached, King praised the white merchants with whom they had negotiated and announced a voter registration drive in Birmingham. The evening after he spoke, the Ku Klux Klan held a meeting near Birmingham, and a bomb exploded under the room where King had stayed at the Gaston Motel.

Focused on restricting the power of southern governments that had done so much to subvert civil liberties, King sought ways to generate support for a civil rights bill before Congress. The result was the March on Washington, set for August 28, 1963, and sponsored by King, Wilkins, James Farmer of the Congress of Racial Equality, John Lewis of SNCC, Andrew Young of SCLC, and A. Philip Randolph of the Brotherhood of Sleeping Car Porters. Bayard Rustin was the principal organizer.

"I have a dream," King told the crowd, "that one day this nation will rise up and live out the true meaning of its creed—we hold these truths to be self-evident, that all men are created equal. I have a dream that one day on the red hills of Georgia, the sons of former slaves and the sons of former slave-owners will be able to sit down together at the table of brotherhood. . . . I have a dream that my four little children will one day live in a nation where they will not be judged by the color of their skin but by the content of their character. . . . When we allow freedom to ring . . . we will be able to speed up that day when all of God's children—black men and white men, Jews and Gentiles, Protestants and Catholics—will be able to join hands and sing in the words of the old Negro spiritual, 'Free at last, free at last; thank God Almighty, we are free at last.'"

Signed into law by Lyndon Johnson who became president after John F. Kennedy's assassination, the Civil Rights Act went beyond striking down laws maintaining compulsory segregation. It established the Equal Opportunity Employment Commission, which was empowered to suppress any voluntary association deemed discriminatory. Considering the barbarism of southern state and municipal governments, it was understandable that King would seek a federal remedy, yet expanding government power has always been dangerous for minorities who, because of their comparatively small numbers, couldn't count on controlling it, as had been the case in the South.

King went on to help blacks secure the right to vote, so they would be better protected from politicians and bureaucrats. "The problem in the South," explained deputy attorney general Nicholas Katzenbach, "was primarily the problem of the literacy tests and the way in which they were administered. You had black Ph.D.'s who couldn't pass a literacy test and you had whites who could barely write their name who had no problem being registered to vote."

The issue came to a head in Selma, Alabama. It was a town of about twenty-nine thousand people, and only about 2 percent of voting-age black people were registered to vote. In February and March 1965, King led demonstrations for voting rights. Sheriff Jim Clark's men punched demonstrators, beat them with billyclubs, and jolted them with electric cattle prods. More than four thousand people were arrested, and King was jailed. He wrote "A Letter from Martin Luther King from a Selma, Alabama Jail," which appeared as a *New York Times* advertisement and attracted national attention. More than twenty-five thousand people joined a march from Selma to Montgomery. They were attacked by Clark's men and shot at by snipers, but they reached Montgomery, and King addressed the multitude gathered at the capitol building. The Voting Rights Act was signed into law on August 6, 1965.

King courageously opposed the Vietnam War. He denounced conscription as "involuntary servitude" and expressed some disillusionment with political power. "No president has really done very much for the American Negro," he lamented, "though the past two presidents have received much undeserved credit for helping us. This credit has accrued to Lyndon Johnson and John Kennedy only because it was during their administration that Negroes began doing more for themselves."

Yet King had the mistaken idea that more speeches, marches, and laws could somehow get rid of poverty. He went to Chicago and demanded that local officials "end slums," housing discrimination, and high-rise housing projects, but this got him nowhere. He didn't seem to realize that government programs are driven by the self-interest of those in power, not the interest of the people supposedy being served. He tried launching a "Poor People's Campaign" in Memphis, but it turned into a riot.

At about 6:01 P.M. on April 4, in room 306 of the Lorraine Motel, Dr. King stepped onto the balcony. There was a shot. A bullet blew away a piece of his jaw as big as a man's fist, then severed his spinal cord, ripped through his chest and came to rest in his back. He slumped to the balcony floor. An ambulance took him to St. Joseph's Hospital. The general surgeon, neurosurgeon, chest surgeon, lung specialist, and kidney specialist tried various emergency measures, but his heart gave out. Official time of death was 7:11 P.M.

Ebenezer Baptist Church was packed for the funeral service, as Daddy King preached over his son's casket. Then it was placed on a flat-bed farm wagon and drawn by two mules three and a half miles through the streets of Atlanta to Morehouse College, as an estimated fifty thousand people paid their respects. At Morehouse, there was a two-hour memorial service. Dr. King was buried at South View Cemetery under a marble monument inscribed, "Free at Last, Free at Last, Thank God Almighty, I'm Free at Last."

The FBI launched what was described as the most intensive manhunt in U.S. history—some fifteen-hundred FBI agents were assigned to the case, and, altogether, about three thousand worked on various aspects of it. Investigators identified the prime suspect as escaped convict James Earl Ray and followed his trail to London. He was apprehended en route to white supremacist Rhodesia. He confessed and was sentenced to ninety-nine years in Tennessee State Prison.

Since then, "civil rights" leaders have abandoned the dream of equal rights and behaved like every other interest group, seeking special favors. They promoted affirmative action for blacks who never were slaves at the expense of whites, Hispanics, Asians, and others who never owned slaves, provoking resentment and conflict. Moreover, noted Thomas Sowell, "It is an often cited statistic that the number of blacks in professional and other high-level occupations increased significantly in the years following passage of the Civil Rights Act of 1964, but it is an almost totally ignored fact that the number of blacks in such professions increased even more rapidly in the years *preceding* passage of the Civil Rights Act of 1964." Dramatic early gains occurred as southern blacks helped themselves by migrating North. It is no wonder more people are returning to King's original vision of equal rights.

With courage and goodwill, Martin Luther King, Jr., reaffirmed the vision of a "higher law," the idea that government laws must be judged by moral standards, a bedrock for liberty going back more than two thousand years.

LIBERTY IN THE NEW MILLENNIUM

AS THESE STORIES make clear, liberty begins with an idea: Individuals are born with a natural right to liberty that cannot be swept away by a decree, a law, or a regulation. This idea took hold in the West and electrified the world.

Critics have belittled liberty as an idea that favors the rich. How, then, to explain the fact that so many great champions of liberty were poor? Desiderius Erasmus, Hugo Grotius, Roger Williams, John Lilburne, John Locke, Sam Adams, Thomas Paine, Mary Wollstonecraft, Friedrich Schiller, Frederick Douglass, Lysander Spooner, Elizabeth Cady Stanton, Susan B. Anthony, Albert Jay Nock, Ludwig von Mises, and Murray Rothbard, for instance, never had much money. A number of others, including William Graham Sumner, F. A. Hayek, George Stigler, Milton Friedman, and James M. Buchanan, lived on a professor's salary. Among the major figures, only a few, like Algernon Sidney, Thomas Jefferson, James Madison, and Lafayette, qualified as aristocrats, but they all had financial troubles. A few authors, such as Thomas Babington Macaulay, William S. Gilbert, Victor Hugo, Louis L'Amour, Robert Heinlein, and Ayn Rand, eventually earned good money from their work, but this came after a life of struggle. Mark Twain went bankrupt despite the popularity of his books. Benjamin Franklin and Antony Fisher were the only successful businessmen among the heroes, and devotion to liberty cost them plenty. Liberty does indeed lead to a more prosperous society, but these individuals clearly cherished liberty because it means the opportunity to pursue one's dreams and live in peace.

People gained liberty when they fought for it. That hundreds of millions have quietly endured tyranny testifies to the terrible risks of rebellion. A dozen of the heroes I wrote about were exiled: Marcus Tullius Cicero, Desiderius Erasmus, François Rabelais, Roger Williams, Algernon Sidney, John Locke, William Penn, Francisco Goya, Ayn Rand, F. A. Hayek, Ludwig von Mises, and Thomas Szasz. More than a dozen were jailed or imprisoned: Edward Coke, Hugo Grotius, John Lilburne, Algernon Sidney, William Penn, Thomas Paine, Lafayette, Daniel O'Connell, William Lloyd Garrison, Henry David Thoreau, John Stuart Mill, Raoul Wallenberg, and Martin Luther King, Jr., and Algernon Sidney were beheaded, and King was shot to death.

Although there have been many rebellions throughout history, most were aimed at overthrowing one man and securing power for another. Ordinary people were not any better off than before. It was in the West that friends of liberty managed to establish essential institutions of a free society: private property, free markets, a rule of law, a separation of powers, an independent judiciary, and a written constitution with a bill of rights.

Secure private property is the most fundamental institution of a free society, because it's a domain where individuals can go about their business without interference from anybody. Secure private property means that individuals can voluntarily cooperate with each other, do business with each other, and build communities together. The more that people can keep the fruits of their labor, the freer they are. Freedom is reduced by tax laws preventing individuals from pursuing the occupation of their choice, laws limiting the freedom of individuals to spend their money as they wish, and laws restricting freedom of movement. Freedom of religion is impossible unless individuals can establish safe places for worship. There cannot be freedom of the press if government owns all the printing presses and paper supplies. Similarly, freedom of speech will thrive only when individuals can use their property as forums for unpopular views. Protecting freedom to compete and trade is the most effective way to undermine monopolies. Overall, the more property that is in private hands and the more widely it is dispersed, the more effective are the limitations on government power.

A rule of law means that laws apply equally to everybody. If politicians know that any laws they pass will apply to them, they will be less likely to pass truly oppressive laws. Reducing discretion in the application of laws reduces the prospects for corruption.

A separation of powers is intended to prevent one person or a few people from monopolizing government power. Failure to establish a separation of powers resulted in the Reign of Terror during the French Revolution. Political monopoly was even more catastrophic during the Russian Revolution. Murderous political monopolies plagued Europe, Asia, Africa, and the Americas during the twentieth century.

The most successful constitutional vision was expressed in the U.S. Constitution. It limited government to specific enumerated powers, established a separation of powers, and reserved important rights to individuals and the states. The Constitution included an independent judiciary, which, as things evolved, asserted the power to strike down laws violating the Constitution. While judges have always been appointed by politicians, and many judges have undermined liberty, nonetheless the inability of politicians to fire judges meant that they could uphold liberty, and often they have done this. Finally, the Constitution has made possible peaceful change through the amendment process.

The greatest threat to liberty continues to be government power. Promoted as the cure for social ills, it has turned out to be immensely destructive and difficult to control. In recent years, far more property value has been destroyed by U.S. government environmental regulations than by arson, as investigative reporter James Bovard has pointed out. Far more property has been lost to U.S. government asset seizures than to bank robbers. It has become difficult to throw out corrupt politicians even in a democracy like the United States because laws limit the ability of challengers to raise money, get on the ballot, and achieve name recognition.

Fortunately, the stories in this book show that there have been many occasions when a single individual or a few individuals made a big difference for liberty. Remember how the bookseller Atticus paid Cicero's bills during his years of exile. The Dutch Quaker merchant Benjamin Farley helped William Penn, John Locke, and Algernon Sidney when they were in trouble. Lafayette, a great transmitter of libertarian ideas, corresponded with Greeks, Hungarians, Poles, Portuguese, Spaniards, and people in South America who were friends of liberty. Arthur Tappan and other Quaker merchants did much to fund the abolitionist movement. Ellen Winsor, Rebecca Winsor Evans, and Edmund C. Evans made it possible for Albert Jay Nock to write some of his best books. H. L. Mencken helped pay Emma Goldman's medical bills. Harold Luhnow paid Ludwig von Mises' salary at New York University and F. A. Hayek's salary at the University of Chicago, so these great thinkers could continue to teach. Surely there would have been less support for a free society if Adam Smith, Thomas Jefferson, and others had not committed their mighty talents to the cause. Anyone who still wonders what a single individual can do for liberty needs only contemplate the amazing achievements of Raoul Wallenberg.

The struggle for liberty will never end. The future will undoubtedly bring more threats from politicians, terrorists, and conquerors. But I am confident that in the new millennium, new heroes and heroines will emerge to defend our precious legacy of liberty.

A SELECTIVE BIBLIOGRAPHY

Although I long dreamed of writing a big book, everybody tells me that readers have limits. Accordingly, I have devoted as many as possible of the pages allotted me to stories, which has meant no footnotes and a selective rather than an exhaustive bibliography.

The following books and articles are principal sources for this work. For the reader's convenience, I have favored the easiest-to-find, most authoritative English-language editions. In a surprising number of cases, though, the best sources are out of print. A reader who wishes to see these must either use a major academic library or do an extensive book search. In building my personal library on liberty, currently around five thousand volumes, I've worked with the biggest out-of-print book sellers in the United States, with specialized book searchers (such as those who get material from Europe) and with the Internet out-of-print book databases like Bibliofind and mxbf. Without question, the most exciting development is the ease and speed of acquiring out-of-print material through the Internet.

In a number of cases, especially some twentieth-century subjects, there are few, if any, published biographies or supporting materials such as letters and diaries. Interviews, original documents, and articles are the principal sources for these stories. I've indicated the sources' reporting style in the text.

The typical biography ends with an individual's death, so I have had to chronicle the subsequent ups and downs of an individual's reputation mainly by interviewing specialized scholars and consulting journal articles. Again, principal sources are indicated in the text.

LORD ACTON (1834–1902)

Fears, J. Rufus, ed. *Essays in the History of Liberty* (Indianapolis: LibertyClassics, 1985).
———. *Essays in the Study and Writing of History* (Indianapolis: LibertyClassics, 1985).
———. *Essays in Religion, Politics, and Morality* (Indianapolis: LibertyClassics, 1988).
Figgis, John Neville, and Reginald Vere Laurence, eds. *Lectures on Modern History*, by John Emerich Edward Dalberg-Acton (London: Macmillan, 1950).
———. *Lectures on the French Revolution*, by John Emerich Edward Dalberg-Acton (New York: Noonday Press, 1959).
Himmelfarb, Gertrude. *Lord Acton: A Study in Conscience and Politics* (Chicago: University of Chicago Press, 1952).

Mathew, David. *Lord Acton and His Times* (Tuscaloosa: University of Alabama Press, 1968).

Paul, Herbert, ed., *Letters of Lord Acton to Mary Gladstone* (New York: Macmillan, 1904).

Schuettinger, Robert. *Lord Acton: Historian on Liberty* (Lasalle, Ill.: Open Court, 1976).

Tulloch, Hugh. *Acton* (New York: St. Martin's Press, 1988).

SAMUEL ADAMS (1722–1803)

Beach, Stewart. *Samuel Adams: The Fateful Years, 1764–1776* (New York: Dodd, Mead, 1965).

Canfield, Cass. *Sam Adams' Revolution* (New York: Harper & Row, 1976).

Cushing, Harry Alonzo, ed. *The Writings of Samuel Adams* (New York: Octagon Books, 1968). 4 vols.

Lewis, Paul. *The Grand Incendiary: A Biography of Samuel Adams* (New York: Dial Press, 1973).

Miller, John C. *Sam Adams: Pioneer in Propaganda* (Boston: Little, Brown, 1936).

Wells, William V. *The Life and Public Services of Samuel Adams* (Boston: Little, Brown, 1865). 3 vols.

FRÉDÉRIC BASTIAT (1801–1850)

Goddard, Arthur, ed. *Economic Sophisms,* by Frédéric Bastiat (Princeton, N.J.: D. Van Nostrand, 1964).

de Huszar, George B., ed. *Economic Harmonies,* by Frédéric Bastiat (Princeton, N.J.: D. Van Nostrand, 1964).

———. *Selected Essays on Political Economy,* by Frédéric Bastiat (Princeton, N.J.: D. Van Nostrand, 1964).

Palmer, R. R. *J-B Say: An Economist in Troubled Times* (Princeton, N.J.: Princeton University Press, 1997).

Roche, George. *Free Markets Free Men: Frédéric Bastiat, 1801–1850* (Hillsdale, Mich.: Hillsdale College Press, 1993).

Russell, Dean. *Government and Legal Plunder: Bastiat Brought Up to Date* (Irvington-on-Hudson, N.Y.: Foundation for Economic Education, 1985).

Teilhac, Ernest. *L'Oeuvre Economique de Jean-Baptiste Say* (Paris: Librairie Felix Alcan, 1927).

LUDWIG VAN BEETHOVEN (1770–1827)

Burton, Humphrey. *Leonard Bernstein* (New York: Doubleday, 1994).

Eaglefield-Hull, A., ed. *Beethoven's Letters* (New York: Dover, 1972).

Kinderman, William. *Beethoven* (Berkeley: University of California, Press, 1995).

Kolodin, Irving. *The Interior Beethoven: A Biography of the Music* (New York: Knopf, 1975).

Robbins Landon, H. C. *Beethoven: His Life, Work and World* (New York: Thames and Hudson, 1993).

Solomon, Maynard. *Beethoven* (New York: Schirmer Books, 1998).

Thayer, Alexander Wheelock. *The Life of Ludwig van Beethoven* (London: Centaur Press, 1960). 3 vols.

JAMES M. BUCHANAN (B. 1919)

Brennan, Geoffrey, and James M. Buchanan. *The Power to Tax: Analytical Foundations of a Fiscal Constitution* (Cambridge: Cambridge University Press, 1980).
——. *Reason of Rules—Constitutional Political Economy* (Cambridge: Cambridge University Press, 1985).
Buchanan, James M. *Better Than Plowing and Other Personal Essays* (Chicago: University of Chicago Press, 1992).
——. *Public Finance in Democratic Process: Fiscal Institutions and Individual Choice* (Chapel Hill: University of North Carolina Press, 1987).
——. *The Public Finances: An Introductory Textbook* (Homewood, Ill.: Richard D. Irwin, 1960).
Buchanan, James M., and Gordon Tullock. *The Calculus of Consent: Logical Foundations of Constitutional Democracy* (Ann Arbor: University of Michigan Press, 1965).
Buchanan, James M., and Robert D. Tollison, eds. *The Theory of Public Choice II* (Ann Arbor: University of Michigan, 1984).
Buchanan, James M., and Richard E. Wagner. *Democracy in Deficit: The Political Legacy of Lord Keynes* (New York: Academic Press, 1977).

MARCUS TULLIUS CICERO (106 B.C.–43 B.C.)

Bailey, D. R. Shackleton. *Cicero: Classical Life and Letters* (New York: Charles Scribner's Sons, 1971).
Cicero. *Letters to Atticus* (Cambridge: Harvard University Press, 1953). 3 vols.
——. *The Letters to His Friends* (Cambridge: Harvard University Press, 1958). 3 vols.
——. *De Officiis* (Cambridge: Harvard University Press, 1990).
——. *De Re Publica, De Legibus* (Cambridge: Harvard University Press, 1959).
——. *The Speeches, In Catilinam I–IV, Pro Murena, Pro Sulla, Pro Flacco* (Cambridge: Harvard University Press, 1959).
Cowell, F. R. *Cicero and the Roman Republic* (London: Isaac Pitman & Sons, 1948).
Grant, Michael, ed. *Cicero on Government* (London: Penguin, 1993).
Rawson, Elizabeth. *Cicero: A Portrait* (Ithaca, N.Y.: Cornell University Press, 1975).

RICHARD COBDEN (1804–1865)

Bright, John, and J. E. Thorold Rogers, eds. *Richard Cobden: Speeches on Questions of Public Policy* (New York: Kraus Reprint, 1970). 2 vols.
Cobden, Richard. *Political Writings* (New York: Kraus Reprint, 1969). 2 vols.
——. *Speeches on Peace, Financial Reform, Colonial Reform and Other Subjects* (New York: Kraus Reprint, 1970).
Edsall, Nicholas C. *Richard Cobden, Independent Radical* (Cambridge: Harvard University Press, 1986).
Hinde, Wendy. *Richard Cobden* (New Haven: Yale University Press, 1987).
Hobson, J. A. *Richard Cobden, the International Man* (New York: Henry Holt, 1919).
Morley, John. *The Life of Richard Cobden* (London: T. Fisher Unwin, 1906).
Trevelyan, George Macauley. *The Life of John Bright* (London: Constable and Co., 1913).
Walling, R. A. J. ed. *John Bright, Diaries* (New York: Morrow, 1930).

EDWARD COKE (1552–1634)

Bowen, Catherine Drinker. *The Lion and the Throne: The Life and Times of Sir Edward Coke* (Boston: Little, Brown, 1957).

Coke, Edward. *The First Part of the Institutes of the Laws of England* (Birmingham, Al.: Legal Classics Library, 1985).

———. *The Second Part of the Institutes of the Laws of England* (London: W. Clark & Sons, 1817). 2 vols.

Lyon, Hastings, and Herman Block. *Edward Coke: Oracle of the Law* (Boston: Houghton Mifflin, 1929).

White, Stephen D. *Sir Edward Coke and the Grievances of the Commonwealth* (Manchester, England: Manchester University Press, 1979).

BENJAMIN CONSTANT (1767–1830)

Cruickshank, John. *Benjamin Constant* (New York: Twayne, 1974).

Dodge, Guy H. *Benjamin Constant's Philosophy of Liberalism: A Study in Politics and Religion* (Chapel Hill: University of North Carolina Press, 1980).

Fontana, Biancamaria. *Benjamin Constant and the Post-Revolutionary Mind* (New Haven: Yale University Press, 1991).

———, ed. *Benjamin Constant, Political Writings* (Cambridge: Cambridge University Press, 1988).

Herold, J. Christopher. *Mistress to an Age: A Life of Madame de Staël* (Indianapolis: Bobbs-Merrill, 1958).

Nicholson, Harold. *Benjamin Constant* (Garden City, N.Y.: Doubleday, 1949).

Schermerhorn, Elizabeth W. *Benjamin Constant: His Private Life and His Contribution to the Cause of Liberal Government in France, 1767–1830* (Boston: Houghton Mifflin, 1924).

Wood, Dennis. *Benjamin Constant: A Biography* (New York: Routledge, 1993).

FREDERICK DOUGLASS (1818–1895)

Foner, Philip S. *Frederick Douglass: A Biography* (Boston: Beacon Press, 1964).

———. *The Life and Writings of Frederick Douglass* (New York: International Publishers, 1950–1955). 4 vols.

Gates, Jr., Henry Louis. *Frederick Douglass Autobiographies* (New York: Library of America, 1994).

McFeely, William S. *Frederick Douglass* (New York: Norton, 1991).

Oberholtzer, Ellis Paxson, ed. *Frederick Douglass,* by Booker T. Washington (New York: Argosy-Antiquarian, 1969).

Quarles, Benjamin. *Frederick Douglass* (New York: Da Capo Press, 1997).

DESIDERIUS ERASMUS (1469?–1536)

Augustijn, Cornelis. *Erasmus: His Life, Works, and Influence* (Toronto: University of Toronto Press, 1993).

Collected Works of Erasmus (Toronto: University Toronto Press, 1974–).

Erasmus, Desiderius. *Praise of Folly* (New York: Penguin, 1971).

Faludy, George. *Erasmus of Rotterdam* (London: Eyre & Spottiswoode, 1970).

McConica, James. *Erasmus* (New York: Oxford University Press, 1991).

Rummel, Erika, ed. *The Erasmus Reader* (Toronto: University of Toronto Press, 1996).

Smith, Preserved. *Erasmus: A Study of His Life, Ideals, and Place in History* (New York: Frederick Ungar Publishing, 1962).

CHARLES JAMES FOX (1749–1806)

Derry, John W. *Charles James Fox* (New York: St. Martin's Press, 1972).
Lascelles, Edward. *The Life of Charles James Fox* (New York: Octagon, 1970).
Rude, George. *Wilkes and Liberty* (London: Oxford University Press, 1962).
Schweitzer, David. *Charles James Fox, 1749–1806: A Bibliography* (Westport, Conn.: Greenwood Press, 1991).
Trevelyan, George Otto. *George the Third and Charles Fox* (London: Longmans, Green, 1912). 2 vols.

BENJAMIN FRANKLIN (1706–1790)

Clark, Ronald W. *Benjamin Franklin: A Biography* (New York: Random House, 1983).
Fleming, Thomas. *The Man Who Dared Lightning: A New Look at Benjamin Franklin* (New York: Morrow, 1971).
Hawke, David Freeman. *Franklin* (New York: Harper & Row, 1976).
Huang, Nian-sheng. *Benjamin Franklin in American Thought and Culture, 1790–1990* (Philadelphia: American Philosophical Society, 1994).
Labaree, Leonard W., Ralph L. Ketcham, Helen C. Boatfield, and Helene H. Fineman, eds. *The Autobiography of Benjamin Franklin* (New Haven: Yale University Press, 1964).
Labaree, Leonard W., et al., eds., *The Papers of Benjamin Franklin* (New Haven: Yale University Press, 1959–1970). 14 vols.
Lemay, J. A. Leo, ed. *Benjamin Franklin Writings* (New York: Library of America, 1987).
Van Doren, Carl. *Benjamin Franklin* (New York: Viking Press, 1938).

MILTON FRIEDMAN (B. 1912)

Friedman, Milton. *Capitalism and Freedom: A Leading Economist's View of the Proper Role of Competitive Capitalism* (Chicago: University of Chicago Press, 1962).
———. *Essays in Positive Economics* (Chicago: University of Chicago Press, 1953).
———. *There's No Such Thing as a Free Lunch: Essays on Public Policy* (La Salle, Ill.: Open Court, 1975).
Friedman, Milton, and Rose Friedman. *Free to Choose: A Personal Statement* (New York: Harcourt, Brace, 1980).
———. *Two Lucky People: Memoirs* (Chicago: University of Chicago Press, 1998).
———. *Tyranny of the Status Quo* (New York: Harcourt Brace Jovanovich, 1984).
Friedman, Milton, and Ann Jacobson Schwartz. *A Monetary History of the United States, 1867–1960* (Princeton, N.J.: Princeton University Press, 1963).
Jordan, Jerry L, Allan H. Meltzer, Anna J. Schwartz, and Thomas J. Sargent. "Milton, Money, and Mischief: Symposium and Articles in Honor of Milton Friedman's 80th Birthday." *Economic Inquiry* (April 1993): 197–212.
Lucas, Jr., Robert E., "Review of Milton Friedman and Anna J. Schwartz's 'A Monetary History of the United States, 1867–1960.'" *Journal of Monetary Economics* 34 (1994): 5–16.

WILLIAM LLOYD GARRISON (1805–1879)

Cain, William E., ed., *William Lloyd Garrison and the Fight Against Slavery: Selections from* The Liberator (Boston: Bedford Books, 1995).
Grimke, Archibald H. *William Lloyd Garrison: The Abolitionist* (New York: AMS Press, 1974).

Korngold, Ralph. *Two Friends of Man: The Story of William Lloyd Garrison and Wendell Phillips* (Boston: Little, Brown, 1950).

Kraditor, Aileen S. *Means and Ends in American Abolitionism: Garrison and His Critics on Strategy and Tactics, 1834–1850* (New York: Vintage, 1969).

Merrill, Walter M. *Against Wind and Tide: A Biography of William Lloyd Garrison* (Cambridge: Harvard University Press, 1963).

———. et al., eds., *The Letters of William Lloyd Garrison, 1822–1879* (Cambridge: Harvard University Press, 1971–1981). 6 vols.

Nelson Truman, ed., *Documents of Upheaval, Selections from William Lloyd Garrison's The Liberator, 1831–1865* (New York: Hill and Wang, 1966).

Stewart, James Brewer. *William Lloyd Garrison and the Challenge of Emancipation* (Arlington Heights, Ill.: Harlan Davidson, 1992).

Thomas, John. *The Liberator, William Lloyd Garrison, A Biography* (Boston: Little, Brown, 1963).

WILLIAM S. GILBERT (1836–1911)

Baily, Leslie. *Gilbert & Sullivan: Their Life and Times* (New York: Viking Press, 1973).

Benford, Harry. *The Gilbert & Sullivan Lexicon* (Ann Arbor, Mich.: Sarah Jennings Press, 1991).

Bradley Ian, ed. *The Complete Annotated Gilbert & Sullivan* (New York: Oxford University Press, 1996).

Jacobs, Arthur. *Arthur Sullivan: A Victorian Musician* (New York: Oxford University Press, 1984).

Ellis, James, ed. *The Bab Ballads,* by W. S. Gilbert (Cambridge: Harvard University Press, 1970).

Pearson, Hesketh. *W. S. Gilbert: His Life and Strife* (New York: Harper, 1957).

Stedman, Jane. *W. S. Gilbert: A Classic Victorian and His Theatre* (New York: Oxford University Press, 1996).

Young, Percy M. *Sir Arthur Sullivan* (New York: Norton, 1971).

WILLIAM EWART GLADSTONE (1809–1898)

Foot, M. R. D., and H. C. G. Matthew. *The Gladstone Diaries* (Oxford: Clarendon Press, 1968–1974). 4 vols.

Jenkins, Roy. *Gladstone* (New York: Random House, 1997).

Magnus, Philip. *Gladstone* (New York: Dutton, 1954).

Matthew, H. C. G. *Gladstone, 1809–1874* (Oxford: Clarendon Press, 1986).

———. *Gladstone, 1875–1898* (Oxford: Clarendon Press, 1995).

Morley, John. *The Life of William Ewart Gladstone* (New York: Macmillan, 1903). 3 vols.

Shannon, Richard. *Gladstone, 1809–1865* (Chapel Hill: University of North Carolina Press, 1984).

———. *Gladstone, 1865–1898* (Chapel Hill: University of North Carolina Press, 1999).

Stansky, Peter. *Gladstone: A Progress in Politics* (Boston: Little, Brown, 1979).

FRANCISCO GOYA (1746–1828)

Gassier, Pierre, and Juliet Wilson. *The Life and Complete Work of Francisco Goya* (New York: Reynal & Co., 1971).

Glendinning, Nigel. *Goya and His Critics* (New Haven: Yale University Press, 1977).

Hull, Anthony. *Goya: A Man Among Kings* (New York: Hamilton Press, 1987).

Licht, Fred. *Goya: The Origins of the Modern Temper in Art* (New York: Universe Books, 1979).
Lopez-Rey, José. *A Cycle of Goya's Drawings: The Expression of Truth and Liberty* (London: Faber and Faber).
Muller, Priscilla E. *Goya's "Black Paintings": Truth and Reason in Light and Liberty* (New York: Hispanic Society of America, 1984).
Vallentin, Antonina. *This I Saw: The Life and Times of Goya* (New York: Random House, 1949).

HUGO GROTIUS (1583–1645)

Campbell, A. C., ed. *The Rights of War and Peace, including the Law of Nature and of Nations*, trans. from the original Latin of Grotius (London: B. Boothroyd, 1814). 3 vols.
Dumbauld, Edward. *The Life and Writings of Hugo Grotius* (Norman, University of Oklahoma Press, 1969).
Edwards, Charles S. *Hugo Grotius, the Miracle of Holland, A Study in Political and Legal Thought* (Chicago: Nelson-Hall, 1981).
van Someren, Liesje. *Umpire to the Nations, Hugo Grotius* (London: Dennis Dobson, 1965).
Vreeland, Hamilton. *Hugo Grotius, the Father of the Modern Science of International Law* (New York: Oxford University Press, 1917).

F. A. HAYEK (1899–1992)

Ebenstein, Alan. *Friedrich Hayek and the Revival of Liberty* (New York: St. Martin's Press, 2000).
The Collected Works of F. A. Hayek. vol. 1, W.W. Bartley III, ed., *The Fatal Conceit: The Errors of Socialism* (Chicago: University of Chicago Press, 1988).
Hayek, F. A. *Individualism and Economic Order* (Chicago: University of Chicago Press, 1958).
———. *The Constitution of Liberty* (Chicago: University of Chicago Press, 1960).
———. *Law, Legislation and Liberty: A New Statement of the Liberal Principles of Justice and Political Economy* (London: Routledge, Kegan Paul, 1982).
———. *The Road to Serfdom* (Chicago: University of Chicago Press, 1944).
———, ed. *Capitalism and the Historians* (Chicago: University of Chicago Press, 1960).
———. *Collectivist Economic Planning* (London: Routledge, Kegan Paul, 1963).
Kresge, Stephen, and Leif Wenar, eds. *F. A. Hayek: Hayek on Hayek* (Chicago: University of Chicago Press, 1994).
Machlup, Fritz, ed. *Essays on Hayek* (New York: New York University Press, 1976).
Raybould, John, ed. Hayek: *A Commemorative Album* (London: Adam Smith Institute, 1998).

ROBERT A. HEINLEIN (1907–1988)

Heinlein, Robert A. *Citizen of the Galaxy* (New York: Ballantine, 1957).
———. *The Moon Is a Harsh Mistress* (New York: Tom Doherty Associates, 1996).
———. *The Past Through Tomorrow* (New York: Putnam's, 1967).
———. *The Puppet Masters* (New York: Ballantine, 1951).
———. *Stranger in a Strange Land* (Ace/Putnam, 1991).
Heinlein, Virginia, ed. *Robert A. Heinlein: Grumbles from the Grave* (New York: Ballantine, 1989).

Kondo, Yoji, ed. *Requiem: New Collected Works by Robert A. Heinlein* (New York: Tom Doherty Associates, 1992).

Panshin, Alexei. *Heinlein in Dimension* (Chicago: Advent Publishers, 1968).

Stover, Leon. *Robert A. Heinlein* (Boston: Twayne, 1987).

VICTOR HUGO (1802–1885)

Edwards Samuel. *Victor Hugo: A Tumultuous Life* (New York: David McKay, 1971).

Hugo, Victor. *The Last Day of a Condemned Man* (New York: Oxford University Press, 1992).

———. *Les Misérables* (New York: Modern Library, 1992).

———. *The Man Who Laughs* (New York: H. M. Caldwell).

———. *Ninety-Three* (New York: Carroll & Graf, 1988).

Josephson, Matthew. *Victor Hugo: A Realistic Biography of the Great Romantic* (Garden City, N.Y.: Doubleday, Doran, 1942).

Juin, Hubert. *Victor Hugo* (Paris: Flammarion, 1980–1986). 3 vols.

Maurois, André. *Victor Hugo* (London: Jonathan Cape, 1956).

Robb, Graham. *Victor Hugo* (New York: Norton, 1997).

THOMAS JEFFERSON (1743–1826)

Boyd, Julian O., et al., eds. *The Papers of Thomas Jefferson* (Princeton, N.J.: Princeton University Press, 1950–).

Cappon, Lester J. *The Adams-Jefferson Letters: The Complete Correspondence Between Thomas Jefferson and Abigail and John Adams* (Chapel Hill: University of North Carolina Press, 1959). 2 vols.

Cunningham, Noble E. *In Pursuit of Reason: The Life of Thomas Jefferson* (Baton Rouge: Louisiana State University Press, 1987).

Maier, Pauline. *American Scripture: Making the Declaration of Independence* (New York:, 1997).

Malone, Dumas. *Jefferson the Virginian* (Boston: Little, Brown, 1948).

———. *Jefferson and the Rights of Man* (Boston: Little, Brown, 1951).

———. *Jefferson and the Ordeal of Liberty* (Boston: Little, Brown, 1962).

———. *Jefferson the President, First Term, 1801–1805* (Boston: Little, Brown, 1970).

———. *Jefferson the President, Second Term, 1805–1809* (Boston: Little, Brown, 1974).

———. *The Sage of Monticello* (Boston: Little, Brown, 1981).

Mayer, David N. *The Constitutional Thought of Thomas Jefferson* (Charlottesville: University Press of Virginia, 1994).

Peterson, Merrill D. *The Jefferson Image in the American Mind* (New York: Oxford University Press, 1960).

———, ed. *Thomas Jefferson Writings* (New York: Library of America, 1984).

Smith, James Morton, ed., *The Republic of Letters: The Correspondence Between Thomas Jefferson and James Madison, 1776–1826* (New York: Norton, 1995). 3 vols.

MARTIN LUTHER KING, JR. (1929–1968)

Branch, Taylor. *Parting the Waters: America in the King Years, 1954–63* (New York: Simon & Schuster, 1988).

———. *Pillar of Fire, America in the King Years, 1963–65* (New York: Simon & Schuster, 1998).

Carson, Clayborne, ed. *The Autobiography of Martin Luther King, Jr.* (New York: Warner Books, 1998).

Frank, Gerold. *An American Death: The True Story of the Assassination of Dr. Martin Luther King, Jr., and the Greatest Manhunt of Our Time* (Garden City, N.Y.: Doubleday, 1972).

Garrow, David J. *Bearing the Cross, Martin Luther King, Jr. and the Southern Christian Leadership Conference* (New York: William Morrow, 1986).

King, Coretta Scott. *My Life with Martin Luther King, Jr.* (New York: Holt, Rinehart & Winston, 1969)

Washington, James M., ed. *A Testament of Hope: The Essential Writings and Speeches of Martin Luther King, Jr.* (San Francisco: HarperSanFrancisco, 1991).

LAFAYETTE (1757–1834)

Chinard, Gilbert, ed. *The Letters of Lafayette and Jefferson* (Baltimore: Johns Hopkins Press, 1929).

Gottschalk, Louis. *Lafayette in America* (Arveyres, France: L'Esprit de Lafayette Society, 1975). 3 vols.

——, ed. *The Letters of Lafayette to Washington, 1777–1799* (Philadelphia: American Philosophical Society, 1976).

Gottschalk, Louis, and Margaret Maddox, *Lafayette in the French Revolution* (Chicago: University of Chicago Press, 1969).

——. *Lafayette in the French Revolution: From the October Days Through the Federation* (Chicago: University of Chicago Press, 1973).

Idzerda, Stanley J., ed. *Lafayette in the Age of the American Revolution: Selected Letters and Papers, 1776–1790* (Ithaca: Cornell University Press, 1977). 5 vols.

Kramer, Lloyd. *Lafayette in Two Worlds: Public Cultures and Personal Identities in an Age of Revolutions* (Chapel Hill: University of North Carolina Press, 1996).

Maurois, André. *Adrienne, the Life of the Marquise de La Fayette* (New York: McGraw-Hill, 1961).

Whitlock, Brand. *La Fayette* (New York: D. Appleton, 1929). 2 vols.

LOUIS L'AMOUR (1908–1988)

Elton, J. C. *Louis L'Amour: The Long Trail: An Unauthorized Biography* (Mattituck, N.Y.: Amereon House, 1989).

Gale, Robert L. *Louis L'Amour* (Boston: Twayne, 1985).

L'Amour, Angelique, ed. *A Trail of Memories: The Quotations of Louis L'Amour* (New York: Bantam, 1988).

——. *Bendigo Shafter* (New York: Bantam, 1993).

——. *Education of a Wandering Man* (New York: Bantam, 1989).

——. *Flint* (New York: Bantam, 1997).

——. *Hondo* (New York: Fawcett, 1953).

——. *Jubal Sackett* (New York: Bantam, 1985).

——. *The Walking Drum* (New York: Bantam, 1985).

Weinberg, Robert, ed. *The Louis L'Amour Companion* (New York: Bantam, 1994).

ROSE WILDER LANE (1887–1968)

Holtz, William. *The Ghost in the Little House: A Life of Rose Wilder Lane* (Columbia: University of Missouri Press, 1993).

——, *Dorothy Thompson and Rose Wilder Lane: Forty Years of Friendship, Letters, 1921–1960* (Columbia: University of Missouri, 1991).

Lane, Rose Wilder. *Woman's Day Book of American Needlework* (New York: Simon & Schuster, 1963).

————. *The Discovery of Freedom* (New York: Arno Press, 1972).

————. *Give Me Liberty* (Mansfield, Mo.: Laura Ingalls Wilder–Rose Wilder Lane Home Association, 1977).

————. *Old Home Town* (Lincoln: University of Nebraska, 1963).

————, and MacBride, Roger Lea. *Rose Wilder Lane* (New York: Stein & Day, 1977).

MacBride, Roger Lea, ed. *The Lady and the Tycoon, The Best of Letters Between Rose Wilder Lane and Jasper Crane* (Caldwell, Ida.: Caxton Printers, 1972).

JOHN LILBURNE (1614?–1657)

Christopher Hill, ed. *H. N. Brailsford, The Levellers and the English Revolution* (Nottingham, England: Spokesman, 1983).

Frank, Joseph. *The Levellers: A History of the Writings of Three Seventeenth Century Social Democrats: John Lilburne, Richard Overton, William Walwyn* (Cambridge: Harvard University Press, 1955).

Gibb, M. A. *John Lilburne, the Leveller: A Christian Democrat* (London: Lindsay Drummond, 1947).

Gregg, Pauline. *Free-Born John: A Biography of John Lilburne* (London: J. M. Dent, 1986).

Haller, William, ed. *Tracts on Liberty in the Puritan Revolution, 1638–1647* (New York: Columbia University Press, 1938). 3 vols.

Pease, Theodore Calvin. *The Leveller Movement: A Study in the History and Political Theory of the English Great Civil War* (Gloucester, Mass.: Peter Smith, 1965).

Wolfe, Don M., ed. *Leveller Manifestoes of the Puritan Revolution* (New York: Humanities Press, 1967).

Woodhouse, A. S. P., ed. *Puritanism and Liberty: Being the Army Debates (1647–9)* (Chicago: University of Chicago Press, 1951).

JOHN LOCKE (1632–1704)

Cranston, Maurice. *John Locke, a Biography* (London: Longmans, 1957).

Huyler, Jerome. *Locke in America, The Moral Philosophy of the Founding Era* (Lawrence: University Press of Kansas, 1995).

Laslett, Peter, ed. *Locke's Two Treatises: A Critical Edition* (Cambridge: Cambridge University Press, 1963).

Locke, John *An Essay Concerning Human Understanding* (Amherst, N.Y.: Prometheus, 1995)

Ramsay, I. T., ed. *John Locke, The Reasonableness of Christianity with A Discourse of Miracles and Part of A Third Letter Concerning Toleration* (Stanford, Calif.: Stanford University Press, 1989).

Tarcov, Nathan. *Locke's Education for Liberty* (Chicago: University of Chicago Press, 1984).

Tully, James H., ed. *John Locke: A Letter Concerning Toleration* (Indianapolis: Hackett Publishing, 1983).

Wootton, David, ed. *Political Writings of John Locke* (New York: Mentor, 1993).

THOMAS BABINGTON MACAULAY (1800–1859)

Beatty, Richmond Croom. *Lord Macaulay, Victorian Liberal* (Norman: University of Oklahoma Press, 1938).

Clive, John. *Macaulay: The Shaping of an Historian* (New York: Knopf, 1973).

Edwards, Owen Dudley. *Macaulay* (New York: St. Martin's, Press, 1988).

Firth, Charles. *A Commentary on Macaulay's History of England* (New York: Barnes & Noble, 1964).
The Life and Works of Lord Macaulay (New York: Longmans, Green, 1896). 10 vols. (Includes a biography by George Otto Trevelyan.)
Millgate, Jane. *Macaulay* (London: Routledge, Kegan Paul, 1973).
Pinney, Thomas, ed. *The Letters of Thomas Babington Macaulay* (Cambridge: Cambridge University Press, 1974–1981). 5 vols.

JAMES MADISON (1751–1836)

Bailyn, Bernard, ed. *The Debate on the Constitution: Federalist and Antifederalist Speeches, Articles, and Letters During the Struggle over Ratification* (New York: Library of America, 1993). 2 vols.
Banning, Lance. *The Sacred Fire of Liberty: James Madison and the Founding of the Federal Republic* (Ithaca, N.Y.: Cornell University Press, 1995).
Elliot, Jonathan, ed. *The Debates in the Several State Conventions on the Adoption of the Federal Constitution as Recommended by the General Convention at Philadelphia in 1787, Together with the Journal of the Federal Convention, Luther Martin's Letter, Yates's Minutes, Congressional Opinions, Virginia and Kentucky Resolutions of '98–'99 and Other Illustrations of the Constitution* (New York: Burt Franklin Reprints, 1974). 5 vols.
Hutchinson, William T., et al., eds. *The Papers of James Madison* (Chicago and Charlottesville: University of Chicago Press and University of Virginia Press, 1962–).
Ketcham, Ralph. *James Madison: A Biography* (New York: Macmillan, 1971).
Kramnick, Isaac, ed. *The Federalist Papers,* by Alexander Hamilton, James Madison, and John Jay (New York: Penguin, 1987).
Madison, James. *Notes of Debates in the Federal Convention of 1787* (Athens: Ohio University Press, 1965).
Mathews, Richard K. *If Men Were Angels: James Madison and the Heartless Empire of Reason* (Lawrence: University Press of Kansas, 1995).
Rutland, Robert A. *The Birth of the Bill of Rights, 1776–1791* (New York: Collier, 1962).
Storing, Herbert J., ed. *The Complete Anti-Federalist* (Chicago: University of Chicago Press, 1981). 7 vols.

H. L. MENCKEN (1880–1956)

DuBasky, Mayo, ed. *The Gist of Mencken: Quotations from America's Critic* (Metuchen, N.J.: Scarecrow Press, 1990).
Fitzpatrick, Vincent. *H. L. Mencken* (New York: Continuum, 1989).
Manchester, William. *Disturber of the Peace, the Life of H. L. Mencken* (New York: Harper & Brothers, 1951).
Mencken, H. L. *The American Language* (New York: Knopf, 1962).
———. *The American Language, Supplement I* (New York: Knopf, 1962).
———. *The American Language, Supplement II* (New York: Knopf, 1962).
———. *A Mencken Chrestomathy* (New York: Knopf, 1949).
———. *Happy Days, 1880–1892* (New York: Knopf, 1940).
———. *Newspaper Days, 1899–1906* (New York: Knopf, 1941).
———. *Heathen Days, 1890–1936* (New York: Knopf, 1963).
Rodgers, Marion Elizabeth. *The Impossible Mencken: A Selection of His Best Newspaper Stories* (New York: Doubleday, 1991).
Teachout Terry, ed. *H. L. Mencken: A Second Mencken Chrestomathy* (New York: Knopf, 1995).

JOHN STUART MILL (1806–1873)

Hayek, F. A. *John Stuart Mill and Harriet Taylor: Their Friendship and Subsequent Marriage* (Chicago: University of Chicago Press, 1951).

Mill, John Stuart. *Autobiography* (New York: Columbia University Press, 1944).

———. *Dissertations and Discussions Political, Philosophical and Historical* (London: Longmans, Green, Reader & Dyer, 1875), 4 vols.

———. *Principles of Political Economy* (New York: Augustus M. Kelley, 1987). (Reprint of 1848 edition.)

———. *The Subjection of Women* (Cambridge: MIT Press, 1970).

———. *Utilitarianism, Liberty, and Representative Government* (New York: Dutton, 1951).

Packe, Michael St. John. *The Life of John Stuart Mill* (New York: Macmillan, 1954).

Spitz, David, ed., *On Liberty*, by John Stuart Mill. (New York: Norton, 1975). Annotated text.

Wood, John Cunningham, ed., *John Stuart Mill: Critical Assessments* (London: Croom Helm, 1987). 4 vols.

LUDWIG VON MISES (1881–1973)

Greaves, Bettina Bien, ed. *MISES: An Annotated Bibliography, 1982–1993 Update* (Irvington-on-Hudson, N.Y.: Foundation for Economic Education, 1995)

———, and Robert W. McGee, eds. *MISES: An Annotated Bibliography: A Comprehensive Listing of Books and Articles by and About Ludwig von Mises* (Irvington-on-Hudson, N.Y.: Foundation for Economic Education, 1993)

Mises, Ludwig von Mises. *Human Action: The Scholar's Edition* (Auburn, Ala.: Ludwig von Mises Institute, 1998). A new introduction by Jeffrey M. Herbener, Hans-Hermann Hoppe, and Joseph T. Salerno.

———. *Liberalism in the Classical Tradition* (Irvington-on-Hudson, N.Y.: Foundation for Economic Education, 1985)

———. *Notes and Reflections* (South Holland, Ill.: Libertarian Press, 1978)

———. *Socialism* (Indianapolis: LibertyClassics, 1981)

———, *The Theory of Money and Credit* (New Haven: Yale University Press, 1953)

Mises, Margit von. *My Years with Ludwig von Mises* (New Rochelle, N.Y.: Arlington House, 1976).

Rothbard, Murray N. *Ludwig von Mises: Scholar, Creator, Hero* (Auburng Ala.: Ludwig von Mises Institute, 1988)

Sennholz, Mary, ed. *On Freedom and Free Enterprise: Essays in Honor of Ludwig von Mises on the 50th Anniversary of His Doctorate* (Princeton, N.J.: D. Van Nostrand, 1956).

BARON DE MONTESQUIEU (1689–1755)

Conroy, Peter V., Jr. *Montesquieu Revisited* (New York: Twayne, 1992).

Hulliung, Mark. *Montesquieu and the Old Regime* (Berkeley: University of California Press, 1976).

Loy, J. Robert. *Montesquieu* (New York: Twayne, 1968).

Montesquieu. *The Persian Letters* (Indianapolis: Bobbs-Merrill, 1964).

———. *The Spirit of the Laws* (Cambridge: Cambridge University Press, 1995).

Pangle, Thomas L. *Montesquieu's Philosophy of Liberalism: A Commentary on "The Spirit of the Laws"* (Chicago: University of Chicago Press, 1973).

Shackleton, Robert. *Montesquieu: A Critical Biography* (Oxford: Oxford University Press, 1961).

Shklar, Judith N. *Montesquieu* (New York: Oxford University Press, 1987).
Spurlin, Paul Merrill. *Montesquieu in America, 1760–1801* (New York: Octagon Books, 1969).

MARIA MONTESSORI (1870–1952)

Boehlein, Mary Maher, ed., *The NAMTA* [North American Montessori Teachers Association] *Montessori Bibliography," NAMTA. Quarterly* (Summer 1985).
Kramer, Rita. *Maria Montessori* (New York: Putnam, 1976).
Montessori, Maria. *The Absorbent Mind* (New York: Delta, 1967).
———. *The Advanced Montessori Method* (New York: Schocken Books, 1965), 2 vols.
———. *The Montessori Method* (New York: Schocken Books, 1964).
———. *The Secret of Childhood* (Notre Dame, Ind.: Fides Publishers, 1966).
Standing, E. M. *Maria Montessori: Her Life and Work* (New York: Plume, 1984).

ALBERT JAY NOCK (1870–1945)

Chodorov, Frnk. *Out of Step: The Autobiography of an Individualist* (New York: Devin-Adair, 1962).
Crunden, Robert M. *The Mind and Art of Albert Jay Nock* (Chicago: Henry Regnery, 1964).
Hamilton, Charles H. *The State of the Union, Essays in Social Criticism by Albert Jay Nock* (Indianapolis: Liberty Press, 1991).
Hubesch, B. W., ed., *The Freeman Book* (New York: B. W. Huebsch, 1924).
Letters from Albert Jay Nock, 1924–1945. (Caldwell, Idaho: Caxton Printers, 1949).
Nock, Albert Jay. *Jefferson* (New York: Harcourt, Brace, 1926).
———. *Memoirs of a Superfluous Man* (Chicago: Henry Regnery, 1964).
———. *Our Enemy, The State* (Caldwell, Idaho: Caxton Printers,
Nock, Francis Jay, ed. *Selected Letters of Albert Jay Nock* (Caldwell, Idaho: Caxton Printers, 1962).
Turner, Susan J. *A History of The Freeman: Literary Landmark of the Early Twenties* (New York: Columbia University Press, 1963).
Wreszin, Michael. *The Superfluous Anarchist: Albert Jay Nock* (Providence: Brown University Press, 1971).

DANIEL O'CONNELL (1775–1847)

Edwards, R. Dudley. Edwards, *Daniel O'Connell and His World* (New York: Thames and Hudson, 1975).
Gwynn, Denis. *Daniel O'Connell, the Irish Liberator* (New York: Frederick A. Stokes Publishing).
Macintyre, Angus. *The Liberator: Daniel O'Connell and the Irish Party, 1830–1847* (New York: Macmillan, 1965).
Moley, Raymond. Daniel O'Connell: *Nationalism Without Violence* (New York: Fordham University Press, 1974).
Nowlan, Kevin B, and Maurice R. O'Connell, eds. *Daniel O'Connell: Portrait of a Radical* (New York: Fordham University Press, 1985).
O'Ferrall, Fergus. *Catholic Emancipation: Daniel O'Connell and the Birth of Irish Democracy* (Dublin: Gill and Macmillan, 1985).
Trench, Charles Chenevix. *The Great Dan: A Biography of Daniel O'Connell* (London: Jonathan Cape, 1994).

THOMAS PAINE (1737–1809)

Aldridge, Alfred Owen. *Man of Reason: The Life of Thomas Paine* (London: Cresset Press, 1960).
Fruchtman, Jack. Jr. *Thomas Paine: Apostle of Freedom* (New York: Four Walls Eight Windows, 1994).
Hawke, David Freeman. *Paine* (New York: Harper & Row, 1974).
Keane, John. *Tom Paine* (Boston: Little, Brown, 1995).
Paine Thomas. *The Writings of Thomas Paine* (New York: Burt Franklin, 1969). 4 vols.

WILLIAM PENN (1644–1718)

Dunn; Mary Maples et al. *The Papers of William Penn* (University of Pennsylvania Press, 1981–1986). 5 vols.
Dunn, Richard S., and Dunn, Mary Maples, eds. *The World of William Penn* (Philadelphia: University of Pennsylvania Press, 1986).
Fantel, Hans. *William Penn, Apostle of Dissent* (New York: William Morrow, 1974).
Peare, Catherine Owens. *William Penn* (Philadelphia: Lippincott, 1957).
Wildes, Harry Emerson. *William Penn* (New York: Macmillan, 1974).

FRANÇOIS RABELAIS (C.1490–1553)

Bakhtin, Mikhail. *Rabelais and His World* (Bloomington: Indiana University Press, 1984).
Frame, Donald. *François Rabelais: A Study* (New York: Harcourt Brace Jovanovich, 1977).
Le Clercq, Jacques. *The Five Books of Gargantua and Pantagruel* (New York: Modern Library, 1936).
D. B. Lewis, Wyndham. *Doctor Rabelais* (New York: Sheed and Ward, 1957).
Nock, Albert Jay. *A Journey into Rabelais's France* (New York: Grosset & Dunlap, 1934).
Nock, Albert Jay, and Wilson, C. R. *François Rabelais: The Man and His Work* (New York: Harper & Brothers, 1929).
———, eds. *The Works of François Rabelais* (New York: Harcourt, Brace & Co., 1931). 2 vols.
Plattard, Jean. *The Life of François Rabelais* (New York: Humanities Press, 1968).
Zegura, Elizabeth Chesney, and Tetel Marcel. *Rabelais Revisited* (New York: Twayne, 1993).

AYN RAND (1905–1982)

Berliner, Michael S, ed. *Letters of Ayn Rand* (New York: Dutton, 1995).
Binswanger, Harry. ed. *The Ayn Rand Lexicon: Objectivism from A to Z* (New York: Meridian, 1988).
Branden, Barbara. *The Passion of Ayn Rand: A Biography* (Garden City, N.Y.: Doubleday, 1986).
Branden, Nathaniel. *Judgment Day, My Years with Ayn Rand* (Boston: Houghton Mifflin, 1989).
Harriman, David, ed., *Journals of Ayn Rand* (New York: Dutton, 1997).
Peikoff, Leonard. *Objectivism: The Philosophy of Ayn Rand* (New York: Meridian, 1991).
Rand, Ayn *Anthem.* With a new introduction and appendix by Leonard Peikoff (New York: Dutton, 1995).

————. *Atlas Shrugged.* With a new introduction by Leonard Peikoff (New York: Dutton, 1992).

————, ed. *Capitalism: The Unknown Ideal* (New York: New American Library, 1962).

————. *The Fountainhead* (New York: Macmillan, 1986).

————. *We the Living* (New York: Random House, 1959).

Sciabarra, Chris Matthew. *Ayn Rand, the Russian Radical* (University Park, Pa.: Pennsylvania State University Press, 1995).

LEONARD E. READ (1898–1983), ANTONY FISHER (1915–1988),
AND EDWARD H. CRANE III (B. 1944)

Boaz, David, and Edward H. Crane, eds. *Market Liberalism: A Paradigm for the 21st Century* (Washington, D.C.: Cato Institute, 1993).

Cockett, Richard. *Think Tanks and the Economic Counter-Revolution, 1931–1983* (London: HarperCollins, 1995).

Fisher, Antony. *Must History Repeat Itself?* (London: Churchill Press, 1974). Issued in the United States as *Fisher's Concise History of Economic Bungling* (Ottawa, Ill.: Caroline House Books, 1978).

Kelley, John L. *Bringing the Market Back In: The Political Revitalization of Market Liberalism* (New York: New York University Press, 1997).

Read, Leonard E. *Anything That's Peaceful* (Irvington-on-Hudson, N.Y.: Foundation for Economic Education, 1992).

Sennholz, Mary. *Leonard E. Read, Philosopher of Freedom* (Irvington-on-Hudson, N.Y.: Foundation for Economic Education, 1993).

Towns, Barnaby. *Time Line of Sir Antony George Anson Fisher, AFC, 1915–1988.* November 7, 1998. Unpublished.

RONALD REAGAN (B. 1911)

Anderson, Martin. *Revolution* (New York: Harcourt Brace Jovanovich, 1988).

D'Souza, Dinesh. *Ronald Reagan: How an Ordinary Man Became an Extraordinary Leader* (New York: Free Press, 1997).

Hannaford, Peter. *Recollections of Reagan: A Portrait of Ronald Reagan* (New York: William Morrow, 1997).

Morris, Edmund. *Dutch: A Memoir of Ronald Reagan* (New York: Random House, 1999).

Reagan, Ronald. *An American Life: The Autobiography* (New York: Simon & Schuster, 1990).

————. *Speaking My Mind: Selected Speeches* (New York: Simon & Schuster, 1989).

Schweitzer, Peter. *Victory: The Reagan Administration's Secret Strategy That Hastened the Collapse of the Soviet Union* (New York: Atlantic Monthly Press, 1994).

Shultz, George P. *Turmoil and Triumph* (New York: Charles Scribner's Sons, 1993).

Stockman, David A. *The Triumph of Politics: Why the Reagan Revolution Failed* (New York: Harper & Row, 1986).

MURRAY N. ROTHBARD (1926–1995)

Block, Walter, and Llewellyn H. Rockwell, Jr. eds. *Man, Economy, and Liberty: Essays in Honor of Murray N. Rothbard* (Auburn, Ala.: Ludwig von Mises Institute, 1988).

Rockwell, Llewellyn H., Jr. ed. *Murray N. Rothbard: In Memoriam* (Auburn, Ala.: Ludwig von Mises Institute, 1995).

Rothbard, Murray N. *America's Great Depression* (Auburn, Ala.: Ludwig von Mises Institute, 1999).

———. *An Austrian Perspective on the History of Economic Thought* (Hants, England: Edward Elgar, 1995). 2 vols.

———. *Conceived in Liberty* (New Rochelle, N.Y.: Arlington House Publishers, 1975–1979). 4 vols.

———. *The Ethics of Liberty* (New York: New York University Press, 1998).

———. *For a New Liberty* (New York: Macmillan, 1973).

———. *Man, Economy and State* (Princeton, N.J.: D. Van Nostrand, 1962). 2 vols.

———. *Power and Market* (Menlo Park, Calif.: Institute for Humane Studies, 1970).

———. *Making Economic Sense* (Auburn, Ala.: Ludwig von Mises Institute, 1995).

FRIEDRICH SCHILLER (1759–1805)

Biermann, Berthold. *Goethe's World as seen in Letters and Memoirs* (New York: New Directions, 1949).

Friedenthal, Richard. *Goethe: His Life And Times* (Cleveland: World Publishing, 1963).

Garland, H. B. *Schiller* (New York: Medill McBride, 1950).

von Heiseler, Bernt. *Schiller* (London: Eyre & Spottiswoode).

Mann, Thomas. *Last Essays* (New York: Knopf, 1956).

Sammons, Jeffrey L. "Friedrich Schiller 1759–1984: Quasi-Heretical Assertions on His 225th Birthday." *Yale University Library Gazette* (April 1985).

———. "Friedrich von Schiller (1759–1805)." In Jacques Barzun, ed., *European Writers, the Romantic Century* (New York: Scribner's, 1985).

———. "The Schiller Centennial: 1859, Some Themes and Motifs." *University of Dayton Review* (Fall 1990).

Schiller, Friedrich. *Don Carlos and Mary Stuart* (New York: Oxford University Press, 1996).

———. *Intrigue and Love, Don Carlos* (New York: Continuum, 1983).

———. *The Robbers and Wallenstein* (New York: Penguin, 1979).

———. *Wilhelm Tell* (Indianapolis: Bobbs-Merrill, 1964).

Sweet, Paul R. *Wilhelm von Humboldt: A Biography* (Columbus: Ohio State University Press, 1978). 2 vols.

Waldeck, Marie-Luise. *The Theme of Freedom in Schiller's Plays* (Stuttgart: Verlag Hans-Dieter Heinz, Akademischer Verlag, 1986).

ALGERNON SIDNEY (1622–1683)

Blom, John, Eco Haitsma Mulie, and Ronald Janse. *Court Maxims,* by Algernon Sidney (Cambridge: Cambridge University Press, 1996).

Carswell, John. *The Porcupine: The Life of Algernon Sidney* (London: John Murray, 1989).

Houston, Alan Craig. *Algernon Sidney and the Republican Heritage in England and America* (Princeton, N.J.: Princeton University Press, 1991).

Scott, Jonathan. *Algernon Sidney and the English Republic, 1623–1677* (Cambridge: Cambridge University Press, 1988).

———. *Algernon Sidney and the Restoration Crisis, 1677–1683* (Cambridge: Cambridge University Press, 1991).

West, Thomas G., ed. *Discourses Concerning Government,* by Algernon Sidney (Indianapolis: LibertyClassics, 1990).

SAMUEL SMILES (1812–1904)

Briggs, Asa. *Victorian People* (Chicago: University of Chicago Press, 1954).

Jarvis, Adrian. *Samuel Smiles and the Construction of Victorian Values* (Phoenix Mill, England: Sutton Publishing, 1997).

Mackay, Thomas, ed. *The Autobiography of Samuel Smiles* (New York: Dutton, 1905).

Smiles, Aileen. *Samuel Smiles and His Surroundings* (London: Robert Hale Ltd., 1956).

Smiles, Samuel. *Character* (New York: Harper & Brothers, 1878).

———. *Duty* (New York: A. L. Burt).

———. *Life and Labour* (London: John Murray, 1887).

———. *Lives of the Engineers* (New York: Augustus M. Kelley, 1968). 3 vols.

———. *Self-Help* (London: IEA Health and Welfare Unit, 1996).

———. *Thrift* (Chicago: Belford, Clarke & Co., 1883).

ADAM SMITH (1723–1790)

Bryce, J. G., ed., *Lectures on Rhetoric and Belles Lettres by Adam Smith* (Indianapolis: LibertyClassics, 1983).

Cannan, Edwin, ed., *An Inquiry into the Nature and Causes of The Wealth of Nations*. With a new preface by George J. Stigler. (Chicago: University of Chicago Press, 1976).

Meck, R. L., Raphael, D. D., and Stein, P. G., ed. *Lectures on Jurisprudence by Adam Smith* (Indianapolis: LibertyClassics, 1978).

Mossner, E. G., and Ross, and I S., ed. *Correspondence of Adam Smith* (Indianapolis: LibertyPress, 1987).

Rae, John. *Life of Adam Smith* (New York: Augustus M. Kelley, 1965).

Raphael, D. D., and Macfie, A. L., eds. *The Theory of Moral Sentiments*, by Adam Smith (Indianapolis: LibertyClassics, 1976).

Ross, Ian Simpson. *The Life of Adam Smith* (Oxford: Clarendon Press, 1995).

Skinner, Andrew S., and Thomas Wilson. *Essays on Adam Smith* (Oxford: Clarendon Press, 1975).

Wightman, W. P. D., ed., *Essays on Philosophical Subjects*, by Adam Smith (Indianapolis: LibertyClassics, 1980).

West, E. G. *Adam Smith, the Man and His Works* (Indianapolis: LibertyPress, 1976).

HERBERT SPENCER (1820–1903)

Duncan, David. *Life and Letters of Herbert Spencer* (New York: D. Appleton, 1904). 2 vols.

Peel, J. D. Y. *Herbert Spencer, the Evolution of a Sociologist* (New York: Basic Books, 1971).

Spencer, Herbert. *An Autobiography* (New York: D. Appleton, 1904). 2 vols.

———. *Education* (New York: D. Appleton, 1896).

———. *The Man Versus the State, with Six Essays on Government, Society, and Freedom* (Indianapolis: LibertyClassics, 1981).

———. *The Principles of Ethics* (Indianapolis: LibertyClassics, 1978). 2 vols.

———. *The Principles of Sociology* (Westport, Conn.: Greenwood Press, 1975). 3 vols.

———. *Social Statics* (New York: Robert Schalkenbach Foundation, 1970).

LYSANDER SPOONER (1808–1887)

Brooks, Frank H. *The Individualist Anarchists: Anthology of Liberty (1881–1908)* (New Brunswick, N.J.: Transaction Publishers, 1994).

Martin, James J. *Men Against the State* (Colorado Springs: Ralph Myles Publisher, 1970).

Smith, George H., ed., *The Lysander Spooner Reader* (San Francisco: Fox & Wilkes, 1992).

The Collected Works of Lysander Spooner (Weston, Mass.: M&S Press, 1971). 6 vols.

ELIZABETH CADY STANTON (1815–1902)

Banner, Lois. *Elizabeth Cady Stanton: A Radical for Woman's Rights* (Boston: Little, Brown, 1980).

Barry, Kathleen. *Susan B. Anthony: A Biography of a Singular Feminist* (New York: New York University Press, 1988).

DuBois, Ellen Carol, ed. *The Elizabeth Cady Stanton–Susan B. Anthony Reader: Correspondence, Writings, Speeches* (Boston: Northeastern University Press, 1991).

Gordon, Ann D., ed. *The Selected Papers of Elizabeth Cady Stanton* (New Brunswick, N.J.: Rutgers University Press, 1997).

Griffith, Eleanor. *In Her Own Right: The Life of Elizabeth Cady Stanton* (New York: Oxford University Press, 1984).

History of Woman Suffrage, 1848–1861. Edited by Elizabeth Cady Stanton, Susan B. Anthony, and Matilda Joslyn Gage (Rochester, N.Y.: Susan B. Anthony, 1889).

History of Woman Suffrage, 1861–1876. Edited by Elizabeth Cady Stanton, Susan B. Anthony, and Matilda Joslyn Gage (Rochester, N.Y.: Susan B. Anthony, 1881).

History of Woman Suffrage, 1876–1885. Edited by Elizabeth Cady Stanton and Matilda Joslyn Gage (Rochester, N.Y.: Susan B. Anthony, 1886).

The History of Woman Suffrage, 1883–1900. Edited by Susan B. Anthony and Ida Husted Harper (Rochester, N.Y.: Susan B. Anthony).

Stanton, Elizabeth Cady. *Eighty Years and More: Reminiscences 1815–1897* (Boston: Northeastern University Press, 1993).

———. *The Woman's Bible* (Boston: Northeastern University Press, 1993).

GEORGE J. STIGLER (1911–1991)

Becker, Gary S. "George Joseph Stigler: January 17, 1911–December 1, 1991." *Journal of Political Economy* (October 1993): 761–767.

Leube, Kurt R., and Thomas Gale Moore, eds., *The Essence of Stigler* (Stanford, Calif.: Hoover Institutition Press, 1986).

Stigler, George J. *The Citizen and the State: Essays on Regulation* (Chicago: University of Chicago Press, 1975).

———. *The Economist as Preacher and Other Essays* (Chicago: University of Chicago Press, 1982).

———. *Essays in the History of Economics* (Chicago: University of Chicago Press, 1965).

———. *Memoirs of an Unregulated Economist* (New York: Basic Books, 1985).

———. *The Intellectual and the Marketplace and Other Essays* (Glencoe, Ill.: Free Press, 1963).

A SELECTIVE BIBLIOGRAPHY [549

WILLIAM GRAHAM SUMNER (1840–1910)

Bannister, Robert C. *On Liberty, Society, and Politics: The Essential Essays of William Graham Sumner* (Indianapolis: Liberty Fund, 1992).
Curtis, Bruce. *William Graham Sumner* (Boston: Twayne, 1981).
Keller, A. G. *Reminiscences (Mainly Personal) of William Graham Sumner* (New Haven: Yale University Press, 1933).
Keller, Albert Galloway, ed. *The Challenge of Facts and Other Essays,* by William Graham Sumner (New Haven: Yale University Press, 1914).
———, ed. *The Forgotten Man and Other Essays,* by William Graham Sumner (New Haven: Yale University Press, 1918).
———, ed., *Earth-Hunger and Other Essays,* by William Graham Sumner (New Haven: Yale University Press, 1913).
———, ed. *War and Other Essays,* by William Graham Sumner (New Haven: Yale University Press, 1914).
Starr, Harris E. *William Graham Sumner* (New York: Henry Holt, 1925).
Sumner, William Graham. *Folkways* (Boston: Ginn, 1940).
———. *What Social Classes Owe to Each Other* (Caldwell, Ida.: Caxton Printers, 1963).
———, and Keller, Albert Galloway. *The Science of Society* (New Haven: Yale University Press, 1927). 4 vols.

THOMAS SZASZ (B. 1920)

Szasz, Thomas. *Ceremonial Chemistry* (Garden City, N.Y.: Anchor Press, 1975).
———. *Law, Liberty and Psychiatry* (Syracuse, N.Y.: Syracuse University Press, 1989).
———. *The Manufacture of Madness: A Comparative Study of the Inquisition and the Mental Health Movement* (Syracuse, N.Y.: Syracuse University Press, 1997).
———. *The Myth of Mental Illness: Foundations of a Theory of Personal Conduct* (New York: Harper & Row, 1961).
———. *Our Right to Drugs: The Case for a Free Market* (Westport, Conn.: Praeger, 1992).
———. *The Therapeutic State: Psychiatry in the Mirror of Current Events* (Buffalo, N.Y.: Prometheus, 1984).
Vatz, Richard E., and Lee S. Weinberg. *Thomas Szasz: Primary Values and Major Contentions* (Buffalo, N.Y.: Prometheus, 1983).

MARGARET THATCHER (B. 1925)

Harris, Robin, ed. *Margaret Thatcher: The Collected Speeches* (New York: Harper-Collins, 1997).
Jenkins, Peter. *Mrs. Thatcher's Revolution: The Ending of the Socialist Era* (Cambridge: Harvard University Press, 1988).
Mikdadi, Faysal. *Margaret Thatcher: A Bibliography* (Westport, Conn.: Greenwood Press, 1993).
Ogden, Chris. *Maggie: An Intimate Portrait of a Woman in Power* (New York: Simon & Schuster, 1990).
Pepper, Gordon. *Inside Thatcher's Monetarist Revolution* (London: Macmillan Press, 1998).
Thatcher, Margaret. *The Downing Street Years* (New York: HarperCollins, 1993).
———. *The Path to Power* (New York: HarperCollins, 1995).

Young, Hugo. *The Iron Lady: A Biography of Margaret Thatcher* (New York: Farrar, Straus, and Giroux, 1989).

HENRY DAVID THOREAU (1817–1862)

Atkinson, Brooks, ed. *Walden and Other Writings of Henry David Thoreau* (New York: Modern Library, 1992).
Canby, Henry Seidel. *Thoreau* (Gloucester, Mass.: Peter Smith, 1965).
Harding, Walter. *A Thoreau Handbook* (New York: New York University Press, 1976).
———. *The Days of Henry Thoreau: A Biography* (Princeton, N.J.: Princeton University Press, 1982).
Miller, Perry. Afterword, Walden—The Secret Center. In Henry David Thoreau, *Walden* (New York: New American Library, 1960).
Richardson, Robert D., Jr. *Emerson: The Mind on Fire* (Berkeley: University of California Press, 1995).

ALEXIS DE TOCQUEVILLE (1805–1859)

Boesche, Roger, ed. *Alexis de Tocqueville: Selected Letters on Politics and Society* (Berkeley: University of California, 1985).
Bradley, Phillips, ed. *Democracy in America,* by Alexis de Tocqueville, with a new introduction by Daniel J. Boorstin (New York: Vintage Classics, 1990). 2 vols.
Jardin, André. *Tocqueville, a Biography* (New York: Farrar, Straus, and Giroux, 1988).
Furet, François, and Françoise Melonio, eds. *Alexis de Tocqueville: The Old Regime and the Revolution* (Chicago: University of Chicago Press, 1998).
Lamberti, Jean-Claude, *Tocqueville and the Two Democracies* (Cambridge: Harvard University Press, 1989).
Mayer, J. P. *Alexis de Tocqueville: A Biographical Study in Political Science* (Gloucester, Mass.: Peter Smith, 1966).
———. *The Recollections of Alexis de Tocqueville* (London: Harvill Press, 1948).
Palmer, R. R., ed. *The Two Tocquevilles, Father and Son, Herve and Alexis de Tocqueville: On the Coming of the French Revolution* (Princeton: Princeton University Press, 1987).
Pierson, George Wilson. *Tocqueville in America* (Baltimore: Johns Hopkins University Press, 1936).

JACQUES TURGOT (1727–1781)

Dakin, Douglas. *Turgot and the Ancien Régime in France* (New York: Octagon, 1965).
"Turgot." In John Morley, *Biographical Studies* (London: Macmillan, 1923).
Stephens, W. Walker. *The Life and Writings of Turgot, Controller General of France 1774–6* (New York: Burt Franklin, 1971).
Turgot, Anne Robert Jacques. *Reflections on the Formation and Distribution of Riches* (New York: Augustus M. Kelley, 1971).

MARK TWAIN (1835–1910)

Branch, Edgar Marquess, et al. *Mark Twain's Letters* (Berkeley: University of California, 1988–).
Geismar, Maxwell. *Mark Twain: An American Prophet* (Boston: Houghton Mifflin, 1970).
Kaplan, Justin. *Mr. Clemens and Mark Twain: A Biography* (New York: Simon & Schuster, 1966).

Lorch, Fred W. *The Trouble Begins at Eight: Mark Twain's Lecture Tours* (Ames: Iowa State University Press, 1968).

Neider, Charles, ed., *The Complete Essays of Mark Twain* (Garden City, N.Y.: Doubleday, 1963).

———. *The Complete Travel Books of Mark Twain* (Garden City, N.Y.: Doubleday, 1967). 2 vols.

———. *The Outrageous Mark Twain: His Rare Controversial Writings with 'Reflections on Religion' Appearing in Book Form for the First Time* (New York: Doubleday, 1987).

Zwick, Jim, ed., *Mark Twain's Weapons of Satire: Anti-Imperialist Writings on the Philippine-American War* (Syracuse, N.Y.: Syracuse University Press, 1992).

RAOUL WALLENBERG (1912–?)

Anger, Per. *With Raoul Wallenberg in Budapest: Memories of the War Years in Hungary* (New York: Holocaust Library, 1981).

Bierman, John. *Righteous Gentile, the Story of Raoul Wallenberg, Missing Hero of the Holocaust* (New York: Viking, 1981).

Marton, Kati. *Wallenberg: Missing Hero* (New York: Arcade Publishing, 1995).

Rosenfeld, Harvey. *Raoul Wallenberg, Angel of Rescue* (Buffalo: Prometheus, 1981).

Wallenberg, Raoul. *Letters and Dispatches, 1924–1944* (New York: Arcade Publishing, 1995).

Werbell, Frederick E., and Thurston Clarke. *Lost Hero: The Mystery of Raoul Wallenberg* (New York: McGraw-Hill, 1982).

BOOKER T. WASHINGTON (1856–1915)

Harlan, Louis R. *Booker T. Washington: The Making of a Black Leader, 1856–1901* (New York: Oxford University Press, 1972).

———. *Booker T. Washington: The Wizard of Tuskegee, 1901–1915* (New York: Oxford University Press, 1983).

——— et al., eds. *The Booker T. Washington Papers* (Urbana: University of Illinois Press, 1972–1989). 14 vols.

Hawkins, Hugh, ed. *Booker T. Washington and His Critics: Black Leadership in Crisis* (Lexington, Mass.: Heath, 1974).

Scott, Emmett J., and Stowe, Lyman Beecher. *Booker T. Washington: Builder of a Civilization* (Garden City, N.Y.: Doubleday, Page, 1916).

Washington, Booker T. *Character Building, Being Addresses Delivered on Sunday Evenings to the Students of Tuskegee Institute* (New York: Doubleday, Page, 1902).

ROGER WILLIAMS (1603–1688)

Chupak, Henry. *Roger Williams* (New York: Twayne, 1969).

Covey, Cyclone. *The Gentle Radical: Roger Williams* (New York: Macmillan, 1966).

Ernst, James E. *The Political Thought of Roger Williams* (Seattle: University of Washington Press, 1929).

Hall, Timothy L. *Separating Church and State: Roger Williams and Religious Liberty* (Urbana: University of Illinois Press, 1998).

LaFantasie, Glenn W., ed. *The Correspondence of Roger Williams* (Providence: Brown University Press, 1988).

Miller, Perry. *Roger Williams: His Contributions to the American Tradition* (Indianapolis: Bobbs-Merrill, 1953).

Morgan, Edmund S. *Roger Williams: The Church and State* (New York: Harcourt, Brace, 1967).
Winslow, Elizabeth. *Master Roger Williams* (New York: Macmillan, 1957).

MARY WOLLSTONECRAFT (1759–1797)

Brody, Miriam, ed. *A Vindication of the Rights of Woman* (London: Penguin, 1992).
Ferguson, Moira, and Janet Todd. *Mary Wollstonecraft* (Boston: Twayne, 1984).
Flexner, Eleanor. *Mary Wollstonecraft: A Biography* (New York: Coward McCann & Geoghegan, 1972).
Tomalin, Claire. *The Life and Death of Mary Wollstonecraft* (London: Penguin, 1992).
Wardle, Ralph M. *Mary Wollstonecraft: A Critical Biography* (Lincoln: University of Nebraska Press, 1966).
Wollstonecraft, Mary. *A Vindication of the Rights of Men, in a Letter to the Honourable Edmund Burke* (New York: Facsimiles & Reprints, 1959).
———, and William Godwin. *A Short Residence in Sweden and Memoirs of the Author of "The Rights of Woman"* (London: Penguin, 1987).

ACKNOWLEDGMENTS

I'M GRATEFUL TO Daniel J. Boorstin, Charles M. Gray, Earl J. Hamilton, Donald F. Lach, William H. McNeill, Ronald Coase, George J. Stigler, and Milton Friedman, who, at the University of Chicago, introduced me to high standards of scholarship. Dr. Boorstin's books *The Discoverers* (1983) and *The Creators* (1992) suggested a way to organize my material.

I thank Hans F. Sennholz who, as president of the Foundation for Economic Education in the early 1990s, provided encouragement when I wanted to write about the history of liberty through the lives of heroes and heroines. Thanks as well to Beth Hoffman and Mary-Ann Murphy at FEE for editing stories that appeared in *The Freeman.*

I've been working on this project for more than five years, and many people pointed out errors and made helpful suggestions along the way—in particular, Randy Barnett, Boston University School of Law; John Blundell, Institute of Economic Affairs; David Boaz, Cato Institute; James Bovard; Allen Dillard Boyer, New York Stock Exchange; James M. Buchanan, George Mason University; Alejandro Chafuen, Atlas Economic Research Foundation; Edward H. Crane, Cato Institute; Guy von Dardel; Alan Ebenstein; Richard Ebeling, Hillsdale College; Daniel A. Evans, Skillman Library, Lafayette College; Mike Fisher; Vincent Fitzpatrick, Enoch Pratt Free Library (Baltimore); Milton Friedman, Hoover Institution; Charles M. Gray, University of Chicago; Bettina Bien Greaves, Foundation for Economic Education; Virginia Heinlein; Robert Hirst, University of California Library (Berkeley); Guido Huelsmann, Ludwig von Mises Institute; Robert D. Kephart; Stephen Kresge; David M. Levy, George Mason University; Kathy L'Amour; Leonard Liggio, George Mason University; Sam Peltzman, University of Chicago; Richard Pipes, Harvard University; Ralph Raico, State University College at Buffalo; Greg Ransom; Llewellyn H. Rockwell, Jr., Ludwig von Mises Institute; Jeffrey R. Sammons, Yale University; Ron Schoeffel, University of Toronto Press; Mark Skousen; Stephen M. Stigler, University of Chicago; Thomas S. Szasz, State University of New York Health Science Center; Joan Kennedy Taylor; Jeffrey Tucker, Ludwig von Mises Institute; Linda Whetstone; and Fredric Woodbridge Wilson, Harvard University.

I'm grateful that my literary agent of fifteen years, Julian Bach, a gentleman if ever there was one, found a home for this book. I'm glad it's with Bruce Nichols and Dan Freedberg at Free Press.

Thanks to Rosalynd Manley and Marissa Ferguson for taking care of Justin and Kristin when I most needed extra hours. I appreciate the patience of Andrea Millen Rich, publisher of Laissez Faire Books, who juggled priorities so I would have more time.

Thanks to Madeline Powell, Marisa Manley, and Paul DeRosa for providing financial support at crucial points in the project.

And thanks to Marisa, Justin, and Kristin for making it all worthwhile.

INDEX

ABOUT THE AUTHOR

FOR MORE THAN thirty years, Jim Powell has gathered material for *The Triumph of Liberty*. He has interviewed scholars, pursued research in major libraries, visited booksellers, museums, and historic sites around the world.

Powell has written for several dozen publications including the *Wall Street Journal, New York Times, Esquire, Connoisseur, Architectural Digest, American Heritage/Audacity, The Freeman, Liberty,* and *Reason*; and has lectured in England, Germany, Japan, Argentina, and Brazil as well as at Harvard University, Stanford University, and other universities across the United States.

A senior fellow at the Cato Institute (http://www.cato.org) since 1988, Powell is editor of Laissez Faire Books (http://www.laissezfaire.org), the world's largest source of books on liberty, with readers in ninety countries. Since 1991, he has presided at the Junto, the largest New York area forum for authors on liberty. He is the editor of http://www.libertystory.net, a website about the history of liberty.

Powell graduated from the University of Chicago in history. There, as an editor of *New Individualist Review*, he helped publish articles by future Nobel Laureates F.A. Hayek, Milton Friedman, and George J. Stigler as well as other libertarian authors like Ludwig von Mises, Henry Hazlitt, and Murray N. Rothbard.

Powell lives with his family in Westport, Connecticut.